ELIZABETH GASKELL:
A HABIT OF STORIES

'You know I can tell stories better than any other way of expressing
myself.'

In November 1848 a first novel by an unknown author took Britain
by storm: *Mary Barton*, a tale of love, murder and industrial misery.
Its anonymous writer was Elizabeth Gaskell, a Unitarian minister's
wife from Manchester, aged thirty-eight with four small girls. In
private, she had been writing for years: she seemed a 'born story-teller'
and Charles Dickens called her his 'dear Scheherazade', but her
unquenchable habit of stories was more than an escape, it was also a
way of exposing the truth of her world.

High-spirited, witty, a shrewd observer, quick to laugh and easily
moved, Elizabeth Gaskell (1810–65) wrote fiction of great variety: the
social protest of *Ruth* and *North and South*, the comedy of *Cranford*,
the historical romance *Sylvia's Lovers*, the mature and brilliant *Wives
and Daughters*, as well as the impassioned biography of her friend
Charlotte Bronte. In this widely acclaimed biography Jenny Uglow
traces Gaskell's youth in rural Knutsford, her married years in the
tension-ridden city of Manchester, her wide networks of friends in
London, Europe and America and her sensitivity to the political,
religious, scientific and feminist arguments of the day. *Elizabeth
Gaskell* shows her enjoyment of life and love of the ridiculous, her
compassion and anger at injustice, and her own deep conflicts about
her role as a woman and a writer.

From this exhilarating and sympathetic reappraisal Elizabeth
Gaskell emerges as an artist of unrecognised complexity, and a
compelling personality-endearing, maddening and vividly alive.

Jenny Uglow grew up in Cumbria, and has worked in publishing since
leaving Oxford. She has written widely on Victorian literature, from
Walter Pater to Margaret Oliphant, Anthony Trollope to sensation
novels and ghost stories. Her previous books include *Macmillan
Dictionary of Women's Biography* and *George Eliot*. She has four
children and lives in Canterbury.

ELIZABETH GASKELL

A Habit of Stories

JENNY UGLOW

faber and faber

LONDON · BOSTON

First published in 1993
by Faber and Faber Limited
3 Queen Square London WC1N 3AU
This paperback edition first published in 1994

Photoset by Wilmaset Ltd, Wirral
Printed in England by Clays Ltd, St Ives plc

© Jenny Uglow, 1993

Jenny Uglow is hereby identified as author of this work in
accordance with Section 77 of the Copyright, Designs and
Patents Act 1988

A CIP record for this book
is available from the British Library
ISBN 0–571–17036–6

2 4 6 8 10 9 7 5 3 1

Contents

v

CONTENTS

List of Illustrations

A Note, and Acknowledgements

Most of us still talk of 'Mrs Gaskell'. That 'Mrs' sounds so comfortable, fit for the author of *Cranford*. Yet Elizabeth Gaskell's first novels, *Mary Barton* and *Ruth*, shocked Victorian readers: the blazon of matronly respectability set its face against controversy just as much as the male pseudonyms Currer Bell and George Eliot.

I had always admired Gaskell's fiction and the vigour and humour of her letters. I liked the way she stood at odds with orthodoxies and eluded pigeon-holes. Conservatives and radicals, Christians and sceptics, Marxists and feminists, all acclaimed different aspects of her work, but all in the end seemed to tap their pens in frustration: she somehow did not 'fit'. I wanted to trace her life, out of curiosity. But in reading her work I became increasingly intrigued by her notorious 'charm' – a word which, when applied to her writing, at once praises and diminishes, and partly explains why such an original, passionate and sometimes rather strange writer is so often taken for granted. Virginia Woolf read Gaskell while recovering from her breakdown in 1915; 'What a modest, capable woman,' she wrote. Yet a fortnight later she grew impatient: 'what I object to in the mid Victorians is their instinctive fluency – as if Mrs G. sat down to write with the cat on her knee'. One knows what she meant. Gaskell's fiction seems so easy; she is the quintessential mid-Victorian, constantly described as 'a born writer', 'a natural artist', 'an instinctive storyteller'.

What do those phrases imply? That she was somehow gifted with a ventriloquist facility for telling other people's tales? Up to a point this rings true – she described her technique in *Mary Barton* as being to SEE the scenes I tried to describe', and then to relate them as if talking to a friend by the fire on a winter night. An intimate, oral, winter's tale tradition certainly lies behind her work. She was, however, very conscious of her craft, aware of the limits of realism, alert to cultural traditions and linguistic history; she saw writing as hard *work*. Furthermore, hers is a fiction of ideas, acting out the dilemmas that preoccupied her time.

Gaskell herself said she could never express herself so well as through stories. It was because of this doubleness, the sense of something learnt so thoroughly that it comes to seem 'second nature', that I called this book 'A Habit of Stories'. (Habits, of course, can be compulsive.) Then, because Elizabeth loved clothes, I found myself thinking of a habit as a garment, a feminine cloak, a dress for action like a riding-habit, a badge of vocation like a nun's. And since she grew up among women who incessantly explained the world through narrative – in gossip, letters and folk-tales – I began to see storytelling less as a habit than a habitat, subject to its own evolutionary laws. Our ways of reading, like Gaskell's writing, have their roots in the mental landscapes of our age. But words from the past are still eloquent: we may accept 'the death of the author', but the habit of stories does not die.

This book was prompted by Will Sulkin, and I should like to thank him, and Stephen Gill, for encouraging me at the start. Since the publication of *The Letters of Mrs Gaskell* in 1966 the principal debt of anyone exploring Gaskell's life must be to the editors of that collection, J. A. V. Chapple and Arthur Pollard. I owe a special debt to John Chapple, who has generously shared his research, sent transcripts, told me of new discoveries, answered queries and read my text – his patience and joviality never seem to flag. Joan Leach, knowledgeable local historian and tireless secretary of the Gaskell Society, has been invaluable in showing me Knutsford and in supplying details of Cheshire history. John Geoffrey Sharps has been a great support: his book *Mrs Gaskell's Observation and Invention*, with its spreading, meticulous notes, is a hoard of information, and he has also kindly allowed me to use his private collection of letters. Others working in this field have provided assistance or inspired ideas, particularly Barbara Brill (with her work on William Gaskell and her study of the Portico Library Archives), Angus Easson, John Gross, John Hodgson, Gunnel Melcher, Alan Shelston, Arthur Pollard, R. W. Webb and Patsy Stoneman.

I am grateful, too, to the following people: Rosemary Ashton and Kenneth Fielding for clarifying details about G. H. Lewes and the Carlyles; Hugh Cunningham, David Kynaston and David Turley for specific historical background; Andrew Motion for comments on early work; Janet Allen, formerly of the Portico Library, Manchester, for her warm hospitality and assistance with picture research; Deborah Rogers for practical and moral support; Jane Turner for her sustained interest; Susanne McDadd, Ron Costley, Helen Jeffrey and my witty, supportive editor, Julian Loose, for seeing the work to press; and Steve, Tom, Hannah, Jamie and Luke Uglow for being themselves. And finally – for reading everything, in bits and pieces and bundles, and for making me think things through – I especially want to thank my friends Hermione Lee, and Francis Spufford.

Mrs R. Trevor Dabbs has very kindly given permission to quote from the Gaskell family's unpublished correspondence and to reproduce portraits in her possession. I am also grateful to J. A. V. Chapple, Arthur Pollard and Manchester University Press for quotations from *The Letters of Mrs Gaskell*, and to Oxford University Press for quotations from *The Letters of Charles Dickens* (Pilgrim edition). I owe thanks to many librarians, notably Dr Iain Brown of the Department of Manuscripts, National Library of Scotland, Christine Lingard of Manchester Central Library, Kate Perry of Girton College Library, Martin Phillips of the University of Keele, Jennie Rathbun of the Houghton Reading Room, Harvard, and Dr C. J. Sheppard of the Brotherton Special Collection, University of Leeds. I am also most grateful for the generous help of many members of the library staff at the University of Kent.

The following institutions and individuals have allowed me to use, quote from or reproduce material in their possession or in which they own the copyright: Birmingham University Library (Martineau Collection); the Bodleian Library, Oxford; University of California, Los Angeles; Christchurch College Library, Canterbury; Cambridge University Library; Columbia University Library, New York; Cornell University Library, Ithaca; the Mistress and Fellows, Girton College, Cambridge; the Houghton Library, Harvard University; the Huntington Library, San Marino, California; the late Dr R. R. Jamison; the John Rylands University Library of Manchester; Keele University Library for the Wedgwood–Mosley Collection, by courtesy of the

A NOTE, AND ACKNOWLEDGEMENTS

Trustees of the Wedgwood Museum, Barlaston, Stoke-on-Trent, Staffordshire; Knutsford Public Library; the Brotherton Special Collection, University of Leeds; Mrs Susan Lowndes Marques; Manchester Central Reference Library; the New York Public Library (Berg Collection); New York University Libraries (Fales Collection); Nottingham Public Library; the Pierpont Morgan Library, New York; the Morris L. Parrish Collection, Princeton University Library; Mr J. G. Sharps; Royal Holloway and Bedford New College Archives (Reid Papers); Rutgers University Library, New Jersey; the National Library of Scotland; the Shakespeare Birthplace Trust, Stratford-upon-Avon; Michael Silverman; Smith College Library (Sophia Smith Collection); and Yale University Library.

References in the Text

WORKS

Elizabeth Gaskell revised her work for new editions as well as for the transfer from periodical to volume publication. For consistency, I have quoted throughout from the only complete edition of the fiction, the Knutsford edition of *The Works of Mrs Gaskell*, ed. A. W. Ward, 8 vols (London, 1906), and for *The Life of Charlotte Brontë* I have used the Penguin Classics edition, ed. Alan Shelston (Harmondsworth, 1975). To allow easy reference to other editions, references are to chapters rather than page numbers.

LETTERS

All quotations are from *The Letters of Mrs Gaskell*, ed. J. A. V. Chapple and Arthur Pollard (Manchester, 1966), unless otherwise indicated in the end-notes. At Professor Chapple's suggestion only the longer, displayed extracts from the *Letters* have references, and these are to the page number (for example, L200, rather than to the somewhat complicated individual letter numbers. Following Chapple and Pollard, I have retained Gaskell's sometimes idiosyncratic spellings and punctuation, and have used braces to indicate her deletions { }, and solidi for her insertions \ /.

To J. A. V. Chapple
and the Gaskell Society

I

LEARNING VOICES
— 1810–48

'We have only to look at a portrait of Mrs Gaskell, soft-eyed, beneath her charming veil, to see that she was a dove . . . she was all a woman was expected to be; gentle, domestic, tactful, prone to tears, easily shocked. So far from chafing at the limits imposed on her activities, she accepted them with serene satisfaction.

Lord David Cecil, 1934

I feel a stirring instinct and long to be off . . . just like a bird wakens up from its content at the change of the seasons . . . But . . . I happen to be a woman instead of a bird . . . and . . . moreover I have no wings like a dove to fly away.

Elizabeth Gaskell to Mary Howitt, 1838

[1]

Far and Near

On a wintry day in October 1831 Elizabeth Stevenson, soon to be Elizabeth Gaskell, was writing to her friend Harriet, scribbling at speed, her curling script crossing and recrossing the crowded page: 'Oh this windy miserable weather; I am writing near a window where puffs of wind come through every now & then, & chill my intellects – you will ask why I don't move – I suppose it is my vis inertia, and my being in a most comfortable arm chair – but I am squeezing myself into as small a compass as I can to collect all the warmth.'[1]

The draughts did not matter. She could write anywhere, under any conditions – in a freezing or a sun-filled room, at a desk or in a field, 'gay with bright spring flowers ... crunching up my paper, & scuttering my pencil away, when any one comes near'. In later life, while her husband retreated to his study and firmly shut the door, she wrote in the dining-room with the doors open to all the demands of children and guests, like Jane Austen in the midst of the household, only hiding her papers when visitors came. With no sign of inertia or a chilled intellect, Elizabeth Gaskell squeezed six long novels, a major biography, dozens of short stories and hundreds of letters into the compass of an extremely active life.

She was always hungry for stories, for involvement in other lives. From Woodside, Liverpool, where she was staying with cousins, she begged Harriet for news: 'Remember, every little, leetle, particular about yourself, and your concerns, and gossipry, and scandal, are most welcome to me, but especially all that interests you, and Elizabeth personally, down to the uninteresting in general basons [sic] of tapioca you have at lunch.'[2] How are the Rankins? she asks. What is become of Marianne Reed? How is Mr Turner's cold?

3

In return Elizabeth pours out her own news – of bonnets and bazaars, phrenology and fashions, shipwrecks on the Mersey, cholera and Coronation Balls. Into the buzz of news there creeps now and then a note of longing, an impatience to be on the move: 'I suppose we shall make wings to ourselves, and fly away, in the course of the next month, to our real home.' The same feeling rises six years later in a letter to the writers William and Mary Howitt. Writing from Manchester, where the May sun gleams only feebly through the smoke, she explains that at the coming of spring:

'I feel a stirring instinct and long to be off into the deep grassy solitudes of the country, just like a bird wakens up from its content at the change of the seasons and tends its way to some well-known but till then forgotten land. But as I happen to be a woman instead of a bird, as I have ties at home and duties to perform, and as, moreover I have no wings like a dove to fly away . . . why I must stay at home and content myself with recalling the happy scenes which your books bring up before me.' (L14)

A feeling of frustration and reined-in energy was often to mark her flight into this inner world, even when she was an established writer, for although she could write anywhere, she was not always free to: 'I . . . was writing away vigorously at Ruth when the Wedgwoods, Etc came: and I was sorry, *very* sorry to give it up my heart being so full of it, in a way which I can't bring back. That's *that*.'

Involvement in the near, yearning for the far, marked Elizabeth Gaskell's life from its earliest days, a pattern established even before she was born. The story of her parents and their families bears directly on her life and work; when she came to write fiction, she returned again and again to the times they lived through, the movements they took part in, the ideas they were stirred by. Even in pictures of apparently static communities like *Cranford*, and still more in a novel like *North and South*, she is preoccupied with the pressure of change, with its losses and gains, painting the energy as well as the misery of the new towns, and the hardship as well as the beauty of the countryside.

Elizabeth Cleghorn Stevenson was born, on 29 September 1810, in Lindsey Row, Chelsea, at the house which is now 93 Cheyne Walk.

Chelsea was still a village, not a fashionable neighbourhood, but it was already an area for writers and artists, many of them, like her parents, newly arrived from elsewhere. With their small son, John, the Stevensons had come to the city four years before after a series of moves which had much to do with the character of Elizabeth's brilliant but erratic father, William. Both her parents were Unitarians, and this faith – a way of thinking and an attitude to life as much as a set of beliefs – was to be a central force in their daughter's life.

The faith Elizabeth learnt was a simple one. Unitarians, as the name suggests, rejected as unknowable, and therefore impossible, such mystical doctrines as the Trinity and the divinity of Christ. In England, after the Dissenting ministers were ejected from the Church in 1662, Unitarianism developed within a strain of Presbyterianism strongly influenced by the ideas of Hobbes, Locke and Newton and by the rationalism and science of the Enlightenment. Unitarians followed Locke in believing the mind to be blank at birth, a *tabula rasa*, and grasped the psychology of David Hartley (developed in his *Observations on Man*, 1749) to explain how personality was formed. Hartley's belief that ideas and attitudes are developed from an early age from the 'associations' of sensations led to a preoccupation with education and upbringing – a theme of Elizabeth's writings from her earliest stories to her final novel, *Wives and Daughters*.

Unitarian doctrines were clarified and strengthened in the late eighteenth century by Joseph Priestley, Theophilus Lindsey (who resigned from the Church of England to found Essex Street Chapel in London) and Lindsey's successor, Thomas Belsham, a brilliant organizer and spokesman, if not an inspired theorist. Unitarianism was a very open church, which asked of its members only a belief in the one God, an acceptance of the divine mission of Jesus and a reliance on the scriptures (although the Bible too was subject to reason and historical criticism). The nature of Jesus remained a matter of debate – he could be a lesser form of God, a man with a divine authority or, indeed, a human being, divinely chosen, yet physically vulnerable and morally fallible. Unitarians refused to accept the notion of original sin or the doctrine of atonement: Jesus was revered as a teacher and example, not a vehicle of grace. No one was 'chosen' and there was no elect. (Many believers – including other Dissenters – felt that in holding to one God and denying the divinity of Christ Unitarians had no right to call themselves Christians at all.)[3]

5

Above all they believed in freedom of thought and stressed the role of reason in the quest for truth. In the Dissenting Academies one of the texts studied was Locke's *Essay Concerning Human Understanding* and they held by his sanguine belief: 'I doubt not but how that a man, by the right use of his natural abilities, may, without any innate principles, attain a knowledge of God, and other things that concern him.'[4] Priestley argued that the universe was ruled by immutable laws which originated from God and applied to both the physical and moral spheres: these laws were, however, within the reach of man's understanding and once understood they could be followed to advance God's plan. This did not deny freedom of will, as he explained by quoting the image from Hobbes's *Leviathan* of water flowing through a channel, at once free and determined. Men have *liberty* to act and yet,

'because every act of man's will, and every desire and inclination, proceedeth from some cause, and that from another cause, in a continual chain (whose first link is in the hand of God, the first of all causes), all things proceed from *necessity*.'[5]

One weakness of this rational, necessitarian framework was that it could feel constricting and arid, denying feeling and mystery. In a galloping list of Coleridge's enthusiasms William Hazlitt (whose father was a Unitarian minister) summed up both its excitement and limitations. Coleridge, he said, became obsessed by 'the great laws of association that binds all things in its mystic chain, and the doctrine of Necessity (the mild teacher of Christ) and the Millennium, anticipative of a life to come – and he plunged deep into the controversy on Matter and spirit'. Then 'as an escape from Dr Priestley's materialism, where he felt himself imprisoned by the logician's spell, as Ariel in the cloven pine tree', he had to move on, to poetry and cloudy transcendentalism.[6]

The faith might lack mystery, but it did not lack fire. Hazlitt's mention of a millennium in this world, not the next, points to Unitarianism's radical, inspiring power. It was essentially optimistic, assuming a dynamic of gradual progress to perfection, both in individuals and societies, and emphasizing personal action. Everyone should promote progress by questioning the status quo. Intellectual and scientific discovery was to be welcomed. Unitarians took the lead in founding the Literary and Philosophical Societies which sprang up in several English towns and cities in the 1780s and 1790s. Debate and experiment were encouraged, as the preface to the first volume of *Memoirs* of the Manchester 'Lit. and Phil.' makes clear: 'Science, like fire, is put in motion by collision.'[7]

In ethics this challenge to convention put equality before hierarchy, moral justice before legal judgement. Unitarians asked, as Gaskell does in so many novels and stories, 'Why do we live in an unjust world if we are all equal in the eyes of God?' To the predominantly Anglican establishment, this made them suspect on political as well as religious grounds. They were identified with revolution because they believed that men and women should speak openly against the things they felt were wrong, in personal and social life as well as on issues of faith. This too was part of Elizabeth's inheritance. Although their numbers were relatively small compared with other sects (there were only twenty declared Unitarian congregations by 1810, the year of Elizabeth's birth), their influence was great. From Unitarian families came a succession of passionate reformers – men like William Roscoe, who voted for the abolition of the slave trade even though he knew he would lose his seat as MP for Liverpool, which lived off the trade. In the nineteenth century Unitarian women were as influential as men in social reform. Florence Nightingale, Harriet Martineau, Barbara Bodichon, Bessie Parkes, Emily Shaen and Mary Carpenter all shared a Unitarian background to some degree, and most were Elizabeth Gaskell's personal friends. Like them, she believed that the witness to truth should be taken, if needs be, to the point of martyrdom. In every fierce controversy about her work – over *Mary Barton, Ruth*, even *The Life of Charlotte Brontë* – she would revert to this deep justification: she had to tell the truth.[8]

Despite its proud radicalism Unitarianism was also the most tolerant of all Nonconformist sects, embracing many shades of opinion. Elizabeth's father and mother belonged to two different phases of the Church, the new and the old. While William Stevenson was a radical, a man of the modern world, his wife, Elizabeth, came from the old-established Dissenting congregations which had taken root in Lancashire and Cheshire in the seventeenth century. Her family, the Hollands, formed part of a community with traditional, even conservative views. Her father, Samuel, farmed at Sandlebridge,

7

near Knutsford in Cheshire, on land which had been in the family since 1718.

The Hollands were known in the area not only as farmers but as doctors, lawyers, bankers and businessmen. They were typical of the solid middle classes who formed the main body of the Unitarian Church in the provinces – where 'a small but highly respectable body' is a frequent description of a congregation.[9] Shared beliefs were buttressed by education and by business and political alliances, forming a nationwide network: Hollands were linked by friendship and marriage to Wedgwoods, Darwins and Turners. Two black basalt vases gleamed in the parlour of Samuel Holland's farmhouse, a wedding gift from Josiah Wedgwood.

Samuel's farm was large, over three hundred acres, and he combined his work as a land-agent and farmer with that of a lay preacher, as Farmer Holman does in Gaskell's pastoral novella, *Cousin Phillis*. His son Swinton felt Samuel's life was 'smooth and easy, happy and contented, but not brilliant; he was fond of farming, improved his estate, was respected by all the neighbourhood and those who knew him, and was remarkable for his strict integrity', while his grandson Henry described him as 'an admirable example of old age rendered venerable by all the gentler qualities of human nature. He was the most perfect practical optimist I have ever known.'[10] He remembered him 'walking cheerfully over his fields, or tranquilly smoking his pipe in an arm-chair coeval with himself'. Samuel's wife, Anne Swinton, also came from a family linked to Knutsford for over two hundred years. She was far less placid than her husband, sharp with her servants and, like her granddaughter, 'a person of extraordinary energy and will'.[11] Elizabeth, their fourth daughter and sixth child, met her future husband in the early 1790s while he was working as a minister at Dob Lane Chapel in Failsworth, near Manchester, sixteen miles from her home. From then on she was swept from her settled life into his wanderings, physical and intellectual.

William Stevenson also came from an old Dissenting family, one tied not to the land but to the sea. His father is said to have been a naval post-captain at Berwick-upon-Tweed, and two of his brothers became naval officers: both died during active service in the Napoleonic wars. When he was eight, his mother, writing to her husband, told him that the children gave her no trouble, except William, who hardly ever attended school and was constantly running about the old city walls of Berwick which overlooked the sea.[12] He must have tamed this restlessness; in 1787, after leaving Berwick Grammar School, he began training for the Unitarian ministry at Daventry, moving with the Academy to Northampton and then to Manchester.

William was a student in stirring times: since 1688 the Unitarians had drunk an annual toast to 'civil and religious liberty the world over', and many of the current leaders greeted the French Revolution with enthusiasm. Mary Ann Galton (daughter of the chemist Samuel Galton, a friend of Joseph Priestley) recalled a typical scene when young Harry Priestley burst through the door, waving his hat and crying, 'Hurrah! Liberty, Reason, brotherly love for ever! Down with kingcraft and priestcraft. The Majesty of the People for ever! France is free, the Bastille taken.'[13] But by 1791 news of the Terror in France brought a backlash of opinion in England. Anyone suspected of republican sympathies was a target, and feelings reached such a height that a mob attacked the Meeting Houses in Birmingham, where Joseph Priestley was a minister, set fire to his house and wrecked his laboratory. Three years later he left England for good, to settle in America. In Manchester, as elsewhere, arguments flared. Radical societies were formed and in 1792 the *Manchester Herald* was launched, supporting Tom Paine's *Rights of Man*; the Unitarians of Manchester Academy and Cross Street Chapel were keenly involved. Amidst this turmoil William Stevenson graduated, at the age of twenty. He made a brief foray abroad, as tutor to an English student at Bruges, before the outbreak of war against France led to his return in 1793, when he took the post in Failsworth and met Elizabeth Holland. He preached at Failsworth and in the surrounding countryside on Sundays and, like many ministers on small salaries, taught during the week at the Manchester Academy as a classical tutor. By 1797, however, about to marry and begin a family, he had rebelled against both occupations. He had come to the conclusion that a paid ministry was wrong, and resigned. He had also decided that the study of classics was meaningless for a modern world, and that his teaching was therefore not only useless but positively harmful. In *Remarks on the Very Inferior Utility of Classical Learning* (1796) he declared that to spend seven years, as most boys did, on intensive Greek and Latin could only lead to 'an overgrown memory and a weak and puny judgement; a blind and bigoted attachment to authorities, names and antiquity; disputes merely verbal; and, consequently the continuance

9

of error and prejudice'.[14] The pamphlet, influenced by Priestley's writings on education, tells us much about Elizabeth's father. He writes boldly and clearly, briskly dismissing all counter-arguments, impatient with forms, hierarchies and traditions, and looks not to ancient learning but to new – modern languages, engineering, physics, chemistry, natural history. The word 'utility' in the title is significant, for the practical, reforming aspect of Unitarianism closely resembled the Utilitarian ideas developed by Jeremy Bentham in the last quarter of the eighteenth century. (In fact Bentham's most famous phrase, 'the greatest happiness of the greatest number', came from a passage in Priestley's writings.)

It is not surprising, then, that when William Stevenson looked for a new way of life to fit his ideals, he turned from the abstract to the practical and took up scientific farming.[15] After a six-month apprenticeship in East Lothian, he and Elizabeth took a farm at Saughton Mills, near Edinburgh. Here their first son, John, was born in 1798. William farmed with his friend James Cleghorn, a successful 'scientific farmer', who later edited the *Farmer's Journal*, for which William wrote.[16] The Stevensons could not match Cleghorn's success. William became ill with 'a severe leprous complaint, approaching almost to elephantiasis . . . which completely disfigured a countenance previously handsome'.[17] In 1801, after four years of poor harvests, they gave up the farm and moved to Edinburgh, where they let lodgings to students in Drummond Street.

Edinburgh was then alight with debate – political, philosophical, literary, scientific. Debating societies, such as the Academical and the Speculative, founded in 1796 and 1799, saw passionate clashes between older Tories and younger Whigs, like Henry Cockburn, Francis Horner, Henry Brougham and Francis Jeffrey. This circle, with Sydney Smith, founded the *Edinburgh Review* in 1802. 'The force of the shock was increased on each subsequent discharge,' wrote Jeffrey of the *Edinburgh*. 'Its talent, its spirit, its writing, its independence were all new.'[18] William joined in the vigorous, convivial life of the dining clubs and informal salons.[19] He coached at the university, worked on his *System of Land Surveying* (1805) and wrote reviews for the *Edinburgh*. In 1803 he became editor of the *Scots Magazine*, Edinburgh's only monthly until *Blackwood's*, in 1816; his contributors included the young Walter Scott, a lawyer in the city.[20]

The Edinburgh sojourn ended three years later when the possibility of a new adventure arose. The hot-tempered, clever Whig peer, James Maitland, 8th Earl of Lauderdale, newly appointed by Fox as governor-general of India, had admired William's articles and now asked him to become his private secretary. The Stevensons sailed south from Leith with all their belongings, but just as they arrived in London the East India Company blocked Lauderdale's appointment. William was left with no job, a wife and child to support and an expensive Mayfair address. Lauderdale came to the rescue, finding him a post as keeper of the records at the Treasury. Instead of travelling the world he came to rest in this quiet London backwater where he stayed until his death.

When the family moved to Chelsea, William's wanderlust faded. He could have moved on: one story suggests that he refused an offer from the tsar of a chair of technology at Kharkov.[21] On behalf of the new Board of Agriculture and Improvement, he toured Surrey (and, later, Dorset) examining crops, land and methods and interviewing farmers for his detailed, forthright and forward-looking *General View of the Agriculture of Surrey* (1809). Like William Hale White, author of *The Autobiography of Mark Rutherford*, a later radical whose principles barred him from becoming a minister, and who also finally became a clerk in the Admiralty, William worked steadily in the civil service, but poured his restless energy into a string of articles, pamphlets and books on subjects ranging from topography to naval history, all marked by clarity, energy and a strong, subtle understanding of economics and politics.

While William's activities are chronicled in the *Annual Obituary*, about his first wife there is silence. As so often – as with Charlotte Brontë, George Eliot, Elizabeth Barrett Browning – it is her father who dominates accounts of Gaskell's parents. We know about William, but have to speculate about her mother, Elizabeth. We can imagine, for example, that when she first married and was still near home, in many ways her life must have continued in familiar patterns; or that on the Scottish farm her childhood experience would have proved useful, although William's experimental ideas were very different from her father's traditional ways. But we cannot know. Certainly the failure of the farm was a hard blow, Edinburgh was an unfamiliar city and, to add to loneliness and struggle, Elizabeth was almost always pregnant. In the space of thirteen years she had eight children, of whom only the first and last, John and Elizabeth, survived.

For most of her married life she was far from her Holland relations, although by 1808, in London, one of her family was near. Her younger brother Swinton had travelled widely abroad in his youth and had settled in Trieste, where he was briefly imprisoned during the Franco-Austrian war. On his return he became a merchant in Liverpool and then moved into banking in London (in 1814 he would become a partner in Baring Brothers). Swinton was now living in the Unitarian heartlands of Newington Green and Hackney, but his sister was not to enjoy his company for long. She was forty when her last child was born and she never fully recovered. In the following summer the Stevensons moved to a larger house nearby, 3 Beaufort Row, but within a few months she was gravely ill. When her condition worsened, Swinton wrote to Knutsford and their sister, Hannah Lumb, came down to nurse her. Hannah was there when Elizabeth Stevenson died, on 29 October 1811.

Hannah, Aunt Lumb, 'my more than mother', was to be the central figure in Elizabeth Gaskell's early years. Her life had its own tragedies; soon after marrying a wealthy Yorkshireman from Wakefield she 'discovered that he was insane, and fled back to Knutsford, her old home'.[22] As if this were not hard enough, her daughter, Mary Anne (sometimes called Marianne), had been a cripple since early childhood after jumping from her nurse's arms out of a window in excitement when she saw her mother coming towards the house. Mary Anne was now twenty, and it was from her that the suggestion came to take baby Elizabeth to Cheshire. She was loving, she had no occupation and she had money, or at least the immediate prospect of it, for when her father died, he had made her his heir, providing an allowance until she came into full inheritance at twenty-one. The day after she heard the news she wrote to her mother: 'Poor little Elizabeth! What will become of her? She has almost been the constant subject of my thoughts ever since – and it is about her I have taken up my Pen, to write to you. Do you not think she could come to us?'[23]

She explains how she could care for Elizabeth herself, brushing aside all objections:

'I know you will remind me of the *time and attention* such a charge will oblige me to sacrifice. I know it (for I have, I think, thought of everything); but can I not rise early in a morning, and by giving up some of my more trifling employments, such as practising for my own amusement only, working fancy-work, and by giving over keeping plants, surely I may find time for all that is needful.'

She had indeed thought of everything. She had carefully measured the space between her bed and the door. 'I find there is ample room for a pretty *large* Crib,' she wrote, but if her mother thought it was too crowded, or would be disturbed, she would take the baby 'up into the Garret and sleep there'. She could even make her clothes, which, she added persuasively, 'will teach me about contriving and planning, which is what I am least acquainted with of anything in the work-line'.

William Stevenson welcomed the idea and shortly afterwards a neighbour, Mrs Whittington, took Elizabeth to Cheshire. From now on, despite his evident concern for her, her living father was almost as absent from her early childhood as her dead mother.

So, at the age of thirteen months – a sturdy infant with brown curly hair and blue eyes, who had walked from the age of ten months – Elizabeth, soon to be known as Lily, came to Knutsford, the place she was to re-create nearly forty years later as Cranford. Sadly, Mary Anne, who so wanted to care for the baby, died the following spring. She had never been strong and may have been consumptive, for she is said to have died of 'spasms', a common description of the final tubercular agony. Her death came in Halifax, where she went with her mother to see the Lumbs' solicitors about her will, planning to divide her money between her mother and Elizabeth. She died before her wishes could be carried out: Aunt Lumb was left to tend for her new charge on her own small income.[24]

Her house stood slightly apart from the main town of Knutsford, opposite the broad triangular heath which stretched away into the countryside around. Knutsford races were held on the heath from the seventeenth century until 1873, and in Elizabeth's childhood a fair was held in race week, with 'wild beasts and beautiful birds'. Here too the local people kept their cows, horses and flocks of geese. (The ladies of *Cranford*, however genteel, were 'quite sufficient', for 'rushing out at the geese that occasionally venture into the gardens if the gates are left open'.) The Heath, now named Heathwaite, was a Queen Anne house of red brick with fine oak-panelled rooms. It had a square of garden in front and its drawing-room windows at the back looked out over lawns surrounded by flower-beds and shaded by a huge cedar, with vegetables, fruit trees, poultry and a paddock with two cows and a pony beyond.

After Mary Anne died the youngest Holland sister, Abigail, who had been living with her brother Sam in Liverpool and teaching his children, joined the household.[25] The Heath was therefore a house of single women, but this was a source of strength rather than deprivation. While Abigail was known for her flaring temper, Hannah was kindly and sociable. Two years before little Lily arrived a young neighbour and relative by marriage, Sarah Whittaker, told her brother about the local parties, including Mrs Lumb's, where 'we are sure of having a pleasant evening where all are unconstrained & merry, which is I think pleasanter than formal tea & Card parties, which are in general very *Stupide*'. And in 1811 she declared that they had been uncommonly gay in Knutsford that winter with balls and suppers and a '*Concert*' at the Lumbs', 'and Danced about Ten or Twelve couples and the Evening finished with a little spouting from some Young *Ladies*'.[26]

Cranford ladies, we are told, were sufficient not only for chasing geese and holding card parties but for 'obtaining clear and correct knowledge of everybody's affairs in the parish' and for 'kindness (somewhat dictatorial) to the poor'. In 'The Last Generation in England', a factual article which Elizabeth wrote in 1849, this well-meaning interest in the parish verges on downright interference. Remembering the town where she grew up, Elizabeth writes: 'Eleven widows of respectability at one time kept house there; besides spinsters innumerable.'

'You may imagine the subjects of conversation amongst these ladies; cards, servants, relations, pedigrees, and last and best, much mutual interest about the poor of the town, to whom they were one and all benefactresses; cooking, sewing for, advising, doctoring, doing everything but educating them.'[27]

Even at the end of Hannah Lumb's life, when she was seriously ill, she fretted about others, as Elizabeth tenderly recorded in a letter to Eliza Gaskell, her future sister-in-law. Although it took Aunt Lumb five minutes to gasp out the sentence, she insisted that a bottle of scent be dispatched to Eliza's sick mother. (Elizabeth added, more realistically: 'I fear the scent wd not be worth the carriage or I would get it.') Another day, although apparently asleep, she picked up bedside whispers of a local woman who had lost her baby, and was soon heard asking the nurse what was 'good to assuage the milk'.

Hannah's busyness and good deeds were part of the Holland tradition. In Cheshire Elizabeth found herself one of a vast, intricate, extended family, whose centre was the farm at Sandlebridge where old Samuel and Anne Holland lived. Sarah Whittaker told her brother about this too:

'their common sitting parlour is a delightful old fashioned room; a stone floor, half of which near the fire is carpeted; a nice large old fashioned chimney piece, with a monstrous grate always well heaped up with Coal; and a "goody Cupboard", always well stocked with mince pies, buns & tarts, pleased me much. We had a fire in our bedroom night & day, which we took care to get up twice in the night to stir.'[28]

Anne died when Lily was four and Samuel two years later, but their farm remained in the family. Its smithy and mill (now converted into houses) still shelter in their hidden valley by the brook, although the old three-storeyed Colthurst House – always known as Sandlebridge, the name of the village – was demolished in the 1960s. It was as familiar to Elizabeth as her own home, and remained a cherished retreat when she was older and had children of her own. There were several large bedrooms with room for three or four beds in each, and she often stayed there with her cousins. She loved its neat parlours, oak beams and flagged passages, huge loft, and casement windows and walls overrun with roses and honeysuckle. She was proud of the house and of its past. In 1849 she told Geraldine Jewsbury the story of the young Robert Clive (who had Holland relations) jumping across the gap between the great stone balls on the entrance gate: 'Of course this made him into a hero before I knew there was such a place as India.' This anecdote, like so much of her fiction, makes the past intimate, giving us a sense of the accessibility, almost the continuing presence of eighteenth-century lives.

It would be wrong, however, to think of this childhood as a rural idyll, with no wider outlook than 'a quaint Cheshire village'.[29] Knutsford had a population of over three thousand. It was the home of one of the two MPs for Cheshire, Sir William Egerton, and was the base for the Quarter Sessions. When Elizabeth was eight, the imposing classical Sessions House was begun, and later a gaol was built for seven hundred prisoners. The town's prosperous past still shows in its two main streets, Princess Street and King Street ('Top Street and Bottom Street'), with their houses of mellow Georgian brick. These streets run parallel along a gentle hill sloping down to a marshy valley known as 'the moor', where Tatton Mere peters out among tall reed beds, and they are linked by cobbled alleys whose names recall their past – Red Cow Yard, Slater's Yard, Silkmill Street. By 1820 the silk mill had failed, but there were still five small cotton mills. Knutsford was far from sleepy. It had its cottages with neat front gardens, but it also had grand country houses: Tabley House, Toft Hall, Booths Hall and Tatton Park, the home of the Egertons, At the back of the Royal George, where the Royal Mail, the Bang Up and the Umpire drew up in the paved yard, were fine Assembly Rooms built by joint subscription of all the county families, with chandeliers, moulded ceilings and Adam fireplaces. The town was thriving and the Holland family were among its leading citizens.

The whole 'Holland clan', as their friends called them, played a part in Elizabeth's early years. Her uncle Peter Holland, an irascible, humorous man, who limped from a leg injured in a fall from a gig, was the local doctor. He lived in Church House at the other end of town and when Elizabeth was small, she travelled in his dog-cart on his rounds in the country practice – much as George Eliot, nine years younger, was to travel with her land-agent father. His practice flourished, and his apprentices (like those of Mr Gibson in *Wives and Daughters*) lodged in Church House with his large family. His first wife, Mary Willetts, who died in 1803, was a niece of Josiah Wedgwood, and Peter, linked to the wider Unitarian network, was an influential figure, more involved with political and mercantile life than the term 'local doctor' implies. He cared for the apprentices at the Gregs' model cotton mill, Styal Mill, a few miles away, but as surgeon to the Cheshire Yeomanry he is thought to have been present when the Manchester workers, with their wives and children, were cut down by the troops at Peterloo in 1819. This terrible day roused outrage in members of the Hollands' circle, like his sister-in-law Mrs Sarah Whittaker, who saw the magistrates as 'abettors of the Ferocious Yeomanry in their brutal attack upon a quiet & orderly assembly' (though she was equally worried that moderate reformers might now be confused with militants).[30]

Peter was a Radical, whose forthright views (and downright

rudeness) often caused family storms. One of his wife's aunts had bitter memories of his *'odious sneering'* at people who could not answer back. Although she saw that he loved his wife, Mary – *'there* he *shone'* – she felt sorry for his children. She remembered him ordering his daughter Bessy to read Hume, a 'wretched man' in her Anglican view: 'his immorality is dreadful, as well as his creed. Dr Holland I fancy from what I saw of him, has profitted by his pupillage.' On one occasion, in 1821, his eldest son, Henry, was called in 'to give his father the advice he often stands in need of in matters of *civility* & temper &c'.[31]

Cousin Henry was renowned for his smooth 'civility' and his career shows just how high provincial Unitarians could rise (usually dropping their Dissenting faith on the way). A medical student in Edinburgh when Elizabeth came to Knutsford, he was Princess Caroline's doctor and gave evidence for her at her trial, and eventually became Physician in Ordinary to Queen Victoria; he was knighted in 1857. His *Recollections* drop names like confetti.[32] He was a terrible snob and compulsive traveller: 'Dr Holland *has* been at Moscow since you saw him, & *is* at Knutsford on his way to Algeria,' Elizabeth wrote laconically in 1852. In the 1820s and 1830s Henry really was at the centre of radical and intellectual circles. His close friends included politicians like Brougham, writers like Walter Scott and Joanna Baillie, and especially scientists such as Humphry Davy, Joseph Banks, John Herschel and Mary Somerville. He himself was made a fellow of the Royal Society in 1816. Henry was married twice – his second wife was Saba, Sydney Smith's daughter – but at various times his sisters Bessy and Mary kept house for him in London. Through him Mary became friends with Maria Edgeworth, whom Henry had met in Ireland in 1809. Maria visited Knutsford in 1813 and the two women exchanged frequent letters until her death in 1849 – including a long letter from Maria about *Mary Barton.*

The Church House family, therefore, were far from narrowly provincial in outlook. Nor were they solemnly intellectual, to judge by the account given by Catherine Whittaker, another of Peter Holland's sisters-in-law, of Mary's birthday party, shortly after Henry returned from an expedition to Iceland in 1810:

'We had a Lottery for prizes of Bags, pincushions, little Memorandum books – everyone had something; Bessy was dressed in a suit of clothes, as it may be called, of Icelandic fashion – consisting of a head-dress, neck-collar, jacket, Apron & gloves, which Henry brought over with him, & she look'd a very outlandish figure. After tea we had a famous game of romps, in which Mrs Holland, Mrs Sharpe, & Mr Sam Holland join'd, with as much activity and spirit as any of the young ones – the game was blind man's Buff, & when ever the blinded one cou'd catch Mrs Sharpe, there was great delight, & hints were given when she was near. If Sarah had been there, she wou'd have enjoyed it very much, altho' she wou'd have betray'd herself frequently, by wishing to stifle a bursting laugh.'[33]

As young women Mary was 'clever' (at the age of fifty-four Elizabeth still smarted when snubbed by her), Bessy was 'pleasing' and 'amiable', while their sister Lucy was 'rather a curiosity, a jumble of untrained ideas, of cleverness in some things, & stupidity in others, no tact, & a simplicity in speaking whatever she thinks, that is very amusing; her perfect good temper makes her take well the laughter, which it is impossible to restrain at her odd speeches, without wishing to make her ridiculous'.[34]

Mary and Lucy have been cited as originals for Deborah and Matty Jenkyns in *Cranford* and, though the point is debatable since they were only eighteen and ten years older than Elizabeth, these older cousins must have seemed more like young aunts and uncles than cousins. Charles and Susan, on the other hand, the children of Peter's second marriage to Mary Whittaker, were nearer her own age. So were the children of her other uncles, Swinton, the London banker, and Samuel, a Liverpool merchant and owner of slate quarries in North Wales. Both these brothers had a talent for making money (though Sam had an equal talent for losing it). They were a contrasting pair: Sam speculative and jovial, Swinton cautious and dour 'with a reputation for diligence and rock-like probity'. When Swinton obtained a place with Baring Brothers in December 1814, he wrote in his diary: 'Omnipotent ruler of the Universe, may I be grateful to Thee, for this mark of Thy goodness in elevating my situation in life' (the 'progressive' Unitarian faith could dovetail very neatly with the aims of the man on the make).[35] Both these uncles, gentleman capitalists in very different ways, had large and lively families, and as the years passed Lily's cousins would become her precious friends.

We have to search hard to see the small Elizabeth Stevenson in the midst of this clan. We can imagine her, perhaps, at two, gazing from the window at the race ground opposite, where 'one of the finest Bonfires that ever has been' blazed away and an effigy of Old Boney was committed to the flames amid wild 'Huzzas', in celebration of Wellington's Peninsular victories. Or at three, wrapped up well in weeks of frost and snow so terrible 'as never was remembered except by those who happen to be old enough to remember the *great frost*'. We catch a glimpse of her at five, when she and little Edmund Sharpe were being 'drawn about by a servant girl of Mr Hollands in a very nice little Carriage with four wheels, which we all thought it imposs-ible cou'd be turned over, by which all the Children by turns have been drawn hundreds of times – it was in Mr Holland's garden, & we conclude that as he was running very fast, she turn'd the corner so very quick as to get the front wheel under the Carriage, & so overset it'. (Poor Edmund broke his arm, but Mrs Lumb's little niece emerged unscathed.)[36] Her life merged with that of the family: she played with her dolls, went on picnics and walks in summer, and in winter slid with the girls down the sand-pits in the snow (while the boys skated on pools at the bottom). She went to the family parties, where the children danced 'Roger de Coverley' and the older girls were 'gay as larks, with Quadrilles, Concerts and Beaux'.

Elizabeth was loved and cared for and never without friends as she grew up within these great clusters of aunts, uncles, cousins and second cousins, embracing almost three generations at once. Yet in a corner of her mind she felt alone. Knutsford was full of reminders of the mother she had hardly known. The intensity of her yearning still echoes in a letter she wrote when she was nearly forty to the Unitarian minister George Hope, who had sent some old correspondence:

'I will not let an hour pass, my dear sir, without acknowledging your kindness in sending me my dear mother's letters, the only relics of her that I have, and of more value to me than I can express, for I have so often longed for some little thing that had once been hers or touched by her. I think no one but one so unfortunate as to be early motherless can enter into the craving one has after the lost mother . . . I have been brought up away from all those who knew my parents, and therefore those who come to me with a remembrance of them as an introduction seem to have a holy claim on my regard.' (L796–7)

19

William Stevenson had married again when Elizabeth was four. His new wife, Catherine Thomson, was the sister of Dr Anthony Todd Thomson, the doctor who had attended her birth and her mother's death. The daughter of a colonial official (at one time Postmaster in Savannah, Georgia), Catherine seems to have felt superior to her husband and to have taken little interest in his daughter, especially after her own children, William and Catherine, were born in 1815 and 1816. Elizabeth did pay them quite long visits, sometimes with her Stevenson cousins. In a letter of 1820, when she is ten, her brother, John, writes that their stepmother 'has been proposing that if you can manage to come up this summer she will ask your cousin Isabella to come up to meet you, and my father will take you down in the Autumn'.[37] But to a small girl the London streets were strange after the leafy lanes and open heaths of Knutsford. The loneliness of a similar country child among city relatives is felt in *North and South*, when Margaret Hale looks back on her arrival at her aunt's house in Harley Street:

'She remembered the dark, dim look of the London nursery, presided over by an austere and ceremonious nurse, who was terribly particular about clean hands and torn frocks. She recollected the first tea up there – separate from her father and aunt, who were dining somewhere down below, an infinite depth of stairs . . . Oh! well did the tall stately girl of eighteen remember the tears shed with such wild passion of grief by the little girl of nine, as she hid her face under the bed-clothes in that first night.' (Ch. 1)

Although Elizabeth returned to Beaufort Row several times over the next few years, she was always wretched there, as she told Mary Howitt many years later:

'Long ago I lived in Chelsea occasionally with my father and stepmother, and *very, very* unhappy I used to be; and if it had not been for the beautiful, grand river, which was an inexplicable comfort to me, and a family of the name of Kennett, I think my child's heart would have broken.' (L797–8)

Of the London family only John, twelve years her senior, seemed to care for her deeply and she saw him only rarely, although in Knutsford he was fondly welcomed by Aunt Lumb and even won the heart of

Aunt Ab. John was lively, warm-hearted and romantic, thrilled when
an aunt in Berwick gave him his grandfather's sword and his uncle
Robert's pistols, and full of pride when he received the Freedom of the
City of Berwick, at the age of twenty-one. He had always wanted to go
to sea like his Stevenson uncles and in 1821, when his sister was
twelve, he left on his first voyage, as a 'free mariner' on the private
vessels working the India route.

Elizabeth went to London to see him sail. They wrote often and met
on his shore leaves. But although John remained a vital figure in her
imagination, the chief memory she passed on to her daughters was of
this first momentous parting. 'When I was about ten years old,' wrote
Marianne Gaskell, 'my mother told me that she could only just
remember her brother [and] that he went to sea. I think she said that
when she was quite a young girl, that she remembered coming up on a
visit to her father from Knutsford to wish her brother goodbye.'[38]

Chelsea seemed even gloomier after John left. Catherine Stevenson
found her stepdaughter impulsive and outspoken – not at all her model
of a feminine young lady. The children, now aged five and six, were
too young to be friends and she never did become close to them,
referring years later to 'my little miss of a $\frac{1}{2}$ sister'. Her isolation was
intensified because it was so hard to build any real relationship with
her father. William was too preoccupied with his work to spare much
time and, despite the clear mind and direct approach he reveals in his
writing, he seems to have lacked the spontaneous warmth she needed
in these early years. A rare picture of him around this time is, I believe,
given in the work of his sister-in-law Katherine, the wife of Dr
Anthony Thomson.

Katherine wrote novels and historical biographies, in her own name
and under the pseudonym Grace Wharton, and among the portraits in
her *Recollections of Literary Characters* is one of John Galt, who lived
in Lindsey Row and whom she met, she says, just round the corner in
Beaufort Row, in the house of his friend, 'a clerk in the Record Office'.
The date would be 1820 or early 1821 (the time of her marriage to Dr
Thomson) as Galt was then writing *The Ayrshire Legatees*. In a letter
of 1820 John told his aunts that the Galts had recently moved in next
door and 'their children being about the age of William form nice
playfellows for him'.[39]

The description of Galt's unnamed friend fits William senior well,
although it is hardly flattering. The Record Office clerk is cultivated

but taciturn, receiving Galt's wild stories with 'a philosophic incredulity, never expressed, but pictured in a face to which nature lent no charm' (William was disfigured by his illness in Scotland). He is a good listener, one 'who rarely grunted an approval, yet was too canny to differ openly', and he also displays a touch of eccentricity, or perhaps just austerity. Katherine describes him entering the drawing-room after his evening stroll: 'He was the last wearer of the willow hat; a blessed but not a becoming invention: on the same principle a gambroon coat was assumed in summer. He neither smoked, nor talked, nor played at cards.' Yet he was, she acknowledged, a man of culture and learning, 'a literary receptacle of knowledge, a man brimful of acquirement, rich in quality as the first champagne, but bottled and collared up with much care. He was a specimen of the pure literary man of the olden time.'[40]

This portrait bears a suggestive likeness to one aspect (but one only) of Mr Gibson, in *Wives and Daughters*, who bottles up his feelings after his second marriage so that his manner grows 'dry and sarcastic' and he becomes 'hard and occasionally bitter in his speeches and his ways'. Gaskell makes wryly devastating comedy out of the new Mrs Gibson's trivial snobbery and obtuseness. Less comically, she traces their effect on Mr Gibson's good nature. Watching, his daughter Molly struggles with love for her father and despair at the way his marriage has taken him from her. Of course, like the picture of Margaret Hale's loneliness in *North and South*, this is fiction not autobiography, imagined not remembered. The most one can safely say is that Molly's keen awareness of the undercurrents shows that Gaskell well understood the buried feelings of a young girl in such a household.

It is particularly tempting to look to the fiction because Elizabeth so rarely wrote of her childhood directly. Her letters to George Hope and Mary Howitt are exceptional. Is this silence significant, a ban on the tongue, a withholding of the mind? Or is it simply an accident of what survives? Did she, perhaps, write about her early years in the many letters which her daughters burnt after her death? Did her own mother's letters, so precious to her, also perish in that blaze? Was she more open in speech than on paper?

We may never know. But her silence did not stem from indifference. Her novels and stories show how much she remembered and how deeply she felt. On the simplest level, she draws on memories of her childhood and youth in Knutsford, of its characters, buildings, stories and scandals, and uses them, especially in *Cranford*, to create a world at once humdrum and exceedingly strange, real and surreal. Her eye for the bizarre was as sharp as it was for the mundane, and many of *Cranford*'s most peculiar stories are true. An old woman told Henry Green (Unitarian minister in Knutsford from 1827 and a close personal friend of Elizabeth in later life) that she immediately recognized the cow which fell into a lime-pit and was given a flannel waistcoat and drawers: the name of the cow's owner, Miss Harker, is flimsily disguised as Miss Betty Barker.[41]

Some of the oddest stories were left out, like the carriage full of dogs, who were driven out in style, each dressed in the male or female fashion of the day, each 'with a pair of house-shoes, for which his carriage boots were changed on his return'.[42] As Gaskell explained to John Ruskin when he wrote to say how much his mother enjoyed the book, fact was really sometimes too ridiculous to make good fiction. The truth would stretch a reader's credulity. For example, she told him, two old ladies had a niece who made a grand marriage (by Knutsford standards), so when the couple came to visit, they bought a new dining-room carpet in their honour. The visitors' first meal was a little disconcerting:

'All dinner time they had noticed that the neat maid servant had performed a sort of "pas-de-basque", hopping & sliding with more grace than security to the dishes she held. When she had left the room, one lady said to the other: "Sister! I think she'll do!" "Yes", said the other, "she managed very nicely!" ' (L748)

The explanation, given as if the most natural thing in the world, was that the servant was new and the carpet was new, 'with white spots or spaces on it, and they had been teaching this girl to vault or jump gracefully over these white places, lest her feet might dirty them!'

Cranford, however, is about interior as well as exterior worlds and is far from just a series of comic anecdotes. Elizabeth Gaskell was not formed as a novelist simply by what she saw and heard. Growing up in Knutsford, she was part of a small world yet in touch with a wider one, through her father and through the far-flung Unitarian web. From her earliest years she absorbed a set of teachings and beliefs: in tolerance, in justice, in the equal worth of all people rich and poor, in the force of conscience and in the importance of searching for the truth and bearing witness to what she found.

Hannah Lumb, in true Unitarian (and Holland) style, taught Elizabeth that kindness and nurture belonged not only in the family, but should be extended to the world at large. Moreover she could be 'more than mother' because – although Peter Holland was head of the family – in their actual household there was no husband or father whose needs must be met, whose whims obeyed. However much Gaskell may poke fun at the women of Cranford, remembering the women of Knutsford, her opening lines are not altogether a joke:

'In the first place, Cranford is in possession of the Amazons; all the holders of houses, above a certain rent, are women. If a married couple come to settle in the town, somehow the gentleman disappears; he is either fairly frightened to death by being the only man in the Cranford evening parties, or he is accounted for by being with his regiment, his ship, or closely engaged in business all the week in the great neighbouring commercial town of Drumble, distant only twenty miles on a railroad. In short, whatever does become of the gentlemen, they are not at Cranford.' (Ch. 1)

Male professions are explanations for an absence. Although men may *seem* to inhabit a sphere of movement and action while women sit still and gossip, this is to look at the appearance, not the reality. Elizabeth Gaskell, observing the world more closely, never made such crude distinctions. The lives of such women were far from sheltered. Widows and spinsters had to be self-reliant and in the unstable 1820s they were particularly vulnerable. When Sam Holland's business faltered, his oldest daughters were busily 'fitting themselves out for situations as governesses', and one Whittaker relation gave a moving account of the collapse of Worswicks Bank in Lancaster, whose most distressing aspect was 'the number of *females*, who have lost their *all*, and are left utterly destitute, without the means of obtaining support'.[43]

Gaskell's fiction is full of single, self-sufficient women, creating the shape of their own lives, earning their living often, at the same time, caring for adopted children. In her short story 'The Grey Woman' two women even act as a couple, one taking the role of 'husband' and father to the child. Sometimes adoption is by choice, sometimes by chance: thus Alice in *Mary Barton* takes in her brother's child, while in 'Lizzie Leigh' Susan Palmer loves and tends a baby that is simply thrust into her arms by a weeping woman in the street. Often, however, their act helps to heal the loneliness of the present and the miseries of the past, as it does for Miss Galindo in *My Lady Ludlow*, when she adopts the daughter of her early suitor.

Gaskell is realistic about the cost of choosing to be mother to another's child. She has no illusions about the sweetness and light of childhood and she confronts the most difficult choice imaginable in the story 'Half a Lifetime Ago', where Susan Dixon's decision to keep her idiot brother at home destroys her chances of marriage. Susan's ultimate consolation is not only the knowledge that she was right, and that she kept faith with her dead mother and her brother, but the realization that she can extend this caring to strangers. At the end she takes in the widow and children of the man who rejected her to 'fill up the haunted hearth with living forms who should banish the ghosts'.

Perhaps, for Aunt Lumb, Elizabeth herself banished the ghost, though not the memory, of Mary Anne. Perhaps Aunt Lumb in turn kept at bay some of the pain of Elizabeth's loss of her mother, and estrangement from her father. Elizabeth called Knutsford her home, and also 'her dear *adopted native* town'. Adoption turns loss into gain, and one of the most noticeable of all the patterns which pervade her fiction is the pattern of the negative which turns out to be a positive. She almost never writes about 'normal' families, or at least about the standard version, with paterfamilias, loving mother, blossoming children.[44] For Gaskell such a norm may never have existed, or not in the world she knew well. The person dearest to her was a single woman, while many of her cousins, her closest friends, had either lost their mothers or were the children of second marriages. For Mary Barton, Ruth and Molly Gibson she could invent an idyllic maternal relationship of tenderness and understanding, but this almost always, significantly, takes place before the real stories begin and in nearly all her novels the heroine is either the only child of one parent (usually the father) or an orphan. Those 'normal' families who live happily together at the start of a novel – the Robsons in *Sylvia's Lovers*, the Hales in *North and South*, the Hamleys in *Wives and Daughters* – are, as the story develops, torn apart, broken by death and disaster.

And over and over again, within these broken families, Gaskell writes of women who find that in the end they must rely on their own strength, not the illusory strength of father or husband. They have to learn to step out from the shadow and speak and act for themselves, according to their conscience: 'Father I will speak,' says Jemima Bradshaw in *Ruth*. 'I will not keep silence.'

The shape of her childhood helped to structure Elizabeth Gaskell's imagination and art. A lover of fairy stories, old rhymes and local legends, which lie embedded like fossils in the layers of her fiction, she had her own folk-tale pattern: the lost mother; the absent father; the stepmother who rejects her; the good woman who takes her in; and the sailor brother, the wandering prince who may never return. She belonged to two places, two families – Cheshire and London, Holland and Stevenson – and her principal subject was to be the struggle of opposing worlds, dependent yet in conflict: country and city, North and South, masters and workers, men and women, present and past. She was fully a part of the 'little, clean, kindly country town' where she grew up, and one of the joys of returning to Knutsford after she was married was simply that she 'knew everybody'. Yet beneath the security lay an awareness of loss, and this too finds a place in her work in the dead or absent figures who haunt the background of scenes filled with the immediacy of daily life. Beyond those city streets and rural farms, so solidly envisioned, lie foreign lands and distant shores, the flow of powerful rivers and the thunder of the dangerous, ever rolling sea.

[2]

Books and the World

Even as a child Elizabeth was fascinated by magic and mystery. She read early. She learnt poetry by heart. She liked fairy tales, proverbs and old folk stories. She also read the didactic children's books of the day, like Thomas Day's *Sandford and Merton* (1783–9), a blend of Rousseau and liberal morality, and Mrs Trimmer's *Fabulous Histories or the History of the Robins* (1786), warning against cruelty to animals, constantly reprinted until the 1870s.[1] And she certainly knew Anna Laetitia Barbauld's famous *Lessons for Children* (1780), and the *Hymns in Prose for Children* (1781), which were translated into five languages. Harriet Martineau too learnt them by heart at the age of seven 'and there were parts of them which I dearly loved, but other parts made me shiver with awe'.[2]

These were books Elizabeth's aunts themselves had read as girls. Until she was eleven she was largely taught at home by Hannah and Abigail and the pattern of her early schooling repeated their own. Unitarians felt strongly that girls, as well as boys, should be educated and should be encouraged to make their own moral judgements at an early age. They favoured a child-oriented teaching, like that advised by Maria Edgeworth and her father Richard in their *Practical Education* (1795), which opposed 'tasks' and suggested that 'by kind patience, and well timed, distinct, and above all, by short lessons, a young child may be initiated in the mysteries of learning, and in the first principles of knowledge without fatigue, or punishment, or tears'.[3]

Both the Edgeworths and Anna Barbauld, an equally influential educationalist, were part of Henry Holland's London circle. In 1874 when Mary Sibylla Holland came to visit her aunts, the now elderly Mary and Lucy, she told her sister:

'This evening we are to read old letters – Edgeworth's, Barbauld's, Aitken's, Darwin's, Wedgewood's, all that old set. Sir Henry Holland always figures as the fashionable young man in the vortex of London society. Miss Edgeworth's letters are charming, and there are drawers full of them.'[4]

Elizabeth's early education, though influenced by these reformers, was conventional in content, and domestic in style – like that described in her story 'My French Master', whose narrator recalls:

'My mother undertook the greater part of our education. We helped her in her household cares during part of the morning: then came an old fashioned routine of lessons, such as she herself had learnt when a girl – Goldsmith's "History of England", Rollin's "Ancient History", Lindley Murray's Grammar, and plenty of sewing and stitching.'

This story is set twenty years earlier than Elizabeth's own childhood, but the works it mentions remained standard fare: she is deliberately listing books which all her contemporaries would recognize and smile at. Every schoolroom had the four substantial, vivid and enjoyable volumes of Goldsmith's *History of England* (Jane Austen used it and it was still a staple of girls' education as late as the 1860s). The Rollin was also constantly in use – when the father of Emily Davies (founder of Girton College) banned Scott's novels from his house, he restricted the family's reading aloud to 'such improving works as Rollin's *Ancient History* and *Paradise Lost*'. The grammar too was equally venerable; good teachers like Mrs Garth in *Middlemarch* 'in a general wreck of society would have tried to hold their Lindley Murray's above the waves'.[5] Such were the 'old books' used by her aunt. She did have other teachers. M. Chalabré, the central figure in 'My French Master', an émigré from revolutionary France, was partly based on Knutsford's own M. Rogier, who gave extremely popular dancing classes in the Assembly Rooms and *may* have taught Elizabeth French.

French émigrés were a noticeable group, even in the provinces, and many lived by teaching. Gaskell's heroine praises M. Chalabré's patience and 'the untiring gentleness with which he made our stubborn English tongues pronounce, and mis-pronounce certain words'. Rogier was remembered more as a colourful local character than as a teacher: a good raconteur, a keen amateur botanist and a model of style, who amused the neighbourhood by the agility with which he kept his highly polished boots out of the Knutsford mud. He had been in the town for years and had even taught William Pitt the Younger when he stayed with Cholmondely relatives in Knutsford (allegedly declaring 'there was nothing whatever in Pitt's dancing to indicate what a great man he would become').[6]

Whether Rogier was the teacher or not, 'My French Master' does give an impression of classes at the Heath:

'Our life was passed as much out-of-doors as in-doors, both winter and summer – we seemed to have our French lessons more frequently in the garden than in the house; for there was a sort of arbour on the lawn near the drawing-room window, to which we always found it easy to carry a table and chairs, and all the rest of the lesson paraphernalia, if my mother did not prohibit a lesson *al fresco*.'

This relaxed approach was like that recommended by Erasmus Darwin, who had stressed pleasant surroundings, fresh air and exercise as antidotes to study, in his *Plan for the Conduct of Female Education in Boarding Schools* in 1788. Such views (plus a pretty patronizing view of women's intellect) are felt in the story when the father bursts in while the mother is teaching:

' "It was a shame to coop such things up in a house", he would say, "when every other young thing was frolicking in the sunshine. Grammar! – what was that but the art of arranging words? – and he never knew a woman but could do that fast enough. Geography! – he would undertake to teach us more geography in one winter evening, telling us of the countries where he had been, with just a map before him, than we could learn in ten years with that stupid book, all full of hard words." '

(When she grew up, Elizabeth always found stories of travel spellbinding – but she never could cope with geography.)

Aunt Lumb believed in handing on proven knowledge: Knutsford Library has a well-thumbed copy of *The Monitor, or a Collection of Precepts, Observations etc*, published in 1804, fondly inscribed to Elizabeth 'from her affectionate aunt Hannah Lumb, Sept. the 29th, 1821' – her eleventh birthday. Beneath the inscription are the pencilled ghosts of another, suggesting the little book had already done service to other relations. The sixty precepts, many firmly marked in the margins, are earnestly divided into sections: Principle, Virtue, Truth,

Fortitude, Social Affections, Manners, Prudence, Religion, with Happiness last of all. The same values were instilled at Sunday school at the beautiful, peaceful Brook Street Chapel at the far end of town. Built of weathered red brick, one of the oldest Nonconformist chapels in the district, it was established in 1689, the year of the Toleration Act, which allowed Dissenters from the Anglican Church to gather for worship and erect their own meeting houses. Elizabeth would describe Brook Street in *Ruth* as Thurstan Benson's chapel, a small building sheltering in a hidden part of town, looking more like a cottage than a church, with outside staircases at each corner where lookouts were posted in the early days of persecution. Beneath its uneven roof old oak pews formed three sides of a square round the minister's raised pulpit. Its windows, clear now, were covered in ivy 'filled with nesting birds', creating a green gloom inside.

The ways of Brook Street, like those of the Heath and Sandlebridge, looked to the past. Elizabeth had an old-fashioned upbringing, as she explained to her publisher George Smith in 1859, when he sent her a new edition of *The Fool of Quality*, Henry Brooke's Rousseau-esque novel, first published in the 1760s. 'I was brought up by old uncles and aunts, who had all old books,' she told Smith, 'and very few new ones; and I used to delight in *The Fool of Quality*, and have hardly read it since.'[7] But Knutsford was not cut off from new ideas. The women of her family, like the men, read the reviews, lent each other new novels and discussed their reading knowledgeably and in detail. Nor were their interests purely literary, to judge from a letter of Catherine Whittaker in 1814:

'We have in Knutsford a Mr Dalton who is giving a course of Lectures on Mechanics, Hydrostatics, Hydraulica and Optics – of the nine, we have already had four with which we have been much pleased – he is but an indifferent Orator, but his Apparatus & Models are very good.'[8]

John Dalton, the famous scientist, was only one of many such lecturers who toured the country districts during these years.

Different strands mingled in Elizabeth's upbringing. On the one hand she was surrounded by busy, intelligent women, who may have loved gossip and matchmaking, and quibbled over their card-games, but who never felt confined to the domestic sphere. They spoke their minds freely – to men as much as to other women. They held strong opinions of their own on such issues as reform, or Catholic emancipation. They were far from sheltered. They travelled to Liverpool, Manchester, Newcastle and London, and at home they took an active, philanthropic role in the community. In 1806 Peter Holland's wife, Mary, founded a Female Benefit Society in Knutsford and in 1821 her sister Martha Sharpe joined a 'Committee of Ladies' to find employment for female prisoners in the local gaol, putting forward proposals to the judges at the Quarter Sessions. Martha's very human attitude shows her balancing home and public duties and (like all people who are nudged on to committees) hoping it won't take up *too* much time:

'We have very high sounding Names, Lady Maria Stanley, Mrs Egerton, Mrs R. Leycester, Miss Ross, Mrs Leigh, & myself. I was very warmly pressed into the service, & as the attendance will be trifling when we have got a Matron & our plans well arrang'd, I could not well plead my home duties as a reason for refusing, & I shall be very glad to aid so very necessary a thing, if I can be useful, without neglecting my own Chicks.'[9]

Mrs Leigh, an organizer of the Benefit Society as well as a member of the Prison Committee, left money in the Knutsford Savings Bank to provide 'an annual dinner for ladies'. As she grew up Elizabeth could see women, both Anglicans and Dissenters, actively engaged in the life around them; but she also saw others cowed by overbearing fathers or husbands, or declining into deep depressions. And if pressed to say what the 'natural' role of women was and what a girl's education was for, all these aunts – Hannah Lumb, Mary Holland, Martha Sharpe – would have answered without hesitation, marriage and motherhood. In the years when she went to school (perhaps, as Harriet Martineau suggested, because the relative prosperity of the middle classes during the Napoleonic wars had led them to 'ape gentility') this assumption that women's role was primarily domestic was overlaid with a new emphasis on 'femininity' which belittled intellectual and practical achievement. She was given conflicting models of female independence and womanly subservience.

This duality, of course, was far from new. The two positions overlap even in the ideas of the radical educationalists of the 1790s, when girls' education had come under fire from Evangelicals like Hannah More and when passionate radicals like Catherine Macaulay and Mary Wollstonecraft expressed horror at the different teaching of boys and girls and recommended enlightened co-education. Wollstonecraft trounced the conservatives, but also ruthlessly dissected the fashionable views of Rousseau: in *Émile* the boys were educated for independence, but their mates, the Sophies of this world, must remain relative creatures, 'turning to men like sunflowers'.[10] (Many Unitarians disapproved of Wollstonecraft's life, but saw the sense of her words. When the Hollands' relation, the Newcastle minister William Turner, wrote to his daughter Mary on the eve of her marriage in 1812 about the mutual responsibilities of husband and wife, he naturally assumed she had 'perused the strong and often coarse, though too often well-founded strictures of Mary Wollstonecraft'.)[11] But even Wollstonecraft, while she felt women could be carpenters and sailors and doctors as well as wives, saw their most important role as motherhood. More moderate reformers, closer to the Hollands, like the Edgeworths and Anna Barbauld, stressed this still more. A girl's education should not be an end in itself. 'In no subject is she required to be deep,' wrote Barbauld, although 'of none ought she to be ignorant'.[12] She should know just enough to make her appeal to 'a man of sense' and provide recreation for a solitary hour.

The education designed to make a girl appeal to 'a man of sense' was a matter of dispute. Different educational approaches simply led to confusion. In the 1850s Elizabeth wrote a comic critique of the conflicts inherited from the eighteenth century which lingered on into her youth. In her story 'Morton Hall' Cordelia Mannisty is in the charge of three aunts, who look after her for a week in turn. The first is busy writing 'The Female Chesterfield: or Letters from a Lady of Quality to her Niece'. She believes in manners and rote-learning: 'good little girls can learn anything they choose, even French verbs'. (The narrator finds this unnerving: ' "That child is cowed by somebody," said I to Ethelinda. "But she knows a deal of geography," ' her sister replies.) The second is a fan of Rousseau who talks of 'the charms of nature, and tears and grief' and encourages her niece to read romances aloud, play the spinet and meditate in the country ('it was very dull,' poor Cordelia confesses). The third aunt changes her mind from one minute to the next: Cordelia is dizzied by arbitrary rules: she must eat her food standing, never say 'red', never mention a 'stomach ache'.

In the 1820s the standard schooling was often a 'phrenzy of accomplishments' mixed with facts learnt by rote with no idea of context, or sometimes, even, of meaning. Forty years later Harriet Martineau looked back hotly at the 'mushroom growth of Ladies Seminaries – a byword for pretension, vulgarity and cant', staffed by women as ignorant as their pupils:

'Those were the days when saucy girls invented names of European capitals, and found the most extraordinary places on the map, with full approbation from a short-sighted teacher. Those were the days when the Sunday morning lesson might be learning four lines of Paradise Lost by heart, leaving off whether there was a full stop or not.'[13]

Such an approach, fiercely attacked by John Stuart Mill and the mid-century feminists, was brilliantly summed up by Elizabeth Barrett Browning in *Aurora Leigh* in 1857. Aurora's aunt (aunts turn up so often as the principal educators) prescribes the following: a little French and German, 'because she liked/ A range of liberal education'; algebra and mathematics, 'because/She misliked women who are frivolous'; a smattering of genealogy, geography and dates, 'because she liked/A general insight into useful facts'; and a great deal of music, dancing and modelling in wax, 'Because she liked accomplishment in girls'. Most of all, Aurora remembers:

> I read a score of books on womanhood . . .
> . . . books that boldly assert
> Their right of comprehending husband's talk
> When not too deep, and even of answering
> With 'may it please you' or 'so it is' . . .
> As long as they keep quiet by the fire.

Not much had changed since the 1770s when Dr Gregory advised his daughters: 'if you have any learning, keep it a profound secret, especially from the men, who generally look with a jealous and malignant eye on a woman of great parts and cultivated understanding'.[14] (Dr Gregory is read aloud by the girls in Gaskell's *My Lady Ludlow*, together with Mrs Chapone's *Letters on the Improvement of the Mind, Addressed to a Young Lady*, 1773, and Sturm's *Reflections*, translated in 1788, which 'told us what to think about for every day in the year, and very dull it was'.) The danger of ostentatious learning was endlessly harped upon, for example in the much used *New Female Instructor: or Young Woman's Guide to Domestic Happiness* (1806).

33

The worst sin – worse even than obvious intellect – was a tendency to argue. 'So it is' was the correct response. A wife should stay quiet by the fire, and girls should keep out of a dispute, said Hannah More, 'even if they know themselves in the right. I do not mean, that they should be robbed of the liberty of private judgement but they should by no means be encouraged to contract a contentious and contradictory turn.' Instead they should 'acquire a submissive temper, and a forbearing spirit'.[15] This deep-seated ruling partly explains why the authorial voice of so many women writers wavers and falters – as Gaskell's would when she challenged accepted opinion in *Mary Barton* and *Ruth* – even when they are sure, at heart, that their 'contentious' argument is right.

A blend of progressive and conservative was a feature of Elizabeth's more formal education, when she was sent away to boarding school in Warwickshire at the age of eleven, in the autumn of 1821.

It may well have been her stepmother's sister-in-law, Katherine Thomson, who determined this step. Before her marriage in 1820 Katherine had taught for nine years with her sisters Maria, Anne and Jane Margaret Byerley at their school in Warwickshire. She and her husband were still closely involved; letters and advice flew to and fro and they took pupils on holidays to Belgium, Switzerland and France. The Byerleys' school was an obvious choice for the Stevensons, and the Hollands would also have approved since the sisters' grandmother was a Wedgwood, an aunt of Peter's and Swinton's wives. Margaret Byerley (the kind of strong woman who could have stepped out of a Gaskell story) had supported her family by setting up shop as a milliner and mantua-maker. Her brother Josiah Wedgwood helped, educating her son Tom and eventually making him a partner (after Tom ran off with strolling players and spent six years in America).

Tom and his wife Frances had five sons and eight daughters. All were well educated and in 1809, using a legacy of £200 each from Josiah, the three oldest girls, Fanny, Maria and Anne, decided to open a school in Warwick. Within two years Fanny married and Maria, aged twenty-two, took over as headmistress, gradually bringing her younger sisters in to help. All the girls were involved at some stage, although the youngest, Charlotte, died in 1814 and Elizabeth and Katherine had married and left by 1821.[16] In the early nineteenth century England was dotted with girls' boarding schools, many merely incompetent, some, like Charlotte Brontë's Cowan Bridge, cruelly starved of comfort and feeling. Many of the better schools were run by Dissenters like the Byerleys, with their modern subjects and humane, warm approach. As their reputation grew during the next thirty years, the Byerley sisters taught girls from leading Unitarian families – Harriet Martineau's niece, Joseph Priestley's granddaughters (sent from America), Julia Leigh Smith – while their Anglican pupils included Jessie Boucherett and Effie Grey, Ruskin's future wife.

In the 1820s many Unitarians were arguing passionately for a more liberal girls' education: the young Harriet Martineau's article 'On Female Education' appeared in the *Monthly Repository* in 1821. But the Byerleys' regime was conservative, broad-ranging – and Anglican. Despite their Dissenting background, the sisters were realists and as most of their pupils belonged to the Church of England, they firmly kept pews in the local church. They banked on their social acceptability: through their Wedgwood connections they had known the most brilliant minds of the day (one of Katherine's earliest memories was of Coleridge reading aloud) and had an entrance to society denied to most Nonconformist families: their father, for example, paid an annual visit to the Queen as the Wedgwood representative.

When Elizabeth arrived, the school was at Barford House, a low neo-classical mansion on the outskirts of a village three miles from Warwick, where the sisters had moved in 1817. Many of the pupils were day girls, but there were seven bedrooms for a small, select group of boarders. Lessons were probably held in the long drawing-room overlooking the garden, but there was also a library, rather grand and very dark, lightened by a large mirror over the fireplace. The house was set among large gardens (boasting a classical temple), with parkland and open fields beyond. Elizabeth remembered the countryside fondly, and the river Avon snaking slowly through grassy meadows near the mill. In 'Lois the Witch' Lois recalls this peaceful scenery when she lands in the alien wilderness of New England, remembering the 'old low grey church' of Barford. Elizabeth worshipped in the church on Sundays and she always liked the Anglican liturgy. When she was away from home, she often went to church even if there was a Unitarian chapel nearby.

The school was welcoming, but at the age of eleven she must have missed her home, the affection of Aunt Lumb, the freedom of Sandlebridge, the busy Knutsford streets on market day. Her early biographer Mrs Chadwick could be right in identifying her with Margaret Dawson in *My Lady Ludlow* who has 'long hard fits of crying' when she first goes to Hanbury Court, feeling that she ought to be at home, and is comforted with jams and jellies by the kindly housekeeper (allegedly based on Anne Byerley, who was deaf and took charge of the domestic side of the school). But Margaret soon settles in and so did Elizabeth: the three years she spent at Barford left no recorded unhappy memories.

In May 1824, when she was nearly fourteen, the school moved to Stratford-upon-Avon, and took over Avonbank, an eighteenth-century mansion rebuilt from a rambling Tudor house which had once belonged to Shakespeare's cousin. At an earlier stage still it was a medieval priory. The ten bedrooms and nine smaller rooms upstairs meant the school could take more boarders, and at one time the number of pupils, including day girls, rose to nearly sixty. The main schoolroom was the oval ballroom, part of the eighteenth-century renovations. In its chilly, elegant spaces under the high domed roof the girls sat on wooden forms behind long desks. The walls around them were hung with maps, and the tall windows, catching the morning sun, looked across sloping lawns to the Avon. Many of the rooms had nicknames and one of the oddest features was a covered way leading from the road to the house, which the girls called 'the elephant's trunk'.

The curriculum Elizabeth followed here was largely unchanged from that of 1810, when Fanny and Maria had advertised 'Instruction in English Reading, Spelling, Grammar and Composition, in Geography and the Use of the Globes, and in Ancient and Modern History'. The extras – a standard part of the course but listed separately to make the main fees less painful – included 'the French Language, Music, Dancing, Drawing and Writing, and Arithmetic'. (Accomplishments still rank higher than numeracy.) Later Italian was added, but the list did not change much: an 1836 school bill lists Italian, French, English and Composition, Dancing, Drawing, Writing and Arithmetic, Lectures and – in accordance with the principles of healthy exercise – Drilling.

Some extras were more expensive because they were taught by outside masters: two émigrés, again, taught French and dancing. And of course there was music. Elizabeth spent long hours carefully copying pieces into her music books.[17] Most of these, copied in pencil and carefully inked over, have the name of the person who passed on the tune, either at school – 'copied from Miss Lord', 'Sophia Smith', 'Mary Ann Lynn', 'Sara Priestley' – or in Chelsea and Knutsford – 'Louise Kennett', 'Louisa Holland'. There are Scottish airs, Swiss marches and waltzes and plenty of sad French songs of unrequited love. Copying music was a bond of friendship, something she deeply enjoyed, unlike Frances Power Cobbe, who lamented that 'the piles of endless music, and songs never to be sung, for which our parents had to pay, and the loss of priceless time for ourselves, was truly deplorable, and the result of course in many cases (as in mine) complete failure'.[18]

Life at the Byerleys' was undemanding. Elizabeth was friendly and effervescent: she may have been taught 'propriety', but she never quite managed 'decorum'. Her only frustration was that she was so confined to school: she told Margaret Howitt that 'as a schoolgirl I could not see much, but I heard of many places that I longed to know more about'. She did collect stories of nearby houses, like 'a mysterious old farm-house near Clifford', once the family mansion of the Grevilles, or the grander Compton Wynyates, Shottery and Charlecote, and in 1838 she sent William and Mary Howitt an account of a trip to Clopton Hall, home of the Wyatts, a fellow-pupil's family. The Howitts reprinted 'Clopton Hall' almost unchanged in their *Visits to Remarkable Places* (1840). It may well have been based on something she wrote at school,[19] since it has a distinct touch of 'composition' about it, like a set piece on 'our day out': 'we set off one beautiful autumn afternoon, full of delight and wonder respecting the place we were going to see' etc. And it gives a wonderful self-mocking picture of schoolgirls wallowing in Gothic shivers. After the tragic story of Charlotte Clopton, locked in the burial vaults, desperately gnawing at her own smooth white shoulder, comes the *Northanger-Abbey*-like discovery of a carved chest with a heavy lid:

'and when it was opened, what do you think we saw – BONES! – but whether human, whether the remains of the lost bride, we did not stay to see, but ran off in partly real and partly feigned terror.'

'Clopton Hall' has touches of authentic Gaskell alchemy, bringing history alive through anecdote, humour and atmosphere. Although it was put into its final form in the late 1830s, it suggests that even at school she was drawn to dark images of women – buried alive, silenced, self-devouring and struggling to be free.

Avonbank girls were encouraged to write – all the Byerley sisters did. The women writers of the day were held in high esteem, like the elderly dramatist Joanna Baillie and the famous poet Felicia Hemans, or Mary Russell Mitford, whose 'Our Village' began in the *Lady's Magazine* in 1819, and Katherine Thomson's friend Letitia Landon, 'L.E.L.', a new star on the horizon from 1824. But Elizabeth and her fellows were not expected to star so much as shine demurely. They were being prepared not for scholarship or fame but for affluent, charitable, gently pious, mildly cultured lives.

The world the girls of Avonbank were expected to enter is vividly evoked by a book which Fanny, one of its founders, wrote in 1825 after fourteen years of marriage to William Parkes. *Domestic Duties: or Instructions to Young Married Ladies, on the Management of Their Households and the Regulation of Their Conduct* contains five hundred pages of solid advice, divided into sections under headings such as 'Social Relationships', 'Household Concerns', 'Regulation of Time' and 'Moral and Religious Duties'. ('Occupations at Home' includes notes on 'Light Reading, Drawing, Music, Light and Ornamental Needlework – Folly of Neglecting these Accomplishments in the Married State'.)

Elizabeth escaped this kind of married life, although she knew its manners well and described them brilliantly in *Cranford*, *North and South* and *Wives and Daughters*. While Fanny never says so openly, it becomes clear that she herself saw the conventional marriage as something of a challenge. Her book is full of pictures of family evenings spent in languid conversation and listless magazine reading, with everyone present 'yawning respectfully until the wished for hour of bed arrives'.[20] Or, worse still, the husband could be devoid of religious principles, addicted to vice, a rake, a wastrel – and only a good woman could save him.

Fanny's stance is direct, and moral, but also humane: she is alert to the isolation of the young wife and, when writing of childcare, she recommends responsive sympathy rather than rigid rules. But from the beginning two voices battle for dominance in *Domestic Duties*, one telling the bride to suffer and be still, the other issuing a clarion call to arms and emphasizing women's rights as well as duties:

38

'It is not the desire, nor the intention of the author to maintain, unmodified, the doctrine of passive obedience in the married female to the wishes of her husband. Such a doctrine may be regarded as incompatible with that spirit which woman assumes as her right; nor is it to be expected that, in the individual who possesses energy of character, a yielding disposition should also predominate. Utopian dreams may portray a state of connubial life, in which the temper of each party so happily blends with that of the other, that no struggle for supremacy can arise between them. But reality and experience present a less pleasing, though truer picture to our view.'[21]

Within the limits of marriage she always maintains the right of women to govern their own lives and direct those of others. Individually, she writes, 'our power is limited', but 'collectively we hold in our hand the happiness or misery of living multitudes'. And when she died in 1842, aged fifty-six, she left her property to her sisters, 'for their separate use & benefit, independently & exclusively of any present or future husband, & without being in any wise subject to his debts, control or management'.[22] Her daughter Maria nursed with Florence Nightingale at Scutari, and her niece Bessie Parkes, a friend of Elizabeth Gaskell and of George Eliot, was at the forefront of the mid-century women's movement. Fanny's beliefs in the combined importance of domestic duty and personal integrity pervaded the school she founded.

There is something of the closet scholar about Fanny Parkes (as there would be about Elizabeth Gaskell). She expects that women will find time to scurry away and study privately in the mornings, but guards against any 'appearance of pedantry' and advises that the only books fit for display in the drawing-room are those which can 'afford topics for conversation when that which is afloat seems either to be declining in interest or to be turned to painful and disagreeable subjects'. Regretfully, she notes that the works of Beaumont and Fletcher, Rousseau's *Confessions* and Fielding's novels are now 'becoming obsolete' and would look out of place in the home of the young and fashionable.

She also warns against dubious matter – 'which, I think will afford you little gratification' – such as the works of Byron.[23] 'I think' is nice – it was well known that although girls were not supposed to read Byron, almost all of them did. Elizabeth often quoted Byron and a year after she left school her brother John praised a criticism of his poetry that she sent to her father. Her music books, begun the year after Byron's death at Missolonghi, have their due sprinkling of fervent songs about Greek independence. The Stevensons were broad-minded: many girls found that only after their weddings was their reading uncensored, as Mr Brooke in *Middlemarch* recognized when he said of Dorothea, 'She may read anything now she is married.'

Unitarian families did not, like some sects, take a firm line on the evils of imaginative literature – either poetry or fiction. Elizabeth never had to shiver with guilt when reading good novels or say, as the nineteen-year-old Mary Ann Evans did in her most Evangelical phase, 'I shall carry to my grave the mental diseases with which they have contaminated me.'[24] The most popular novelist of Elizabeth's youth was Walter Scott, whose *Waverley* novels were exempt from moral disapproval in all but the strictest households (a few years after her outburst the future George Eliot was reading Scott aloud every night to her father). After *Waverley* in 1814 his novels appeared at the rate of at least one a year until his death in 1832. In 1820 Sarah Whittaker wrote from Knutsford, with a typical mixture of insight, prejudice and sly humour:

'We have been reading Ivanhoe: what do you think of it, compared with the Scotch novels – I seem to miss the Scotch character & Language, but the *Jews* are admirable, & the contention of a *naturally good character* with *habitual avarice* in Isaac of York, reminded me of a departed friend of our own – it is admirably imagined.'[25]

In Manchester, after her marriage, Elizabeth had a brush with a fellow-minister's wife for having 'five minutes conversation with one or two girls' about *Kenilworth* during Sunday school (to illustrate the character of Queen Elizabeth):

'Mrs. J. J. Tayler is shocked at such a subject of conversation on a *Sunday*, – so there I am in a scrape – well! it can't be helped, I am myself and nobody else, and can't be bound by another's rules.' (L63–4)

Her father had fostered this independence. Sometimes she went to Chelsea in the holidays, where he was busily writing: articles for *Blackwood's* and material for the *Annual Register*. Perhaps John's voyages revived his old love for the sea, since in 1824 he published his

40

most substantial work, *A Historial Sketch of Discovery, Navigation and Commerce*. As Lily grew older William took an increasing interest in her schooling, coaching her in languages and Latin, and encouraging her reading, giving her Cowper's *Poems* in 1823 and Gray's *Poems* in 1825. He had no patience with the 'submissive' school of girls' education. In a fascinating review in the *Westminster* in January 1826 he declared that women should be seen as 'companions and co-operators' with men in intellectual pursuits:

'Women, therefore, ought to discountenance every kind of treatment and behaviour which, proceeding on the supposition that they are helpless, dependent and frivolous in their thought and pursuits renders them so, and bestow their approbation only on those men who regard and trust them as equal to themselves in their capacity for knowledge and usefulness.'[26]

In 1827, after Elizabeth left school, William told her that he was glad she was still studying on her own:

'you must, however, work a large portion of the day if you have little or no time to read – as you have now been at Knutsford above a month. I hope you are again applying to your Latin and Italian; Let me know, when you write, in what manner you spend your day – I mean, so far as work or study is concerned.'[27]

He sent the latest number of the *Literary Gazette*, containing a review of Scott's *Life of Napoleon*, 'or rather long extracts from it', and a review of Moore's *Epicurean*.

But although William Stevenson was an important influence, Knutsford was Elizabeth's real home and during the holidays she still read her favourite books from the stock at the Heath, Church House or Sandlebridge. The Hollands had a wide, if old selection, as Angus Easson points out: 'Cervantes, Defoe, Fielding, Sterne, Smollett, Richardson and Goldsmith were obviously among them, and the *Arabian Nights* and those oriental tales that ornament the *Spectator*'.[28] Aunt Lumb's neighbours, the Sharpes, were typical of this circle, and this is how Martha Sharpe describes her girls, in November evenings, after watching a 'grand display of fireworks':

'Emily is reading Pilgrim's Progress, & enters into it very fully. Molly was devouring Guy Mannering last night to herself – but reads the English History to me, in which she seems much interested. I have promised to read a few of Shakespeare's historical Plays with her, in an Evening, when Aunt Kate is gone, & we are quite alone, as a great Treat.'[29]

They also read Spenser's *Faerie Queene* and Thomson's *Seasons*, and their letters are full of rhapsodies about Scott and scandalized gossip about Byron (though *The Corsair* was read with enthusiasm).

A different idea of the kind of reading the Hollands enjoyed is given by a contemporary of Elizabeth, Hannah Macaulay, sister of the historian. Remembering how her father read aloud to them, Hannah says:

'Among the books selected I can recall Clarendon, Burnet, Shakespeare (a great treat when my mother took the volume), Miss Edgeworth, Mackenzie's Lounger and Mirror, and, as a steady diet The Edinburgh and The Quarterly Reviews.'[30]

(Interesting that in both families it is a great treat when the mother reads the Bard.) The Macaulays also read Pepys, Addison, Horace Walpole and Dr Johnson, and the novels of Richardson, Burney, Austen and Bulwer-Lytton. All these names appear in Elizabeth's reading: the *Edinburgh* and *Quarterly* were taken in most Unitarian homes as well as in Evangelical households such as the Macaulays', and her family, like Hannah's, read poetry as much as prose.

She continued to read poetry for pleasure all her life: the epigraphs to her novels show that she knew the poets of her time – Wordsworth, Coleridge, Southey, Landor, Byron, Hemans, Tennyson – but they also reveal a great fondness for the poets (and prose writers) of the sixteenth and seventeenth centuries. This seems to have been an early taste, perhaps fostered by the popular books of extracts such as Lindley Murray's *The English Reader, or Elegant Selections in Prose and Poetry*. In the commonplace book which she kept when she was twenty-one ballads and seventeenth-century poems intermingle with Shakespeare, Burns and Wordsworth.[31]

After she left school she read a wider variety of new books. In Newcastle, in 1829, her friend Harriet Carr lent her William Massie's three-decker *Sydenham* 'one rainy day', and a year later she was reading the sequel, *Alice Paulet*. One of her favourite novels, which she claimed to have read three times in 1831, the year it appeared, was Susan Ferrier's *Destiny, or The Chief's Daughter*. Like her friend

Walter Scott, Ferrier combined excitement, romance and local colour with a keen awareness of the dilemmas facing women, and pungent irony and comedy. Another 'new' novelist was Bulwer-Lytton: *Pelham* was all the rage in 1828, and *Paul Clifford* in 1830. 'I have been reading Paul Clifford over again and am delighted with it,' she tells Harriet, 'as I believe I am with all Bulwer's works in spite of their alleged immorality.'[32]

It may have been the alleged immorality that attracted her – the same letter refers to a current pamphlet which clearly both fascinated and shocked her: *Facts Relating to the Punishment of Death in the Metropolis* by the extraordinary Edward Gibbon Wakefield (later a moving spirit in the development of New Zealand). Gibbon had become interested in capital punishment while serving three years in prison for abducting a fifteen-year-old-heiress and persuading her, by lies and force, to marry him at Gretna Green. Furthermore this was a local scandal, since the heiress lived near Macclesfield, her father was Sheriff of Cheshire and she was at school in Liverpool when abducted. Elizabeth asked Harriet what she made of Gibbon Wakefield's pamphlet, adding in a pursed-lip tone: 'Can any good thing come from such a polluted source?' She always had a weakness for tales of desire, crime, bigamy, detection – themes which run through her own short stories and novels – and in 1832, like the rest of the reading public, she was deep in Bulwer-Lytton's new novel, *Eugene Aram*.

She also dipped into newly published memoirs. Sometimes these were by famous people known to her family, like Lafayette, sometimes by unfamiliar authors like Alexander Mackenzie, whose *A Year in Spain by a Young American* she read three times, finding its egotistical style made it even more 'entertaining and romantic'. (She was less keen on Thomas Moore's serious biography of Lord Edward Fitzgerald, published the same year.) The book that pleased her most in May 1832 was Fanny Trollope's outspoken and observant *Domestic Manners of the Americans*: 'It is so very amusing and by abusing the Americans has won my heart. I don't mean their more solid moral qualities but their manners which I have always disliked.' (How many Americans had she known?)

By the time she married her likes and dislikes were already strong. She was never a literary snob. In 1849 William Gaskell became chairman of Manchester's Portico Library and could borrow books for his wife and daughters as well as himself (women could not be members). Elizabeth hopped impatiently as she waited for each new novel – *Esmond* in 1852, *Adam Bede* in 1859. In the first decade of the Revd Gaskell's borrowings, among hundreds of novels, memoirs, travels, histories, new scientific works and treatises on the poor and education are a host of books by women writers like Mrs Gore, Frederika Bremer, Julia Kavanagh, Fanny Trollope, Mrs Craik (Dinah Mulock), Margaret Oliphant, Miss Mitford and the popular Mrs Anne Marsh, author of *Emilia Wyndham*, *Evelyn Marston* and of the enticingly titled *Time the Avenger* (1851). (Perhaps the most startling of these varied titles, however, is *Perversion: or the Causes and Consequences of Infidelity. A Tale for the Times*, borrowed in June 1856.)[33]

As a schoolgirl Elizabeth had responded eagerly to books and to her teachers, but she showed no passionate hunger for learning; she was no Mary Ann Evans seeking fuel for her devouring intellect; no Harriet Martineau complaining that she had to sit in the parlour and sew instead of learning Greek. Nor did she, like the Brontë sisters, create her own imaginary world built from the books she read, the distant wars she heard of. She was a clever child, but those warnings against displayed learning seem to have had their effect, since for many years, as an adult, she hid her cleverness, claiming not to have read economics, not to understand science, not to like sermons, not to be 'metaphysical'. But she did escape into literature and drew on her reading constantly, for comparisons with other lives, for different visions of the world – and for ways of telling stories.

She left Avonbank before she was sixteen. A letter of June 1826 from Jane Byerley, who was sending on her books, regrets that Elizabeth cannot visit the school on her way north to Knutsford from London: 'we should have been happy to have seen you once more an inmate here, and to have known you in the new character of visitor'.[34] Two other ex-pupils have just been back, 'Jane Pickard and Sophy', and in the person of Sophy we find the ideal Avonbank product. Sophy, says Miss Jane, 'gives promise of being an honor to our sex: she is a noble minded intelligent ingenuous creature', a girl of warm affections and strong principles who has, to her teachers' delight, shown herself unaffected by the temptations of fashionable Cheltenham – 'she has left the place sick of its miscalled pleasures' – and who still prefers a country walk to 'the gaiest ball or rout'. Jane writes more mournfully about Marianne and Sarah Priestley: Marianne is consumptive, while Sarah is showing her true religious spirit by sticking loyally to her fiancé, even though his family have lost their fortune. Jane said she looked forward to watching the progress of these girls through life. She watched Elizabeth's too; in 1847, writing to Mrs Montagu, Elizabeth mentions hearing recently from 'dear Miss Jane'. 'Do you ever see Kate Thomson?' she asks, 'or any of our old schoolfellows. It is 20 years since I have been at dear Avonbank.'

'Dear Avonbank' helped form her taste and her character, but its teaching was ambivalent. It presupposed a life in which women were expected to be at once pillars of strength and models of meekness. While Elizabeth later chose to speak out rather than be silent, these contradictory values vibrate like tightened strings through her letters and her fiction. As a reader she might be able to say, 'I am myself and nobody else, and can't be bound by another's rules', but such a stand was harder to hold as a writer: if domestic duties were paramount, writing must come second. As late as 1850, the mother of four children and the acclaimed author of *Mary Barton*, she was still debating these opposing roles with her friend Tottie Fox. Tottie, a painter, had been studying in Paris, excited by the freedom she found there. Now she wanted to spend six months in Munich. Her father was ageing. Who would look after him while she was away? How could she resolve the conflict of 'home duties and individual life'? Elizabeth responded with feeling: 'It is just my puzzle; and I don't think I can get nearer to a solution than you have done.'

'One thing is pretty clear, *Women*, must give up living an artist's life, if home duties are to be paramount. It is different with men, whose home duties are so small a part of their life. However we are talking of women. I am sure it is healthy for them to have the refuge of the hidden world of Art to shelter themselves in when too much pressed upon by daily small Lilliputian arrows of peddling cares . . . I have felt this in writing. I see others feel it in music, you in painting, so assuredly a blending of the two is desirable (Home duties and the development of the Individual I mean) . . . I have no doubt that the cultivation of each tends to keep the other in a healthy state, – my grammar is all at sixes and sevens I have no doubt but never mind if you can pick out my meaning.' (L106)

She knew that for Tottie and herself art was more than a refuge. Painting and writing were an expression of their inner beings. As such, they might be seen as self-indulgent, the opposite of proper womanly self-sacrifice. Having slept on the puzzle, she wrote on the following day:

'If Self is to be the end of exertions, those exertions are unholy – there is no doubt of *that* – and that is part of the danger in cultivating the Individual Life; but I do believe we have all some appointed work to do, whh no one else can do so well; Wh. is *our* work; what *we* have to do in advancing the Kingdom of God; and that first we must find out what we are sent into the world to do, and define it and make it clear to ourselves, (that's *the* hard part) and then forget ourselves in our work, and our work in the End we ought to strive to bring about.' (L107)

At that very moment she had to cut her letter short: their servant, Hearn, was away and 'the little ones come down upon us like the Goths on Rome; making inroads and onslaughts into our plans'. As she was later to say of Charlotte Brontë, the separate duties of the woman and of the artist were 'not impossible, but difficult to be reconciled'.

[3]

Changing Places:
1826–31

'Who – What, Where, Wherefore, Why – oh! do be a woman, and give me all possible details.' (L540)

Thus Elizabeth badgered Tottie's father, W. J. Fox, in 1859 when she heard that her friend had married in Rome. (Tottie married a painter, cleverly settling Art v. Domestic Duties). For Elizabeth the mere news was not enough: she needed every minute particular.

This thirst for detail, which she judged so feminine, struck at an early age. She began by finding out all she could about her family and friends, rich and poor, their past histories and their daily habits. Her first concerns are often unabashedly, conventionally female – clothes and cookery. But a world can be evoked through a wardrobe and meals can embody a whole way of life. The detail which makes Gaskell's fiction so alive is also found in her letters, and those of the women she grew up with. Their fascinated interest in apparent trivia and in the small concerns of the moment tended to be joked about by men. Elizabeth's cousin Henry Holland called her letters 'a heterogenous mass of nonsense', just as Martha Sharpe's husband laughed at her marvellously vital and immediate scribblings. 'I am sure, my dear William,' Martha told her nephew jokingly, 'that it is high time either for My Husband *or his Rib*, to thank you for all your kindness to us & ours.' She felt 'agreeably compelled' to take on the task herself, she said, since Mr Sharpe was

'now too busy to write any but scraps, & moreover highly compliments that Rib, on her superior talent for compiling chit-chat intelligence out of nothing.'[1]

From such small chit-chat intelligence Elizabeth's interest fanned into a curiosity about the patterns of history, politics and faith which made people what they were. She became a superb social reporter and collector of oral history, traditions and customs. She quizzed everyone she met and sometimes she kept journals or made notes. When Charlotte Brontë told her how her father received *Jane Eyre*, Gaskell wrote it down next day. When she heard that Lady Hatherton's gardener had worked for the Shah of Persia, 'I was so much interested in the details he gave me that I made notes at the time.'[2] We follow her grilling Mr Burton, his vegetables untended as she runs through her list: housing, clothes, travel, weather, food (very important), politics, festivals, public executions and the mysteries of the harem.

She began this tactful – or not so tactful – delving for detail when she was a girl. All the time she was noting the life of the town, its traditions and its intricate rules. Even the avid card-games, as she records in 'The Last Generation in England', had a strict etiquette which it was fatal to transgress. The curtains were drawn, the candles lighted, the tables set out with two new packs of cards, for which everyone placed a shilling under the candlestick.

'Cards were a business in those days, not a recreation. Their very names were to be treated with reverence. Some one came to — from a place where flippancy was the fashion; he called the knave "Jack" and everybody looked grave, and voted him vulgar; but when he was overheard calling Preference – the decorous, highly respectable game of Preference, – Pref., why, what course remained for us but to cut him, and cut him we did.'[3]

Card-players like these told Elizabeth tales of local characters, such as Lady Jane Stanley, who left money for a footpath on condition it should only be broad enough for one, to discourage the indecent new habit of linking arms, and bequeathed her sedan chair to the women of the town, causing problems for the next generation, whose arrivals and departures had to be so carefully timed that they were like 'Adam and Eve in the weather-glass'. One favourite source of stories was 'a very clever old lady of one hundred and twenty – or so I thought her; I now think she, perhaps, was only about seventy', who told the young Elizabeth about her Shropshire youth and passed on – like family treasures – mysterious stories of ghosts and disappearances that she herself had heard as a girl.[4] As well as local gossip and old memories, national events had a hold on Knutsford imaginations. For two decades British life had been dominated by the French wars: stories of spies were rife and Bonaparte loomed like a black figure of legend. In 1821 Martha Sharpe asked her nephew: 'I wonder whether, like me, you feel hardly persuaded that Napoleon is *really dead*, & has died a natural death – & can no more disturb the world by his restless spirit?'[5] She had always imagined he would escape, and return in disguise.

Elizabeth listened and noted and remembered. With a curiosity about people went a passion for local places. There were endless family gatherings, like these of 1828: 'a family party of fourteen at Mr Holland's dinner table every day – & those chiefly young ones, could not but be very joyous – & we had Gigs, & ponies, 2 Sailing parties on Tabley Mere.'[6] Tabley, the estate of the Leicester family a couple of miles outside Knutsford, was one of Elizabeth's most frequent outings. An early letter to the Howitts (in the mannered style she must have thought they approved of) is full of nostalgia for the days she spent there with her cousins and friends: 'Here on summer mornings did we often come, a merry young party, on donkey, pony, or even in a cart with sacks swung across – each with our favourite book, some with sketch books, and one or two with eatables.' They walked or lounged on the grass and read or drifted on the Mere, singing, 'in the old crazy boats, that would do nothing but float on the glassy water'. When it rained, they sheltered in the Old Hall, built on an island in the lake and abandoned by the family for the new mansion in 1744. The Jacobean house had kept its medieval hall, forty feet long, with a gallery on three sides and walls hung with weapons and armour. Elizabeth remembered a quartet singing Shakespeare's ballads here, two singers in the gallery echoed by two below. It appealed to the lover of Scott and Romantic poetry – and its fate would have suited her own ghost stories. Today, ruined by subsidence, its tumbled walls are screened by a dense tangle of trees, rising from the spreading water lilies of the ancient moat.

Elizabeth soon began to put her impressions in writing. In the summer of 1827, hearing that the Hollands were planning a visit to Wales, her father advised her to keep a 'regular journal of what you see and remember.'[7] Her brother John had suggested a journal two years before in a letter to Aunts Hannah and Abigail. His motive was partly self-interest – if she kept a diary, it might provide more matter for her letters and 'the difficulty of filling up her paper would soon cease'. In June 1827 he was still encouraging her journal-keeping, saying he was sure she could make it 'very amusing as well as interesting', and asking for 'good long extracts.'[8] John wrote to her often, teasing her as 'a saucy girl', asking about her chilblains, sending her books. His breezy love of literature and his own skills as a writer affected hers. He suggested she read *Paul and Virginie* and *The Exiles of Siberia* and sent lighter reading, like *Friendship's Garland*.

John adored parodies, and his letters were full of them, mingled with jolly (if sometimes hair-raising) dramas of ship-board life: crossing the line, enormous sharks, men lost overboard. He too had clearly been begged to give every detail: his routine, his fellow-sailors and passengers. He dutifully described the new second-mate, tall, dark, with very long whiskers, 'rather good-looking – are you satisfied?' In more serious vein, he evoked each place where his ship docked, the food, customs, dress, economy and local politics. With an inquiring radical bent, he wrote of the mud huts and palaces of Calcutta, of the evils of the caste system, of the bloated dead bodies in the Ganges. Letters came from India, China, Burma, bearing the romance of the East. The very names of his ships had a touch of glamour: the *Earl Kelly*, the barque *Marianne Sophia*, the *Recovery*. His sea-stained missives were also part of Elizabeth's education.

In 1827 her own horizons widened, though not as far as John's. That summer she spent a month in North Wales with her Uncle Sam Holland's family. Two years before, to the fury of local landlords, Sam had sold the lease of his Ffestiniog quarry to a government syndicate promoted by Nathan Rothschild, and he was now running a copper mine near Tremadoc. His son, another Sam, also became a quarry-owner, one of the most advanced of his day, and would later become MP for the area.[9] In 1827, after three years of negotiations, 'young Sam', at the age of twenty-four, had just moved into Plas Penrhyn, a large white house on the hillside at Minffordd, near Penrhyndeud-raeth, with sweeping views north-east up the valley towards Snowdon and west across the recently drained estuary to Portmadoc and Cardigan Bay. Plas Penrhyn became home for his mother and sisters and, from 1832, for his father. It was a favourite holiday place for Elizabeth both before and after her marriage; she would flee there in 1848, the week *Mary Barton* was published.

Sam was busy renovating and adding to his house (an obsession of all the younger Hollands). So his family, joined by the usual cluster of relations, spent a month at Aber, three miles from Bangor. From there they explored Snowdonia, visited Conway and crossed to Anglesey. Nine years later, in 1838, Elizabeth described her trip, 'with 17 aunts and uncles and cousins and such Like', in a letter to her sister-in-law Eliza Gaskell, who was staying at the Anglesey resort of Beaumaris:

'I wish you would go to Priestholme or Puffin's Island – It is such a singular place & to a botanist (*like you* Ma'am) would be a great treat – Many ships returning from Foreign ports – used to make offerings at the monastery there, – and cast out their ballast, which often contained curious seeds which took root – The old monastery is in ruins – but there is a telegraph station; the man who kept it years & years ago in my youth, had fought in the *Victory* with Nelson – the Puffins too are queer uncanny looking animals.' (L20–1)

A romantic list, despite the casual style. In the heat of a Manchester July she confessed: 'I *long* to be in those wild places again, with the fresh sea breeze round me, so thoroughly exhilarating.' But she wished, she said, that Eliza were in 'a wilder more Welshy place'.

Wild Wales was an encounter with the Romantic landscapes of her reading, a parallel to the highlands of Scott, the lakes of Wordsworth. Although it was near to home – she could see blue mountains in the distance when she stood on a Cheshire hill – it seemed like a foreign land. Its history, customs, legends and language as well as its craggy mountains and encircling seas fired her imagination. Her second music book, begun on 12 June 1827 and continued for the next two years, reflects the new passion. Into the mix of English folk-songs, quadrilles, mazurkas, French and Italian songs come numerous Welsh tunes, sometimes accompanied by notes translating the title or identifying the place or the story: 'Men of Harlech', 'The Death of Llewellyn', 'The Free Sons of Cambria'. Less familiar songs have the words carefully written in Welsh, like 'Codiad yr Haul', 'Morfa Rhuddlan', 'O Swyth Edwart', 'Llwynon', 'Tri chant o' binnau.'[10]

Elizabeth and her cousins were especially fascinated by the Welsh gentry, who, she would write decidedly four years later, seemed

'not to have progressed beyond what the English were two centuries ago. The Lord of the Manor is so completely a little King, and may do what he likes, without being questioned, for everybody seems to consider justice and revenge in their own hands, and the scanty population make their crimes not to be heard of.'[11]

'My cousin Anne and I,' she continued, 'are intending some day to publish a book, a history of *crimes* of *innocent* people.' The innocent people and their crimes would provide material for 'The Doom of the Griffiths' and 'The Well of Pen-Morfa', stories set in the Lleyn peninsula and the country round Tremadoc, near Plas Penrhyn. Snowdonia would be the backdrop for the abandonment of Ruth, whose response to the mountains conjures up their impact on an impressionable girl:

'It was opening a new sense; vast ideas of beauty and grandeur filled her mind at the sight of the mountains, now first beheld in full majesty. She was almost overpowered by the vague and solemn delight; but by-and-by her love for them equalled her awe.' (Ch. 5)

Ruth was published in 1853, when Gaskell knew this landscape well. Yet even at seventeen Wales inspired her. In her 1838 letter she asks Eliza about a figure she remembered from her first Welsh holiday: 'You never mention Captain Barton. Is he "to the fore" yet?' This captain had intrigued her so strongly in 1827 that she built a story around him and sent it to her brother, combined with an account of her cousin Kate's adventure on some shifting sands. John replied that she had made 'a very pretty story' of it – 'it would almost make the foundations of a novel.'[12] She was on her way to becoming a writer.

John always kept her in touch with Stevenson news. By the late 1820s all was not well in Chelsea and Elizabeth's stable life was threatened, at first imperceptibly, by her father's troubles. During this decade, while the Hollands had prospered, the Stevensons had found life increasingly difficult. William's finances were insecure and he also had to untangle the financial affairs of his wife, Catherine, and her sister (her partner before her marriage). He took on more work, however ill paid, writing for the *Reviews* and constantly suggesting new books to his publisher, William Blackwood. His letters to Blackwood often apologize for not turning work in on time – and equally often appeal for money. The pressure did produce some fruits, especially the series of articles 'The Political Economist', in which he tried to work out a sound theoretical basis for this new science, and appealed (as his daughter would) for ethical values to replace market demands.[13] But his money troubles grew. Blackwood had to lend him money for his son William's education and in June 1827, with Catherine's agreement, he sold stocks, worth £800, which had made up part of her dowry, stipulating in his will that this should be repaid before any legacies to his older son and daughter.[14]

The following July John reported that Catherine and the children were 'going down to Scotland where they intend to remain till the end of September'. In mid-August he told Elizabeth about Colonel Kennett and his boisterous sisters. Far more important, he wrote of his own dashed hopes of being a published writer:

'I have just got the final answer from Smith and Elder – they are extremely sorry to decline taking my book &c &c, but dare say Longman would take – as a sort of douceur for thus disappointing me, they enclosed a friendship offering and a book on the present state of slavery in the West Indies – to end my hopes of being an author.'

Restless and uncertain of his future, unable to rely on his father for financial support, John had decided to quit England, give up the sailor's life and settle in India. His letter sounds almost desperate in its resignation; 'You yourself seem convinced that nothing is to be done in England – thus it seems I must be contented to be a banished man for what use is it returning and having nothing to do.' His only sure income was £3 a month, probably from investments, and on that, 'What can I save – What can I do?' The letter ends:

'And now, my dearest Elizabeth farewell – Should we never meet again, accept my very best wishes for your welfare through life and may every blessing attend you –, with Love to all enquiring

Believe me to be
Your ever affectionate brother
Jno. Stevenson'[15]

His premonition proved fearfully accurate. These letters of July and August 1828 are the last which survive, almost certainly the last Elizabeth received. That winter John vanished from her life. He was lost, either at sea or after his arrival in India: no definite news ever came of his fate. She never wrote or talked about this loss, just as she never openly reflected on her childhood. But the figure of the sailor in peril moves through her fiction with the power of a recurring dream – like the vision which haunts Mrs Hale, in North and South, longing for news of her son:

53

'I dream of him in some stormy sea, with great, clear, glass-green walls of waves on either side his ship, but far higher than her very masts, curling over her with that cruel, terrible white foam, like some gigantic crested serpent. It is an old dream, but it always comes back on windy nights, till I am thankful to waken, sitting straight and stiff up in bed with my terror.' (Ch. 14)

Like the frail, feminine ship itself, Elizabeth could not protect her brother; she did not know if he was dead, she dared not hope he would return. In her novels and stories the sailors are strong, reckless, warm-hearted. Whether they return or not, they are figures of loss and longing, mingled fear and hope: Will Wilson in *Mary Barton*, Peter in *Cranford*, Frederick in *North and South*, Kinraid in *Sylvia's Lovers*. 'Disappearances' was the title of one of her first articles for *Household Words*, and such stories of people who vanished without trace, she said, 'haunted her imagination longer than any tale of wonder'.

During the winter of 1828–9 Elizabeth went to Chelsea. Her father was devastated by John's disappearance and was ill and anxious. On Friday, 20 March, at tea with his family, he suffered a stroke and was temporarily blinded, and although he recovered slightly, a second stroke came two days later, which he did not survive. On 27 March 1829 his funeral was held at St Luke's, Chelsea. He was buried beside his first wife in King's Road Cemetery. As with her brother, Elizabeth's grief, and her complex feelings about her father, are never mentioned in her letters. In her fiction fathers would often be ambivalent figures, whose strength conceals weakness and who are viewed by their children – especially their daughters – with mingled tenderness and resentment, longing and anger.

Elizabeth stayed in London for three long months while her father's chaotic will was sorted out (not only was it undated and unsigned, but William had called his executor, Dr Anthony Thomson, by his father's name, Alexander Thomson). On 15 June, the day after the weary process ended and the will was finally proved, Catherine Stevenson wrote to Hannah Lumb about Elizabeth:

'I often think how fortunate it was her being with us, when her poor father died; and it must always be a source of comfort to her to think that she had seen him. Often did he intend writing to you about Elizabeth and frequently spoke to me about her. Indeed both he and I considered her much improved altogether and although he said little, I could easily see that he felt proud of his daughter. I do not recollect at present in any one instance he was either hurt or vexed about her. Her conduct at the time of her Father's and my distress was certainly very beautiful and more like a person much older. Indeed she was a very great comfort to me, my own girl being young and consequently not so thoughtful. I shall ever love Elizabeth as my own child, and trust that nothing will ever break that friendship which I trust is between us at this time, and also the love that she and her brother and sister have for each other.'[16]

The voice in this letter is uncannily like Mrs Gibson of *Wives and Daughters* in its backhanded compliments, its implied vexations, its emphatic, guilty 'indeeds', its egocentricity. Despite the fulsome ending there was no real love between Catherine and Elizabeth. The Chelsea connection was broken for good; the house was sold and in September Catherine returned to her family's home town, Dumfries, 'She will have much to contend with in her new way of life,' wrote Jane Byerley to Elizabeth in November.[17] Elizabeth did visit her there – but not until twenty-five years had passed.

When her father died, Elizabeth was still a minor, technically (and uncomfortably) dependent on an uncongenial stepmother. Once more, as after her mother's death, the Hollands took charge. The whole family offered shelter and support, homes where she could rest and face the future. There was no sense of hurry: with her reduced inheritance, Elizabeth was hardly a sought-after heiress and no one expected her to marry at once. The Heath was still her home, but over the next two years, to continue her education and broaden her experience, it was arranged that she should visit various relations, often (as was the custom of her class) for weeks or months at a time.

At first, in the summer of 1829, she stayed in the south, visiting the Holland families there and entering briefly into their prosperous lives. Her cousin Henry was well established at 25 Brook Street, earning £5,000 a year and being firmly attached to the highest social circles (he eventually attended six prime ministers as well as the royal family).[18] Elizabeth does not seem to have spun into his elevated sphere – nor to have liked him much (almost all her passing references are mildly sarcastic). She preferred her other cousins, 'the good people at Park Lane', the home of Swinton's son Edward. Swinton had died the previous year, but 'Aunt Swinton', and Edward, Louisa and Charlotte, often appear in Elizabeth's letters. She stayed with them in London and at Dumbleton Hall in the Vale of Evesham, bought by Swinton in 1823 and now inherited by Edward. She must have told her old teacher Jane Byerley how much she enjoyed it, for Jane replied in November, sounding like Miss Bates in *Emma*: 'you describe a most happy kind of life, such as realizes one's idea of felicity in the country.'[19]

By late autumn she was back in Knutsford, but not for long. That winter, and the next, she spent at the house of the Revd William Turner in Newcastle-upon-Tyne. Turner was a third-generation Dissenting minister: both his grandfather and his father had been ministers for short periods at Brook Street Chapel, and in the bewilderingly entwined Unitarian community he was trebly related to Elizabeth. His mother was the eldest sister of her grandfather, Samuel; his first wife Mary was her mother's cousin (the daughter of Thomas Holland of Manchester); his second wife, Jane Willetts, was the sister of her uncle Peter's first wife, Mary, and of Swinton's wife, Anne. Jane had died in 1826 and he now lived with his unmarried daughter, Ann, who was in her early thirties.

Peter Holland's children had all spent time with the Turners: Henry Holland lived with them for four years, from 1799 to 1803, from the age of eleven to fifteen, and Mary, Bessy and Lucy paid lengthy visits. Henry remembered fondly that in his Newcastle days 'there was very little constraint upon me, quiet instruction and a cheerful home'. Tyneside was a great contrast to rural Cheshire and he was profoundly impressed by everything he saw, 'the collieries with their vast and varied machinery – the Tyne, with its crowded navigation and its then perilous opening to the sea – the chemical and other manufactures (now multiplied fourfold) which already lined its banks.'[20]

When Elizabeth arrived, industry and commerce had not yet multiplied fourfold (the great shipyards rose later in the century), but they had greatly expanded. In 1801 William Turner had called Newcastle 'a country town'; by 1830 it was the second port to London, handling over 200,000 tonnes of merchant shipping.[21] Coal was the basis of its wealth, and mining syndicates and marriage settlements linked the old landed families to the new merchants and industrialists. There were chemical works and soap and glass factories on the river, whose banks were also lined by the yards of small shipbuilders and repairers. A set of engravings, by J. W. Carmichael, made in 1828–9 shows the city exactly as Elizabeth would have seen it, with the narrow lanes and crooked cottages giving place to broad thoroughfares and grand stone buildings. Through and beyond the city the Tyne swirled down to the North Sea, with many kinds of craft crowding across the treacherous Tynemouth bar: the famous London traders taking coal to the south; barques bringing goods from the Baltic, the Mediterranean and the West Indies; local sloops serving the east coast ports.[22]

After the end of the French wars the reduction of the navy put many Newcastle keelmen out of work, and in the 1820s there was still great hardship. William Turner's ministry bridged rich and poor and during her stay with him Elizabeth met the kind of work, and the kind of people, she would find in her future life as a Manchester minister's wife. In 1829 Turner, now nearly seventy, was one of the most respected figures in Newcastle. He had been minister of the Hanover Square congregation for nearly half a century, since he came there at the age of twenty-one in 1783. Like his friends Joseph Priestley and Theophilus Lindsey, he had played a major part in the development of Unitarianism. For many years he had his own school in Percy Street and led the way in Newcastle's educational and intellectual life, starting the first Sunday school in the north of England in 1784, founding the Newcastle Literary and Philosophical Society in 1793, opening Jubilee Schools for the poor in 1810 and establishing the Mechanics Institute in 1824.

Yet despite his power and energy, Turner was a modest man. He could command fees of £200 for each session of twenty lectures at the Lit. and Phil., but he lived simply and was compulsively generous. Indeed he had to be forcibly stopped from giving all he earned away, as his exasperated nephew, the Manchester businessman James Aspinall Turner, said, 'to assist in enriching some knave who has imposed on your good nature'. The practical, long-suffering Ann despaired when she discovered her father's secret transactions, such as the selling of stocks (actually left to *her* by her mother) to pay off a poor man's debts. She pointed out acerbically that while *she* could survive, he himself might be penniless in his old age. He nearly was, for he tried three times to renounce his pension.[23] But although he may have been lacking 'in worldly wisdom and business-like prudence', William Turner's transparent integrity and boundless charity won him respect among all denominations, and he must have been canny enough in his way if he could deal with local factions and intrigues successfully for fifty years.

Turner was liked by all, including children – even by the seven-year-old Harriet Martineau, who disliked all clerics on principle (chiefly because they ignored her):

'The first of the order who took any direct notice of me was, as far as I know, good Mr Turner of Newcastle, my mother's pastor and friend before her marriage. At Newcastle we usually went to tea at his house on Sunday evenings; and it was then we began the excellent practice of writing recollections of one of the sermons of the day.'[24]

'One of the sermons' – how many did this small girl have to sit through? Any strain, however, was dispelled by Ann Turner, then fourteen, who went back to Norwich with the Martineaus and became Harriet's mentor and friend, as she was to be Elizabeth's twenty years later.

The Turners lived at 13 Cumberland Terrace, in a small red-brick terrace house, every detail of which Elizabeth Gaskell remembered when she described the house of Thurstan Benson, the minister at Eccleston, in *Ruth*.[25] She called *Ruth* 'my Newcastle novel' (although *Sylvia's Lovers* has more direct connection with 'Newcassel' and the Tyne, and Eccleston is clearly not Newcastle but a Lancashire town). Benson resembles Turner only in his kindness and charity, but his relationship with his realistic sister Faith does sound remarkably like that of William and his daughter Ann.

From the windows of her room on the top floor of Cumberland Terrace Elizabeth could see the Rothbury Hills beyond the city. Downstairs the minister's room opened directly on to the street, so that people needing help could come in and out without anyone knowing. The centre of the household was the back parlour, which looked out on to a small yard. In the novel Ruth comes down on her first morning to this parlour, 'bright and still and clean', full of the scent of mignonette and stocks, to find Miss Benson arranging China and damask roses in an old vase, while her brother reads 'in some large folio'. All is peace – for a moment:

'With gentle morning speech they greeted her; but the quiet repose of the scene was instantly broken by Sally popping in from the kitchen, and glancing at Ruth with sharp reproach. She said –

"I reckon I may bring in the breakfast, now?" with a strong emphasis on the last word.' (Ch. 3)

Such servants, loyal but tough, often act as useful counters to sentiment in Gaskell's fiction.

Elizabeth liked the sturdiness of Newcastle, which Sally evokes, and was affected by the goodness, quietness and order of the Turners' household. Other sides of the minister's life were equally impressive. Turner was still secretary of the Literary and Philosophical Society, which had moved to a new building in 1825 and now had eight hundred members. In 1828 the society marked his long association by commissioning a portrait and bust, and in 1831 his fiftieth year in the city was celebrated by a dinner for over a hundred people. Although he had also started a literary society in 1814, his real passion was science: by 1830 Newcastle had three scientific societies, including the Natural History Society, launched the previous year. Turner himself lectured at the Lit. and Phil., and the subjects on which he spoke during Elizabeth's visits included 'The Vegetable Kingdom', 'Mineralogy and Geology' and 'Optics and Astronomy.'[26]

Historians of science see William Turner as a pioneering figure, 'linking the scientific movement with a wider scientific audience, and with local society generally', and point out that for his audience he looked to the new men of power, 'the merchant, the manufacturer, the engineer, the shipwright and the navigator.'[27] Many new ideas and inventions, idealistic and practical, were explored at the society, from Sir George Cayley's paper 'on the possibilities of an apparatus for flying' to vital new safety lamps for the local collieries. Turner's interest was practical as well as theoretical, and one of his most famous tributes came from George Stephenson, whom he helped as a struggling engineer. 'Mr Turner,' said Stephenson, 'was always ready to assist me with books, with instruments, and with counsel, gratuitously and cheerfully. He gave me the most valuable assistance and instruction; and to my dying day I can never forget the obligation which I owe to my venerable friend.'[28] From 1828 to 1830 the society's members were proudly following the construction of Stephenson's pioneering Liverpool to Manchester railway.

Elizabeth would later encounter a similar scientific fervour in Manchester. In her novels the passion for science cuts across classes and generations, inspiring Job Legh, the artisan-scholar in *Mary Barton,* as much as Lord Hollingford with his private laboratory in *Wives and Daughters.* In *Cousin Phillis* a shared interest in railway engineering connects the narrator's father, Mr Manning, a workman inventor with hands blackened by the foundry who shows 'the same genius for mechanical invention as that of George Stephenson', to the new professional, Edward Holdsworth, with his university degree, southern drawl and elegant clothes.

Gaskell also shows how the work of the new generation, like Holdsworth and Roger Hamley in *Wives and Daughters*, took them overseas: building railroads in Italy and Canada, seeking botanical specimens in the heart of Africa. Her engineers and scientists resemble her sailors, touched by romance and danger. And when sailor and scientist meet, in *Mary Barton*, the world uncovered by science seems even stranger than that of the seafarers' myths, with its own outlandish language. To Mary's amazement Job Legh discredits Will Simpson's tales of mermaids (which she has heard of), but believes his accounts of flying fish (which she has not):

'"Ay! Ay! young man. Now you're speaking truth,"

"Well, now, you'll swallow that, old gentleman. You'll credit me when I say I've seen a critter half fish, half bird, and you won't credit me when I say there be such beasts as mermaids, half-fish, half-woman. To me, one's just as strange as t'other." . . .

"It's the Exocetus; one of the Malacopterygii Abdominales," said Job, much interested.

"Ay, there you go! You're one o' them folks as never knows beasts unless they're called out o' their names. Put 'em in Sunday clothes, and you know 'em, but in their work-a-day English you never know nought about 'em. I've met wi' many o' your kidney; and if I'd ha' known it, I'd ha' christened poor Jack's mermaid wi' some grand gibberish of a name, Mermaidicus Jack Harrisensis; that's just like their new-fangled words. D'ye believe there's such a thing as the Mermaidicus, master?" asked Will, enjoying his own joke uncommonly, as most people do.' (Ch. 13)

Will is right to poke fun (as Gaskell always does at jargon), since the grand Latin name takes one no further than the visually accurate 'flying fish'. But she is making another point, that Mary is excluded from the 'strange language' of science, while she is attuned to that of romance; her first explanation of the 'wizard-like' scientific paraphernalia in Job's room is that he must be a fortune-teller.

In Gaskell's books women half glimpse the transforming power of scientific perceptions and languages, but the prevailing culture conspires against them. In *Wives and Daughters*, set in the late 1820s, Miss Browning and her sister Phoebe are intrigued by Roger Hamley's 'kindness' to Molly Gibson:

"'Now, Phoebe, attend! How was he kind to you, Molly?'"

"Oh, he told me what books to read; and one day he made me notice how many bees I saw – "

"Bees, child! What do you mean? Either you or he must have been crazy!"

"No, not at all. There are more than two hundred kinds of bees in England, and he wanted me to notice the difference between them and flies. – Miss Browning, I can't help seeing what you fancy," said Molly, as red as fire, "but it is very wrong; it is all a mistake".' (Ch.13)

Yet Miss Browning is right. Love, not knowledge, is the Victorian heroine's fate. Science, like industry, is the province of men. In fact in the late 1820s Elizabeth did know women in both spheres. By then Jane Marcet had published two *Conversations* written specially for women, on *Natural Philosophy* and *Vegetable Physiology*, and Mary Somerville (another Unitarian) was giving papers to the Royal Society. Both women were patients and friends of Henry Holland. As for industry, in Newcastle Elizabeth knew the forceful Miss Losh, who inherited her father's ironworks and ran them extremely successfully until 1847.[29] But in fiction she wrote of the norm, not the exception.

Women were not excluded from the Newcastle Lit. and Phil.; in the 1790s it was the first society to open its doors to them. By the more conservative 1820s this caused something of a problem: an enormous fuss arose over the huge male sculptures by John Graham Lough, a local mason, which were exhibited at Hanover Square in 1827: the cast of *Milo* had to be moved to the Committee Rooms, 'where female delicacy might not be exposed to that trial to which it is now subjected.'[30] In January and February 1829, while Elizabeth was there, an equally fierce row brewed over the issue of 'proper books', spurred by the committee's purchase of *Don Juan*. Finally, like poor *Milo*, *Don Juan* was expelled from the library.

Newcastle provided Elizabeth with a different education. There was a buzz of excitement in the air: the hum of ideas as well as the clatter of industry and trade. And she was living for the first time in an atmosphere of active politics. One of Turner's chief allies in Newcastle was James Losh, a prominent barrister on the Northern Circuit, an organizer of the anti-slavery campaign, a friend of Brougham and passionate supporter of parliamentary reform. The 1820s, after the long period of anti-Jacobin feeling, had seen much repressive legislation swept away: the repeal of the Combination Act in 1824, and the Test and Corporation Acts in 1828, meant that trade unions could develop more freely and Dissenters could hold public office for the first time. At the end of the decade the Catholic Emancipation Act tumbled Peel's government from power and let in an uneasy alliance of liberal Tories, Whigs and Radicals committed to the extension of the franchise. In 1830, while regimes toppled abroad, unrest erupted in Britain, first in the south among the agricultural workers with 'Captain Swing' and the rick-burners and then, in the following January, among the militant factory workers of the north. Demand for the Reform Bill grew increasingly fierce and the ups and downs of the debate in parliament, the upheavals at Westminster, the petitions, parades and marches in the country at large filled the papers. In Newcastle the carrying of the second reading of the first Bill in the Commons caused a sensation: bells rang in every parish, bonfires were lit, bands paraded, cannon were fired.[31] Elizabeth embraced the reformers' cause.

At this age, however, she was really more interested in parties and dancing than science and politics, however heady the atmosphere. The wealthy merchants in William Turner's congregation were very sociable, and Elizabeth made many local friends, whom she always remembered with affection. Just after she was married she asked William Turner to give 'my kind love to Ann, the Rankins, the Eldonites, Mrs Welbank, Althusens, Mortons and Carrs'. Many of the names she mentions in her letters to Harriet Carr – Losh, Cayley, Brandling, Collinston, Headlam and Reed – figure large in the history of the city at this time. Harriet herself was the best friend of all. Carrs had been distinguished on Tyneside for many generations, but Harriet's father, George, had only recently moved north from London. He had been a Baltic merchant in St Petersburg and was now agent for the new branch of the Bank of England, opened in 1828; his salary exceeded £1,000 a year.[32] The Carrs lived in Clavering Place, in the old heart of the city near Hanover Square, although many of their set were already moving out to villages like Jesmond, soon the smartest of the new suburbs. After she left Elizabeth wrote happily about tea with the Carrs on rainy days, when they practised the mazurka and she went through her repertoire of popular songs, 'with a voice that was much better suited to "Sleep no more, my voice doth murder sleep" ', or of evenings at Jesmond where she could not keep a straight face when a 'fraud' of a man began to sing. Harriet was rich and she was fun: '*Harriet Carr* and *giddiness* (synonyms)', according to Elizabeth.

She was clearly quite giddy herself. 'You used to complain of me being a "general liker",' she wrote. She made an impression on everyone, and it was probably while she was in Newcastle (not, as is generally thought, in Edinburgh) that a bust of her was sculpted by David Dunbar. Dunbar was working in Newcastle during these years (he presented his bust of 'Earl Grey of the Reform Bill' to the Literary and Philosophical Society in 1833) and later became famous for his sculpture of the local heroine, Grace Darling.[33] His elegant public style makes Elizabeth look rather matronly, though it catches a hint of her eagerness. She was teased about this dignified portrait: 'Mr Losh told my cousins in town that he thought my bust so very like Napoleon – do you?'

Yet she could be restrained and proper, as she is in one letter to Anne Burnett, a member of the wealthy family who owned lead mines near Newcastle. Elizabeth thanks Anne for a kind note, and 'the accompanying book which I have long wished to see' (she does not say what it is), and continues:

'I hope I shall never require anything to remind me of any of my kind Newcastle friends, or of the many pleasant hours I have spent here, but, as a token of your regard, you may be very sure I shall always value it exceedingly.'[34]

('Far too demure to be at all typical,' notes John Chapple, joint editor of Gaskell's letters.)

Elizabeth spent two successive winters at Newcastle, and at some point she also went with Ann Turner to Edinburgh. Later Elizabeth's daughter Meta quashed a suggestion that the two women were sent north to escape the cholera (which did not reach Newcastle until autumn 1831). Instead, she said, her mother simply went to stay with 'friends of her parents.'[35] We know little about this visit, although it is generally accepted that Gaskell used some of her memories when she wrote the prologue to *Round the Sofa* in 1859. Four years before, in 1855, she had visited relations in Scotland and her thoughts may also have turned to Edinburgh after the death in 1858 of her old friend Eliza Fletcher, who had known William Stevenson there at the turn of the century.

Round the Sofa is a collection of disparate pieces, and to provide a framework Gaskell invented an Edinburgh salon, whose members tell a story each week. She rarely, if ever, wrote about settings she did not know and one can recognize her own brand of impatience in the portrait of the young country girl who comes to the Scottish capital with her companion, 'poor grave Miss Duncan', and has to dress neatly and go for 'stiff walks in the streets' instead of the country rambles she is used to. Perpetually evading the sly old landlord's demands for money (a former tutor to university entrants, like her father), and perpetually hungry because the meals are so meagre, she feels bored, lonely and 'longs for company'. The evenings are the worst, until they are asked by kindly Mrs Dawson to her Monday evenings 'at home' ('if it had been to spend an evening at the dentists, I believe I should have welcomed the invitation'). At Mrs Dawson's they enter a different world:

'In came Edinburgh professors, Edinburgh beauties and celebrities, all on their way to some other gayer and later party, but coming first to see Mrs. Dawson, and tell her their *bon-mots*, or their interests, or their plans. By each learned man, by each lovely girl, she was treated as a dear friend . . .

It was very brilliant and very dazzling, and gave enough to think and wonder about for many days.'

Gaskell may have been drawing here more on the memories of Mrs Fletcher, who had held such a salon, than on her own.[36] But she would have had an entry into 'brilliant' society through connections of the Turners and the Hollands, Stevensons and Thomsons. Scotland's leading miniaturist, William John Thomson of Edinburgh, painted Elizabeth, and there has been speculation as to how this came about since she was far from rich and could not have commissioned him.[37] There is no mystery – Thomson was the elder brother of her stepmother, Catherine. His family may therefore have been the 'friends of her parents' to whom Meta referred. William Thomson, however, was a prominent figure in the Scottish art scene, a member of the Royal Scottish Academy and the holder of several official posts. He had just declined a knighthood and his house in Northumberland Street was a far cry from the dingy Old Town lodgings where the narrator and Miss Duncan stay in *Round the Sofa*. In Thomson's conventionally romantic portrait Elizabeth looks back over round white shoulders, her face framed by soft brown hair falling from a rich coil piled on top of her head. Her small waist, amid billowing sleeves and stole, is tightly circled by a black belt, but while the effect is sensual, the sideways glance of the blue-grey eyes is alert, intelligent and cool.

At the start of the 1830s Edinburgh saw itself as a Scottish metropolis, a cultural centre rivalling London. The city's latest idol (or object of abuse, depending on your point of view) was George Combe, the phrenologist, who began his extremely popular lectures there in 1825; around the time of Elizabeth's visit these had been temporarily suspended, following the disputes over his book *The Constitution of Man*.[38] Phrenology was just one of the crazes ranging from hydropathy and vegetarianism to mesmerism and spiritualism which swept Britain in the 1830s to 1840s. Its devotees argued that each separate intellectual and temperamental faculty – reason, sensuality, affection – had its precise position in the brain, and that these, and character as a whole, could be calculated by measuring a person's skull. It appealed particularly to women, because it countered suggestions of mental inequality between the sexes, and Elizabeth could hardly escape the theory which held Edinburgh in thrall, although (unlike George Eliot a few years later) she did not take it very seriously. Her sense of the absurd got the better of her. In 1831 she told Harriet:

'I have been studying Spurzheim on Phrenology during my retirement and intend to illuminate the world in the character of Lectures soon, so completely am I convinced of it, more especially as I have the organ of causality, alias the reasoning faculty, so very strongly developed, and you know what a reasonable person I am.'[39]

The retirement which drove her to read Spurzheim followed her return to her Holland relations. Her polite thank-you letter to Anne Burnett was one of farewell: 'I am looking forward with great pleasure to reading your most acceptable present when settled for the Summer at Woodside, where I hope to join my Aunt the day after tomorrow.'[40] Her days of travelling were almost over. She remained very fond of William Turner until the end of his life. He baptized her second daughter in 1837 and after he retired in 1840, he and Ann moved to Manchester, where his daughter Mary lived. Elizabeth read aloud to him in his old age and when he died, aged ninety-seven, her husband preached the funeral sermon.[41]

In June 1831 Hannah Lumb was already at Woodside, Birkenhead, with Samuel Holland's family, and Elizabeth stayed there with her until September. She complained to Harriet, who had been enjoying the 'pomps and vanities' of London, of the terrible weather and the quiet life: 'unless I told you how the hay crops &c were going on and what show of fruit there is I could send you little news'. Glumly she turned to the books she had read so often. At the end of August, on a day of such rain that muddy streams were running down the road she groans: 'Fancy our agreeable situation – not a book but what we have all read hundreds of times', such as 'odd volumes' of Dante and Shakespeare and a few old newspapers. Perhaps 'hundreds of times' is overdoing it, for in the same letter she writes of Mme de Sévigné, 'eternal woman – how often have I begun both her and Sir Chas. Grandison, and never finished either'. *Sir Charles Grandison* may have stayed unread but Mme de Sévigné became her heroine, to the extent of planning to write her biography. The old books made their impact.

Elizabeth did not spend all the time at Woodside reading. Her laments about lack of news are misleading – like most people, she was a chameleon correspondent. Writing to Harriet, with her smart social life, she always put on her most worldly face. In reality she showed no sign of languorous ennui. It is clear that she thoroughly enjoyed Birkenhead and Liverpool, as she seemed to enjoy herself everywhere. She liked her teasing uncle Sam and sensible aunt Katherine. Her cousin Charles was a merchant in Buenos Aires and young Sam was busy with his house in north Wales, but Anne and Fanny, now in their early thirties, and Kate, six years older than herself, were witty and lively companions. It did not rain all the time (but she wrote her letters when it did) and far from sitting alone, Elizabeth went to dances and concerts, dinners and regattas, and sails on the river, letting slip in an unguarded moment: 'I do like Liverpool and the Mersey and the accent and the people very much.'

Liverpool had trebled in size in thirty years, its ships trading with ports across the globe, from Calcutta to New York and Rio de Janeiro. Crowded quays were piled with bales of raw cotton destined for the textile towns inland and with finished goods for the markets overseas. By the 1820s 'the country mansions of merchant princes were to be found dotting the country side, scattered over Everton Hill, frequent in the southern part of Toxteth Park, and even as far afield as Childwell and Allerton.'[42] Until recently the Hollands had lived in the Toxteth area, in Wellington Road. But the slums had mushroomed as fast as the mansions and one of the worst districts was not far away, at the north end of Toxteth Park.

Liverpool Unitarians responded philanthropically to the over-crowding and disease of the growing city. Among the people Elizabeth dined with was Dr Traill, soon to become professor of medical jurisprudence at Edinburgh, and a moving spirit behind Liverpool's Royal Infirmary School of Medicine, founded in 1834. Elizabeth took part in the inevitable 'good works', which sometimes made her groan. The great preoccupation of August 1831 (almost eclipsing William IV's coronation on 8 September) was

'the *bazaar* for the benefit of the Infirmary and oh! how I wish the name of bazaar like that of Macgregor might perish for ever! there is to be a Ball one of the nights, a much more sensible way of being charitable I think — Feet versus Hands.'[43]

In these letters frivolity is uppermost. Events are filtered through the lens of social life and even tragedies are the stuff of dinner-party chat, like the loss of *Rothsay Castle*, sunk on its way to Beaumaris. Outraged as she was by the way the irresponsible owners had grossly overloaded the boat, a certain flippancy creeps into her eager account of the news:

'I had a slight dining acquaintance was on board and he survived. I dined with him on Monday at Dr. Traills but as he said he had been a hero nine times that day I could not, much as I longed, make my enquiries as to his feelings, him having been quite insensible when taken up he must have experienced all the sensations of drowning!'[44]

She dashes on to gossip of mutual friends. On the next page the heroic survivor is merely identified, in passing, as 'the drowned gentleman'.

Friends, clothes, music, books, weddings – these are the subjects she likes best. Despite Sam Holland's ups and downs in trade, money did not seem to be lacking. When they set out to buy wedding presents, there was a 'grand dispute': 'I am for a magnificent dressing box for it is a thing I always long for, with plenty of cut glass and silver about it – but I am quite in the minority, and a timepiece is the conqueror I fear. A cousin of mine here has just had a commission to buy sixty pound worth of jewellery for a wedding present.' The contrast between such extravagance and the agony of the poor would become one of her great themes, but in 1831 her reforming zeal had temporarily faded: 'Oh! how tired I am of the Reform Bill – and my Aunt, and most of my cousins, are quite anti-reformers and abuse Lord Brougham and think him superficial.' Hearing that Harriet was going to Ascot, she confessed that she would quite like to see the royal family, 'proper and improper. In spite of my political principles I can not help admiring high blood and aristocracy.' Instead of her social anger, these early letters show her love of glamour and romance and her playful, free-ranging imagination, spinning across space and time from tiny details of shared women's lives:

'The other day being in Liverpool, I thought I would get some coloured cloth to work upon for stools, à la mode of some we saw the other day: so stept into a shop to ask for some fine cloth – to my great astonishment the man quite seriously asked me if I wanted it for *pantaloons*! . . . Do you know that at Buenos Ayres, very large combs for the hair behind are quite the fashion, but as they have them all from Paris, they can't afford to have one a piece, so three or four subscribe for one amongst them and take it in turns to be in the fashion – It is pretty much the case with *the* pen in this house for we have but one fit to write with among us, and can none of us mend one were our lives at stake – Or it is like the reign of Edward the third where some antiquary has rummaged out that one needle was the common allowance among four or five sisters, and when one tore her gown the needle was brought forth like the pen now – which good pen as you have probably found out is monopolized by another scribbler, so that poor I have in good sooth, sometimes one little better than a stick.'[45]

(She was at home in this sisterhood of dress, of sewing, of writing – but all her life she would moan about her pens.)

She borrowed stories from everywhere. For lack of news she pads one letter with a vivid account of the emigration to America of Colonel Murat, whom 'my Aunt' (probably Swinton's wife, Anne) knew when she was 'living in Naples'. Charles sent his gossip from South America and Edward (Swinton's son) from Prussia. Other friends went to Russia – in August 1831 Edward's sister Louisa joked that it is 'a point of dispute as to whether Mr. Wm. Cayley is gone to get a wife or Cholera Morbus in St Petersburg'.

This joke turned sour. A second wave of Asiatic cholera, which had reached Russia in 1830, was driving its way across Europe. Elizabeth was wrong when she rejoiced with Harriet, who feared for her St Petersburg friends, that the disease was now abating. By midsummer of 1831 it had reached Riga, by early autumn it was ravaging Hamburg and the Baltic ports and in October, crossing by the ships to the Tyne, it took its first British victim, a Sunderland keelman. Despite desperate attempts at containment, including blockades on the roads, cholera spread through Britain, killing over thirty-two thousand people in the next two years.[46] The Hollands and their circle escaped – it was mostly the poor who died – but Elizabeth, despite her great capacity for sympathy, recorded little of their suffering. In Knutsford the following summer she felt only the lurking shadow of the epidemic, when she learnt that it had reached some nearby villages or heard a man cursing in anger, *'Cholera seize Thee!'*

In September 1831 Elizabeth and Aunt Lumb left Liverpool, and went home. There had been plans for Lily to spend a month or so at Plas Penrhyn, but these were shelved due to more work on the house. It was good to be back after so long. She went out to Sandlebridge with Peter Holland's daughter Susan, and in beautiful weather they rose and went to bed *'almost'* with the sun and spent nearly all day outdoors. There were no interruptions except 'now and then, when the carriage came from Knutsford bringing letters and *meat* and an importation of cousins for an hour or two'. In October Aunt Swinton and cousin Charlotte were due to descend and, to prepare for them, she returned to the Heath. 'I am now settling down to the winter,' she wrote, 'and mean to be very regular and quiet – I really am glad of it for it is a long time since I was steadily settled at home with my various books, writing materials and "helps to learning" about me.' Her time was hardly quiet: as well as her London relations, Peter Holland's daughters were all at home until Christmas, when two were to go to Henry in Brook Street. Elizabeth taught them the mazurka: 'I keep my pupils at first step however having forgotten the figures, though I don't acknowledge it.'

At twenty-one she was lively, gregarious, restless. Love affairs filled her mind. She was intrigued when her cousin Louisa told her of a grand ball at Park Lane with 'capital "flirting places" in the balcony'. Matters often went beyond flirtation, to judge by this Jane Austenish comment: 'What do you think of my knowing forty-three *couples* engaged – couples, not single people.' A touch of exaggeration perhaps. She teases Harriet about a certain Matthew who is building a house, saying she thought he had one 'and only wanted a Mrs Matthew to complete his decorations'. (It appears that Harriet did eventually marry Matthew Andersen, a Russian merchant.) And she may have dallied with the idea of a Newcastle marriage herself, though it was only a passing fancy:

'I shall like to hear your opinion of *my* house in Jesmond, since mine it will be, without doubt, and your present (you are a very interested creature) *when* the happy event takes place, shall be even unto the half of my kingdom. I never knew such a week as this has been for marriages – no less than three intimate friends of ours became fiancées during this last fortnight, and what is more extraordinary I am not one of the number!'[47]

This was soon to change. That autumn Elizabeth went with Ann Turner to Manchester, to stay with William Turner's elder daughter, Mary, who was married to John Gooch Robberds, minister of Cross Street Chapel. It was probably at the Robberds's house in Greenheys that she met the assistant minister, a brilliant man only five years older than herself, extremely tall, extremely thin, extremely attractive – the Revd William Gaskell.

[4]

Love, Marriage and Manchester

By the following spring William and Elizabeth were engaged. By the end of summer they were married. It was not an obvious match and, although William said that a Manchester friend, Alma Worthington, had told him that she had 'predicted what the consequences would be, if Elizabeth and I saw much of each other', there was some truth in Aunt Lumb's teasing question, 'Why Elizabeth how could this man ever take a fancy to such a little giddy thoughtless thing as you?' In 'The Doom of the Griffiths' Elizabeth would ask: 'How often do we see giddy, coquetting, restless girls become sobered by marriage? A great object in life is decided, one on which their thoughts have been running in all their vagaries.'

Elizabeth was lively and open. William, until people knew him well, appeared grave, scholarly, rather austere. Yet these contrasts strengthened their relationship. She drew him out, finding his warmth and humour, and touching a romantic vein in his nature, while he gave her a fixed point in the compass of her emotions, a stability which she sometimes resisted but never undervalued. At times she wished he was more demonstrative, less dry, less rule-bound, less busy. When he was away, she confessed she breathed more freely – but she always yearned for his return. She turned to William not to make decisions for her, but to reinforce or question those she made for herself. He became a valued critic and a stalwart support against the criticism of others, upholding her right to publish the truth as she found it. He would stand by her when *Mary Barton* enraged the wealthy mill-owners, when members of his congregation burnt their copies of *Ruth*, when *The Life of Charlotte Brontë* led to angry letters and libel suits. The Gaskells' marriage was not untroubled, and in later years its strength

71

depended as much on distance as on closeness. But it was a strong, complex relationship tested over time.

Towards the end of *The Life of Charlotte Brontë* Gaskell firmly shuts the door on Mr Nicholls and Charlotte, implying that it would be wrong to pry inside. In some ways time and the loss of her private letters have done her the same courtesy. Only one letter from William to Elizabeth survives, and none from her to him, although they wrote constantly to each other when they were apart. Some of their shared interests and concerns are clear to see, especially their enjoyment of music, art and literature. They were also – and this was to be central to Elizabeth's early career as a writer – both fascinated by language. Elizabeth was interested in modes of expression and in the way speech revealed personality, attitudes, class and history. William, a classicist, loved etymology and enjoyed words in themselves: he was notorious for his puns (signing himself 'Mr Goosequill' to his children and to his friend John Relly Beard) and gave lectures on the Lancashire dialect, on which Elizabeth drew when writing *Mary Barton*.[1]

After his death a pupil at William's literature classes wrote of his intense, physical enjoyment of language, describing him as a man who 'licked his intellectual lips after a dainty reading from Herrick' and who relished the individual word. 'Now and then he showed a marked preference for a fine word, and I remember how he used to gloat over Gray's use of "redolent", and how other such similar words seemed to have a great fascination for him.' The same writer recalled that William was renowned for his reading, which was not fiery or rhetorical, but

'clear and sweet, and no word was ever uttered by him but you could hear it all round as it were. This gave his reading of poetry a peculiar charm, for while he had a keen ear for the subtleties of rhyme, rhythm and metre, nothing was ever lost of the meaning or the beauty of the words.'[2]

With William, Elizabeth found a renewed delight in reading and a new impetus to write: it was partly through their work together in the 1830s (and also in reaction to it) that she evolved her individual style.

A fundamental bond between them was their faith, allied to a broad (but not absolute) tolerance of other opinions, a progressive vision of history and a liberal position in politics. Both the Gaskells held to a version of Unitarianism which was essentially optimistic, trusting in the innate goodness of human nature, warped though human actions might become in response to material, emotional or spiritual deprivation. It was against social evil, not original sin or the works of the devil, that the Gaskells took their stand. If such evil was humanly created, it must, they felt, be open to human remedy through practical measures and through the power of the word to awaken conscience and modify behaviour. The opportunity to share William's work seemed to offer Elizabeth a practical role in tune with these beliefs (although she quickly insisted on defining the nature of that role for herself). In later years her many-sided commitments devoured her time and she sometimes burst out in frustration or weariness, but she rarely expressed self-pity. On the contrary, the people she pitied were those who cut themselves off from involvement, like the wife and daughters of Carson, the mill-owner in *Mary Barton*, with their genteel airs and languorous headaches. Activity was essential to her, as it was to William.

William Gaskell was born in 1805 at Latchford, on the outskirts of Warrington, where his father was a sail-canvas manufacturer.[3] He was the first of seven children and he seems to have had the solemnity and sense of responsibility often found in an oldest child, reinforced by the deaths of his sister Margaret, aged six, in 1816, of his father in 1819 and his youngest brother, John, in 1821.

The Gaskells were an old, many-branched Lancashire Dissenting family whose name appears in the earliest records of Sankey Street Chapel, Warrington, and Cross Street, Manchester. But while William's forebears on his father's side were solidly middle class, prosperous and well educated, his mother, Margaret Jackson, came from a different background: according to one story, his father had one day noticed a remarkably beautiful housemaid working on a doorstep, and became so intrigued that he paid for her schooling and later married her.[4] Margaret was warm and unaffected and was deeply loved by her children. Three years after her first husband died she married the Revd Edward Dimock, minister of Sankey Street Chapel, a well-meaning but pompous man who was often the butt of his stepchildren's jokes. 'Tell my dear mother,' Elizabeth once wrote ironically to her sister-in-law Eliza, 'how I did enjoy the pears. My blessing (and there are two senses to that word) to Mr Dimock.' On another occasion she composed a long Johnsonian parody aimed, she said, to satisfy Dimockian tastes.

William had already left home when his mother remarried. At fifteen he went to Glasgow University, much favoured by Dissenters, who were not admitted to Oxford or Cambridge. William was a natural scholar. He worked swiftly through the curriculum (first year Latin, second Greek, third logic, fourth year ethics and modern philosophy) and, after taking his BA in 1825, he continued with a wide-ranging final year of natural philosophy, physics, mathematics, history and geography. On the way he collected prizes in all subjects, including the prestigious Blackstone prize in Greek in 1822; the classics remained one of his private passions.

In 1825, aged twenty, he took his MA and began training for the ministry at Manchester New College, which was then situated in York, under the tutelage of Charles Wellbeloved and James Turner (William Turner's son). While Elizabeth was copying Italian songs and practising quadrilles at Avonbank and Knutsford, her future husband was a member of a highly regulated community, one of whose rules read: 'Dancing in public is altogether prohibited.'[5] His courses included classics and science as well as divinity and as a student he also began preaching in the surrounding villages (the fine speaking voice which so many people admired may have been helped by the college's weekly elocution class, 'sometimes taken by an actor from Covent Garden or Drury Lane'). During his student years William made friendships which lasted all his life. At Glasgow he came to know Henry Green, who became minister at Knutsford in 1827 and was a friend of the Hollands, and Edmund and Sidney Potter, from the wealthy calico-printing family, a major force in Manchester life. In later years he spent many holidays in Scotland with Edmund Potter (but always on his own – he too needed escape, less, one sometimes feels, from the city than from his growing family).[6]

At York he lived even more in the ambit of the leading Dissenting families, for whom the college was almost a mini-university. Many of his contemporaries there, like John Relly Beard, Edward Tagart and James Martineau, were destined for the ministry, but there were also many lay students. The list of pupils during the college's time at York reads like a roll-call of the aristocracy of Dissent, containing the names of almost all the powerful manufacturing and commercial families: Strutts, Marslands, Houldsworths and McConnells (the four largest cotton-spinning firms); Ashtons and Fieldens (great factory-owners);

Darbishires, Philips, Potters (Manchester industrialists and merchants); as well as brewers, bankers, iron-workers and ship-owners.[7]
The broad syllabus, which took in maths, science and political
economy, was designed to form men who would be leaders of the
coming age and who could overcome the barriers their sectarian faith
created. Even the emphasis on elocution was intended to help them in
the public sphere.

William never deviated from his intention of becoming a minister
and when he left York in 1828, he was offered a choice of four posts, a
tribute to his ability and promise.[8] After some hesitation he picked
Cross Street, the major Unitarian chapel in Manchester. It was a bold
decision for a young man taking up his first ministry. At Cross Street
he faced a long-established, influential and highly educated congregation who would expect high standards of preaching and an active
commitment to the social and political causes which they espoused. In
addition he was to work in a rapidly expanding city where the
majority of workers were immigrants from elsewhere, where the
factories produced immense poverty as well as immense wealth and
where the slums bred disease and distress on a scale which no one, as
yet, had fully fathomed. William confessed he was daunted, but he was
lucky in his senior minister, John Robberds, a hard-working, jolly,
sympathetic man full of practical advice and moral support. In his
memoir of Robberds the Revd J. J. Tayler described him as 'ever
inclined to pass a favourable judgment and to look on the bright side
of things', and when William himself preached his funeral sermon, he
specifically referred to his old friend's lively conversation, with its
'sparkling turn and witty jests'.[9] With John Robberds and his
forthright wife, Mary, William thawed and relaxed, and it was in their
easy-going household that he came to know Elizabeth Stevenson.

Over the winter of 1831–2 William saw Elizabeth often and in March
he went to Knutsford to meet Aunt Lumb. While he was there, she fell
ill, as Elizabeth explained: 'the very morning after he came, she broke
a small bloodvessel which alarmed us very much'. Before her illness
she had already welcomed William, he told his sister Eliza, 'in the
kindest and most affectionate manner, and expressed the great
pleasure which she felt that Elizabeth had been led to form an
engagement with me'. His deep feelings, surface formality and humour
emerge in this letter, written after his sudden recall to Manchester on

the death of John Robberds's mother. 'I have called Mrs. L's illness unfortunate,' he wrote, 'and yet in one respect I can hardly deem it so. It served to present Elizabeth to me in a still more lively and endearing light than I had before beheld her, and did more perhaps to knit our souls together than months could have done, without it. You can't imagine how lonely I feel without her.' He was writing, he said, with her rings on his fingers and her portrait in front of him.[10]

He sounds a bit bemused. Rumours about the engagement had spread like fire in Manchester, and he was deluged with congratulations, while in Knutsford he had to parry the curiosity of the whole Holland family about their future relatives. 'One of the Miss Hollands enquired of me whether you drew,' he told Eliza. 'I answered "a little", another whether you played, I replied "a little". I hope to the last you will soon enable me to reply "Yes".' Eliza Gaskell (usually addressed as Lizzie or Lizzy) – was then twenty. She had been acting as William's housekeeper in Manchester and was highly accomplished, widely read and almost as good a classical scholar as her brother, with whom she also shared a keen interest in natural history. A letter of the 1840s describes her as 'a very striking woman . . . very clever, energetic and animated' (noting, intriguingly, how like her sister-in-law Elizabeth she looked, and how unlike her brother).[11] In this letter of March 1832 William enclosed a note from Elizabeth, a precursor of the many breathless, crowded pages she was to send Lizzy over the next ten years. She wrote with her usual headlong irreverence, declaring that William 'may finish his half at Ardwick, and as I shan't be there to see, he may say what scandal he likes of us all, and give me as bad a character as he chooses. N.B. I have been behaving very well so don't believe a word of it.' The appeal made to Harriet Carr is heard again: 'and do you, dearest, pray write again to me, and that right speedily – tell me anything that interests you – and oh! don't forget how to fight with pillows and "farm yard noises" when Edward heard you laughing so plainly'. (It appears that the Gaskell family were not all scholarship and solemnity.) She also sends her 'warmest thanks' for a letter from William's older sister, Anne, who was living at home with the Dimocks in Warrington. Anne, who would marry the Warrington postmaster, William Robson, also became one of Elizabeth's dearest friends, the person she would write to most intimately about her husband and children until the end of her life.

William came back to see his future bride in Knutsford at the end of

March and then began to plan their married life with great efficiency. He took a house, 14 Dover Street (at a rent of £32 a year), a few doors from no. 1, where he had lived with Eliza. Elizabeth stayed in Cheshire to nurse Aunt Lumb, who did not fully recover until early May. She was happy, but often tired, and her letters to Harriet are full of remedies for the headaches that plagued them both. All around her more friends and cousins were marrying and moving to new places. She was already drawing slightly away from the close-knit Holland clan, and did not, for instance, take part in the family production of *The Rivals* that July, although she was caught up in the excitement, which took over 'the drawing room part' of their lives, 'and Lucy Holland for some days was "great" as Mrs. Malaprop, making some really capital travesties of words'.[12]

She told Harriet all about *The Rivals* in a long letter of 8 August. Married life was approaching fast:

'I am in the middle, or rather I hope, three quarters through the bustle of wedding-gowns, though in the opinion of some sage people preparations for a marriage should not be *begun* before the last fortnight, and it wants rather more than that to the day, when I am to learn obedience the 30th of this month. Never having received a letter from any lady similarly situated, I don't the least know how to express myself on the reason but I fancy "to learn obedience" is something new: to me at least it is. I have got the very prettiest bonnet for the occasion that ever was, and cannot help trying it on every time I go into my room. I smell nothing but marking-ink, and see nothing but E.C.S. everywhere.'

The tone is light, the details trivial, the sequence spontaneous and careless. But in Gaskell's writing casual juxtapositions and minor details are often keys to vital issues, and here, as she tries on her bonnet and looks at her old initials, she is watching herself indelibly changing her identity. Her nervousness about obedience was real as well as assumed; she was never to play a submissive role. Once married, she always signed herself Elizabeth Gaskell, not Mrs William Gaskell. In 1838, when Eliza Gaskell married Charles Holland, she chided her for not doing the same: 'It is a *a silly piece of bride-like affectation* my dear, not to sign youself by your proper name . . . so goodbye my dear Mrs. Elizabeth Holland.'

Unitarians believed that marriage should be based on give and take, not rule and submission. Twenty years earlier, when Mary Turner married John Robberds, her father William had written: 'You are neither of you, I trust, disposed to be jealous of each other's rights, or grudging in the discharge of mutual obligations.'[13] Elizabeth was determined to run her own life. When she wrote to Tottie Fox in 1856, agreeing to sign the petition for the Married Women's Property Act, she still had reservations about marriage: 'a husband can coax, wheedle, beat or tyrannize his wife out of something and no law whatever will help this that I see'. In her novels, and especially in her short stories, Gaskell drew many dominating husbands capable of crippling their wives and children: in 'Lizzie Leigh,' for example, where the mother denies her longing to find her erring daughter because of her humble adherence to the spirit of Milton's line, 'He for God only, she for God in him'. Perhaps the fiercest portrait is of the intransigent Mr Bradshaw in *Ruth*, a pillar of the congregation, so proud of his fine bass voice and sure of his inner righteousness:

'He was a tall, large-boned, iron man; stern, powerful and authoritative in appearance; dressed in clothes of the finest broadcloth, and scrupulously ill-made, as if to show that he was indifferent to all outward things. His wife was sweet and gentle-looking, but as if she was thoroughly broken into submission.' (Ch. 14)

Elizabeth had no intention of being broken. Not that she saw William as an autocrat: it was neither in his nature, nor in his creed. The alarm her letter hints at seems to be based more upon a dread of what *might* have been, had William's character not pre-empted the question of obedience by making it irrelevant. As it was, although she felt the pressure of his opinions, especially in regard to her writing, he helped propel her into a sphere of pragmatic self-assertion which called out her own self-reliance. Sometimes she even felt slightly ambivalent about her freedom. In the interesting correspondence with Tottie about the difficulties women face in finding a role, she admits:

'Yes, that discovery of one's exact work in the world is a puzzle: I never meant to say it was not. I long (weakly) for the old times when right and wrong did not seem such complicated matters; and I am sometimes coward enough to wish that we were back in the darkness where obedience was the only seen duty of women. Only even then I don't believe William would ever have *commanded* me.' (L109)

This suggests how ingrained the notion of submission was. Even while she chafed against it and portrayed it so bitterly in her fiction, she held to some model (a romantic fantasy as much as a social belief) of the strong, stern man ruling the impulsive, imaginative woman – a pattern which provides the dramatic and sexual tension of *North and South*. In 1854, when she was writing that novel, she wrote a curious letter to John Forster about Charlotte Brontë's forthcoming marriage to Arthur Bell Nicholls:

'I fancy him very good, but *very* stern & bigoted; but I dare say that is partly fancy. Still it arises from what she has told me . . . However, with all his bigotry & sternness it must be charming to be loved with all the strength of his heart as she sounds to be. Mr Shaen accuses me always of being "too much of a woman" in always wanting to obey somebody – but I am sure that Miss Brontë could never have borne not to be well-ruled & ordered – well! I think I have got a "fiasco" and I have hardly any right to go on discussing what she could or she could not do – but I mean that she would never have been happy but with an exacting rigid, law-giving, passionate man.' (L280–1)

In the summer of 1832, as her own marriage approached, Elizabeth's own fears may have included another element. She never writes openly about sex or sexuality, but at the very end of the August letter to Harriet she slips in a bizarre Cranfordian anecdote. For post-Freudian readers, it may, perhaps, speak for itself:

'Did you see that account of a lady & gentleman who were struck with lightning on their wedding tour. They were cousins of Mrs Edward Holland's, a Mr and Mrs Boddington, and are nearly recovered now; but for some time it made us very much afraid of putting up a umbrella for fear of lightning, as in their case the brass point served as a conductor, and afterwards the steel in Mrs. Boddington's stays, conveyed the fluid to within a straw's breadth of a vital part in her leg.'[14]

Without obvious fire from heaven Elizabeth Stevenson married William Gaskell in St John's Parish Church, Knutsford (since Dissenters could not marry in their own chapels until 1837), on 30 August 1832. Her uncle Peter Holland gave her away, her cousins Kate and Susan were bridesmaids and William's brother Sam was best man. The wedding breakfast took place next door, at Church House. All went smoothly – or seemed to. A fortnight later Elizabeth told Lizzy that Kate had just sent her a 'long, long letter . . . and among other things made us laugh exceedingly with telling us one *report* of which I dare say neither you nor Sam were aware. Pray ask him with my love whether he knew that Sue put his shoulder out of joint by pulling him to her at the altar, and that so much force was required on *Susan's* part because Kate was pulling so at his other arm. Since hearing this Wm & I have felt rather anxious to hear of his health.'

On her wedding day Knutsford paid tribute to Elizabeth with its old custom of sanding (which she thought was derived from medieval well-dressing). The ground outside almost every house was strewn with red sand, sprinkled with white in patterns of flowers and verses.[15] The number of houses sanded was a clue to the bride's popularity and, as she later told Mary Howitt,

'When I was married, nearly all the houses in the town were sanded, and these were the two favourite verses:

> Long may they live,
> Happy may they be,
> Blest with content,
> And from misfortune free.

> Long may they live,
> Happy may they be,
> And blest with a numerous
> Pro-ge-ny.'

(L29)

(Years later, in *Sylvia's Lovers*, she would give the second verse to the farm servant Kester, to recite at Sylvia's wedding.)

Leaving the messages of goodwill behind them, the couple left for Wales. William described their wedding trip in a letter to Eliza in which the language of united souls gives way to something altogether warmer and more direct. After spending three weeks at Aber, they took the coach to Conway, 'as beautiful a ride as heart could desire':

'On the left we had Beaumaris and the sea shining and sparkling in the morning light, and on our right the hills covered with the richest and warmest tints, and the air so fresh and pure, and Lily looking so very well, and two bugles playing all the way – wasn't it enough to make one very happy? We went through the fine old castle at Conway and, as I cannot tell you fully our feelings as we wandered through it and thought of departed greatness and all that – why I shall only tell you that we felt very properly – and I (but I did not tell this before) felt very hungry.'[16]

Hunger pangs were compensated for by the beauty of the drive to Llanrwst (where William remembered they had brought some cake), and then through even finer country to Capel Curig. Here disaster struck, for 'on the way Lily's boa took a fancy to some little nook or other, & though we stayed a considerable time at Capel Curig, consoling ourselves for its absence by eating our dinners, it made not its appearance before we left, and no tidings of it have reached us up to the present'. Giving up the search, they continues their journey over the pass of Llanberis, 'and here boa and everything else, but my own Lily, was forgotten in the wondrous wildness and rugged grandeur of the scene'.

At Beddgelert Elizabeth had to overcome her terror of umbrellas, at least the mundane variety. The weather closed in and lashing rain and wind pursued them to Samuel Holland's house at Plas Penrhyn. William, however, was in a mood to think well of everyone and everything, despite the rain: 'Mrs Holland is kindness itself – and Sam I like very much – and Ann I am quite in love with. My bonny wee wife – *My* bonny wee wife – grows I do think more bonny than ever.' Kept inside by the weather, the party must have gathered, as usual, around the piano, inspiring William (whose thoughts were now turning to Manchester) to cast aside all notion of thrift and to ask Lizzy to go straight away 'to Hargreaves and Hime, in the Square, and ask if they have disposed of the piano which Mr. Shore recommended to me. It was one of the Broadwoods, Patents – price £55 for cash. If they have it still – get them to send it up, and say I will pay for it on my return.' (The piano, and music generally, were to play an important part in their future family life.) More practical instructions followed: to get the remainder of the wedding cake, to put saucers under the plants, to earth up the celery. The Gaskells were on their way home.

Once again Lily filled up her half of the letter, writing 'helter-skelter' with 'thanks upon thanks from the very bottom of my long heart, for yr letter which was *so* welcome, as we had been longing for news from *our* home'. 'As you justly conjecture,' she added, 'I *have* a *great* deal of trouble, in managing this obstreperous brother of yours, though I dare say he will try and persuade you the trouble is all on his side.' Her spirits high, she too writes of their health and their joint appetites, her jokes slipping into a suggestive conceit, signed off with a hasty flourish:

'You would be astonished to see our appetites, the dragon of Wantley, "who ate churches of a Sunday, whole dishes of people were to him, but a dish of Salmagunde" was really a delicate appetite compared to ours. If you hear of the principality of Wales being swallowed up by an earthquake, for earthquake read Revd. Wm. Gaskell – How very good you are to be staying at home by yourself while

here's post

your most affect[ionate] Sister

E. C. Gaskell'

(L2–3)

William and Elizabeth returned via Knutsford, where they stayed while Elizabeth shook off a sore throat. They arrived at 14 Dover Street on 29 September, Lily's twenty-second birthday. She was still 'in a whirl' as she told William Turner, to whom she wrote on 6 October, 'seizing the first leisure moment'. As soon as the formal bridal calls were over, she said, William had promised to introduce her to the families under his care, 'as the minister's wife, and one who intends to be their useful friend.'[17] Mary Robberds (William Turner's daughter) would advise her on her duties. (Mary doubtless passed on the advice she herself had received from her father: making her small income 'support a respectable appearance', setting an example of propriety and decorum, helping in charity and Sunday schools and also, more alarmingly, trying to make peace when petty quarrels, gossip and general busybodiness created rifts among the womenfolk of the congregation.) But although she wrote so dutifully to the old Newcastle pastor, Elizabeth rather resisted full involvement. In the words of A. Cobden Smith, 'she no sooner settled in Manchester than she steadily and consistently objected to her time being considered as belonging in any way to her husband's congregation', in the way of visiting, or giving leadership as a minister's wife. 'What she did was of her own choice and desire. The one place she did unite in willing service was the Sunday School.'[18]

Elizabeth may have set her own terms, but in the first years of marriage, as throughout her education, she was pulled by conflicting voices – the Unitarian call to independence and the conventional appeal to submission. That second voice echoed through the 1830s and 1840s in countless books of advice to young women and wives, like Mrs John Sandford's *Woman in Her Social and Domestic Character* (1831) or Sarah Stickney Ellis's influential tomes *The Women of England: Their Social Duties and Domestic Habits* (1839) and *The Daughters of England* (1842). The introduction to the latter spells out the fundamental creed:

'I must now take it for granted that the youthful reader of these pages has reflected seriously upon her position in society as a woman, has acknowledged her inferiority to man, has examined her own nature, and found there a capability of feeling, a quickness of perception, and a facility of adaptation, beyond what he possesses, and which, consequently, fit her for a distinct and separate sphere.'[19]

Despite her evident 'capacity of feeling' and 'quickness of perception' Elizabeth was already ambivalent about the notion of separate spheres, and was to become increasingly resistant to the doctrine. But she did believe she should adapt her life to her husband's. That September she was still receiving presents (like 'a very handsome fish-slice', from James Turner), but the honeymoon was over. Responsibilities loomed.

She would not be lonely in Manchester. Mary Robberds was kind and welcoming and the Hollands had many other friends in the city (Peter Holland had even thought of moving there in 1828); William's lively, always joking brother Sam, eighteen months his junior and now a Manchester doctor, visited Dover Street regularly. Elizabeth was proud and happy to have her own house at last. Aunt Lumb had promised to come and stay soon, and she was pleased that she could 'in some means provide for her comforts, as she has so often done for mine'. But the whole experience of marriage and settling in was slightly overwhelming. She sympathized with Ann Turner, who was in the throes of moving house, 'for I am just now feeling so doubtful as to the success of my housekeeping, and little *daily* cares, that the very idea of a removal sounds alarming'.[20]

Elizabeth told William Turner that she was particularly relieved about one thing: 'I like my new home very much indeed – for

Manchester it is very countrified, and so very cheerful and comfortable in every part.' This points to another anxiety, the commitment she must make not only to her husband but to the city in which he worked. William, like Elizabeth, was drawn to open landscapes and hills, across which he liked to stride at a great pace, but he had grown up in Warrington and, as one ex-pupil said, 'Much as he liked Nature and everything that was beautiful in scenery and art, he was most at home in cities.' Elizabeth's childhood memories, on the other hand, were of the leafy lanes and open heaths of Cheshire. Would she be able to breathe in the spreading city, notorious, even by the 1820s, for its lack of green spaces?

Dover Street was on the south-west side of the town off the busy Oxford Road, in the Ardwick district. In 1816 Ardwick Green had been described as 'a delightful suburb'[21] and although the slums and factories of Ancoats were now only a few streets away, there were still green fields nearby, like those of Greenheys Farm, described at the opening of *Mary Barton*. It was just on the edge of the smoke: most of the middle classes lived to the south-west rather than the east or north-east, as Engels noted, 'because ten or eleven months of the year the west and south-west wind drives the smoke of all the factories hither, and that the working-people alone may breathe.'[22] Nevertheless Elizabeth breathed factory air. Later she was often found puzzling over which garden flowers could survive the city smoke, and her picture of Mrs Hale in *North and South*, despairing over the fate of the muslin curtains, has a heartfelt ring.

The Gaskells were to move house twice, staying on the lapping fringe as Manchester surged outwards. Their first move, in 1842, was to a slightly larger house in the next road, 121 Upper Rumford Street. There, Elizabeth told Tottie Fox,

'our home is a mile and a half from the *very* middle of Manchester; the last house countrywards of an interminably long street, the other end of which touches the town, while we look into fields from some of our windows; not very pretty or rural fields it must be owned, but in which the children can see cows milked and hay made in summer time.' (L81)

Their second and final move, eight years later, was to 42 (now 84) Plymouth Grove, still within the same square mile. It was a substantial house with a large garden, which Lily made as much like a small farm as possible. Her friend Catherine Winkworth was amused that she 'was more proud of her cows and poultry, pigs and vegetables, than of her literary triumphs'.[23] She eventually grew used to 'dear, ugly, smoky, grim old Manchester', but still clung to the thought of escape to the countryside; her letters show how her spirits rose on holidays at Sandlebridge and later at Silverdale in Lancashire, in Wales or the Lake District.

Over the years she spent more and more time away from the city. So much so, in fact, that it becomes increasingly hard to see her, as she is often described, as 'the Manchester novelist' *par excellence*. Early works such as 'Libbie Marsh's Three Eras', *Mary Barton* and 'Lizzie Leigh' do indeed deal with Manchester life graphically and sympathetically but after 1850 she used this setting for only one major work, *North and South*, in 1854, and one story, 'The Manchester Marriage', in 1858. In both of these much of the action takes place in the south or in London. When she writes of Manchester, she vividly conveys the feel of its streets, courts and houses, the crowded pavements, the slap of wet washing in the face as girls hurry through cobbled courtyards, the twang of its mingled accents. But it is noticeable that the city as a whole is nearly always approached – by narrator and reader, literally and metaphorically – from the outside: from the pastoral Greenheys fields at the start of *Mary Barton*, from the Rochdale farm in 'Lizzie Leigh', from the generalized 'South' of *North and South*.

Although she knew it so intimately from within, when Gaskell tries to describe 'Manchester' as an entity, as opposed to painting particular scenes, she begins to write like her predecessors and contemporaries, who saw the city with mingled fear and admiration, as a new phenomenon, but always from *without*. From the late eighteenth century the spreading industrial town seemed almost to have a life of its own, as Wordsworth implied in Book VIII of *The Excursion* in 1814:

> Meanwhile, at social Industry's command,
> How quick, how vast an increase! from the germ
> Of some poor hamlet, rapidly produced
> Here a huge town, continuous and compact,
> Hiding the face of earth for leagues.

In the 1820s observers like James Butterworth saw Manchester as a vortex, sucking in 'art, science, industry, activity and wealth' from the neighbouring counties. In 1832, the year Elizabeth arrived, the doctor James Kay humanized it by analogy with the body, but a body riddled with fear and contagion, where factories 'vomit forth' smoke. Kay saw the dark areas of the city, the underside of its wealth, as a primitive wasteland inhabited by thieves and desperadoes, 'resembling savages in their appetites and habits'. And at the end of this decade Thomas Carlyle endowed it with the energy of nature at its most awesome. The noise of Manchester's thousand mills was 'like the boom of an Atlantic tide . . . sublime as a Niagara, or more so.'[24]

The sense of something created by men but out of man's control, of a grandeur built, in Carlyle's words, 'on infinite abysses', remains beneath Gaskell's realistic pictures of the place she came to know and in part to love, but also in part to dread. A volcanic, hell-like threat is felt, for example, in the description of the foundry in *Mary Barton*:

'Dark, black were the walls, the ground, the faces around them, as they crossed the yard. But, in the furnace-house, a deep and lurid red glared over all; the furnace roared with mighty flame. The men, like demons, in their fire-and-soot colouring, stood swart around, awaiting the moment when the tons of solid iron should have melted down into fiery liquid, fit to be poured, with still, heavy sound, into the delicate moulding of fine black sand, prepared to receive it. The heat was intense, and the red glare grew every instant more fierce.' – (Ch.19)

Elizabeth's home, in art as in life, was on the edge of this turbulent city, but the pivot around which the Gaskells' life revolved, Cross Street Chapel, was indeed in 'the *very* middle of Manchester'. Founded in 1689, the chapel now stood on one of the busiest streets in the commercial heart of the town, encircled by concentric rings of factories, warehouses and slums which crowded along the banks of the canals and the rivers Irk, Irwell and Medlock. Cross Street was a paradox, a building which breathed the quiet of past centuries, yet a focus of energy and change.

On Sundays, judging by the memory of one unnamed elderly minister who was a student during the Gaskells' early days at Cross Street, the old-fashioned air predominated. He had clearly yawned through the simple, austere services, redeemed in his view only by the fine organ music, the 'earnest eloquence of the senior minister and the graceful elocution and elegant style of his young colleague.'[25] When his eye wandered, he saw 'a large, quaint-galleried building, dimly illuminated by candles in brass candlesticks, with an atmosphere savouring entirely of the eighteenth century. It had a two-decker pulpit, great square oaken pews, and a fine flavour of decaying worthies.' There, 'in the large old-fashioned table pew where the Lord's supper was duly administered on the first Sunday of every month, sat the wives of the two ministers', Mary Robberds and Elizabeth Gaskell, 'then a young and handsome woman, whose first book was not published until a few years later'. Even before she was a well-known writer she was very much on display.

As in Newcastle and Liverpool, Birmingham and Bristol, Unitarians were at the forefront of city life. Cross Street, as Valentine Cunningham succinctly puts it, 'was where the bourgeoisie of Manchester worshipped God . . . The Trustees and members were the millocracy, the benefactors, the leaders of Manchester society: corn millers, silk manufacturers, calico printers, patent-reed makers, engineers; bankers and barristers; founders of hospitals, libraries, educational institutes, charitable funds, missions to the poor. The cousinhood extending outwards from the chapel was powerful indeed.'[26] Radicals they might be, but these Manchester Unitarians held to an ideal of individualism rather than one of equality, to the ethic of the market as much as to that of the Gospels. Elizabeth's attack on mercantile ethics and callous masters in *Mary Barton* was brave indeed. Out of the five best known 'enlightened' factory-owners – Robert Owen, the Fieldens, the Gregs, the Strutts, the Ashtons – all but Owen were Unitarians. Even they often resented outside interference: the Unitarian MPs Mark Philips and John Potter spoke vehemently in the Commons against government legislation on factory hours and conditions. *Laissez-faire* economic principles, naturally allied to a demand for free trade and tariff reform, helped to make Cross Street the base for the Manchester Anti-Corn Law Association in 1838 (the national Anti-Corn Law League followed in 1839). Free trade and factory reform continued to be hotly debated during the next decade, as Cross Street worshippers took an increasing part in public life, local and national. After the Municipal Reform Act of 1835 and the 1838 charter of incorporation Thomas Potter became Manchester's first mayor and at one time there were five MPs in the congregation.[27]

Yet the ethic of 'self-help' was also a spur to reform, to solidarity as well as division. Unitarians had formed the core of the Literary and

87

Philosophical Society since it was founded in 1781 in a room adjoining Cross Street Chapel. In the decade before Elizabeth came to Manchester they had initiated numerous projects, such as the Natural History Society (1821), the Royal Manchester Institution (1823), the Mechanics Institute and the Royal Medical College (both 1824) and the *Manchester Guardian* (started in 1821 by John Edward Taylor as a response to the Peterloo Massacre of 1819). Susanna Winkworth, an active Unitarian in the 1840s despite her Anglican background, found them both cultured and energetic. 'The Unitarians in Manchester,' she declared, 'were, as a body, faraway superior to any other in intellect, culture and refinement of manners, and certainly did not come behind any other in active philanthropy and earnest efforts for the social improvement of those around them.'[28] Susanna also noted that 'most of the German merchants who were among our more intelligent and agreeable acquaintances belonged either to Mr Gaskell's or to Mr Tayler's congregation.' (J. J. Tayler was the minister at Brook Street, another Manchester chapel.) Merchants and industrialists like the Gaskells' friends the calico printers Adolf and Salis Schwabe, the Schunks, Meyers and Leislers were well established in the town and their presence fostered the exchange of ideas with Europe.

In the late summer of 1832, when the Gaskells began their married life, the immediate concern was with the city's health. The previous November Manchester had set up a special board of health to prepare for the expected onslaught of cholera. The board's secretary, James P. Kay, was a young Non conformist doctor who had been educated in Edinburgh and was familiar with urban health problems from his work in the poorer quarters of Edinburgh and Dublin and his visits to European cities; he took the post of medical officer at the new Ardwick and Ancoats dispensary at the same time as William became junior minister at Cross Street. In the winter of 1831 Kay collected information and when the disease finally reached the city in May 1832, he organized the local doctors and took over abandoned factories and warehouses as hospitals. These measures could not contain the disease, and in the atmosphere of fear wild rumours spread – even that doctors were killing patients. On 2 September, three weeks before the Gaskells moved to Dover Street, a serious riot broke out at the temporary hospital in Swan Street. Only the coming of winter halted the epidemic.[29]

In the aftermath of the cholera the medical board summarized their experiences in a pamphlet which was to influence national as well as local views of the relationship between poverty and disease: *The Moral and Physical Condition of the Working Classes Employed in the Cotton Manufacture of Manchester* (1832). Despite the stress on 'moral', the Unitarians (with the Quakers) stood apart from other denominations in their attitude to the epidemic, holding that it was largely created by the filth and overcrowding of the cities, and denying – in contrast to the Established Church and many Nonconformist sects – that it was an act of God, a punishment for sin. A belief in divine retribution absolved society of responsibility (and proved a useful argument to the government of the day), while the Unitarian view that the epidemic was aggravated by men implied that it could also be eradicated, or at least ameliorated, by human endeavours. This attitude led Kay, with the brothers Samuel and William Rathbone Greg and Benjamin Heywood, to found the Manchester Statistical Society in 1833, initially to gather the information which would pave the way for reform. All four men were closely associated with Cross Street Chapel and were well known to the Gaskells, as were the other great public health campaigners, Edwin Chadwick and Thomas Southwood Smith (a Unitarian doctor and minister and the grandfather of Octavia Hill). William himself later became drawn into similar work, and sat for many years on committees for sanitary and housing reform.

Although William's pastoral work inevitably drew him into such campaigns, he always avoided public platforms. In 1852, when he was due to speak at the British Association in London, Elizabeth wrote to their daughter Marianne:

'Speechmaking, public meetings and such noisy obtrusive ways of "doing good" are his dislike, as you know; but oh! he is so good really in his own quiet way, beginning at home and working outwards without noise or hubbub – I am more & more convinced *be* good, & *doing* good comes naturally, & need not be fussed and spoken about. It is so funny, Papa's fright of that great *form* of the British Association!' (L187–8)

William's work usually began less in his own home than in those of his poorest parishioners, in overcrowded lodging-houses and dank cellars, ill-ventilated courts and back-to-back-terraces. Social and educational work, as opposed to factory reform or free trade, was always his preferred field. In 1833, for example, he was one of the founders of the Manchester Domestic Home Mission, inspired by a Boston minister, Joseph Tuckerman, who visited England in the autumn of 1833 and called for 'a ministry of intelligent and philanthropic men', whose efforts would encourage Christian responsibility in the rich as well as relieve the poor. The funds were raised by Unitarians, but the mission was non-denominational; it did not aim to convert but to give practical help – coal, bedding, soup tickets, food, clothes and infirmary tickets. This would be followed (or so it was hoped) by spiritual and moral guidance.[30]

Elizabeth was never a home visitor, but she discussed the mission's work with William, who was its secretary for many years, and she undoubtedly read the committee's short annual reports, which give a grim picture of the lower depths of city life. She herself came into personal contact with the working class more through the Unitarians' educational programme, especially the Mosley Street Sunday schools, the one place, as Cobden Smith said, that she gladly played 'minister's wife'. In 1832 William and John Robberds sat on a committee to move these schools (which were attached to Mosley Street Chapel, a few streets away from Cross Street) into better premises. Teachers were appointed by the chapel, and supported by volunteers. Both William and Elizabeth taught in the crowded old schoolrooms – the boys studied in the chapel cellar and the girls in a separate room at the back. (To the chagrin of the more devout chapel members, they were taught arithmetic and writing in addition to religion.) Parents flocked to send their daughters as well as their sons. When the new, larger schools opened in Lower Mosley Street in 1836, the girls' school alone had a hundred pupils, and by 1847, under the dedicated headmaster, John Curtis, the combined numbers of boys and girls had reached four hundred. The students paid 4d a week and were mostly in their teens, although some were as young as six and a few as old as thirty.[31] Here William preached on alternate Sundays, and began to give lectures, his first steps in what was to become almost a second career after 1840.

Elizabeth was most involved with these Sunday schools during the 1840s, visiting the girls at home and inviting them to her house on Sunday afternoons. Before then family life took precedence over the campaigns which preoccupied Cross Street. She was pregnant within a few months of her marriage, looking forward eagerly to motherhood.

But it was motherhood bitterly denied, or at least postponed – on 10 July 1833 she gave birth to a stillborn girl. She saw the baby, but did not give her a name.

All her life, as her letters show, Gaskell had a great capacity for putting disasters, great or small, behind her and writing 'That's *that* ', or even 'hang 'em!' Yet the tensions probably contributed to her frequent illnesses and evident exhaustion. By December 1833 she seemed to have recovered, and to be caught up again in the small social life of the congregation, having 'Miss Taylor and Miss Crook and the Robberds' to tea and passing on gossip of engagements, marriages and births to Lizzy. William was supportive, but did not like her to brood and tried to direct her interest outward; he himself was busy with chapel affairs and committees – discussing the future of the Sunday schools, the establishment of the mission. At this difficult time Elizabeth looked for comfort to her family circle. Lizzy and Anne Gaskell were frequent visitors. Holland cousins came to stay and she noted all their comings and goings: Lucy to Newcastle and London, Bessy to Gloucestershire, Kate to Everton. She wrapped herself in family concerns and even looked back to her Chelsea days, hearing the news of her half-sister's wedding and confessing: 'I long for news of the Thomsons.'

She kept the misery of her baby's death to herself, but inwardly she chose to remember rather than forget. Three years later, after marking the day by visiting the baby's grave, she wrote this sonnet:

> On Visiting the Grave of My Stillborn Little Girl
> Sunday, July 4th, 1836
>
> I made a vow within my soul, O Child,
> When thou wert laid beside my weary heart,
> With marks of death on every tender part
> That, if in time a living infant smiled,
> Winning my ear with gentle sounds of love
> In sunshine of such joy, I still would save
> A green rest for thy memory, O Dove!
> And oft times visit thy small, nameless grave.
> Thee have I not forgot, my firstborn, thou
> Whose eyes ne're opened to my wistful gaze,
> Whose sufferings stamped with pain thy little brow;
> I think of thee in these far happier days,

> And thou, my child, from thy bright heaven see
> How well I keep my faithful vow to thee.[32]

The pain is still sharp, but her faith allows her to write with tender intimacy: she believes that the child, though lost to her, is safe in its 'bright heaven'. Her sonnet can be set in a long tradition of women's poetry which goes back, for example, to Mary Cary's seventeenth-century poem 'Upon the Sight of My Abortive Birth'. But although it follows a convention, it is also unconventional. The opening at once establishes a relationship, through its direct address and through its explanatory yet loving tone. The dead baby, so clear to her mind's eye, shares equal place with the grieving mother. Serene, not submissive, realistic, not pious, the poem is remarkable for the honesty with which Gaskell accepts without guilt that the joy of another child has a healing power as great as, if not greater than the religious consolation.

By 1836 the 'living infant', Marianne, was a sturdy toddler. Safely born on 12 September 1834, she was the object of her mother's intense, anxious and joyful attention. The delight of a first baby, 'nuzzling and cooing by one's side', which she recalled in her letters years later, is often expressed in Gaskell's novels: in the pictures of Sylvia Robson with her baby, of Mrs Hale remembering Frederick's infancy and, perhaps the most moving of all, of Ruth with her illegitimate son, a mark of shame in the eyes of society, but a source of wonder to her:

'It was her own, her darling, her individual baby, already, though not an hour old, separate and sole in her heart, strangely filling up its measure with love and peace, and even hope. For here was a new, pure, beautiful, innocent life, which she fondly imagined, in that early passion of maternal love, she could guard from every touch of corrupting sin by ever watchful and most tender care.' (Ch. 15)

For mother, as well as child, a new life can begin.

[5]

Finding a Voice

When she was forty, Elizabeth would tell Tottie Fox that she had a great number of 'me's, and lament: 'How am I to reconcile all these warring members?' In her early twenties she was not so self-aware, but she was already conscious, in a way that may seem strikingly modern, of having several 'selves' which needed to find expression in different ways.

Everyone has a multiple life to some degree and each self has its own story, the narratives flowing together, separate yet overlapping, like threads in a weave. Elizabeth Gaskell's life and writing were such a woven cloth, the surface highly patterned and brightly coloured, but the web on the underside darker, subdued and tangled. Her ghost stories (a form which, in Henry James's phrase, always uncovers 'the other side of the tapestry') display this sombre streak, intensified by personal tragedies and by the distress she saw around her. She explained the 'morbid' element in *Mary Barton* by attributing it to her own dark mood, which had led, she said, to 'there being too heavy a shadow over the book; but I doubt if the story could have been deeply realized without these shadows'. The variety of her fiction has often baffled those who wish to pigeon-hole her neatly: social comedy, protest novel, domestic drama. Such labels sacrifice her richness and complexity to false gods of order and unity. Each of her selves, at various times, found its own voice and form, and sometimes the voices blend – or clash – within a single work.

On a Tuesday evening, 10 March 1835, two days before Marianne was six months old, Elizabeth began a diary. It was a serious undertaking, and she had a reader other than herself in mind:

'To dear little Marianne I shall "dedicate" this book, which if I should not live to give it to her myself, will, I trust, be received for her as a token of her Mother's love, and extreme anxiety in the formation of her little daughter's character. If this little daughter should in time become a mother herself, she may take an interest in the experience of another, and at any rate she will perhaps like to become acquainted with her character in its earliest form.'[1]

Elizabeth's record of her daughter's earliest years and her own anxieties and hopes is also a way of asserting her belief in the continuity of motherly love in the face of death.[2] In time Marianne did inherit the diary; she gave it to her daughter, who passed it on to hers. It now belongs to Elizabeth's great-granddaughter.

But such dedications were not exclusively feminine. They were used in the nineteenth century by men as well as women, almost as an excuse for indulging in the self-absorption of purely personal writing. As she described her daughter's growth, Elizabeth was surprised to find how much she was writing about herself: 'I had no idea the journal of my own disposition and feelings was so intimately connected with that of my little baby, whose regular gentle breathing has been the music of my thought all the time I have been writing.' She not only felt with her daughter and cried when she cried, but found that Marianne's babyhood made her reach back to her own early days: the baby is active early, as she was, kicking and moving on the floor, or 'goes to bed *awake*: another practice I began very early'.

Her anticipation of death was a genuine anxiety. Mothers *did* die. Her own mother had died when she was one; Mary Anne Lumb, who first adopted her, was dead within a year of her coming to Knutsford. Her sense of responsibility was genuine too: her Unitarian teaching had stressed the importance of nurture as well as nature, and to the end of her life, in stories and novels as late as *Wives and Daughters*, and in her biography of Charlotte Brontë, she continued to explore the balance between 'materials' of character and the influence of upbringing. At twenty-four she felt the burden deeply. 'The materials put into my hands are so excellent and beautiful,' she wrote. And, like new mothers in any era, she was bemused by conflicting theories – 'Books do so differ,' she sighed.

'One says, "Do not let them have anything they cry for;" another (Mme. Necker de Saussure, "Sur l'Education Progressive," the nicest book I have read on the subject) says: "Les larmes d'enfants sont si amères, la calme parfait de l'âme est si nécessaire qu'il faut surtout épargner des larmes." So I had to make a rule for myself.'[3]

Elizabeth felt joy as well as worry as she watched her daughter. She wished she had begun the diary earlier, 'though I should have laughed at the idea twelve months ago', because so many small details were already hard to remember clearly. She notes everything: how many teeth Marianne has, what she eats, the 'little triumphing noises' she makes when she thinks she is going to be picked up from her cot. She watches her reflecting adult expressions: 'When I laugh, she laughs', but when Elizabeth is listening to William reading, 'it is quite ridiculous to see her little face of gravity, as if she understood every word'. She records her baby's love of movement, and the way her babbled nonsense takes on the rhythms and tones of speech 'just like conversation'. Her fascinated absorption is that of all parents. And her own complex reactions are instantly recognizable too, like the pang she feels when Marianne clings to her nurse, Betsy, and pushes her away: 'William told me the other day I was not of a jealous disposition; I do not think he knows me . . . This was hard to bear; but I am almost sure I have never shown this feeling to anyone; for I believe Betsy fully deserves and returns her love.' We sympathize later too when Marianne is learning to talk and can say, 'pretty plainly, "Papa, dark, stir, ship, lamp, book, tea, sweep", &c leaving poor Mama in the background'. (The list itself suggests the style of life at Dover Street.)

The more she loved her child, the more she feared she might lose her. Terrified that Marianne might die and frightened of investing too much in her, of making her 'an idol', she came to see her diary in a different light. As with her sonnet to her stillborn child, writing could be a means of holding on to the beloved. In February 1836 she wrote:

'This morning we heard a sermon from the text. "And his mother kept all these sayings in her heart". Oh! how very, very true it is – and I sometimes think I may find this little journal a great help in recalling the memory of my darling child if we should lose her.'[4]

The text is taken from the story in St Luke's Gospel of Mary and Joseph finding their lost son in the temple when he is twelve, and of his rebuke, 'Wist ye not that I must be about my Father's business?' Mary does not understand, but ponders on the words: the will of the Father, however benign, is mysterious, unpredictable and threatening. In her fiction Gaskell would write repeatedly of the death, or possible death, of a child, and of the mother's guilt and fear of failure. And in this diary she prays continually for her daughter to live and be happy: 'Do with her, O Lord, as seemeth best with thee, for thou art a God of love and will not causelessly afflict!'

She also prays for help for herself, dreading her own impatience and tendency to anger. 'Lord,' she confesses, 'thou knowest that "the sin that doth so easily beset me" hath overtaken me once or twice even with this dear child – but thou knowest too how bitterly I have repented, and how earnestly I mean to try for the future.' Elsewhere she prays: 'make me even tempered. With her I do try a great deal, but Oh my Father, help me to regulate my impatient temper better.' Her worries show that even though Unitarians had replaced a God of wrath with a merciful Father, they retained the self-scrutinizing anxieties of traditional Nonconformity. Gaskell's stories often treat the tendency to violent emotion, and the terrible consequences of loss of control, a theme, for example, of both the melodramatic 'Doom of the Griffiths' and the light-hearted 'Christmas Storms and Sunshine'. The latter story is comic, but at its centre are a young mother's fear for her child, who is ill with croup, and her fear for herself. In despair one day she beats the neighbour's cat, and, 'feeling very angry and very guilty', slams the door with such a bang that she wakens her baby:

'Everything was to go wrong with Mary to-day . . . She took the child in her arms and tried to hush him off to sleep again, and as she sung she cried, she could hardly tell why, – a sort of reaction from her violent angry feelings. She wished she had never beaten the poor cat; she wondered if his leg was really broken. What would her mother say if she knew how cross and cruel her little Mary was getting? If she should live to beat her child in one of those angry fits?'[5]

The memory of the mother's love is both a check and a support.

Elizabeth had her own black moments, as the diary shows. She felt young and inadequate, frightened that she might 'misguide from carelessness or negligence: *wilfully* is not in a mother's heart'. She was often sorely puzzled about the right course of action and bothered by her inconsistency: 'But though I have laid down rules, I fear I have not sufficiently attended to them!' She was not entirely isolated, since William was as passionately involved with the baby as she was, and they quickly decided together that, whatever the books on childcare said, the most important things were responsiveness and respect for Marianne's individual character. She must be left to grow at her own pace: 'as I am not anxious for her to walk or talk earlier than her own nature prompts, and as her Papa thinks the same, we allow her to take her own way'.

The same principle, however, could not be applied to moral development, which troubled the Gaskells greatly. Elizabeth ascribes a definite character to her daughter even at six months: good-tempered, but prone to fits of passion and impatience. Poor Marianne sounds no more demanding than most babies, yet Elizabeth writes that at eleven months 'her little passions are terrible and give me quite a heavy heart'. As a toddler she aroused increasing alarm when her 'little fits of obstinacy' turned into 'whole hours of wilfulness'. Lily and William debated earnestly how to control her. They tried putting her in a corner, but (like Eppy in *Silas Marner*) she made this into a game. When she was small, they solved this by putting her in a high chair and making 'grave and sorrowful' faces until she showed small signs of repentance. After she grew out of the chair she was banished to 'a light room' (not Eppy's coal-hole) while they shut their ears to her wails. The worst moment came when she was three, learning her alphabet and stubbornly refusing to say 'A'. Banishment, with the inevitable crying, might wake their new baby, Meta:

'So William gave her a slap on the hand, every time she refused to say it, till at last she said it quite pat. Still I am sure we were so unhappy that night that we cried, when she was gone to bed. And I don't know if it was right.'[6]

It sounds like more of a punishment to the parents than to the child, and Marianne certainly came out the winner: after that there were no more lessons until she decided to get out the reading-book herself.

The interpretations of Marianne's behaviour illustrate Elizabeth's underlying assumptions. She believes strongly that moral judgements should come from within, and should be learnt from example not from dictation. She connects bad moods with physical conditions like illness, cold or tiredness, just as she later attributes the violence of factory workers to their conditions rather than their characters. And, most revealing of all, when she notes Marianne's 'acute sensibilities' and shyness with strangers, she describes her as 'remarkably observing, watching actions, things, &c, with such continued attention. She is very *feminine*. I think, in her quietness, which is as far removed from inactivity of mind as possible.'[7]

Elizabeth's diary and letters also continue the narrative of her outer life, showing, for instance, what a great deal of time she actually stayed away from Manchester. Summer holidays were spent on the coast at Poulton in Lancashire and several months of 1835 and 1836 were passed in visits to Knutsford and Warrington, where Aunt Lumb and Mrs Dimock played doting great-aunt and grandmother. In Knutsford Elizabeth kept up with old friends and visited the familiar places, thinking nothing of an eighteen-mile ride to lunch with Mr Davenport at Capesthorne Park. She was happiest when she could link her old and new lives, as she did when she, Aunt Lumb and Marianne stayed at Sandlebridge in May 1836. From there she wrote ecstatically to her sister-in-law, stressing her escape from any touch of urban life:

'My dearest Lizzy
I wish I could paint my present situation to you. Fancy me sitting in an old-fashioned parlour, "doors and windows opened wide", with casement window opening into a sunny court all filled with flowers which scent the air with their fragrance – in the very depth of the country – 5 miles from the least approach to a town – the song of birds, the hum of insects the lowing of cattle the only sounds – and such pretty fields & woods all round.' (L5–6)

So she runs on, mixing pleasures of the mind with those of the body. They wake with the birds and sit on the old stone steps, breathing the scent of flowers, '"far from the busy hum of men", but *not* far from the busy hum of bees. Here is a little standard library kept: Spenser, Shakspere, Wordsworth, & a few foreign books & we sit & read & dream, our time away – except at meals when we *don't* dream over cream that your spoon stands upright in, & such sweet (not sentimental but literal) oven-cakes, and fresh butter.'

It was an entirely female household, consisting of Elizabeth, Marianne, Betsy, Aunt Lumb and Peter Holland's daughter Bessy. They seemed to be almost on an island, with Sue Holland as their messenger, rowing across from Knutsford bringing 'news of the civilized world – in the shape of letters &c'. To Elizabeth this female Eden, primitive, in touch with nature, cried out to be painted in words.

Identifying with her toddler, who was at the 'very tip-top of bliss', she provided a list, the simplest of all modes of description:

'There are chickens, & little childish pigs, & cows & calves & horses, & *baby horses*, & fish in the pond, & ducks in the lane, & the mill & the smithy, & sheep & baby sheep, & flowers – oh! you would laugh to see her going about, with a great big nosegay in each hand, & wanting to be *bathed* in the golden bushes of wall-flowers – she is absolutely fatter since she came here, & is I'm sure stronger.'

Although the women seem to be 'far from the busy hum of men', male voices do enter Elizabeth's account through the works of poets, who give a literary colouring to this sensual, 'literal' world. While the nurse, Betsy, is teaching Marianne to 'call the pigs, & grunt like any old sow', Elizabeth is studying another language:

'I have brought Coleridge with me, & am *doing* him & Wordsworth – *fit place for the latter* ! I sat in a shady corner of a field gay with bright spring flowers – daisies, primroses, wild anemones, & the "lesser celandine", & with lambs all around me – and the air so full of sweet sounds, & wrote my first chapr of W. yesterday in pencil – & today I'm going to finish him – and my heart feels so full of him I don't know how to express my fullness without being too diffuse. If you were here, I think your advice, & listening would do me so much good – but I have \ to / do it all by myself alone, crunching up my paper, & scuttering my pencil away, when any one comes near.' (L4)

She had already done 'all my *composition* of Ld B—', finished Crabbe 'and got up Dryden and Pope'. It sounds as though she had a substantial project on hand, one of her own rather than notes to help William with his classes: 'If I don't get much writing done here, I get great many thoughts on the subject – for one can't think any thing but poetry & happiness.'

It is not only the lesser celandine, beside her in the field, that conjures Wordsworth's presence. His language and rhythms pervade this letter, especially those of the ode 'Intimations of Immortality', where the earth adorns herself in 'the sweet May morning'.[8]

> And the Children are culling
> On every side,
> In a thousand valleys far and wide,

Fresh flowers; while the sun shines warm,
And the Babe leaps up on his Mother's arm:-
I hear, I hear, with joy I hear!

With her own female babe demanding attention Elizabeth found it hard to express her fullness: she needed Lizzy to help her crystallize her thoughts. Her literary interests were almost a guilty secret, to be hidden away, just as she scrunched her paper and scuttered her pencil out of sight when people came near. There were always other priorities. Even on the magic isle of Sandlebridge there were intrusions, visitors from the mainland: 'The worst is tomorrow evening – Mrs Robt. Greg & her sisters are coming to see Bessy being her great cronies, & I don't care an atom for them, yet shall have to be tidy and civil.' Such outbursts of frustration would be constantly repeated in years to come as her 'proper' womanly duties pushed writing aside. Yet it must be said that she was hardly a bluestocking: '*I bought* Bessy's bonnet for 15s – (*Aunt Lumb* paying for it) and people say it suits me!'

In 1836 Elizabeth was writing poetry as well as reading it. And she had begun to write of the town as well as the country. The name of Crabbe, one of the poets 'done' at Sandlebridge, crops up in connection with another scheme undertaken in this year, one that aroused no conflict since she wrote as William's partner and her aim was not 'selfish' but social and moral. Two years later, after telling Mary Howitt that William had been giving four lectures 'to the very poorest of weavers in the very poorest district of Manchester, Miles Platting, on "The Poets and Poetry of Humble Life" ', she outlined what they had been trying to do:

'As for the Poetry of Humble Life, that, even in a town, is met with on every hand. We have such a district, and we constantly meet with examples of the beautiful truth in that passage of "The Cumberland Beggar:"

> Man is dear to man; the poorest poor
> Long for some moments in a weary life
> When they can know and feel that they have been
> Themselves, the fathers and the dealers out
> Of some small blessings; have been kind to such

> As needed kindness, for this simple cause
> that we have all of us a human heart.

In short, the beauty and poetry of many of the common things and daily events of life in its humblest aspect does not seem to me sufficiently appreciated.

We once thought of *trying* to write sketches among the poor, *rather* in the manner of Crabbe (now don't think this presumptuous), but in a more seeing-beauty spirit; and one – the only one – was published in *Blackwood*, January 1837. But I suppose we spoke of our plan near a dog-rose, for it never went any further.' (L33)

'Sketches among the Poor, No. 1', a poem in rhyming couplets of 153 lines, was almost certainly written in the summer of 1836. It appeared in *Blackwood's Edinburgh Magazine* the following January, sandwiched between 'The World We Live In' (an article about Peel and the constitution) and the final piece in a satirical series called 'Alcibiades the Man'.[9] The placing is oddly appropriate since the Gaskells' poem is about the world they lived in – a world light-years from Westminster – and it is about wisdom, the unspoken philosophy of a woman, not an articulate man.

Its subject is an old woman named Mary, a character drawn from life, as Elizabeth explained, who had come to Manchester from the Lake District as a young girl. An exile in the city, far from her family, Mary always hopes to return home, but is kept in the alien streets by her work and her concern for others. Her one solace is her memory of the farm with its dim panes, its grey moss and houseleeks on the roof and of the sister she played with, now long dead and buried under a grassy mound. In old age she grows deaf and blind, and finally slips into a dream, oblivious to all around her:

> Fancy wild
> Had placed her in her father's house a child;
> It was her mother sang her to her rest;
> The lark awoke her, springing from his nest;
> The bees sang cheerily the livelong day.

The poem pursues Crabbe's aim as well as employing his form. The Gaskells planned to paint a community and to draw moral lessons through portraits of individuals as Crabbe had done thirty years earlier in 'The Parish Register' and *The Borough*: the words of the Suffolk Anglican vicar could apply to the Manchester Unitarian minister and his wife:

> The year revolves, and I again explore
> The simple annals of my parish poor.[10]

William and Elizabeth transferred the essential loneliness of Crabbe's figures in a rural landscape to an isolated individual in the crowded city. Their poem, however, does not match Crabbe's strength, lacking his irony, his challenging direct speech and telling details, while it does, unfortunately, inherit some of his weaknesses, particularly the use of generalized epithets to describe character: 'A wife grown feeble, mourning, pining, vexed'.[11] Mary can hardly come alive when portrayed in this style:

> A single, not a lonely woman, sage
> And thoughtful ever, yet most truly kind.

The other clear influence in the poem, that of the 'more seeing-beauty spirit', is, of course, Wordsworth. The Preface to the *Lyrical Ballads* has been read, learnt and thoroughly digested. Although William and Elizabeth did not use 'the language really used by men' (but then nor did Wordsworth), they were trying to take situations from common life and 'throw over them a certain colouring of the imagination, whereby ordinary things should be presented to the mind in an unusual aspect'.[12] The 'Sketch' sets out to dignify Mary's mundane life – 'to some she might prosaic seem, but me / She always charmed with daily poesy' – and looks back from age to childhood innocence, and from the streets to the country, in order to define a state where 'the passions of men are incorporated with the beautiful and permanent forms of nature'. Mary's retreat into childhood is seen as positive. 'Fancy wild' is not escapist fantasy but the Wordsworthian working of powerful memory which releases the imagination into a world of its own making.

The 'Sketch' recalls Wordsworth's 'Reverie of Poor Susan', in which Susan sees visions of mountains, mist and trees as she walks through 'the vale of Cheapside':

> Green pastures she views in the midst of the dale,
> Down which she so often has tripped with her pail;

And a single small cottage, a nest like a dove's
The one only dwelling on earth that she loves.

But influences mix and blend. The stranger in the city, the nostalgia for
the country and for a pre-industrial life, and the idealized childhood
darkened by separation or death (motifs which run all through
Gaskell's work) were constant themes of the 'poetry of humble life'.
Wordsworth's Susan is matched, for example, by the narrator of
Bamford's 'Farewell to My Cottage', who is forced to the city to earn a
living:

Here all seemeth strange, as if foreign the land,
A place and a people I don't understand;
And as from the latter I turn me away,
I think of old neighbours now lost, well-a-day,
I think of my cottage full many a time,
A nest among flowers at midsummer prime;
With sweet pink, and white rock, and bonny rose bower,
And honeybine garland o'er window and door.[13]

Samuel Bamford was a leading figure among the local poets whom
William and Elizabeth admired. After working as a civil servant in
London, he retired to Manchester, where the Gaskells knew him well.
A man of great physical force and vigour, he had been imprisoned
several times in his youth for his political activities, and his early
poems, written at the end of the Napoleonic wars and at the time of
Peterloo, are proudly radical: their tone of outrage at the exploitation
of labour and the gulf between rich and poor as affronts to justice and
common humanity would be echoed in a modified form in *Mary
Barton*. But Bamford also wrote in a milder strain, pleading for
recognition of the dignity of the poor, and of their resilience,
endurance and mutual support. This is the verse with which the
Gaskells shared common ground. They too wanted to offset the
patronizing stereotypes that self-taught poets like Bamford resented so
much, and that the *English Chartist Circular* scourged:

'whenever sketches of the poor are given in any literary periodical, it is
generally the composition of some clever, irresistible humorist, seeking
to raise, it may be, a good natured smile, or even a broad grin at
provincialisms; the peculiar habits and usage of trade, the eccentricities of individuals remarkable in some other mode than their poverty,

but how rarely do we hear of the benevolence, the active sympathy, or charities of the poor.'[14]

In the end, though, and this is where one feels the presence of Elizabeth rather than William, the strongest impression left by the 'Sketch' is not of Mary's practical selflessness (although the stoic spirit of single women would be one of Gaskell's major themes) but of the power of memory and imagination as a means of escape and self-healing. Mary's final lapse into unconsciousness before her death is evoked in very 'female' language, as a state that both encloses and releases her inner being:

> And all the outward fading from the world
> Was like the flower at night, when it has furled
> Its golden leaves, and lapped them round its heart,
> To nestle closer in its sweetest part.

Although we can read her hand in this collaboration with her husband, Elizabeth's true voice, like Mary's hidden poetry, is still silent:

> Never heard,
> E'en as the mate of some sweet singing-bird,
> That mute and still broods on her treasure-nest,
> Her heart's fond hope hid deep within her breast.

The 'nest' here, as in the quotations from Wordsworth and Bamford, is ostensibly the longed-for rural home. But the lines also suggest private treasures of the imagination laid up for the future, when the 'singing-bird' will be mute no longer.

Ten years later Gaskell would retell Mary's story as that of Alice Wilson in *Mary Barton*. The emotions remain, but the sentiment falls away. Here is Mary, always believing she will see her home soon:

> A few short weeks, and then, unbound the chains
> Which held her to another's woes or pains.

And here is Alice, remembering how she saved and planned to go home for a week when she was in service, 'but first one thing came, and then another'. First the children got measles.

'Then missis herself fell sick, and I could go less than ever. For, you see, they kept a little shop, and he drank, and missis and me was all there was to mind children and shop and all, and cook and wash besides.' (Ch. 4)

Here is Mary's childhood home, where bees sang in the heather and a gnarled hawthorn stood in a nook by the stream.

> And if you passed in spring-time; you might see
> The knotted trunk all coronal'd with flowers,
> That every breeze struck down in fragrant showers.

And here is Alice, among the same moss-covered rocks,

'and the ground beneath them knee-deep in purple heather, smelling sae sweet and fragrant, and the low music of the humming-bee for ever sounding among it. Mother used to send Sally and me out to gather ling and heather for besoms, and it was such pleasant work! We used to come home of an evening loaded so as you could not see us, for all it was so light to carry. And then mother would make us sit down under the old hawthorn tree (where we used to make our house among the great roots as stood above th' ground) to pick and tie up the heather. It seems all like yesterday, and yet it's a long long time agone.' (Ch. 4)

The change from poetic diction to a selective use of local speech and the pinning of feeling to the daily round of women's work vividly conjure up the individual life. In the pressure of the city streets, and in woman's strength, Gaskell had found a subject, but not a medium; her characters would come to life not in verse but in a prose that echoed the speech of the people themselves.

When Elizabeth was in her own rural retreat, studying Wordsworth in the May sunshine at Sandlebridge in 1836, her world seemed almost too perfect: 'Oh that life would make a standstill in this happy place.' But life could not stand still. On she went to Warrington and after that, for Marianne's health to Grange-over-Sands on Morecambe Bay. Rather to her alarm Sam Gaskell had prescribed sea-bathing for Marianne, but, luckily, 'Aunt Anne, a capital bather, was with us, and undertook the charge of her, which was so much better than being frightened by being given over to a strange woman in an uncouth dress . . . I stood on the rocks with a shawl ready to receive her and gave her a biscuit.'[15] (The diary is endearingly punctuated by biscuits, ready for every emergency.)

The unsettled summer over, Elizabeth returned to Dover Street, to the oaken pews, the Sunday schools and the social whirl. That winter she was pregnant again and in poor health until Margaret Emily (known as Meta) was born, on 7 February 1837. In January Aunt Lumb, now sixty-nine, took Marianne to stay with her in Knutsford until the new baby arrived. Hannah's eyesight had failed and so she could write no letters, but Elizabeth later gleaned scraps of stories about their time together: how MA (as she was often called) slept in a cot by her aunt's bed; how 'Aunt Lumb gave her breakfast, sitting on her knee, by a window, with many loving jokes between them'; how they went for walks together and how Marianne clung to her 'in any little distress'. The careful recounting of Aunt Lumb's pleasure may have soothed an unstated fear on Elizabeth's part that this extra charge was too much for her. Every story was cherished the more because, by the time she noted them in her diary, Hannah Lumb, her 'more than mother', was dead.

On 8 March Hannah had a severe stroke. Elizabeth, hardly recovered from childbirth, rushed to Knutsford and spent the next eight weeks in lodgings with Marianne, the baby and the invaluable Betsy. Dashing back at intervals to feed Meta, she spent all day with her aunt, watching her pain (which the leeches prescribed by Peter Holland did nothing to relieve), torn between wanting to keep her and longing for her death to end her suffering. 'Oh! Lizzy! is it not sad,' she wrote. 'Oh! there will never be one like her.'

Yet even in this intense emotion she recorded what she saw with bitter, tender accuracy:

'When she wakens the pain is nearly as violent, catching her breath in deep gasps, & her head is dreadful . . . This morning she surprised us all by asking for a bit of what we call muffin & you pikelake . . . Lucy went out & searched the town over for one, and she ate about this much of the whole thickness of a penny one, which I can not help fancying a good sign.' (L9)

After 'penny one' comes a tiny diagram, a segment of a circle.

She would often use similar observations, subtly tied to a woman's world ('not sentimental but literal'), to heighten moments of acute feeling, for example in the moving description of John Barton's state after the death of his wife:

'Barton sat on, like a stock or a stone, so rigid, so still. He heard the sounds above, too, and knew what they meant. He heard the stiff unseasoned drawer, in which his wife kept her clothes, pulled open. He saw the neighbour come down, and blunder about in search of soap and water. He knew well what she wanted, and *why* she wanted them, but he did not speak, nor offer to help.' (Ch. 3)

During the weeks of Aunt Lumb's illness Elizabeth, as befitted a woman, was practical and busy, but inwardly she was stricken and numb. Marianne too was understandably disturbed. Used to being with Aunt Lumb and getting into her bed in the morning, she begged to see her, but fled, terrified at the sight of the thin, pale figure, her head bound like a corpse after the leeches. Next time Elizabeth and her aunt knew better: Aunt Lumb wore her best nightcap and hid the ubiquitous 'sponge biscuit' under her pillow. But there was little time left, as Elizabeth knew. 'On May 1st,' she later wrote in her diary, 'I lost my best friend. May God reward her for all her kindness to me!'

The entries which look back on these weeks have a note of desperation and claustrophobia. Birth and death are too close. In their different ways Elizabeth, Aunt Lumb, Marianne and baby Meta had all experienced 'confinement', immured in sickrooms and small lodgings.[16] In her grief Elizabeth found it impossible to tell the three-year-old Marianne that Aunt Lumb was dead; the belief that language should be truthful, so often repeated in the diary, finally failed her. She and William tried to think of a way to explain, but sidestepped the issue by saying Aunt Lumb had gone to sleep, a euphemism for death which they had used when Marianne suffered night-terrors after Betsy's too literal explanation of a passing funeral, 'a poor girl that they were going to put into a hole & cover her up with earth' (the ultimate confinement). Perhaps the evasion reflected Elizabeth's own reluctance to face her loss, as much as the desire to protect her child from pain. In the end, after staying in Knutsford that September, Marianne solved the problem for herself, simply stating in a matter-of-fact way that 'Aunt Lumb didn't live with Aunt Ab now'.

[6]

Beginnings

In her will Hannah Lumb left Elizabeth an annuity of £80 and specified that half of her property was to go to her niece on Abigail's death, the rest being divided among other Holland relations.[1] The annuity was welcome since William's earnings were not high, even when supplemented by private pupils. Mrs Lumb's death signalled the end of Elizabeth's days at the Heath. Aunt Ab, with her difficult moods, was not so welcoming. A year or two later Elizabeth hoped wistfully that Abigail would, as she had once suggested, allow them to look after the house while she was away, but 'she repented and cooled in her invite!' This was probably just as well, as her cousin Susan reminded her, 'for Aunt Ab would be sure to find faults with everything we did in her absence, and we should only get into scrapes'.

After the strain of Meta's birth and Aunt Lumb's long illness Elizabeth's health collapsed and in September William took her to stay for three weeks at Plas Penrhyn. They left the girls behind, Marianne in Knutsford with Susan, who had married Peter Holland's partner Dr Deane, and Meta with Mrs Dimock in Warrington. The weather in Wales was wild and wet, but Elizabeth went on outings with her cousins and one day she and Lucy walked from Ffestiniog up to Cwm Morfyn Lake.

As she told Lizzy:

'I could fancy that in dry weather it would be a very pleasant place for a picnic. When we were there it was as wet and boggy as heart could desire, and I sopped my feet completely, and went into one of those little cottages to take off my shoes & stockings and give them a thorough drying, and the woman cd not speak English or we Welsh,

108

but we had merry laughs and some conversation, and a good piece of oat cake notwithstanding.' (L17)

Her thirst to communicate was rarely balked.

The holiday revived her interest in the Welsh and their ways, providing a much needed change from Dover Street, where the combined demands of family, chapel and social life put her under constant pressure. She had not yet learnt the art of organization which so impressed later visitors. Guests, like William's relations, the Holbrook Gaskells of Prospect Hill, who threatened to arrive without warning might find her 'during a regular rummaging, brushing, carpet taking up, cleaning day; and 10 – 1 we should have been caught in the middle of our hubbub as we have been aforetime'. One week in March 1838 she was looking forward to Lizzy coming to stay. So was Marianne: 'She is to be your little maid, and help you dress (such dressing,) and run your errands.' Lily and William had just had to cope with Marianne's croup, in those days a dangerous complaint, from which little Eddie Deane died in Knutsford the same week. Both parents were alarmed. After giving her '24 drops Ipec wine' William rushed to get Sam, reaching the infirmary in ten minutes. Sam was out, but William sent a note after him, '& by 11 he was here, – he sat quietly enough till she coughed when he flew upstairs, & said we must send for Mr Partington instantly; it was ½p.12. Mr P. came & He & Sam got it under, – Sam & Wm sat up all night – & I was up till 2.' These Gaskell men did not turn their backs on the domestic sphere.

Marianne soon recovered and was allowed downstairs, muffled in a blanket. Able to face the world again, Elizabeth braced herself to help Mrs Robberds as one of the 'standers' at the bazaar. Staying in or venturing out seemed equally daunting: 'Wm says I look *miserable* – which remark he repeats about 20 times a day – but I have not been out for a week – we stand from 10 till 5 – But Oh what teas we must & will have.' She longed for Lizzy – and for William's brother Robert and his wife, Anne – to come and 'talk over Wales':

'*When* shall we meet. I wish with all my heart you were coming here instead of going home to talk parlevoo to little petticoats. Could not you manage it ? *Do* if you possibly can; & bring Anne with you. Bob says she is gone to Beaumaris to join you, and we will so talk all three at once if you will. And why the d— (Honi soit qui mal y pense) should not you – it would save expense to come straight from Lpool – And now must I tell you something about ourselves – We are "here today, & gone tomorrow", as the fat scullion maid said in some extract in Holland's Exercise book.' (L17)

Although she describes herself as 'most unfit from fatigue', she seems to have had boundless reserves. By the summer of 1838 her spirits had revived, though her health was still fragile. Her letters are peppered with descriptions of visits and prominent Manchester names: Taylers, Marslands, Gregs, Carvers, Worthingtons and Alcocks. These manufacturers, bankers and lawyers lived in far grander style than their ministers, having left the town centre for new mansions on the 'breezy heights' of Cheetham Hill, Broughton and Pendleton.[2] They had conservatories, crystal chandeliers and holidays in Paris and Scotland, and Elizabeth found their wealthy lives intriguingly exotic. At the Dukinfield Darbishires, for example, she saw a night-blooming Cereus, a rare plant from the West Indies, 'such a flower – a splendid white flower with a golden glory around it'.

Samuel Dukinfield Darbishire, a prosperous Manchester solicitor, was a trustee of Cross Street and although he was nearly twenty years older than William, they became good friends and worked closely together. The Darbishires lived nearby in Emden Street, Greenheys, and had been particularly kind to Lily ever since her marriage, exchanging music and books and visits. An early note suggests how touchingly grateful she was, especially when William was so busy with his work:

'My dear Mrs Darbishire,
I quite intended to call on you this morning with these songs, & to give you and Mr Darbishire our very best wishes for the season. But I was prevented by the rain, and so I must send you them on paper, which never seems half so warm & real. I had only time to copy you these two songs, as we were shopping till ½ past 4 on Friday, though we went out directly after breakfast . . . I am having my 3rd lonely evening this week as Mr Gaskell is gone to dine at B[?] Hill.

I return you Brockedon's appendix with many thanks. May I beg for "little Frank", and the Dublin Penny Magazine which I will return you tomorrow without fail.

I remain my dear kind friend

Yours very affectionately
E. C. Gaskell'[3]

In the 1830s Elizabeth spent many weekends at the Darbishire's second house, in the country, recouping her energy. 'This Rivington air has done wonders; and made me so strong and hungry. Good air for ever!' she exclaimed to Lizzy. She longed for that country air and continually escaped to Knutsford (staying on for an extra week in July 1838 to watch the festivities for Victoria's coronation), but back in smoky Manchester she had hardly a moment to spare. No wonder she wrote: 'I am in a whirl', 'such a bustle', 'you have no idea how overwhelmed I have been with business since I came home'. The ins and outs of the Unitarian community amused as well as exhausted her:

'Mrs J J Tayler has got an impromptu baby at Blackpool; – went there and lo & behold a little girl unexpectedly made her appearance, & clothes have had to be sent in such a hurry. Bathing places do so much good. Susan & Mary went to Blackpool last year, but did not derive the same benefit . . . So ends Mrs J J Tayler's *delicate state of health, arising from some internal complaint,* as Mr Ransom called it.' (L20)

This anecdote, rapid, gleeful, pointed, is in striking contrast to the anxious self-probing and religious tone of her diary. Elizabeth had a worldly as well as a spiritual side. She sparkled in society and made many new friends. One couple she came to like greatly were John and Julia Bradford, and a description of a christening party at the Bradfords' illustrates exactly why Elizabeth found them so attractive – and they her. She and William set out for the two-hour walk across the city to Pendleton, arriving about six at 'a large handsome house'.

'Ushered in with much astonishment, heard scuttering away to dress – and found that the Christening had been in the morning, and that we were dreadfully too early. However when Mr. & Mrs. Bradford were dressed – (she in a *beautiful* worked white muslin over white satin shoes, brussels lace, & flowers in her hair looking so very pretty,) I in the very gown I am now sitting in, great thick shoes, & Wm in boots & without gloves) they came in & very agreeable he was & very lovely she. He is a great friend of Bryant the poet, so W. & he had some pleasant confabulation – about 8 oclock full dressed people began pouring in, and we went into a large dancing room – windows open, hot-house plants, muslin curtains &c, & there we danced till supper at 12, & such a supper! I suppose the Bradfords are very rich, – for wine & grapes, & pines, & such cakes my mouth waters at the thought, & ducks &

green peas, & new potatoes & asparagus & chickens without end, & savoury pies, & all sort of beautiful confectionery – & we wended our way home by day*light* – ½ past 3 when we got home walking to be sure. You would have enjoyed it – waltzing, galloppes, &c &c.' (L18)

All in those 'great thick shoes'.

Julia was Manchester born, but John was a wealthy American who had settled in the city. Elizabeth was fascinated by his American past (he knew Washington Irving and van Buren), his acquaintance with British statesmen and aristocrats and his international connections: 'it seems funny to dine with a man who has dined with the Pope, who always seems such a queer, unreal, faraway sort of personage'. Despite the gulf in income – the Bradfords owned a priceless collection of paintings and antiques – the two families remained close throughout the next decade. The only problem, she told Lizzy, was how to repay their hospitality: 'Not room enough for dancing, – and people get tired of bagatelle else we have got the Mason's bagatelle board – So what *are* we to do – Well! that job will be jobbed before you get this letter.'

She liked to take things in hand. In this summer of 1838 she was again caught up in family affairs: her cousin Charles Holland – 'very clever, a great traveller, a great quiz and a great Radical', as Susanna Winkworth later described him – had fallen in love with Lizzy Gaskell. Lizzy was hesitating, and Elizabeth, with the wisdom of six years of marriage, was acting as intermediary, cajoling, reasoning, darting over to Warrington for lengthy talks. She argued away Lizzy's doubts about short engagements, the ups and downs of trade, even the duty to parents. 'As to your mother – finish yourself first, and then wonder if your mother would consent.' Impatient as ever, she wanted them to marry soon, before the summer passed: 'As you love me don't have it in the winter – Fancy slip, slop, splash splash to the chapel, or going in pattens to the carriage – and red noses and blue cheeks, and a great swelled finger to wriggle out of the glove, and present for the ring.' However teasing she sounds, she urgently wanted to bind the Hollands and Gaskells even more closely together. Her persuasion worked. In November Charles and Lizzy were married.

Elizabeth's letters to Lizzy and other women friends are so packed that at first it seems she wrote about every aspect of her life. But there is one noticeable gap. She writes of the rich of Manchester but not of the poor, of handsome houses but not of alleys and courts and tenements. She could not deal with these in the same light-hearted style: they demanded an effort of sympathy and imagination, a different voice. This too she had been slowly discovering, through her writing of the sketch and other literary apprenticeships.

Since 1832 William's activities had widened. As one of his obituaries put it with dry understatement, 'Mr. Gaskell was not one who could abstain with pleasure from active work.'[4] His work also drew Elizabeth, more and more, into an attempt to understand the city she had made her home – and into finding a way to describe the lives of its poorer inhabitants. At this stage, to use the imagery of their poem, Elizabeth was hardly 'mute or still', but it was certainly her mate, William, who seemed to be the 'singing-bird'. In 1837 he contributed seventy hymns to the collection edited by his friend and fellow-student at York, John Relly Beard, now minister at Strangeways Chapel, Salford. Some of William's hymns are still sung today. They illustrate his faith, his pacifism, his tolerance and his belief in the dignity of labour. They also advocate Christian resignation of a kind which both he and Elizabeth came to question after their experience of the depression of the 1840s. In a handwritten addition to his own copy he inserted a 'Hymn for the Cottage', in the tradition of Herbert's 'Who sweeps a room as for thy laws'. It contains these verses:

> Child of labour! lift thy head
> Think not meanly of thy state
> Let thy soul be nobly fed
> Thine shall be a noble fate.
> . . . .
> Meekly take thy part assigned
> Let its evils be withstood
> And thy soul ere long shall find
> Holy use turns all to good.

This is a long way from the passionate recognition in *Mary Barton*, and in William's 'Manchester Song' which precedes chapter 6 of that novel, that it is hard to accept poverty meekly while you watch your children starve.[5]

Two years later William again tried to adapt his poetry to the life of the poor, displaying a typically Victorian desire to combine literature and philanthropy. In 1839 he published his *Temperance Rhymes*, [6]

dedicated, with an appropriately industrial image, 'to the working
men of Manchester . . . in the hope that they may act as another small
weight on the right end of that lever which is to raise them in the scale
of humanity'. The rhymes range from stirring narratives to quiet
hymn-like ballads. All are marked by sympathy and respect for the
individual: it is drink, not the drinker, that William blames. Some
contain vivid sketches of city characters, an exhausted worker, a
drunken wife, a youth educating himself alone at night, dreaming of
his rural home. The language is plain, and even the tempting demon
has an audible smack of Lancashire:

> But his day has been hard, and, tottering by
> The fire from the Dragon blazed full in his eye
> Right tempting it looked; for a moment he stood:-
> And I whispered, 'A glass might do him much good'.

The collection won an approving letter from Wordsworth, who wrote:
'I have read your Temperance Rhymes with much pleasure and cannot
but think that they must do good.'⁷ He approved of the inclusion of
pictures of the virtuous as well as the wretched, and particularly liked
'Heaven to Thee', a poem based on an old Welsh funeral custom of
wishing heaven to the dead. (Both points suggest how closely William's literary aims were linked to Elizabeth's, in the depiction of the
virtues, rather than just the miseries of the poor and the lasting interest
in collecting and noting rural customs.)

William's poems are written in a style which echoes the broadside
ballads of the street and the local poetry on which he had lectured the
previous year. Although Elizabeth told Lizzy that his lectures dealt
with 'a new subject', William's interest in 'Poets and Poetry of Humble
Life' was not unique. Since Southey's *Lives and Works of Our
Uneducated Poets* had appeared in 1831, such writing had been the
subject of intense interest to the middle classes. Southey's study,
originally a 180-page introduction to the poetry of John Jones, had
drawn a long review from T. H. Lister in the respected *Edinburgh
Review*. More articles followed, the most influential being Carlyle's
'Corn Law Rhymes' (1832), also in the *Edinburgh*. Typically (but
inaccurately), Carlyle described Ebenezer Elliott, the author of the
Rhymes, as 'a voice coming from the deep Cyclopean forges, where
Labour, in real soot and sweat, beats with his thousand hammers "the
red sun of the furnace" . . . an intelligent voice from the hitherto Mute

and Irrational, to tell us at first hand how it is with him'.[8] This dark, romantic vision of labour and emphasis on the documentary and autobiographical elements of artisan poetry was characteristic of the 'educated' critical response.

Carlyle had already written on Burns, who was always discussed in the context of 'poetry of humble life' and who ranked high (beside Milton, Shelley and Byron) in the pantheon acclaimed by the self-taught writers themselves. William certainly lectured on him; 'Wm is famously clapped, bless him, finishing his lecture on Burns,' wrote Elizabeth. These lectures remained part of William's repertoire for several years. A note in the *Macclesfield Courier* (1 January 1842) reports that William gave his 'Poets of Humble Life' at Brook Street Chapel, Knutsford, and the next day, by popular request, lectured on 'The Poetry of Burns': 'Both lectures were highly interesting and gave general satisfaction.'[9] Sadly, the lectures have not survived, but there is evidence of William's interest in J. F. Bryant, one of Southey's subjects, and there were plenty of contemporary poets for him to study in Manchester alone, Samuel Bamford, Elijah Ridings, John Rogerson, Charles Swain and J. C. Prince being the most admired. These five men and thirteen more – a sizeable number – met regularly in the Sun Inn in Long Millgate, forming a group which was celebrated in Alexander Wilson's drinking song of 1842, 'The Poet's Corner'.

William's talks were a great success. Deputations arrived on the doorstep from the teachers of Mosley Street Sunday School and from the Salford Mechanics Institute to ask him to repeat them. He planned four new lectures for the winter, 'and in the meanwhile,' Elizabeth told Mary Howitt, 'we are picking up all the "Poets of Humble Life" we can think of'. She knew that the Howitts would share their interest. They came from Quaker backgrounds and when William Howitt had worked as a chemist in Nottingham, they belonged to a group of self-educated writers known as 'The Sherwood Foresters'. The elegant, quiet Mary was widely praised for her verse (some admirers even compared her to Felicia Hemans) and William's *Book of the Seasons, or Calendar of Nature* (1831) went through seven substantial editions. William was an interesting (and to some people infuriating) man, dapper, bustling, combative, a fierce supporter of every radical, Chartist and feminist cause. His *Popular History of Priestcraft in All Ages and Nations* (1833) set out to prove that the Anglican clergy were not only overpaid and underworked (if not absent from their livings altogether), but were in a direct line from the propagators of phallic, Bacchanalian and orgiastic cults of the past. Not surprisingly, this thesis caused something of a stir.

After moving to Esher in 1836, the Howitts published works for the kind of working-class readers who were flocking to William Gaskell's lectures. They were addressing a receptive audience, as an article on William's later classes at the Working Men's College makes clear:

'many people wondered that workmen and clerks and people who had to work hard for their living should care for belles lettres, but the fact was then as it is now, the keenest appreciation of the best things are often to be found among those who work and work hard. The class was by far the largest in the college.'[10]

William Howitt's *Homes and Haunts of English Poets* (1847) aimed (like William Gaskell's lectures) to introduce such readers to the British poetic heritage and, at the same time, to make them proud of the great oral tradition and published poets of their own class: 'Burns, Hogg, Bloomfield, Clare, Elliott, Alan Cunningham, Nicoll, Thom, Massey; our Thomas Miller and Thomas Cooper'. 'It is with pride,' Howitt wrote, 'and more than pride, that I call the attention of my countrymen to this great and unique section of their country's glorious literature.'[11]

But *all* the stars in Howitt's galaxy, and all the writers discussed in William's classes, were men. Here was another 'male tradition' after that of the great poets. Although women did contribute to Chartist journals and popular magazines, their work was never collected or acclaimed in the same way. Such artisan poets influenced Elizabeth Gaskell, but they could not offer accepted models of women's writing, or help her develop a language born of her own experience and that of other women. When she told Lizzy about the deputations who came to Dover Street, she noted drily that they would not pay: 'Whilk is a pity – but *if* the Manchester M. Institution came – shan't they pay for all. In the meantime we look gracious & affable as a new made Queen, and are "most happy" &c.' In all the excitement Elizabeth, like a modest wife, sat back and admired: 'Wm read his 2 first lectures on poetry &c aloud which people seemed very much to like & I lay on the sofa & enjoyed myself in listening.'

She would not remain a listener for long, but in these first years, despite encouragement, William somehow subdued her confidence in her own style. Even in the rapid note attached to his account of their wedding trip she joked that he had 'taken such a time to his eloquence that poor I must write helter-skelter'. One weekend in August 1838 William was away preaching; Lily missed him, and could not help thinking of 'those old absences when I had dear Aunt Lumb to care about and open my heart to'. Instead she opened her heart to Lizzy:

'When I had finished my last letter, William looked at it, and said it was *"slip-shod"* – and seemed to wish me not to send it . . . the consciousness that Wm may at any time and does generally see my letters makes me not write so naturally & heartily as I think I should do. Don't begin that bad custom, my dear! and don't notice it in your answer. Still I chuckled when I got your letter today for I thought I can answer it with so much more comfort to myself when Wm is away which you know he is at Buxton!' (L34)

However mildly, she was using his absence to evade his authority, and she knew it – witness the guilty 'don't notice it in your answer'. And on the day he left, 18 August, she sat down to write to Mary Howitt. Mary was currently her model of a professional but socially motivated woman writer. Was this the hope 'hid deep within her breast'?

If Elizabeth was already writing with an eye to publication, the Howitts were the right people to help her. She had written to them in May, thanking them very formally for the pleasure their books had given her 'by their charming descriptions of natural scenery and the thoughts and feelings arising from her happy circumstances of rural life', and adding, in explanation: 'I was brought up in a country town, and my lot is now to live in or rather on the borders of a great manufacturing town.' Her early letters to the Howitts are all inspired by nostalgia for the country and lost youth. This August she sent Mary a long account of rural customs and superstitions, preceded by a description of some of the Warwickshire houses she had heard of at Avonbank: 'I am giving but vague directions, but I am unwilling to leave even in thought the haunts of such happy days as my schooldays were.'

The notes on customs are motivated by a desire to record and thereby in some sense conserve a disappearing past. 'Many poetical beliefs,' she writes, 'are vanishing with the passing generation.' Some of the traditions are seasonal, like carols at Christmas and simnel cake in Lent, but most are tied to women's lives. She writes of the Knutsford 'sanding' at weddings and the blessing for 'numerous progeny'. She tells of Cheshire's 'Riding Stang', the communal humiliation of any woman, 'a wife more particularly', who 'has been scolding, beating or otherwise abusing one of the other sex', when the townsfolk 'hunt out the delinquent from her resting place' and make her ride facing backwards on 'an old, shabby, broken down horse' to the rough music of pots and pans. She mentions 'Lifting Monday and Lifting Tuesday', part of the Easter festivities, still kept up in their full vigour, when the man of the household is 'lifted' or 'heaved'. ('My husband has had to run hard to escape'). May Day, above all, is a female festival: 'I never heard of its being kept as it is by the common people in Lancashire and Cheshire.' Branches are hung at the door to symbolize the characters of the women within:

'A branch of birch signifies a pretty girl, an alder (or owler they call it) a scold, an oak a good woman, a broom a good housewife. But I am sorry to say there are many symbols hung up in spite, which have anything but a good meaning. If gorse, nettles, sycamore or sawdust are placed at the door, they cast the worst imputation on a woman's character, and vary according as she be girl, wife or widow.' (L30)

Elizabeth had been talking eagerly to her servants about such customs and (as servants so often do in her work) their comments bring a wry note of realism. The maidservants buy 'Dragon's blood', a druggist's powder sure to win the man they love: 'A pretty servant once told me it always had the desired effect with her.' They curtsy to the full moon and turn the money in their pockets, 'which *ought* to be doubled before the moon is out'.

William Howitt used verbatim extracts from this letter in the second edition of his *Rural Life of England*. And in 1840, in his *Visits to Remarkable Places*, he included the description of old Clopton Hall, which Elizabeth also sent in 1838 when she heard that he was planning a book on historic houses.[12] 'Clopton Hall' is usually glanced at in passing as an indication of Gaskell's antiquarianism and early skill at Gothic scene-setting. Yet it is, in many ways, remarkable – entirely her own, looking back to her youth, before she met William and moved to Manchester. The hovering spirits here are not those of male poets, but of Mrs Radcliffe, of *Northanger Abbey* and of the popular women's novels of the 1820s. Although she may have reworked a schoolgirl essay, the four short pages also suggest Elizabeth's anxieties in the late 1830s: her fears about sex, death, entrapment, man's power and woman's weakness. Indeed it is hardly a topographical piece at all, but a meditation on the fate of women, trapped for ever in the rigid 'old house of their fathers'. Clopton Hall is a mausoleum haunted by the girls, mothers and vanished children of the past.

The house itself, approached through desolate half-tilled fields, is 'a large, heavy, compact, square brick building, of that deep, dead red almost approaching to purple' (strikingly like the square, dark house behind its screen of trees which shelters the quivering spirit of Mrs Transome in *Felix Holt*, and her 'woman's keen sensibility and dread'). Its pillars are topped 'with two grim monsters', the walls of its formal court are broken and flowers are entangled with nettles: 'the grass grew as rank and wild within the enclosure as in the raised avenue walk down which we had come'. This is the castle of Sleeping Beauty, with its single yellow rose and Austrian brier. Inside, instead of sleeping courtiers, are ranks of uncannily lifelike portraits of people two hundred years in their grave, and beside them hangs a reminder of formalized violence, a map of the Civil War, its armies eternally poised for battle.

Allowed to wander freely through the house, Elizabeth climbs the wide stair, noting the 'crumbling and worm-eaten balustrade' and finds herself, in the shadows of approaching evening, in a bedroom said to be haunted. The room contains only the portrait of a beautiful girl, her eyes filled with unshed tears – Charlotte Clopton, who was thought to have died of the plague in the seventeenth century and was buried 'with fearful haste' in the family chapel attached to Stratford Church. A few days later another body was carried to the ancestral vault;

'but as they descended the gloomy stairs, they saw by the torchlight, Charlotte Clopton in her grave-clothes leaning against the wall; and when they looked nearer she was indeed dead, but not before, in the agonies of despair and hunger, she had bitten a piece from her white round shoulder! Of course she had *walked* ever since.'[13]

Entombed alive, a young woman devours herself, free to move only after death.

Images of decay – dust, creepers, broken glass – are accompanied by ones of enclosure and regression. Elizabeth enters an old chapel, 'walled up and forgotten', moving on her hands and knees 'for the entrance was very low'. Significantly, the only book that catches her eye (and the only male poet mentioned) is Dryden's *All for Love, or The World Well Lost*. In this dreamlike, labyrinthine house staircases branch off endlessly and 'so numerous were the crooked, half-lighted passages, that I wondered if I could find my way back again'. Here she finds that chest full of 'BONES!', perhaps, she says, the remains of the 'lost bride'. The lost bride is unexplained. But by faultless logic the next room – 'the last, the most deserted, and the saddest' – is the nursery, 'a nursery without children, without singing voices, without merry chiming footsteps!' As before only portraits remain; no one knows the fate of the painted children. Then, without a pause or a paragraph, comes a final anecdote whose language needs no decoding:

'Behind the house, in a hollow now wild, damp, and overgrown with elder-bushes, was a well called Margaret's Well, for there had a maiden of the house of that name drowned herself.'[14]

'Clopton Hall' is an enjoyable Gothic exercise full of ghoulish pleasures and it ends with a history of the family's decline, tailing off in a mass of lawsuits. The decaying house is identified with the decaying line, as it is in Edgar Allen Poe's 'The Fall of the House of Usher' (published at almost exactly the same time, in 1840), in which Madeline Usher, like Charlotte Clopton, is also buried alive in an ancient vault. This is the first appearance of those houses haunted by the past, and by stories, which will recur so often in Gaskell's fiction, like the fantastical château of 'Curious if True', in whose empty galleries the narrator hears 'a mighty rushing murmur (like the ceaseless sound of a distant sea, ebbing and flowing for ever and ever) . . . as if the voices of generations of men yet echoed and eddied in the silent air'. And the fate of the Clopton women anticipates a host of tales with oppressed yet defiant heroines: 'The Old Nurse's Story', 'The Grey Woman', 'Morton Hall', 'Crowley Castle'. From the beginning Gaskell's stance was both radical and feminist, and she continued all her life to make use of these Gothic conventions to link the cruel repression of wives and daughters to the pressure of history and the patriarchal power of the aristocracy, in contrast to the tenderness of women, the mutual care of the poor, the rough, loving loyalty of servants.

When he read 'Clopton Hall' William Howitt felt the force of the extraordinary piece without, perhaps, examining its implications. In one way he could see that he was right; when he visited the house himself in the autumn of 1838, he found that everything *was* changing. The hall had a new owner and 'the house was undergoing a thorough metamorphosis, from an old haunted house to a good substantial, monotonous, well-furnished family mansion'.[15] All the old fireplaces and wainscoting had been ripped out and the ancient furniture removed. He met the new owner on the stairs, his arms full of pictures, ready to hang in the gallery, but the Clopton family portraits had vanished, no one knew where.

William thought Elizabeth's writing so impressive that he 'urged his correspondent to use her pen for the public good'. But in her letters to the Howitts, although she mentions the plan for 'Sketches among the Poor' and 'The Poets of Humble Life', the public good is not in the foreground. Instead – like Charlotte Clopton, – she feeds on her own life. And she was consciously *practising* her writing. This Elizabeth is subtly different from the one who pours out a slapdash tumble of news to Lizzy. Each letter is carefully composed, the prose measured, ladylike and far from *'slip-shod'*. The style is set in the May letter in which she describes her youthful outings to Old Tabley Hall:

'Here we rambled, lounged and meditated: some stretched on the grass in indolent repose, half reading, half musing with a posy of musk roses from the old-fashioned trim garden behind the house, lulled by the ripple of the waters against the grassy lawn.' (L15)

Such conventional eighteenth-century 'charm' and cliché (at Tabley Hall the young people 'warble like birds') would occasionally creep into her later work, but this studied prose was not her natural style, any more than the verse of the 'Sketch'. The contrasting letters to Lizzy and the Howitts show a woman already aware of her facility, if not of her full talent. Revelling in her versatility, she can turn in a moment from lyrical description to swift character sketches, from gossip to the parodies she had once enjoyed sharing with her brother John. Her long letter to Lizzy, when the latter was staying in Anglesey in July 1838, ends with

'a grand Johnsonian sentence which I beg you will read aloud to elevate me in Dimockian eyes. He who can wander by the melodious waters of the Menai and partake of the finny tribes that gambol in the translucent current, and can disport himself at pleasure in the lunar-governed tide; the man who can do this, I say . . .' (L21)

And on it rolls, holding the main verb to the very end, when she gasps; 'Find out my meaning if you can, for I can't.' But her convoluted sentence, if splendidly silly, makes perfect sense.

Wales inspired more than parody. In December 1857, when 'The Doom of the Griffiths' was about to appear in *Harper's Monthly Magazine*, Elizabeth wrote to her American friend Charles Eliot Norton, placing its genesis in the 1830s: 'The story, per se, is an old rubbishy one, – begun when Marianne was a baby, – the only merit whereof is that it is founded on fact.'[16]

'The Doom of the Griffiths' is melodramatic, with showers of exclamation marks in climactic scenes, but it is not 'rubbishy'. The plot was probably based on a local scandal heard at Plas Penrhyn and the setting strives hard for authenticity: the topography is accurate, the text is sprinkled with historical references, allusions to songs like 'Men of Harlech' and 'Tri chant o' binnau' and Welsh phrases and proverbs (sadly mangled by Harpers' compositors). There are almost anthropological accounts of farmhouse interiors, inns, local dress and food, such as the dried kid's flesh, 'with a liquor called "*diod giofal*", made from the berries of the sorbus ancaparia, infused in water and then fermented'.

This realism gives ballast to a supernatural story. Long ago a member of the Griffith family had betrayed the Welsh leader Owen Glyndwr, who placed a curse upon them: for nine generations the Griffiths will never prosper, and in the ninth 'the son shall slay the father'. Gaskell's hero, Owen, is the son of the ninth generation, and at one point he reads 'the old Greek dramas which treat of a family foredoomed by an avenging Fate. The worn page opened of itself at the play of Oedipus Tyrannus.' But Sophocles is a point of departure rather than a model to be imitated. The implication that the tragedy of an unknown family in a remote country area can be as poignant as the fate of kings is typical of Gaskell's adaptation of high culture to the lives of ordinary people. And the sins of the fathers are visited upon the sons, but not in the commonly understood sense, for Unitarians did not believe that God was vengeful or that a child could inherit guilt.

The curse of the Griffiths is not divinely but socially constructed, carried through generations by patriarchal pride.

Both Owen and his father have great natural tenderness – Owen plays lovingly with his son just as his father had cared for him, after his mother's death:

'That part of the Squire's character, which was so tender and almost feminine, seemed called forth by the helpless situation of the little infant, who stretched out his arms to his father with the same earnest cooing that happier children make use of to their mother alone.' (Ch. 1)

Gaskell believed that much of the harshness of society could be overcome if men would only free the feminine side of their nature. Owen and Squire Griffith are mild, imaginative, indolent men, liable to 'vehement and fearful passions when roused'. Both dread losing self-control. If only they could recognize the maternal softness in each other, their doom would be averted, but instead, ruled by pride, they become hardened and violent.

While Owen is small, the family is held together by his sister, who replaces the lost mother, the force for life. After she leaves to be married, the house becomes dark, as in a folk-tale: 'the very fires burned dim, and were always sinking down into heaps of dull grey ashes'. The scene is set for the entrance of a witch, in the person of Squire Griffith's second wife. Owen's alienation from his father and the later disaster which leads to the final tragedy both stem, paradoxically, from love – from Squire Griffith's remarriage, and from Owen's secret union with a local peasant girl, Nest. These marriages are threatening not only because sexual relationships set up exclusive bonds, rivalling those of parent and child, but also because in this class marriage is inextricably entwined with property and status. The beautiful but ill-intentioned stepmother (ironically named Mrs Owen) works to replace Owen in the Squire's affections with her own son, Robert. She deliberately separates father and son, employing a Lamia's guile, 'so slight, so imperceptible to the common observer, yet so resistless in its effects'. At first Owen is spellbound, watching 'with a sort of breathless admiration. Her measured grace, her faultless movements, her tones of voice, sweet, until the ear was sated with her sweetness, made Owen less angry at his father's marriage.' Yet her charm is hollow: 'Almost too obtrusive was the attention paid to his wishes; but still he fancied that the heart had no part in the winning advances.'

The key to Owen's fate is the banishment from family love; he becomes moody and soured and his isolation makes him feel Nest's attraction more keenly. His clandestine domestic happiness consoles (and conceals) his jealousy of his father's second marriage and his longing for his own dead mother. When the Squire calls Nest a harlot, Owen cries out in defence:

'She is as pure as your own wife; nay God help me! as the dear, precious mother who brought me forth and then left me – with no refuge in a mother's heart – to struggle through life alone.' (Ch. 2)

In his rage the Squire hurls Owen's baby across the room to his death; Nest tries to catch him, but her son too fails to find refuge in a mother's arms. The mother gives life, the father takes it away. Love is replaced in Owen's heart by a desire for revenge, which he tries desperately to subdue. Returning to collect his belongings, he attacks his taunting stepbrother: 'Had Owen been left to his own nature, his heart would have worked itself to love doubly the boy whom he had injured; but he was stubborn from injustice, and hardened by suffering.' He refuses to clear himself. The Squire pursues him – they struggle by the sea's edge and fall together into the waves:

'Down went the Squire, down into the deep waters below – down after him went Owen, half-consciously, half-unconsciously . . . Owen knew nothing save that the awful doom seemed ever now present. He plunged down, he dived below the water in search of the body . . . he saw his father in those depths; he clutched at him; he brought him up and cast him, a dead weight, into the boat; and, exhausted by the effort, he had begun himself to sink again before he instinctively strove to rise and climb into the rocking boat.' (Ch. 2)

In their emotional turbulence these dark Welsh waters resemble the rising flood of *The Mill on the Floss*, or the Mediterranean depths where Grandcourt drowns as Gwendolen looks on in *Daniel Deronda*. 'Wild, despairing, fate pursued', Owen and Nest, clutching her dead baby, set off into the night, hoping to reach Liverpool and sail to new lands. But the sea, that powerful unpredictable element, engulfs and hides them for ever: 'They sailed into the tossing darkness and were never more seen of men.'

This story, 'begun when Marianne was a baby', not only illustrates Gaskell's lasting attraction to death and melodrama, but also shows how early key figures enter her work – the dead mother, the stubborn father, the dangerous second wife, the supportive sister. And it introduces ideas to which she would constantly return, moral conflicts expressed figuratively through masculine and feminine oppositions: revenge and love, rigid 'justice' and flexible sympathy, proud silence and open dialogue. These oppositions are explored again in a second story set in the same landscape, 'The Well of Pen-Morfa', which was possibly conceived at the same time.[17] Here another local beauty (also called Nest) is rejected by her lover after she is crippled from a fall near a mountain well. This, however, is a story of mothers and daughters, not fathers and sons, and its theme is love, not violence. Burnt by her rejection, Nest in turn rejects her mother's fierce protective love, understanding its value only after her death. As a gesture of reparation she takes in an idiot girl, an action prompted by a visiting preacher's words: 'I tell you if no one loves you, it is time for you to begin to love.' Companion pieces in setting, the two Welsh stories complement each other in argument and resolution.

The contrast of stern father and loving mother is found in a longer story, 'Lizzie Leigh', also probably begun in the late 1830s, although not published until 1850.[18] Lizzie is a figure who appears in William's *Temperance Rhymes*, a young prostitute,

> Pale, pale through the winter nights
> Trying to barter her stale delights.

Like Mary in the 'Sketch', Lizzie leaves a country farm to go into service in Manchester. When she is seduced and becomes pregnant, she is dismissed by her employers and, after a time in the workhouse, goes on the streets. Her father disowns her, decreeing 'that she should be as one dead, and her name never more be named at market or at meal time, in blessing or in prayer'. His deathbed repentance frees his wife, bound hitherto by marital obedience, to go to search for Lizzie in the unfamiliar city. There her son Will falls in love with a young teacher, Susan Palmer, who lives with her father and a two-year-old girl, Nanny, whom she calls her niece. Nanny is Lizzie's baby, thrust into Susan's arms one night in the street and recognized by Mrs Leigh when she sees the frocks in a parcel of baby clothes, 'made out of a part of a gown that she and her daughter had bought at Rochdale'.

125

When Will fears that Susan will reject him because of Lizzie's disgrace, his mother has more faith: 'Will, Will! If she's so good as thou say'st she'll have pity on such as my Lizzie. If she has no pity for such, she's a cruel Pharisee, and thour't best without her.' It is he, not Susan, who is the Pharisee. In an exchange about Lizzie's sufferings Susan's balanced, even rhymed, retort to Will's harshness formally underlines the point (and makes one speculate if this story too may have begun as a verse 'sketch'):

'He made answer, low and stern, "She deserved them all; every jot."
"In the eye of God, perhaps she does. He is the Judge; we are not." '
(Ch. 4)

The Pharisaic, Old Testament sternness of the men is once again contrasted with the sympathetic mercy of the New Testament, shown by the women, a contrast made explicit by references to both the Prodigal Son and Mary Magdalen. But although Gaskell stresses forgiveness, her underlying attitude is ambivalent, as it always would be to sexual error. Woman's nature embraces both sinner and saint, mother and whore: the narrative is punitive as well as merciful. Lizzie has not entirely abandoned her child. She leaves packets of money from time to time, and is nearby at the crisis, when the baby dies after falling downstairs. Susan and Lizzie, the good daughter and the bad, embrace over the child's body. At the end Lizzie returns to the farm and helps her neighbours, 'a sad, gentle-looking woman', who rarely smiles, while Susan marries Will and blossoms like the countryside itself: 'Children grow around her and call her blessed.' But the harsh price exacted for Lizzie's redemption is the death of her innocent child, 'a little unconscious sacrifice whose early calling home had recalled her poor wandering mother'.

The terrible theme of the child's death, and the buried guilt of the mother who is helpless to save it, invaded Elizabeth's own life again at the end of this decade. It was a tragedy that has only recently come to light through the discovery of a letter to Harriet Carr, written in March 1856, when Harriet had long been Mrs Andersen.[19] The friends had been out of touch for years, and Elizabeth wrote: 'Ah! you don't know my children yet.' First, she said, came Marianne and Meta and then 'my two *little* girls. We make that distinction, because, owing to the death of a little son while yet a baby there is six years difference in age between Meta and Florence, the next girl.' This first son, not named, must have died very early: no record has yet been found of his birth or his death.

In the 1830s she had known the joy of childbirth, but also the grief of loss – her stillborn daughter, Aunt Lumb, her baby son. She had two small girls to care for and her days were consumed by family affairs, parish duties and social engagements. Yet she found time to write: her imagination could not be constrained. We do not know exactly how much she wrote and stored away over the next few years, but by the late 1840s and 1850s, when her work was much in demand, she produced her stories suspiciously quickly, even for someone who wrote at speed. Her voice, though still unheard, was being rehearsed in private.

Over twenty years later, in 1862, she would offer advice to a young wife who aspired to be a writer. She is full of helpful tips on housework and organizing time and ends with a wild attempt to link domesticity and art: 'making the various household arts into real studies (& there is plenty of poetry and association about them – remember how the Greek princesses in Homer washed the clothes &c&c&c&c)'. But the nub of her message is this:

'The exercise of a talent or power *is* always a great pleasure; but one should weigh well whether this pleasure may not be obtained by the sacrifice of some duty. When I had *little* children I do not think I could have written stories, because I should have become too much absorbed in my *fictitious* people to attend to my *real* ones.' (L694–5)

Her correspondent wanted to earn money to help her husband, a laudable object, Elizabeth agreed, but one that might make her feel sorry if she was

'unable to give your tender sympathy to your little ones in their small joys & sorrows; and yet, don't you know how you, – how every one, who tries to write stories *must* become absorbed in them, (fictitious though they be,) if they are to interest their readers in them. Besides viewing the subject from a solely artistic point of view a good writer of fiction must have *lived* an active & sympathetic life if she wishes her books to have strength & vitality in them. When you are forty, and if you have a gift for being an authoress you will write ten times as good a novel as you could do now, just because you will have gone through so much more of the interests of a wife and mother.'

Yet she herself had never really stopped writing stories when her children were small. As in this letter, the nurturing of real and fictitious people was inextricably linked – both 'absorbed' the woman – and although they seemed to compete, it was the experience of being 'a wife and mother', she felt, that brought out the writer's 'gift'.

[7]

Light and Darkness

In the early 1840s, while Elizabeth cared for her children at home, she still paid close attention to wider issues – of faith, morality, politics. The world around her, and her own life, were full of startling contrasts. In Manchester she saw suffering and unrest, riots and starvation; on holiday in Germany she dined amid scenes of lavish wealth. In public she seemed confident and busy; in private she was often lonely and anxious. She moves like an actress from a bright stage into the private dark of the wings and then suddenly out into the glare again.

One major factor in the Gaskells' lives at this stage was the opening of Manchester New College, when the Unitarian academy in York moved back to Manchester, its original base. Funds had run low in the 1830s and when the principal, Charles Wellbeloved, was due to retire in 1839, the trustees wondered if the college should move to London and train divinity students, affiliating to the new, non-denominational London University, founded in 1836. In the end they settled on Manchester, where local dissent (and financial support) were strong. When the college opened in 1840, William became its clerical secretary and lectured in literature; in 1846 he would become professor of history, literature and logic. His friends and fellow-ministers were also closely involved: John Robberds was professor of pastoral theology and Hebrew and J. J. Tayler professor of ecclesiastical history.

The college brought a striking new figure into Elizabeth's orbit – James Martineau, the new professor of mental and moral philosophy. Martineau was the same age as William and had been his fellow-student at York. In 1832, after four years in Dublin, he became minister at Paradise Street Chapel, Liverpool, and still kept this post after 1840, travelling into Manchester to teach. Combative, passionate and eloquent, he was the most assertive among the leaders of a new school of Unitarian theology which generated controversy so heated that it almost threatened to split the sect in two. James Martineau was a romantic, an idealist, strongly influenced by Kant (in contrast to his sister Harriet, who was drawn increasingly to secularism). He saw this Manchester appointment as a watershed in his life since the need to revise his lectures and rethink his position clearly finally gave him the chance, he said, 'to escape from a logical cage into open air'.[1]

Martineau was enormously influential because he offered a direct challenge to Priestleyan rationalism, the core of Unitarian belief. He defied the notion of a predetermined universe, stressed the role of free will and insisted that belief, rather than relying on 'evidence', sprang from an inner, emotional impulse. In a brilliant sermon on 'The Communion of Saints', in November 1840, he declared that 'worship is an attitude which our nature assumes, not *for a purpose*, but *from an emotion*'.[2] Preaching on St Paul in 1841, Martineau had stated his belief that true moral power did not come from will and reason but

'from a new affection, so deep, so pure, so entrancing, as to bring us back to that self-oblivion which guilt had destroyed . . . and surprise us into devotedness to some fresh object of confidence and love.'[3]

A new emphasis on feeling was already present in Unitarian thinking during the 1830s, influenced partly by American ministers like William Ellery Channing and Joseph Tuckerman, and partly by the absorption of Methodist congregations, who brought with them their different tradition of 'vigorous, unconventional preaching' and religious fervour.[4] William and Elizabeth were swept up in the philanthropic tide which followed Tuckerman's visit, and they welcomed the warmer, more spiritual style of preaching. Elizabeth always disliked the dogmatic, hard Unitarianism of the Priestleyan or 'Hampstead' school. In 1859 she would write: 'Oh! for some really devotional preaching instead of controversy about doctrines, – about which I am more and more certain we can *never be certain* in this world.'[5] But they were more conservative than Martineau. Most of William's closest friends and associates – like William Turner, John Robberds or J. R. Beard – held traditional views, and William himself stayed a Priestleyan at heart, convinced that rational inquiry was the surest route to understanding the laws of God. He clung to a 'necessitarian' view of causes and consequences, and two years before his death, in a sermon of 1878, he was still insisting that errors of plan were 'sure' to lead to defects of execution, improper actions 'infallibly' produced 'mischievous consequences', vice 'inevitably' brought punishment and virtue reward:

'In the nature of things, it cannot be otherwise; if it might, the world would be a chaos, without law, without order, without object, without anything intelligible or certain – a mere wreck drifting blindly and hopelessly on to destruction and oblivion. As, however, in all its departments it is pervaded by universal relations and dependencies, their foundation is laid for our instruction and guidance.'[6]

From this foundation, he said, the sciences are developed, the 'object of the world's existence' is discovered, 'and by these means we turn from the present to the past, and bring back to us lessons of an important and valuable kind'.

Although Elizabeth's heroines are often Anglicans, and the allegiance of her 'Dissenters' is usually vague, this sterner aspect of Unitarianism is found in fiction (especially in *Mary Barton, Ruth* and *Sylvia's Lovers*) in her tracing of consequences and her emphasis on education, truth and lies, atonement and regeneration. But the influence of the new school of thought, which gave priority to feeling, is equally strong, if not stronger. Again and again she shows characters progressing from guilt, misery or self-obsession, through love (or sympathetic identification with another) to positive involvement with the whole community. Her stories act out Martineau's 'great moral truth' of the contrast between 'the emancipating energy of the unconscious affections and the feebleness of the self-interested will'.[7] Sometimes they even resemble the 'devotional preaching' she admired, and had a similar effect. In 1854 the feminist journalist Frances Power Cobbe, who thought of herself as a pragmatic rationalist, bent on acquiring truth through knowledge, read 'a pretty little story by Mrs Gaskell'. 'Suddenly,' Cobbe wrote, 'it came to me that Love is greater than knowledge – that it is more beautiful to serve our brothers freely and tenderly, than to hive up learning with each studious year.'[8]

But although Elizabeth liked Martineau's ideas, she did not exactly like *him*. He could be savage to opponents and she was suspicious of his charismatic power. In 1853, staying in Wales, she complained to

Marianne: 'All the James Martineaus come tomorrow . . . I wish they weren't coming – I like to range about ad libitum, & sit looking at views &c; not talking sense by the yard.' She herself dearly liked to talk 'ad libitum', though in a different style, preferring to talk about people than abstract ideas, but she took everything in and her close friends were well aware of the searching mind beneath the apparently casual chatter. When Susanna Winkworth first met James Anthony Froude and his wife, she told her sister Selina that she felt quite oppressed by 'those mountains of intellect', adding: 'I never was with anybody half so clever before, except Lily; and she, you know, has always plenty of women's subjects to talk about.'[9]

If James Martineau overwhelmed Elizabeth (and sometimes bored her), she loved his friend Francis Newman, the new professor of classics, who satisfied her sense of fun as well as her concern with religion. Newman was a talented eccentric, the irresistible prey of students' practical jokes. Tall and angular, with piercing blue eyes set deep in an aquiline face framed in long dark hair, he appealed to Elizabeth's delight in the bizarre, often dressing, as an early biographer pointed out, 'in the onion fashion – three coats one over the other, and the last one – green!'[10] Elizabeth noticed these coats, but also the attractiveness beneath: 'He dresses so shabbily you would not see his full beauty, – he used to wear detestable bottle green coats, which never show off a man.' His colourful past intrigued her as much as his strange appearance: in 1830 he had set out with a group of idealistic friends to convert the Muslims in Baghdad. Inevitably the venture failed, bringing not only disillusionment but tragedy – all the women in the party died and Newman himself barely survived. He married on his return to England, and both Elizabeth and Mary Robberds found his wife, who belonged to the Plymouth Brethren, rather alarming. Mary said that the religious samplers which hung on the Newmans' walls reminded her of 'the scripture denunciations which were placarded on the walls of Albion Street in Race week',[11] and Elizabeth, although she grew fond of Mrs Newman, defined her creed as 'a sort of community-of-goods-and-equality-of-rank-on-religious-principles and *very* Calvinistic'.

Newman himself (whom George Eliot later called 'our blessed St Francis')[12] held highly unorthodox religious views which were far from Calvinistic. Just as Harriet and James Martineau had moved in opposite directions, so the brothers John Henry (later Cardinal) and

Francis Newman took widely divergent routes in their search for a faith. (A contemporary called the former 'a spiritual Tory', the latter 'a spiritual radical'.)[13] Like Martineau, Francis Newman stressed the imaginative, intuitive basis of faith, explored in his books *The Soul* (1849) and the autobiographical *Phases of Faith* (1850), but he rejected the divinity of Christ altogether, insisting that if Jesus was not as vulnerable and prone to sin as other men, this deprived his life of any moral example and sympathy.[14] Elizabeth's position was not so radical. She certainly did not see Christ as equal to God, but she did feel that he was in some sense divine, as well as human. In 1854 she told Marianne that the Anglican Litany made her feel more 'devotional' than the plain chapel services, but she saw this as a danger, since the prayers to the Trinity obscured the single nature of God:

'Then the one thing I *am* clear and sure about is this that Jesus Christ was not equal to His father; that, however divine a being he was *not* God; and that worship as God addressed to Him is therefore wrong in me.' (L860)

Newman was a radical in every sense. He was an inspiring, unconventional teacher, who taught Greek as a living language; a vegetarian (but one who felt that plants too could feel pain) and a fervent campaigner for the Anti-Corn Law League, relief of the Irish problem, women's rights. In Manchester his outright views made enemies, like the Sunday school inspector who, said Elizabeth, 'roundly abused our Mr Newman' for trying to acquire 'various branches of knowledge', which, he said, savoured of vanity, and was a temptation of the devil. Elizabeth did not always agree with Newman, but in 1850, four years after he left Manchester, she told Tottie: 'Yes I *do* know my dear Mr Newman, we all here reverence him with true reverence as you would if you know him. He is so holy!'

'We first knew Mr Newman from his coming here to be a professor at the Manchester College – and the face and voice at first sight told "He had been with Christ". I never during a 6 years pretty intimate acquaintance heard or saw anything which took off that first conviction. Oh dear! I long for the days back again when he came dropping in in the dusk and lost no time in pouring out what his heart were full of, (thats the secret of eloquence) whether it was a derivation of a word, a joke or a burst of indignation or a holy thought.' (L87–8)

The advent of Manchester College enriched Elizabeth's life in many ways, and clarified the structure of her beliefs. And it seems as if she took from both strands of Unitarianism – unconsciously rather than artfully – those elements that helped her, imaginatively, as a novelist: the chain of cause and consequence which appears in her fiction (as in George Eliot's) as the workings of poetic, as much as divine, justice; the feeling that humanity is engaged in a continuous process of learning, of unravelling the puzzle of life (an idea at the heart of the liberal tradition of the novel); the emphasis on enlightenment through feeling and personal relationships; the idea of Christ as nearer in nature to man than to God, which hallowed the artistic 'incarnation' of spiritual truths in the daily life of fallible mortals. By using her art as the vehicle for her belief, writing became a religious exercise and therefore 'permissible', reflecting a feeling which had lingered on from the eighteenth century that novels were somehow frivolous and corrupting unless they had a clear moral or spiritual message.

Theology was not the only area currently rocked by new theories and forceful personalities. Scientific circles were alight as well, and the ideas canvassed here also formed a significant element in the culture from which Elizabeth Gaskell wrote. Until recently Manchester had seemed a scientific backwater, but it had rapidly created a reputation, particularly for applied science. Discussion flourished and new societies bloomed: the Natural History Society (1821); the Royal Manchester Institution (1823); the Mechanics Institute (1824); the Statistical Society (1834); the Geological Society (1838). The centre of all this activity was still, however, the Manchester Literary and Philosophical Society; William Gaskell became a member in January 1840, near the end of the long presidency of the eminent John Dalton.

Two years later the Lit. and Phil. was the main centre when the town played host to the annual meeting of the British Association in June 1842, bringing a constellation of scientific stars from London, Oxford, Cambridge, Scotland – Herschel, Buckland, Whewell, Roget and many more. Exhibitions, banquets, lectures, soirées were held all over the city. At the Association Dinner, the Revd Adam Sedgwick, Woodwardian professor of geology at Cambridge, told the assembled company how astounded he had been, walking the streets of Manchester: 'in talking to men whose brows were smeared with dirt and whose hands were black with soot, I found upon them the marks of intellectual minds, and the proofs of high character'. He urged the learned, affluent members of the association to mingle with these artisans in the 'overlooked corners of our great cities', reminding them that customs and formal institutions too often 'draw a great and harsh line between man and man'. But Sedgwick was quick to add:

'Do not suppose for a moment that I am holding any levelling doctrines. Far from it. I seek but to consolidate the best institutions of society. But I do wish that the barriers between man and man, between rank and rank, should not be harsh, and high and thorny; but rather that they should be a kind of sunk fence, sufficient to draw lines of demarcation between one and another, and yet such that the smile of gladness and the voice of cheerfulness might pass over, and be felt and heard on the other side.'[15]

Sedgwick was a conservative at heart, in science as well as politics; he would have no talk of evolution and was later a vehement opponent of his former protégé Charles Darwin. His image of the sunk fence, the ha-ha – with its aristocratic, eighteenth-century nuance and unstated desire to obtain a pleasant prospect while keeping the animals (or lower orders) off the private lawns – gives him away. But few of those present at this dinner would have chafed at his patronizing tone; a 'sunk fence', as working-class radicals knew, was a harder barrier to demolish, precisely because it was invisible.

As a member of the Lit. and Phil. William followed scientific innovations closely. Since Charles Lyell's *Principles of Geology* (1831–3) and *Elements of Geology* (1838) had attempted to replace the current view of the 'catastrophic' development of the earth (held by men like Sedgwick) by new theories of gradual development, many people, especially those who looked to the Bible as a fount of truth, had been dismayed by the findings of geologists. In the coming decade still more alarm was aroused by the Edinburgh publisher Robert Chambers, whose *Vestiges of the Natural History of Creation* was published anonymously in 1844. This dazzling, journalistic work put into popular form startling new ideas about the evolution of the universe, from the birth of the planets to the development of man; and although Chambers held that the cosmos was governed by mathematical laws, implying an external intelligence, he argued that God had not created a world of fixed forms but one whose 'laws' depended on constant change.

To Unitarians, almost alone among Christian sects, such ideas posed no threat. They meshed with their optimistic notion of material laws set in motion by God and with the vision of nature already proclaimed, for example, by Thomas Southwood Smith in his *Divine Government* – an endless progression, with organisms, plants, animals and men 'continually advancing from one degree of knowledge, perfection and happiness to another'. For William Gaskell, as for Smith, each scientific advance was therefore a step towards understanding God's plan: 'the more we come to know of His working, the more clearly shall we see how marvellous it is, and the more profoundly be led to adore'.[16]

William's increased outside interests meant that Elizabeth found herself more often alone. She seemed the domestic one, while he was involved in the outer world. Even when he was at home, he was busy with sermons, reports and private teaching. Among his new pupils in 1841 were the three older daughters of a silk merchant who lived at the Polygon, Ardwick: Emily, Selina and Susanna Winkworth. They had heard of William from his other students, the Paterson sisters: 'they like and admire Mr Gaskell beyond measure; they say he is "beautiful", about twenty-nine and has a very nice wife and two pretty little children'. He taught them history, composition, chemistry, German and music, 'over all which,' wrote Susanna, 'we were in the highest state of delight and excitement'.

From 1843 William also taught their younger sister, Catherine,[17] and in time the Winkworths would be among Elizabeth's closest friends and confidantes. But in 1841 their classes were yet another thing which absorbed William's attention. Sometimes, especially when she was ill, the desire to confide her worries overwhelmed her. On one such evening, two days before Christmas 1840, she wrote to her sister-in-law Anne Robson, her 'dearest Nancy'.[18] Marianne had been ill and though she was now recovering (on 'broth & eggs'), Elizabeth confessed:

'one can't help having 'Mother's fears', and Wm I dare say kindly won't allow me ever to talk to him about anxieties, while it would be SUCH A RELIEF often. So don't allude too much to what I've been saying in your answer. William is at a minister's meeting tonight, – and tomorrow dines with a world of professors and college people at Mark Philips.' (L45)

Once again, with William away, she could say what she felt, while keeping it a secret from him. She was brooding on Marianne's sensitivity and shyness, compared with little Meta's independent, open spirit. Lack of love might, she felt, make MA 'sullen and deceitful', while tenderness would bring her out.

'Now Anne, will you remember this? It is difficult to have the right trust in God almost, when thinking about one's children – and you know I have no sister or near relation whom I could entreat to watch over any peculiarity in their disposition. Now you know that dear William feeling most kindly towards his children, is yet most reserved in *expressions* of either affection or sympathy – & in case of my death, we all know the probability of widowers marrying again, – would you promise, dearest Anne, to remember MA's peculiarity of character, and as much as circumstances would permit, watch over her & cherish her.' (L46)

This is eloquent and revealing, about William's reserve, her own isolation and her dread of second marriages like the one which had overshadowed her own childhood. She would always need women confidantes acutely. Two years earlier, telling Lizzy how much she missed Aunt Lumb, she had written: 'Thank you dear Lizzy for telling me so nicely all about your feelings &c – you cannot weary me by so doing, for I take the greatest interest in every particular, and I heartily wish you were here, with your sweet comforting face, and I would listen, and talk, & talk, & listen.' Her appeal to Lizzy, and to Nancy in 1840, anticipates many others, like this to her cousin Fanny in 1847: 'I *want* you; I don't know if I can offer any inducements but you wd be such a comfort and help to me.'[19] This enduring need is felt even behind that letter of advice to the young woman writer in 1862: 'Have you no sister or relation who could come and help you for a little while till you get stronger – no older friend at hand who would help you to plan your work so that it should oppress you as little as possible?' William could never play this role. His reticence was not due to lack of feeling (if anything, he worried more about the girls than she did). It was the dwelling on such worries that he disliked. Finding it hard to express his own feelings, he discouraged introspection and when Elizabeth was depressed, he tried to direct her attention away from herself, and urge her to be active. Yet he was far from insensitive, and was, in his way, highly perceptive: she did need action to lift her from the slough of despond.

In 1840 events forced Elizabeth to look outward, away from the family. Her own anxieties, however intense, seemed small beside those of the first victims of the 'hungry forties'. The early 1830s had seen a boom in Manchester trade. Cotton goods and yarn made up half of Britain's exports (equal to twice the total export of the Russian empire).[20] The need for machinery boosted the local engineering works and banks sprang up like mushrooms to fund the expansion: fifty joint stock banks were opened in 1836 alone. But the boom was followed by a crash: even a major Manchester bank, the Northern Central, had to be bailed out by the Bank of England.

After a brief recovery a second crash followed in 1839. American banks had been giving credit to planters so that they could hold back cotton and demand high prices. Lancashire manufacturers retaliated by refusing to order and slowing production. Workers were laid off by the thousand and hundreds of mills lay idle. Other pressures heightened potential unrest. There was nationwide agitation against the new Poor Law of 1834, which had introduced the harsh workhouse system (the target of *Oliver Twist* in 1837–8). Chartism took root and spread, issuing its eight demands, including universal suffrage, in the People's Charter of 1838. In the same year the Anti-Corn Law campaigners began to mobilize the merchants against the protective tariffs which, they claimed, served only the landed interests; their propaganda made a double appeal to middle-class self-interest and humanitarian concern.

These simultaneous movements converged and clashed. In Manchester on 23 September 1838, at the same time as a great Chartist gathering was taking place on Kersal Moor, a meeting was being held in one of the city's hotels which marked the start of the Anti-Corn Law League campaign. Within a year Chartists and Leaguers were in conflict with each other, as well as with the government. There was fear of revolution, for this was part of the rhetoric of many activists. The Revd Joseph Rayner Stephens, speaking to a vast rally of over forty thousand people on Newcastle Town Moor on New Year's Day 1839, urged that if their demands were ignored they should burn the city to the ground and proclaimed himself 'a revolutionist by fire, a revolutionist by blood, to the knife, to the death'.[21] Fear and rumour spread. In Lancashire, it was said, nearly forty thousand men were armed with picks, staves and even guns. General Napier, sent north to command the troops, saw Manchester as 'the chimney of the world. Rich rascals, poor rogues, drunken ragamuffins and prostitutes form the moral, soot made into paste by rain the physique, and the only view is a long chimney. What a place! The entrance to hell realised!'[22] The rumbling threat of violence was increased by poor harvests and higher prices. The Chartist petition, signed by over a million people, was presented to the House of Commons on 14 June. After a month of suspense, on 12 July the House refused to consider it, by a vote of 189 to 92. The delegates (like Gaskell's John Barton) returned to their towns embittered and disillusioned.

While Chartism was rudely rebuffed, the Anti-Corn Law League was girding itself for battle. Its base, and its symbol, was Manchester. The Manchester Leaguers extolled their city's glories, comparing it to the great city states of the past, even to Jerusalem, the rallying point of the crusades. They held their meetings in a vast wooden pavilion, capable of holding banquets for four thousand people, on the site of the future Free Trade Hall. Throughout 1840 and 1841 their public gatherings were constantly disrupted by the Chartists and on 2 June 1841, after months of tension, the two sides clashed in Stevenson Square. Chartists surrounded a League platform, waving banners which were broken and turned into weapons by League supporters, including ranks of Manchester Irish, marshalled by the Radical MP Daniel O'Connor. (The Irish population, among the most poverty-stricken in the city, numbered over thirty thousand, and were so strictly organized 'that in the twinkling of an eye, one or 2,000 can be collected at any given spot'.)[23]

After this the Manchester Chartists were less powerful, but the brawls did not cease. When the Chartist leader Feargus O'Connor visited the city in March 1842, there was 'a tremendous fight – all the furniture was smashed to attoms'. O'Connor himself was felled three times and others were badly hurt, including 'Revd. Schofield – black eye – loose teeth – cut lip'.[24] The riots in Gaskell's fiction seem mild by comparison.

Ten days after Stevenson Square Elizabeth wrote to the American Unitarian minister John Pierpont, who had visited Manchester in the mid-1830s. Pierpont was a man of many causes, including the abolition of slavery, the peace movement and temperance; in 1841 he was involved in a fierce battle with the rum merchants in his Boston congregation. Elizabeth had corresponded with him since his visit: thanking him for a copy of his poems, she assured him of their support in his struggles and sent him William's *Temperance Rhymes*. But, she told him:

'We are feeling as indeed all English people *must* do, that we are at a great crisis, and that there is a great struggle going on in the matter of the Corn Laws. Perhaps it may have been decided before this reaches you; if not peacefully decided, at least by agitation and distress which is most painful to think of. The manufacturing classes around us are in very great trouble, and if it were winter the lower classes would find it almost unbearable; as it is the early warmth of the season has been a great blessing.'[25]

William and Elizabeth held back from political campaigning, preferring to put their efforts into relief work. Innumerable contemporary accounts describe the suffering in Lancashire from 1840 to 1842. Archibald Prentice, a leader of the Anti-Corn Law movement, cited visits to 258 families, consisting of 1,009 individuals, whose average earnings were 7½d per week. Joseph Adshead, the founder of the Night Asylum for the destitute, found that under a fifth of households in some districts had any member in full employment, and counted over 2,000 cellar dwellings in a single area, where children under twelve numbered 3,479.[26] Many of these children were starving. Penniless families sold their furniture, or were turned out of their houses: their diet was oatmeal, skimmed milk and water. Engels, who arrived in Manchester in late 1842, vividly described one of the worst areas around the Medlock, 'Little Ireland', south-west of the Oxford Road, not far from the Gaskells' home:

'The race that lives in these ruinous cottages behind broken windows, mended with oilskin, sprung doors, and rotten doorposts, or in dark, wet cellars, in measureless filth and stench, in this atmosphere penned in as if with a purpose, this race must really have reached the lowest stage of humanity . . . in each of these pens, containing at most two rooms, a garret and perhaps a cellar, on the average twenty human beings live.'[27]

There was no sanitation. The narrow lanes and courts were filled with filth and excrement, added to by the family pigs – the poor's only source of meat – which roamed the streets at large. As Engels pointed out, conditions had hardly changed since Kay's report of 1831 and although the cholera did not return, typhus was rife in 1837 and again in 1842: this is the fever which stalks *Mary Barton*.

Engels's book *The Condition of the Working Class in England* was not published in Britain until 1892, long after Elizabeth's death. William, who was fluent in German, could have read the original when it appeared in 1844, but he did not need to: all accounts, and his own experience, revealed the same picture. At the annual general meeting of the Domestic Home Mission in 1840 (chaired by William) one of the visitors, George Buckland, described a typical cellar, lit only by the raking of the meagre fire:

'I saw a woman lying on a few bits of dirty sacking upon the bare flags, and herself almost in a state of nudity, and who had been delivered of a child only three or four hours. The infant was living, and all but naked, as was also another little child that crept out from beneath the slender covering . . . The husband said that he had neither candle, food nor money.'[28]

This was truly naked poverty.

The Gaskells were also involved with the District Provident Society, founded by William Langton and James Kay, which had 250 voluntary visitors. Relief work united all denominations and ministers worked together, dividing the city into relief districts and organizing the distribution of soup tickets, food and clothing. Better off families like the Gaskells and Winkworths fed long queues of hungry people who came to their kitchen doors each morning. Elizabeth felt for the cellar-dwellers, the homeless and the vagrants, but she was almost more concerned at the change in feeling among the 'respectable' working class. These were people she knew well through her chapel work, the kinds of families who could afford the luxury of 4d a week for Sunday school. She was deeply disturbed by the alienation of this group, whose settled lives were disrupted and incomes lost. In *Mary Barton* she would make a special point of showing that even men like the weaver Job Legh, who could understand the economic causes and who distrusted union antagonism, had now become polarized in their attitudes. Job could say, with justice:

'I'm wanting in learning, I'm aware; but I can use my eyes. I never see the masters getting thin and haggard for want of food . . . it's in things for show they cut short; while for such as me, it's in things for life we've to stint. For sure, sir, you'll own it's come to a hard pass when a man would give aught in the world for work to keep his children from starving, and can't get a bit, if he's ever so willing to labour.' (Ch. 37)

When she wrote to John Pierpont in June, Elizabeth described the distress, but also told him about their own plans to escape, briefly, by using William's month of summer leave to travel abroad. William had toured Europe for ten weeks with a friend in the autumn of 1839, travelling through France and Switzerland as far as Florence and Venice. But as for herself, 'I have never been out of the Island before.'[29]

On the Continent Elizabeth put the turmoil of Manchester behind her. She gave a full account of her trip to Lizzy, beginning with the 'practical poetry' of the old cathedrals of Flanders; she had enjoyed Bruges, Ghent and Antwerp, she said, 'more than I can tell – while every bit was so solemn and sublime, appearing so deserted and lonely, as if the world had stood still with them since the 14th century'. On the other hand the Rhine, when they reached it, was not quite 'sublime' enough:

'We got to the Rhine at Cologne which smells of the bones of the 3,000 virgins. The Rhine (very sub rosa) was a disappointment. To be sure it rained cats & dogs – but the hills & rocks are round not pointed in their outline.' (L41)

They dutifully climbed the Drachenfels, where they met some Coleridge relations ('I should like to tell you of *our* conversation it was so high-toned & so superior'). Then they left the tourists behind and headed for Heidelberg. This ancient town in the beautiful Neckar valley had everything she liked, fine scenery, sunshine, ancient legends – and high society.

William and Lily stayed just outside the town as paying guests of Frau von Pickford, sister of their Manchester friend Mrs Schwabe. To their astonishment the very first people they met were Mary Howitt and her daughter. In 1840 the Howitts had taken their large family to Heidelberg, where they stayed for three years, translating German works and also, rather oddly, learning Swedish and Danish (Mary later translated Frederika Bremer and introduced her Scandinavian

brand of feminism to Britain). This first meeting was sprung on the
Gaskells as soon as they arrived. It was dusk, remembered Elizabeth,
'& I could only see instead of the simple Quaker I had pictured to
myself, a lady in a gay-coloured satin, black satin scarf & leghorn
bonnet with a plume of drooping white feathers. It was such a funny
feeling of astonishment, and Miss Howitt was equally unquakerish.'
The whole group 'sallied forth' along the river bank and walked
through the pine-woods to a clearing, lit by coloured lamps, where
boards were laid on the grass, and a group of whirling students and
peasant girls danced to a spirited band. This unexpected evening was
followed by many more:

'We never drank tea alone I think. Sometimes some of the students
when we had music dancing & all manner of games; sometimes the
Howitts – when we all told the most frightening & wild stories we had
ever heard, – some *such* fearful ones – all true – then we drank tea out
at the Howitts, – looking over all the portfolios of splendid engravings,
casts &c they had collected – (My word! authorship brings them in a
pretty penny) – at the Webers – he a Dr of Philosophie – grave German
& philosophical, to say nothing of politico-œconomical evenings – at
the Schlosser's, & Nie's, two gay balls.' (L44)

One of Gaskell's most extraordinary short stories suggests the kind
of tales she and the Howitts enjoyed – of robber bands roaming the
north-west banks of the Rhine at the end of the eighteenth century, of
cruelty and murder. In 'The Grey Woman' a loyal servant helps her
desperate mistress to escape a robber husband and the two women
then live together as man and wife; the 'wildness' includes cross-
dressing and, at the end, bigamy. The heroines break every rule. 'The
Grey Woman' appeared in 1861, but it is introduced by the finding of a
bundle of old letters, in the summer of '184–', and its genesis does
seem to lie in this first German holiday. Another story, 'Six Weeks at
Heppenheim', also contains an affectionate reminder of 1841. In this
gentle pastoral, set around the southern Rhine, the name of the servant
heroine is Thekla – that of the elegant, stylish daughter of the Gaskells'
landlady, Frau Pickford.

Elizabeth and Mary Howitt shared a fondness for the Gothic. At the
Schlosser's ball Mary mysteriously led her away from the dance, down
to a river bank where noble nuns lay buried under stone escutcheons
and sculptured tombs in a vault 'still as death', hidden from the gay

crowd outside; 'Was it not a picturesque contrast between the dead and the living?' Nine years later, on Christmas Day 1850, Mary wrote to her daughter:

'Last night Eliza Fox wrote proposing for them and Mrs Gaskell to come to us this evening. Meggie suggests that we should not be grand and intellectual – but ghost stories and capital tales shall be told, and that we should even play at blind-man's buff. We may be merry and tell tales, but I doubt the playing at blind-man's buff.'[30]

There were no such undignified games at Heidelberg parties, where the balls were exceedingly grand. Elizabeth gave a rapturous account of the one at Mme Schlosser's 450-year-old mansion, complete with panelling, terraces, conservatories, fountains (and nuns). She made sure she knew the customs; no one under forty, she informed Lizzy, wears anything but muslin, and the flowers in their hair (a signal that one wanted to dance) must be real, not artificial. 'Mine was geranium – Thekla wove it, – but the prevalent & fashionable flower was the intensely scarlet pomegranate blossom with its deep green leaves – Matilda had ivy and looked like a Bacchante.' She occasionally slipped up: after two turns round the room in an extra-quick waltz she was 'desperate dizzy', and on the point of taking her partner's arm ('a Baron, my dear'), when Thekla Pickford stopped her:

' "Don't be offended with me, Mrs G. – but I forgot to tell you no one takes a gentn's arm & I have heard English ladies so much remarked upon for this", so I very properly stood holding & being held by the tips of my fingers in the most decorous manner, thinking of the funniness of morality which in one place makes it immoral to be taken by the waist, in another to be taken by the arm.' (L821)

A characteristic observation. She danced every dance until the end of the evening, when, dizzy and tired, she refused 'a very ugly man'. This was a mistake, since he was Goethe's grandson, and 'Wm said I shd have danced with the *name*'.

The escapist holiday had to end, and on her return, after brief stays in Warrington and Knutsford, Elizabeth had to face Manchester again. The Anti-Corn Law campaign was reaching a new pitch of fervour and on 17 August 1841 a major conference took place in Manchester of ministers of religion in support of the League, which brought together all denominations (although Anglicans were a noticeable minority). William had grave doubts about such involvement, and his attitude was probably close to that of James Martineau, on receiving a circular about the meeting;

'*This* and Dr Hutton's Corn-Law Sermon have led me to think a good deal about the duty of our order in relation to political action. The question is grave and difficult; but I think I have made up my mind that, *in our capacity of ministers*, we ought to stand aloof from all controversies of which the *essence and* subject-matter do not lie within the province of religion and morals.'[31]

Martineau could not see the issue as a 'sacred war'; it was not the same as the American war against slavery, where he would have been conscious bound to join the battle. Other Unitarians felt differently, John Relly Beard was one of the conference organizers, while Mrs Robberds and Mrs Tayler sat on the vast committee (360 names) set up that November to plan a grand bazaar, in an attempt to involve all 'the ladies who had taken a deep interest in the question as affecting the welfare of suffering millions'. Soon 'thousands of feminine fingers were instantly at work'.[32] Elizabeth's may have been among them, but she was not on the committee. When the bazaar was held the following February, it was on a scale which looked forward to the Great Exhibition of 1851, raising £10,000 not for 'the suffering millions' but for funds and propaganda for the League.

Neither of the Gaskells formally identified with the Anti-Corn Law cause. *Mary Barton* suggests that Elizabeth's sympathies lay as much, if not more, with the Chartists than the Leaguers, although she thought their actions misguided, and felt that unions could be as tyrannical as masters. The winter of 1841–2 had seen intensified distress and no sign of effective parliamentary action. Both Chartists and the Anti-Corn Law League were frustrated and desperate for action. Early in 1842 some of the Leaguers, led by John Bright, had suggested closing the factories to threaten the government (an idea first mooted by the Chartists in 1839). But in August the tables were turned: it was the workers, not the owners, who struck, and Manchester was plunged into the Plug Plot Riots – (so called because the workers removed the plugs from the great steam boilers in all the factories that cut wages).

The dramatic events which followed anticipate Gaskell's 1854 novel

North and South as well as *Mary Barton*, although the attack on
Thornton's mill in *North and South* stems from a grudge against a
particular owner rather than a general strike. The movement began on
5 August in the satellite towns of Stalybridge, Oldham, Ashton and
Dukinfield. Over twenty thousand workers marched on Manchester,
gathering men from every mill they passed. Briefly held back by troops
and police at Holt Town, they poured on into the city and whenever
they met resistance, violence flared – Birley's mill was stormed and two
policemen and a bystander killed. In his history of the Anti-Corn Law
League Archibald Prentice recalled the scenes of the evening, in the
area where the Gaskells lived:

'About nine o'clock, in the whole of the South-eastern part of the
borough, including Garrett Road, Brook Street, Oxford Road and
Green Heys, the shops were closed, and bands of from twenty to fifty
youths were parading the streets and knocking at doors to ask for
food, and seldom went away empty handed.'[33]

During the next two weeks rioting spread throughout Cheshire,
Lancashire and the Potteries, with disturbances in every industrial
town from Tyneside to Leicester. By 16 August Manchester was held
by three battalions, and the Royal Dragoons and heavily armed
artillery stood by. Faced by such force, the riots ceased. The distress,
however, did not. That winter hungry men still gathered on every
street corner.

By then Elizabeth had withdrawn into family life: on 7 October
1842 the Gaskells' third daughter, Florence Emily, was born. Few
letters survive from this time and we have no early decriptions of
Florence (who soon became Flora, then Flossy or Flossie). The first real
glimpse of her is at the age of three, 'not a bit shy', displaying her toys
to the Darbishire children and reluctant to leave, 'but she manfully
choked down her crys and came away like a very good dear little girl'.

As often as she could Elizabeth took her children out of Manchester,
and in July of 1843 they stayed for a month at Gibraltar Farm in
Silverdale, a village of farmers and fishermen on Morecambe Bay
which was to become a regular holiday home. Many Manchester
families stayed in the area, so it was far from a complete retreat: this
time the Winkworth family were there and William could not quite
escape his teaching, giving the girls a volume of Coleridge, Shelley and

Keats when he met them at church (the Gaskells always went to Anglican churches on holiday if there was no chapel near).

In 1850, describing their 'annual pilgrimage to the seaside' to Lady Kay-Shuttleworth, Elizabeth admitted that 'Silverdale can hardly be called the sea-side, as it is a little dale running down to Morecambe Bay, with grey limestone rocks on all sides which in the sun or moonlight, glisten like silver'. Silverdale, with its curious glacial boulders and wide sea views, brought out her love of strangeness and mystery as North Wales had done. The view to the west, with 'meadow green and mountain grey, and the blue dazzle of Morecambe Bay', appears at the opening of her story 'The Sexton's Hero', almost certainly written before 1845, and its crisis takes place on the treacherous sands between Lancaster and Ulverston, where the swift tides had claimed many lives.[34]

Like 'The Doom of the Griffiths', this story was probably based on a local tale (perhaps heard on her earlier stay at Grange in 1836). And once more its underlying theme is the pressure on men to abandon gentleness in favour of 'manly' self-assertion. Two friends are resting in the sun in the peaceful chuchyard above the bay, discussing the nature of a 'hero'; one defines heroism as acting according to the 'highest idea of duty' and, when pressed, accepts that this includes military heroes. The narrator challenges this: 'A poor, unchristian heroism, whose manifestation consists in injury to others!' Gaskell is reflecting on Carlyle's *On Heroes, Hero Worship and the Heroic in History*, published in 1841. Many Unitarians were staunch pacifists: where, Gaskell asks, is the scope for male courage, without war or fighting?

The village sexton, working nearby, answers this question. He is a Wordsworthian figure whom the friends have overlooked 'as though he was as inanimate as one of the moss-covered headstones', and the man he proposes as a hero is Gilbert Dawson, his rival in love forty years before. Gilbert had refused to fight for the flirtatious Letty, 'because,' he said, 'I think it is wrong to quarrel, and use violence'. In consequence he is shunned by the rough lads of the neighbourhood and laughed at as a 'Quaker', but the children, recognizing his true character, cluster round him like a swarm of bees. Letty and the Sexton marry and one evening, having taken their cart across the wide bay to collect a pig, they foolishly try to return in the same tide. As they pick their way between the holes and quicksands in the rising darkness, while the mist swirls around them like 'a ghastly curtain', they are caught by the rushing tide. In their terror a rescuer comes – Gilbert Dawson. His strong bay horse carries the couple to safety, but he himself is lost in the swirling waters. The Sexton knows the sacrifice involved: 'if he had ridden off with Letty, he would have been saved, not me'. 'Of a surety, sir,' he concludes, 'there's call enough for bravery in the service of God, and to show love to man, without quarrelling and fighting.'

In 'The Sexton's Hero' Gaskell achieves a new flexibility of style, presenting her narrative in a version of plain local speech, which does not attempt an accurate transcription of dialect but keeps the rhythms, and some of the diction, of the vernacular. This lets her establish the character and class of the speaker, and yet move when she needs to from earthiness to drama. She can use the prosaic, even the quasi-comic, to heighten the impact, as she does when the Sexton feels the last moment has come:

'We were longer than we should ha' been in crossing the hollow, the sand was so quick; and when we came up again, there, again the blackness, was the white line of the rushing tide coming up the bay! It looked not a mile from us, and when the wind blows up the bay it comes swifter than a galloping horse. "Lord help us!" said I; and then was sorry I'd spoken, to frighten Letty; but the words were crushed out of my heart by the terror. I felt her shiver up by my side, and clutch my coat. And as if the pig (as had screeched himself hoarse some time ago) had found the danger we were all in, he took to squealing again, enough to bewilder any man. I cursed him between my teeth for his noise; and yet it was God's answer to my prayer, blind sinner as I was.'[35]

Gilbert Dawson is 'the Sexton's hero', but there is another type of bravery hidden in this text, a different terror to be faced. Letty's greatest horror, as the waves rise around her, is that she will never see her baby again. She later has a son, named Gilbert after their rescuer, but we learn, almost in passing, that she was never the same after that night. Within two years both she and her daughter were dead: 'our girl was carried off in teething; and Letty just quietly drooped, and died in less than a six week. They were buried here; so I came to be near them and away from Lindal, a place I could never abide after Letty was gone.' The Sexton turns back to his work, digging a grave for a child. His lonely life has its own stoical heroism, the courage not of action but of endurance. This was the courage Elizabeth would have to learn, and cling to, among the surging currents of ideas, politics and private tragedy that swirled around her in her busy life.

[8]

Emerging from Shadows

In the late autumn of 1842 the Gaskells had moved house, just round the corner to 121 Upper Rumford Street, an 'interminably long street' running from the heart of the city to the straggling fields at its edges. The new house was slightly larger, with views over the fields, and here Elizabeth ran the household with the help of their servant, a country girl, Ann Hearn. Hearn, as she was always known, became a 'dear friend' and stayed with the family for over fifty years, caring for them long after Elizabeth died.

At Upper Rumford Street life was as crowded as ever, with family, work, Sunday school, parties, lectures and concerts. In the summer they took the girls to the seaside and from time to time Lily escaped to visit relations in Warrington, Knutsford and Liverpool. Charles and Lizzy Holland (far richer than the Gaskells) had also just moved, leaving Liverpool itself for a grand mansion in Liscard Vale, Wallasey, with sweeping lawns down to the Mersey. They already had five children, including twins, and their latest son, born in 1843, was called William Gaskell Holland.

The following year, on 23 October, the Gaskells too had a son, also named William after his father, an engaging, healthy, red-haired boy who gave Elizabeth intense joy. In the summer of 1845, dating her letter only 'Sunday morning. Willie asleep everyone else out', she wrote blithely to Lizzy, who was worn out by her lively little daughter Alice – labelled a typical Holland:

'My dearest Lizzie,
I have just received your letter & if one does not answer a letter directly when the impulse is on one there is no knowing how long one

150

may wait for a "convenient season". So here goes though I've nothing to say very particular except I want your mother to come & wonder I don't hear . . . *And* I am so sorry to hear about Alice feeling responsible as I ought to do; & she does sound proudly without order. She would *so* fidget here; all the Holland fidgetiness would blaze out in crossness. I am so busy & so happy. My laddie is grunting so I must make haste. I can't make out what you do with *five* ponies. Such a great number. You say "at present I can see after her" (i.e. Alice). Can't you nine months hence my lady? Are things in *that* state? Where do you get your pretty gowns from? tell me? You said they were all taken up by the Robsons? Was that a tally diddle? I wish I had been inside of home (articles & pronouns very useless parts of speech to mothers with large families aren't they?)' (L823)

Then she gave a vivid account of her own daily routine. Florence and the baby slept in her room, 'which is also nursery'. At six she called Hearn, who gave Florence breakfast, and then she herself got up at 7.30. After that there was no peace: '8 Flora goes down to her sisters & Daddy, & Hearn to her breakfast. While I in my dressing-gown dress Willie. ½ p. 8 I go to breakfast with parlour people, Florence being with us & Willie (ought to be) in his cot. Hearn makes beds etc in nursery only.' At nine came family prayers, first with the servants and next with the children. At half past (while the upstairs rooms were aired) the two little ones came down to the drawing-room. At 10.30 Elizabeth would 'go in kitchen, cellars & order dinner. Write letters; ¼ p. 11 put on things; ½ p. 11 take Florence out. 1 come in, nurse W. & get ready for dinner; ½ p. 1 dinner.'

The afternoon was quieter. Florence and William were brought down for half an hour while the servants had their lunch, then from three o'clock 'I have two hours to kick my heels in (to be elegant & explicit)'. Then, when Marianne and Meta came back from lessons,

'Papa when he can comes in drawing room to 'Lilly a hornpipe', i.e. dance while Mama plays, & make all the noise they can. Daddy reads, writes or does what he likes in dining room. ½ p. 5 Margaret (nursemaid) brings Florence's supper, which Marianne gives her, being answerable for slops, dirty pinafores & untidy misbehaviours while Meta goes upstairs to get ready & fold up Willie's basket of clothes while he is undressed (this by way of feminine & family duties).

Meta is so neat & so knowing, only, handles wet napkins very gingerly.' (L824)

(Marianne was now ten and Meta eight.)

After Florence and Willie were asleep, Elizabeth read to the two older girls while they learnt more feminine duties: sewing, knitting and worsted work. Then at last Lily collapsed: 'From 8 till 10 gape.' As she said to Lizzy, 'we are so desperately punctual that now you may know what we are doing every hour'.

Theirs was a conventional, lively Victorian family. In her two free hours Elizabeth read: poetry, essays, new novels like Harriet Martineau's *Deerbrook* and *The Hour and the Man* and foreign writers such as Androwitch, noting, 'is it not well translated? Using old fashioned plain spoken words in all simplicity.'

When she sent this packed timetable to Lizzy, Marianne and Meta were about to go and stay at Liscard Vale. Among Elizabeth's instructions (such as keeping Meta's feet warm in bed) comes the request, '*please*, (though not likely at all) don't let them come into contact with the Martineau children. You need not ask why but please *don't*.' It is unclear whether she feared for their moral or physical health – she may have felt that both were at risk. In 1844 James Martineau and his family had moved to a new house, Park Nook, in Princess Park, escaping the fumes of central Liverpool for 'the pleasant quiet, the pure air, the outlook on grass and foliage and flowers'.[1] In early 1845, despite the pure air, nine-year-old Herbert fell seriously ill with an undiagnosed fever. He died in his father's arms in March 1846.

Elizabeth may well have feared contagion: her early diary is full of alarms for her children's health. But however hard she tried, she could not protect them for ever. In late July 1845 she and William took Marianne and nine-month-old Willie, with their nurse, Fergusson, on holiday to Wales. They stayed at an inn in Ffestiniog, in the heart of Snowdonia. But, unknown to them, the mountain villages were as full of infection as the city and within days Marianne fell ill with scarlet fever. She soon recovered and ten days later they took her to convalesce at Portmadoc, but there, just as the danger seemed over, Willie suddenly showed alarming symptoms. The landlady, Mrs Hughes, helped all she could, but the disease was fatal to so small a baby. On 10 August Willie died.

After her son was buried in Cairo Street Cemetery, Warrington, Elizabeth collapsed. It was during these terrible months that William, searching desperately for something to distract her, encouraged her to write a novel. As she explained in the preface to the first edition of *Mary Barton* in 1848, 'Three years ago I became anxious (from circumstances that need not be more fully alluded to) to employ myself in writing a work of fiction.' She began a short story set on the Yorkshire borders in the early eighteenth century, but in the aftermath of Willie's death flight to another period and place would not suffice. She needed involvement with the real, present lives which pressed on her – almost physically – day by day. 'I bethought me,' she wrote, 'how deep might be the romance of those who elbowed me daily in the busy streets of the town where I resided.'[1]

Her words echo those to the Howitts describing 'Sketches among the Poor', but this time her sympathy with the people of Manchester, whose children so often died in epidemics, was intensely personal: before the story opens John Barton's son has died of scarlet fever, and several of the subsequent deaths are from fever, probably typhus. Maria Edgeworth was not alone in complaining of the many deathbed scenes in the novel.[2] They come thick and fast: the grim passing of Ben Davenport in the chapter 'Poverty and Death' is immediately followed by the deaths of Jem Wilson's small twin brothers. The second twin to die, gasping with effort, has to be taken from his mother's knee as she 'wishes' him to live. 'Ay; donno' ye know what "wishing" means?' says old Alice Wilson. 'There's none can die in the arms of those who are wishing them sore to stay on earth. The soul o' them as holds them won't let the dying soul go free; so it has a hard struggle for the quiet of death. We mun get him awa fra' his mother.' Such powerful wishing cut across all barriers of class: Elizabeth's infant son had not died in her arms, but in those of his nurse.[3]

Willie's death simultaneously filled her mind and was mercifully blotted out by her writing:

'The tale was formed, and the greater part of the first volume was written when I was obliged to lie down constantly on the sofa, and when I took refuge in the invention to exclude the memory of painful scenes which would force themselves on my remembrance . . . Perhaps after all it may be true that I, in my state of feelings at that time, was not fitted to introduce the glimpse of light and happiness which might have relieved the gloom.' (L74–5)

Within the novel she explains her belief in activity as therapy: 'Oh! I do think that the necessity for exertion, for some kind of action (bodily or mental) in time of distress, is a most infinite blessing, although the first efforts at such seasons are painful.' Action implies hope, and hope for others can drown personal sorrow, better than any well-meaning counsel of resignation. She writes in the first person when she makes this bitter comment:

'Of all trite, worn-out, hollow mockeries of comfort that were ever uttered by people who will not take the trouble of sympathising with others, the one I dislike the most is the exhortation not to grieve over an event, "for it cannot be helped!" Do you think if I could help it, I would sit still with folded hands, content to mourn?' (Ch. 22)

She tried to be patient and accept God's will, but her anger rose at glib consolations – 'mock me not, or any other mourner with the speech, "Do not grieve, for it cannot be helped. It is past remedy".'

  Writing helped her survive her misery and as her book approached publication she could look back over the blackness. In March 1847, writing to her cousin Fanny, she sent her love to her uncle Sam at Plas Penrhyn: 'I don't forget his coming to Ffestiniog, and noticing my lost darling so much that day. All those awful days are stamped in my heart, and I don't believe even Heaven itself can obliterate the memory of that agony.'[4] The following year she wrote emotionally to Annie Shaen:

'I have just been up to our room. There is a fire in it, and a smell of baking, and oddly enough the feelings and recollections of 3 years ago came over me so strongly – when I used to sit up in the room so often in the evenings reading by the fire, and watching my darling *darling* Willie, who now sleeps sounder still in the dull, dreary chapel-yard at Warrington. That wound will never heal on earth, although hardly anyone knows how it has changed me. I wish you had seen my little fellow, dearest dear Annie. I can give you no idea what a darling he was – so affectionate and *reasonable* a baby I never saw.' (L57)

At times she had wanted to die. At least such is the implication of her original dedication, which seems to look back to both her dead sons:

Take, good ferryman, I pray,
Take a triple fare today:
The twain who with me touched the strand
Were visitants from spirit-land.[5]

The same note is struck more lightly in a letter to Tottie, written in
1850, during the chaos of carpet-cleaning, cornice-choosing and
cabbage-planting when the Gaskells were about to leave Upper
Rumford Street for Plymouth Grove:

'Do come to us soon! I want to get associations about that house; *here*
there is the precious perfume lingering of my darling's short presence
in this life – I wish I were with him in that "light, where we shall all see
light", for I am often sorely puzzled here – but however I must not
waste my strength or my time about the never ending sorrow; but
which hallows this house. I think that is one evil of this bustling life
that one has never time calmly and bravely to face a great grief, and to
view it on every side as to bring the harmony out of it. – Well! I meant
to write a merry letter.' (LIII)

With that typical squaring of the shoulders she got on with her letter –
as she had with her life, and with her novel.

Once she had decided on her subject, Elizabeth immersed herself in her
novel. It was not only the prostration following Willie's death which
led to much of *Mary Barton* being written from her couch: by the
spring of 1846 she was pregnant again. Her fourth daughter, Julia
Bradford (named after her rich friend) was born on 3 September 1846.
And as the baby grew into 'a very big, healthy, merry, plain child', the
mother wrote faster than ever.[6]

While Elizabeth worked in private, exploring the problems of her
city in her imagination, William was becoming a well-known public
figure. After eighteen years at Cross Street the Revd Gaskell was
known throughout Manchester as minister, teacher and charity
worker. His eloquent sermons were much admired and he was often
asked to preach in the outlying towns and villages. When John Evans
published *Lancashire Authors and Orators* in 1850, he described
William as one of the best orators the Unitarians possessed in the
neighbourhood, a man who went 'far into the high-ways and by-ways'
and was known as a practical good Samaritan, as well as a brilliant
preacher. In the pulpit William had a powerful, theatrical presence. He

was tall and thin and by his early forties his dark hair had already turned iron grey, while his pale, angular face emphasized the effect of his eyes, 'which nearly approach a jet black in hue and are strikingly full and impressive'. Each of William's sermons was a performance, written at home behind the firmly shut study door and learnt by heart, impressing his hearers by forceful arguments, careful use of analogies and the 'strong confident tone with which he gave vent to his opinions'.[7]

He was equally impressive, but far more relaxed, as a teacher. When John Kenrick became principal of Manchester New College in 1846, William took his place as professor of history, literature and logic, a post he held until the college moved to London in 1853. He also taught at the Mechanics Institute in Copper Street, a few streets away from Cross Street, and he was now campaigning hard for greater education for the working classes, founding the Lancashire Public Schools Association with his fellow-ministers J. R. Beard and J. J. Tayler in 1847. He brought his New College students home, and they had fond memories of walks in the country and evenings with Elizabeth. At Upper Rumford Street they might be joined by William's older pupils from the Mechanics Institute, who included amateur scientists in addition to lovers of literature: when William gave a course with J. J. Tayler in the winter of 1847, his lectures included not only 'Poets and Poetry of Humble Life', and 'Books' and 'Reading', but also 'Animal-culae' and 'Insect Life'.

William was fiercely committed to his work. Indeed all the Unitarian ministers of Manchester, and many of the laymen who worked with them, seem to have been driven men: passionate polemicists like James Martineau, unworldly idealists like Francis Newman, tormented, energetic enthusiasts like Travers Madge or the elderly prison visitor Thomas Wright. These last two men were frequent visitors at Upper Rumford Street in the late 1840s. Travers Madge was a strange, intense young man in his mid-twenties, the son of a Unitarian minister, a former student at Manchester New College and a great friend of William Shaen. He was a tireless worker, who tramped the countryside to preach but rejected the idea of a paid ministry, and was drawn to the more fervent sects on the fringes of Unitarianism. In 1848 he began working with the Mosley Street Sunday schools and roused Elizabeth into far greater involvement than before.[8]

Thomas Wright, a very different personality, also spurred her into action. He was a foundry-worker who had taken up the cause of prisoners after a religious revelation turned him from a dissipated youth. Nearly all his leisure time (despite two marriages and nineteen children) was devoted to this voluntary work and Elizabeth paid tribute to him in *Mary Barton* as the 'overseer of a foundry, an aged man, with hoary hair' who spends his Sundays 'in visiting the prisoners and the afflicted at Manchester New Bailey' and finding them employment after their release. Later she suspected Wright's stories were exaggerated, but until the late 1850s she was his firm supporter and, on his prompting, began to visit the New Bailey herself.[9]

People like Madge and Wright helped to pull Elizabeth out of her depression. William's work involved her, her daughters needed her, friends called, visits must be paid. Gradually, during 1846, she returned to her sociable, lively self. For her daughters' sake, in particular, she shrugged off the cloud of grief. She took her parental responsibilities no less seriously than she had when Marianne and Meta were babies, and the intensity of the mother-image in her writings of these years may be partly linked to her anxious sense of the 'ideal', unselfish, loving mother and the sheer difficulty of living out such an ideal in practice.

Her worries about the girls' upbringing came to a head in March of 1847. As Marianne and Meta grew older she felt that Fergusson (who had advanced from nanny to governess) was no longer able to manage them properly, and after much heart-searching decided to dismiss her. As she told Fanny Holland, while she could see the bad effects of Fergusson's regime, she could hardly bear to think of her 'dear household friend' not being there any more, 'and sometimes I can not keep down the feeling which I yet know to be morbid, that it is ungrateful to even part with one who was *so tender* to my poor darling boy, and that makes me most miserable. However I do try to look steadfastly to the *right* for my children.'[10] Any break with the past was a sore wrench, but she was comforted by the fact that 'Miss F. understood and agreed'.

She and William briskly organized a new routine for the girls, although she wanted to leave some ideas to develop naturally: 'I want them very much to act from inner sense, rather than from outward force of either scolding or reminding.' They called in outside teachers: Mme Frielot for French twice a week and Miss Hooley, a Knutsford acquaintance, for writing and arithmetic on Friday evenings. William taught his girls history and natural history, while their friend Rosa Mitchell (with whom old William Turner now lodged) took Meta for music and, 'for the present', Emily Winkworth taught Marianne the piano. They also went to dancing classes, and studied drawing at the School of Design. Elizabeth had a role, though she played down its importance:

'My part will be reduced to general superintendence & help-giving in the preparation of their lessons; we shall work together, & read some book aloud at nights. I shall give them dictation & grammar lessons; walk out with them (to be regular in *this* will be one great difficulty,) and make myself as much as possible their companion and friend.'[11]

One wonders how those grammar lessons went, given William's strictures about her own *'slip-shod'* style: as late as 1860 William was teasingly complaining that Marianne's spelling was a touch too phonetic.[12] In 1857 Elizabeth was still lamenting that it was hard for her to write a 'proper' letter, 'with Dear Sir in the right place, & verbs agreeing with their nominatives, & (agreeing with [crossed out]) governing their accusatives; and it is letters of that kind I dread receiving, because of the knowledge of grammar, & good pens required to answer them'. Her narrator in 'Morton Hall' writes a history of the Morton family but says: 'for fear of mistakes, I showed it to Mr Swinton, our young curate, who has put it quite in order for me'. She seemed to see the rules of syntax as the province of men, a kind of straitjacket on the spontaneity of women. When the girls were small, she did try some gentle chivvying in her letters, but confined herself to presentation rather than grammar: 'It is ungrateful to *'look a gift horse in the mouth'* (Aunt Lizzy will tell you what this means) but my Dear Miss Meta do you know your epistle was *rather* of the untidiest. You *can* write nicely & tidily, & do try love, to do so *habitually.*' But she soon slipped back more comfortably into 'companion and friend'.

Elizabeth refused to talk down to her daughters and treated them as individuals, whose opinions should be heard. One letter from around the time of Julia's birth deals with an issue common with new babies – finding the right name. 'My dearest girls,' she writes reassuringly, 'I think we shall subscribe the shilling necessary (I believe,) to have the name of Laetitia altered. I don't think we should any of us like it, and I cannot think what made Papa think of it.' She also sent news of three-year-old Flossy, who was being terribly spoilt while her sisters were away, loaded with presents by Marianne Marsland ('Noah's ark; a box of pewter tea-things, an apple &c &c') and playing with the Dukinfield Darbishire children, who made her paper boxes and boats. 'The next day *we* had Louy, Emily, Agnes, Francis and Charlie (only 2 years old;) they came at three o'clock, and Florence displayed all her playthings, and we did very well, and they were very unwilling to go at ½ past 6.'

Flossy had her father's full attention too. He made her two kites: 'the first went up into some trees where it stuck but the last is still to be seen & flown when the wind bears. She & Papa are very happy together flying it sometimes.' William loved his daughters, but could be wry about the chaos of family life: when James and William Turner's dogs yelped at being driven off in a cart, 'Daddy said it was a noisy enough turn out even for you Meta'. All Elizabeth's enjoyment of life emerges in these affectionate, gossipy letters to Marianne and Meta. She wrote to amuse, and knew what would interest them, like the time when Florence visited Miss Marsland and 'had a funny dinner, 1 fowl, 1 Partridge 7 snipes and 4 plovers', or the bat which young Robert Darbishire had found in a turf stack and fed with a candle-lighter, and which 'has a sort of hand-claw at the end of its wings, by which it hangs itself up very tidily'. One of the nicest, written from Southport in 1848, where she was staying with the Winkworth sisters, shows that even at the seaside Elizabeth could not escape the enthusiastic inventors of Lancashire:

'I met such a droll man in the omnibus. He gave me a receipt for making "sun pictures" as he called them.

> Take of bi-chloride of potash
>   An ounce to a gill,
> Mix them as you like to stand as
>   long as you will,
> Expose them to the light where
>   the sun doth forth shine,
> And you may have a picture
>   before that you dine.

He meant it for poetry but it's not very like it I think. However he was a very kind old man and spoke nicely to everyone. I often wish for you here to run up and down these steep stairs for me; they are very tiring.' (L59)

Sometimes the combination of family, social life and writing involved hectic juggling, as it did when she took Florence to stay with the Samuel Gregs at Bollington, near Macclesfield, in 1847. She had known the Greg family from her youth, when her uncle Peter had been the doctor to the apprentices at Styal Mill. Samuel's wife was also a friend from Knutsford days, when, as Mary Needham, she sang duets with her sister at Tabley Old Hall. But Elizabeth felt slightly guilty about this particular visit as she had left William ill at home. Since he objected to her fussing, she enrolled Marianne and Meta as spies: 'tell me exactly how Papa is. I begged him yesterday to promise to write and tell me how he was this morning, but he would not; so you must be my correspondents and tell me every particular.'

After this stab of wifely concern she described their arrival, saying that when they got to Macclesfield, they took a 'fly' from the station, 'a word which puzzled Florence extremely; and which she talked about, for an hour I think'. Just as tea was announced, and Elizabeth was preparing to be a gracious guest, one of Flossy's shoe buttons came off, and she suddenly had to revert to being mother:

'I had desired Hearn particularly to see after them, and in the hurry, and desire to be punctual on first arriving it was very provoking. I wanted Florence to be content to wear her slippers at tea, but I found she did not like the idea so I rang for some black thread, & at last we made our appearance downstairs.' (L53)

'I found she did not like the idea' was putting it mildly. The battle continued. Flossy would not let the nurses put her to bed, 'so I did, and she would sleep in the cot prepared for Baby. However I took her into bed when I went.' Then at last she could escape into being a writer: 'I worked till bed-time; and sometimes Mr Greg was in the room, and sometimes he went into another.' Her daughters and friends were clearly used to seeing her write, if unaware, as yet, of what her work was leading to.

After Willie's death old friends like the Gregs helped to ease Elizabeth back into the social round. The Gaskells' Manchester acquaintance was rich and varied and cosmopolitan, ranging from the Potters and Gregs to Americans like John Bradford and Jewish merchants from Germany like Adolf and Salis Schwabe (both converts to Protestant Unitarianism). The Schwabes were as much at home in Paris or Berlin as in Manchester or London. After several years in Glasgow Salis Schwabe had come to Manchester in 1832, like the Gaskells, and was now among the city's biggest employers (and also the proud owner of its tallest chimney, famed throughout the industrial north – 321 feet high, costing £5,000). He and his wife, Grace, one of Elizabeth's closest friends in years to come, lived at Crumpsall House, a fine Georgian building with extensive grounds and an ornamental lake, and were great philanthropists and patrons of the arts, especially music. Neukomm, Haydn's best pupil, lived with them in the mid-1840s and Chopin and Jenny Lind (a personal friend) stayed at Crumpsall when they gave charity concerts for the infirmary in 1848.[13]

And Manchester had Italian, Greek and Turkish as well as German communities. The Gaskells, for example, knew the journalist Antonio Gallenga and his family and the Greek Dilberbogues with their beautiful daughter, Calliope. In 'Modern Greek Songs', in 1854, Elizabeth described a Greek Easter Day feast, with a table in one corner of the very English drawing-room, 'covered with mellow-looking sweetmeats, as if all the glow of sunset rested on their amber and crimson colours and there were decanters containing mysterious liquids to match'.[14]

Of all their many friends, the Dukinfield Darbishires were especially kind. Everything the 'D.D.s' did was on a large scale, including their family, which now ranged from adolescents down to two-year-old Charlie. Anne Darbishire had much of Elizabeth's zest and refused to let her personality be swamped: in the 1850s Edward Herford remembered how people had laughed at her 'with her fifteen children, or so, setting to work upon German'.[15] Elizabeth rejoiced in her stylish exaggeration. In the sweltering summer of 1846 she arrived at Upper Rumford Street with early grapes from her hothouse, carefully arranged in a beautiful basket under flowers and cool green vine-leaves, and made Elizabeth laugh, as she told the girls, 'by telling me what she had had to bring from London. 10 children, six servants, three horses, *one cow* & 27 hundred weight of luggage'. She was always planning parties and dances, even when the house was being decorated and the drawing-rooms were stripped of furniture; Elizabeth supposed they were 'to sit in the white-washers' pails and on steps of ladders, which will be original'.

Older women like Grace Schwabe and Anne Darbishire were valued friends, but from 1846 to 1848 Elizabeth's circle widened to include younger women like the Winkworth sisters. She grew particularly close to Emily and Susanna, now in their mid-twenties, and to Catherine, who was nearly nineteen in 1846. Catherine adored William, once she got over her fear of his high standards. She felt that her own mind was stimulated by his 'rich and varied culture, rare critical power, and exquisite refinement of taste'.[16] All the Winkworths regretted that his duties left him so little time for original work of his own, especially in history and criticism.

To begin with the girls were slightly in awe of Elizabeth. Many years afterwards Susanna described her as she was in the 1840s, before she became famous. Perhaps with the benefit of hindsight, she said that she and her sisters were struck with Mrs Gaskell's 'genius', and 'used to say to each other that we were sure she could write books, or do anything else in the world that she liked'. Susanna thought her 'noble-looking, with a queenly presence', but added that 'her high, broad, serene brow, and finely-cut mobile features, were lighted up by a constantly varying play of expression as she poured forth her wonderful talk'. In company (if not in her letters) Elizabeth was free of 'restlessness and eagerness . . . There was no hurry or high-pressure about her'. Instead she had an air of 'ease, leisure and playful geniality'.

'When you were with her, you felt as if you had twice the life in you that you had at ordinary times. All her great intellectual gifts, – her quick keen observation, her marvellous memory, her wealth of imaginative power, her rare felicity of instinct, her graceful and racy humour, – were so warmed and brightened by sympathy and feeling, that while actually with her, you were less conscious of her power than of her charm. No one ever came near her in the gift of telling a story. In her hands the simplest incident, – a meeting in the street, a talk with a factory-girl, a country walk, an old family history, – became picturesque and vivid and interesting.'[17]

When they read her novels, the sisters felt that her work was 'a mere fraction of what she might have written, had her life been a less many-sided one'.

The Winkworths were Anglicans, but Susanna became a Unitarian, teaching at the Lower Mosley Street Sunday schools and working as a visitor for the Ancoats District Provident Association. Her description of one Chartist family she visited on her rounds in 1846 shows that the governing belief of *Mary Barton* – dialogue and sympathy as the route to removing class tension – was common in Gaskell's circle. Susanna found her Chartists 'nice people', but so prejudiced against the upper classes in general that she almost 'despaired of getting them to listen to reason':

'However quite to my surprise last Tuesday, the man began to praise me and said that if all the middle classes took as great an interest in the working classes as I did, they could soon come to an understanding with each other and get their grievances redressed.'[18]

(A few years later she lent this couple *Mary Barton*. They were delighted with it, cried over it and considered Jem Wilson – who had the same first name as their own son – to be the undoubted hero of the book.)[19]

Susanna worked with Elizabeth, but it was the young Catherine who became especially devoted. Catherine had been severely shaken by her mother's death and then by her father's remarriage in 1845, and had gone to live for some months in Dresden, where the new ideas she encountered caused a crisis of faith. She was now, as Susanna put it, 'in the Sturm und Drang' period of her life: highly impressionable, a prodigious reader, whose frequent collapses of health were blamed by her father on too much studying (a familiar Victorian tale), although her sister stoutly averred that, on the contrary, the trouble was too much physical exercise. From 1846 onwards she and Susanna were urgently trying to plan independent lives. Their cast of mind was intellectual, their German was excellent and they were passionately interested in current theological and philosophical debates. But they felt life was so much more difficult for an intellectual woman than for a man: 'He has so many paths to turn to. She often has difficulty finding *one* on which she can work without doing more harm than good.' Elizabeth listened sympathetically – 'She and her friends seem to have just such notions about these matters as we have,' wrote Susanna – and actively set about using her connections within the Manchester German community to find them work as translators.[20]

Elizabeth's friendship was not entirely unselfish. When the Gaskells spent a month at Silverdale in June 1847, she was keen for Susanna, Emily and their younger sister, Alice, to stay nearby, since 'she knows they are very good walkers, and they must take long expeditions with Mr G., which she is not strong enough to do'.[21] Meanwhile, she suggested, the youngest sister, Alice, could play with her children. (And would she herself be left alone to write?) A year or two later Susanna was busy running errands and writing letters: 'Lily as usual brought me various commissions.' Using younger women as secretaries (as she later used her own daughters) was a useful strategy for cramming so much into so little time.

If Elizabeth's interest was partly maternal – she was a good fifteen years their senior – she also gathered these young women into her orbit because of her longing for confidantes. In November 1848 she told Catherine:

'Do call me Lily, and never mind respect to your elders. *Ils sont passés ces beaux jours là*, when old people were looked upon as people who could do no wrong; and were to have all outward and inward respect paid to them; so let me for one of the body, have affection instead of respect. I wish I had five sisters, who were bound to love me by their parents' marriage certificate; but as I have not, I mean to take you for sisters and daughters at once.' (L62)

She had always sought these elusive sisters, in Harriet Carr, in Lizzy and Nancy, in her Holland cousins, and her translation of friendships into family relationships – sisters, daughters – may have been some recompense for her adoptive childhood. But it was also a way of making closeness 'safe'. She sensed the deep emotions in men, but even in her father and her husband she saw how they bottled up their feelings, holding them down by rules (like their letters, 'with Dear Sir in the right place'). She could only talk and write freely to other women. With them she could laugh and cry, gossip and worry, share longings and ambitions as well as problems. And women together could be sensual, touching and embracing in a way which, given the contemporary social codes, was impossible between the sexes without misinterpretation.

Elizabeth's friendships were typical of her century. Two generations later, when the feminist composer Ethel Smyth was wondering why women were generally so much more excited about friends of their own sex, her friend Harry Brewster suggested that 'probably there are several reasons; among others this one, that these affections entail no duties, no sacrifice of liberty or of tastes, no partial loss of individuality; whereas friendships of equal warmth with men have that danger (and others) in the background.'[22]

In her fiction Gaskell gives full due to female rivalry, jealousy, cruelty and pettiness, but the closeness of women is still one of her great subjects, from 'Libbie Marsh' and *Cranford* to stories like 'The Poor Clare', where the heroine takes refuge in a literal 'sisterhood', or 'The Grey Woman', where Anna Scherer and her servant, aptly called Amante, live together disguised as a man and wife. Scenes between women call forth stronger language and more direct physical expression than those between lovers or married couples: 'hearts full of love' and 'fast embraces'.[23] The context, however, is often the safe maternal one of giving comfort in distress, as it is in a late scene (written in the last weeks of Elizabeth's life) between Molly Gibson and Cynthia Kirkpatrick in *Wives and Daughters*. Here Cynthia is wretched, determined to extricate herself from a misguided engagement to Roger Hamley, the man whom Molly loves. Mr Gibson leaves the room:

' "Go to Cynthia!" he whispered, and Molly went. She took Cynthia into her arms with gentle power, and laid her head against her own breast, as if the one had been a mother, and the other a child.

"Oh, my darling!" she murmured. "I do so love you, dear, dear Cynthia!" and she stroked her hair, and kissed her eyelids; Cynthia passive all the while, till suddenly she started up, stung with a new idea, and looking Molly straight in the face, she said –

"Molly, Roger will marry you! See if it isn't so! You two good" –

But Molly pushed her away, with a sudden violence of repulsion. "Don't!" she said. She was crimson with shame and indignation. "Your husband this morning! Mine tonight! What do you take him for?"

"A man!" smiled Cynthia. 'And therefore, if you won't let me call him changeable, I'll coin a word and call him consolable!' (Ch. 51)

The physical and emotional harmony between the stepsisters (an image of sisterhood without a blood relationship) is violently disturbed by the mention of Roger – the lover, the potential husband. A swarm of negative feelings arise: 'repulsion, 'shame', 'indignation'.

The sense of intrusion is due to Molly's unacknowledged love for Roger, but suggests how threatening and unstable male love seems in contrast to the female bond.[24]

Elizabeth needed women to comfort her in moments of misery, as Molly comforts Cynthia, and to share the minutiae of life that she poured into her letters. But she also urgently wanted a different kind of closeness, a woman friend who understood her urge to write. This was the kind of sister she sought in Mary Howitt or Eliza Fox, and in Charlotte Brontë, someone who shared her pleasure in poetry and novels and could help her sort out her ideas. 'Read "Jane Eyre",' she told one young friend, Annie Shaen, in 1849, 'it is an uncommon book. I don't know if I like it or dislike it. I take the opposite side to the person I am talking with always in order to hear some convincing arguments to clear up my opinions.' The Winkworths could not really meet this need: apart from the more domestic, tender-hearted Emily, they were too intellectual, too morally earnest. They did not really like the women's novels she gave them, like Anne Marsh's *Emilia Wyndham*, one of the most popular books of 1846, 'wherewith we are not altogether captivated (as Mrs Gaskell had told us we should be)'. Susanna detested *Wuthering Heights*, finding it too disagreeable to finish, its characters were so intolerably wicked and unhappy. She and Catherine liked Charlotte Brontë's novels no better than Emily's and could not understand Elizabeth's enthusiasm.[25]

Despite these differences the motherless Winkworth sisters touched her, and as single women seeking fulfilling work they roused her latent feminism. So did Annie Shaen, who came to stay with the Gaskells in November 1847. The Shaens were a wealthy Unitarian family from Essex; Samuel Shaen was a lawyer, one of the first Unitarians to be made a magistrate after the repeal of the Test and Corporation Acts in 1828, and his wife was a witty, educated woman, prone to sprinkling her conversation with French and Italian phrases. In 1847 their son William (who would marry Emily Winkworth) was a young lawyer of twenty-six, a friend of Mazzini and a keen anti-slavery campaigner, and later, as an MP, he became a leading supporter of female suffrage and women's education. From an early age his sisters – Annie, Louey and Emma – were equally vehement about political and social rights.

When Elizabeth first visited their home at Crix, near Colchester, in December 1847, she spent the morning with the Shaen girls, 'with books in our hands, but not reading much, only talking'. Six months later Emily Winkworth reported the kind of conversation Elizabeth might have had. In a 'good long talk' of two or three hours Emily had argued with Emma Shaen over the equality of man ('she is a great Republican'), human rights, government, capital punishment and the nature of the human will. Emma's views, thought Emily, came entangled with all the submissive conditioning of a gentlewoman's schooling:

'She is a decided Chartist and "Rights of Woman" personage, but has her aristocratic education to thank for a very strong dislike to all improprieties and oddnesses. She quite recognises the wickedness of making self-development the object of life – to my surprise, for she joins in so many things with the party who do this; yet even goes further in condemning it than I should dare to do – for she has the impudence to "hate and despite Goethe" for it!'[26]

The contradictions resembled those which Elizabeth had inherited from her upbringing and her Avonbank education, and which she would try to unravel in her letters to Tottie Fox. Yet it took a long time for her to take these much younger and more intellectual women fully into her confidence about writing. Normally open and frank, she kept her work very much to herself during these first years, like a treasure which might crumble into dust if exposed to the air.

Until 1849 she had little direct contact with women authors apart from Mary Howitt. There were writers, however, among her Manchester acquaintances – in particular Geraldine Jewsbury, only two years younger, who kept house for her brother nearby in Carlton Terrace, Greenheys. Geraldine's older sister Maria Jane, who had died in 1833, had also been a writer, a Manchester celebrity who rose to be leading writer for the *Athenaeum* and was a close friend of Wordsworth's daughter Dora and of the poet Felicia Hemans. Geraldine loved to mix with the colourful foreign settlers in the city – Germans, Italians, Greeks – and in the 1840s her house was a centre for local journalists, theatre folk and American visitors like Ralph Waldo Emerson, or the actress Charlotte Cushman. Since 1842 she had been wrapped up in a passionate friendship, amounting to hero-worship on her side, with Thomas Carlyle's wife, Jane. Their joint voices are a useful counter to Elizabeth's letters, as they were suspicious of Unitarian ideals of self-control and tolerance. Geraldine, for example, felt it was better to express her anger than to 'suppress it and allow it to work in the system, from no matter what "Unitarian" motive, universal benevolence and "welfare of others" principle . . . better to scold, scold, scold!'²⁷

Geraldine had achieved fame (and notoriety) in 1845 with her sensational first novel, *Zöe*, which brought together two controversial subjects – religious doubt, in its hero, Everhard, and female passion in Zöe herself. Yet although she seemed daring and confident, her severe reaction to her Calvinist upbringing had almost led to a nervous breakdown, and, like the Winkworth and Shaen sisters, she felt anger and frustration at the current plight of intellectual women. She wrote movingly to Jane Welsh Carlyle:

'I do not feel that either you or I are to be counted failures. We are indications of a development of womanhood which as yet is not recognised. It has, so far, no ready-made channels to run in, but still we have looked, and tried, and found that the present rules for women will not hold us – that something better and stronger is needed'.²⁸

There could have been fellow-feeling between Elizabeth and her neighbour, but Geraldine was almost shockingly outspoken and flamboyant. Ella Hepworth Dixon, the daughter of the *Athenaeum* editor, vividly remembered her mass of red-brown hair, her spectacles and endless supply of cigaritos, her clothes made by a modish dressmaker and her earrings like miniature parrots which swayed as she talked.²⁹ She was rather condescending to the more conventional Gaskells and once, as she lay on the floor at Upper Rumford Street reading Lamb's *Essays of Elia*, she told them their drawing-room was so ugly that they could never be happy there. Although they moved in overlapping circles, the two writers were not friends: in unusually stilted letters Elizabeth addressed her as Miss Jewsbury, and in November 1848 she complained: 'the Darbishires come tonight with "Zoe", Dr Hodgson, Mr Green (shan't we be intellectual, that's all?) and a few others. I wish myself well thro' it.' By then her own novel was published and was the subject of furious debate, but she was clinging hard to anonymity. She did not want to declare herself 'an author' and to be classed with independent single women like Geraldine, whom, anyway, she did not much like.

Part of Elizabeth's unease was due to her difficulty in diagnosing her own restlessness. Unlike Geraldine, she *did* partly identify with a notion of womanhood that had 'ready-made channels'. She was happy to be a wife and mother. Even so, she wanted something more, something which she hardly admitted to herself. Although her writing was a secret joy and a refuge from grief, she could not let herself see it as 'self-development'; in *Mary Barton* and her other early stories she was 'using her pen to the public good' as William Howitt had advised. But pride, and a desire that her own voice be heard, were beginning to play a part, none the less.

[9]

Into Print

By the end of 1847 Elizabeth Gaskell was already, in a small, anonymous way, a published writer. That year she found her way into print (as she had seven years before with 'Clopton Hall') through her friendship with Mary and William Howitt. She had kept in touch with them after they returned from Germany in 1843 and watched their reputations grow: Mary was now known for translations of Fredrika Bremer and Hans Christian Andersen and for her poetry, while William was busily touring England for his *Homes and Haunts of English Poets*.

The Howitts' circle was far more radical and unconventional than that of the Gaskells. Their house, the Elms, in Clapton, was a focus for every new cause from Swedenborgism and mesmerism to the rights of women, the abolition of slavery and revolutionary socialism. Visitors from overseas included Freiligrath, the associate of Marx, the American abolitionist Lloyd Garrison and the freed slave Frederick Douglass, and the imposingly intellectual Boston Transcendentalist and feminist Margaret Fuller. Local friends included Southwood Smith, Tennyson, Leigh Hunt, Dickens and some of the more conspicuously radical Unitarians and their associates. Prominent among these was W. J. Fox, Tottie's father. Fox had been the Unitarian minister of South Place Chapel for twenty-eight years, until a row over his relationship with his ward, the talented musician Eliza Flower (a friend of J. S. Mill's future wife, Harriet Taylor, and the object of Robert Browning's young romantic dreams); when he resigned, his congregation seceded with him. A popular leader in the 1832 reform movement, Fox edited the *Monthly Repository* until 1836 and in the 1840s had put his considerable powers of oratory behind the Corn Law cause. In 1847 he had just been elected MP for Oldham.

Another of the Howitts' close friends was Fox's successor at the *Monthly Repository*, Richard Henry Horne, whose adventurous past included a spell in the Mexican navy during their wars of independence. Horne was a poet and dramatist as well as a journalist: Elizabeth Barrett Browning collaborated with him on the essay on Tennyson in *New Spirit of the Age* in 1844. Even more flamboyant was the young publisher and bookseller John Chapman, currently living in an uneasy *ménage à trois* with his wife and mistress. He was soon to be a key figure in the personal and professional life of Mary Ann Evans (now calling herself Marian), whom he installed as the brilliant (unpaid and unacknowledged) editor of the *Westminster Review* in 1851.

With devoted admirers, and furious detractors, the Howitts were the centre of a constant flurry of activity. Mary's friends included women like the art historian and feminist Anna Jameson, and Elizabeth Barrett Browning admired her poems, although Robert Browning, an early supporter, grew to distrust the Howitts after hearing stories about William scribbling surreptitious notes on Wordsworth's conversation. When William asked Elizabeth to write for the *People's Journal*, Robert dissuaded her vehemently: 'Come out from them my soul, neither be a partaker of their habitations.'[1]

William Howitt had begun to write for John Saunders's *People's Journal* in 1846, and soon he became its principal owner. Having long wanted to publish a journal of his own, he then withdrew from the agreement, but immediately found himself entangled in financial arguments and lawsuits. His new *Howitt's Journal* was doomed before it started, and ran for only eighteen months, but in those months it published three stories by Elizabeth Gaskell. 'Libbie Marsh's Three Eras' appeared in three parts in June 1847, 'The Sexton's Hero' in September and 'Christmas Storms and Sunshine' on New Year's Day 1848.[2]

The context of Elizabeth's first published fiction is worth remarking. *Howitt's Journal* contained every kind of radicalism, its varied ingredients boiled down into a rather bland soup with a dominant flavour of romantic, high-minded reformism, salted by Samuel Smiles's self-help. It set out to entertain, but nothing could disguise its didactic taste. 'Working,' said Mary Howitt in her *Autobiography*, 'with gifted and popular writers, we sought, in an attractive form, to urge the labouring classes, by means of temperance, self-education and moral conduct, to be their own benefactors.'[3] Even the opening manifesto managed somehow to turn rights into duties, and socialism into petty capitalism:

'We shall say to the people, inform your minds on your rights; combine to maintain them; be industrious and get money; be prudent and invest it to the best advantage; but learn at the same time to respect the rights of your fellow men.'[4]

Howitt's Journal claimed to be 'bound to no class' and the list of its causes (to which it wished 'a great and glorious time!') included peace, temperance, sanitary reform, public education, free trade, free opinion and civil liberties – including the rights of women. The editors might have done better to heed the warning of the Corn Law poet, Ebenezer Elliott, that 'men engaged in a death-bed struggle for bread will pay for amusement when they will not for instruction. If you were able and willing to fill the journal with fun, it would pay.'[5] It was not filled with fun, and it did not pay. Elizabeth's stories were among the liveliest contributions, appearing in the closely printed double columns next to Mary Howitt's long ballads, the worthy stories of Edward Youl, the feminist fables of Eliza Meteyard ('Silverpen') and the 'Weekly Report' of co-operative meetings and sanitary legislation.

Elizabeth wrote under the name Cotton Mather Mills, a complex cover which reminds one of William Gaskell's love of puns and linguistic subtleties. Cotton Mather was an American Puritan minister of the late seventeenth and early eighteenth centuries, who was known for his part in the Salem witchcraft trials, a subject of great interest to Unitarians fighting obscurantism in the 1840s. In the annals of Unitarianism he was also renowned for a famous sermon, warning that ministers were neglecting to preach the word of Christ.[6] The name is male, yet the style and the concentration on domestic life must have seemed transparently female. It suggests the setting – cotton mills – yet the central 'Mather', with its unconscious echo of 'mother', points to the buried central image of all three stories.

The pseudonym hints at the way Gaskell kept subjects in her mind; Salem would be the focus of 'Lois the Witch', not published until 1859. The three *Howitt's* stories may themselves have been held by for some time. 'The Sexton's Hero', with its Silverdale connection, stands apart from the other two, which are both set in Manchester – but a Manchester of the 'decent poor' and the respectable lower-middle classes, free of the starvation and unemployment of the 1840s. 'Christmas Storms and Sunshine', in particular, is set 'a dozen years earlier', in the mid-1830s, and recalls Elizabeth's panic when Marianne had croup at the age of eighteen months, like the baby in the story. In 1849, when Mary Howitt wrote asking if Elizabeth could give her a quick piece for *Sartain's Union Magazine*, she said:

'perhaps you can send me the article – for I presume it is already written and is one of the many manuscripts which lie in a certain desk drawer, & may have lain there for years.'[7]

Had the *Howitt's Journal* stories come from this hidden store?

The ease and confidence of Gaskell's writing are striking from the start. In 'Libbie Marsh's Three Eras' each episode is linked to a holiday – St Valentine's Day, Whitsuntide and Michaelmas. The simple story tells how a young seamstress gives a canary to a crippled boy as a Valentine present, and so wins the friendship of his embittered mother. At Whitsun they take him on an outing to Dunham Woods. At Michaelmas he dies, and after his funeral the two women agree to share a house together. It opens as naturally and colloquially as if Gaskell were writing to a friend: 'Last week there was a flitting in the neighbourhood: hardly a flitting at all for it was only a single person changing her place of abode.' Only the last phrase has a ring of formal writing. In a single paragraph, as Gaskell describes Libbie walking listlessly through the streets with her one wooden box, she evokes her rootlessness, her isolation, her anonymity and total unimportance to the world at large. Soon she fills in her past: mother, father and brother dead, friends moved away, days spent ignored by kindly bustling employers 'except when they wanted gowns turned, carpets mended, or household linen darned'. Bleakest of all, Libbie has no lover, and does not expect one, for she is very plain. Gaskell was already writing the fiction of 'ordinary, unheroic lives' that George Eliot would aim at ten years later in *Scenes of Clerical Life*.

Settings are as deftly sketched as character, from the houses of skilled spinners like the Dixons, with whom Libbie lodges, who can afford ham and cream and other little luxuries, to the barber's back room lined with birds in wicker cages: 'for many of the weavers know and care more about birds than anyone would easily credit'. The Dixons live in a narrow Manchester 'court', built in parallel round a square, where each side 'looked at its exact likeness opposite, as if it were seeing itself in a looking-glass'. The court is not, however as it was for Engels, a site of oppression and misery. It is more like the alleys and courts in *Bleak House*, with their feasts and funerals, leaders and scapegoats, friendships and feuds, a small world of its own, where boys play marbles and get underfoot and women at home care for the children of those who work. The style of life is caught in an early morning scene before the Whitsun outing when men in shirtsleeves shout to each other through the open windows. Dunham Park is too old-fashioned, claims one, Alderley's the place to go now.

' "Ay, that's because there's only thee and thy missis. Wait till thou hast gotten four childer, like me, and thou'lt be glad enough to take 'em to Dunham, oud-fashioned way, for fourpence a-piece."

"I'd still go to Alderley; I'd not be bothered with my children; they should keep house at home."

A pair of hands, the person to whom they belonged invisible, boxed his ears on this last speech, in a very spirited though playful manner, and the neighbours all laughed at the surprised look of the speaker, at this assault from an unseen foe. The man who had been holding conversation with him cried out –

"Sarved him right, Mrs Slater; he knows nought about it yet: but when he gets them he'll be as loth to leave the babbies at home on a Whitsuntide, as any on us. We shall live to see him in Dunham Park yet, wi' twins in his arms, and another pair on 'em clinging at daddy's coat tails, let alone your share of youngsters, missis." ' (Ch. 2)

Here are the economic realities of the workers' lives, but also their energy and closeness, emphasizing, by contrast, Libbie's own lack of family or prospect of children.

This kind of encapsulating scene is characteristic of Gaskell, and of the period. She uses figurative language sparingly, achieving the same effect through description and dramatization. Rather than saying, 'the fire and warmth had left John Barton's life', she will show Barton actually sitting in front of an empty hearth, filled with dead ashes. Rather than comparing Ruth to a lily or a water-nymph, she will show Ruth's lover, Bellingham, braiding her hair with water lilies as she sits by a deep pool in a hidden glade. Even in this early story realistic detail acquires the force of metaphor as Libbie sits on her 'Noah's ark' of a chest, gazing at the stars, like a fugitive seeking solid ground amid the restless flow; across the court she sees the shadow of Franky Hall's hand waving against a drawn blind in 'constant, weary motion'. Like her, the crippled boy finds solace in nature, gazing at a bunch of Michaelmas daisies from the market, until 'by and by one or two of the constellation of lilac stars faded'. The canary which Libbie gives Franky is not a prize-winner, just a dull-coloured bird which mopes in the corner of its cage, grandly named Jupiter in compensation for its lack of song. The bird in the cage hints at the caged lives of the child and the women and their lack of a heard voice. (It deeply upset the elderly Leigh Hunt when Elizabeth sent him a copy of the story, reminding him of his own imprisonment.)[8] But the gift brings happiness to Franky and breaks the hostile silence of Margaret Hall.

The Dunham episode dramatizes two kinds of good. The first is the Wordsworthian power of nature, 'lapping the soul in green images of the country', creating harmony among quarrelsome neighbours and providing a foretaste of 'heaven' to the dying child. The second is the nurturing ethos of the working class, especially of the men, who carry Franky in a shawl slung like a hammock up to the top of the hill. Here another convention takes over; the view of Manchester from the hilltop reproduces those contemporary landscapes so beloved of rich manufacturers, showing picnicking groups on a wooded ridge with chimneys and warehouses in a hazy, softened distance:

'They had taken Franky there to show him Manchester, far away in the blue plain, against which the woodland foreground cut with a soft clear line. Far away in the distance, on that flat plain, you might see the motionless cloud of smoke hanging over a great town, and that was Manchester, — ugly, smoky Manchester; dear, busy, earnest, noble-working Manchester; where their children had been born, and where, perhaps, some lay buried; where their homes were and where God had cast their lives, and told them to work out their destiny.' (Ch. 2)

Generalizations replace sharp particulars. The effusive adjectives protest too much, belying the experience of the characters.

The passage is imbued with the call to resignation of William Gaskell's hymn: 'Meekly take thy part assigned'. The final Michaelmas episode qualifies this, demonstrating Gaskell's belief that people *choose* the way they work out their destiny even within a foreordained lot. After Franky's funeral Margaret must still work: 'And I mun go washing, just as if nothing had happened . . . And I mun come home at night, and find his place empty, and all still where I used to be sure of hearing his voice, ere ever I got up the stair. No one will ever call me mother again!' This is harder stuff altogether. The feeling that grief is a middle-class luxury and that stoicism is almost forced on the poor links Gaskell to the Wordsworth of 'Michael', or to Scott's *Antiquary*, with its contrast between the 'ancient forms of mourning' in Glenallan House, and the way that the Mucklebackits have to return straight away to their fishing after Steenie's death. Yet good comes from pain; Margaret's bleak self-pity prompts Libbie to ask if she can live with her.

Libbie's decision follows immediately after her landlady's daughter Anne Dixon has decided to marry her lover, a potential drunkard:

'After all, what is marrying? just a spree, Bob says. He often says he does not think I shall make him a good wife, for I know nought about house-matters, wi' working in a factory; but he says he'd rather be uneasy wi' me, than easy wi' anybody else. There's love for you! And I tell him I'd rather have him tipsy than anyone else sober!' (Ch. 3)

When Libbie responds with horror, explaining that her own father had killed her baby brother in a fit of drunkenness, Anne counters, 'Dear, what a preachment!' and dismisses Libbie as 'as born an old maid as ever I saw'. For the first time Libbie is angry. As she sees it, if God has kept her out of 'women's natural work' as wife and mother, she must find work for herself:

'I can see many a one misses it in this. They will hanker after what is ne'er likely to be theirs instead of facing it out, and settling down to be old maids, and, as old maids, just looking round for the odd jobs God leaves in the world for such as old maids to do. There's plenty of such work, and there's the blessing of God on them as does it.' (Ch. 3)

Gaskell is not saying that women should choose *not* to marry. Like her heroine, she undoubtedly considers this women's 'natural' work, but she makes it perfectly clear that a marriage like Anne's is unlikely to be happy and she is bold in her declaration of the value of 'old maids'. As a result of Libbie's choice, the 'fierce and unwomanly' Margaret becomes as tender to Libbie as her dead mother, while 'Libbie herself has such peace shining on her countenance, as almost makes it beautiful, as she renders the service of a daughter to Franky's mother — no longer the desolate, lonely orphan, a stranger on the earth'. Love is a social virtue, not a biological instinct. It can exist between strangers and need not be confined to the family. Margaret and Libbie cannot change their external conditions, but by acting as mother and daughter they alter the quality of their inner lives. Neither is 'only a single person' any longer.

'Christmas Storms and Sunshine', Elizabeth's third story for *Howitt's Journal* (following 'The Sexton's Hero'), also urges female solidarity, but this time between married women. Her stories often form complementary pairs (like 'The Doom of the Griffiths' and 'The Well of Pen-Morfa'), and here, in place of an angry widow helped by her young neighbour, Mary Hodgson, a naïve young mother, is saved by the splendidly sour Mrs Jenkins. This is a comic story with a serious centre, which turns once again on the threatened death of a child. Often called Dickensian, it shows Gaskell moving towards the style of *Cranford*; witty yet affectionate, its characterization approaching caricature, yet avoiding cruelty. The move to comedy is linked to a shift in the social class of her subjects, as if Gaskell could poke fun at the middle class in a way she could not at the poor, and could deal with them in language less burdened with Sunday-school phrases.

The story opens with brisk, satirical economy:

'In the town of — (no matter where) there circulated two newspapers (no matter when). Now the *Flying Post* was long-established and respectable – alias bigoted and Tory; the *Examiner* was spirited and intelligent – alias new-fangled and democratic. Every week these newspapers contained articles abusing each other, as cross and peppery as articles could be, and evidently the production of irritated minds, although they seemed to have one stereotyped commencement – "Though the article appearing in our last week's *Post* (or *Examiner*) is below contempt, yet we have been induced," &c &c.'

Each week their respective readers congratulate themselves on victory, and declare their rivals 'at last gasp'. The chief compositors of the competing papers live in the same lodgings, but while the young Radical, Mr Hodgson, is an individualist prone to flights of fancy who inserts his own unlikely compositions into blank spaces ('announcements of a forthcoming crop of green peas in December'), the older Tory, Mr Jenkins, has 'a proper reverence for all in authority, from the King down to the editor and sub-editor' and would never dream of taking such liberties. These 'heroes' are at daggers drawn.

Each has a wife, 'to finish the completeness of the quarrel', and each wife has her darling – the Hodgsons a baby, the Jenkinses a cat. The crisis comes on Christmas Eve when Mary Hodgson beats the cat, who has gnawed her husband's dinner, and then has to appeal to a furious Mrs Jenkins for help with her baby's croup. The lodging-house hierarchy is effortlessly conveyed – from Mrs Jenkins's contempt for Mary (who has been in service and has no fine lace cap) down to the landlady's daughter Fanny (whose concern for the sick baby vies with her excitement at the drama). In the end, though, Gaskell cannot see these women as comic. Mrs Jenkins's childlessness is 'the great unspoken disappointment of her life'; Mary adores her child but is isolated and frightened. Yet both women cherish the image of their mothers and, as in 'Libbie Marsh', maternal feeling unlocks tenderness – this is a tale for Christmas, the Nativity. Mrs Jenkins is listening to carol singers outside:

> 'He neither shall be born in purple nor in pall,
> But all in fair linen, as were babies all:
> He neither shall be rocked in silver nor in gold,
> But in a wooden cradle that rocks on the mould.'

The story attains a new seriousness when Mary knocks at her door uttering an elemental plea, 'Let me have water for my baby, for the love of God!' and Mrs Jenkins, after curtly refusing, not only brings the water, but relieves the attack before the doctor comes. Meanwhile, the unfeeling (male) cat has eaten the Jenkins's own sausages ('he would have eaten his own father if he had been tender enough'). The quarrel is forgotten when the two families share Christmas dinner, baby on Mrs Jenkins's knee, well-fed cat on Mary's, but while the women have come to understand and like each other, nothing can puncture the comic self-importance of the men.

The casual ease of 'Christmas Storms and Sunshine', with its implicit contrast of male and female values, conceals considerable skill, blending humour and sentiment, and combining the vivacity of oral traditions of storytelling with literary mock-heroic:

'So saying, Mary Hodgson caught up her husband's Sunday cane, and despite pussy's cries and scratches, she gave him such a beating as she hoped might cure him of his thievish propensities; when, lo! and behold, Mrs Jenkins stood at the door with a face of bitter wrath.'

This works wonderfully when read aloud, as does Mrs Jenkins's subsequent tirade, sliding between political and personal animosity:

' "There is such a thing as a law for brute animals. I'll ask Mr Jenkins, but I don't think them Radicals has done away with that law yet, for all their Reform Bill, ma'am. My poor precious love of a Tommy, is he hurt? and is his leg broke for taking a mouthful of scraps, as most people would give away to a beggar – if he'd take 'em!" wound up Mrs Jenkins, casting a contemptuous look on the remnant of a scrag end of mutton.'

The three *Howitt's* stories, while in no obvious sense autobiographical, show Elizabeth's experience filtering into her fiction, from the anecdotes with which she amused her friends ('a meeting in the street, a talk with a factory-girl') to her deep fears about motherhood and the deaths of children. By contrast, the other *Howitt's* piece attributed to her – a report of Emerson's Manchester lectures in November 1847 – evokes the style of her public, rather than private, life.[9]

In the 1830s Ralph Waldo Emerson had turned from the 'corpse-cold' Unitarianism of New England to develop his own Transcendentalist philosophy, emphasizing the truth of the 'heart', of nature, of mystical love, and the leading role of inspired men. He was now internationally known both for his writing and as an itinerant lecturer. After landing in Liverpool on 22 October 1847, he visited his friend Carlyle in London and then came north again to lecture on 'Representative Men of Great Ideas' at the Manchester Athenaeum and on miscellaneous subjects such as 'Eloquence', 'Domestic Life', 'Reading' and 'The Humanity of Science' at the Mechanics Institute. He refused to be lionized, but Manchester society crowded to hear him. On the second night Elizabeth and William went along to the Athenaeum with the Winkworth sisters and Annie Shaen.[10] That afternoon they had showed Annie the city's commercial life – the Houldsworth and Winkworth warehouses – and in the evening they set out to display its culture. Arriving ten minutes before the door opened, they found the crush so great that they had to 'press upwards as best we might' and were almost carried up the flights of stairs to the lecture room.

Elizabeth thought Emerson a compelling figure as he stood under the glaring jet of gas, his face in shadow, disconcerting his audience by his wooden expression and offhand, almost rude delivery (very different from pulpit eloquence). 'So much for the outward husk,' she wrote. But the husk seems to have interested her more than the kernel. In her view,

'Swedenborg the mystic was a misty subject, treated in a misty manner. Some man near me gravely asked his neighbour if he did not think he could understand it better if they stood on their heads?'

'Montaigne the Sceptic' on the following night (just as crowded) and 'Shakespeare' on the third were more to her taste, and that of the Manchester public.

Gaskell did not mean to be dismissive of Emerson. The issues raised in 'Representative Men of Great Ideas' were of great concern to her, particularly in her questioning of 'heroism', but she saw the *scene* as almost more significant than the lectures themselves. What we sense here – as in her reaction to James Martineau – is her prickliness about intellectual pretension, her dislike of obscurantism and cant, her feeling that people are shamming understanding. She likes the blunt men who admit they cannot follow a word, in contrast to those who pretend they can. She is not suspicious of Emerson's ideas so much as of his status as the fashionable thinker of the day (on a par with the latest song), whom shallow-minded girls like the daughters of Carson, the mill-owner in *Mary Barton,* feel they should be seen reading, even if his work bores them:

'The elder two had been at a dancing-party the night before, and were listless and sleepy in consequence. One tried to read "Emerson's Essays", and fell asleep in the attempt; the other was turning over a parcel of new songs, in order to select what she liked.' (Ch. 18)

Of all Emerson's lectures the lecture which roused the greatest enthusiasm in Manchester was not at the Athenaeum at all, but at the Mechanics Institute. It had a far more accessible-sounding title: 'On Domestic Life' – 'so large a subject,' wrote Gaskell, 'on which we wander so much astray'. So far Elizabeth's own stories had concentrated largely on domestic life. *Mary Barton*, however, now almost finished, dealt with a larger canvas and treated issues of passionate practical interest to the kind of Manchester men so bemused by Emerson's abstractions. And although she had set her story at the beginning of the decade, recent events were making it appear increasingly topical. By 1844 it had seemed that the worst distress was over:

trade expanded and incomes rose. The new municipal associations began to provide public parks and, spurred by Edwin Chadwick's devastating reports of 1842 and 1843, work started on Manchester's sanitation and water supply.

In 1846 hard times returned. In Ireland the potato crop failed for two years running; thousands died of starvation and fever. In England the harvests were ruined by storms, the price of food rose sharply and a long winter brought new misery. By June 1847 fifty thousand Manchester workers were on short time, and tensions grew between desperate Irish immigrants and unemployed workers. Mrs Greg told William Gaskell that the magistrates feared riots against the Irish over the Whitsun holiday and that the yeomanry were drilling in secret.[11]

That danger passed, but in November *Howitt's Journal* once again declared that 'distress is the great topic of the day'. Manchester operatives reported a ten per cent cut in wages, with most mills working only two or three days a week and thirty-three completely idle.[12] According to the mission visitors, 'the Poor Office (as it was called) and the soup-kitchens were besieged, the pawnbrokers' shops were full to overflowing, houses were stripped of nearly every article which could be dispensed with'.[13] Typhus returned and all the hospitals in Manchester, Salford and Chorlton-on-Medlock were full. The long awaited repeal of the Corn Laws in June 1846 had done little to help the poor. Middle-class reformers expressed their alarm and looked for someone – but not the free traders or capitalists – to blame. In the same week as Emerson's lectures a typical argument broke out among the Gaskells' friends, as Catherine Winkworth reported to Susanna:

'Last Thursday I was asked to the Darbishires' to meet Cobdens, Leislers, Hawkshaws, Gaskells, Mr. Kenrick &c. It was an eating-tea in the Pompeii room, and we were fortunate enough to have the principal gentlemen at our table, so of course, before tea was half-over, they were deep in a discussion on the present state of the commercial world, which lasted a great part of the evening, and to which we ladies were, as you may suppose, very glad to listen with all our ears.'[14]

'A regular pitched battle' developed between Cobden and Hawkshaw about parliament's intervention in the railway boom. (Railway entrepreneurs had criss-crossed Britain with over three thousand new miles of track since 1843.) Cobden, betraying his free-trade principles, as Hawkshaw took pains to point out, supported government action to slow down the rapid expansion, but Hawkshaw argued that if thousands of mechanics and navvies were being laid off daily – 'by far the most turbulent classes of the community' – riots must be expected over the winter. Cobden retaliated by claiming that the cotton trade would revive, providing work for the unemployed railwaymen. Feelings ran high. Possibly Elizabeth was at another table, but it is curious to think of her, among the silent ladies, on this and other evenings, knowing that her own book, now on its way to finding a publisher, dealt with the rift between the classes to which such arguments inevitably returned.

She hoped to remain anonymous, but she did not keep her book completely secret. As it neared completion she anxiously sent the first volume to chosen friends or relatives who might advise her. One of these was her stepmother's sister, Katherine Thomson, by now a well-known figure in literary London. According to Elizabeth Barrett Browning, who said she heard it from an acquaintance of the Anthony Todd Thomsons (probably her friend Mrs Ogilvie), ' "Mary Barton" was sent in manuscript to Mrs Thomson, and failed to please her; and, in deference to her judgement, certain alterations were made. Subsequently it was offered to all or nearly all the publishers in London and rejected.'[15] She thought, for example, that the publisher Moxon had had it for some time, but although Gaskell later admitted that it had been refused by Moxon 'as a gift', she herself never spoke of such a wholesale rejection.

The Howitts also read the manuscript. William Howitt liked handing out advice to young authors and was not backward in claiming credit if they succeeded. A couple of years later he wrote smugly: 'Have you read *Mary Barton* ? The book was written at my suggestion and disposed of by me. The authoress never wrote a book before.'[16] It was natural for Elizabeth to turn to the man who was currently publishing her work in his journal. When she sent Howitt the first volume, she told him, according to Mary, that it had been written as 'the result of his advice. We were delighted with it, and a few months later Mrs Gaskell came up to London, and to our house, with the work completed.'[17]

Fortunately for Elizabeth, one of the people to whom William Howitt showed it was John Forster, the influential reader for the publishers Chapman and Hall. (Dickens had introduced him when they were publishing the *Pickwick Papers* in the 1830s.) The history of the firm describes Forster as 'bridging the gulf between the Patron of the eighteenth century and the Literary Agent of the twentieth', and records memories of him 'swinging into the office as though the whole place belonged to him, and carrying off the proofs of half the publications, to read at his leisure in his chambers'.[18] He was largely responsible for building their impressive list of the 1840s and 1850s, bringing in, among others, Gaskell, Kingsley, Thackeray, Carlyle, Browning, Clough, Harrison Ainsworth and Trollope. He thought *Mary Barton* had weaknesses (which he later offered to list for Elizabeth, if she could stand it, an offer she gratefully accepted), but he recommended publication.[19] Chapman and Hall offered £100 for the copyright – and later, of their own accord, gave Elizabeth another £100 for the second edition. 'Two hundred pounds is a good price – isn't it?' wrote the sharp Elizabeth Barrett Browning to Mary Russell Mitford, 'for a novel, as times go. Miss Lynn had only a hundred and fifty for her Egyptian novel, or perhaps for the Greek one.'[20]

Elizabeth was more than happy with Howitt's arrangements and, despite his self-importance, he proved a shrewd negotiator, telling her that he would 'take great care that Messrs Chapman and Hall do not imagine that you would have been satisfied with less. Of course, I took the proposal quite coolly, and as a matter of business.' He also realized that he had a writer in his care whose talent, once unleashed, would not stop here. Should she declare her identity?

'What is to be done in drawing the agreement? It should be done in your own name, and in that case it must be confided to them in strict confidence. If you have any objection to that we must see whether they will be satisfied to have it made in the name of Cotton Mather Mills. But it seems to me that as you will write (I trust many) other works, it would be as well for them to be known as the works of a lady. I think they would be more popular; and in that case the question still arises what will you do? Pray let me know.'[21]

The contract was made in her name, but it is clear, from her search for a male pseudonym up to the time of publication, that she was reluctant to be identified with the book and did not want it to seem 'the work of a lady'. Authority meant more to her than 'popularity'.

As the Gaskells were then planning to stay with the Shaens in Essex, Howitt suggested they spend a night in Clapton on their way 'and then you could have as much talk as you liked'. The following month the visit was paid. After the long railway journey (during which William, hungry as ever, was extremely glad of the sandwiches 'put up in Mrs Darbishire's bag') they arrived at Euston. Their response to the capital brings out their different characters: William's stubborn Mancunian loyalties, and his wife's delight in the new, and unerring eye for small, bizarre, differentiating detail:

'Then when we got to London we took a cab and went driving through wide lighted streets – Papa said very much like Oldham Road in Manchester, but I thought much handsomer. They sell geese here with their necks hanging down at full length, instead of being tucked up like Lancashire geese, – and the shops are full of them against Xmas, & you can't think how funny they look.' (L49)

The Howitts' house showed Elizabeth how comfortable a literary life could be: 'Such a blazing fire – such a crimson carpet – such an easy chair – such white dimity curtains', such a fine garden and so many fine casts and paintings. They had their promised talk ('we went on talking till 12 o'clock. What do you think of *that*?'), but the real business matters were left until January, when she and William would meet Edward Chapman in person.

From the Howitts' William and Elizabeth went on to the Shaens'. It was their first visit to Crix, and William, who disliked being away from home, promptly collapsed with a cold, while Elizabeth was excited and curious. She gave her 'dearest girls' a precise account of the house and grounds, down to the six oak trees, 'the largest measuring 22 feet round'. Crix had just the easy, affluent atmosphere she liked. Mr Shaen read a sermon aloud on Sunday afternoon, but most of the time was spent in 'talking, laughing and singing', with walks round the village with the girls, and vast family meals: 'You should have seen the sirloin of beef (more than 40lb) we had at the bottom of the table and 2 *turkeys* at the top yesterday – but then we were 10 in the parlour and 32 in the servants hall.' There is no doubt that Elizabeth thoroughly enjoyed good living, good food, concerts and carriages – all the things the mill-owning Carsons take for granted in *Mary Barton*, and which Mary dreams of in her dangerous 'Alnaschar visions'. Crix was far from Lancashire distress and she could enjoy it without guilt, just as she had her visit to Heidelberg during the misery of 1841. But her criticism in *Mary Barton* reaches beyond the unfeeling ignorance of individuals to the whole style of life of the rich: in her picture of the Carsons she not only attacked the world of her friends (as some of them bitterly pointed out), but turned the beam of conscience on herself.

The Shaens and her other friends knew nothing of this yet, although they would within a year. On 9 January 1848 Mary Howitt wrote to say that as soon as she and William had read the conclusion of the novel 'we *immediately* sent it to Chapman and Hall, but we have heard nothing. Publishers are slow. We will, however, "poke them up". I feel sure they will take it.'[22] They did. An undated letter from Mary shows her working on Elizabeth's behalf, and also shows that Gaskell already saw her tale as 'a love story' and was not, as has been hitherto presumed, forced to consider this subtitle by her publisher:

'Dear Sir,
    I send you the remainder of our friend's "Manchester Love Story". I think it beautiful – I hope you will do the same & let us know very soon that you will publish it & also what you incline to offer for it as the author is very impatient to know what you say in this part of the business.'[23]

Soon the Gaskells returned to London, where Edward Chapman gave Elizabeth the impression that her novel would appear that spring, following Geraldine Jewsbury's *The Half-sisters*. By the end of March there was no sign of it and Elizabeth wrote anxiously, appealing to her publisher's sense of timing. The overthrow of Louis Philippe's government in February was forcing the pace of popular movements in Austria, Germany and Italy. In Britain, on 10 April, a new Chartist petition was presented to parliament and a huge demonstration in its support was swiftly broken up. The papers were full of the agitation at home and abroad. Would it be wise to seize the moment – or not?

'I can not help feeling that the tenor of my tale is such as to excite attention at the present time of struggle on the part of work people to obtain what they esteem their rights; on the other side it is very possible that people are now so absorbed by public work as to have very little time or interest to bestow on works of fiction.' (L54)

More letters followed, with growing impatience. 'I begin to think it probable you never received a letter, which I addressed to you about 10 days ago,' she wrote on 2 April. A fortnight later, her tone perceptibly sharper, she referred Chapman to his original agreement with Howitt, before retreating into modesty: 'of course, I defer to your superior knowledge, only repeating my own belief that the tale would bear directly upon the present circumstances'. Within days she had a reply, but found she also had to make a hard decision. On 17 April she agreed to change the title from 'John Barton' to 'Mary Barton'. Chapman (or Forster) may have been reluctant to shock the public by having the name of a murderer, John Barton, as the title, but Elizabeth resented this bitterly because it defied her conception of the novel. All her books (even *Cranford*) are dramas of character, springing from intense identification with individuals. This was true of *Mary Barton*, even though she spoke for a whole class, as she explained in 1849:

' "John Barton" was the original name, as being the central figure to my mind; indeed I had so long felt that the bewildered life of an ignorant thoughtful man of strong power of sympathy, dwelling in a town so full of striking contrasts as this is, was a tragic poem, that in writing he was my "hero"; and it was a London thought coming through the publisher that it must be called *Mary B.*' (L70)

Chapman was not so imperceptive. As the novel progresses Mary does move to centre stage and so does Gaskell's enduring subject – a different kind of psychological drama, the violent jolting into maturity and sexual awareness of a young, idealistic and innocent girl.

In the same letter – full of 'London thoughts' – Chapman had also raised doubts about the dialect, and here William came to her aid, as Elizabeth told him: 'It is so difficult living in Lancashire to decide upon words likely to be unintelligible in another county; but my husband has put notes to those we believe to require them.' She now sent Chapman the verses of the ballad of 'The Oldham Weaver', and enclosed her choice of epigraphs, including several of William's poems. Soon afterwards she fell seriously ill with measles and, according to William, was in real danger for a day or two and feared she was dying. She was still not well by the summer, and was on tenterhooks about her book. In July she told Chapman resignedly that she was happy to leave the date of publication to him. They finally compromised on the title, adopting the more neutral, all-inclusive 'Mary Barton, A Tale of Manchester Life'. At last, having met all Chapman's demands, all that Elizabeth had to prepare for was publication itself.

While she was making these finishing touches, her life followed its familiar course: parties at the Darbishires, visits to relatives and friends, a short holiday in the Lakes and parish duties. Still, she was nervous and impatient. In September she celebrated her thirty-eighth birthday and at the end of that month, knowing her book would soon be out, she fled to Wales rather than face the reaction in Manchester.

First, however, she went to see Catherine Winkworth, who had been ill all year and had been sent to recuperate at Southport. Although Elizabeth herself was still not well, 'very thin and pale', she could talk as energetically as ever. One morning Catherine started a letter, 'but Mrs Gaskell began to talk very nicely and I have been sitting here an hour and a half listening to her instead, and now she and Emily are talking away instead'.[24] (The Winkworths only met one person who could talk faster, and that was the Prussian ambassador Chevalier Bunsen; Elizabeth was quite put out and complained that she could not remember a word he said.)[25] Far from being numb with exhaustion, Catherine reached new heights of adoration:

'Southport has a halo of glory round it in my eyes now, because of Mrs Gaskell's visit to us. It *was* so delightful having her here all to ourselves and we got so intimate together. Everything I see of her makes me admire and love her more. She is so full of information on such various subjects, has seen so many clever and curious people, so much life altogether; – and then she is so thoro'ly good. Her thoughtful kindness and gentleness to me, because I was ill, was as great as if I were one of her own children. Well! she certainly is as near perfection as anyone I know.'[26]

At Plas Penrhyn her cousins doubtless quickly removed the halo.

In Wales she saw the first advertisement in the *Edinburgh* and, as if finally convinced of the book's reality, suddenly suggested a pseudonym, asking Chapman if he would object to Stephen Berwick. This male disguise was a tribute to her father, William Stevenson, and to Berwick, the town where he was born, a rather backhanded compliment, given the tangled emotional relationship of father and daughter in the novel. She may have felt that a man's name (like the proposed title, 'John Barton') would make readers take the politics of the book more seriously, but it is intriguing that she wished to retreat behind a *fatherly* pseudonym. Was she perhaps remembering Stevenson's *Blackwood* articles of the 1820s on 'The Political Economist', in which he denied that free-market mechanisms would benefit all, and argued instead for an ethos of mutual support? Or were there further unacknowledged reasons?

It was, in any case, altogether too late, as Chapman pointed out. On 18 October *Mary Barton* was published, anonymously, in two volumes. Elizabeth pretended that nothing had happened and wrote to Katie Winkworth about the laziness of life at Plas Penrhyn – apart from the scramble for the postbag. She enclosed her letter in one from Emily, who had gone with her to Wales and had very different news:

'What do you think? "Mary Barton, a Story of Manchester Life" is by Mrs Gaskell, or "I'm a blackie!", as Aunt says! I got hold of it last night going to bed, and knew by the first few words it was hers – about Green Heys Fields and the stile she was describing to Kate and me the other day; – but we haven't talked a word about it yet, and I don't mean to say I guess it, till I have said all I want about it first. The folks here know it I am sure – they all turned so silent when I began to talk about it at breakfast time, and Mrs Gaskell suddenly popped down under the table to look for something which I am sure wasn't there.'[27]

It was useless to duck: from now on she could hide in the shadows no longer.

II

SPEAKING OUT
1848–56

Do they want to know why? Then let them read Mary
Barton. *Do they want to know why poor men, kind
and sympathising as women to each other, learn to
hate law and order, Queen, Lords and Commons,
country-party, and corn law leagues, all alike – to hate
the rich in short? Then let them read* Mary Barton.

Charles Kingsley, Fraser's Magazine, 1848

*I did feel as if I had something to say about it that I
must say, and you know I can tell stories better than
any other way of expressing myself.*

Elizabeth Gaskell on Ruth, 1853

*Oh, Mrs Gaskell – fearful – fearful! If I were Mr G.
O Heaven how I would beat her!*

Charles Dickens, 1854

[10]

Exposure: *Mary Barton*

In that summer of waiting in 1847 Edward Chapman suggested that Elizabeth should write an 'explanatory preface' to *Mary Barton*. She said she did not quite know what he meant:

'The only thing I should like to make clear is that it is no catch-penny run up since the events on the Continent have directed public attention to the consideration of the state of affairs between the Employers, & their work-people.

If you think the book requires such a preface I will try to concoct it; but at present, I have no idea what to say.' (158)

In October, though, she did write a preface, refuting any charge of opportunism by stressing that the story was begun three years ago, and was born of her own experience. And when Chapman asked for six thousand words to make up the pages of the third volume, she used the space to insert a crucial conversation debating the rights and wrongs of masters and workmen. She anticipated criticism. She had dared to write about Manchester and expose the suffering of the workers; she knew her book would strike directly at many of her friends.

The growing antagonism between rich and poor had been a matter of heated argument since the 1830s, voiced in Carlyle's *Past and Present* in 1843, and in Disraeli's *Coningsby* and *Sybil* in 1844 and 1845. Gaskell was not the first woman to tackle industrial strife in fiction. Charlotte Tonna's *Combination* and Harriet Martineau's 'A Manchester Strike' in *Illustrations of Political Economy* had appeared as early as 1832. More recently, Frances Trollope's *Michael Armstrong, the Factory Boy* (1839) had forwarded the cause of Tory reformers in support of the Ten Hours Bill, and Tonna's Evangelical *Helen Fleetwood* (1841) had graphically exposed the horrors of child labour. A still closer novel to Elizabeth's was *William Langshawe. The Cotton Lord* (1842) by Elizabeth Stone, whose father owned the *Manchester Chronicle*. Stone's plot, like that of *Mary Barton*, was partly based on the murder of Thomas Ashton by striking workers in 1831, and she gave a similar, although more hostile picture of conspiring unionists. When Elizabeth was trying to hide her authorship, she pretended that Marianne Darbishire had given her 'convincing proofs' that *Mary Barton* was written by Mrs Stone.[1]

To ward off her critics, Elizabeth explained in her preface that she always felt 'a deep sympathy with the care-worn men, who looked as if doomed to struggle through their lives in strange alternation between work and want'. She could see their resentment of the rich, 'the even tenor of whose seemingly happy lives appeared to increase the anguish caused by the lottery-like nature of their own', and understand how their sense of neglect, however mistaken, had tainted 'resignation to God's will', and turned them to revenge. 'The more I reflected on this unhappy state of things between those so bound to each other by common interests, as the employers and the employed must ever be, the more anxious I became to give some utterance to the agony which, from time to time, convulses this dumb people.' Appealing to self-interest as much as sympathy, she depicted the workers' belief that their suffering was ignored as a danger 'to all parties':

'At present they seem to me to be left in a state, wherein lamentations and tears are thrown aside as useless, but in which the lips are compressed for curses, and the hands clenched and ready to smite.

I know nothing of Political Economy, or the theories of trade. I have tried to write truthfully; and if my accounts agree or clash with any system, the agreement or disagreement is unintentional.'[2]

With the remark, 'I know nothing of Political Economy, or the theories of trade', she deliberately distanced herself from Harriet Martineau and other professed experts. She was defiant as well as modest: 'truth' must come before 'systems'. The biblical rhythms of the first sentence show a writer at one with her subject: the cautious formality of the second shows a woman braced for attack.

Elizabeth allegedly told Travers Madge of the moment which inspired *Mary Barton*. One day, visiting a poor family, she was trying,

like Susanna Winkworth, to argue against their suspicion of the rich,
'when the head of the family took hold of her arm, and grasping it
tightly said, with tears in his eyes, "Ay, ma'am, but have ye ever seen a
child clemmed to death?" '³ This is the question which John Barton,
the weaver-hero of her novel, hurls at the rich: have they ever seen
their children starve? The story may be apocryphal, but the book has
all the urgency of such a confrontation; the father's voice literally
gripped her. How could she reconcile, in her own conscience, those
'fine, well lit shops' lining the Oxford Road with the starvation which
lay just a few yards behind them? The book was born of her own shock
and guilt, and the words 'bewildered', 'mysterious', 'uncertain' and
'desperate' occur on almost every page. Her own profound questioning is expressed by her hero:

'John Barton's overpowering thought, which was to work out his fate
on earth, was rich and poor; why are they so separate, so distinct,
when God has made them all? It is not His will, that their interests are
so far apart. Whose doing is it?' (Ch. 15)

As Barton pursues his search, 'bewildered and lost, unhappy and
suffering', it drives him to become 'a Chartist, a Communist, all that is
commonly called wild and visionary'. But, Gaskell comments, 'Ay! but
being visionary is something. It shows a soul, a being not altogether
sensual; a creature who looks forward for others, if not for himself.' In
the course of writing she too was driven from the practical towards the
visionary. In 1849 she told Mrs Greg that John Barton had been her
central character, 'with whom all my sympathies went',

'because I believed from personal observation that such men were not
uncommon, and would well reward such sympathy and love as should
throw light upon their groping search after the causes of suffering, and
the reason why suffering is sent, and what they can do to lighten it.'
(L74)

Her own search led her beyond the immediate troubles of industrial
Lancashire. *Mary Barton* turned a drama of conflict between classes
into an examination of humanity's essentially divided nature. As
Gaskell delved into the question of suffering her book became an
exploration of the Fall, of innocence and guilt, asking continually,
'Whose doing is it?' Moral absolutes became blurred. Is it a 'sin' for a
father to steal to feed his dying son? For a mother to give opium to

starving children, or turn to prostitution to buy medicine for her daughter?

Mary Barton touched and shocked its middle-class readers to an unprecedented extent because it showed how the poor suffered not in the mill or the factory but in their homes, with their wives and children, as the settled rhythms of their lives were shaken and destroyed. Gaskell described their furniture, their crockery, their trivial family arguments, their small moments of pride or hurt feelings. She let them tell their own stories in their own rich language, but at the same time she insisted that they were *not* so different: rich and poor were not two nations but one, split by ignorance and misunderstanding. And she lured her readers gently into this unfamiliar world; her study of conflict and hardship began with a vision of a better time, a gentler place, a holiday outing and a tea-party.

The story opens in the mid-1830s, a time of relative plenty. Through Green Heys Fields, on the fringe of Manchester, wander groups of work-people on holiday: independent factory girls and families out for the day, among them the Bartons and the Wilsons. In the Bartons city and country join. John Barton is 'a thorough specimen of a Manchester man; born of factory workers, and himself bred up in youth, and living in manhood, among the mills'. He is short, stunted, pale, bearing the marks of childhood deprivation, but his features are strong 'and their expression was extreme earnestness; resolute either for good or evil; a sort of latent, stern enthusiasm'. His pregnant wife, by contrast, has 'the fresh beauty of the agricultural districts' (and, Gaskell adds, something of the 'deficiency of sense in her countenance' which marks rural folk in contrast to natives of the manufacturing towns).

Green Heys Fields, with their farm, stile and deep, clear pond, were real enough. Yet they also belong to a vanished literary Pastoral, where the May day of sun and showers is 'the April of the poets' and flowers grow 'in most republican and discriminate order'; Gaskell evokes the older genre to guide her readers into her new industrial novel. But the city dwellers she depicts are exiled from this Eden. They have fled for work to the city and many live in dread of being flung back on the harsh new Poor Law of the country parish. And within the city commercial values replace the 'natural'. As the mill-owner's 'rosebud' daughter, Amy Carson, points out, here each flower has its price: half a guinea for a small rose, half a crown for lilies of the valley.

In fact the opening idyll is already tainted, but not by industrial

EXPOSURE: *MARY BARTON*

strife – as in the first Eden, a woman is to blame. The first line of dialogue is George Wilson's sympathetic question to John Barton, 'Any news of Esther yet?' Mrs Barton's sister, Esther, has disappeared, leaving the Bartons' house after John attacked her vanity:

'Says I, "Esther, I see what you'll end at with your artificials, and your fly-away veils, and stopping out when honest women are in their beds; you'll be a street-walker, Esther and then, don't you go to think to darken my door, though my wife is your sister." ' (Ch. 1)

It is amid such talk that we first hear of John's daughter, Mary; his real grudge against Esther (who has left to follow a rich officer) is her suggestion that she might return and 'make a lady' out of Mary. He would rather see his daughter earning her bread by the sweat of her brow than being a 'do-nothing lady, worrying shopmen all morning and screeching at her pianny all afternoon, and going to bed without having done a good turn to any of God's creatures but herself'. In response to Wilson's amused remark. 'Thou never could abide the gentlefolk', John launches into a bitter attack upon the rich. What have they ever done for the poor? Do they nurse them when sick? Do they bring broth when a child is dying, as his son Tom had died? Do they share their plenty in the weeks of black frost when the poor are out of work?

' "No, I tell you, it's the poor and the poor only, as does such things for the poor. Don't think to come over me with the old tale, as the rich know nothing of the trials of the poor. I say, if they don't know, they ought to know. We are their slaves as long as we can work; we pile up their fortunes with the sweat of our brows; and yet we are to live in two separate worlds; ay, as separate as Dives and Lazarus, with a great gulf betwixt us: but I know who was best off then," and he wound up his speech with a low chuckle that had no mirth in it.' (Ch. 1)

The men turn homewards, speaking of George's sister, Alice Wilson, who has devoted her life to caring for others. Only then do we see Mary, a girl of thirteen, gathering hawthorn buds while Jem Wilson snatches a kiss, prompting a blush and a rapid slap.

The characters are thus introduced within a network of family relationships, endowed with pasts and stories that make them individuals, not representative 'workers'. Oppositions are established that will echo through the novel – between country and city, past and

195

present, rich and poor, callousness and care. And the opening suggests too a deeper split within men and women themselves. John Barton is loving to his wife and daughter, yet stern towards Esther and bitter about the rich; Mary may follow the paths of either of the 'sisters' – the 'selfish' Esther or the selfless Alice Wilson.

From the open country Gaskell follows the Bartons and Wilsons into a maze of 'half-finished streets, all so like one another that you might easily have been bewildered and lost your way'. In the Bartons' house, lit by the glowing fire, the blue and white curtains are drawn 'to shut in the friends met to enjoy themselves'. The minute description of this room, seen through Mrs Barton's proud eyes, displays the harmony that will be lost. It is crammed with furniture, 'sure sign of good times', and holds romance at its heart. On a table, resting against the wall, is 'a bright green japanned tea-tray, having a couple of scarlet lovers embracing in the middle'. Then the mood is broken – by Alice's unlucky toast to 'absent friends', a reminder of Esther – and that night Mrs Barton dies in premature labour.

The years pass. Driven in upon himself, John throws himself into politics, while Mary – 'the light of his hearth, the voice of his otherwise silent home'– becomes an apprentice dressmaker, spurning the attentions of Jem for the flattery of Harry Carson, the mill-owner's son. It was Gaskell's intention in *Mary Barton*, as in 'Sketches among the Poor', to show the strengths as well as sorrows of the poor. In these slow-moving early chapters she does so by giving Mary three friends: Alice Wilson, Margaret Legh and Margaret's grandfather Job. Each is true to life, yet also emblematic: Alice, like 'Mary' in the *Blackwood's* poem, brings to the city her healing herbs and country innocence; Job, the naturalist, embodies the learning and passion of the self-taught artisan – typical of the many weavers who work while 'Newton's "Principia" lies open on the loom', he copies out Bamford's 'Hymn to the Poor' for Barton. His granddaughter Margaret, blinded by work as a seamstress, is a singer, voicing the hidden music of the poor, 'the poetry of humble life' itself. Her first song is 'The Oldham Weaver', the rebellious local ballad about silence and starvation:

'Oi've howden my tung, till oi've near stopped my breath,
Oi think i' my heeart oi'se soon clem to deeath.'

Her singing has something of the author's own involvement and urgency:

'Margaret, with fixed eye, and earnest, dreamy look, seemed to become more and more absorbed in realising to herself the woe she had been describing, and which she felt might at that very moment be suffering and hopeless within a short distance of their comparative comfort.

Suddenly she burst forth with all the power of her magnificent voice, as if a prayer from her very heart for all who were in distress, in the grand supplication, "Lord, remember David".' (Ch. 4)

That distress does not reach its peak in the novel until a fire at Carson's mill, in which Jem, poised on a ladder high above the street, rescues his father, watched by a swooning Mary. The fire, like a primal force, breathes life into dormant antagonisms. Since trade is slack and the mill-owners are well insured, they take the opportunity of laying off workers, saving wages and refitting their factory. They can lounge over breakfast and enjoy getting to know the agreeable and accomplished daughters on whom they have lavished their money. But, Gaskell tells us:

'There is another side to the picture. There were homes over which the Carsons' fire threw a deep, terrible gloom; the homes of those who would fain work, and no man gave unto them – the home of those to whom leisure was a curse. There, the family music was hungry wails.' (Ch. 6)

The long rhetorical passage that follows, with its sonorous diction and rolling rhythms, asserts at once the destruction of family life and the strength born of suffering:

'There were desperate fathers; there were bitter-tongued mothers (O God! what wonder!); there were reckless children; the very closest bonds of nature were snapt in that time of trial and distress. There was Faith such as the rich can never imagine on earth; there was 'love strong as death'; and self-denial, among rude, coarse men, akin to that of Sir Philip Sidney's most glorious deed. (Ch. 6)

Sidney, dying in battle, passed a cup of water to a wounded man whose need he thought was greater – the poor are true 'gentle-folk' under pressure.

The succeeding chapter, describing the efforts of John Barton and George Wilson to help the family of Ben Davenport, one of Carson's workers dying of fever in a nearby cellar, is shocking even today. Gaskell drew here upon the reports of the Mission to the Poor, but the impact is heightened by her juxtaposition of the squalid cellar to the casual ease of the mill-owner's house.[4] Going to seek help, Wilson is greeted in the Carsons' kitchen by servants who would gladly have fed him had they *known* he was hungry. The cook complains of the price of salmon; Mrs Carson orders a carriage for an afternoon lecture; Mr Carson and Henry lazily read newspapers over breakfast in the library. When Wilson asks for an infirmary order for Davenport, Carson does not even know the sick man's name:

' "He's worked in your factory better nor three years, sir".

"Very likely; I don't pretend to know the names of the men I employ; that I leave to the overlooker. So he's ill, eh?" ' (Ch. 6)

He hands out an out-patient order for a dying man.

Fiction restores the names to 'hands' and 'factory girls', replacing generalizations and Blue Book statistics with real people. But what really shocks the reader in this brief exchange, almost more than the plight of Davenport, is the rough, slick turn of phrase of Carson. Gaskell's ear, as always, is unerring. Catching each tone of voice, she identifies the inhabitants of her industrial city as carefully as Job Legh tickets his specimens. Her documentary accuracy reflects the moral aim of a particular kind of realism, which George Eliot would define in her essay on Riehl, 'The Natural History of German Life':

'Art is the nearest thing to life, it is a mode of amplifying experience and extending our contact with our fellow men beyond the bounds of our personal lot. All the more sacred is the task of the artist when he undertakes to paint the life of the People. Falsification here is far more pernicious than in the more artificial aspects of life.'[5]

Fiction, however (as Eliot was pre-eminently to show), also displays its truth metaphorically. Every dwelling Gaskell describes could be found in Manchester, yet each expresses the values of those within: Alice's basement, with its bunches of healing herbs; Job's rooms, like 'a wizard's dwelling' full of impaled insects and cabbalistic instruments; the Carsons' mansion, whose mirrors and portraits reflect their complacent self-importance. The cellar is exactly as the mission visitor described it, yet it is also the lowest depth of human life, approached through alleys awash with stagnant slops and urine, crossed by stepping-stones of ashes. It is like a Bosch painting, where naked children crawl in darkness and a dying man lies on rotten straw, with only sacking to cover his 'worn skeleton of a body'. This very real Manchester is also a kind of hell, where Esther stands in Milton's 'darkness visible'; where the poor 'need only a Dante to describe their woes'; where workmen in a foundry are silhouetted like 'demons' against the blazing furnace.

At the darkest point, when Davenport's death is followed by that of the Wilson twins, the stories of John and Mary Barton converge. Both harbour dreams of escape: John's hopes are public, Mary's private. As a Chartist delegate, John accompanies the great petition of 1839 to London, 'an argosy of the previous hopes of many otherwise despairing creatures', while Mary dreams of marrying Henry Carson, and thereby helping her father and friends. Both are castles in the air. Disappointed in London and then enraged by Harry Carson's intransigent rudeness, John and his fellow unionists plot to murder the young mill-owner. John, chosen by lot, borrows Jem's gun and shoots Harry Carson. Jem, who has been seen fighting with Harry in the street, is arrested. When Mary discovers the truth, through the intervention of Esther, she knows that she must save Jem without incriminating her father.

This theatrical crisis had always been part of Gaskell's scheme. She used melodrama to express concepts of innocence, guilt and justice in ways which realism — or cool economic analysis — could not encompass. *Mary Barton*'s appeal stems both from the slow first half in which the lives and deaths of the poor are so vividly depicted and from the impulsive, rushing, pausing narrative which then takes over. When Elizabeth began to write, she had made a plan.[6] She kept to its basic elements, but gradually began to shape her themes more dramatically, her major structural change being the introduction of Jem's sailor cousin Will Wilson (who falls in love with Margaret). His part in providing Jem's alibi leads to some of the most suspenseful episodes of the closing chapters, like Mary's dramatic chase down the Mersey against the wind and tide, pursuing the ship which is carrying him away:

'Mary stood up, steadying herself by the mast, and stretched out her arms, imploring the flying vessel to stay its course by that mute action while the tears streamed down her cheeks.' (Ch. 28)

On the 'glorious river', with its white-sailed ships carrying the commerce that brings both wealth and exploitation, Mary appears like the iconic heroines of Victorian engravings, a solitary individual crying against the winds of trade and the tides of time.

In such an image, and in the portrait of Mary in the witness box, looking like Guido's 'Beatrice Cenci', facing the court with 'mute imploring agony', Gaskell's sympathy is entirely with the suppliant. So it is with the action of the novel as a whole. Once her imagination is engaged, she expresses the 'dumb agony' of the poor so powerfully that her book cannot fail to move. Yet when she stands back and tries to argue rationally, her intellectual confusion – as opposed to her imaginative certainty – becomes uncomfortably evident. Her nervousness is most apparent in the early chapters, which are sprinkled with the phraseology commonly used by those who saw the poor as largely responsible for their own misery. This language is particularly marked when she tries to analyse the bewilderment of 'the poor weaver':

'Why should he alone suffer from bad times?

I know this is not really the case; and I know what is the truth in such matters: but what I wish to impress is what the workman feels and thinks. True, that with child-like improvidence, good times will often dissipate his grumbling and make him forget his prudence and foresight.

But there are earnest men among these people, men who have endured wrongs without complaining, but without ever forgetting or forgiving those whom (they believe) have caused all this woe.' (Ch. 3)

The defensive vagueness, the imputation of 'improvidence', the parenthetical 'they believe', the reductiveness of 'grumbling' and the infantilization of the worker are at odds with the picture she herself is painting. As the story progresses the apologetic interventions drop away and each detail seems to strengthen the case of the poor. Moral and spiritual meanings cluster strongly around basic necessities. Bread, for example, is more than a staple of life: the new loaf Mary buys for the Bartons' party embodies their temporary prosperity and hope; Alice's fragile clap-bread, which breaks in her hands, is her offering to Mary and Margaret of 'the bread of her childhood', her memories and faith; Mrs Carson's casually ordered roll stands in stark contrast to the single crust which Wilson and Barton give to the starving Davenport children (the crumbs which Lazarus craved from the rich man's table).

Clothing, in particular, defines rich and poor – Dives in his 'purple and fine linen', Lazarus in his rags and nakedness – while also underlining the gap between appearance and illusion. Clothes are the dress of dreams: John Barton puts on his best to go to London; Job Legh remembers bringing Margaret north to Manchester as a baby, when (in a comic version of the theme of men as mothers) his companion borrowed the nursemaid's cap, 'but I laughed outright at t'auld bearded chap thinking he'd make hissel like a woman just by putting on a woman's cap'; Jem dresses up to woo Mary, 'as if one waistcoat or another could decide his fate in so momentous a thing'. Such small things matter to people. Mary is right to spend all night sponging and lengthening her old gown for Mrs Davenport to go to Ben's funeral; the widow's neat black dress is 'a satisfaction to her poor heart in the midst of her sorrow'. Yet Mary's dressmaking also fosters her fantasies, and her final indifference to her appearance marks her inner growth. 'How can I think on dress at such a time?' she asks before Jem's trial.

Dress is linked to another illusory division, that between 'high' and 'low' culture. In comparison to the rough-looking Jem, Harry Carson thinks himself 'Hyperion to a satyr'; but Jem remembers a counter-quote from Burns: 'A man's a man for a' that.' ('Our toils obscure, an' a' that/The rank is but the guinea's stamp/The man's the gowd for a' that.') Again, when Harry listens to the shabbily clad trade-union delegation, he draws a cartoon of the ragged army in *Henry IV, Part 2*; 'food for powder, they'll fill a/pit as well as better'. The nub of this passage is actually the fundamental *equality* of men: 'Tush man,/ mortal man, mortal men'. Carson turns individuals into a mob, yet forgets their common humanity. He complacently appropriates Shakespeare to strike at the people, but in Gaskell's view Shakespeare, like Burns, is a poet *of* the people. Harry's insult seals his fate: the unionists tear his cartoon into strips to draw lots for his murderer..

The chapter epigraphs to *Mary Barton* are taken from radical verse, like Caroline Norton's 'Song of the Islands' or Ebenezer Elliott's rhymes as well as from Gaskell's favourite seventeenth- and eight-eenth-century and Romantic poets. Some direct comparisons within the text, such as that of the dying Davenport to 'the prophet in the plague picture' (Poole's painting, hung in the Royal Academy in 1843) or of Margaret to Mrs Knyvett (an Oldham singer, popular in London until the 1840s), translate the 'uncultured' world of the poor into forms Gaskell expects her readers to respect. At the same time they also point up those readers' prejudices, insisting that the poor *share* the national inheritance; even their dialect is shown by William's notes to derive from the English of Chaucer, of Langland, of Shakespeare, of the Book of Common Prayer. Furthermore they have a rich culture of their own. Among themselves they are not 'dumb'. They have their stories, their ballads and their poetry, and can speak to their peers, as John Barton does, with 'rough Lancashire eloquence coming out of the fullness of his heart'. The problem (as the cultural references emphasize) is that the poor speak a language to which the rich are deaf.

The novel constantly returns to the difficulty of speaking. Again and again the characters fail to find the words they need. In both the political and the personal stories their voices die in their throats or the act of speech is physically painful. If they do gain the courage to speak, they encounter a terrible gulf between themselves and their audience. 'Well thou'lt speak at last,' says a neighbour to John when he takes the petition to London. Parliament will not listen. John Barton himself will not listen when Esther tries to warn him about Mary and Harry Carson: 'He would not listen to me; what can I do?' Next she turns to Jem, but he too rebuffs her. Trembling, she holds him in a 'firm and unusual grasp':

' "You must listen to me, Jem Wilson," she said, with almost an accent of command.

"Go away, missis; I've nought to do with you, either in hearkening or talking."

He made another struggle.

"You must listen," she said again authoritatively, "for Mary Barton's sake."

The spell of her name was as potent as that of the mariner's glittering eye. "He listened like a three-year child." ' (Ch. 14)

When men will not listen, confrontation replaces dialogue.

Gaskell hoped that her story would exert an Ancient Mariner's spell, breaking the listeners' resistance. She was making herself the voice of the outcast, deliberately confronting revulsion and fear: 'To whom shall the prostitute tell her tale! . . . Hers is the leper sin, and all shall stand aloof dreading to be counted unclean.' Sometimes a tale *must* be told, and a woman must speak out regardless of modesty, just as Mary speaks at Jem's trial, facing massed male ranks of lawyers, jury and judge: 'Now, when the beloved stood thus, abhorred of men, there would be no feminine shame to stand between her and her avowal.'

Gaskell knew that stories had a persuasive power beyond that of rational exposition: this is why she filled *Mary Barton* with inset tales, not, as is sometimes implied, because she lacked artistic self-control.[7] Each story contributes to and qualifies the whole. Alice's tale of exile from her rural 'home' evokes the country as a source of faith, as 'healing' as her gathered herbs. Job's story of bringing Margaret from London illustrates the potential tenderness of men. Margaret's account of a dormant scorpion roused to dangerous life by the heat of the fire suggests the suppressed violence of the workers. Esther's tale of her seduction shows her not as sinner but victim, her prostitution an act of maternal unselfishness.

Some of the stories and allusions function in a different way, summoning themes which lie beneath the surface narrative. Thus Will's sailor yarns and his dispute with Job over the existence of flying fish and mermaids, which may appear superfluous, suggest the different forms of truth which can be expressed by romance as opposed to investigative 'science'. They raise questions of language, evidence, appearance and metamorphosis which are integral to Gaskell's theme of division. And the story of the mermaid, set as it is in a land where women go 'half-naked', where muslin is too hot to wear and the sea is 'milk-warm', is crucial too in relating such duality to female desire.

Mary is ready to believe Will's tales, rather than Job's science, just as she is ready to believe the romances she reads at Miss Simmonds', even if his mermaid's comb did turn out to be a plain tooth-comb, not coral studded with pearls. She cannot see that she herself may be like the mermaid on the rock, a being of two natures, a 'fickle jade as did not rightly know her own mind'. The image hovers behind the ballad-like description of her misery when she awakens from her romantic dreams after Jem's arrest:

'She threw herself on the ground, yes, on the hard flags she threw her soft limbs down; and the comb fell out of her hair, and those bright tresses swept the dusty floor.' (Ch. 20)

It lingers too beneath the description of her despair on the Liverpool dock as she gazes into the water below, with the 'spectral thought' drifting in the depths of her mind that beneath that cold dismal surface there might be rest from the troubles of the earth. At last, in court she leaves the mermaid self behind when she hides 'the bright treasure of her hair' beneath her cap and tells of her love for Jem.

The theme of a double nature pervades *Mary Barton*, and images from fantasy, like the mermaid or Frankenstein's monster, locate this duality below rational understanding. They also display the author's own deep prejudices and fears – about sexuality, violence and political unrest. The mermaid in *Mary* is counterpointed by the monster Gaskell sees in John Barton, a sympathetic man, whose lack of education deprives him of wisdom: 'He acted to the best of his judgment, but it was a widely-erring judgment.'

'The actions of the uneducated seem to me typified in those of Frankenstein, that monster of many human qualities, ungifted with a soul, a knowledge of the difference between good and evil.

The people rise up to life; they irritate us, they terrify us, and we become their enemies. Then, in the sorrowful moment of our triumphant power, their eyes gaze on us with mute reproach. Why have we made them what they are; a powerful monster, yet without the inner means for peace and happiness?' (Ch. 15)

Part of the tragedy of Mary Shelley's monster, if read in Gaskell's sense, is his desperate search to understand his origins, his identity, the purpose of his creation. She sees the people in the same light, as neglected children turning on their creators. The monster, we remember, has no mother, only a 'father'.[8] Fathers, of course, can be loving too: in Green Heys Fields the infants are 'mostly carried by their fathers'; John Barton and George Wilson are 'rough and tender nurses'; Job caresses Margaret like a mother; Mary, waking new born from fever, gazes at Jem, 'as a baby does when it sees its mother tending its little cot'. And the mothers we actually see are far from perfect. When Mary dreams of the protecting mother of her child-hood, Gaskell points out that in reality the daughter was the stronger personality. Although the one 'seed of the future soul' in Mary's garrulous, intriguing friend Sally Leadbetter is her love for her aged mother, we are quickly told that 'the mother was lightly principled like Sally herself'. The actual is not the point; the image transcends reality. Mrs Wilson may be fretful and jealous, but when Jem thinks of enlisting or turning to drink, 'the thought of his mother stood like an angel with a drawn sword in the way to sin'. The ghosts of her mother and sister haunt Esther's guilty dreams; and when Mary falls for Henry Carson, Gaskell asks us to remember how 'motherless' she is.

The 'mother' is at once the sword of conscience and the fountain of mercy, who gives to a child 'tender words of comfort, be her grief or error what it might'. (Despite all external evidence, Mrs Wilson never doubts Jem's innocence: 'Mother-like!' says Job Legh.) The link of mother and child takes precedence over all, defying circumstance and language: on his way to murder Harry Carson John Barton restores a child to its mother and receives a deluge of 'Irish blessings'; Mary, reeling under the news of Jem's arrest, stops to give food to a hungry boy, caught by a cry of 'Mama mia'. But the workers, crying out in hunger and distress, are met not by maternal kindness but by stubborn patriarchal authority. In response they too become hard and aggressive and the tender discrimination of the mother is replaced by the inflexible 'Law of the Fathers' – an eye for an eye, or, as Job puts it, 'a Death for a Death'.

The ethic of revenge is pre-Christian and as she strips her characters to the core, Gaskell exposes a desire for vengeance which mocks her age's supposed allegiance to the Gospels:

'Are ye worshippers of Christ? or of Alecto?

O, Orestes! you would have made a very tolerable Christian of the nineteenth century!' (Ch. 18)

The unions follow the New Testament when they care for their weaker members, but the ancient law of the Judaic Old Testament – or of the Greek Alecto – when they turn to intimidation and revenge. At one point a union agitator praises Lucius Brutus, who condemned his son to death for conspiring with his enemies – in the same way, Gaskell suggests, the unionists are ready to kill their brothers, the blacklegs who take their jobs.

Oppression breeds oppression, violence breeds violence. This is a primitive 'law' : when John Barton seeks revenge for his people, or

Carson blindly pursues the murderer of his son, they become 'wild beasts'. As an instrument of Carson's vengeance even the 'civilized' legal system turns into a creature with 'fangs'. And the opposing impulses of gentleness and sternness struggle for dominance within individuals as well as societies. In her delirious fever after the trial Mary recoils from her father's double nature:

'mingled even with the most tender expressions of love for her father, was a sort of horror of him; a dread of him as a blood-shedder, which seemed to separate him into two persons, – one, the father who had dandled her on his knee, and loved her all her life long; the other, the assassin, the cause of all her trouble and woe.' (Ch. 33)

Mary's own story expresses the theme of a dual nature not in familial but in sexual terms. The narratives of father and daughter, and the themes of death and love, are inextricably linked by coincidence of people and place. Their interdependence is shown by a single device, the Valentine which Jem gives Mary. On the reverse side of this card covered in hearts and flowers Job Legh copies the 'Song of the Poor' for John Barton, and then, carrying its double message, it becomes the wadding for the gun which kills Harry. Finally the paper is retrieved from the hedgerow by Esther, providing Mary with the evidence of her lover's innocence and her father's guilt.

In the romantic plot questions of innocence and guilt are explored within the individual psyche, felt, bodily, on the individual pulse. *Mary Barton* is an intensely sensual novel, concerned with taste, touch, texture, smell, sight. Much of its urgency comes from this physical force, the language of 'dizziness', beating hearts, swoons of fever or intense emotion, and from the variations in pace, with bursts of violent physical action or emotional conflict interspersed by long periods of 'waiting'. The elements themselves provide an overarching structure: the earth of Green Heys from which the action slowly grows; the blazing warehouse surrounded by the swarming crowds, which heralds destruction; the waters and winds of the Mersey which sweep towards the dramatic conclusion.

Elemental forces without mirror passions within; desire is felt in the rhythms of the prose and the mixed emotions of Harry, Jem, Mary, Will and Margaret. Gaskell's overt concern is the way that in a materialist society a girl like Mary confuses love and sex with dreams of wealth and status. Mary's beauty is her only hope. 'I wish I could

sing', she says, looking at Margaret's first earnings, 'I wish I were a
boy. I'd go to sea with you,' she tells Will. Like the manual skill of the
workers, her body is her sole asset, and is priced as such by her
employer and by Harry. Beneath Gaskell's analysis, however, lurks the
feeling that women, like men, have their darker side. The key figure in
Mary's inner conflict is Esther, the prostitute. After Mary has been
dreaming of her childhood, longing for her mother's comfort and love,
she hears a knock and a voice with the country accents she remembers:

'So, without fear, she rose and unbarred the door. There, against the
moonlight, stood a form, so closely resembling her dead mother that
Mary never doubted the identity, but exclaiming (as if she were a
terrified child, secure of all safety when near the protecting care of its
parent) —
"O! Mother! Mother! You are come at last?" she threw herself, or
rather fell into the trembling arms, of her long-lost, unrecognised Aunt
Esther.' (Ch. 20)

Esther's life and death open the narrative; not only is she the dark
'mother' of the heroine, but she is like a shadow of the author, a veiled
figure, hard to recognize, who follows the action from outside, who
peers through windows, tracking the partipants through the maze of
lanes, crying her warnings like Cassandra, intervening at crucial
moments of the plot.
  In John Barton's view it is Esther who causes his wife's death and
begins his own fatal hardening of heart: 'her giddiness, her lightness
had wrought this woe'. From this early attribution of blame, sexuality
and death brush closely together, as in the fatal device of the Valentine.
Jem thrills guiltily to Mary's touch even in his grief at his twin
brothers' deaths; Harry Carson flings five shillings to George Wilson
for the dying Davenport, as he leaves in a hurry, hoping to meet 'lovely
Mary Barton'; at Harry's death Mary feels guilty relief to be free of his
advances, while Harry's sisters are casually discussing his flirtations at
the moment his corpse is carried into the house. Filled with jealousy of
Harry, Jem warns Mary that the denial of her love may make him a
drunkard, a thief or a murderer. Just as John Barton is both tender
father and brutal murderer, so Jem can be both lover and avenger:

'Then uprose the guilty longing for blood! – the frenzy of jealousy! –
Some one should die. He would rather Mary were dead, cold in her

grave, than that she were another's. A vision of her pale, sweet face, with her bright hair, all bedabbled with gore, seemed to float constantly before his aching eyes.' (Ch. 14)

The sexuality of Esther and Mary, like that of Eve 'who wroughten all this woe' and brought death into the world, is linked throughout to men's propensity to violence. It is as if desire is inherently dangerous, an urge akin to rage that can only be tamed if transformed into unselfish protectiveness.

The fusion of sex and violence, love and cruelty, reaches its height in a rapid sequence of scenes in the middle of the narrative. Despair has 'settled as a heavy cloud' over the city, caught in a long winter frost. The Bartons' house is stripped of its much prized possessions and John has paid his fruitless visit to London. Both he and Mary are caught up with secret assignations, his with the union, hers with Harry Carson. As their closeness turns to hostility, John strikes her 'a hard blow', which 'blistered and reddened Mary's soft white skin with pain'. At this critical point Esther accosts John to warn him about Mary and Harry. Although John rejects her approach with loathing, the language of the scene, insisting on the woman's weakness and the man's rough strength, gives it a troubling undertone of sexual assault:

'He gripped her arm – the arm he had just before shaken off, and dragged her, faintly resisting, to the nearest lamp-post. He pushed the bonnet back, and roughly held the face she would fain have averted, to the light, and, in her large unnaturally bright grey eyes, her lovely mouth, half open, as if imploring the forbearance she could not ask for in words, he saw at once the long-lost Esther.' (Ch. 10)

He shakes her 'with passion' despite her appeals: 'In vain did her face grow deadly pale around the vivid circle of paint, in vain did she gasp for mercy – he burst forth again.' Finally he flings her 'trembling, sickening, fainting, from him' and strides away.

The sexual ambivalence is compounded by the references to 'Mary', the name of John's wife as well as his daughter, and then by his immediate identification of Mary with Esther, because of their 'very bodily likeness'. As he grows uncomfortably aware of his daughter's maturity John's previous indifference turns to anxious, possessive watchfulness. As Jem later suggests, we feel that there could be an alternative plot, in which the murder was motivated not by political bitterness but by John's jealous anger at Carson's pursuit of Mary, which he had 'bloodily resented'.

The scene in which Jem declares his love, in the following chapter, is also full of 'deep and violent emotion', alternating between threatening despair and 'fond, passionate entreaty'. It is a traumatic encounter which leaves Mary (like Esther, after her meeting with John) trembling and faint. In her ensuing exhaustion, as after some initiation, she first becomes aware of her own doubleness:

'It was as if two people were arguing the matter; that mournful desponding communion between her former self, and her present self. Herself, a day, an hour ago; and herself now.' (Ch. 11)

Almost immediately afterwards she has to struggle with Harry Carson. This is the only time we see the two together, and instead of a love scene it is yet another form of assault in which Harry not only grips and hurts Mary, but exposes the true value of his love, his feeling 'that at any price he must have her, only that he would obtain her as cheaply as he could'.

Mary finally escapes: 'with a wrench, for which she had reserved all her strength, she was off like a bolt'. While she eludes Harry, and rejects the Esther side of herself, her good looks make it impossible for her not to be judged in sexual terms. Even Mrs Sturgis, the Liverpool boatman's kindly wife, is suspicious that so beautiful a girl should be alone in the city at night. Despite her doubts she, at last, offers the 'motherly' sympathy which Gaskell suggests should be given to the Esthers of the world:

' "Perhaps" (sinking her voice a little) "thou'rt a bad one; I almost misdoubt thee, thou'rt so pretty. Well-a-well! it's the bad ones as have the broken hearts, sure enough; good folk never get utterly cast down, they've always getten hope in the Lord; it's the sinful as bear the bitter, bitter grief in their crushed hearts, poor souls; it's them we ought, most of all, to pity and to help. She shanna leave the house to-night, choose who she is, – worst woman in Liverpool, she shanna." ' (Ch. 31)

Like Mrs Sturgis, Mary learns to separate the sin from the sinner. She cannot 'reconcile the two ideas, of her father and a blood-shedder', but she pities and helps him: 'his crime was a thing apart, never more to be considered by her'.

John Barton escapes the courts, but, as Gaskell told Mrs Greg, his 'course of action, violating the eternal laws of God', brings 'its own punishment of an avenging conscience far more difficult to bear than any worldly privation'. Even this is not enough. Mary and Jem might be willing to set the crimes of John and Esther aside and care for the person, but Gaskell, their creator, must punish their guilt. Both must die. Both crawl back to their old home, John like a ghost, Esther like a wounded animal. Defined throughout by her 'bedraggled finery', Mary and Jem find her on the pavement: 'fallen into what appeared simply a heap of white or light-coloured clothes, fainting or dead lay the poor crushed Butterfly – the once innocent Esther'.

John Barton has already died, in the arms of a reformed Mr Carson, turned from revenge to pity. When Gaskell forces her tale to a suitably reformist conclusion, the nervous accommodations of the opening return. Few readers in the 1840s or since have been convinced by Carson's conversion or have felt that his unspecified improvements in 'the system of employment in Manchester' will be more than a drop in the ocean. In a rather terrible way it is suggested that the rich are reformed by witnessing the suffering of the poor, a suffering which they themselves have caused; even the innocent Jem and Mary are driven to emigration.

The deeper implications of the ending are expressed less through the reformation of Carson than through the deaths of John and Esther, a psychic catharsis which clears the stage and allows the living to start afresh. Only by annihilating one side of their natures – the violent father and the sexual, narcissistic 'mother' – can men and women be freed from the maze to escape to a 'New World'. In Canada Jem and Mary settle outside a town, in a clearing where only one of the 'old primeval trees' remains. Here they wait with their child for Margaret, Will and Job to join them – the art, imagination and science of the world they have left. Balancing the opening rural paradise of Green Heys, this is an Eden not of innocence but of experience, a fitting symbolic conclusion for 'a tragic poem'.

Elizabeth Gaskell felt, as she said of Francis Newman, that the secret of true eloquence was in pouring out what the heart was full of; rephrasing the Romantic notion of art, defined by Wordsworth as 'the spontaneous overflow of powerful feelings'. She felt too that fiction and poetry could be both more accurate and more powerful than argument because they dealt in the complexities of feeling as well as with ideas and facts. She strove to submerge her own emotions while conveying those of her characters, as if she had internalized William's disapproval of introspection as 'morbid' and incorporated it into her theory of art: *Mary Barton* was born of a mother's grief, but it is also a vehement public statement.

Theoretically, Gaskell's model of the writer was as an objective recorder; like John Ruskin in the first volumes of *Modern Painters*, also in the 1840s, she merged the expressive ideal with an older aesthetic, inherited in part from the eighteenth century, of a literal 'truth' to nature, of the accurate representation of facts and events. When she praised the writing of Mary Howitt's daughter in 1850, it was because, as Mary explained, 'she says you do not make the reader see things with your eyes but you present the scene itself to him'.[9] Her most explicit statement of this ideal (in which one sometimes feels she protests too much) appears in a long letter of 1859 giving advice to Herbert Grey on a novel, *The Three Paths*.[10] Is the form being used, she asks, merely to convey opinions? 'If so you had better have condensed them into the shape of an Essay.' But if the writer wishes to 'narrate', as she suspects.

'I think you must observe what is *out* of you, instead of examining what is *in* you. It is always an unhealthy sign when we are too conscious of any of the physical processes that go on within us; & I believe in like manner that we ought not to be too cognizant of our mental proceedings, only taking note of the results. But certainly – whether introspection be morbid or not, – it is not \ a / safe {for a nov} training for a novelist. It is a weakening of the art which has crept in of late years. Just read a few pages of De Foe &c – and you will see the healthy way in which he sets *objects* not *feelings* before you. I am sure the right way is this. You are an Electric telegraph something or other.' (L541)

She sounds startlingly modern in her reference to the telegraph, a new and still semi-magical-seeming means of direct, instantaneous communication. Her first concern is with technique; Herbert Grey must write about the life he knows, must keep the language simple and, most vital of all, must find a good plot. She offers a metaphor: a novel is not like a body but like an 'anatomical drawing' – the skeleton must be outlined before the artist can add flesh and muscle and then, finally, clothes. This is an 'outside' image, in contrast to the involuntary origins and organic inner development she had attributed to *Mary Barton*. She told Lady Kay-Shuttleworth that its dark tone was due to 'the choice of the subject; which yet I did not *choose*, but which was as it were impressed upon me'. Elsewhere, describing its composition, she wrote:

'The whole tale grew up in my mind as imperceptibly as a seed germinates in the earth, so I cannot trace back now why or how such a thing was written, or such a character or circumstance introduced.' (L74)

While writing, she said, she felt the story growing almost of its own accord, governed by a single overriding idea: 'I can remember now that the prevailing thought in my mind at the time when the tale was silently forming itself and impressing me with the force of a reality, was the seeming injustice of the inequalities of fortune.'

Saying that the tale 'formed itself', of course, usefully absolved her of responsibility – we know that she made a careful plan before she started writing – but her 1859 letter, despite its emphasis on objectivity, evokes a similar process. After the conscious effort of planning and developing the plot the story exerts its own force; it is as if the author were a conduit rather than a creator:

'Then set to & imagine yourself a spectator & auditor of every scene & event! Work hard at this till it becomes a reality to you, – a thing you have to recollect & describe & report fully & accurately as it struck you, in order that your reader may have it equally before him. Don't intrude yourself into your description. If you think but eagerly of your story till *you see it in action*, words, good, simple words, will come, – just as if you saw an accident in the street \ that impressed you strongly/ you would describe it forcibly.' (L542)

In 1849 Elizabeth insisted to Tottie Fox, who was struck by the verisimilitude of Mary Barton, that 'nobody and nothing was real (I am sorry for you, but I must tell the truth) in M. Barton' except the character of John: the circumstances are different but the character and some of the speeches, are exactly a poor man I know'. She was glad Tottie liked Mary – 'I do, but people are angry with her just because she is not perfect.' Then she added:

'I told the story according to a fancy of my own; to really SEE the scenes I tried to describe, (and they WERE as real as my own life at the time) and then to tell them as nearly as I could, as if I were speaking to a friend over the fire on a winter's night and describing real occurrences. I am at the end of my paper, and the girls are waiting with lessons to say.' (L82)

Her own imagined scenes rose up and possessed her. From *Mary Barton* onwards Elizabeth's writing provided a second, competing world, as vivid and demanding as her daily life, which she could enter and leave at will.

Fame and New Friends

In 1850 Elizabeth wrote to the American critic John Seely Hart:

'The writing of "Mary Barton" was a great pleasure to me; and I became so deeply, sometimes painfully, interested in it, that I don't think I cared at the time of its publication what reception it met with. I was sure a great deal of it was truth, and I knew that I had realized all my people to myself so vividly that parting with them was like parting with friends. But the reception it met with was a great surprize to me. I neither expected the friends nor the enemies which it has made me. But the latter I am thankful to say are disappearing while the former are (some of them,) friends for life.' (L115)

As soon as it appeared *Mary Barton* sparked off furious arguments, especially, of course, in Manchester. Elizabeth was not quite so surprised as she protested, but she had been living among like-minded people – the Winkworths, the Robberdses, the Darbishires – for so long that she was shocked by the vehemence of the outcry against the book from other quarters. Many local people, including some of the rich manufacturers in the Cross Street congregation, were outraged and mortified. They felt the novel vilified the masters and glorified the workers, wilfully ignoring market forces and the capitalists' share of the risks. By remaining silent about the charitable efforts of recent years, it cast a slur on their whole city. It was an incitement not to greater understanding but to greater class tension.

Anger was matched by curiosity, since the wealth of local detail made it clear that the anonymous writer must live among them. Chapman had been sending Elizabeth copies through a local bookseller, Simms and Dinham of Queen Ann Square, and it seems that it was Simms who first pointed the finger at her: within weeks she found herself in the limelight. At first she tried hard to remain incognito, fending off inquiries by fostering the rumour that the author was Elizabeth Stone, now Mrs Wheeler, 'author of some book called "The Cotton Lord" '.

The ruse worked, briefly, and she wrote wryly to Chapman that she feared he too would be convinced, 'and transact that part of the business that remains unaccomplished with her'. If she did not want the publicity, she did want her money. But, as Mary Howitt had said, 'Publishers are slow.' In December Elizabeth dropped the coyness and demanded payment outright, almost as compensation for the distress she was feeling:

'Hitherto the whole affair of publication has been one of extreme annoyance to me, from the impertinent and unjustifiable curiosity of people, who have tried to force me either into an absolute denial, or an acknowledgement of what they must have seen the writer wanted to keep concealed.' (L64)

It seems hard to berate Chapman for the assaults on her privacy. He responded calmly, sending the first half of her payment, promising to correct the errors in printing the dialect and attempting to soothe her alarm about the public interest. Curiosity extended beyond Lancashire: her London cousin Henry Holland and his friend Lady Coltman soon guessed she was the author and spread her name among their circle. Mary Ewart, a Manchester friend who was then staying with Lady Coltman, certainly knew. '*I cannot imagine how*?' Gaskell asked ingenuously, admitting that now she saw the reaction she was almost frightened by her boldness. By early December, increasingly uncomfortable at the deceit involved in protecting her anonymity, she gave in and admitted the truth.

She had already faced several reviews in November, including the *Athenaeum*, the *Examiner* and the *Literary Gazette*. All were complimentary.[1] 'Who writes the literary reviews in the Examiner?' she asked Chapman, guessing rightly that it was John Forster. Gleeful acquaintances forecast (correctly) that she would be praised by the *Westminster* and attacked by the *British Quarterly*. The thought of adverse criticism shook her less than the 'angry feeling towards me personally among some of those I live amongst' and some people's insistence that her book would do harm: 'I am sure in the long run it will not; I have faith that what I wrote so earnestly & from the fulness of my heart must be right.'

Her faith sometimes wavered, although everyone acknowledged the power of her novel; most readers seem to have cried. The drama and pathos were heightened when the book was read aloud, as nineteenth-century novels so often were. Mary and William Howitt had read it to each other in manuscript for two hours each evening (William had to take over when Mary's eyes were weak from crying); Lucy Holland read it to her father Peter; Maria Edgeworth's sister read it to her.[2] The emotional impact was not always quite what the author intended: one reader, the wife of Thomas Bayley Potter (a prominent member of the Cross Street congregation), was the sister of Thomas Ashton, murdered during the strike of 1831. According to her son, 'on coming to the chapter of the murder she suddenly realised that it was a description of her own brother's assassination, and she fainted'.[3]

The whole book was too close to home for many Manchester people and Elizabeth smarted under their disapproval. From November to January she was on edge, boosting her spirits with news that Edmund Potter was going to buy the book for his men, 'since he thinks it is so true'. She confided to Katie Winkworth, 'some say the masters are very sore, but I'm sure I *believe* I wrote the truth', and wrote defensively to Mary Ewart: 'No one can feel more deeply than I how *wicked* it is to do anything to excite class against class, and the sin has been most unconscious if I have done so.' She had simply drawn attention to ills which must be recognized. To sympathizers like Julia Lamont and Mary Greg she explained the underlying concepts at length, and in January, having withdrawn to the safety of Southport for a week, she told her cousin Edward:

'My poor Mary Barton is stirring up all sorts of angry feelings against me in Manchester; but those best acquainted with the way of thinking & feeling among the poor acknowledge its *truth*; which is the acknowledgement I most of all desire, because evils being once recognised are half way on towards their remedy.' (L827)

An early testimony to the novel's truth came from a valued source: Thomas Carlyle. Before publication she had asked for copies to be sent to writers she admired, Dickens and Carlyle among them. Dickens never acknowledged his – a poor start to their future relationship.

Elizabeth was piqued but shrugged off the omission by claiming she had sent the copies more for her own satisfaction than for thanks. Carlyle, however, wrote almost at once. Just before the novel appeared Chapman had asked: 'Am I at liberty to tell your name to anyone? Dickens or Carlyle should they ask? I will, if you wish it, preserve a profound mystery.'⁴ She opted for mystery, but Carlyle may, as Elizabeth thought, have heard her name mentioned by the Holland set. At any rate he at once identified the writer as a woman, opening his letter: 'Dear Madam . . . (for I catch the treble of that melodious voice very well)'. Both he and Jane, he said, had read the book with real pleasure, and he praised her 'cheerfully pious, social, clear and observant character' as well as the astute choice of a new and important field. In his view *Mary Barton* stood 'far above the ordinary garbage of Novels', and fulfilled the aims of its preface:

'I gratefully accept it as a real contribution (about the first real one) towards developing a huge subject, which has lain dumb too long, and really ought to speak for itself, and tell us its meaning a little, if there be any voice in it at all. Speech or literature (which is, or should be, select speech) could hardly find a more rational function, I think, at present.'⁵

His letter was comforting too in its certainty that she would write more, and that *Mary Barton* would open the way: 'May you live long to write good books.'

Carlyle's praise was a source of strength in the agitation of the next few months. She tried to immerse herself in daily life, in Sunday-school work, concerts and visits to friends, and there were occasional high spots, like the excitement at Christmas over Emily Winkworth's engagement to William Shaen, but the reception of her book clouded her spirits, like the Manchester weather itself: 'the perfection of dreariness, grey black fog close to the house; clinging to everything and penetrating to one's very soul'. She was becoming quite notorious, as Geraldine Jewsbury (who thought the novel 'most powerful') told Arthur Hugh Clough in January:

'I know the author of Mary Barton. She is a very nice woman and was much admired before any of us suspected her of writing a book. It has however raised a great clamour, for it is said to be dreadfully *one sided*.'⁶

In February a third edition had brought fierce criticism of that 'one-sidedness' in the *Manchester Guardian*, and at the same time the expected blast came from the *British Quarterly*, which called *Mary Barton* 'mischievous' and complained of the exaggerated picture of industrial misery and strife and the 'very great injustice to the employers'.[7] Elizabeth was downcast despite the support of men like Samuel Bamford, who wrote her a long letter in early March, saying he had read the book at one go: 'I care not what the critics say . . . It seems to me that you have begun a great work and I hope you will not be discouraged from going on with it.'[8] He found it true to his experience: 'of John Bartons, I have known hundreds, his very self in all things except his fatal crime'. These were comforting words, but the climate was still dreary: she needed a change.

This time, when she thought of escaping Manchester, her mind did not turn as it usually did to the country but to London, the home of those who had encouraged her most; the Howitts, Shaens, Chapman, Carlyle. She made up her mind, booked lodgings (on the Darbishires' advice) and wrote to Edward Chapman. He was delighted and immediately sent out for 'orders' on her behalf – special tickets to concerts, lectures and plays – but he also warned her, like a cautious uncle, against the danger of being 'lionized'. It is hard to believe that she was so naïve, but celebrity in London, like ostracism in Manchester, seems hardly to have crossed her mind. She promised to be on her guard, and assured him that Anne Holland, who was to accompany her, would swiftly puncture any bubble of vanity: 'Luckily for me Miss Holland possesses excellent sense, and a very fair proportion of satirical power, which she is not at all unwilling to exert.' She claimed that she only wished to come as a tourist: 'Oh dear! I wish poor Mary Barton could be annihilated in this month; and then I might go where I liked, & do & see what I liked naturally & simply.'

In February she found time for distractions like G. H. Lewes's lectures on speculative philosophy at the Athenaeum. Unlike Emerson, Lewes pleased his Manchester audience, greatly. They liked his 'contemptuous treatment of metaphysics and exaltation of science . . . It was pleasant to be told that though you had never troubled yourself about the "problems of life and mind", you were just as wise as any of the long series of sages who had wended their way along the "high *priori* road", which, according to Lewes, led nowhere.'[9] Lewes also gave his sympathetic portrayal of Shylock at the Theatre Royal in March, and Elizabeth, suspicious at first, decided that she rather liked him. She was later to change her mind.

Meanwhile plans were laid in London and Dickens invited her to dinner on 31 March.[10] Then, it seems, the visit was postponed for a week or two (one of the girls was ill), and it was not until mid-April that Elizabeth and Anne arrived in Bloomsbury, in their 'little, dusty, noisy lodgings in Panton Square'.[11]

Elizabeth had plenty of close connections in London. Her brother-in-law Sam Gaskell was now working there for the Lunacy Commission, and Edward Tagart, William's old friend, was minister at Little Portland Street Chapel; his boisterous, outspoken family welcomed her warmly. She met the Howitts, who had recently moved into town from Clapton, and, most important of all, she renewed her acquaintance with her distant relations, Fanny and Hensleigh Wedgwood. Hensleigh was a kindly, unworldly man (to the distraction of his family, he had lost his job as a magistrate by refusing, on principle, to take the oath). While he withdrew to his study to follow his passion for etymology, his wife, Fanny, daughter of the influential Whig MP Sir James Mackintosh, loved politics, parties and literary society. Although she was ten years older than Elizabeth, she immediately took her under her wing, and the Wedgwoods' daughters Julia and Euphemia (known as Snow and Effie) would later become lifelong friends of Marianne and Meta.[12] Through Fanny and Hensleigh Elizabeth met other family connections again, especially Hensleigh's cousins Charles and Erasmus, or Ras, Darwin (with whom Fanny was rumoured to have maintained a long and discreet affair). The Wedgwoods were close friends of Harriet Martineau and the Carlyles, and, like Harriet, Fanny had long been an advocate of women's rights.

On this trip to London Elizabeth also met Anna Jameson, another of the older generation of feminists. Irish born, intelligent and sensible, Mrs Jameson was a greatly liked figure who had first won fame for her novel *The Diary of an Ennuyée* in 1826, and for her 1832 study *Shakespeare's Heroines. Characteristics of Women, Moral, Poetical and Historical.* Now a respected art critic, she was almost equally well known for her unhappy marriage (she had separated from her husband in 1836) and for her views on women – her article 'Women's Mission and Women's Position', included in her *Memoirs and Essays* in 1846, had mounted a straightforward attack on the notion of the 'angel in the house'.

Anna Jameson's support would prove important to Elizabeth, particularly in her anxieties over *Ruth*, but during this stay, at least at first, she was more interested in sightseeing than politics or feminism. In late April she teamed up with Emily Winkworth, who was staying with her aunt in Islington to be close to her fiancé, William Shaen. Together they visited Lincoln's Inn and the Temple, where Elizabeth became quite dizzy with rapture, declaring she was sure her character would change if she could only live in oak-roofed halls and gaze through Gothic windows. London seemed full of romance. She thought the city and the parties exhilarating, in complete contrast to Charlotte Brontë, who would find the same process such an ordeal later in 1849, or to the young John Ruskin, who would moan to his mother about literary life the following year: 'terrible party last night – stiff – large – dull – fidgety – strange – run-against-everybody-know-nobody sort of party!'[13]

Even Elizabeth was slightly overwhelmed. The words 'whirled about' and 'confused' recur in her letters and she found it difficult to recall every moment, however hard she tried: the sparkling conversation of an 'intoxicating evening' at the house of the poet Bryan Procter (who wrote as Barry Cornwall) was forgotten in the morning light, she said: 'the foam has faded from the Champagne'.

There was one initial disappointment. Jane Carlyle asked her to 'a *quiet tea*', saying how much Carlyle would like to meet her. The sage himself, apparently, had not been consulted. Elizabeth sat an hour in the dining-room while Jane peered anxiously out at the garden, where, according to a furious Emily Winkworth, 'her great rude husband was walking backwards and forwards in a dirty Scotch plaid smoking'. Despite four appeals he would not come in, and at last Jane went out herself, 'but it was no use, and she came back looking *so* mortified'. Carlyle behaved better on later occasions and Elizabeth, in any case, would have forgiven him anything. At the end of her stay he made up for his earlier silence by 'spouting for a good hour . . . a regular Jeremiad on the condition of England, Ireland and the rest of the habitable globe'. 'Wasn't it good of Lily to take me?' asked Emily.[14]

Anne and Emily accompanied Lily on most occasions (although she would doubtless have sailed through on her own), and she soon found a new ally and lasting friend in Eliza Fox, who lived with her father in Charlotte Street, a few minutes' walk from Panton Square. Tottie (as all her friends called her) was now twenty-eight, and just as unconventional as might be expected of the daughter of W. J. Fox. Fox had long argued for liberal education for women and for changes in the divorce and marriage laws (it was he, incidentally, who introduced Harriet Taylor to John Stuart Mill in 1830). Eliza grew up a feminist, like many daughters of this circle: Annie and Emma Shaen, Anna Mary Howitt, Adelaide Procter, Bessie Parkes and the leader of them all, Barbara Leigh Smith (later Barbara Bodichon). She had wanted to go on the stage – friends remembered her as a great reader, a talent inherited from her father, who used to lie on the sofa, 'his big head with long greyish locks thrown back on the cushions', giving spellbinding impromptu Shakespearian readings.[15] Fox was nervous about a theatrical career for Tottie and, after being dissuaded by his actor friend Macready (who said she was too small), at the age of twenty she took up art instead: 'rather an unusual and independent step for a girl to take, when I was young'.[16] She had studied with Anna Mary Howitt at Sass's school and was now a successful portrait painter, exhibiting at the Royal Academy in 1848.

Tottie had first heard of Elizabeth one evening at the Howitts' the year before. Half a century later she still remembered that summer evening, and how Mary's 'busy needles used to fly, turning out roll after roll of pretty lace edging':

'Mrs Howitt was describing the new novel which was expected to make such a sensation. She and her husband had read it in manuscript and had been appealed to by the yet unknown author to help find a publisher. They were full of sympathy for the authoress, the sweet Manchester lady who had roused herself from her bitter grief for the loss of her little son.'[17]

When they met in the spring of 1849, Tottie was entranced by Elizabeth's 'radiant smile and clear blue eyes'. She got a copy of *Mary Barton* from a library and was sitting in the studio reading when she was surprised by a knock and 'a bell-like voice', and Elizabeth entered. They found much in common. Tottie sent her the first issue of *David Copperfield*, published on 1 May. Thanking 'Miss Fox', on 5 May, Elizabeth wrote:

'I don't know if you did *finally* ask us to dinner at five on Wednesday; but the Fates (in the shape of Mr Forster,) seem to have determined it for us, whether you will or no, my dear! And we mean to Sadlers-Wells it afterwards, as you proposed. May we?' (L77)

The note of diffidence soon vanished, and the letters began, 'Dear Eliza': '(I sha'nt Miss Fox you any more. I wish you were here I am so lonely, for Emily is gone to the opera.)' Tottie had joined the ranks of the confidantes.

Elizabeth found her vitality and informality a relief from the more boring aspects of lionizing. Tottie recalled one party, where the hostess was determined to show her off and 'Mrs Gaskell determined not to be victimised'. She spotted a sofa in the corner, well protected by a large table:

'In an unguarded moment she ensconced herself at the farthest end of it, motioning to myself and another young friend to follow and protect her in her retreat . . . She made us sit between herself and the rest of the party, thus keeping them at bay for a great part of the evening, while engaging us in continuous and delightful conversation. We felt very naughty, and I believe we all three enjoyed ourselves very much.'[18]

Another new confidant was John Forster, who had arranged that dinner with Tottie. Forster was also a Unitarian and had been born and brought up in Newcastle, where he attended William Turner's Hanover Square Chapel and acquired an early love of debate at the Newcastle Lit. and Phil. He had left Tyneside for Cambridge, London and the Bar, in early 1829, only a few months before Elizabeth came to live with the Turners. She had read his reviews and journalism in W. J. Fox's *Sun*, and in Dickens's *Daily News* and the *Examiner* (of which Forster became editor in 1847), and she admired his *Lives of Eminent British Statesmen* and recent biography of Oliver Goldsmith. She appreciated his championship of *Mary Barton* and was equally grateful for, if subdued, by his criticism:

'I wish people wd tell author's privately & *fully* what are their real faults. I, for one, should be thankful. I try and find out the places where Mr Forster said I strained after commonplace materials for effect, till the whole book dances before my eyes as a commonplace piece of effect.' (L69)

She thought the best course might be simply to forget writing and follow Carlyle's advice to 'do silently good actions which is far more indispensable'.

Forster became a friend as well as a mentor. They liked each other at once. 'Lily is deep in love with Mr Forster,' reported Emily, adding that 'Mr. F. himself is little, and *very* fat and affected, yet *so* clever and shrewd and good-hearted and right-minded'.[19] He was the perfect guide to the London literary scene, a complex man who had offset his loneliness and sense of being an outsider at the Bar (he was a Newcastle butcher's son) by close friendships with older men – Leigh Hunt, Lamb, Bulwer-Lytton, Macready, Landor, Carlyle – and with contemporaries like Dickens, Browning and Tennyson. While these younger friends provided a host of godchildren, they all saw Foster as a confirmed bachelor: when he finally married Eliza Colburn in 1856, Dickens wrote, 'After I knew it (from himself) this morning, I lay down flat, as if an Engine and Tender had fallen upon me.'[20]

Bewhiskered and rotund, studious and high principled at this stage of his life John Forster was also gregarious, jolly and unpredictable, capable of sweeping Jane Carlyle into a dance, breaking into a comic turn or acting (extremely well) in amateur theatricals. He did like to dominate and his pomposity could drive his friends to fury (years later Dickens caricatured him cruelly as Podsnap in *Our Mutual Friend*), but he was consistently generous with his legal and editorial advice. In Thackeray's words, sardonic but not untrue, he was 'Great and Beneficent like a Superior Power . . . whenever anybody is in a scrape we all fly to him for refuge. He is omniscient and works miracles.'[21]

Forster worked his miracles for Gaskell. He squired her round town and had her to dine at his book-lined rooms in Lincoln's Inn Fields. For the next five years they wrote to each other frequently; Forster published extracts from William's lectures on the Lancashire dialect in the *Examiner*, and fulfilled a host of small requests. More significantly, he advised Elizabeth on her dealings with her publishers, especially Dickens. She respected him, but was never 'awe stricken', as (with a certain air of satisfaction) she indiscreetly told him that Geraldine Jewsbury was: ' "I never dare to say anything that is not profound sense before him", she says: so I (in private) wince and shrink up at the idea of all I have said that is not sensible.' They met whenever she came to London, losing touch only after he married and partially retired from literary life to become secretary to the Lunacy Commission.

John Forster was not the only one to pronounce on her work. When she spent a couple of nights with the Howitts, the music critic Henry Chorley gave her 'a great dose of literary advice', managing at the same time to prophesy that if she took all the advice offered, her next book would be a failure. Her next book, however, seemed happily distant; *Mary Barton* was still uppermost in her mind. In April new reviews appeared. One was a biting, forcefully argued attack in the *Edinburgh* by the Gaskells' Manchester friend William Rathbone Greg, who followed earlier critics in castigating her biased picture of the masters, her exaggeration of the animosity between the classes, her unfair picture of Manchester and her total ignorance of economics. To balance this, however, the novel won high praise from William and Mary Turner Ellis in the *Westminster* for its reformist aims and new-style heroine, 'One of Labour's daughters', while Charles Kingsley, in *Fraser's Magazine*, declared roundly: 'we would placard its sheets on every wall, and have them read aloud from every pulpit, till a nation, calling itself Christian, began to act upon the awful facts contained in it'.[22]

Both criticism and praise made Elizabeth even more of a celebrity. She was taken up by the elderly poet Sam Rogers, now eighty-six, but still determined to keep his finger on the pulse of literary gossip. At dinner with Dickens he asked Jane Welsh Carlyle quite openly if her husband was still infatuated with Lady Asburton. Jane thought he 'ought to have been buried long ago, so old and ill-natured is he grown . . . Very devilish old man! but he got no satisfaction to his devilishness out of *me*.'[23] (Elizabeth, after the same dinner, merely remarked mildly that the old poet looked very unfit to be in such a large party.) He treated her courteously, inviting her to breakfast on 7 May, with Forster, Catherine Dickens and Mrs Macready. His breakfasts at 22 St James Place, to which he never asked more than three or four people, were 'celebrated throughout Europe for their particular refinement and taste', as Charlotte Brontë explained to her father in 1851.[24]

Breakfasts were smart social events. One notable day, 12 May, began at Richard Monckton Milnes's, 'a very short two hours which everyone said was the proper number of hours to stay at breakfast'. The throng included, according to Anne Holland, 'the House of Lords', as well as such dignitaries as François Guizot, the historian and former prime minister of France, ousted in the revolution of 1848, William Whewell, scientist, professor of moral philosophy and Master of Trinity College, Cambridge, and Archdeacon Hare, an eminent theologian. Typically, the conversation Elizabeth liked best was a long gossip with Whewell (before she knew who he was) 'about Silverdale and all our dear places in the North'. Emily noticed that she also spoke at length to the Christian Socialists F. D. Maurice and John Ludlow, 'all about the right things and nothing else'.[25]

Later on, dropping with tiredness after visiting the Royal Academy and the picture-gallery at Stafford House, Elizabeth dressed for the grand dinner given by Dickens to celebrate the opening issue of *David Copperfield*. Among the guests were Rogers, Forster, Douglas Jerrold of *Punch*, the illustrator Hablot Browne, the Tagarts, the poet and philanthropist John Kenyon, Thackeray and the Carlyles. After dinner they were joined by many more. The whole occasion roused great indignation in Jane Carlyle. It was her first visit to Devonshire Terrace, and she pursed her lips at Dickens's 'getting up of steam', so unbecoming to a literary man, and the way that the dinner 'was served up in the new fashion – not placed on the table at all – but handed round – only the dessert on the table and quantities of *artificial* flowers – but such an overloaded dessert! pyramids of figs raisins oranges – ach!' Amid this ostentation Jane saw Elizabeth as a victim: 'I had already seen her at my house: a natural unassuming woman whom they have been doing their best to spoil by making a lioness of her.'[26]

Elizabeth rather enjoyed being spoilt. Lacking Jane's acid, she wrote to Annie Green in Knutsford about Dickens's study, not his dessert, his guests, not his grandeur. The man himself she found harder to describe, although at dinner she was placed between Dickens and Jerrold, while Anne sat between Carlyle and Rogers: 'Anne heard the most sense, and I the most wit.' It was Jerrold's wit and odd appearance, not Dickens's, that she mentioned: 'I never heard anyone so witty as Douglas Jerrold, who is a very little deformed man with grey flowing hair, and very fine eyes.' By the next day his remarks had slipped from her memory, but what she *did* remember, characteristically, was a woman's story, featuring two strong, odd women – Jane Carlyle and her Annandale servant, who could never get used to titles:

'so when Count Pepoli called she announced him as Mr Compilloly; Lord Jeffrey as Lorcherfield; and simply repeated it louder & louder each time; till at last Mrs Carlyle said "What is it – man, woman or beast?" to which the servant answered "a little wee gentleman

Ma'am." Miss Fanny Kemble called in a hat & a habit, and when Mrs C. spoke to the servant about bringing Miss K. in, unannounced, the servant said "I did not know if it was a Mr or Mrs." ' (L828–9)

This anecdotal kind of humour, focusing on character, situation and speech ('woman's talk', as Susanna Winkworth once described it) appealed to Elizabeth, and was used by her far more than the competitive 'male wit' of epigram and *bon mot*. With its oddity, exasperation and marvellous scrambling of language Jane's story could almost be a Scottish version of an incident in *Cranford*.

Elizabeth continued to see the Dickens family, going with Catherine Dickens and her sister, for example, to Tothill Fields Prison to inspect the 'silent associated system' recommended by Thomas Wright. Forster came too and in Emily's view the trip degenerated rapidly from social concern to 'a matter of mere amusement'.[27] Dickens took her to the opera, thus missing a meeting with Thomas Talfourd: 'I am engaged, (for my sins) to go with Mary Barton to the German opera and to dine with her first.'[28] If Dickens found it a chore, Elizabeth too had had enough by now. She packed in a final visit to Hampton Court, and a dinner at the Whittington Club for Louis Blanc, but the rest of this week was spent in farewells – including visits to Sam Rogers, to see his Etruscan and Egyptian treasures and his famous collection of pictures, among them works by Raphael, Titian, Rembrandt, Rubens, Velázquez, Poussin and Watteau. She also went to say goodbye to the Carlyles in Chelsea. Here she stopped to look once more at her father's old home in Beaufort Row, the site of the lonely visits to London as a girl, a great contrast to this adult triumph.

She had been dazzled by London but not blinded. Her reactions were those of a true provincial, wide-eyed but wary, and her suspicion of metropolitan gloss can be felt in the glib dinner-table talk of *North and South*. One of her strengths as a writer was that she felt herself to be, and deliberately remained, an outsider. She had been thrilled, however, to meet authors whose books she had admired from afar, and from now on she keenly solicited autographs from London acquaintances. (The Gaskell collection of autograph letters, now in the John Rylands Library, is suggestive both of Elizabeth's mingled modesty and impudence – in the way, for instance, that she begged John Kenyon to send her a letter from Elizabeth Barrett Browning in

1853 – and of the complex, overlapping circles of Victorian literature, philanthropy, politics and religion.)[29]

The Londoners, for their part, had liked her precisely because she was unaffected. When Crabb Robinson met her at breakfast with Edward Chapman on 22 April, he described her in his notebook as 'a woman of agreeable manners, with a hale florid complexion with nothing literary about her appearance – she pleased me'.[30] She made a similar impression on Charles and Mary Cowden Clarke, whose Bayswater neighbour Helen Tagart came round one day to say that Mrs Gaskell was coming to lunch: would they like to meet her?

'Joyfully did we accept; and delightful was the meeting. We found a charming, brilliant complexioned, but quiet mannered woman; thoroughly unaffected, thoroughly attractive – so modest that she blushed like a girl when we hazarded some expression of ardent admiration of "Mary Barton".'[31]

They liked her enthusiasm and the way she talked vividly and freely on subjects of 'humanity and benevolence' – but they thought she looked so young that they could hardly believe she had two teenage daughters.

On 16 May Elizabeth left London, not to go home, but to stay with her Worcestershire cousins at Shottery near Stratford-upon-Avon, another place full of memories of her girlhood, the Avonbank years. Bessy Holland joined them from Knutsford and in an old-fashioned cottage with the scent of sweet-brier and lilies of the valley drifting through the windows Elizabeth and Anne poured out their London news.

This was a strange interlude: she was thrust abruptly not only back into her family, her youth and the depths of rural England, but back into an older world. She and her cousins (great believers in ghosts) exchanged 'capital ghost-stories'. She had her fortune told by a gypsy and in an overgrown house, fit for Sleeping Beauty, deep in tangled woods, she told Eliza Fox, 'I SAW a ghost! Yes I did; though in such a matter of fact place as Charlotte St I should not wonder if you are sceptical.' Describing the encounter twenty years later to the young A. C. Hare, she said that they had been one afternoon to Compton Winyates – a local house well known to be haunted – and on their return the talk turned naturally to ghosts. Hearing that a local carter was supposedly haunted by the spirit of his wife who had died in

London ('the seat of all wickedness'), Elizabeth, typically, wanted to talk to the man himself. The doors of his cottage were locked and no one answered, but they could see a woman at the windows. When they asked next door, they were told the carter was away for the day:

' "Oh", said Mrs Gaskell, "but we have *seen* a woman in the house in a lilac print gown". "Then", they answered, "you have seen the ghost: there is no *woman* in the house; but there is *she*".'[32]

One can think of a less mystical explanation for the woman's elusiveness and the carter's sleepless nights, but a ghost made for a better story.

At Shottery she suddenly felt homesick and within a week she was back in Manchester. Her husband met her at the station and when she reached home, her daughters rushed upon her and almost smothered her. All six of them, parents and children, 'talked at once, upon different subjects, incessantly till bed-time for the younger ones; when the elder two had a little peace, and did really talk'. By the following evening, after telling her news all over again to Susanna Winkworth, Lily was exhausted:

'my ancles ached with talking at the end of the day; it's a *true* and not a figurative expression; they did ache, and I had (not) walked a step only talked. The next day I fairly settled down to home life, lessons till 12 – lunch walk etc; and so we've gone on ever since.' (L181)

The London lioness had reverted to Manchester mother.

Once she settled in, Elizabeth dutifully did the rounds of all her friends: Mary Ewart, the Darbishires, the Taylers. While she had been away, a new figure had begun to dominate the scene, the thirty-year-old James Anthony Froude, currently tutor at the Darbishires'. According to his daughter, Elizabeth had shared a railway carriage with him on her journey north, and had a long, grave talk about the problems of faith.[33] Froude's father was archdeacon of Totnes, and his older brother, Richard Hurrell Froude, who died in 1836, had been a close friend of John Henry Newman, collaborating with him in the *Lyra Apostolica* and *Tracts for the Times*. J. A. Froude himself had also been influenced by Newman, almost to the verge of Catholicism, but during the 1840s, especially after Newman's conversion to Rome in 1846, he endured a period of anguished doubt, which he explored in two semi-autobiographical novels, *Shadows of a Cloud* (1847) and

The Nemesis of Faith (1849). *The Nemesis*, describing the turbulent
spiritual and emotional struggles of a young clergyman, caused such
outrage on publication that a copy was openly burnt by the senior
tutor at Exeter College, Oxford, where Froude was a fellow. (Instead
of stifling the book, the publicity ensured a swift second edition.)
Froude resigned his fellowship and took refuge with Charles Kingsley
and his wife, Fanny, in Lynmouth, Devon, where he met and became
engaged to Charlotte Grenfell, Fanny's sister. After abandoning the
idea of a post in Tasmania, he gratefully accepted the Samuel
Darbishires' offer of employment, and was living with them until his
marriage in October, when he planned to settle in Greenheys.

In Froude's story, as in those of James and Harriet Martineau and
John Henry and Francis Newman, Elizabeth saw another example of
how religious arguments could split families apart (a theme she would
explore in 'Traits and Stories of the Huguenots' and 'Lois the Witch').
In another way his situation as a displaced southerner found a place in
her fiction, in the plight of Mr Hale in *North and South*, who resigns
his Anglican living on the grounds of conscience and comes north to
work as a tutor, putting his classical education at the service of the rich
families of Milton. Although the fictional character and situation are
quite different, Elizabeth undoubtedly had Froude in mind. When he
read *North and South*, Froude told her, 'it gave me such a strange
feeling to see our drawing room in Greenheys *photographed*' as that of
Mr Hale.[34] His daughter Georgina was later convinced that the
spirited, idealistic Margaret Hale was a portrait of her mother,
Charlotte.

Froude, though, was no gentle scholar like Mr Hale. His impact on
the Darbishires' household was immediate and comically dramatic:
'they've got into a very helter-skelter way of spending Sundays ever
since they read the *"Nemesis"* ,' wrote Elizabeth. She herself found
him fascinating, as she did so many strong, peculiar characters:

'If anyone under the sun has a magical, magnetic, glamour-like
influence, that man has. He's *"aut Mephistopheles aut nihil"*, that's
what he is. The D.D.'s all bend and bow to his will, like reeds before
the wind, blow whichever way it listeth. He smokes cigars constantly,
Père, Robert, Arthur, Vernon (nay, once even little Francis), smoke
constantly. He disbelieves, they disbelieve; he wears shabby garments,
they wear shabby garments; in short it's the most complete taking

away their own wills and informing them with his own that ever was. I stand just without the circle of his influence; resisting with all my might, but feeling and seeing the attraction. It's queer!' (L83–4)

Elizabeth was intensely curious about his future wife, and told Tottie the 'very romantic story' of how Charlotte, 'a strict Puseyite' who 'confesses to a priest etc.', had planned to enter a convent but 'instead of a nunnery she had chosen a marriage'. When she met her, Charlotte proved something of a let-down: 'not a heroine of romance-looking woman'. She was 'kind hearted and hearty though, and that's a great deal in this cold world. But I don't know what age she is – and that was a blow.' They became fast friends.

When she described Froude's magnetism to Catherine Winkworth, Elizabeth had known him four months. On her return from London in May, as part of their duty to the industrial north, she and Mrs Darbishire had taken him to see Aspinall-Turner's mill in Liverpool. Another day they went on an odder mission, to consult a clairvoyante at Bolton, recommended by Harriet Martineau, who was then staying with the Darbishires.[35] Mrs D.D. was now caught up by a new enthusiasm, mesmerism, and was busily conducting experiments and hypnotizing her son Vernon, a convinced believer. The whole affair intrigued Elizabeth. The widespread interest in mesmerism and spiritualism in the 1840s seemed in some ways to be linked to the loss of faith; the interest expressed by Froude and Harriet Martineau, both avowedly sceptical of miracles, was typical. In *The Nemesis of Faith* Froude had remarked on the child's capacity for belief in the 'Wonder Tales' heard in Sunday school, a credulity which adults outgrew while they kept the outer forms of faith. The combination of scepticism with a 'childlike' readiness to accept other kinds of supernatural evidence seemed to Elizabeth to express a kind of longing for at least some form of belief.

Elizabeth herself had *not* lost her faith (she stood outside Froude's charmed circle). She was suspicious of mesmerism and later wrote to her friend Mrs Scott; 'I have rather a dread of it altogether, I *think* because I have a feeling that it *twisted* Miss Martineau's mind; but it may not be that, & it may be a superstitious feeling (& consequently a faithless one) of mine.'[36] What fascinated her most of all was credulity itself, the openness to the fantastic and 'unreal', even in those who prided themselves in being rational (from Harriet Martineau to Miss

Pole in *Cranford*). She began to ponder the essential attraction of 'Wonder Tales' in themselves and the persuasive power of those who borrow their spell, whether it be the priest, the fanatic, the clair-voyante, the magician-like Froude or Cranford's conjuror Signor Brunoni – or the simple storyteller.

Elizabeth's other concern was that faith should be of *practical* effect in the world. For this reason she was drawn to the new Christian Socialism, telling Tottie of 'my *hero* Mr Kingsley' and inquiring if the Fox's knew of a co-operative tailor's shop established by F. D. Maurice and others on Louis Blanc's principle. With a certain sly humour, she disclaimed understanding of intellectual or theological arguments, although she clearly enjoyed being in the thick of them:

'We drank tea at the Froudes last night. *Is* Miss Jewsbury's review shallow? It looked to me very deep, but then I know I'm easily imposed upon in the metaphysical line, and could no more attempt to write such an article than fly ... Meanwhile Marianne is practising gorgeous Litanies to the Virgin with Mrs Froude which she has brought from Rome; and I am going through a course of John Henry Newman's sermons. *Our* own Mr Newman is just going to publish something on public worship and Mr Froude's Life of Tacitus gets on grandly (in imagination his wife says) And now I must copy Mr Kingsley's lines.' (L91–2)

The intensity of contemporary arguments about belief, all taking place within the same small circles and communities, is hard to convey today. In July 1849 Harriet Martineau looked in amazement, for instance, at the residents and tourists gathered around the Lake District village of Ambleside, marvelling at

'the diversities of faith within our valley! Let us see. We have High Church, Low Church and Middle Church families; Catholics, both in and out of communion; Independents, Unitarians, Quakers, Sweden-borgians, Wesleyans, Plymouth Brethren, and some who belong to no Christian sect at all.'[37]

The Gaskell family were among the Lakeland Unitarians that summer. In June they went to stay at Skelwith in Little Langdale, two miles from Ambleside, where lodgings had been found for them by the Wordsworths and Arnolds. Their landlady, Mrs Preston, was a 'Stateswoman', as the independent farmers of the region were called, and her family had lived there for two hundred years, with 'no ambition but much dignity'. In 1859 Elizabeth would tell a young friend, Charles Bosanquet, that Mr Preston sometimes drank, but his wife was 'a fine true friendly sensible woman . . . N.B. She would *make* you change your stockings if you got your feet wet, and such like motherly and imperative cares.' She loved the old house, Mill Brow, and its 'dear charming farm-kitchen', with warming-pans on the wall and spurs hanging beside the crockery on the dresser.

The Gaskells had escaped the city heat but not its society. Selina Winkworth came with them, her brother Stephen visited, and the Darbishires (plus Froude) stayed in a farmhouse nearby. Both households had a stream of visitors, including the sixteen-year-old Julia Wedgwood, Frank Holland, the Bonamy Prices and Froude's friend the Oxford orientalist, Max Müller. It was all very jolly: years later Müller asked Elizabeth if she remembered 'the German serenade with which we disturbed your slumber, – Mr Froude, Mr Monier and myself – when we arrived at the middle of the night at Skelwith'.[38] (It sounds hardly likely she'd forget.)

During the holiday Elizabeth paid visits of her own and made another new friend, Mary Fletcher, who had known her father, William Stevenson, when she was a hostess to the Edinburgh radical set at the turn of the century.[39] Now seventy-nine, still beautiful, witty and full of anecdotes, she had settled at Lancrigg, in the lovely hidden valley of Easedale near Grasmere. Her daughter Margaret and husband, Dr John Davy (brother of scientist Humphry Davy), lived in Ambleside and her other daughter Mary also lived nearby with her husband, Sir John Richardson, the Arctic explorer (Elizabeth dubbed her 'Lady (North-Pole) Richardson').

The Fletchers knew the Arnolds and Wordsworths and this summer Elizabeth finally met Wordsworth, in the year before his death. She had tea with Edward Quillinan, the widower of Wordsworth's daughter Dora, who told Crabb Robinson he had 'got Mr W to meet her and her husband . . . she is a very pleasing interesting person'.[40] And at the Davys' house, Lesketh How, which Quillinan was renting for the summer, she collected Wordsworth's autograph, one of the most precious in her collection:

He that feels contempt
For any living thing, hath faculties
Which he hath never used.
        Lesketh How, 20 July 1849.[41]

The time at Skelwith was a complete success. In baking weather the
Gaskells and friends climbed in the Langdales, scrambled over
Loughrigg to Grasmere or walked south to Coniston. On their last day
they got lost on Loughrigg Fell behind Mill Brow and limped home in
the dusk past the Arnolds' house, Fox How: 'Mrs G. quite done up.'[42]
Life was not always so strenuous. Sometimes they merely lazed and
read, borrowing books from Mrs Nicholson's circulating library at
Ambleside. Mrs Nicholson, the postmistress, had known the country
round about, Elizabeth told Bosanquet, 'for years and years; and
though short and stern till she sees you are really good for something,
she is true and sound at heart, and very interesting from her
recollections of so much worth remembering'. At Ambleside, as in
Wales, Silverdale and Shottery, she was hungry for local tales.

The Gaskells returned to Manchester in late August and Elizabeth
tried to adjust to making flannel petticoats, pickles and preserves, and
putting '192 tucks' into her daughters' clothes. Marianne was now
fourteen, needing 'the debauchery of a white tarlatane frock' for
Christmas dances. All the girls were growing, and William and
Elizabeth decided Upper Rumford Street was too small. That autumn
they started to look for houses. When Tottie came to stay in
November, they saw several and even considered having one built in
Victoria Park.

Over the winter Elizabeth was often unwell, but would astonish her
friends by rising suddenly from her sickbed to put on a silk gown when
Mrs Wedgwood called without warning, or to dash off to dinner with
the new bishop of Manchester at the Schwabes'. In addition to the
prestige of being married to William Gaskell, an eminent local figure,
she was now a celebrity in her own right and used her new influence
where she could, negotiating with Chevalier Bunsen, the Prussian
ambassador, for example, for Susanna Winkworth to translate the life
of Niebuhr, or getting John Forster to send a signed copy of
Tennyson's poems for Samuel Bamford. Arthur Clough, meeting
Elizabeth in February 1850 'chez the Jewsbury', thought her 'neither

young (past 30) nor beautiful; very retiring but quite capable of talking when she likes – a good deal of the clergyman's wife about her. Rather hard featured in the Scotch style.'[43]

She could be intimidating. When she met Bishop Lee's wife the next April, she and William (dreaded Unitarians) had paid a surprise call in the middle of 'a visitation or a something-ation, and upwards of 20 clergymen were there':

'Such fun! we were tumbled into the drawing room to them; arch-deacons and all (Florence stay'd in the carriage). Mrs Lee is a little timid woman – *I* should make a better Bishop's wife if the Unitarians ever come uppermost in my day: and she thinks me "satirical" and is afraid of me Mrs Schwabe says. So you may imagine the mal aproposness of the whole affair. Mr Stowell was there and all the cursing Evangelicals.' (L112)

The bishop won praise for not skirting the subject of Unitarianism but pouncing on it at once, while the Evangelicals 'looked as if a bombshell was going off amongst them'. She withdrew her approval, though, on seeing a painting in his study of a baby, who had died in agony, two days after being severely burnt: 'I would not send my child to be educated by the man who could hang up such a picture as that for an object of contemplation . . . not all his pleasant tattle with Florence set him right with me. He's got something wrong with his heart.' She was a woman of decided opinions, but she judged by the heart, as much as the mind, as *Mary Barton* had shown.

Mary Barton was behind her, but Elizabeth had not stopped writing. In July 1849 she gave 'Hand and Heart' to Travers Madge's new *Sunday School Penny Magazine*, a moral tale of an orphaned child's good influence on his uncle's chaotic household, which has much in common with her earlier *Howitt's* stories.[44] The Howitts' influence persisted. Mary suggested Elizabeth's name to the American *Sartain's Union Magazine*, for which she herself wrote, and that July *Sartain's* published a very different piece by Gaskell, 'The Last Generation in England'.[45] This article was inspired, Elizabeth said, by a mention in an 1848 *Edinburgh Review* that Southey had planned 'a history of domestic life'. In recording her recollections of the town of '—' she promised that 'every circumstance and occurrence . . . is strictly and truthfully told without exaggeration', set down just as it arose in her memory. The unnamed town is unmistakably Knutsford, and the semi-comic account of the town's intricately hierarchical, predominantly female society takes us one step towards *Cranford*.

Her next piece of writing was different again, a Lakeland tale, 'Martha Preston'. This was sent to Mary Howitt in October and appeared in *Sartain's* the following February.[46] The setting is Loughrigg Fell, behind Mill Brow, and Preston, of course, was the name of their landlady. Six years later Elizabeth would rewrite this short piece, expanding it into one of her most powerful short stories, 'Half a Lifetime Ago', changing the heroine's name to Susan Dixon and moving the setting slightly south to avoid identification.[47] But the link with Skelwith was re-established when the story was collected in *Round the Sofa* in 1859, where it is told by 'Mrs Preston, wife of a Westmoreland Squire, or as he preferred to be called, Statesman'.

'Martha Preston' is presented as fact, 'Half a Lifetime Ago' as fiction. But in both a young woman loses the man who had promised to marry her because she insists on caring for her idiot brother. Martha Preston, after a harsh, monotonous life, finds her former lover's son lost in the snow; they become friends and when he grows up, she gives him the money to marry and acts as 'Granny' to his children. In 'Half a Lifetime Ago' the victim of the snow is the suitor himself, dead from exposure, and Susan Dixon then takes in his widow and children. One can see the appeal of the original tale, with its strong, solitary heroine, its theme of self-sacrifice and final extension of 'maternal' love outside the family, healing the pain of the past. And how vividly Gaskell imagined the winter bleakness of the fells, known to her only in their summer beauty. Passing the farmhouse, she writes, 'you seem to have left all human habitation behind – the very fences disappear, as if the moorland and bog were not worth enclosing'.[48] The barren landscape – under misty rain, or black and frost-bound under 'the cruel east wind', or swept by blinding snow with drifts in the gullies – mirrors the desolate loneliness of Martha, and of Susan.

As she wrote about these three familiar settings – Manchester, Knutsford and the Lakes – Elizabeth began to enjoy her work again. By 1850, with the encouragement of her new friends, she had come to terms with fame, and could start to consider her future as a writer.

[12]

A Habit of Stories

'I did feel as if I had something to say about it that I *must* say, and you know I can tell stories better than any other way of expressing myself.'[1]

This was how Elizabeth would explain *Ruth* to her friend Mary Green. Her new fame forced her to ask herself why she wrote. Until the late 1840s writing had been a private hobby, and she could justify the publication of the *Howitt's* stories and *Mary Barton* by her Unitarian belief in the moral function of art and in the duty to state the truth and expose social evils. Writing fiction was permissible as a branch of philanthropy. But what if it was just fun in itself? A personal need? A virtual career? While part of her shrank from the taint of professionalism, at the same time Elizabeth was briskly counting her earnings, studying her contracts and moaning about her publishers.

1850 was the year of her letters to Eliza Fox about the conflict of home duties and art. It was also the year she met Charlotte Brontë, and the year that she began to write for Dickens. A good time, then, to consider how completely she lived in an atmosphere of stories. In 1850 she published 'Lizzie Leigh', 'The Well of Pen-Morfa' and 'The Heart of John Middleton' and a novella, *The Moorland Cottage*. These were forerunners of a wealth of shorter works, stunningly varied and accomplished, which would pour from her pen in the next fifteen years, most of them destined to appear in Dickens's *Household Words*.

From time to time after *Mary Barton* was published Elizabeth would proclaim to the world at large that she was *not* working on another book. The fact was, however, that she simply could not cease writing. Stories were intrinsic to her cast of mind. Her letters are studded with swift character sketches and condensed narratives. Some flash past in a few suggestive phrases, like the placing of the yet unknown Charlotte Froude as a heroine of romance, or this description of a local murder in 1850: 'such a tragedy here yesterday, which you will see in the papers. We knew Mrs Novelli! She was a madonna-like person with a face (and character I believe) full of thought and gentle love, Miss Maistaid's faithful servant and friend.' Other letters are instinctively composed to produce an effect, like the long description of giving Tennyson's poems to Bamford, with its structure of quest, discovery, climax and final tableau. She told Forster of her great joy in hunting across Manchester for the 'great, grey stalwart man', pouncing on him as he emerged from a pub and leaving him, red with pleasure, reading aloud in the middle of the street in a 'sleep-walking state', in grave danger, she feared, of being run over.

The habit marked her talk as well as her letters, as Emily Winkworth had noted when Elizabeth visited Catherine at Southport in 1848: 'all those nice long stories and that very factual style of conversation that Katie likes so much'. In late 1349 Emily mentioned this again, bemoaning the fact that she could not entertain her sick sister half so well: 'Oh! what would I give to be able to tell long stories like Lily, or to speak out all my actual present little feelings in that simple picturesque way she does.'[2]

Elizabeth loved rich, wide-ranging talk, as full of stories as a Christmas cake is of fruit, nuts, spices and peel. Her idea of social misery was a stuffy dinner party, or a 'grave and serious' tea of the kind she described in 'Company Manners' in 1854.[3] At this tea-party the talk was as heavy as the food, and in every ponderous silence the hostess would say, 'eat another macaroon'. The first macaroon she revelled in, the second she enjoyed, the third she got through – but after the sixth she got up to go. She was met with a burst of indignant surprise: ' "You are surely never going before supper!" I stopped. I ate that supper, hot jugged hare, hot roast turkey, hot boiled ham, hot apple-tart, hot toasted cheese. No wonder I am old before my time.' It was not the food which weighed on her so much as the boredom. She longed for word-games to be played – 'Wit, Advice, Bout-rimés, Spanish Merchant, Twenty Questions'. She yearned for rules to be transgressed. She delighted when one of these 'rational parties', where everyone wore sedate, anxious expressions, was brilliantly disrupted by 'a beautiful, audacious but most feminine romp' who made them play a ridiculous game of puffing to keep a feather in the air. A far better use of their breath, in Elizabeth's view, than earnestly reporting new scientific discoveries ('the details of which were all and each of them wrong').

What she liked best was 'a slightly gipsy and impromptu character' and in 'Company Manners' she gave an example of her ideal five o'clock tea. It was held in a large old schoolroom, which could have been doleful but was thoroughly romantic: the trees moaned outside, Irish staghounds bayed in the stables, a Spanish parrot talked continuously from its perch in a dark corner and 'the walls of the room seemed to recede as in a dream, and, instead of them, the flickering firelight painted tropical forests or Norwegian fiords, according to the will of our talkers'. The old black kettle, long banished from the kitchen, sputtered and leaked, and 'did everything that was improper'. They ate only thick bread and butter:

'Who ate it I don't know, for we stole from our places round the fireside to the tea-table, in comparative darkness, in the twilight, near the window, and came back on tiptoe to hear one of the party tell of wild enchanted spicy islands in the Eastern Archipelago, or buried cities in farthest Mexico; he used to look into the fire and draw and paint with words in a manner perfectly marvellous . . . Our host was scientific; a name of high repute; he, too, told us of wonderful discoveries, strange surmises, glimpses into something far away and utterly dream-like. His son had been in Norway, fishing; then, when he sat all splashed with hunting, he too, could tell of adventures in a natural racy way.'

But in the formal dining-room that night the magic vanished:

'At dinner the host talked of nothing more intelligible than French mathematics; the heir drawled out an infinite deal of nothing about the "Shakespeare and musical glasses" of the day; the traveller gave us latitudes and longitudes, and rates of population, exports and imports, with the greatest precision; and the girls were as pretty, helpless, inane fine ladies as you would wish to see.'

Conversational storytelling can take many forms. At its simplest it is just recounting what has happened, to oneself, one's family, one's friends. A degree further on these accounts become embroidered and shaped – memories crystallize into anecdotes through frequent repetition. At some stage in this process, in the hands of particular people, storytelling becomes an art and the teller is valued for the gift, especially when the tales conjure up different worlds, like the travellers' yarns, or re-create a vanished past. This latter quality was what Elizabeth treasured as a girl in Knutsford, where, as she says in 'The Last Generation', 'the old ladies were living hoards of tradition and old custom'. At another remove some stories become increasingly fantastical in the telling, slipping from experience towards fantasy. Such are the ghost stories and wild tales Elizabeth swapped with Mary Howitt and her cousins, but even here the tellers would still claim truth to 'fact' as a pledge of authenticity.

Because her conversation vanished with her, critics tend to ignore the links between Gaskell's spontaneous, spoken stories and her written work. Yet she herself often refers to this context. She saw social storytelling as an art and in her view one of the great qualities of Mme de Sablé and her circle (the starting point for 'Company Manners') was that 'they knew how to narrate':

'Very simple, say you? I say, no! I believe the art of telling a story is born with some people, and these have it to perfection; but all might acquire some expertness in it, and ought to do so, before launching out into the muddled, hesitating, broken, disjointed, poor, bald, accounts of events which have neither unity, nor colour, nor life, nor end in them, that one sometimes hears.'

Hard words.

In her own short stories and novellas Gaskell likes to present herself and her narrators as telling stories to a friend by the fire, or as part of a community of storytellers, like those who gather in Mrs Dawson's salon in *Round the Sofa*, each promising to 'narrate something interesting, which we had either heard, or which had fallen within our own experience'. A convention like this – used in so many Victorian collections – reflected real social practice. Skilfully used, this context of talk, of unplanned entertainment, allowed freedom from strict rules of form. The varied personalities of the 'speakers' hover behind each piece and the unspoken story of their own lives enriches the readers' response to their narration – one 'teller' might present something as dense and tight as an academic paper, like an 'An Accursed Race', while another might spin a long, loosely structured tale of reminiscence, like *My Lady Ludlow*, which Mrs Dawson declares to be 'no story: it has, as I said, neither beginning, middle, nor end'.

Part of the fun of reading Gaskell is watching her subtle play with the figure of the narrator, and with the inevitable claims of veracity: there is a tongue-in-cheek irony in the very title of a comic story like 'Mr Harrison's Confessions'. She knew the lure of the good story, and in real life she was alert to the perilous frontier between accuracy and invention, the slippery, heady slide from dramatic reporting to a heightened and selected version of the truth and finally to a lie.

In 1859 she wrote a worried letter to her young friend Charles Bosanquet about the danger of getting the 'bible-women' who were encouraging the poor to subscribe to bibles, to keep journals 'of more than mere statistics'. She noticed that when this happened, the temptation was that conversations were 'thrown into dramas, as it were – with little accounts of looks, & gestures which seemed "touched up" as it were'. Instead of an accurate picture of the poor, all individuality was lost – they all seemed to say the same thing. She explained her odd fear – for she supported the cause – by referring to her disillusionment with 'a *very* good man' (almost certainly her old friend Thomas Wright). Some years ago, she said, he was

'brought into much notice for his philanthropy, and many people were only too glad to learn something of the peculiar methods by which he certainly *had* reclaimed the erring. So he was asked about his "experiences", and told many *true* interesting histories. Lately I have observed that it was difficult to "bring him to book" as it were about his cases, he would tell one of a story that made one's heart bleed, – tell it dramatically too, whh faculty is always a temptation, & when, unwilling to let emotion die without passing into action, one asked for the address &c, – it always became vague, – in different ways. For some time I have suspected that he told *old* true stories, as if they were happening *now*, or had happened *yesterday*. And just lately I have found that this temptation to excite his hearers strongly, has led to *pure invention*.' (L588)

Wright knew how to narrate too well. Storytelling gives power, and power corrupts the teller.

When she laid passionate claim to the truth of her own controversial novels, *Mary Barton* and *Ruth*, Gaskell was, of course, appealing not to the accurate representation of facts – although she felt these were not distorted – but to a truth of feeling, attitudes, experience. And within her fiction lies a major cause of psychic crises. Often these untruths are not wilful inventions, but 'white lies' forced on people to *cover up* the truth: Thurstan and Faith Benson inventing a past life for Ruth to protect her and her illegitimate child; Margaret Hale lying to protect her brother from arrest; Ellinor Wilkins in 'A Dark Night's Work' colluding with her father's lies after he has killed his clerk, Dunster. The pressure is terrible: the truth will out. As Ellinor says, after eighteen years of suppression, 'I knew it would come out in the end.'

In a more light-hearted vein in her short stories Gaskell plays knowingly with that borderline between invention and fact (fact which we, as readers, and she, as author, already know to be fiction). In 'My French Master', for example, a Paris friend tells the narrator about the marriages which, as in a Shakespearian comedy, end the sad exile of the hero, M. Chalabré, and return him to his ancestral estates. The teller bears a marked resemblance to Elizabeth's own friend, Mary Clarke Mohl – 'English by birth, but married to a German Professor, and very French in manners and ways'. Mme Mohl had a well-known love of matchmaking and we are warned, in the story, against this narrator's inevitable claims of truthfulness since 'she was rather in the habit of exaggerating trifles into romances'. We are also alerted to other perils:

'I sank back in my easy chair. Some of my friends are rather long-winded, and it is well to be settled in a comfortable position before they begin to talk.'

The real danger of such talk is that it trembles on the edge of gossip, turning private tragedy or triumph into public entertainment. Gaskell was well aware of this. She gives us splendid gossips, both malicious and harmless, like the cynical Miss Horsman of 'Mr Harrison's Confessions' and the bustling Miss Pole of *Cranford*. Both are a-quiver with nosiness, bursting to be first with the news. On one dreadful occasion in *Cranford* when Mrs Forrester arrives at Miss Matty's house in the midst of the gratifying excitement caused by Miss Pole's announcement of Lady Glenmire's engagement to Mr Hoggins, the unhappy Miss Pole is seized with a terrible fit of coughing. Knowing her so well, Matty and Mary Smith generously hold back the news, until her choking has passed:

'I shall never forget the imploring expression of her eyes, as she looked at us over her pocket handkerchief. They said, plain as words could speak, "Don't let Nature deprive me of the treasure which is mine, although for a time I can make no use of it". And we did not.' (Ch. 11)

Elizabeth herself was not a compulsive gossip, but she could certainly identify with *Cranford*'s narrator Mary Smith, who confesses:

'In my own home, whenever people had nothing else to do, they blamed me for want of discretion. Indiscretion was my bugbear fault. Everybody has a bugbear fault; a sort of standing characteristic – a *pièce de resistance* for their friends to cut at; and in general they cut and come again.' (Ch. 12)

Her own indiscretions sometimes tripped her up. In 1851, for instance, she was happily passing on rumours about the splendour of Dickens's house. Writing to Emily Tagart, she hotly disputes the notion that her informant is an ignoramus from, of all places, Lancaster. 'Tell Helen,' she writes, 'my informant, who lives in *London* I beg to say, and in a capital circle in London too, writes me word that the Dickens have bought a dinner-service of *gold* plate. My informant dined with the Dickens the very day when he wrote to me, and told me this; so after *that*, let Helen doubt me as she will.' She should have known better: Dickens added a teasing postscript to his next letter:

'We have just bought a neat little dinner service of pure gold for common use. It is very neat & quiet.'[4]

He kept the joke running for months, from references to Catherine and Kate Dickens wearing dresses of gold and silver thread to the tender announcement of the birth of Edward Dickens in 1852 as a golden baby, 'his silver skin laced (internally) with his golden blood'.[5]

Elizabeth did not learn from experience. In 1855 she was caught repeating some scandal about 'Mr Hawkes' 2 wives', which seems to have started with Jane Carlyle and Fanny Wedgwood and found its way back to Thomas Carlyle via Mazzini, who demanded an explanation.[6] A more serious tangle arose in 1859 when she was swept into the controversy about the authorship of *Scenes of Clerical Life* and *Adam Bede*. One camp (led by Florence Nightingale's friends Charles and Selina Bracebridge, and abetted by the imposter himself) declared

George Eliot to be a certain Joseph Liggins of Nuneaton. Elizabeth was taken in, reluctant, at first, to believe that the books she so admired were written by the Marian Evans who lived openly with G. H. Lewes (of whom, by then, she thoroughly disapproved). She was desperately curious and soon her whole network of contacts was humming. Her 'informants' were legion, but all her evidence was second, third or even fourth hand. She relied on vague contacts such as Miss Ewart's cousin-in-law, Mr Bacon, a clergyman near Nuneaton, or Mrs Sandars's friend Mrs Fisher, 'unknown to me', who had allegedly sat next to Liggins at dinner. To explain her credulity she was reduced to citing Blackwood's bookseller in Edinburgh, who had been sharply cross-examined by Meta:

'And Meta (1st week in August, when everyone was discussing Miss Evans' claims) being in Blackwoods shop, plumped the question to the head young man "Who wrote Adam Bede" "I do not know. But I know it was not written by a lady – " (observe this last clause was volunteered.) Meta said "Do you *know* it was not written by a lady?" "Yes, I do".' (L585)

Harriet Martineau, the recipient of this story, had taken a great interest in the affair: letters flew back and forth (with Elizabeth's handwriting becoming faster and larger in every one). By October 1859 Harriet, and other friends, including Elizabeth's current publisher, George Smith, had convinced her of her error. When she knew the truth, she was full of remorse. The whole incident gives a gripping impression of Elizabeth's burrowing curiosity and love of a good story, and also of the extraordinary intensity of such rumour-mongering. At one point we find members of a house-party busily copying letters to one of the guests and bearing them off to show other friends and relations, thus spreading the ripples of falsehood wider and wider.[7] This was an accepted practice, but when one realizes how busily these worthy Victorians talked about each other and how freely letters could become public property, Elizabeth's adamant instructions to Marianne make very good sense: '*Pray* burn my letters. I am always afraid of writing much to you, you are so careless about letters.'

She was not alone in her fears. R. K. Webb describes the same fierce anxiety in Harriet Martineau: 'Injunctions about her letters went out to all her correspondents: they were either to return them or suffer excommunication, and she did what she could to prevent any publication of her letters after her death.'[8] 'Letters are talk,' said Harriet. How could she write freely if all the world might read them? Victorian correspondences, especially those of women, are littered with urgent notes like Geraldine Jewsbury's to Jane Carlyle: 'for pity's sake take care of your letters. I have burned all yours which could be misunderstood'.[9] Elizabeth herself carefully edited the letters of Charlotte Brontë when she presented her life to the public, but in private she was as great a sinner as any. In one letter to John Forster she enclosed not only Charlotte's intensely personal note about her engagement to Arthur Nicholls ('to make up for my dull letter') but also two of Mary Mohl's letters from Paris: 'Don't you like reading letters? I do, so much. Not grand formal letters; but such as Mme Mohl's I mean.'

She was on safer ground, one would think, when she passed on stories which were *not* about people she knew, like wild adventures or ghost stories. She told these constantly, with great relish. Charlotte Brontë once had to stop her hastily when she was about to launch into a particularly dismal ghost story, just before bedtime, by explaining that she was superstitious and dreaded 'the involuntary recurrence of any thoughts of ominous gloom which might have been suggested to her'.[10] (The *frisson* of ominous gloom was just what thrilled Mrs G.)

One of Elizabeth's own special tales was about a young married woman haunted to the point of illness and breakdown by the face of a man. Eventually, while convalescing in Rome, she vanishes completely, last glimpsed weeping in a carriage – and 'by her side there sat a strange man, with the face she had so often described'. Elizabeth saw such stories as heirlooms, treasures like old lace or family jewels, to be protected and cared for and handed on to the next generation. Three weeks before she died she told this tale to A. C. Hare, saying that it had been told to her as a girl in Knutsford. She impressed on him that

'she felt so greatly the uncertainty of life, that she wished a story which might possibly be of consequence, and which had been intrusted to her, to remain with someone who was certain to record it accurately.'[11]

Her strong feelings over this particular story led to a dusty exchange with Dickens, who also loved to talk about 'the latest murder and the newest thing in ghosts'.[12] When she discovered that he had included a version (getting the ending wrong) in 'To be Read at Dusk' for *Heath's Keepsake* (Christmas 1851), she was furious: 'wretch that he is to go and write MY story of the lady haunted by the face; I shall have nothing to talk about now at dull parties'. Dickens sent flamboyant, comic apologies, pleading in mitigation: 'I never yet met anybody who read the Keepsake.' He clearly felt no guilt and pointed out that the same thing had happened to him: 'Yet I never complained!' Casting a sideways glance at Catherine Crowe's immensely successful two-volume anthology of 1848, *The Night Side of Nature*, he went on:

'More than that, Crows have plucked at the fleeces of other Ghosts of mine before now – but I have borne it meekly. Ghost stories, illustrating particular states of mind and processes of the imagination, are common property, I always think – except in the manner of relating them, and O who can rob some people of *that*!'[13]

The rebuke was fair. Such tales were indeed common property, and if Dickens pinched one, Gaskell had more to hand.

Dickens was right to point out the collective ownership of stories. He was right too in his throw-away words about the 'manner of relating them'. Gaskell's stories, spoken and written, always bore the stamp of her style and were invariably recast to bring out the ideas that most preoccupied her. Many were based on real life. She could be extremely discreet, but she could also be free with people's private lives if she found a good story or a colourful detail; the danger she saw in Thomas Wright was not altogether absent in herself. When *Cranford* was published, the good folk of Knutsford fell over themselves in their eagerness to find the originals of her characters. Part of the 'evidence' in the Liggins affair in 1859 would turn on the eager pursuit of local models for George Eliot's characters, and Elizabeth told Harriet Martineau (who had experienced the same fuss after *Deerbrook*) that she herself had been

'complimented or reproached, as the case might be, with having used such or such an incident, or described such & such a person, & never seem able to understand how one acquires one's materials unconsciously as it were.' (L909)[14]

1850 offers two examples of the way Elizabeth acquired her materials 'unconsciously as it were' and used real lives imaginatively –

one in fiction, the other, more dubiously, in biography. The first is a young prostitute, whom we know only as Pasley. Elizabeth had visited her in Manchester's New Bailey Prison in 1849 and when Tottie came to stay that December , she too became concerned with Pasley's case; Elizabeth later wrote to her about 'our girl'. On 8 January 1850 she wrote to Dickens, at the suggestion of his brother-in-law Henry Burnett, who lived near her in Manchester. She knew of Dickens's involvement in the refuge for fallen women that he had established with Angela Burdett Coutts at Urania Cottage in Shepherd's Bush. Could he or Miss Coutts advise her, she asked, or accept Pasley in one of their emigration schemes?

Elizabeth's letter, while accurate (as far as we know), gives a distinctive Gaskellian shape to the girl's life. Pasley is a girl of good family; her father is an Irish clergyman who dies when she is two, and her mother ignores her, remarries and sends her out to nurse. At six her uncle puts her in an orphanage and at fourteen she is apprenticed to a dressmaker. When the business fails, her employer sends her to another dressmaker, who connives at her seduction by a doctor, called in when she is ill. Pasley appeals to her mother in vain, and in her despair enters the penitentiary. There she is picked up by a woman who visits specifically to decoy the inmates into prostitution. For months she has lived on the streets

'in the hopes, as she tells me, of killing herself, for "no one had ever cared for her in this world" – she drank, "wishing it might be poison", pawned every article of clothing – and at last stole.' (L99)

Almost as if for effect, after signing the letter, Elizabeth scrawled 'Turn over'. Now comes a postscript, a dramatic, ironic coda: 'I have not told you one incident.' In prison Pasley is confronted 'face to face' by her seducer, now the prison doctor. As she faints, he whispers, 'Good God, how did you come here.' (Gaskell adds, in good storytelling vein: 'The chaplain can guarantee the truth of all I have said.')

It may be unfair to stress the style of narration and structure, since there is no doubt of Elizabeth's real concern. Dickens replied at once, using a wonderfully suggestive image: Miss Coutts could not take responsibility, since 'the Voyage Out has been, and still is, our great difficulty'.[15] He did, however, send a page of advice from Angela Burdett Coutts which Elizabeth gratefully took. She found a couple sailing for the Cape, organized the master of a local ragged school to take her to London and found a 'whole *nest* of good ladies' to take care of her until the ship sailed. What became of the real Pasley we do not know, but her plight, and some aspects of her story, took fictional shape in Gaskell's next novel, *Ruth*.

The second figure, by odd coincidence, was also the daughter of an Irish clergyman: Charlotte Brontë. She too had a hard childhood, although of a different kind, and she too, in Elizabeth's eyes, appealed in some ways to be 'rescued'. If Pasley was cast as heroine-victim (under the heading 'fallen woman'), so was Charlotte (under the class of 'lonely genius'). The image was fixed before Gaskell even set eyes on her.

The writers already admired each other's work: Gaskell was fascinated and puzzled by *Jane Eyre* and Brontë thought *Mary Barton* 'a clever though painful tale', but feared its theme might anticipate *Shirley*, which she was working on at the time.[16] Before *Shirley* was published, in November 1849, she sent an early copy to Gaskell and was moved by her prompt letter of congratulation: 'The note brought tears to my eyes. She is a good, she is a great woman.' The support of writers like Mrs Gaskell and Harriet Martineau, she said, took the sting out of other criticism.[17] Meanwhile (despite her rage at the impertinence of those who had tried to pierce her own anonymity) Elizabeth was, of course, consumed with curiosity about Currer Bell. She pursued her quest through Tottie and other friends, and by late November was telling Catherine Winkworth: 'Currer Bell (aha! what will you give me for a secret?) She's a she – that I will tell you – who has sent me "Shirley".' In December, her goal reached, she was able to tell Annie Shaen about Charlotte's meeting with Harriet Martineau, describing her (unseen) as 'a little, very little, bright haired sprite, looking not above 15, very unsophisticated, neat & tidy . . . Her father a Yorkshire clergyman who has never slept out of his house for 26 years; she has lived a most retired life.' When she read the romantic account in the biography, describing how Charlotte, after slight hesitation, went straight to her side, Harriet – who was very deaf and well known for her bizarre ear-trumpets – just wrote tartly in the margin: 'Seeing the trumpet'.[18]

Charlotte and Elizabeth were finally brought together in the summer of 1850 by Sir James Kay-Shuttleworth, the James Kay who had tackled the Manchester cholera in 1832; he had been made a baronet, and added his wife's surname on inheriting the

Shuttleworth estates. Assiduous in pursuit of the famous, he called at Haworth after the publication of *Shirley* and invited a reluctant Charlotte to their splendid Elizabethan house, Gawthorpe Hall, near Burnley, on the East Lancashire border. She went in June. The stay was not as bad as she feared and she agreed to stay with them at Windermere that summer. By then Lady Kay-Shuttleworth, a small, energetic woman of thirty-two, had met Elizabeth, while staying at Capesthorne. They had exchanged long letters, about the restless age, the search for purpose, the growth of sisterhoods – and about Charlotte Brontë, to whom Elizabeth said she was drawn not only by her books but by 'the glimpses one gets of *her*, and her mode of thought, and, all unconsciously to herself, of the way in which she has suffered. I wonder if she suffers *now*?' In August Lady Kay-Shuttleworth gave her the chance to find out, by inviting the Gaskells to Briery Close.

William has just returned from Scotland and was about to set off for Birmingham so Elizabeth went alone. Both she and Charlotte found the worldly, talkative Sir James hard to take. (Marianne Gaskell later got the measure of his self-importance perfectly: 'watch his left eye, & provide him with Savoy biscuits'.) Charlotte particularly disliked him. She respected his intellect and 'marked kindness', but decided that 'the substratum of his character is hard as flint' and that he had a natural antipathy to imaginative writers: 'Their virtues give him no pleasure – their faults are as wormwood and gall in his soul: he perpetually threatens a visit to Haworth – may this be averted!'[19]

Briery Close stands on the hillside above Lowood, just south of Ambleside, looking westward to the fells across the shimmering lake. As their hostess had a cold, Charlotte and Elizabeth were thrown together, talking over needlework in the drawing-room, driving in the countryside and boating on the lake. They also paid a visit to the Arnolds at Fox How, which revealed Charlotte's chronic shyness. In long conversations they explored each other's tastes, finding that they agreed on some things, such as liking Ruskin, but were far apart on others. Afterwards Elizabeth told Charlotte Froude: 'she and I quarrelled & differed about almost everything – she calls me a democrat, & can not bear Tennyson – but we like each other heartily I think/ & hope we shall ripen into friends'. In her turn Charlotte Brontë found Elizabeth 'a woman of the most genuine talent – of cheerful, pleasing and cordial manners and – I believe – of a kind and good heart'.[20] On returning home they immediately wrote to one another and Charlotte sent Wordsworth's *Prelude* and a 'little book of rhymes' – the *Poems* of Ellis, Acton and Currer Bell.

By virtually the same posts that carried her mail to Haworth, Elizabeth was dispatching a flurry of letters to different friends, including Charlotte Froude and Tottie, describing her Windermere stay. In these, her first introduction to Charlotte has the sense of a puzzle, a dark shape she cannot yet make out: 'a little lady in black silk gown, whom I could not see at first for the dazzle in the room'. As she wrote her letters the picture became focused and detailed, and she mixed what she had learnt of her past directly from Charlotte with the untrustworthy gossip of Lady Kay-Shuttleworth, much of it gleaned from 'an old woman of Burnley' (an embittered nurse dismissed by Patrick Brontë in his wife's last illness). Miss Brontë, Elizabeth reported, was 'altogether *plain*' (like many Gaskell heroines), tiny, 'undeveloped'. She saw a child within the woman:

'Her hands are like birds' claws, and she is so shortsighted that she cannot see your face unless you are close to her. She is said to be frightfully shy, and almost cries at the thought of going amongst strangers.' (L127)

Patrick Brontë was already defined, sight unseen, as 'strange and half mad'. He sawed up chairs and set fire to hearthrugs when enraged, ate by himself, did not educate his daughters and ignored their writing; Mrs Brontë had died of a broken heart; Emily and Anne had been denied a doctor's care and Charlotte herself had been stunted by starvation at school and was probably 'tainted with consumption', living in the lonely Parsonage, so bleak that no flowers could grow because of the biting winds: 'the wonder to me is how she can keep heart and power alive in her life of desolation'. Seen thus, it was undoubtedly a tragic story; the pattern was set for the *Life*.

Elizabeth could not help turning lives into stories, and Charlotte Brontë's seemed the opposite of her own. Charlotte wrote in solitude, in the wild isolation of the moors, while she scribbled amid the chaos of family life in the heart of a city. In 1850 the puzzle was not only how to find time but whether she could, or should, try to reconcile her 'selfish' compulsion to write with the demands of motherly, wifely and parish duties.

Charles Dickens had written in early January, asking if she would contribute to the new weekly journal he was planning, *Household Words*, declaring: 'there is no living English writer whose aid I would desire to enlist, in preference to the authoress of *Mary Barton* (a book that most profoundly affected and impressed me)'. (This tribute is often quoted to illustrate Dickens's high opinion of Gaskell, but, alas, he wrote in this vein to all his potential contributors.) In addition to flattering her, he cleverly appealed to her conscience as well as her pride. The aim of his journal, he said, would be 'the raising up of those that are down, and the general improvement of our social condition'.[21] The causes Dickens particularly wanted to publicize – education, housing, sanitary reform – were dear to the Gaskells' hearts. But Elizabeth still felt torn between home and writing, a dilemma which Dickens (who had no such worries) smartly brushed aside, saying that he was 'not at all afraid of the interruptions necessary to your domestic life, and that I think you will be far less sensible of them in writing short stories than in writing a long one'.[22] For this year, at least, she took his advice, and wrote shorter – if not short – fiction.

In response to his January request she sent 'Lizzie Leigh'. This tale of prostitution, sombre in tone, seems a strange offering for a family journal, but she knew of Dickens's interest and had only recently written for advice about Pasley. She may not have known, however, that just before her story arrived he had promised Angela Burdett Coutts he would try to deal with the 'sad' subject in *Household Words*.[23] Gaskell's timing was good – she did the work for him. The truth was, also, that the magazine was flung together in something of a rush, and Dickens, who wrote much of the paper himself, was grateful for a lead story.

'Lizzie Leigh' appeared in the first issue, dated 30 March 1850, following, appropriately, immediately after the stirring 'Preliminary Remarks', where Dickens proclaimed that 'in all familiar things, even in those which are repellent on the surface, there is Romance enough, if we will find it out'.[24] The rest of the issue was made up of an article by Dickens and Wills on the new General Post Office, another Dickens piece on popular theatre, a dramatic poem by Leigh Hunt, a profile of the French tragedienne Clairon and 'A Bundle of Emigrants Letters' by the campaigning Caroline Chisholm. For her story, which ran for three issues, Elizabeth received £20, a generous payment by contemporary standards. She was delighted: 'I stared, and wondered if I was swindling them but I suppose I am not; and Wm has composedly buttoned it up in his pocket. He has promised I may have some for the Refuge.'

This little incident has been taken to show that William ruled his wife and took her earnings. Given his character, what it really shows is how he liked to tease in the face of her excitement. While he helped to manage her affairs, signing contracts and receipts, William certainly never asserted his legal right over Elizabeth's property; many payments were sent straight to her. Over the years the small sums from *Household Words* – 10 guineas here, £5 there – were a useful bonus, and she would later dash off a quick story or two when she needed money urgently. Dickens's magazine promised to be an ideal outlet. Payment was good, publication swift and, since the articles carried no names, she was freed from fear of criticism. In fact, as Dickens was mentioned on every page as 'Conductor' (not anonymous but '*mononymous* throughout', said Douglas Jerrold), most stories were credited to him, and 'Lizzie Leigh' even appeared under his name in the American *Harper's* that June.[25]

Although she liked the idea, Elizabeth had little time to write for *Household Words* in early 1850. Plaintively, Dickens wrote in July:

'This is a brief letter, but – if you only knew it! – a very touching one in its earnestness.

Can't you – won't you – don't you ever mean to – write me another story?'[26]

It was not until early November that she dug in her desk and sent him 'The Well of Pen-Morfa'. Until then her attention had been occupied elsewhere. To her own annoyance she had promised Edward Chapman a Christmas book. When she finished it in August, she told Tottie it had been 'a *very foolish* engagement of mine, which I am angry with myself for doing, but I promised it and I have done it'. The whole affair irritated her. She was sore with Chapman, who never told her about sales or new editions of *Mary Barton*. She felt that he simultaneously ignored her and bullied her. He asked her to write, she complained, 'recommending benevolence, charity, etc . . . However I could not write about virtues to order, so it is simply a little country love story called Rosemary.' The title was the next battle. Chapman discarded

'Rosemary' for 'The Fagot', at which Elizabeth was understandably appalled: 'I will disown that book if you call it The Fagot; – the name of *my* book is December Days'.

In the end it was called *The Moorland Cottage*.²⁷ It is, as she said, a country love story, telling of the slow-growing romance between the daughter of a clergyman's widow and the local squire's son, threatened by the squire's pride and the criminal activities of the heroine's spoilt brother, but dramatically saved by her unselfish courage. The melodramatic climax packs in a fire and a shipwreck, but on the whole the pace is leisurely, with the moorland landscapes lovingly described. It could not have been more different, in subject and tone as well as setting, from *Mary Barton*, and some of her friends were disappointed; Emily Winkworth dismissed it as 'a sweet, poetical, simple, sketchy story' which she could safely give her younger sister. Other readers, however, bathed happily in its sentiment. Matthew Arnold's sister, Mary Forster, told a friend how he was spending the week after Christmas at Fox How: 'Matt is stretched out full length on the sofa, reading a Christmas tale of Mrs Gaskell's which moves him to tears, and the tears to complacent admiration of his own sensibility.'²⁸ It was redeemed in Elizabeth's eyes by the fact that Charlotte Brontë liked it, declaring that it opened like a daisy and 'finished like a herb – a balsamic herb with healing in its leaves . . . The little story is fresh, natural, religious. No more need be said.'²⁹

The Moorland Cottage is a gentle book, with an interesting feminist tinge, but there was no gentleness in 'The Heart of John Middleton', which Gaskell sent to Dickens in early December.³⁰ This is a sternly moral tale in which a fierce man is turned from vengeance on an old enemy by the intervention of his dying wife. In a central incident, before they marry, Nell is crippled when hit by a sharp stone aimed at John by his rival. Gaskell's fondness for such accidents made Dickens sigh. He had already had the death of little Nanny in 'Lizzie Leigh' and the crippling of Nest in 'Pen-Morfa'. He also thought the death of Nell unnecessary. He told Wills that he found the story 'very clever' –

'I think the best thing I have seen, not excepting Mary Barton – and if it had ended happily (which is the whole meaning of it) would have been a great success. As it is, it had better go in the next No., but will not do much, and will link itself painfully, with the girl who fell down at the well and the child who tumbled down stairs. I wish to Heaven, her people would keep a little firmer on their legs'.[31]

Writing to Elizabeth, he diplomatically called it 'a story of extraordinary power, worked out with a vigour and truthfulness that very very few people could reach', but he still said he wished she had not killed the wife, an infliction of unnecessary pain.[32]

'The Heart of John Middleton' is indeed powerful and, as Dickens also acknowledged, very clever. In it Gaskell works out with a single stroke how to dramatize the conflict of (masculine) revenge and (feminine) love, making her narrator-hero the son of a violent father who never knows his mother and who comes to religion through falling in love with a tender, pure woman. At first his religion is still vengeful: he becomes a 'ranter', a member of a fanatical sect, wishing he had been present at Christ's death to take vengeance on 'the wicked Jews'. He is drawn naturally to the old stories of Ishmael, Joseph and Pharaoh, Jael and Sisera, taking the Bible's message as a personal one and reading 'the mighty act of God's vengeance, in the Old Testament, with a kind of triumphant faith that, sooner or later He would take my cause in hand and revenge me on mine enemy'. Only when he is given this chance, and rejects it, following the spirit of his wife's dying words, is he redeemed: 'the burning burden of a sinful, angry heart was taken off'.

The story is set on the high moors near Pendle Hill, which separate Yorkshire from Lancashire, and Gaskell gives it a regional quality by combining the Old Testament references with a north-country proverb which Charlotte Brontë had told her: 'Keep a stone in thy pocket for seven years; turn it, and keep it seven year more; but have it ever ready to cast to thine enemy when the time comes.'[33] The stone that wounds Nell is also the stone in John's heart. His narration blends the language of the Authorized Version easily with the local dialect, as he himself explains – 'for we, in Lancashire, speak a rough kind of bible language' – and with the rhythms of the books he finds in the travelling pedlar's packs: *Pilgrim's Progress*, *Paradise Lost*, Byron's *Narrative*. As the moment of confrontation approaches the writing gains a particular intensity which Gaskell would only find again when she came to describe a similar fanatical Puritan, Manasseh in 'Lois the Witch'. Romantic personification of nature fuses with Gothic supernatural and with apocalyptic language in a fearful image of that recurring figure in her fiction, the Grim Father:

'The wind came sweeping down from the hill-top in great beats, like the pulses of heaven; and, during the pauses, while I listened for the coming roar, I felt the earth shiver beneath me. The rain beat against windows and doors, and sobbed for entrance. I thought the Prince of the Air was abroad; and I heard, or fancied I heard, shrieks come on the blast, likes the cries of sinful souls given over to his power.

The sounds came nearer and nearer. I got up and saw to the fastenings of the door, for, though I cared not for mortal man, I did care for what I believed was surrounding the house, in evil might and power.'

From this year on Dickens became the chief publisher of Gaskell's shorter works, and to start with he proved a shrewd and tactful editor. He soothed her initial anxieties about her tendency to detail and her inability to write to a prescribed space: 'Allow the story to take its own length and work itself out,' he said (having complained privately to Wills a week earlier that 'Lizzie Leigh' was 'very good, but long').[34] His editorial suggestions were sensible – that Lizzie herself should put the baby into Susan's arms, so that the contrast between her abandonment of her baby and her mother's maternal tenderness would not disconcert the reader, or that Nell Middleton should not die but live on to be a good influence.[35] Gaskell accepted the first suggestion and would have done the second if it had reached her in time. She was due to come to London the following week and Wills, thinking she was already there, chased all over town to find her. As Dickens was in his usual hurry, he printed it as it stood; by the time she got the message it was too late. Dickens alleged that he rushed to see if he could alter it, but found the magazine 'at Press, and 20,000 copies already printed . . . Never mind. It is a very fine story, nobly written, – and you can put a pleasanter ending to the next one!'[36]

Dickens always tried to avoid depressing his family readership and this mild admonition was in line with his appeal to Wills about the magazine in general: 'Brighten it, brighten it, brighten it!' As it happened – though probably not because of this rebuke – most of what Gaskell sent him over two years was to be much brighter in tone. This was especially true of the Cranford sequence, but also of potentially serious articles like 'Disappearances', written in response to his own pieces on the new detective system:

'Once more, let me say, I am thankful I live in the days of the Detective Police. If I am murdered, or commit bigamy, at any rate my friends will have the comfort of knowing all about it.'[37]

For the first couple of years their relationship was good and, as far as was possible for an editor with such itchy fingers, he left her work alone. The honeymoon did not last. They disagreed, gently, over the first Cranford episode in 1851, then fiercely over 'The Old Nurse's Story' in 1852 and eventually clashed violently, with endless, hair-tearing wrangles, over the serialization of North and South in 1854. What began as a friendly, even flirtatious relationship finally settled into a wary and stubborn truce. But of over forty stories and articles written by Elizabeth Gaskell between 1850 and her death, two-thirds were published by Dickens, either in Household Words or its successor, All the Year Round.

Gaskell's lesser works are inevitably overshadowed by her novels, but a quick glance forward shows what an inventive and innovative short-story writer she was. To call these stories 'short' is somewhat misleading since few are under thirty pages, most are well over fifty and at least five are novellas, like The Moorland Cottage, of over a hundred pages. They vary in subject, style and setting from moral tales to Gothic mysteries and brilliant small-scale comedies. Their relative simplicity allows central themes and favourite character types to leap swiftly into view: wayward sons, stern fathers or husbands, mother-less children, ailing wives, returning wanderers (for good or ill), stalwart servants, heroines forced into self-sufficiency or finding solidarity with other women.

Stories could lie in Elizabeth's mind for years, but she usually wrote the final versions very fast and rarely troubled to correct, which led to her sometimes muddling the characters' names, forgetting the number of their children or repeating favourite details (in Cranford almost everyone drums their fingers on the table). Sometimes, with hindsight, the stories seem sketchy in a different sense, a first outline of ideas developed more thoroughly later: thus 'Martha Preston' is reworked in 'Half a Lifetime Ago', the stone-throwing incident from 'The Heart of John Middleton' becomes a key scene in North and South, the character groupings from The Moorland Cottage reappear in Wives *and Daughters*.[38] In her short stories we see Gaskell consciously practising her craft, playing with it and expanding its possibilities. She mixes real and surreal, comic and tragic. She explores the possibilities of language – making bold use of the vernacular in 'The Heart of John Middleton' and 'The Crooked Branch', or creating a period speech for 'Lois the Witch'. She experiments with structure, from the play-like 'Mr Harrison's Confessions' to the sweeping historical 'Morton Hall' or the loose, enfolding form of *My Lady Ludlow*.

Beneath these variations lies an underlying pattern, which seems to mirror the process of creation, the engagement and full release of her imagination. In almost all Gaskell's works, short or long, author and reader slowly approach the subject and learn the lie of the land until, at a moment of crisis, a door suddenly seems to open, like Sesame, and we step into new terrain – melodrama, mystery, intense emotion or fantasy. Some openings embody the movement into fiction physically – the Bartons and Wilsons walking from Greenheys into Manchester – while others provide a social map, so to speak, of the territory, like the description of the 'Amazons' in *Cranford*. Sometimes map and movement are combined, as in the panorama of Monkshaven and Sylvia's walk into the town with her butter in *Sylvia's Lovers*, or the railway journey to Keighley and the fierce habits and customs of Yorkshire in *The Life of Charlotte Brontë*. The early stages establish the milieu, the characters and their way of life until at some central point narrative itself takes over. From that point on 'truth' is displayed not in realism or analysis but in the symbolic workings of the plot.

Only once did Gaskell suggest what it means to cross this threshold into a self-governing world of fiction. She did so – naturally – in a story, one that is not serious but playful and ironic. In 1860 she wrote her first piece for Thackeray's *Cornhill*, a *jeu d'esprit* whose ambiguous title, 'Curious if True', questions the usual storyteller's claim to be curious *but* true.[39] An earnest Englishman, Richard Whittingham (first clue), travels to Catholic France to trace his solid, austere Calvinist ancestry; but the ancestors he finds are rather different. One night, lost in a dark wood, he sees a lighted château through the trees with 'pepper boxes, and *tourelles* and what not, fantastically growing up into the dim starlight'. A great entertainment is in progress and to his surprise he is greeted as if expected. But where, he is asked, is his friend, Monsieur le Geanquilleur? The bemused Whittingham cannot think who this can be, even when he learns that he is also known as Le

Grand Jean d'Angleterre. Can they mean John Bull? John Russell? John Bright!

The guests seem familiar but exceedingly odd: M. Poucet, with whiskers and very old boots; a beautiful lady 'splendid as dawn' fast asleep on the settee; a fat old lady of twinkling charm, who long ago married a prince despite the efforts of two unkind half-sisters. The hostess is a Madame de Retz, who weeps over the memory of 'the best of husbands', killed in haste by her brothers, and fondly shows the visitor his portrait:

' "You observe the colouring is not quite what it should be."
"In this light the beard is of rather a peculiar tint". said I.
"Yes; the painter did not do it justice. It was most lovely, and gave him such a distinguished air, quite different from the common herd. Stay, I will show you the exact colour, if you will come near this flambeau!" And going near the light, she took off a bracelet of hair, with a magnificent clasp of pearls. It was peculiar, certainly. I did not know what to say. "His precious, lovely beard!" said she. "And the pearls go so well with the delicate blue!" '

'Curious if True' is Gaskell's tribute to the most haunting and popular (in all senses) of storytelling genres. Within its mansion it is the imaginary characters who live 'real' lives, domestic, bustling and down to earth, growing old with their memories, which are also our favourite fairy tales. When, for once, they tell their own tales, these turn out to be different from what centuries of 'gossip' would have us believe. They inhabit the house of story, which is different from the house of dreams, for listeners to stories are wide awake. This house exists in the middle of the dark wood of life, throughout time, alongside the daily rush. Yet some 'rational' people, like Whittingham, will never understand how the imagination can whisper of an ideal world where 'everybody would have their rights and we should have no more trouble'. 'If I were in England', Whittingham says, 'I should imagine Madame was speaking of the Reform Bill or the millennium; but I am in ignorance.'

When the folding doors are thrown open and the long-awaited Madame la Fée-marraine finally arrives, Whittingham is still in ignorance, denied revelation. He awakes on the grass in the clear light of morning to fimd that the château has vanished. Elizabeth Gaskell, however, gathering her 'materials unconsciously as it were', with her lifelong passion for stories and magical gift for telling them, could find and re-enter the castle of fiction at will, unlocking a different door each time. And although she returns to certain themes, characters, incidents and images, the cumulative effect is not of repetition but of subtle variation and advancing skill – no story 'feels' the same as any other. No wonder Dickens pressed her to write for him and called her his 'dear Scheherazade' – because, as he said,

'I am sure your powers of narrative can never be exhausted in a single night, but must be good for at least a thousand nights and one.'[40]

Daily Life

In December 1850, when she was due to meet Elizabeth at a London dinner party, Jane Carlyle received a letter from Geraldine Jewsbury in Manchester:

'The people here are beginning to be mildly pained for Mr "Mary Barton". And one lady said to me the other day, "I don't think authoresses ever ought to marry", and then proceeded to eulogise Mr Gaskell. I want to know how you got along with Mrs Gaskell today? I have a notion that if one could get at the "Mary Barton" that is the kernel of Mrs Gaskell one would like her, but I have never done so yet. Have you?'[1]

This was shrewd as well as sharp. Elizabeth's writing career was unusual, and a bit embarrassing in a minister's wife. Those who did not know her well found it hard to reconcile her public face — sometimes earnest, sometimes frivolous, always frantically busy — with the reflective, impassioned author of the fiction.

This year had made these conflicts clearer, even to herself. That April she and William had finally found their new house, 42 Plymouth Grove. Excitedly Elizabeth promised Tottie that Meta would draw her a plan, but confessed that she was troubled by the selfishness of such a purchase when so many were wanting:

'that is the haunting thought to me; at least to one of my "Mes", for I have a great number and that's the plague. One of my mes is, I do believe, a true Christian — (only people call her socialist and communist), another of my mes is a wife and mother, and highly delighted at the delight of everyone else in the house, Meta and William most especially who are in full exstasy. Now that's my "social" self I suppose. Then again I've another self with a full taste for beauty and convenience whh is pleased on its own account. How am I to reconcile all these warring members? I try to drown myself (my *first* self), by saying it's Wm who is to decide on all these things, and his feeling it right ought to be my rule. And so it is – only that does not quite do.' (L108)

It never quite did.

The Gaskells moved in June, after a holiday in Silverdale. Elizabeth's fictional houses always reflect their inhabitants and to a certain extent 42 Plymouth Grove embodied the contrasts in her own life. From the outside it was (and still is) the personification of Manchester order and solidity, its size and squareness emphasized by the white lines of stucco, topped like classical columns, which divide the façade, its pillared portico standing squarely at the apex of a short carriage drive. The face it presents to the world is sturdy and dignified, wholly suitable for the respected minister of Cross Street Chapel. The inside, however, is very different. The house had been built at the beginning of the century by an eccentric bachelor with his own ideas of design, and all the rooms lead into one another. The dining-room, with its old oak tables and armchairs, which the Gaskells used as a family sitting-room, and where Elizabeth often wrote, had three doors, open to the flow of family, friends and visitors. The whole effect is irregular, encircling, interconnected.

To begin with Plymouth Grove seemed vast. In estate agents' language it had seven bedrooms, two large reception rooms, a study (for William – door kept closed) and two big attics (the one above Hearn's room became a nursery for Flossy and Julia). Besides these there were kitchens, scullery, pantry and outhouses and a large garden with a greenhouse, which filled Elizabeth with delight. The Gaskells finances had improved when Aunt Abigail died in 1847 and her will passed on Hannah Lumb's full bequest to Elizabeth. William had also received some family legacies and in January 1849 Edward Holland had put £1,500 into Catherine Dock shares on their behalf, obviously as part of a wider plan of investment. But the move was expensive; the rent was nearly five times that of their first married home in Dover Street. 'My dear!' Elizabeth exclaimed to Tottie, 'it's 150 a year, and I dare say we shall be ruined; and I've already asked about the ventilation of the new Borough Gaol, and bespoken Mr Wright to visit us'.

Although she made it a joke, the expense was a worry. 'Our house is proving rather too expensive for us,' she told Nancy Robson later. They had decided not to furnish the drawing-room, and meant to be 'very œconomical because it seems such an addition to children's health & happiness to have plenty of room, & above all a garden to play in'. Eventually they would furnish it in style, with Chippendale tables, 'a fine enamelled bedroom suite' in the main bedroom and a new piano to replace the one which William had so proudly ordered on their honeymoon, 'a great event in the family – semi-grand Broadwood'. They kept very up to date, to judge by this little note to Lucy Holland:

'I begin to be anxious about the Refrigerator; it has never made its appearance; and as, although it is not hot weather, yet we are going to be a large party in the house soon, I should be very glad to have it soon.'[2]

The catalogue of the sale at Plymouth Grove held after Meta's death in 1910 shows that over the years the Gaskells acquired the usual heavy curtains, oriental rugs and, like good Victorians (and Wedgwood relations), quantities of china. There were several different tea sets in Wedgwood, Coalport and Staffordshire, including one which must have come from former days: 'Early English Tea Ware, 56 pieces, decorated with red and gold butterflies.'[3] For everyday use they had a willow-pattern dinner service, but grander occasions called for a full-scale Minton set of 127 pieces. There is something poignant about the catalogue's cold list of contents, which hint at so many aspects of their lives – furniture handed on from Knutsford and Warrington, portraits of the family and old friends like William Turner, oil paintings of *Lyn Gwynant* and *The Shining Silverdale*, and even a small sketch by Charlotte Brontë.

The echoing spaces were soon full of people as well as possessions and although she had a large spare room with a dressing-room (useful for babies), Elizabeth could hardly accommodate her stream of visitors. In late 1851, fretting about Christmas guests, she confessed to Marianne, 'the sleeping room is *rather* the puzzle in this plan', and a year later, pressing Nancy Robson to stay, plus baby, she could only offer the nurse '½ a large bed (with Flossy or Hearn could share it with her, and your nurse could sleep with one of the servants)'.

The garden filled up as rapidly as the house. In March 1851 she told Marianne: 'we have got peas, Jerusalem artichokes, cabbages, mignonette etc down, pinks, carnations, campions, canterbury bells & the hot bed is just "set agait" (vide Frank) for cutting the borders etc'. The next letter's list is still longer, with 'Thunderbergias' and gladioli in the flower-beds, and, in the vegetable garden, 'we have sown our first crop of peas. We are giving up beans as they did not answer; we have sown mustard, cress, radishes, lettuces, cauliflowers.' When the first gardener left, her schemes grew even more ambitious:

'James our new man, understands both cows & pigs, and he & I plan it together, and plan to take the field joining our garden for the cow, and the Bellhouses will sell us their cow things, i.e. milking stool, cans &c &c &c.' (L170)

The cow ('such a pet') was, she said proudly, half Alderney, quarter Ayrshire, quarter Holderness. They had eggs from their poultry and made their own butter. One of the outhouses was converted into a dairy; it was still there in 1910, complete with milking stools.

Elizabeth needed considerable help with such an establishment, especially since she was often away for weeks or even months at a time. Apart from the invaluable Hearn, she soon had a cook, two or three maids, a 'waiter' and a gardener. Her letters buzz with the problem of 'staff'. Telling Tottie about the new gardener, she rattled on:

'and I've got a new cook instead of Mary, who is to be married 'by Master' in February and said new cook is coming in January, and her name is Isabella Postlethwaite of Legberthwaite in Tilburthwaite, you may guess her habitat from that; and we have got a Bessy instead of Maria, and a Margaret instead of Margaret, all changes against my will at the time, but improvements I think.' (L171–2)

Shortly afterwards she announced to Marianne, without a trace of irony: 'All of our new servants do very nicely. To be sure we are a very small family, and there is proportionately very little work to be done.' Cooks remained her major headache, taking priority over everything. To Mary Holland she wrote:

> My dear Mary,
>   Cooks are dearer to me than cousins,
>   Of cousins I'll get many an one

> Of cooks perhaps ne'er anither,
> and a cook is coming to see me on Friday afternoon,
> I am sorry: for I like Frank, & I love Sybil.[4]

However much she joked or fretted, during all her married life
Elizabeth was closely involved in her servants' lives. After her first
maid Bessy left in 1837 she wrote: 'we still keep her as a friend, and she
has been to stay with us several weeks this autumn'.[5] In 1851 she sent
this request to her friend Mrs Davenport via Lady Crewe:

'we have a gardener, for whom we [have] a great respect, as he does a
great deal of good amongst the poor &c; I find that he has a great wish
to see the gardens at Capesthorne; and I should be glad to know if this
is ever permitted. He is a very simple, quaint Shropshire man, not very
clever in his business, but singularly good and generous as far as he is
able; giving time and thought as well as what little money he can
spare.'[6]

And in the last year of her life, when she was looking for a place for
Hearn to convalesce after an illness, she called her 'a dear and valuable
friend'.

In a later article, 'French Life', Elizabeth said how much she liked
the French middle-class style of living in an apartment, where 'there is
the moral advantage of uniting mistresses and maids in a more
complete family bond', and praised a London friend who felt she could
have country girls as servants since she lived in a flat:

'if they had had to live in the depths of a London kitchen, she should
not have tried bringing them out of their primitive country homes; as it
was, she could have them under her own eye without any appearance
of watching them; and besides this, she could hear of their joys and
sorrows and, by taking an interest in their interests, induce them to
care for hers. French people appear to me to live in this pleasant kind
of familiarity with their servants – a familiarity which does not breed
contempt, in spite of proverbs.'[7]

This delicate balance between intimacy and superiority, kindness
and self-interest, is very typical of Elizabeth and her circle – another
instance of the invisible 'sunk fence' between the classes. The Gaskells
often had country-born servants and frequently knew them before
they brought them to the city. In December 1851 Mrs Preston from

Skelwith came to stay and shortly afterwards her daughter Margaret became a maid at Plymouth Grove, taking over as cook in the autumn of 1852. And when James (the cow and pig expert) was dismissed for drunkenness, he was replaced as gardener by Margaret's brother Will. In 1854 Elizabeth heard that another Preston sister, Eleanor, was in danger of being seduced in London, and was quick to act. Will, she felt, was too persuadable to be sent to London to bring her back (Eleanor was resisting being 'rescued'), so Margaret was dispatched instead, wringing her hands at her sister's 'passionate wilfulness':

'Margaret is sensible, & spirited, not a very good temper, & I am *afraid* of her & Eleanor falling out; but I have given & will give her many warnings about this, & about the hidden influence that will be pulling on the other side . . . I write all sorts of grammar, & all sorts of spelling, & all sorts of paper, for I am in a great hurry.' (L271)

But if Elizabeth cared for her servants, she also depended on them, and not merely for practical help. Hearn, who had seen her through the black days of grief after Willie's death, remained her chief support. When she was away, all fell apart: servants departed, keys were lost, even the butter woman failed to come. The importance of servants in her life is reflected in her fiction, where they play a more central role than in the novels of any of her contemporaries. Indeed the mistress often seems more like a child, while the servant is a source of strength. Alice Wilson in *Mary Barton* runs her sick mistress's shop; Martha steps in to give Miss Matty a house in *Cranford*; Hester protects Rosamund from the spirits in 'The Old Nurse's Story'; Miss Monro, the governess, provides a home for Ellinor in 'A Dark Night's Work'. At moments of crisis servants constantly take the initiative: Nancy in *The Moorland Cottage*, Sally in *Ruth*, Amante in 'The Grey Woman', Peggy in 'Half a Lifetime Ago', Norah in 'The Manchester Marriage', Betty in *Cousin Phillis*. All are depicted with affection and deep respect.

In 1850 Elizabeth had need of Hearn. She was unwell on and off all year, telling Tottie in April about the foreign trips of all her rich Manchester friends and apologizing for not having read Robert Browning's new poem: 'you see I've been very poorly; and yet we've been dining out at a great rate, bidding good bye to people in the unsentimental way of eating their dinners'. (Her ill health, which was quite genuine, never stopped her going out when she wanted to, although it came in useful when she did not.)

That spring she had also been busy helping Pasley and, with prison visiting on her mind, was wrestling with a scheme on behalf of Thomas Wright. She wanted to get Bishop Lee, Salis Schwabe and other local dignitaries to contribute to a fund to buy G. F. Watts's painting *The Good Samaritan*, which had been exhibited at the Royal Academy with an inscription honouring Wright. Her unreliable London inter-mediary, Tom Taylor, who always missed appointments, drove her to distraction: 'That Mr Tom Taylor is born to get me into scrapes I verily believe!' Wright himself was a frequent visitor at Plymouth Grove, who took tea and 'said "*By Jingo*" with great unction, when very much animated, much to William's amusement, not to say delight'.

During this burst of social responsibility Elizabeth also acted as a link in the chain distributing Christian Socialist tracts, asking her brother-in-law William Robson to give them to working men in Warrington. Sometimes she wearied of all this good work, and longed to satisfy that 'self with a full taste for beauty', but her social conscience pricked her. She envied Tottie her London concerts and galleries, feeling that holy music and grand pictures would be calming and 'take the fretting pain out of one's heart'. There was no beauty of either nature or art in Manchester, she lamented, which might 'take one out of one's little self – and shame the demon (I beg its pardon) Conscience; or to sleep. My idea of Heaven just now is a place where we shan't have any consciences.'

Her conscience was allowed to sleep a bit that summer, which was taken up with holidays and house-moving, with her trip to Winder-mere and the writing of *The Moorland Cottage*. At the end of August Mary Green's daughters, Annie and Ellen, aged fourteen and fifteen and great friends of Marianne and Meta, arrived from Knutsford 'for a month's music mastering'. The house was full, William was away and Elizabeth was ill again: 'I am obliged to lie down on the sofa constantly which I think addles my brains for I feel very stupid . . . I am very happy nevertheless making flannel petticoats and reading Modern painters.' Like so many Victorian women who astonish us with their energy, Elizabeth's intense activity was interspersed with frequent collapses into illness and, like her peers (although not to the degree of Elizabeth Barrett Browning), when she took to her sofa, she sought relief in opiates. This was quite usual, and she openly discussed it with Charlotte Brontë three years later, as she explained in the *Life*:

'I asked her if she had ever taken opium, as the description given of its effects in "Villette" was so exactly like what I had experienced, – vivid and exaggerated presence of objects, of which the outlines were indistinct, or lost in golden mist &c. She replied, that she had never, to her knowledge, taken a grain of it in any shape.' (Ch. 13)

In many ways Charlotte was the tougher of the two. Elizabeth's migraines and neuralgia and feelings of total lassitude were often the results of stress, although at this stage the doctors put the symptoms down to 'spinal irritation'. In 1850, however, judging from a description given by the German writer Fanny Lewald, who was staying with Geraldine Jewsbury in early September and spotted Elizabeth at a concert, one would never guess how strained and tired 'this beautiful woman' really was:

'Rather tall, full figure, robust, with black hair and a lively reddish-brown complexion. You would unquestionably take her for an Italian from the shape of her head, the cut of her features, and from her complexion . . . There is in her appearance such a stamp of vigour and completeness that you do not find the healthy intellectual grasp of things and uniformity of talent exceptional in such a woman.'[8]

Soon after that concert she was sent to the sea to convalesce for a couple of weeks at Poulton-le-Sands near Lancaster, and at the end of October William insisted she go south, since in Manchester there was already 'thick fog till ten or eleven, beginning again at four'. Sir James Kay-Shuttleworth had advised her to move altogether, 'advice which I feel to be good, and yet which I cannot follow; for the work appointed both for my husband & me lies in Manchester'.

She stayed first at Boughton House near Worcester with her cousin Charlotte Holland Isaacs. There she saw other cousins of Swinton Holland's family, from whom, she said, she had 'been separated nearly eighteen years, but with whom are associated some of the happiest recollections of my childhood', and during this stay she found time to write 'The Heart of John Middleton'. In November she went on to London, to find a school for Marianne, which both parents hoped might cure some 'faults of mental indolence' and improve her music, which seemed to be her only talent. At sixteen Marianne was lively but

frivolous, something of a worry to her parents. There is some hint too
that this was a move to get her away from an awkward adolescent
romance. Elizabeth told Tottie, who had offered to have MA to stay,
that William 'should not like her to be without me for so long a time
just now, when we want to examine into the real state of her feelings –
(not much touched I fancy,) – and besides you know Wm's anxiety
about his girls, and I believe he is afraid of her going to London for the
first time without me to take care of her'.

She looked carefully at several schools, rejecting one because it
showed 'the very worst style of dogmatic hard Unitarianism, utilitarian to the backbone' and another because it had too many pupils, '30 I
believe'. Before long she settled on a school in Hampstead run by Mrs
Lalor, the wife of the editor of the Unitarian *Inquirer*. It had been
recommended by Tottie, and although Elizabeth and William hoped
Marianne would be able to go to lectures at Queen's College, they
chose it more for its atmosphere than its academic record. Elizabeth
had been warned that Mrs Lalor had brusque off-putting manners but
was

'told by her old pupils that her power of forming conscientious,
thoughtful, earnest, independent characters is very great, and that her
manners are very soft and tender towards her pupils, whatever they
may be to comparative strangers. Now I like a dark cloud with a silver
lining, far better than one that turns out all its silver to inspection.'
(L138)

In London Elizabeth and Marianne saw a great deal of Tottie, but
stayed mainly with the Shaens: 'Does Marianne Gaskell make too
much noise for you in that tiny room?' Catherine Winkworth asked
Emma Shaen. 'Or is she quiet and good, as she is sometimes, especially
to sick people?'[9] William came down at Christmas, bringing Meta,
who had never been parted from her sister for so long before. They
were very close, and the following April Elizabeth was to tell
Marianne: 'Meta cried sadly last Sunday because you did not write to
her.' After William went home Elizabeth joined in the London social
round, going to 'a Christmas tree' at Chevalier Bunsen's, where she
met Radowitz and Mme Klausen, staying with Hensleigh and Fanny
Wedgwood and the Procters, and dining at the Dickenses with the
Carlyles and Catherine Crowe, of ghost-story renown. Then she spent
the next month at Crix, where in the quiet of the Shaens's 'warm,

267

sheltered home' she finished a new story, the comic 'Mr Harrison's Confessions', which was published in Jane Loudun's *Ladies Companion* that spring.

At the end of January 1851, after almost four months away, she finally returned to Manchester, to plunge into a fever of furnishing and planting at Plymouth Grove and resume her proper place (in Manchester's eyes) at William's side. Marianne was now settled at Mrs Lalor's, where she stayed for the next two years, apart from holidays. Her mother wrote to her weekly and these letters to her 'dearest Polly' (which, fortunately, Marianne did not burn, despite instructions) give an intimate view of the Gaskells' domestic and social life. They were the kind of letters Elizabeth liked to get herself: 'Your yesterday's letter was a charming one,' she told her daughter once, 'full of detail and very satisfactory.' Her own were crowded with such satisfactory detail, relating the progress of garden, greenhouse, poultry and pigs (William buying a new cold frame, Florence and Julia watching a robin building a nest in the greenhouse) and recounting the visits, dinners, parties, marriages, births and deaths of all her circle, until the mind is dizzy with names.

The tone is light, full of mingled affection and frustration with her teenage daughter: Marianne *must* remember to practise her music daily, must do exercises for her 'naughty' shoulders, must *not* go to the Tagarts', where Elizabeth felt there was a 'rude, quarrelsome atmosphere' (although at the end of the year she was busily writing gossipy letters to Helen and Emily Tagart and by 1852, although she still shrank from their 'frightful' bonnets, was telling Marianne she *must* go and see them because they were so kind). Sometimes the advice is more fundamental. Marianne should think, for example, before she speaks on subjects like free trade (she recommends her to read Cobden's speeches and Adam Smith's *Wealth of Nations*). On this last point, perhaps smarting from criticisms directed at herself, she adds:

'Seriously, dear, you must not be a *partizan* in politics or in anything else, – you must have a "reason for the faith that is in you", – and not in three weeks suppose you can know enough to form an opinion about measures of state. That is one reason why so many people dislike that women should meddle with politics; they say it is a subject requiring long, patient study of many branches of science; and a logical training which few women have had, – that women are apt to take up a thing without being even able to state their reasons clearly, and yet on that insufficient knowledge they take a more violent and bigoted stand than thoughtful men dare to do.'

Her advice is clear:

'Have as many and as large and varied interests as you can; but do not again give a decided opinion on a subject on which you can at present know nothing. About yr bonnet get it *large*, and trimmed with white.' (L148)

The heartfelt lecture is exceptional: bonnets are far more common subjects. After a year Elizabeth reports that Hearn, holding up her hands in despair, declares Marianne should be dressed in leather: 'Can't you wear your *blk* jacket to your *green* skirt?' Even clothes can bring out her sense of language (and her ear for small snobberies):

'*Don't* call Shifts Chemises. Take the pretty simple *English* word whenever you can. As Mrs Davenport said the other day "It is only washerwomen who call Shifts '*chemises*', now". But independently of the word we shall be most glad of the *thing*. Flossie is in her last shifts in two senses of the word.' (L181)

The letters are sprinkled with common mother's complaints ('Be sure you take care of MY *cameo* brooch. I find you have got it; now I only lent it to you and value it extremely, and would not have it lost on any account') and there is all the fond fussing over a daughter away from home. An early note brings to mind Peter Jenkyns's plea in *Cranford* when he starts at boarding school: 'Mother, dear, do send me a cake and put plenty of citron in.' This is Elizabeth's version:

'*May* you have a cake, you great Baby? And if we send you a cake, you must have a box, & if you have a box, do you want anything besides compasses, & Shakespeares, & seeds? Send me word about the cake.' (L151)

Elizabeth judged Mrs Lalor's school a success, and, she wrote cryptically, 'a proof of how evil works out good'. She thought Polly more independent, helpful and happy and felt that her singing had improved, although in September, she told Nancy Robson resignedly, she still 'looks at nothing from an intellectual point of view, & will never care for reading, – teaching music, & domestic activity, especially about children will be her forte'. Describing Marianne led her to reflect on her other children. The two younger girls were still being taught at home by Rosa Mitchell. Nine-year-old Florence, who was so often ill, was a problem – 'no talents under the sun; and is very nervous and anxious' – but Julia, nearly five, was 'witty, & wild & clever & droll, the pet of the house'. Meta, however, was clearly the cleverest. Self-critical, good at music, skilled at drawing, she too would be sent away two years later to a school run by Rachel Martineau (James's sister) in Liverpool. Now, at fifteen, she was 'untidy, dreamy and absent; but so brim full of I don't know what to call it, for it is something deeper and less showy than talent'.

Meta was not always quiet. She shone, for example, at their riotous sessions of charades. In March 1851 Tottie, Meta, Florence, Julia and Meta's friend Annie Austin all acted in the 'outer lobby, under the gas; and we stood on the staircase in the inner hall and the folding doors were thrown open'. The first word they chose was highly appropriate, and so, less obviously, were the individual scenes, with their hints of religion, mystery, female sisterhood under threat, usurpation of male divine power and a writer's potential downfall:

'Awe – a nun brought before the Inquisition. Tottie (nun) rushed in from the back stair-case door, was caught by Annie and the doors flew open, and displayed the three judges dressed in black with blk masks on (your 3 sisters.) Thor the Scandinavian god, – a piece of his life &c. Author a scene or tableau of Hogarth's Distressed Author.' (L147)

Less solemnly, in January 1852, Meta acted a tipsy Irish woman so well that Katie Winkworth said they 'nearly died of laughing'.[10]

Throughout the spring of 1851 Elizabeth sent her family news and Manchester gossip to Marianne in London. In the midst of the flow – which covers pages without a paragraph – is a calendar of events: in February a royal benefit concert ('I did not see the Queen. Our box was right over her head'), a visit from Emily Winkworth, a Darbishire family wedding; in March a stay at Capesthorne, William Carpenter's lectures, Papa's lumbago and the arrival of Tottie, who stayed until May; in April news of the Wedgwoods' trip to Paris and a return visit from Mrs Davenport of Capesthorne.

Mrs Davenport had to be shown all Manchester's glories and charities and the account of her stay gives a vivid sense of Elizabeth's life. On the first afternoon they visited a school at Swinton 'to hear the band – 20 boys, playing on trumpets &c every kind of brass wind instrument, a double drum and *four* common drums. You may fancy the noise, as none played piano.' The next morning, with Tottie, they saw the Deaf and Dumb Asylum and, on impulse, Elizabeth offered to take one of the boys, who wanted to be apprenticed to a calico printer, to their next stop, the Schwabes' print works: 'and you can't think what a commotion of talking on the fingers there was directly among all the children'. The tour was completed by lunch at the Schwabes' grand house (deaf and dumb boy still in tow), and the afternoon was filled by shopping. Most of Elizabeth's days were equally full and although Mrs Davenport asked them to stay, to meet Lord Ebrington and Monckton Milnes, 'we seem to have too many engagements to be able to accept of it'.

As summer came round again, Manchester slowly emptied. There was a special migration southwards that May, to the Great Exhibition in London. The Crystal Palace in Hyde Park, with its million feet of glass, was one of the wonders of the age. It held over fourteen thousand separate displays, and during this year would welcome six million visitors. Almost everyone the Gaskells knew seemed to be going, sometimes escorting foreign visitors, like the Swedish novelist Frederika Bremer, who apparently 'annoyed Mrs Davenport and Mrs Stanley a little by her habit of – how shall I express it – *spitting* right and left, in the Exhibition, and not entirely sparing private houses'. The Gaskells must go too – a visit was *de rigueur*. William hoped to take Marianne and Meta in June, but they were worried that Mrs Lalor's holidays might interfere with his plans to go to the British Association meeting in Ipswich in July. 'In short every possible plan is in a whirl; and nothing is settled.'

Matters were further complicated when Florence fell ill and went to recuperate, with Julia and Hearn, at Moss Farm at Bowden, near Knutsford. She was still weak when they returned, despite the fresh air and farmhouse bread:

'She is nursed on the knee just like a baby & does not want to be spoken to or disturbed. Only to put her head against our shoulders & lie still. Papa has given her ½ a glass of port wine at 11 o'clock for some days past which is a good deal for a little girl of her age. Poor darling!' (L836)

It seemed that they would never get away, but one great compensation was a visit from Charlotte Brontë, on the way home from *her* visit to London in late June. And where Elizabeth saw chaos, Charlotte saw domestic bliss.

Charlotte Brontë came to Plymouth Grove three times, in 1851, 1853 and 1854. Gaskell's relationship with her is complex. On one level she saw in her the longed-for literary sister. They exchanged books, complained about publishers and reviewers, and in the next four years she eagerly sought Charlotte's opinion on work in progress – the ending of *Ruth*, the plot of *North and South*. Charlotte never felt the same need for advice. But she was always responsive and generous and in 1853, for example, answering a frantic appeal, asked George Smith to postpone *Villette* so that it would not clash with *Ruth*. She reassured Elizabeth in these moving words:

'I dare say, arrange as we may, we shall not be able wholly to prevent comparisons; it is the nature of some critics to be invidious; but we need not care: we can set them at defiance; they *shall* not make us foes, they *shall* not mingle with our mutual feelings one taint of jealousy; there is my hand on that; I know you will give clasp for clasp.'[11]

Elizabeth did give clasp for clasp. While, as a writer, she respected what she genuinely felt to be Charlotte's superior genius, she set out, as a friend, to help what she saw as a suffering woman, six years younger than herself. One way she showed this was to press her to stay with them in Manchester, to escape her moorland fastness. Far from resenting this as interference, Charlotte appreciated the kindness strongly: 'I wish to see *you*,' she wrote in that letter about *Ruth*. On this first visit the weather was boiling and Charlotte was exhausted after London sightseeing, so they did little but sit indoors and talk. Charlotte told her publisher George Smith that she found her stay with Mrs Gaskell 'very pleasant':

'She lives in a large, cheerful, airy house, quite out of Manchester smoke; a garden surrounds it, and, as in this hot weather the windows were kept open, a whispering of leaves and perfume of flowers always pervaded the rooms. Mrs Gaskell herself is a woman of whose conversation and company I should not soon tire. She seems to me kind, clever, animated and unaffected; her husband is a good and kind man too.'[12]

The girls, she told Mrs Smith, 'scattered through the rooms of a somewhat spacious house – seem to fill it with liveliness and gaiety. Haworth Parsonage is rather a contrast'.[13]

In the *Life* Gaskell describes how Julia, then nearly five, would steal her hand into Charlotte's, and how when she asked her to show Miss Brontë to a room, Charlotte objected, because, she said, she was so pleased to 'have her attention spontaneously'. In one letter Charlotte asked: 'Could you manage to convey a small kiss to that dear but dangerous little person Julia? She has surreptitiously possessed herself of a minute fraction of my heart, which has been missing ever since I saw her.' She told Elizabeth she knew that she would hang back like a fond but bashful suitor on seeing Julia and Florence again: 'Such is the clearest idea I can give you of my feeling towards children I like, but to whom I am a stranger. And to what children am I not a stranger?'[14]

Elizabeth was in the opposite position, all too aware of the demands as well as delights of small girls, longing for time alone. Later that year, determined to find some time each day for herself, and watching her cousins and friends submerged in household cares, she would muse to Annie Shaen:

'Strange is it not that people's lives apparently suit them so little. Here is a note from Miss Brontë oppressed by the monotony and solitude of her life. She has seen *no one* but her Father since 3rd of July last. Here is Mary Holland and Louy at Knutsford absolutely *ill* for want of being more by themselves – each wishing that she could be alone in the evenings. Well! – the world's a puzzle.' (L169)

Charlotte's visit revived Elizabeth's spirits and at last, at the very end of June, once Flossy was better, she went with William, Meta and Marianne to join the exhibition crowds. She went to the Crystal Palace three times and swore never to go again. Like Charlotte (who was taken five times), she found it noisy, crowded, confusing and hectic, and decided firmly that she was '*not* scientific nor mechanical'. William and Meta, by contrast, went often, 'but not enough they say. That's difference of opinion.'

William always loved exhibitions. In June 1854 the re-erected Crystal Palace was opened by Queen Victoria in Sydenham and Elizabeth asked John Forster if he could gain admission for William. Forster came up with an 'Editor's ticket':

'and when once inside he found a friend able & willing to show him more than he had time to see. He heard all the music rehearsed, saw most things very agreeably if only cursorily, was introduced to many people of note, all through the medium of – hold your nose lest you sneeze at the idea! of a worthy *tobacconist* in Manchester who has contracted to supply all the drinckables [*sic*] . . . I know you will be glad to hear he got in & saw so much even through such ignoble means. For my part I am so grateful I mean to take snuff for the future.'[15]

In 1851 the Great Exhibition was William's sole reason for going to the capital, which he never liked, and he absolutely refused to 'have an engagement or *to have it known he is in London*', so Lily's gregariousness was kept in check. Altogether she felt rather downhearted. On 14 July, after a week at home, the family took off again to Holborn Hill on the Cumberland coast, near Duddon Sands. They stayed at a clean little inn, said Elizabeth, '& paid £5 a week for all & everything; had plenty to eat and the house very comfortable'. Elizabeth had hoped to take a holiday in Scotland and by contrast Holborn Hill was a disappointment, an ugly place, two miles down a dull road from the sea, with no good walks nearby, so after ten days they packed up and retreated to their old lodgings with the Prestons at Skelwith, where they stayed until mid-August.

The tone of dissatisfaction – with the exhibition, with Holborn Hill – is a new one in Elizabeth's letters and suggests a tension that was not there before (or had been hidden more successfully). Her home life was happy and busy, as Charlotte Brontë noticed, but Elizabeth was under strain. She thought William was overworked and, like herself, in need of a proper holiday. The previous year she had asked his old friend, Charles Herford, if he could arrange for William to accompany him on a trip to Palestine, since he was 'so fagged with the monotonous exertions of so many years', and at one point rumours spread that the Gaskells were even planning to leave Manchester for good.[16]

From now on she tended to blame her troubles upon Manchester, its climate and its demanding society. All was not sweetness and light in the Gaskells' circles. By the end of 1849 the scholarly Froude had found Manchester directness hard to take. On the one hand he was shocked by Geraldine Jewsbury's flippancy, shown by such things as a 'very coarse story' about the *Nouvelle Héloïse*. On the other hand, he told Max Müller, 'the Unitarians here, partly from dislike of my books and partly from a foolish jealousy of an Oxford man coming down and putting out their lights, show me a cold shoulder, and even look coldly on the Darbishires on my account'. By April 1850 his dislike had become a passion:

'We hate Manchester – Manchester in any form – Unitarian Manchester most of all. Vulgar and insolent: as they practise little virtue among themselves, so they pretend to even less than they possess, by the gracelessness of their manner; and when we leave the place, which we shall do in the summer, we shall leave it without breaking any ties except such as one might form with a prison cell.'[17]

He and his wife left Manchester that June and moved to the romantic quiet of Plas Gwynant at the foot of Snowdon in North Wales.

In early spring of 1851 Elizabeth herself had fallen out with her old friends the Darbishires, deciding, after an '*untrue* conversation at Miss Marslands', that Mrs D.D. was not to be trusted. The breach was slow to heal. She told Emily Tagart in December: 'We are in a *very* uncomfortable state with the DDs, and shall be all our lives long I suspect; we speak but ice would be warmer than our manners.' Not until early 1853 could she write that 'the S.D.Ds and we are *really* I think becoming thick again', and even then she held back warily.

In this dispute Elizabeth felt she was in the right, but in the same letter to Emily Tagart she had to apologize for her own unkind remarks to Robert Darbishire's fiancée, Harriet Cobb: 'I was *really* and *gravely* sorry for what I said.' She said she had been 'fidgetty' about calling on Harriet, but William had made her go and she almost felt like ringing the doorbell and running away, and 'was so uncomfortable that I dare say I was cross, and repelling, as people often tell me I am, where I know in my heart that I have been feeling frightened and miserable'. Intimate letters like this and the torrents of gossip which she virtually telegraphed to Marianne, show how impulsive and touchy Gaskell could be. She was prone to swift judgements which she later regretted, like her view of the Tagarts, or of young Alice Winkworth, of whom she wrote in 1852, after she had become one of William's private pupils: 'Alice Winkworth seems a very nice girl. You know I have had a strong prejudice against her, but now it is being overcome.' A few months later she writes: 'We all like her.'

Conversely she sometimes fell speedily in love with new friends but cooled towards them later. A case in point was Susanna Winkworth, who had moved nearer to the Gaskells in 1850 as housekeeper to her brother, Stephen, in Nelson Street. Although Elizabeth saw her constantly, one detects a touch of tension in their relationship, since Susanna was so clearly what she could never be, a true intellectual whose work was respected by scholars like Chevalier Bunsen and – more significantly – by William Gaskell. Self-doubt hovers behind her gibes that the interest in Susanna's translation of *Niebuhr* had led to *Mary Barton* being called 'frivolous', and beneath this joking appeal to Tottie:

'I wish you could see S.W. she is so funny and cock a hoop about Niebuhr, she snubs me so, and makes such love to William he says "my life is the only protection he has – else he *knows* she would marry him". I wish you could hear him speaking thus in a meek fatalist kind of way, and I believe she *would* too. *Can't* you marry her to Mr. Forster; then I *cd* die in peace feeling that my husband was in safety.' (L190)

In 1853, after *Niebuhr* was admired by the critics, she told Tottie acidly that Susanna 'is wiser than ever since the Times said she was no average woman'.

The sheer closeness of Manchester circles made for irritation. After her rather unsatisfactory summer Elizabeth's September was rushed and fraught, with Emily Winkworth's marriage to William Shaen, at which William officiated, and a visit from the Tagarts, who had to be sent on to the Darbishires' since their arrival clashed with that of Thomas Carlyle, on his way home from Scotland. Jane Carlyle, who was staying with Geraldine, had dined with the Gaskells and been for drives with Elizabeth, and decided that Plymouth Grove would be an ideal hotel for Thomas, 'very large & in the middle of a shrubbery and quite near this' (a note to Elizabeth simply announces that Mr C. will be delivered to the door at ten that night). She gave her husband her latest sharp opinion of Mrs G.: 'a very kind cheery woman in her own house; but there is an atmosphere of moral dulness about her, as about all Socinian women'.[18]

Elizabeth's dullness may have had something to do with the pressure she was under. The only place she could really relax was Knutsford, and she gladly agreed to go there in mid-October to give her cousin

Lucy a rest from looking after the elderly Dr Holland, who was now almost completely blind. From Church House she went on to stay with the Greens, with Mrs Davenport (who was to marry Lord Hatherton the following February) and with the Robert Gregs at Norcliffe. She enjoyed these calls on old friends and Knutsford gave her the breathing-space she so much needed. While there she resolved to order her life more quietly. On her return to Manchester she told Annie Shaen:

'I am so much better for Knutsford – partly air, partly quiet and partly being by myself a good piece of every day which is I am sure so essential to my health that I am going to persevere and enforce it here.' (L168)

She would have no 'poppers in', she would make sure she was out with the children 'all calling time', she would get all her entertaining done in one blow with large parties instead of endless dinners and only write letters when the girls' singing teacher came: 'So don't you approve of these rules for my life; – I don't mean with regard to writing anything like a book, but solely for my own health and mind.' She put her rules into practice at once. Susanna Winkworth had suggested that she come over for the day, 'but I, possessed of my love of solitude – or rather my sense of its *necessity*, savagely declined'. It was now that she compared her position to that of Charlotte Brontë's solitary life.

Her good resolutions were futile. She had returned to a stream of concerts and dinners and children's parties and guests. Edward Holland and family came to stay, and so did Mrs Fletcher from Grasmere, with her daughter Margaret and son Angus. With them Elizabeth went to the huge meeting in the Free Trade Hall where Kossuth, the Hungarian revolutionary leader, addressed an audience of seven thousand people. William, who heard him at a smaller private meeting, told Susanna it was all he could do to refrain from weeping 'and he did see many of the hard Manchester faces covered with tears'.[19] Elizabeth was more suspicious: she thought Kossuth 'a WONDERFUL man for cleverness' and admired his power to move his audience, but fanaticism like his always disturbed her:

'I am not quite *sure* about him, that's to say I am *quite* sure about his end being a noble one, but I think it has so possessed him that I am not quite *out and out* sure that he would stick at *any* means.' (L172)

Amid this whirl came moments of peace, like the day when Susanna found her with her feet on the fender reading Thomas Beddoes's poems and William so enjoying having the house to themselves 'that he chuckled over it every morning at breakfast'.[20] And some of these free days could be used for writing. She was disillusioned with publishers like Chapman and 'that man Marples' at Liverpool who was churning out copies of an edition of *Libbie Marsh* but paying nothing, and told Tottie that she was thinking of reviewing for the *Critic*, which would pay her 3d a line, but 'Wm is very mad about it, and calls me names which are not pretty for a husband to call a wife, "great goose" etc'.

Of course, despite that disclaimer to Annie – 'I don't mean with regard to writing anything like a book' – she *was* in fact writing a book. From March onwards she had been discussing *Ruth* with close friends. She was still wincing at the reception of *Mary Barton* and now that she was about to speak out on the even more sensitive topics of 'fallen women' and illegitimate children, she openly sought support. Her new approach troubled Katie Winkworth, who told Emma Shaen: 'I can't help feeling that Mr Forster and we shall spoil "Ruth" in itself, as well as for ourselves, by talking it all over with Lily and being summoned to give judgement and advice on it.'[21] Their encouragement, however, kept her going. By November she had almost finished the first volume, but after her visit to Knutsford in October a new subject had begun to fill her mind. *Ruth* was put aside while she wrote a very different kind of story, prompted by her memories of that small Cheshire town. At the beginning of December she sent Charles Dickens the opening episode of *Cranford*.

[14]

Making Safe: *Cranford*

When Elizabeth retreated to Knutsford in October 1851, she found it a haven from the rush of Manchester and the stress of writing *Ruth*. But although it was still familiar and dear, much had changed: Aunt Lumb was long gone, Aunt Abigail too, and Peter Holland was old and blind. In the past two years the visits to Chelsea and Warwickshire and her friendship with Mrs Fletcher had made her think of her father and her girlhood, but she was now forty-one, and events like the Great Exhibition made her feel as if science and progress were sweeping away the era of her youth. She could still hear these echoes when she read old family correspondence, like the yellow bundles of letters which Matty Jenkyns brings out in the Cranford candlelight. Writing to Lizzy Gaskell, when she was expecting a baby in 1852, she asked: 'I wonder if odd bundles of old letters would amuse you in your confinement? I dare say you would not care for them, but you *might*.' At the same time she had been reading a succession of books which dealt in different ways with childhood, youth, loss, change and memory: Wordsworth's *Prelude*, Tennyson's *In Memoriam*, Dickens's *David Copperfield*, Southey's *Life and Correspondence*. 'Have you read Southey's memoir?' she asked Tottie in late 1849. Robert Southey, like herself, had been brought up by his aunt, referred to as 'Miss Tyler, of cleanly memory' in the opening pages of *Cranford*.

Cranford was the final stage in a process of recollection, gradually transmuted into fiction, which began with 'The Last Generation in England' in 1849, and continued with 'Mr Harrison's Confessions', in spring 1851. In 'The Last Generation' Gaskell describes the hierarchy of the small town of her youth from the top downwards: the landed gentry; the professional classes; the shopkeepers; the 'usual respectable and disrespectable poor'; and the alienated fringe, hanging on the outskirts of society 'and every now and then dropping off the pit's brink into crime', attacking the old ladies on their way back from card parties. The germ of Cranford's famous opening line is here, as Gaskell notes in passing: 'if ever there was an Amazonian town in England it was —'.[1] But it is when she moves on to behaviour and anecdote that we step into the true Cranford territory of tightly regulated morning calls, passionate games of Preference and eccentric stories which are yet parables of survival – the cow in the lime-pit who is given a flannel coat, the lace which is eaten by (and rescued from) the cat.

Such stories were part of Holland family lore. In 1854, in the middle of a torrent of gossip to John Forster, Elizabeth wrote, completely inconsequentially:

'Shall I tell you a Cranfordism. An old lady a Mrs Frances Wright said to one of my cousins "I have never been able to spell since I lost my teeth".' (L290)

Her cousins were always good sources of anecdotes and in 1858 Marianne repeated one to their American friend Charles Eliot Norton which is typical in its absurdity, its suggestion of nosy interference and its delight in wonderfully silly linguistic invention. 'I remember so well,' writes Marianne, 'the particular Knutsford story that took Mr Wild's fancy, but I am sure we must have told it you.'

'Some cousins of Mama's very often had an old lady staying with them who was most inquisitive and if the cousins had been out of the room or were away from her for some time, on their return this old lady would make a point of saying "Well Mary and what have you been doing". Mary told her, but in time this grew very tiresome, so they determined to invent a word which was to mean anything they chose. So the next time the old lady asked her Everlasting question of "Well Mary and what have you been doing" Oh said Mary I have been "scrattling". The old lady never liked to betray her ignorance of this word so she said "Oh scrattling have you and a very nice employment it is for you".'[2]

Once Elizabeth had turned back to Knutsford for 'The Last Generation', such material was irresistible. Her move from fact to fiction came in 'Mr Harrison's Confessions', where the town, as

Duncombe, takes on full comic character.[3] It is still judged from the
outside, and not without condescension since it is seen through the
eyes of a man, and a stranger, Frank Harrison. Frank arrives from
London expecting provincial peace, only to find that within minutes of
his arrival he is the object of intense speculation and gossip. Any slight
connections he may have with the great are magnified a thousand
times and as an eligible bachelor he is immediately subject to the
marital manoeuvrings of at least three formidable matrons: the fierce
Miss Tomkinson, who marks him down for her sister Caroline; Mrs
Bullock, who sees him as the means of getting rid of her intelligent,
unwanted stepdaughter Jemima, and even his own kind housekeeper
the widowed Mrs Rose. His own heart is given to Sophie, the vicar's
daughter, and after a tangle of misunderstandings (like a provincial
version of Sheridan, whose plays Elizabeth so enjoyed) all is resolved
when Frank saves Sophie's life with a new medicine which the old
doctor has mistrusted as 'poison'. (Newfangled science prevails in the
end.)

Grief does enter Duncombe with the death of Sophie's small
brother, but the story is a comedy, with a play-like structure, its short
scenes pushing the action forward through dialogue. In one of these
Frank eavesdrops on a conversation between Mrs Rose and Mrs
Munton, the leader of Duncombe society, about his gift to Mrs Rose of
a sewing table, bought at an auction by mistake. As Mrs Munton is
deaf, Mrs Rose has to speak rather loudly:

' " . . . a present from Mr Harrison."

Mumble, mumble.

"Who could have told you, ma'am? Miss Horsman? Oh, yes, I
showed it to Miss Horsman."

Mumble, mumble.

"I don't quite understand you, ma'am."

Mumble, mumble.

"I'm not blushing, I believe. I really am quite in the dark as to what
you mean."

Mumble, mumble.'

And so it goes on, the subject changing suddenly to another friend's
'mucous membrane' (which calls forth 'a commiserating mumble')
and finally returning to Frank, by which time we know that Mrs Rose

is well and truly hooked by the rumour that he is courting her. The modern equivalent of this simple, clever scene would be hearing one end of a telephone call. Here, as throughout, Gaskell teases the reader with her first-person narration (often a means of twisting rather than expressing the truth). We slowly begin to wonder if Frank is quite as 'frank' as he pretends to be, or even if his recollections are not true at all, but simply a yarn spun to entertain his friend while Sophie puts the baby to bed. Gaskell's facility and versatility seem particularly striking when this ironic comedy is placed next to 'The Heart of John Middleton', published only a few weeks before.

The social range of 'Mr Harrison's Confessions' is almost as broad as that of 'The Last Generation', extending from the doctors, the Rector, the well-off farmers and shopkeepers down to the respectable poor. The wit is critical as well as affectionate (the gossip-monger, Miss Horsman, has a touch of malice lacking in Cranford's Miss Pole, the Tomkinson sisters show an insensitivity to the poor unthinkable in Deborah or Matty Jenkyns). When '—' and Duncombe became Cranford, Gaskell narrowed her focus and moved closer to the heart of her subject, concentrating on one layer, the community of single women, defined in 'The Last Generation' as the daughters of aristocratic families, 'with their genealogy at their fingers' ends' (Cranford's Hon. Mrs Jamieson), the widows of cadets of these families, 'also poor and proud' (Mrs Forrester), and the 'single or widow ladies' (Miss Pole, the Misses Jenkyns, Mrs Fitz-Adam). In *Cranford* professional men like the doctor, Mr Hoggins and the Rector, or shopkeepers like Mr Johnson, appear solely in relation to the 'ladies', while the dangerous lower orders do not appear at all, except in the women's vivid imaginations.

Elizabeth originally intended to write only one episode. Her first story, 'Our Society at Cranford', which appeared in *Household Words* on 13 December 1851, is complete in itself. It describes the narrator's memories of the small town 'many years' ago, and tells how the genteel life of the ladies of Cranford, especially that of the middle-aged daughters of the town's late Rector, Deborah and Matty Jenkyns, is disrupted by the arrival of the bluff ex-soldier Captain Brown. The Captain has a position on the new railway, which has been 'vehemently petitioned against by the little town':

'and if, in addition to his masculine gender, and his connection with the obnoxious railroad, he was so brazen as to talk of being poor – why, then, indeed, he must be sent to Coventry. Death was as true and as common as poverty; yet people never spoke about that, loud out in the streets.' (Ch. 1)

Captain Brown, despite his blindness to the importance of Cranford's trivial ceremonies, and his even worse blindness, in Deborah Jenkyns's eyes, in preferring Dickens to Dr Johnson, wins the ladies' trust by his kindness (and usefulness) and his evident care for his sick elder daughter. When he is knocked down by a train, having been, as the county newspaper puts it, 'deeply engaged in the perusal of a number of "Pickwick" which he had just received', his death shakes them to the core. Miss Jenkyns, his arch-rival, still thinks of him fondly when she is 'old and feeble' in the months before her death.

The death of Captain Brown was the first time that Dickens ventured to edit without Mrs Gaskell's approval, changing the book that the Captain reads so enthusiastically from *Pickwick* to *Hood's Poems*. This was understandable, as he could not be seen to puff his own book in his own journal, but Elizabeth was extremely upset, also understandably, as the contrast between Johnson's solemnity and Dickens's humorous humanity was integral to her argument. When she objected, he took shelter behind a favourite excuse:

'I write in great haste to tell you that Mr Wills in the utmost consternation has brought me your letter just received (4 o'clock) and that it is *too late* to recall your tale. I was so delighted with it that I put it first in the No. (not hearing of any objection to my proposed alteration by return of Post) and the No. is now made up and in the Printer's hands. I cannot possibly take the tale out – it has departed from me.'[4]

He would do anything (he said) rather than cause her a minute's vexation, and signed himself 'the unfortunate but innocent, Charles Dickens'. There was nothing she could do except put *Pickwick* back as soon as *Cranford* was published in volume form, in 1853.

Within a fortnight (despite her later insistence to John Ruskin in 1865 that she 'never meant to write more, so killed Capt Brown very much against my will'), Elizabeth sent Dickens the story of Matty and Mr Holbrook. He responded with teasing flattery:

'My Dear Mrs Gaskell

If you were not the most suspicious of women, always looking for soft sawder in the purest metal of praise I should call your paper delightful, and touched in the tenderest and most delicate manner. Being what you are, I confine myself to the observation that I have called it "A Love Affair at Cranford", and sent it off to the Printer.

Faithfully Yours Ever

CHARLES DICKENS'[5]

Her subject had pulled her back. Over the next sixteen months she would write six more Cranford stories.[6] The great difference in tone between *Cranford* and 'Mr Harrison's Confessions' is largely due to the fact that Gaskell's narrator is not a male outsider but a young woman familiar with the town, who no longer only half hears, or half understands. In 'Our Society at Cranford' she is merely a nameless intermediary with a distant public, but as the episodes progress she gains a name, Mary Smith, and a history of her own, and begins to take a significant part in the action. Having, as she says, 'vibrated all my life between Drumble and Cranford', she can be both detached and fond, knowing and naïve, as she is when she comments on the Misses Jenkyns's practice of adding new wine to old dregs in their decanters: 'I fancy poor Captain Brown did not much like wine; for I noticed he never finished his first glass, and most military men take several.' (Since she insists Miss Matty open new bottles for the Gordons, we know, despite her innocent tone, that she quite understands the Captain's abstinence.)

We are made to sympathize with, yet stand back from *Cranford*'s comedy, through Mary's fond acceptance but shrewd understanding of such foibles, which are not those of Cranford alone, but can be met everywhere (Miss Matty's conviction that green tea keeps her awake, for example, came from an episode on one of Charlotte Brontë's visits). Through Mary, Gaskell quickly lets us see behind the screens. In the opening episode the circle of friends waits for Mrs Forrester's maid, a little charity girl, to enter grandly with the tea-tray. They know perfectly well that she has just been helped to carry it upstairs by her mistress,

'who now sat in state, pretending not to know what cakes were sent up; though she knew, and we knew, and she knew that we knew, and we knew that she knew that we knew, she had been busy all the morning making tea-bread and sponge cakes.' (Ch. 1)

Although the pretence is funny, it is not fiercely mocked, because we see it for what it is, a necessary strategy for preserving dignity and self-esteem. But some other pretences, as much a principle of Cranford life as 'elegant economy', are more dangerous and must be gently cleared away. These are the great illusions: that the guide to a person's worth is their social status and that the Amazons can survive perfectly well, indeed better, without that unnecessary and annoying species – men.

The women's strengths and weaknesses, the enclosed nature of their world and their defensiveness which masquerades as aggression are all displayed in *Cranford*'s splendid, Johnsonian opening paragraph:

'For keeping the trim gardens full of choice flowers without a weed to speck them; for frightening away little boys who look wistfully at the said flowers through the railings; for rushing out at the geese who occasionally venture into the gardens if the gates are left open; for deciding all questions of literature and politics without unnecessary reasons or arguments; for obtaining clear and correct knowledge of everybody's affairs in the parish; for keeping their neat servants in admirable order; for kindness (somewhat dictatorial) to the poor, and real tender good offices to each other whenever they are in distress, the ladies of Cranford are quite sufficient. "A man," as one of them observed to me once, "is *so* in the way in the house!".' (Ch. 1)

Gaskell does not ridicule: it is an achievement for women – especially single, middle-aged women – to order a world, even a small one, according to their desires, and their real tenderness, casually but carefully mentioned as their final virtue, is much needed in the wider world. But their female independence is illusory. In fact in every single Cranford story, there *is* a man in the house, in spirit or memory if not in body. Despite their protestations, we gradually learn that none of these single women has deliberately set out to live without men. Even Deborah Jenkyns once harboured dreams of marrying an archdeacon, however much she now emulates her namesake the stern Hebrew prophetess and would, in Mary's view, scorn 'modern' notions of women's equality – 'Equal, indeed! She knew they were superior.'

The tongue-in-cheek opening, written in the present tense, suggests a static, unchanging world. This too is an illusion. Cranford does alter in the course of the story and Gaskell shows that change, although painful, is not necessarily bad. The small social group begins to encompass those hitherto banned on grounds of class. By the date at which the main action is set (the 1830s and 1840s) the narrow circle is giving way to pressure from below; the Hon. Mrs Jamieson accepts an invitation from Betty Barker, a retired milliner whose elder sister had been her own maid; her sister, Lady Glenmire, happily drops her title to marry the local doctor. The patriarchal certainties and strict laws of precedence of the eighteenth century that Deborah Jenkyns invokes – those of 'my father, the Rector' and 'the Great Doctor', Samuel Johnson – have been of value in giving the women dignity and providing rules to control their lives. After Deborah's death these start to give way to the more flexible ethos of the nineteenth century, embodied in her kindly, unworldly younger sister, Matty (who takes after her mother), and in Captain Brown, who starts the shocking process of change by being courteous to all, regardless of class.

Good can come out of change, however threatening. The Captain, who at first makes the women moan over the 'invasion of their territories by a man', turns out to have a tenderness equal to that of any woman. His death is not really due (as Deborah persists in believing) to his reading *Pickwick* and failing to see the train but to his instinctive act of jumping on the line to save a small girl, throwing her into her mother's arms. Metaphorically his death also returns the father-dominated Deborah to her mother's arms, unloosing her hidden kindness as she nurses his dying elder daughter and accompanies Jessie, the younger, to his funeral in the interests of both 'propriety and humanity'. But humanity is already overturning propriety. Deborah not only allows Jessie to 'weep her passionate fill' at the graveside, but welcomes her returned lover, Major Gordon. Matty, horrified to see a man in the drawing-room with his arm round Jessie's waist, is dumbfounded when Deborah, the dragon of decorum, tells her that this is 'the most proper place in the world for his arm to be in'.

Humanity will triumph in the future too. Jessie marries Major Gordon and years later their daughter, Flora, the Captain's grand-daughter, is seen dutifully reading Johnson's *Rambler* to a now frail Deborah. But in the intervals, when Miss Jenkyns is reminiscing about 'poor Captain Brown' and Mr Boz, Flora uses the time to 'get a good long spell at the "Christmas Carol" which Miss Matty had left on the table'. *Christmas Carol* is apt, as *Pickwick* was apt, for past, present and future meet in that book on the table.

The *Cranford* stories were written to entertain, and Gaskell has fun adapting the stock conventions of serial fiction: the railway accident, the childhood sweetheart, the servants' romance, the bank failure, the long lost brother.[7] Yet they have a serious argument. The fundamental proposition is that middle-aged women on their own become strong by supporting each other and that their old age need not be bleak and lonely. But we are slowly brought to see how limited their lives and viewpoints are, and are led to suspect too that the women do not understand their *real* strength, which lies not – as they think – in their strict social codes but in their kindness and concern for each other – their 'feminine weakness'. Towards the end of the series, in 'Stopped Payment', when Matty is ruined by the collapse of the Town and County Bank, her first thought is not for herself but for the farmer standing in the shop beside her holding a worthless note, which she exchanges for her carefully saved sovereigns. It is her personality not her position in society that brings out the generosity in others: in the friends who pledge secret donations, in her servant Martha, in the Rector, who buys and tries to give back her books, in the shopkeeper Mr Johnson, whom she consults about her plans to sell tea, contrary to all competitive rules of trade. Respecting her openness, he sends her his customers, who in turn bring presents of cheese, eggs, fruits and flowers. *Cranford* expresses the dream that the meek may inherit the earth, at least in fiction. As Mary comments:

'my father says, "such simplicity might be very well in Cranford, but would never do in the world." And I fancy the world must be very bad, for with my father's suspicion of everyone with whom he has dealings, and in spite of his many precautions, he lost upwards of a thousand pounds by roguery only last year.' (Ch. 15)

A second argument, woven into the first, is that masculine authority, stern pride and rigid rules are not positive strengths but barren weaknesses. Snobbish pride in the Jenkynses' family connection with Arley Hall prevents Matty's marriage to Mr Holbrook, leaving her with a child she holds only in her dreams, not in her arms. The Rector's sense of dignity leads him to flog his son, Peter, when he crosses the border of decorum (and gender) by publicly dressing up as Deborah carrying a baby; when Peter runs away to sea, his mother's heart is broken. After her death Deborah takes her place in caring for their father: 'His eyes failed him and she read book after book, and wrote, and copied, and was always at his service in any parish duties.' Her slavish devotion to her father replaces thought of marriage; there will be no Jenkyns heirs except in Matty's dreams and Peter's mimicry, no line into the future.

Paternal authority, taken to excess, blights rather than fosters life. Gaskell asks us to look elsewhere for male strength and finds it first in the combination of skill and courage with an underrated 'feminine' capacity to care, a quality which saves lives – as the doctor, Mr Hoggins, despite his vulgar bread and cheese suppers and creaking boots, saves Signor Brunoni, as Captain Brown saves Lord Mauleverer in the wars, nurses his daughter and saves the child at Cranford station, as Peter Jenkyns cures the chief of a Burmese tribe and little Phoebe Brunoni in India. And men have other strengths which the women of Cranford, with their meagre education and sheltered lives, sadly lack. They have a wider knowledge of the globe (about which the ladies are woefully muddled) and a familiarity with learning and literature (the Rector's classics, Mr Holbrook's love of poetry). They bring into the women's enclosed lives a hint of transgressive magic (in Signor Brunoni's tricks, in Peter Jenkyns's traveller's tales). The wider sphere in which they move may embrace war, empire and cut-throat trade, but the men who actually enter Cranford's life – from Captain Brown onwards – have a beneficial effect in prompting the women to modify those rules which have bound as well as supported them.

Cranford is not a separatist Utopia, but an appeal *against* separate spheres, an argument for preserving the independence and the precious qualities of this female community, while opening the gates to the boys who gaze at the flowers through the railings. The model of society which it asks us to consider is one where men and women live together side by side and benefit from both 'masculine' and 'feminine' virtues. It is a model of partnership based not on marriage but on a bond where the balance of power is less unequal, that of brother and sister, reunited – like Matty and Peter Jenkyns – after too long apart.

Cranford is a rich and rewarding book. Yet its richness is very subtle and its comedy so delicate that it can seem to repudiate analysis as too heavy, a violation of its mood. We are not asked, as we are with Gaskell's serious novels, to think as we read. Instead we are cajoled into acceptance of underlying arguments by our surrender to the absurdity of inconsequential detail and apparently casual or odd conjunctions. The surface of the text lulls, surprises and distracts; it works by sleight of hand, like Signor Brunoni's conjuring. 'Don't you think Mrs Gaskell charming?' Dickens asked Forster in 1852.[9] 'Charm' is a dread word in Gaskell criticism, often used to belittle her achievement, but in this case it is right. The spell the stories cast comes from the telling, the minutely particular creation of a self-contained world.

Cranford constantly undercuts solemnity, its humour resting on an upside-down sense of priorities which endow 'realism' with the unreality, crazy logic, leaping connections and total divorce between language and meaning later found in Lewis Carroll. Miss Matty, who can never remember the difference between astrology and astronomy, *does* believe astrological predictions but tells Mary confidentially that she can *not* believe 'that the earth was moving constantly, and that she would not believe it if she could, it made her feel so tired and dizzy when she thought about it'. Later, desperately trying to pin down a rumour that Peter Jenkyns had somehow become the 'Great Lama' of Tibet, Mary finds herself listening to a dispute as to whether llamas are carnivores, in which Mrs Forrester admits that she

'always confused carnivorous and graminivorous together, just as she did horizontal and perpendicular; but then she apologized for it very prettily, by saying that in her day the only use people made of four-syllabled words was to teach how they should be spelt.' (Ch. 12)

The women have no suspicion that they might be deemed comic or absurd. They cannot see anything wrong, or even at all odd, in their ignorance and in their preoccupation with the concrete and immediate as opposed to the intellectual. The priorities of the everyday can be just as serious – one of the old Rector's high-flown epistles, enclosing a tender Latin lyric, is endorsed in the margin: 'Hebrew verses sent me by my honoured husband. I had thowt to have had a letter about killing the pig, but must wait.'

The technique of juxtaposing the profound to the everyday is brilliantly employed in *Cranford*, both to puncture pretension and to reconcile comic surface with emotional depth. The shock when Peter runs away is felt in the heap of wilting petals, intended for the cowslip wine that his mother will now never make. Martha's sympathy and love for the ruined Miss Matty is expressed not in tearful consolations but in a pudding, and no ordinary pudding at that, but a 'lion *couchant*' with currant eyes, a creation worthy, Matty says in all seriousness, of being kept under a glass shade. She cannot understand why Mary laughs:

' "I am sure, dear, I have seen uglier things under a glass shade before now," said she.

So had I, many a time and oft, and I accordingly composed my countenance (and now I could hardly keep from crying), and we both fell to upon the pudding, which was indeed excellent – only every morsel seemed to choke us, our hearts were so full.' (Ch. 14)

The whole story of Matty and Mr Holbrook is cast in this vein. Matty does not meet her old lover after thirty years in a romantic setting but in the shop, where she is choosing silk 'to match a grey and black *mousseline de laine*' and he is asking for woollen gloves. The impact of the encounter is shown simply by the way the silks are forgotten and the gloves unpurchased. When Matty visits his house, Woodley, the site of her youthful hopes, Holbrook tries to express his feelings indirectly through poetry, particularly Tennyson's 'Locksley Hall' (1842), a poem which Gaskell does not quote, but which her readers would associate with lost love and youth, with the rejection of modernity, commerce, war and class violence, and also with a bitter taunt against women's inconstancy:

'I am shamed thro' all my nature to have loved so slight a thing

Weakness to be wroth with weakness! woman's pleasure, woman's pain –
Nature made them blinder motions bounded in a shallower brain;

Woman is the lesser man, and all thy passions, matched with mine,
Are as moonlight unto sunlight, and as water unto wine –.'

Matty and Miss Pole, however, are unlikely to hear this message:

'nothing would serve him but he must read us the poems he had been speaking of; and Miss Pole encouraged him in his proposal, I thought, because she wished me to hear his beautiful reading, of which she had boasted; but she afterwards said it was because she had got to a difficult part of her crochet, and wanted to count her stitches without having to talk. Whatever he had proposed would have been right to Miss Matty; although she did fall sound asleep within five minutes after he had begun a long poem called "Locksley Hall," and had a comfortable nap, unobserved, till he ended; when the cessation of his voice wakened her up, and she said, feeling that something was expected, and that Miss Pole was counting –

"What a pretty book!" ' (Ch. 4)

A few days later, fired by youthful vigour, Mr Holbrook sets off to Paris. Before leaving he gives Matty the book she had admired; its contents, its author, are still a blank to her.

'And he was gone, But he had given her a book, and he had called her Matty, just as he used to do thirty years ago.

"I wish he would not go to Paris", said Miss Matilda anxiously. "I don't believe frogs will agree with him; he used to have to be very careful of what he ate, which was curious in so strong-looking a young man".' (Ch. 4)

It is the last time they meet. When Mr Holbrook dies on his return from France, Matty's unspoken grief is expressed only by that most Cranfordian object, a new bonnet. But as she silently reviews that lost opportunity of love, she decides to overturn one of her deepest ingrained codes, inherited from Deborah, and suggests that she *might* allow her maid Martha a follower. The all too real present springs up to replace the past: 'Please, Ma'am, here's Jem Hearn, and he's a joiner, making three-and-sixpence a day, and six foot one in his stocking feet.' 'Though Miss Matty was startled,' the story concludes, 'she submitted to Fate and Love.'

As we would expect of Gaskell, each carefully placed detail – of food, clothing, furniture, books – adds to our understanding of this world. In their concern for propriety Matty and Miss Pole risk losing the good things of life – Mr Holbrook's delicious green peas slip uncontrollably through the ancient two-pronged forks he has given them and they have to give up with a sigh. Only Mary, boldly breaking the rules and using her knife like her host, enjoys the feast. And often the Cranford ladies sleep, deaf to the poetry of life, or, like Miss Pole, count the stitches and fail to see the pattern.

The poignancy of *Cranford* comes partly from this telling use of mundane detail, but even more from the dreamlike shifting and sliding of planes of time; 'more than half a lifetime and yet it seems like yesterday,' says Peter when he is reunited with Matty. In the description of the day at Woodley, and even more in the next episode, 'Old Letters', a past which has been suppressed or locked away invades the present. The central group of women resemble the Assembly Rooms in which they meet to see the conjuror, a little worn and faded now, but brushed by memories of long gone parties and blushing beauties, 'a dusty recollection of days gone by'. The very prose evokes nostalgia: John Forster – who loved these stories – forecast in 1853 that 'the little book which collects them will be a "hit" if there be any taste left for that kind of social painting'.[9] This implies that the writing follows an older tradition, yet it is extremely hard to find any particular model. There are rustling echoes of Mary Russell Mitford's *Our Village*, of Lamb's *Essays of Elia*, and perhaps of Maria Edgeworth and Jane Austen. A. W. Ward, editor of the Knutsford edition, who pondered all these sources, perceptively directs us to Crabbe, one of the earliest and most enduring influences on Gaskell's writing, and quotes 'The Maid's Story':

> Poor grandmamma among the gentry dwelt
> Of a small town, and all the honour felt;
> Shrinking from all approaches to disgrace
> That might be marked in so genteel a place;
> Where every daily deed, as soon as done,
> Ran through the town as fast as it could run; –
> At dinners what appear'd – at cards who lost or won.[10]

The old-fashioned feel of *Cranford*, whose humour is far gentler than Crabbe's, comes less from imitation of any other writer than from its own unusual incorporation of time. The episodic narrative moves like an act of memory itself, overturning chronology, giving distant and near events equal weight – just as one can be lost in a day-dream but aware of the hardness of the chair, the motes of dust in a sunbeam. The narration, even in small passages, has an enfolding quality. Anecdotes are often told backwards, like Mary's early recollection of a Cranford party, which starts by her observing that it was very good of Deborah Jenkyns to keep time to Jessie Brown's out-of-tune singing, then moves backwards to explain what had happened just before (Jessie's ill-considered remarks about her uncle's wool-shop which had made Deborah urgently suggest some music) and then forwards again ('so I say again, it was very good of her'). But of course this is still *not* the present, for the whole incident is set back several years in time. The habit of retrospection, placing present against past, even marks individual lines of dialogue, as in Matty's comment about Paris, frogs and Mr Holbrook's youth, or her seemingly simple inquiry, 'Have you drawers enough dear? . . . I don't know how my sister used to arrange them.'

The overall structure of the story-cycle has a similar backwards–forwards movement, and this is particularly interesting since it was in no sense planned. The first half of the book reveals a scouring of the past that modern psychoanalysts might recognize as having a pattern resembling that of therapy, a process of reaching back to unspoken trauma and then to childhood that enables the subject, in this case Matty Jenkyns, to come to terms with hidden pain and look to the future. Thus the first episode looks back from 1850 to the mid-1830s when Matty is most under Deborah's control, while the next probes further back to the time of her youth (about 1810), before her forced separation from Mr Holbrook, her long illness and the loss of her hoped-for marriage and children. The third, 'Old Letters', takes us even deeper into the past, to her parents' courtship in the 1770s. The opening of her father's letters to her mother is associated with scent, that most powerful memory-inducing sense, 'a faint, pleasant smell of Tonquin beans', and the letters themselves have 'a vivid and intense sense of the present time, which seemed so strong and full, as if it could never pass away'.

Unlike Deborah, who diligently copied her father's words, Matty lets them go: 'We must burn them, I think,' she says. One by one she drops his letters into the fire, 'watching each blaze up, die out, and rise away in faint, white, ghostly semblance'. As she reads of her parents' marriage then of Deborah's birth and of her own, memories are released. At this point a new figure enters *Cranford*, who has so far been exiled from the town, and from the text: her brother, Peter. Gaskell does not appear to have planned to include him when she began to write, and Mary perhaps expresses something of her own surprise:

'It seems curious that I should never have heard of this brother before; but I concluded that he died young; or else surely he would have been alluded to by his sisters.' (Ch. 5)

The story of 'Poor Peter', his practical jokes, his punishment and disappearance and his mother's grief and death, is as sad as that of Matty's lost love. She believes him dead and admits that 'it sometimes fidgets me that we have never put on mourning for him', but at other times she listens for his footstep in the street and her heart flutters – but he never comes.

Matty's open talk of Peter is like exorcism of a ghost, or a formal act of mourning: the retrospective movement of the stories ceases and from now on the momentum is forward. If the episodes so far seem to describe an unconscious therapy for Matty, their writing was also, perhaps therapeutic for Elizabeth herself. Like Virginia Woolf in *To the Lighthouse*, Gaskell intuitively returned in memory to a particular place which allowed her both to explore the world which had formed her – that of the 'old uncles and aunts' – and to face the pain she left unspoken, the loss of her brother, the loss of her child. At this point of discovery, as though some need had been fulfilled, the mood of the Cranford stories altered. The next episode, 'Visiting at Cranford', which appeared in *Household Words* in April 1852 (later divided into chapters 'Visiting' and 'Your Ladyship'), suggests that the world of Matty and her friends is due for an upheaval, although the Amazons now appear at their most snobbish and silly and the action is still firmly anchored in a world of appearances, reverence and ritual. This atmosphere is wonderfully evoked by Mrs Jamieson's drawing-room when she takes the unusual step of giving a party for her sister, Lady Glenmire:

'The chairs were all a-row against the walls, with the exception of four or five which stood in a circle round the fire. They were railed with white bars across the back, and knobbed with gold; neither the railings nor the knobs invited to ease. There was a japanned table devoted to literature, on which lay a Bible, a Peerage, and a Prayer Book. There was another square Pembroke table dedicated to the Fine Arts, on which were a kaleidoscope, conversation-cards, puzzle-cards (tied together to an interminable length with faded pink satin ribbon), and a box painted in fond imitation of the drawings which decorate tea-chests . . . Mrs. Jamieson stood up, giving us each a torpid smile of welcome, and looking helplessly beyond us at Mr. Mulliner, as if she hoped he would place us in chairs, for, if he did not, she never could. I suppose he thought we could find our way to the circle round the fire, which reminded me of Stonehenge, I don't know why.' (Ch. 8)

That stone circle is about to be broken: Lady Glenmire turns out not to be grand at all but poor, kind, good at Preference and fond of lace (exactly like the rest of them), and later jolts the town by marrying Mr Hoggins, muddy top-boots and all.

After this episode Gaskell paused in her writing. So far the first Cranford stories had appeared in *Household Words* in a fairly steady sequence since December 1851. Then after April 1852, there came a long break, while she worked on *Ruth*. One can understand why Dickens scribbled 'Cranford???' at the foot of a letter in December 1852.[11] Gaskell returned to Cranford at the end of that year, as soon as she had finished her novel, with a sense of release and enjoyment; the next episode was published in January 1853 and the final three came in a rush in April and May. The second half of *Cranford* is very different from the first; Lady Glenmire's marriage to Mr Hoggins is only one of the ways in which social rules are broken, boundaries crossed and romance joyfully overturns reality. The town had always had more than a touch of the bizarre, but now Gaskell makes her characteristic leap away from realism, using the women's preoccupation with appearances and the arrival of the conjuror, Signor Brunoni, to emphasize the gap between illusion and reality.

In the chapters 'Signor Brunoni' and 'The Panic', for example, a host of romantic dreams and suppressed fears are, so to speak, wrapped up in the constant Cranford concern with head-gear, beginning with the fashionable sea-green turban that Matty longs to wear at the conjuror's show. When the sensible Mary wisely (but so disappointingly) brings a neat, middle-aged cap and Matty finally sees the Signor's Turkish splendour, she looks through her eye-glass, wipes it and looks again and remarks, 'in a kind, mild, sorrowful tone – "You see, my dear, turbans *are* worn." ' Signor Brunoni's turban is not noticed only by Matty; it leads Mrs Forrester, with impeccable sartorial logic, to blame him for the (entirely imaginary) spate of burglaries. Since Cranford people would not disgrace their upbringings by crime, she argues, the robbers must be strangers, and if strangers, why not foreigners?

'– if foreigners, who so likely as the French? Signor Brunoni spoke broken English like a Frenchman, and, though he wore a turban like a

Turk, Mrs Forrester had seen a print of Madame de Staël with a turban on, and another of Mr Denon in just such a dress as that in which the conjuror had made his appearance; showing clearly that the French, as well as the Turks, wore turbans: there could be no doubt Signor Brunoni was a Frenchman – a French spy, come to discover the weak and undefended places of England.' (Ch. 10)

Mrs Forrester is ridiculously wrong (especially as Brunoni is later unmasked as plain Samuel Brown), but she is also unwittingly right. He has uncovered one of the weak and undefended places, the uncharted territory of the women's own alarms and fantasies. He not only suggests their fear of the violence and fatal authority of men ('He had apparently killed a canary with only a word of command; his will seemed of deadly force'), but releases their dark imaginations. It is a small step from magical disappearances to imagining real ones, and then from defending yourself against imagined burglars, as Matty and Miss Pole do, to telling gruesome tales. 'Before we retired,' says Mary, 'the two ladies rummaged up, out of the recesses of their memory, such horrid stories of robbery and murder that I confess I quite quaked in my shoes.' After telling stories like the one about the pedlar's pack which oozes blood and the brave servant-girl who fights off the robbers, it is easy for the Cranford ladies to be terrified by the rumours of a headless woman who haunts 'Darkness Lane'. And of course it is Miss Pole, who has just asserted that ghosts are born of 'indigestion, spectral illusions, optical delusions', who insists they avoid that lane on their way home from Mrs Forrester's.

Stories express emotional truths. The great Cranford 'robbery' turns out to be merely the theft of a neck of mutton by a cat, but when Signor Brunoni (or plain Sam Brown) is found lying sick at an inn, the 'real' turns out to be miraculous. Signora Brunoni tells Mary her story, of how she walked alone across India with her baby, the sole survivor of six children. She carried a Catholic print of a Raphael madonna, and gave thanks in the temples of the natives, who had previously warned her

'from going into the deep woods, which looked very strange and dark; but it seemed to me as if death was following me to take my baby away from me; and as if I must go on and on – and I thought how God had cared for mothers ever since the world was made, and would care for me!' (Ch. 11)

God, she believes, led her to an Englishman who saved her – 'Aga Jenkyns'. The name blends near and far, exotic and familiar.

The saving of the baby and the solace of the mother on her lonely journey through the dark woods of life presage another miracle, the return of the lost brother, 'Aga Jenkyns', who has become confounded in Cranford mythology with *Lalla Rookh*, oriental hair lotions and Peruvian bonds (let alone Lamas and llamas). After the Signora's story, even before the ruin of Matty, Mary is trying to find Peter. She does so in a way that is entirely 'unrealistic', the act of *writing*. She posts a letter to a lost man and sends it to a place with a strange name that no one can spell, far across the rolling ocean. And as she drops it in the box she allows herself to dream:

'for a minute I stood at the wooden pane, with a gaping slit, which divided me from the letter, but a moment ago in my hand. It was gone from me like life – never to be recalled. It would get tossed about on the sea, and stained with sea waves perhaps; and be carried among palm-trees, and scented with all tropical fragrance; – the little piece of paper, but an hour ago so familiar and commonplace, had set out on its race to the strange, wild countries beyond the Ganges!' (Ch. 14)

Mary's gesture is as irrational as Martha's passionate pudding: 'I'll not listen to reason,' Martha cries. ' "Reason always means what someone else has got to say." ' But the irrational is effective: Peter returns to close the circle of time, appearing at the door of the shop with Indian muslin and pearls for the sister he still thinks of as a girl.

Peter brings happiness to Matty by his very presence. She looks forward to the future, insisting they live together with Jem and Martha, and her new little god-daughter, Matilda. And through Peter she can express her generosity; even Mary is given a handsome bound set of Dr Johnson, in memory of Deborah. But Peter wins the admiration of Cranford less by his presents than by his stories, more wonderful than Sinbad's and, as Miss Pole says, 'quite as good as an Arabian Night any evening'. His last trick is worked by an appeal to magic – bringing the friends together at the Gordons' dinner and reconciling Mrs Jamieson to her sister, now Mrs Hoggins, by asking her to sponsor the return of 'Signor Brunoni, magician to the King of Delhi, the Raja of Onde, and the Great Lama of Tibet, etc, etc.' He teases Miss Pole and rouses the apathetic Mrs Jamieson to unusual animation by telling them of his distress when he discovered he had shot a cherubim in the Himalayas, letting the reader – and Mary – know by the twinkle in his eye that this is the realm of fairy tale. His listeners, however, receive such stories in 'perfect good faith'. Fear and pain are exorcized, and peace is brought to Cranford, by fantasy and fiction.

Elizabeth's memories of Knutsford, she said in 'The Last Generation', arose in her mind in 1849 almost of their own volition. *Cranford* inserted itself between her and *Ruth*, just as *Silas Marner* came between George Eliot and *Romola*. Both books demanded to be written at a time of stress in their authors' lives. (It is a sad irony that because of their surface simplicity these two works, so essentially adult in theme and appeal, should always be set texts for schoolchildren, who generally dislike them.) *Cranford*'s comedy is entirely different in tone from Eliot's poetic fable, just as Matty comes from a different society from that of the lonely weaver. Yet in some ways they are not dissimilar. Both authors contrast the self-interest of the aristocratic past and the industrial present to the mutually supportive values of a small rural village or provincial town, and both do so through stories of childless people who find love at the moment they lose material wealth. Both celebrate the caring and maternal in men and women and both make the dangerous safe, touching the tenderest spots of memory and bringing the single, the odd and the wanderer into the circle of family and community.

Perhaps it was this quality of healing, of salving pain through stories cast into the unknown, like Mary's letter, as well as its affectionate recall of well-loved eccentricities that made *Cranford* Elizabeth's own favourite among her books. Shortly before she died, in 1865, she told John Ruskin:

'I am so much pleased you like it. It is the only one of my own books that I can read again; – but whenever I am ailing or ill, I take "Cranford" and – I was going to say, *enjoy* it! (but that would not be pretty!) laugh over it afresh!' (L747)

Overlapping Circles

Elizabeth Gaskell's life was one of unceasing, immediate activity, and the new year of 1852 began with the usual bustle. Tottie was staying, and so were Annie Austin and the Green girls from Knutsford. While the Cranford stories were delighting her friends, Elizabeth was dashing off 'Bessy's Troubles at Home', 'on the very last day', for Travers Madge's *Sunday School Penny Magazine*.[1] In early February Dickens descended on Manchester with his amateur players, touring the north to raise funds for the improvident Leigh Hunt. John Forster gave Elizabeth a private ticket and she took the Winkworths, only to find that their front row seats at the Free Trade Hall, right under the 'very raised stage', gave her a crick in the neck and a terrible headache. She told Agnes Sandars:

'The play is very long too, 3 hours & a half, & they omitted 1 scene. And very stupid indeed. The farce was capital. Dickens was *so* good, & Mark Lemon, – D Jerrold was not there and Mr Forster was sadly too long over his very moral sentences in the play.'[2]

On evenings out she always preferred laughter to sober instruction.

The social excitements continued into February, when she visited Capesthorne to see Caroline Davenport's trousseau for her wedding to Lord Hatherton. It was good material for a gossipy account and provided memories on which she would draw in the opening chapter of *North and South*, where Margaret Hale stands draped like an eastern princess in Indian shawls, while her aunt's friends exclaim at their cost. Mrs Davenport's wedding finery was 'quite like the Arabian nights . . . six beautiful Indian shawls, endless jewellery . . . including two complete sets of diamonds and opals etc'. Elizabeth was shocked by the wife of the architect Henry Blore, who was 'in ecstasies at every separate piece, & put on rings until she could not bend her knuckles to try & come up to Mrs Davenport's grandeur'. She hoped never to see Mrs Blore again: 'such a testing of everything by money I never heard in my life'. She herself was stirred by the sheer beauty of the shawls, lilac, crimson and blue, embroidered and fringed in gold: 'oh *dear*! they were so soft and delicate and went into such beautiful folds!'[3]

She went back to Capesthorne again to witness Caroline's touching farewell to her tenantry (at which everyone cried), and in March visited Teddesley to inspect the new Lady Hatherton's married splendour (and to grill her gardener for *Household Words*).[4] Capesthorne was a contrast to another February visit, to the Samuel Gregs at Bollington, who were so despondent over the failure of Sam's idealistic industrial schemes that they thought of going to New Zealand.[5] Most Manchester manufacturers, however, were in buoyant mood. There was a grand ball at the Schunks' and another at Park Hall, given by Robert and Mark Philips.[6] (Both brothers were MPs and Mark had allegedly been the model for Mr Millbank in Disraeli's *Coningsby*.) Sharp elbows were needed here as there were nearly three hundred guests and a terrible 'crush & crowd into supper. Mrs Schwabe & I tried 3 times before we got in.'

While Elizabeth was socializing, William, as usual, was immersed in work. He preached as many as three times on Sunday, took evening classes twice a week, taught his private pupils and, with John Beard, was now planning a home missionary college to train would-be ministers from the working classes. He was also liaising with Anglican ministers on a sanitary committee to plan for a feared epidemic of cholera and on another committee for regulating beer-halls. In his spare time he went to lectures at the Lit. and Phil. and was chairman of the Portico Library. It was an energetic, committed life, and William was held in exceptional respect in Manchester, as was shown that autumn when he was invited to give the prizes at the medical school, the first Dissenting minister to be offered this honour.

Elizabeth's only firm commitment to Cross Street was the Sunday school, but she had her own charitable interests. In January and February she was canvassing subscriptions for Thomas Wright, whose health was failing, and in April and May was excitedly supporting the model school at Price's candle factory at Vauxhall, and pressing Dickens to let her write about it in *Household Words*.[7] But Plymouth

Grove was relatively peaceful: William was working, Marianne was at school, Meta was in London for several weeks in March and April, Flossy and Julia were cared for by Rosa Mitchell during the week and Hearn at weekends. For most of the spring Elizabeth settled down to work on *Ruth*.

Yet from April onwards, despite the calm, she felt restless. She and William talked about going to Silverdale again, but the house they liked was booked, so they had to resign themselves to the cramped if romantic tower at Lindeth Farm. With no alternative, she thought they could survive: '3 windows being made to open wide'. Before then they went to London to stay with Emily Shaen, who was expecting her first baby. This time William was surprisingly jolly about facing the city: it was only for two or three days and he was very fond of Emily. He swore that no one would eat the Plymouth Grove eggs – they should all go to her – and even volunteered 'to make his own bed as well as any housemaid if required'.[8] Only after he went back to Manchester, however, did Elizabeth feel really free to enjoy herself: 'Lily in radiant spirits again,' Emily reported, 'half – *I* say – because she has got an espiègle French bonnet', half because F. D. Maurice had asked her to see him again.[9]

She stayed in London until the end of Marianne's term and then returned briefly to Plymouth Grove before the family left for Silverdale. Emily, stuck in the heat of London, thought longingly of them all walking in the woods, having strawberry feasts and bathing in the creek. As usual, however, the holiday was no quiet retreat, although Elizabeth did dissuade Marianne from inviting her favourite teacher, Mrs Lalor's sister, Miss Banks:

'I find Papa does not like the idea of having a *stranger* in the house in holiday time when you know he likes to play pranks, go cockling etc, etc, and feel at liberty to say or do what he likes.' (L850)

This did not stop her from asking her own friends, like Catherine and Stephen Winkworth and Fanny and Hensleigh Wedgwood. Presumably they did not make William feel 'constrained and obliged to be "proper" '. Another guest was Tottie, whom Elizabeth had *begged* to come, glamorizing the 'unhealthy' tower and saying she had made a pact that Tottie would come when she herself gave up the idea of going to Bonn, 'with many sighs because W. was so against it'.

In the mornings Elizabeth worked on her novel, starting early, often before the labourers went to their work. She wrote in the drawing-room at the top of the tower, which had an iron staircase leading to the flat roof, and her room had views all round, of the coast and bays to the south, the open sea to the west and the hazy Lakeland mountains to the north and east. Silverdale's scenery was already part of her novel. Here she imagined Ruth's stay at Eagle's Crag, a house which combined elements of Lindeth Farm and the Cove, a house built on the rocks with zigzag paths down to the bay – where Charlotte Brontë had stayed as a girl, to escape the fever at school.

When Elizabeth wrote of Abermouth, where the Bradshaw children dig channels in the sand and Ruth confronts her former lover, memories of Aber in North Wales blended with Morecambe Bay. When Ruth walks down to the water's edge at one of the great low tides, the view she sees is recognizably that of Silverdale:

'She was perhaps half-a-mile or more from the grey, silvery rocks, which sloped away into brown moorland, interspersed with a field here and there of golden, waving corn. Behind were purple hills, with sharp, clear outlines, touching the sky. A little on one side from where she stood she saw the white cottages and houses which formed the village of Abermouth, scattered up and down; and, on a windy hill, about a mile inland, she saw the little grey church where even now many were worshipping in peace.' (Ch. 24)

Her troubled heroine seems a small, solitary figure, balanced between past and future, as she walks on these vast stretches of sand and hears the moan of the waves 'broken only by the skirl of the grey sea-birds as they alighted in groups on the edge of the waters, or as they rose with their measured balancing motion, and the sunlight caught their white breasts'. In 1910 Gaskell's first biographer, Mrs Chadwick, could still see the black posts on which Ruth fixed her gaze, 'rising above the heaving waters', marking where the fishermen's nets were laid.[10]

Elizabeth was not allowed to write all the time. The Gaskells and friends went on drives to Arnside, the little local port gazing across the estuary to Grange, and to Deepdale, just inland, with its green pool among the trees. William was relaxed and happy and, said Katie Winkworth, 'looks very handsome in his country clothes'. He liked to think up even longer outings, with a great air of mystery. These could be rather daunting. One was a three-day trip across to Yorkshire, involving complicated arrangements with trains and pony carriage, and including tortuous detours. One day William and Meta walked fourteen or fifteen miles across the hills to the top of Airedale, while Lily drove round by a longer road. The road *was* longer and the pony, 'having lived in Manchester all his days, had a strong objection to going down hills, so Miss Fox had to lead him always'.[11] Since the pony was just as reluctant to go up hills as down, in the end they walked almost as much as William and Meta. At last they thought they had reached their goal, only to find that it was the wrong village and they still had to cover six more miles, over what the landlord of the local pub described as 'not a pertikler good road'. 'Lily seemed falling into terrible low spirits at this announcement,' reported Katie, 'but we persuaded her into having some porter and biscuits and she got better and we went on.'

Eventually the two groups met, but then it transpired that William now expected them either to explore the beauty spot at Malham Cove (as he had already done) or to walk with him to the waterfall at Gordale Scar. The more energetic Tottie and Marianne ran after William, who 'darted off at railroad speed'. The rest explored the Cove. Elizabeth opted out completely. This time it was her turn to revive their spirits, if in a rather Spartan fashion: 'When we came back, Lily made us lie down on the floor and drink milk and eat hard biscuits by way of dinner and tea.' They still had eight more miles to go to the inn at Gargrave. Exhausted, convinced they were lost, they traipsed across the billowing moors in the moonlight until long past midnight. It was a day that Elizabeth, and Tottie, remembered all their lives.

The Gaskells returned to Manchester after these wanderings to find half of literary London on their doorstep. On 31 August William was given a last minute ticket to a banquet in honour of the Guild of Literature and Art (founded by Dickens and Bulwer-Lytton). The next day Charles and Catherine Dickens and Georgina Hogarth called very early, and invited the Gaskells down to watch the 'Amateurs', who were performing Boucicault's farce, *Used Up*, J. R. Planché's *Charles XII* and Dickens's own *Mr Nightingale's Diary*. This time Elizabeth avoided a crick in the neck, telling Marianne: 'Papa & I went behind the scenes to see the play and had tea *there*, which was a very luxurious mode of seeing it.'

On 2 September another great event took place, the opening of the Free Library, which placed Manchester proudly in the vanguard of enlightened municipalities. It was one of Britain's first public libraries, the fruits of a bill pushed through parliament in 1850 by the Liverpool merchant and MP William Ewart. John Potter, the mayor of Manchester (and a Cross Street stalwart), raised money by public subscription and the Hall of Science in Campfield, near the city centre, was refurbished and stocked with books (including copies of *Mary Barton*, nervously donated by Elizabeth). The library was a triumph for the city, endorsed by a personal gift of eighteen volumes from Prince Albert, who asked that they should be 'freely accessible to persons of all classes without distinction'.[12] Dickens gave Elizabeth and Meta reserved seats for the grand opening, attended by almost one thousand people. They had excellent places near the speakers, who included John Bright, the Earl of Shaftesbury, Bulwer-Lytton, Dickens, Thackeray, Sir James Stephens and Monckton Milnes.

Afterwards Dickens wrote excitedly to Angela Burdett Coutts:

'I wish you could have seen the opening of the Free Library for the people, at Manchester today. Such a noble effort, so wisely and modestly made; so wonderfully calculated to keep one part of that awful machine, a great working town, in harmony with the other!'[13]

Although the library was 'for the people' and the ceremonies included a special evening session for workers, not one working man appeared on the platform with the local politicians and honoured guests. The event was yet another of those well-intentioned gestures towards democracy which carefully held the people at arm's length, illustrating so clearly the ambivalent attitudes of the milieu in which Elizabeth Gaskell lived. Although Bulwer-Lytton, for instance, talked of a library as a 'mighty arsenal . . . for books are weapons, whether for war or defence', he followed this by a reference to the principles of chivalry, not to the rights of man. Richard Monckton Milnes did mention politics, but his were the defensive politics of appeasement and incorporation, not confrontation:

'It is only, remember, what lies in these books that makes all the difference between the wildest socialism that ever passed into the mind of a man in this hall, and the deductions and careful processes of the mind of the student who will . . . learn humility seeing what others have taught before him.'[14]

Mrs Gaskell, it must be admitted, did not listen very closely to these fine sentiments. In spite of its huge size, the room, she told her 'dearest

Polly', was *'so close*, & the speeches were so long that I could not attend & wished myself at home many & many a time',

'my only comfort being seeing the caricatures Thackeray was drawing, which were very funny. He and Mr Monckton Milnes made plenty of fun, till poor Thackeray was called on to speak & broke down utterly, after which he drew no more caricatures.' (L197)

'Poor Thackeray', tired after his train journey, was stricken into silence within three minutes. He did, however, manage to stutter out his belief that the provision of books was as important as sanitary and social reform, 'and we look to this, as much as we look to air, or as we look to light and water, for benefiting our poor', adding disarmingly that books like his would be a very small part of such a library's collection: novels were 'tarts for the people, and science is bread, and historical and spiritual truth are that upon which they must be fed'.

Despite his failure at public speaking, Thackeray was the hero of the autumn to Elizabeth and her girls. His *Esmond* had just been published (Meta raved about it) and in late September and October he lectured at the Manchester Athenaeum on 'The English Humorists'. Elizabeth and William dined with him before his first lecture at the house of A. J. Scott, the principal of Owen's College, and Elizabeth's birthday present that year was 'Johnson's lives of the people Thackeray is going to lecture about'.

The plans she had made a year before for a quiet life were utterly defeated by the round of visitors and visiting, parties and concerts. That winter, as an indulgence, the Gaskells took out subscriptions to Charles Hallé's concert season. Hallé, who had transformed Manchester music since he took over the old-established Gentlemen's Concerts in 1849, was a personal friend of the Gaskells. He lived near them in Greenheys and became Marianne's music teacher in 1853; thanking him for a letter, Elizabeth once teased him: 'I had no idea you could write – I thought you left that to baser clumsier fingers . . . has anyone in Manchester a similar rarity? I am so pleased – I really never heard of your writing to any one before.'

In the cracks of time left over Elizabeth wrote, and worried about, *Ruth*. At the beginning of October she told Marianne she would give her a copy: 'Only I dislike its being published so much that I should not wonder if I put it off another year.' She had been forced back to work in late September when Chapman told her that Forster had given him the manuscript 'and that the first two volumes *were printed*; all complete news to me! But I set to on the trumpet sound thereof.' Unfortunately, just as she got into her stride, the Wedgwoods came to stay. In mid-October she reeled out of Manchester, to stay with the Davys and Mrs Fletcher in the Lakes, and wrote to Tottie from Lesketh How in a state of collapse:

'Well I'm here! *How* I came, I don't seem to know for of all the weary, killing wearing out bustles in this life that of the last week passed all belief. Thackeray's lectures, two dinners, one concert card party at home, killing a pig, *my* week at the school which took me into town from 9 till 12 every morning – company in the house, Isabella leaving, Wm too busy to be agreeable to my unfortunate visitors (Mr and Mrs Wedgwood, Dot and Jane, their servant, Annie and Ellen Green, closely packed!) so I had to do double duty and talk aesthetically (I dare say) all the time I was thinking of pickle for pork, and with a Ruskian face and tongue I talked away with a heart like Martha's. And at last when Meta's and my cab came to take us to the station not before the house cleared, they smashed into Ruth in grand style. I have not much hope of her now this year, now I've been frightened off my nest again.' (L205)

While she was frightened off her nest, she quickly wrote 'The Old Nurse's Story' for the special Christmas number of *Household Words*.[15] She had visited all her local friends, including the Prestons, and 'The Old Nurse's Story' is told by a woman from the Westmorland fells (like those around Mill Brow). The narrator is a nursemaid at the local parsonage and when the rector and his wife die, she takes her charge, Rosamund, to live with an elderly relation, Grace Furnivall, in Northumberland. The ancient house is lonely and strange, and from the locked east wing wild organ music sounds: 'it rose above the great gusts of wind, and wailed and triumphed just like a living creature'. Here, in the depths of winter, little Rosamund is drawn irresistibly out into the freezing snows by the ghost of a girl of her own age, tapping at the window. It gradually emerges that in her youth Grace lost the man she loved, a foreign music teacher, to her sister Maude and betrayed her to her ruthless father in revenge. Maude and her illegitimate daughter were cast out, to die under a hawthorn bush in the snow. At the climax, amid howling winds, ghostly music and crashing doors, the spirits of the child, Maude and Lord Furnivall suddenly appear and

Grace Furnivall collapses, stricken by remorse: 'Alas! Alas!' she cries, 'what is done in youth can never be undone in age!'

This ghost story is one of the finest Victorian examples of the genre. As if the short form and Gothic, aristocratic setting had released her inhibitions almost without her knowing it, Gaskell produced a bold, sweeping treatment of the same themes – unmarried sex and illegitimacy – that she was currently dealing with so cautiously in *Ruth*. Here she makes no play with 'innocence', but exposes stormy passions in lonely women, attacking the jealous, self-righteous sister and violently punishing the cruel, intolerant father.

Dickens thought it 'a very fine ghost story indeed. Nobly told and wonderfully managed.'[16] But the ending was the cause of a sharp disagreement between him and Elizabeth. He felt strongly that only the little girl, Rosamund should see the phantoms. Elizabeth (having learnt to be swift from her experience with *Pickwick* in the first episode of *Cranford*) replied by return, adamantly insisting that Grace must be *visibly* confronted by her guilt. Both were equally determined. Dickens hung on, proposing to leave the story on one side, 'then to come to it afresh – alter it myself – and send you the proof'.[17] Which he did. She sent it straight back, rejecting his alterations and conceding only that Rosamund should see the ghost-child first. Dickens gave in, but drew himself up to full editorial height:

'I have no doubt, according to every principle of art that is known to me from Shakespeare downwards, that you weaken the terror of the story by making them all see the phantoms at the end. And I feel a perfect conviction that the best readers will be the most certain to make this discovery. Nous verrons.'[18]

Having won, Elizabeth was overcome by nerves at that 'Nous verrons'. Dickens condescended to soothe her. He still thought his ending best, though, and brought out an unanswerable argument: 'All I can urge in its behalf, is, that it is what I should have done myself.'[19]

One of the reasons why Elizabeth was so jumpy was her increasing anxiety about *Ruth*. Now, more than ever, she *had* to believe in her own artistic judgement. Throughout November her nerves were on edge. Forster sent calming letters, telling her to 'have no fears about the book. It will far more than sustain the success of "Mary Barton" – of that I have no doubt.'[20] But she did have fears. In the same week she was telling Marianne that she would *not* give a copy of *Ruth* to Mrs

Lalor, or probably even Miss Banks, 'as I say again, *when* or *if ever* I shall finish it I don't know. I hate publishing because of the talk people make, which I always feel a great impertinence, *if they address their remarks to me* in any way.' She pressed on, alarmed by the fact that the book was announced in the press and that the libraries were expecting it daily. Her panic shows in a long letter to Mary Green, firmly marked 'Private':

'Ruth "has yet to be finished", which is an expression I used only this morning to Wm before your letter came. I mean it is far from completion and I feel uncertain if it will ever be done . . . I am so far from satisfied with it myself, that I don't know how much to re-write, or what to do about it; I was as much startled as you could be by the advertisement. However it will not hurry me, & *until I have thought it out fully* I shall *not* write it, & if I never think it out it will never be either written or (*consequently*) published.'[21]

She promised to warn Mary if it did come out, as 'I doubt it is a book that you will like to have in your family. This is *forced* from me by Chapman's impatience. I don't want to *be* talked to about it, & I don't want it talked about.'

The final chapters were written with great speed and intensity, but then nerves overcame her. She read her work aloud to Katie Winkworth in the evenings, not so much for her listener's comments as to be sure of her own judgement. On 22 November Katie told Emily that *Ruth* was 'not finished yet. Lily is not satisfied with the last 100 pages, and we are going over it very carefully to take out superfluous epithets and sentences, of which there were certainly enough here and there to give it a slightly sentimental twang.'[22] At last, on 20 December, Elizabeth could tell Tottie that 'Ruth is done – utterly off my mind and gone up to the printers, – that's all I know about it'. She was not the only one who had been anxiously finishing a novel. *Villette* was done too, and Elizabeth's words echo Charlotte Brontë's sigh of relief exactly a month before: 'Truly thankful am I to be able to tell you that I finished my long task on Saturday; packed and sent off the parcel to Cornhill. I said my prayers when I had done it. Whether it is well or ill done, I don't know. D.V.'[23] Charlotte, though, could take comfort that her book was not 'of a character to excite hostility'. This was not to be true of *Ruth*.

The novel was finished. Christmas came and went and the new year opened at Plymouth Grove as hectically as the old had closed. There was a servants' party in the kitchen, so family and friends cooked tea on the dining-room fire, 'ham and eggs better than any you have ever tasted'. The fat caught alight and Lily rushed out of doors, blazing pan in hand, past screaming children, to let it go out on the steps:

'The toast was not so first rate . . . I believe we attempted too much for one fire. But the tea was uproarious & then we played at dumb crambo with the children till late bed time & then I whipped them into a hot bath by way of washing made easy. And where Julia's hair is to-day is better imagined than described. Meanwhile the party downstairs went on as joyously. Wm host, Margaret hostess, Hearn heroine, 2 whist tables (great difficulty in finding cards!) I thought it my duty to stay up till company had departed; so it was ½p.11 before I went to bed & what with cutting out in Chapel room, going to Picture Exhibition with Katie cook etc, I *was* tired; I am today too . . . Oh I am so tired.' (L857-8)

Her tiredness is understandable. In the past two years she had been constantly busy and often ill. Yet she had written three strikingly different books – *The Moorland Cottage, Ruth* and most of *Cranford* – as well as several long stories and substantial articles. Her achievement seems almost impossible.

The richness of Gaskell's fiction derives from the very fullness of the daily life which constricted her writing time. She moved in a world where personal contacts and the flow of ideas were so interconnected that the idea of the web will not do, unless one thinks of an autumn hedgerow where web after web glistens in the sun, each so intricately linked to the other that the slightest touch sets them all in motion. A better image is that of overlapping circles, drawn by a compass whose point is fixed in a central circle of Elizabeth's family, marriage and faith. Family relationships shade into a wider Unitarian circle, and this in turn overlaps with others – philanthropic, political, literary, scientific – which embrace people of different religious affiliations: Anglican, Evangelical, Quaker, Christian Socialist, agnostic. Such rings then touch and connect with others, with circles of theologians, writers and radical refugees from Europe, with American Transcendentalists, feminists and abolitionists.

One minor example may demonstrate the mesh of connections.

Nathaniel Hawthorne and Elizabeth Gaskell never met: he will not enter her 'life' in person, but *The Scarlet Letter* appeared in early 1851, when she was beginning *Ruth*. Both novels deal with a sexual fall, social hypocrisy and humiliation, a woman's struggle for autonomy – Gaskell's seducer even bears the name of Hawthorne's governor, Bellingham. Both heroines sew for a living, but Hester Prynne makes her needlework subversive, carrying her scarlet letter openly, while Ruth keeps her transgression secret. Hester is defiant, Ruth penitent, but each woman has a child, the 'badge of her shame', as Faith Benson puts it in *Ruth*, who is also the means of her spiritual self-discovery.

Hawthorne was American consul in Liverpool in 1853 and knew the Martineaus, Henry Bright and other Gaskell friends. Introductions were planned, but not fulfilled, although in 1856 anecdotes about Hawthorne enter Elizabeth's flow of chatter to Marianne. They seem to shadow each other. In 1858 he is in Rome with William Wetmore Story, with whom Elizabeth had stayed the previous year. Later he stays at Redcar in Yorkshire; a few weeks afterwards Elizabeth stays twenty miles away at Whitby. Wetmore's sculpture of Cleopatra, which Elizabeth had admired in Rome, and her own 'stolen' story of the face, which Dickens had told to Emelyn Story and she to Hawthorne, both find a place in *The Marble Faun* in 1860. In 1862 the circle is complete when Gaskell enters Hawthorne's native territory, and the ground of *The Scarlet Letter*, with her Salem story, 'Lois the Witch'.[24]

This kind of close yet indirect exchange is typical. But if we think again of the overlapping spheres, another point emerges. Elizabeth's place within them is always slightly off-centre. She keeps her own perspective, both involved and detached. She is a devoted wife, but her life is separate from her husband's and her writing scandalizes some of his congregation. She is a Unitarian drawn to Christian Socialism and the Anglican liturgy; a Manchester resident who spends most of her time elsewhere; a woman of moderate income who enters the homes of rich and poor but belongs to neither world; a writer who enjoys but is suspicious of the London literary scene. Most relevant to *Ruth*, she holds the same tangential position with regard to the women's movement and to philanthropy, the two 'circles' which bear most closely on her writing at the start of the 1850s.

Both *Cranford* and *Ruth* can be read, with qualifications, as feminist texts. Elizabeth's friends included the older mentors of the emerging mid-century women's movement – Harriet Martineau, Mary Howitt and Anna Jameson – who had been calling for change since the 1830s. And since 1849, through Tottie, she had come to know several younger women in their early twenties, who would become the activists of the next decade. Many of them were the daughters of people she knew, and most had a Unitarian background, like Bessie Parkes, daughter of the Radical Birmingham MP, Joseph Parkes, and great-granddaughter of Joseph Priestley, and her inseparable friend, Barbara Leigh Smith, whose father, Benjamin, had been MP for Norwich. Other members of this group were Adelaide Procter, daughter of the poet Barry Cornwall, who entertained Elizabeth in London in 1849, Anna Mary Howitt, daughter of William and Mary Howitt, and Miranda and Octavia Hill. (Tottie and Octavia both taught at the experimental school which Barbara Leigh Smith opened at Portman Place in 1854.) These were the women who formed the nucleus of the 'Langham Place Group' which organized around the *Englishwoman's Journal* in the late 1850s.[25]

Elizabeth gave them her qualified support. She signed the petition for the amendment of the married woman's property laws organized by Barbara in 1854, and approved their campaigns for education and employment. But she was disturbed as well as attracted by their radicalism. When she tried to take these independent younger women under her maternal wing, she sometimes found herself gently rebuffed, as she was by Dinah Mulock in 1851. Elizabeth was touched by the sight of a 22-year-old trying to make her way alone as a writer in London. In fact Dinah was doing extremely well: she quickly sold the copyright of her first three novels to Chapman and Hall, and when Elizabeth offered to introduce her to friends, she replied, politely but firmly, that she was too busy writing.[26] Elizabeth, slightly put out, set such professionalism against the 'feminine' view of spontaneous, undeniable creativity, which she claimed to share with Charlotte Brontë:

'I wish she had some other means of support besides writing; I think it bad in it's [sic] effect upon her writing, which must be pumped up instead of bubbling out; and very bad for her health, poor girl . . . I think Miss Brontë had hold of the true idea, when she said to me last summer, "If I had to earn my living, I would go out as a governess again, much as I dislike the life; but I think one should only write out of the fulness of one's heart, spontaneously." ' (L167–8)

She was even more startled by the boldness of Barbara Leigh Smith and Bessie Parkes, who travelled unchaperoned on the Continent together in 1850, abandoning convention (and corsets) in a way the Gaskells would never have dreamt of allowing their daughters.[27] Barbara particularly intrigued her. Her father had never married her mother, Anne Longden, and in the words of George Eliot, later Barbara's closest friend, his children were therefore a 'tabooed family'; the Nightingales, their first cousins, refused to have anything to do with them. Gaskell would have no truck with such intolerance and in July 1850 told Tottie rather diffidently: 'Do you know I've taken a great fancy for asking Barbara Smith to come and pay us a visit. *Do* you think she'd come?' She felt that Barbara's battling spirit sprang from her illegitimacy as well as from her father's insistence that she have an educational and financial independence equal to her brothers. In 1860 Elizabeth wrote:

'She is – I think in consequence of her birth, a strong fighter against the established opinions of the world, – which goes against my – what shall I call it? – *taste* – (that is not the word,) but I can't help admiring her noble bravery, and respecting – while I don't personally *like* her.' (L607)

The hesitant search for words underlines her ambivalence. In *Ruth*, when dealing with the unmarried mother and illegitimate child, she herself had fought against 'the established opinions of the world', while also implicitly acknowledging the force of those conventions.

In 1850, when Elizabeth first met Barbara and her friends, there was a new vigour in the fight for women's rights. Transatlantic feminism had reached Manchester: that October an American, Mrs Baxter, lectured at the Mechanics Institute on 'Bloomerism and Dress Reform'.[28] The first Women's Rights Convention in Seneca Falls in 1848 had sent ripples across the Atlantic. Queen's College was founded that year and Bedford College a few months later. Elizabeth had friends connected with both. Frederick Denison Maurice was one of the prime movers of Queen's, and Fanny Wedgwood and Harriet Martineau were on the council of the Ladies College in Bedford Square, founded by Elizabeth Reid, a wealthy Unitarian widow.

A renewed call for political rights soon followed. In 1851 the first women's suffrage petition was presented to the House of Lords, and Harriet Taylor's supporting article 'The Enfranchisement of Women' in the *Westminster Review*. In an apologetic, if curt, exchange with J. S. Mill after *The Life of Charlotte Brontë* Elizabeth claimed not to have read this – which is curious, since she wrote to Charlotte about it (making the common assumption that it was by Mill).[29] Her letter is lost, but in her reply Charlotte said that Elizabeth's words exactly expressed her own view that the article was finely argued but jarred the soul:

'I think the writer forgets there is such a thing as self-sacrificing love and devotion. When I first read the paper, I thought it was the work of a powerful, clear-headed woman, who had a hard, jealous heart, and nerves of bend leather; of a woman who longed for power and had never felt affection. To many women affection is sweet, and power conquered indifferent – though we all like influence won. I believe J. S. Mill would make a hard, dry, dismal world of it; and yet he speaks admirable sense through a great portion of his article – especially when he says that if there be a natural unfitness in women for men's employment there is no need to make laws on the subject; leave all careers open, let them try.'[30]

She concluded: 'In short, J. S. Mill's head is, I dare say, very good, but I feel disposed to scorn his heart.'

The conflict of head and heart, personal rights and loving duties, reverberates through contemporary discussions of women's fitness or unfitness for employment. The 1851 census finally put figures to the problem of the 'superabundant woman', highlighting an issue canvassed throughout the past ten years, particularly in relation to governesses. One of the cries of the 1840s, which Elizabeth heard from the Winkworth and Shaen sisters, was the purposelessness of middle-class women's lives, powerfully stated by Geraldine Jewsbury's heroine Marian Withers in 1851: 'I have nothing to occupy me; nothing to interest me . . . My whole life is stagnating . . . I feel as if I were buried alive. I am good for nothing . . . I am stunned and stupid – nothing seems real, not even I myself.'[31] (The sensation of being buried alive, felt in Gaskell's 'Clopton Hall' several years earlier, is strong in *Ruth*, where stagnation, loss of identity and unreality and a feeling that the world is 'chaotic and strange' form a large part of Jemima Bradshaw's misery.) Florence Nightingale was another who inveighed against the terrible ennui of a life like that of her mother and sister, 'lying on two sofas and telling each other "not to tire by putting flowers into water" '. Her fictional heroine, Cassandra, bitterly questions the position of women: 'Why have women passion, intellectual, moral activity – these three – and a place in society where no one of these can be exercised?' Privately Florence wrote: 'I see the numbers of my kind who have gone mad for want of something to do.'[32]

The most famous of these appeals comes in Brontë's *Jane Eyre*, when Jane goes up to the roof and gazes across the fields, longing for 'a power of vision which might overpass that limit':

'It is vain to say human beings ought to be satisfied with tranquillity: they must have action; and they will make it if they cannot find it. Millions are condemned to a stiller doom than mine, and millions are in silent revolt against their lot. Nobody knows how many rebellions ferment in the masses of life which people earth. Women are supposed to be very calm generally: but women feel just as men feel; they need exercise for their faculties and a field for their efforts as much as their brothers do; they suffer from too rigid a restraint, too absolute a stagnation, precisely as men would suffer.' (Ch. 12)

'It is narrow minded,' Jane continues, 'to say that they ought to confine themselves to making puddings and knitting stockings, to playing on the piano and embroidering bags. It is thoughtless to condemn them, or laugh at them, if they seek to do more than custom has pronounced necessary for their sex.'

It was the jarring, brilliant transition, at the end of this passage, to the crazy laughter of the madwoman in the attic, not yet discovered by Jane, that made Virginia Woolf feel that the book, and Brontë's genius, were distorted by her anger: 'How could she help but die young, cramped and thwarted?'[33] A similar indignation is heard in the passionate appeal to the male sex in *Shirley*:

'Men of England! Look at your poor girls, many of them fading around you, dropping off in consumption and decline; or, what is worse, degenerating to sour old maids, anxious, backbiting, wretched, because life is a desert to them.' (Ch. 22)

In Brontë's view, the only alternative women had was to debase themselves to gain 'a position and consideration by marriage, which to celibacy is denied'.

Elizabeth did have 'a position and consideration by marriage', but she felt profound sympathy for single women. In 1850, writing to Lady Kay-Shuttleworth, she said that while she rather disliked the plot of *Shirley*, she thought the expression of Brontë's own thoughts in it 'so true and brave, that I greatly admire her'. She goes on to mention another woman she admired, Priscilla Sellon, who had founded a lay community, the Sisters of Mercy, in 1848.[34] Surely Lady Kay-Shuttleworth agreed that single women would be happier if they could find work in a community like this?

'I do not think they need to be banded together, or even to take any name, unless indeed such forms strengthened their usefulness; but I think I see every day how women, deprived of their natural duties as wives & mothers, must look out for other duties if they wish to be at peace.' (LI17)

That phrase 'natural duties' is significant. Directing her correspondent's attention to the purposelessness of a life such as that described by Sir James Stephens's daughter Caroline in *Passages in the Life of a Daughter at Home*, she concludes:

'I am always glad and thankful to Him that I am a wife and a mother and that I am so happy in the performance of those clear and defined duties; for I think there must be a few years of great difficulty in the life of every woman who foresees and casually accepts single life.' (LI18)

Elizabeth had, of course, been writing for years about the strength of single women, as well as their struggle, but always within a context of service and mutual support. *Cranford* is a riposte to Brontë's hopeless picture of sour, backbiting old maids, and a protest against inadequate education for girls, but it is not a radical text. While it argues against seeing women only in relation to men and promotes an ideal of brotherly–sisterly partnership, it still upholds the convention of women in the home, men in the world.

Although Elizabeth was too firmly locked in the domestic sphere to be an out and out radical, from 1850 a sharper feminist note enters her fiction, sometimes in unlikely places. It is found, for example, in the picture of Maggie's frustration in the early chapters of *The Moorland Cottage*. Her spoilt brother, Edward, who is sent to school while she stays at home, delivers the conventional view:

'You see, Maggie, a man must be educated to be a gentleman. Now, if a woman knows how to keep a house that's all that is wanted from her. So my time is of more consequence than yours. Mamma says I'm to go to college, and be a clergyman; so I must get on with my Latin.'

Afterwards, as she carries the heavy pail back from the well, Maggie broods: 'I wish I could help being clumsy and stupid. Ned says all women are so. I wish I was not a woman. It must be a fine thing to be a man.' (These chapters anticipate *The Mill on the Floss* in more than the heroine's name.)

A slightly later story, 'Morton Hall' (1853), is more forthright.[35] Its loose trilogy of episodes shows the country swallowed by the city and the declining aristocracy of land giving way to that of trade, but it also offers a history of women, told by women to women; the narrator, her sister and the housekeeper gather round the fire while the father is deliberately sent out on an errand. In the opening episode, set in the Civil War and Restoration, Alice Carr, a powerful Puritan, is betrayed by her husband, who claims her property and sees her as 'a beautiful woman to be tamed and made to come at his beck and call'. When she seeks refuge in austere religion, he seizes, strikes and binds her: 'He unloosed his sash, and bound her arms tight – tight together, and she never struggled or spoke.' Alice is forced from her home and locked away as 'mad'. In the second story, set in the late eighteenth century, Phillis Morton gives up her chance of marriage to care for the hall, ruined by her brother's gambling debts, and eventually dies of starvation. The final, contemporary chapter is a satire on the conflicting theories of women's education. Entrapment, religious mania, silencing, madness, self-sacrifice, starvation, confusion: women's history is a sorry tale.

More current concerns appear in 'My French Master', also 1853, where the heroine, Susan, appeals to her father to let her become a Sister of Charity.[36] In *Ruth*, published in 1853, almost two years before she met Florence Nightingale, Elizabeth was already arguing for the dignity of nursing, then considered a menial occupation, and she later encouraged Meta in this vocation:

'I have told Meta she may begin to prepare herself for entering upon a nurse's life of devotion when she is thirty or so, by going about among the sick now, and that all the help I can give in letting her see hospitals, etc, if she wishes she may have. I doubt if she has purpose to do all this: but I have taken great care not to damp her – and if she has purpose I will help her, as I propose, to live such a life; tho' it is not everyone who can be Miss N.' (L320–1)

'Devotion', however, is still the necessary justification for an independent career. Many people felt that for the single woman fulfilment was best found in philanthropy, an extension of 'natural' domestic responsibility. This was a far better way of getting rid of their frustrations than, say, writing. In this context one of the oddest 'invidious comparisons' between Brontë and Gaskell came at the end of a long review of *Ruth* by the Christian Socialist John Ludlow, in the *North British Review*. Answering the hypothetical questions, 'Why should we have women novelists?' and, if so, '*What* women should write novels?' he declared that married women made excellent novelists but single women did not, and contrasted Mrs Gaskell's 'full and wholesome, and most womanly perfection' with a quality in Miss Brontë which he found 'harsh, rough, unsatisfying . . . unwomanly'. He must have thought his logic unassailable: unmarried women could not write about love since they would either be too 'abstract', working solely from imagination, or too bitter (obvious, since they were unmarried). Writing might be a safety-valve for their 'morbid' frustration or bitterness, but they would do far better to turn to 'living and practical affections and duties'. He goes on:

'The adoptive motherhood of the school may be yours, yours the adoptive sisterhood of the Nurse's Institution, of the Penitentiary, or the simple district visitor. Here, together with the household of your own brothers and sisters, is the sphere within which your heart may preserve itself fresh and lovely, and mellow every year more and more.'[37]

This 'fresh and lovely' prospect is anything but. Yet although Elizabeth, on Charlotte's behalf, took heated issue with Ludlow's point about women writers, she undoubtedly felt some sympathy with the underlying view.

Ludlow ignored another aspect of women's philanthropy, its

enabling power. Through such work they learnt how to organize, form committees, establish networks. They learnt too, as they confronted the plight of poorer women, that the objects of their charity were also subjects, like themselves. All women were victims of economic and sexual exploitation within the prevailing social structure. As Josephine Butler later put it, poor women were merely the base of a pyramid of oppression: the mercenary marriage planned in the drawing-room was little different, in essence, from a brief business transaction in a back alley.[38] *Ruth* depicts both the working-class Ruth Hilton and the well-off Jemima Bradshaw as passive beings, shaped and disposed of by others. In this respect they are sisters. The novel was a daring step in the transformation of working-class women from object to subject, taking the outcast girl with her illegitimate child out of the shadows and making her a heroine with whom middle-class readers were asked to identify.

Writing was Gaskell's most effective form of philanthropy. This was true of her correspondence as well as her fiction. Her letters show her as part of a network extending to London, Scotland, Paris and Boston, discussing ideas, passing on papers, finding addresses, hunting up information. Yet the impression they give of active involvement in a host of initiatives is slightly misleading. She had plenty to say on every good cause, from nurseries and sisterhoods, to ragged schools and workshops. She never said anything she did not mean, but she often replied enthusiastically to correspondents like Lady Kay-Shuttleworth or Mary Cowden Clarke because she knew what they wanted to hear. In practice she had little time, and chose to concentrate on what was near at hand.

For instance, in 1856 the American abolitionist and feminist Maria Weston Chapman visited Manchester: Elizabeth scurried round, gathered up all her friends, set out some chairs and held an impromptu meeting. Maria was left feeling that she was thoroughly immersed in the cause: 'She will, I trust, be a tower of strength to us in Manchester,'[39] In fact Elizabeth was far too busy working on *The Life of Charlotte Brontë* and had quite a different view of the occasion. She told Mary Green:

'I am *very* fond of her, though I know nothing about abolition, & that great interest of hers . . . That night we had a sort of Anti-Slavery conference in the drawing-room and they sighed over my apathy, but I cannot get up an interest in the *measures* adopted by people so far away across the Atlantic.'⁴⁰

Having done her bit, she put all thoughts of anti-slavery on one side as swiftly as she rearranged the drawing-room chairs. Three years later, when her sister-in-law Nancy Robson threatened to bring the black abolitionist speaker Sarah Parker Remond to stay, she positively begged her not to: 'I don't call the use of words *action*: unless there is some definite, distinct, practical *course of action* logically proposed by those words.'

Her own practical involvement was spasmodic, and was usually inspired by individuals as much as causes: Susanna Winkworth and Travers Madge fired her enthusiasm for the Sunday schools, Thomas Wright her prison visiting. She had such energy that once she *was* involved, she pursued her cause to the end, as she did with Pasley. When she was in Manchester, she carried out all her commitments without flagging, and worked herself almost to death during the cotton famine of 1862. A letter to Maria James, written while she was labouring to finish *North and South*, describes a day which may not be typical, but is representative:

'In the first place I had to be at the school 2 miles from here at 9 – till 12; then on to see a family of nine children who had just lost their mother in her confinement, 5 miles from here; back at two to have a meeting by appointment with one or two friends who are taking an interest in poor little Isabel Cameron etc etc.'⁴¹

Isabel, who seems to have been about five, was being physically abused by her father, who was alternately fond and violent. Mr Cameron was clearly paranoid and frighteningly 'deranged': one day 'he wheeled a chair into the darkest corner of the room, saying "Don't look at me! Don't look at me – my nose was growing so large I have pared it all round with my razor" – and his face really was all blood!' Elizabeth was working desperately to have Isabel and her eight-year-old sister, Ida, taken by her mother's relations, although Cameron said he would rather see them dead; if he refused, she would fight to get them made wards of court.

Again and again, from her early married days, her charitable work brought her face to face with women or girls who were abused and exploited. William and his fellow-ministers were pioneers: his drive for temperance in the late 1820s and early 1830s (predating the temperance societies) made Elizabeth confront drunkenness and violence in the home, subjects raised in early stories like 'Libbie Marsh'. His work for destitute women in the 1830s (again predating the Refuge Movement) lay behind her portraits of Lizzie Leigh and Esther. His parish work in the 1830s made her sharply aware of the hardships of the seamstress's life, later brought to public attention by the Second Report of the Children's Employment Commission of 1843. She wrote about it in 'Libbie Marsh' and *Mary Barton*, and gave practical help as well. In 1849 the less philanthropic Geraldine Jewsbury told Jane Carlyle with relief that she was released from making her own petticoats:

' "Mary Barton" has begged me out of charity to give them her for one of her "protégées" to make, whom she wants to find work for! So you see my good deeds are very vicarious. I think doing good for the poor is a somewhat questionable employment.'[42]

Ruth undoubtedly sprang from 'doing good for the poor', but, like *Mary Barton*, it owed a debt to literature as well as life. Numerous stories, articles and poems had followed Thomas Hood's 'Song of the Shirt' (1843) and Caroline Norton's 'Song of the Islands' (1845). Gaskell quoted Norton's poem as a chapter epigraph in *Mary Barton*, and Ruth, like Norton's seamstress, is 'a ruined farmer's daughter'. By the time Elizabeth was helping Pasley in the spring of 1850 a literary image was fixed. Eliza Meteyard's *Lucy Dean: The Noble Needle-woman*, which appeared in *Eliza Cook's Journal* in March and April 1850, contains what has been called 'the iconographic seamstress: lonely garret, sputtering candle, wintry moon, prostitute sister'.[43]

Although Ruth is seduced, she is not a prostitute. But the wintry moon that she gazes at through her workroom window also shines, in contemporary pictures and poems, over the 'fallen woman'. Seamstress and prostitute were often linked – in literature and in life – because, like Pasley, their financial need and uncertain employment often drove them to the streets. And the prostitute, like the seamstress, was a focus of debate in the press and periodicals. Elizabeth and her friends eagerly followed Henry Mayhew's revelatory articles, 'London Labour and the London Poor', in the *Morning Chronicle* of 1849. In 1850 the article 'Woman's Mission' in the *Westminster* specifically noticed the double standard of sexual morality, and that summer the *Westminster* published W. R. Greg's powerful article 'Prostitution'.[44]

Greg took up the contrast suggested in 'Lizzie Leigh' (and used again in *Ruth*) between society's attitude to the Prodigal Son and the 'Prodigal Daughter', and he may have firmed Elizabeth's resolve when he asserted: 'no ruler or writer has yet been found with the nerve to face the sadness, the resolution to encounter the difficulties . . . It is discreditable to a woman to know of their existence.' He also directed attention to what he saw as a crucial moment of choice, 'the very first halting, timid step' which could take a girl either to salvation or 'appalling doom'. He stressed too the 'pure unknowingness' of young girls, whose confidence is won and who are gradually led on, learning too late 'that a lover's encroachment, to be repelled successfully, must be repelled and negatived at the very outset', and criticized the hypocrisy of those who thought that she would be 'made an honest woman again' if only her seducer would marry her.

Here, in the ideas of innocence and encroachment and the sense of tremulous balance between redemption and ruin – like the gulls which Gaskell saw balancing in the gusts at the sea's edge, their white breasts glinting briefly in the sunlight – is the essence of *Ruth*.

[16]

Ruth: Nature, Lies and Sacrifice

Elizabeth confessed that if she were to hear of a new novel with a fifteen-year-old heroine who is seduced and made pregnant, she would be shocked and dismayed. She told Mary Green:

'I am sure I should have been repulsed by hearing that "a tale of seduction" was chosen as a subject for fiction, – *that* was the opinion I dreaded; – I felt *almost* sure that if people would only read what I had to say they would not be disgusted – but I feared & still think it probable that many may refuse to read any book of that kind.'[1]

Many people did refuse to read it, or forbade their womenfolk to – and the author's own hesitation and fear of the subject can also be felt in this novel. One of the reasons she found it so hard to write was quite simply that it dealt with sex. It is, indeed, an unusually sensual book, even more than *Mary Barton*. The scene at Abermouth, amid the swirling tides, where Ruth almost faints at the sound of Bellingham's voice, has such a dragging physical power that it is impossible to escape feeling that Elizabeth had known such emotion, such desire – just as Charlotte Brontë had known the passion which lies behind *Villette*. The effort of identifying with her heroine forced her to face her own sexuality. And sex, despite the hallowing sacrament of marriage, was a site of anxiety and guilt for a respectable Victorian woman. Her unease helps to explain the overwriting, the emphasis on both Ruth's innocence and her guilt and, perhaps, the novel's controversial ending.

Ruth's life falls into three stages. She is a farmer's daughter whose mother dies when she is young, soon followed by her father. At fourteen her guardian apprentices her to a dressmaker, Mrs Mason,

322

and one night, when she is sent to repair dresses at the Shire Ball, she catches the eye of a young aristocrat, Mr Bellingham. They meet again when they rescue a young boy from the river, and, in her loneliness, Ruth values his friendship. One day, when they have revisited her childhood home, Mrs Mason sees them and abruptly dismisses Ruth. Bellingham impulsively takes her to London.

Months later, on holiday with Bellingham in North Wales, Ruth encounters Thurstan Benson, a strange-looking man, crippled and almost deformed, a Dissenting minister from Eccleston, a large industrial town. When Bellingham falls ill, his mother arrives, banishing Ruth from his sickroom and sweeping her son home, leaving the distraught girl with £50 and a curt note advising her to seek a penitentiary. At this point of suicidal despair Thurstan Benson rescues her, summons his stalwart sister Faith, and takes her back to Eccleston. There Faith persuades Thurstan, against his better judgement, to pass Ruth off as a widow, Mrs Denbigh; her son Leonard is born and she becomes a governess to a local family, the Bradshaws. For five years all goes well until two crises arise. First her lover reappears, having taken the name of Donne, as a parliamentary candidate sponsored by the powerful Mr Bradshaw, and she rejects his offer of marriage. Then, in time, Mr Bradshaw discovers her past and dismisses her from her post. Having told her son the truth, Ruth now embarks on a final stage of reparation and is redeemed in the eyes of all by her selfless dedication as a nurse in a terrible typhus outbreak: 'I could fell you,' says one old man, 'for calling that woman a great sinner. The blessing of them who were ready to perish is upon her.'

If the story had closed here, it could have stood as a lesson in successful reclamation of the 'fallen woman'. But it does not. Ruth steps back into the fever to nurse her former lover and perishes herself. In April 1852, when Elizabeth told Charlotte Brontë the outline of her novel, Charlotte praised *Ruth*'s theoretical strength, hoped for practical results and suggested that it might give hope and energy to those who feared they had 'forfeited their right to both'. Then she continued:

'Yet – hear my protest!

'Why should she die? Why are we to shut up the book weeping? My heart fails me already at the thought of the pang it will have to undergo. And yet you must follow the impulse of your own inspiration. If *that* commands the slaying of the victim, no bystander has a right to put out his hand to stay the sacrificial knife; but I hold you a stern priestess in these matters.'[2]

But on what altar is Ruth sacrificed?

In February 1853 Chevalier Bunsen, the Prussian ambassador, a close friend of the Schwabes and the Winkworth sisters and a deeply religious man, explained the necessity of Ruth's death in these terms:

'Ruth *must needs* perish, but atoned and glorified. That is required by man's sense of the Eternal Laws of the World's Order. To anyone who understands this, the last volume will be as valuable and indispensable as the two former ones. It is Psyche in the purifying fire of ordinary life.'[3]

If Ruth is Psyche (and the image is apt), is she the soul or the body? Has she been searching for God or Eros? Are the two incompatible? Is sexual desire in women 'natural' or is it itself the sin, which, like Eve's eating of the apple, brings banishment from Eden and inevitable death? Is it this which brings the exile and grief suggested by the name Ruth, 'weeping among the alien corn'? The flaws in the novel stem from Gaskell's inability to solve, or really to face, these fundamental questions, which inform every stage of the narrative.[4]

Once again, as with Esther in *Mary Barton*, she has deliberately chosen to be the voice of the outcast, the social leper. Her plea is that of Thurstan Benson in a chapter called 'Preparing to Stand on the Truth'. In contrast to the harsh, self-righteous Mr Bradshaw, who appeals to the 'practical wisdom' of the world which 'has decided how such women are to be treated', Benson invokes 'that gentle, tender help which Jesus gave once to Mary Magdalen'. 'I take my stand with Christ against the world,' he says.

'Is it not time to change some of our ways of thinking and acting? I declare before God, that if I believe in any one human truth, it is this – that to every woman who, like Ruth, has sinned should be given a chance of self-redemption – and that such a chance should be given in no supercilious or contemptuous manner, but in the spirit of the holy Christ.' (Ch. 27).

'Such as getting her into a friend's house under false colours,' replies Bradshaw pointedly.

Thurstan Benson's expedient lie, although presented as an error, does not undermine the 'truth' he stands by. He is not the person on trial in this novel. Instead, in order to defend the rights of the seduced girl and the illegitimate child, Gaskell attacks those who have contributed to Ruth's fall, denying her 'tender vigilance and maternal care' – her careless father, her neglectful guardian, her employer Mrs Mason, her lover Bellingham – and those who condemn her without thought, like Mrs Bellingham and Mr Bradshaw. These are the people in the dock. Bradshaw in particular is savagely exposed, and in this portrait one feels something rare in Gaskell's writing, an active, angry dislike. This domestic bully and sanctimonious public figure is the kind of man who would not only damn Ruth in real life, but actually burn the book that told her tale.

She knew, however, that in most readers' opinions the blame would lie with Ruth herself. For this reason she stresses her heroine's purity, her 'gentle downcast countenance', her goodness, patience and piety. But Ruth's innocence creates problems, the most immediate being its threat to credibility. If one accepts the unlikely possibility that Ruth would not hear enough workroom gossip to warn her against going away with a man, then her very ignorance would lead one to suspect that physical sex would be something of a shock. Yet in Wales, after her seduction, Ruth is fulfilled and happy. Her only worry is that she cannot please Bellingham enough. Not until a small boy unnerves her by calling her a 'bad, naughty woman' does she being to feel doubt or guilt. This raises a different sort of question: if sex has seemed natural to Ruth, is female desire itself then 'innocent'?

Gaskell clearly does and does not believe this. The later stages of the novel insist that Ruth's act, even though committed in ignorance, renders her as guilty in the eyes of God as in those of the world. It is for the 'penitent sinner' that Benson appeals to Christ's mercy and when he speaks to Ruth herself, he conjures the severe justice of the Father, the lawgiver. She must learn to accept her social shame meekly 'as but the reasonable and just penance God has laid upon you'. The divine law invoked, indeed, seems even harsher than Mr Bradshaw's 'practical wisdom', and the inevitable, though unintended, comparison between the Pharisaical paterfamilias and the stern Father of the Bible – both of whom condemn regardless of circumstance – is one of the most disturbing aspects of the novel. Gaskell's unstated unease is felt in Benson's wavering between the laws of religion and the needs of humanity:

'I torment myself. I have lost my clear instincts of conscience. Formerly, if I believed that such or such an action was according to the will of God, I went and did it, or at least I tried to do it, without thinking of consequences. Now, I reason and weigh what will happen if I do so and so – I grope where formerly I saw.' (Ch. 27)

When Bellingham reappears, shattering Ruth's calm, she has to confront the ambiguous combination of judgement and mercy in this God. In the church at Abermouth, feeling 'exiled and cast out', she has what almost amounts to a hallucination. Her immediate surroundings recede as she fixes her gaze on a gargoyle, set in deep shadow, frozen in an expression of suffering for long centuries, its anguish part of its beauty. The word 'law' and the male pronoun are repeated like a tolling bell, as she shrinks from the idea of her own future misery.

'And as for the rest, was not the sure justice of His law finding out even now? His laws once broken, His justice and the very nature of those laws bring the immutable retribution; but if we turn penitently to Him, He enables us to bear our punishment with a meek and docile heart, "for His mercy endureth for ever".' (Ch. 23)

Frozen, entrapped suffering; immutable laws. *Ruth* is a novel about confinement and repression in which the truth is buried, particularly the truth about women's emotional history. Faith Benson's early love is sacrificed so that she can care for her crippled brother; Sally's comic story of her proposals is told to an unhearing, sleeping Ruth; the oppressed Mrs Bradshaw indulges in escapist day-dreams, 'after the manner of the Minerva Press'; her daughter Jemima stifles her love for Mr Farquhar. These private secrets, though, are surely more 'innocent' than the election bribery, forgery and self-interest of the public male sphere. The world of *Ruth*, as Jemima Bradshaw says, is somehow inverted, 'chaotic and strange'. Form is accepted more readily than substance: the wedding ring, the widow's cap, the carefully constructed history of Mrs Denbigh, the parchment of Sally's will. Signs and documents are the things which count, yet they can bear false witness, like the signature Mr Bradshaw's son Richard forges on Benson's deed of stock. Words are inadequate to express Ruth's complex history. At her death Benson writes a funeral sermon, but 'words seemed hard and inflexible, and refused to fit themselves to his ideas'. He puts it away unread. When Bradshaw, Ruth's accuser, leads home her weeping son, he cannot speak to his old friend Benson, 'for the sympathy which choked up his voice'.[5]

Gaskell too had struggled over words, working to make the novel's style as 'quiet' and innocent as its heroine, trying to take out, so she told Nancy Robson, 'the slightest exaggeration' and 'over-strained sentiment'. *Ruth* is a study of repression which is itself repressed. Its powerful, unresolved questioning is felt not in direct statements but in tensions, evasions, suppressions and allusions. It opens with one of Gaskell's typical descriptive placings, leading the reader through the streets and doorways, and, metaphorically, through time and society. The first words tell us we are in a world ruled by law: 'There is an assize-town in one of the Eastern Counties.' The grand old houses, built by aristocrats, have been taken over by speculators. In former days their gables and balconies overshadowed the narrow streets, which 'suffered from all these projections and advanced storeys above; they were dark and ill paved with large, round, jolting pebbles'. Such streets were perilous by night and day. Those walking below found that carriages 'hemmed them up against the houses' while the 'inhospitable houses' in turn forced them back into danger. At night the oil-lamps made them visible only for a moment, until they stepped back into the pools of darkness where robbers 'wait for their prey'.

After this suggestive sequence we are abruptly told that past traditions are built into the present and absorbed before we are aware, so that 'daily life . . . forms chains which only one in a hundred has moral strength enough to despise and break when the right time comes'. The liberating strength in this novel will be that of Thurstan Benson, but the ambience of restriction and rebellion colours our first glimpse of Ruth. As she walks, at two in the morning, up the oaken staircase of one of these ancient houses, she passes a stained-glass window 'through which the moonlight fell on her with a glow of many colours' – a Romantic figure, reminiscent of Keats or Shelley. She enters a room full of adolescent girls, imprisoned at their work, all silent, in a suspended life of heavy limbs and sighs. Many are 'stupidly placid', eating their bread and cheese at the brief meal break like 'cows ruminating in the first meadow you happen to pass'.

Ruth is different. Ruth feels her imprisonment; she 'sprang to the large window and pressed against it as a bird presses against the bars of a cage'. She gazes at the moon, the snow, and the larch, once free, now 'pent up and girded about with flagstones', and works in the darkest corner, where she can see an old decorated panel depicting flowers of all seasons, 'profuse and luxuriant beyond description'. The painted flowers rouse her senses, but only in imagination – suggesting fragrance, rustling breezes, silken petals. The 'golden-tressed laburnum' is like Ruth's own mass of auburn hair. The suggestion is not of innocence but restless energy, unfocused yearning and sensuality. The moon Ruth watches symbolizes changeability, motherhood and female power as well as virginity.

The snow is also an ambiguous image. (By a curious coincidence, it links Ruth to Lucy Snowe, in *Villette*, a very different treatment of repression, confinement, unspoken desire.) We know that Ruth's mother had never told her about sex:

'*the* subject of a woman's life – if, indeed, wise parents ever directly speak of what, in its depth and power, cannot be put into words – which is a brooding spirit with no definite form or shape that men should know it, but which is there, and present before we have recognised and realised its existence. Ruth was innocent and snow-pure.' (Ch. 3)

In Eccleston, Ruth's room is white and green, like a snowdrop, its floor brown, like the mould from which the snowdrop springs. But while snow transfigures the world, it does not change the earth beneath. Snow melts. We feel this at the Shire Ball, where Ruth meets her future lover:

'Outside all was cold, and colourless, and uniform, – one coating of snow over all. But inside it was warm, and glowing, and vivid; flowers scented the air, and wreathed the head, and rested on the bosom, as if it were midsummer.' (Ch. 2)

Ruth's whiteness is a protective colouring, like her later widow's black and grey, or like the landscape at her son's birth, when the earth, we are told, 'hides its guilty front with innocent snow'.

Men instinctively sense and are enticed by the gap between Ruth's quiet exterior and her hidden sexuality: at the inn in Wales a man rises from his breakfast to look at her: 'She's a very lovely creature,' he says rashly to his wife, 'very modest and innocent-looking in her white gown!' In the Eccleston chapel Mr Bradshaw looks up from his prayers to watch Ruth at hers. His alarm when he discovers the past of this woman who is quietly teaching his daughters resembles the *frisson* felt by readers of sensation novels like *Lady Audley's Secret* and *East Lynne* ten years later, which uncovered sex, adultery and even murder at the heart of 'the angel in the house'. And Ruth *is* in disguise. As Jemima guesses, she has had 'a black secret shut up in her soul for years'.

Ruth's 'black secret' springs from a source which Victorian society was loath to acknowledge – the natural sexuality of women and, worse still, of 'innocent' young girls. Gaskell's novel is erotic in the manner of Pre-Raphaelite paintings whose women gaze out with pale, enigmatic faces, while their bodies, drapery and surroundings flow with life. Eros is displaced from the heroine and located in her surroundings. Ruth herself hardly recognizes her body as her own and knows she is pretty only because 'many people have told me so'. When she studies her reflection in the mountain pool, at Bellingham's command, she does not associate her beauty with her 'self': 'She knew that she was beautiful; but that seemed abstract, and removed from herself. Her existence was in feeling and thinking, and loving.'

While Ruth has a vivid inner life, she is not, to begin with, self-aware. In the first two volumes Gaskell therefore evokes her emotions and sensuality by embodying them in the natural world outside. Her story is structured by the pattern of seasons. When snow gives way to spring, Ruth departs with Bellingham. A summer of seduction and storm in Wales is followed by autumnal desolation in Eccleston. Her son, Leonard (like the redeeming Christ), is born in midwinter and she begins a new life as a governess when the flowers bud again. But indifferent nature can mock as well as reflect human fates. A glorious August day heralds Ruth's dismissal and an 'unusually gorgeous summer' fosters the fever that overwhelms the town in the autumn damp.

Duality, rather than consistency, marks Gaskell's use of the imagery of flowers, which express both Ruth's sensuality and purity, and are carefully linked to her longing for love. Just as she is fallen woman and pure mother, Magdalen and Madonna, so she is both white and scarlet, lily and rose, the snowdrop and the spoilt flower. Leaving home as a child, she tears off 'in a passion of love whole boughs of favourite China and damask roses, late flowering against the casement window of what had been her mother's room'. Returning to the farm with Bellingham, she still clings to her childhood, seeking out plants 'to which some history or remembrance was attached':

'She wound in and out in natural, graceful, wavy lines between the luxuriant and overgrown shrubs, which were fragrant with a leafy smell of spring growth; she went on, careless of watching eyes, indeed unconscious, for the time, of their existence. Once she stopped to take hold of a spray of jessamine, and softly kiss it; it had been her mother's favourite flower.' (Ch. 4)

But Bellingham, aroused, watches those 'natural, graceful' curves. In Wales, in the sexualized landscape of a deep pool in a mountain cleft, fringed with green trees, he crowns her with different flowers:

'She stood in her white dress against the trees that grew around, her face was flushed into a brilliancy of colour which resembled that of a rose in June; the great, heavy, white flowers drooped on either side of her beautiful head, and if her brown hair was a little disordered, the very disorder only seemed to add a grace.' (Ch. 6)

The Bensons and Sally subdue this languorous wildness; in their walled garden the rich autumnal colours are 'toned down by the clear and delicate air'. The starry sprays of jessamine, her mother's flower, press through their parlour window and the roses are no longer the seductive blooms of June but cut flowers, brought back into the domestic interior: 'Miss Benson was arranging a bunch of China and damask roses in an old-fashioned jar; they lay, all dewy and fresh, on the white breakfast-cloth when Ruth entered.' That evening, in a marvellously evocative scene, Sally mercilessly cuts Ruth's luxuriant hair with her formidable scissors, retrieving the long tresses 'and letting them drop and float on the air (like the pendant branches of the weeping birch)'. Ruth submits to the transformation from a creature of nature into a widow with cropped hair, just as passively as she had submitted to Bellingham when he made her into a water-nymph beside the pool in Wales.

Ruth is passive, and a child of nature, but nature itself is equivocal in this novel, and as she grows up she must learn to be self-reliant and to find other, spiritual values to sustain her. Before her visit to her childhood home with Bellingham, Gaskell summons the shades of Romeo and Juliet: 'They sauntered through the fragrant lanes, as if their loitering would prolong the time and check the fiery-footed steeds galloping apace towards the close of the happy day.' Juliet, we remember, was doomed. When they reach the old farm, the garden is rank and lush, but the house is empty and cold; Ruth cannot return to her childhood. This chapter, called 'Treading in Perilous Places', ends on a sandy heath, 'a green waste', with a lonely pool. To regain the road and inn the couple have to plunge through 'broken ground', and the atmosphere becomes heavy and dreamlike, sensual yet problematic, as they make their way 'hand in hand, now pricked by the far-spreading gorse, now ankle-deep in sand; now pressing the soft, thick heath'. (The biblical sand and rock are recurring images, repeated at the critical moment of choice when Ruth meets Bellingham again on the wide sands at Abermouth and looks back at the rocks and church behind her.) Nature here offers a false sense of freedom. After Mrs Mason sees them together and summarily dismisses her, and Bellingham leaves to find a carriage, Ruth is driven indoors into the inn. Sick and frightened, she opens the window. The scent of sweet-brier reminds her of her mother, but she cannot get outside to reach it since the innkeeper's bulky male frame 'obstructs' the door.

When we next see Ruth, in Wales, she is still imprisoned in an inn. She sits in the window-seat looking at a scene which, unwittingly to her, exemplifies her sexual fall and spiritual rebirth, the rain falling 'like a rush of silver arrows', the purple darkness of the heather, the 'pale, golden gleam which succeeded'. She insists on going out alone on the mountains, but her freedom is still an illusion; at the pool she is merely Bellingham's 'toy', decorated for his pleasure. During his illness, barred from his room, she crouches in a dark corner near windows cut in a thick wall 'where great untrimmed geraniums grew and strove to reach the light'. After he leaves, she lies in a coma, with her window shaded by calico, 'to shut out the light'. Only when she reaches Eccleston are enclosure and freedom reconciled as the scent of flowers drifts into the parlour, and she can gaze calmly from her attic window at the moors rising wave upon wave into the distance.

Ruth's inner struggles are powerfully conveyed by the untamed aspects of the natural world, wild mountains, storm and water. The 'sullen roar of the stream that was ceaselessly and unrelentingly flowing on' when she and Bellingham rescue young Tom from the flooding river in the opening chapters becomes the swollen mountain torrent where she meets Benson, who helps her across the stepping-stones, while 'her eyes were on the current running swiftly below her feet'. These are the 'siren waters' which tempt her to death, and feed the great tides which ebb and flow at Abermouth when her lover returns.

331

The power of the waters is matched by that of the wind – sea and storm being Gaskell's favourite images for loss of control. Ruth is 'the storm-spirit subdued'. After Benson finds her crouching in the hedge-row like a hunted creature and persuades her from suicide, she envies the tattered storm clouds crossing the mountain barrier which separates her from the man she loves, 'with the moon shining like hope through their darkest centre'. Storm, sand and sea surround her at his return as 'Mr Donne' (an ironic name, with its hint of the poet of love and religion and also of something concluded, finished). At the sound of his voice her body betrays her mind. The sands tremble beneath her, she sways with dizziness and the figures round her vanish: 'It seemed as if weights were tied to her feet – as if the steadfast rocks receded – as if time stood still; – it was so long, so terrible, that path across the reeling sand.' Her path is a moral as well as a physical one. That night, as Ruth struggles with the memory of her love and the pain of her abandonment in Wales, the storm rises. She opens the window and tears off her gown, feeling 'as if thought and emotion had been repressed so sternly that they would not come to relieve her stupefied brain. Till at once, like a flash of lightning, her life, past and present, was revealed to her in the minutest detail.' It is left unclear whether it is the storm or her own pulse which she hears as she sinks, 'quite dead', and 'listens as to the sound of galloping armies'.

Ruth comes to understand Bellingham's selfishness when she thinks of her love for her son, and through this she gains the strength to reject his offer of marriage. But although she can now see clearly that Leonard's father is 'a bad man', she cries aloud: 'yet, oh! pitiful God, I love him; I cannot forget – I cannot!' The lure of the window persists:

'She threw her body half out of the window into the cold night air. The wind was rising and came in great gusts. The rain beat down on her. It did her good. A still, calm night would not have soothed her as this did. The wild tattered clouds, hurrying past the moon, gave her a foolish kind of pleasure that almost made her smile a vacant smile. The blast-driven rain came on her again, and drenched her hair through and through. The words "stormy wind fulfilling His word" came into her mind.' (Ch. 13)

The chapter title, 'Recognition', applies to her recognition of this desire as well as to her lover's reappearance. The storm, with its great gusts and unearthly wails, 'like the vanguard of the Prince of the Air' –

as in 'The Heart of John Middleton' and 'The Old Nurse's Story' – is the call of the dark side of herself.

Gaskell uses other devices to dramatize psychic division and repression. In a manner that Freud would recognize, she shows how fear and guilt surface in dreams and illness, both significant indicators in *Ruth*, as in *Mary Barton*. As Sally says, 'What are dreams for but for warnings?' When she is a girl, Ruth dreams that her mother abandons her; at her son's birth she dreams of him falling into a pit, pulled by a clinging girl. Before meeting Bellingham/Donne she has a dream of undefined premonitory terror, while Leonard repeats her own girl-hood dream of separation, seeing his mother disappear on 'feathery wings'. In a later dream, when she thinks that Bellingham will enforce his paternal rights and take Leonard away, she thinks she is on a lonely shore, desperately carrying her son from some unnamed pursuer, whom she hears behind her like 'the roaring tide'. Once more her feet feel weighted down and suddenly a 'black whirlwind of waves' pulls her back, 'to a mysterious something too dreadful to be borne'. She throws Leonard to the shore, not knowing whether he reaches safety or not.

In the later stages of the novel the imagery of water and storm and the symbolism of dreams meet in a series of surreal, supernatural images. The clanking steps behind Ruth on her way to church and the echoing footsteps on the hard sand resemble the fearful tread of a ghost. Life becomes 'a nightmare, where the evil dreaded is never avoided, never completely shunned, but is at one's side at the very moment of triumph in escape'. She cannot talk about 'this mocking echo, this haunting phantom, this past, that would not rest in the grave' but is 'stalking abroad in the world'. After Mr Bradshaw confronts her she is like 'a wild creature at bay' and shakes with 'lightning-fear' as if trembling 'on a precipice'. Her silence has been useless:

'the old offence could never be drowned in the Deep; but thus, when all was calm on the great, broad, sunny sea, it rose to the surface, and faced her with its unclosed eyes and its ghastly countenance. The blood bubbled up to her brain, and made such a sound there, as of boiling waters, that she did not hear the words which Mr Bradshaw first spoke.' (Ch. 26)

But Ruth has found a defender, Jemima. When Mr Bradshaw orders his daughter to leave the room, her refusal is explained in language which links her directly to Ruth:

' "Why, father?" replied she, in an opposition that was strange even to herself, but which was prompted by the sullen passion which seethed below the stagnant surface of her life, and which sought a vent in defiance.' (Ch. 26)

Jemima Bradshaw comes to the forefront of the novel's action at the calmest period of Ruth's life, when she is working quietly as a governess and is absorbed in the education of her small son, before that fatal meeting on the sands. It is as if a single character could not contain the rebellion and division submerged in the novel. The heroine literally splits in two. When we first meet her, the dark-eyed Jemima has 'a warm, affectionate, ardent nature, free from all envy and carking care of self'. Yet, like her brother Richard, she is in awe of her bullying, sanctimonious father, unable to act independently 'according to her own sense of right, or rather, I should say, according to her own passionate impulses'. Five years later, she is no longer free from care; in front of her father she is silent, almost reduced to a corpse by the effort of repression:

'when she thought she was not kindly treated, when a suspicion crossed her mind, or when she was angry with herself, her lips were tight-pressed together, her colour was wan and almost livid, and a stormy gloom coloured her eyes as with a film.' (Ch. 19)

In the chapter 'Jemima Refuses to be Managed' she irritably rejects her father's partner, Mr Farquhar, whom she has loved for years, because of her father's ill-timed intervention. However, when Farquhar, exhausted by her 'uncurbed and passionate' nature, begins to pay attention to the outwardly placid Ruth, she is consumed by despair.

Jemima's defiance and her jealousy of Ruth overlap with Ruth's crisis at Abermouth. As the 'good daughter' Gaskell can endow her with all the anger and frustration which Ruth, who must remain innocent, is not allowed. Jemima too paces restlessly, is confused and silent about her feelings, dismayed by 'the demon' in her heart. Her horror when she discovers Ruth's secret is attributed to her sheltered life, but it is the combined element of sex and lies, the spectre in the depths, that really appals her. Ruth's suppression mirrors her own:

'The diver leaving the green sward, smooth and known, where his friends stand with their familiar smiling faces, admiring his glad bravery – the diver, down in an instant in the horrid depths of the sea, close to some strange, ghastly, lidless-eyed monster, can hardly feel his blood curdle at the near terror as did Jemima now.' (Ch. 25)

Our reading of *Ruth* is inevitably affected by changed social mores, and a diminution of the sense of sin. The most painful aspect for a modern reader is not Ruth's transgression but the way Gaskell shows how women's natural impulses are transformed under the pressure of internalized values into something monstrous. A personality can split under such pressure. Wracked by intense emotion, Jemima too opens the window and sees the clouds ˙hurrying over the moon's face in a tempestuous and unstable manner, making all things unreal'. She too finds life a waking nightmare, and is dizzied by 'the sick, weary notion that the earth was wandering lawless and aimless through the heavens'.

Ruth's exposure and Jemima's defence take place, aptly, in the schoolroom, a place of both innocence and knowledge. From now on the two women are kept apart by the command of Bradshaw, the father. Jemima, reconciled to Farquhar, visits Ruth on the eve of her wedding and on her return from her honeymoon abroad, when Ruth is hoping to find new work as a nurse, but Ruth knows it would not be right for her to visit her respectable friend in her own home. They must remain apart, she says, unless Jemima is ill, or in sorrow. In that case Ruth will come to her in a different spirit from that with which she nurses her usual patients: her words express the closeness between them:

' "But I should come to you, love, in quite a different way; I should go to you with my heart full of love – so full that I am afraid I should be too anxious."

"I almost wish I were ill, that I might make you come at once."

"And I am almost ashamed to think how I should like you to be in some position in which I could show you how well I remember that day – that terrible day in the schoolroom. God bless you for it, Jemima!" ' (Ch. 29)

The imagined scene of fever, love and memory does occur, but not with Jemima. Fever is the last controlling image of Ruth, a poison in the blood and a common Victorian image for 'sexual pollution'. As a seamstress at Mrs Mason's Ruth is already 'feverish', about to succumb to a fatal affliction which she cannot diagnose: 'she had heard of falling in love, but did not know the signs and symptoms thereof'. And as she is both bad and good, so she is both sufferer and healer. She nurses her consumptive work-mate Jenny, her lover Bellingham, and her son, Leonard, who falls victim to 'fever' just as he catches the stigma of her shame. In the epidemic which strikes Eccleston, as if immunized, she can enter the 'poisoned air' of the infirmary without fear. The tables turn. Ruth becomes a public heroine while Bradshaw becomes an object of shame and pity, when his son is exposed as a forger and then injured in an accident. He too attains humanity through love for his child.

In the eyes of all who know her, including Bradshaw, Ruth has completed her penance; there is no practical or moral need for her to nurse Bellingham, lying sick at the inn. It is an internal 'black whirlwind of waves' that pulls her back. As in her dream, Leonard is thrown to the safety of the shore, his future being ensured when the doctor, Mr Davis, offers him an apprenticeship. Davis is himself illegitimate and therefore identifies Ruth not as a sinner but simply as a wronged mother. When she tells him the truth, in order to persuade him to let her nurse 'Mr Donne', it is he who asks the buried, unspoken question: 'Answer me truly – do you love him?' Her fragmented, repetitive answer suggests a force she cannot resist:

' "I have been thinking – but I do not know – I cannot tell – I don't think I should love him, if he were well and happy – but you said he was ill – and alone – how can I help caring for him? How can I help caring for him?" ' (Ch. 34)

In his delirium Bellingham sees no change in her and asks, 'Where are the water-lilies? Where are the lilies in her hair?' In her own fever, caught from him, she retreats to a still earlier stage of innocence, singing the ditties her mother taught her. Her troubled self-knowledge surrenders to 'a sweet, childlike insanity'. Juliet has become Ophelia.

The atmosphere of the final volume of *Ruth* has a peculiar disconcerting intensity. Ruth's guilt and self-torment appear ludicrously out of proportion to her offence, particularly since she has re-created her life through her love for her Leonard and self-sacrificing work. At times the writing, lapsing so often into those images of storm, of monstrosity, of terror, of a stern, guilt-inducing God, seems almost hysterical. George Eliot, a shrewd critic and admirer of Mrs Gaskell, immediately sensed this. Comparing *Ruth* with 'the false and feeble representations' of most women's novels, she said that its style had been 'a great refreshment to me, from its finish and fulness' and that she loved the touches of description, the rich humour of Sally and the 'sly satire' of Bradshaw. But she felt that its achievement was uneven:

' "Ruth", with all its merits, will not be an enduring or classical fiction, – will it? Mrs Gaskell seems to me to be constantly misled by a love of sharp contrasts – of "dramatic" effects. She is not contented with the subdued colouring – the half tints of real life. Hence she agitates one for the moment, but she does not secure one's lasting sympathy; her scenes and characters do not become typical.'[6]

Eliot was right in seeing that this was no work of classic realism. It has an imbalance, a distress which makes one question the deep motive beneath the writing. While *Ruth* remains a 'philanthropic novel', which sprang from genuine social concern, its symbolism and tone suggest a private identification, not altogether acknowledged, with Ruth and Jemima, women who repress, and must be punished by the world and by God for their desire, anger, jealousy and passion.

There is no denying *Ruth*'s emotional power or the pathos of its ending. When he read it in proof, John Forster wrote at once: 'Well done! – yet I am not quite sure either if it is quite dignified in a hardened critic to confess that he had neither more nor less than a good cry over these final chapters.'[7] Ruth had to die, if only to wring a final tear of sympathy from readers and hardened critics. The sacrificial altar is that of literary as well as moral convention: madness or death is the fate of all fallen women. The manner of Ruth's death, however, subtly suggests that she does not perish because of her sin but because of her forbidden love, which could have no place in the Victorian world. She is the Psyche of Greek myth as well as Psyche the purified soul: a woman who embraces death because she returns, against all reason, against all entreaties, to hold up the lamp and look openly – as her author was forced to do in writing her story – on the forbidden face of her own desire.

Ruth brought Elizabeth all the heartache she expected. First reactions were dreadful. Even old friends like Rosa Mitchell expressed 'deep regret' that she should have written such a book. She had isolated herself by 'having *forbidden*' friends to write because their disapproval would be 'very painful and stinging' and she veered between misery and defiance, painting herself with aggrandized self-pity to Nancy Robson as a martyr to the truth:

'An "unfit subject for fiction" is *the* thing to say about it; I knew all this before; but I determined to speak my mind out about it; only how I shrink with more pain than I can tell you from what people are saying, though I would do every jot of it over again tomorrow . . . In short the only comparison I can find for myself is to St Sebastian tied to a tree to be shot with arrows.' (L220–1)

She was in 'a quiver of pain', had 'a terrible fit of crying all Saty night', and, she told Tottie, even dreamt about it. William was firm and she promised him to think of it as little as possible, but it was a promise she could not keep.

Almost immediately Bell's Library in London withdrew the novel as unsuitable for family reading. The *Athenaeum* was equivocal, applauding her courage while disapproving of the 'warped morality' of Benson's lie. Elizabeth listed all the really bad notices for Tottie, like those in the *Spectator* and the *Literary Gazette*, which called it 'insufferably dull' and affected, and spoke of 'deep regret' at her 'loss of reputation'.[8] The only paper that praised it, she said, was the *Examiner*, 'wh. was bound to for Chapman's sake – and that's *that*, and be hanged to it'. (The review was by John Forster.) One of the first reviews, in *Sharpe's London Magazine*, cautioned against *Ruth*'s introduction to the family hearth and upheld the Bradshaw line: surely any *'pater familias'* would have done the same?[9] This view was repeated by *Blackwood's*, and two years later the Anglican *Christian Observer* was still outraged at the suggestion that 'a woman who has violated the laws of purity is entitled to occupy precisely the same position in society as one who has never thus offended'.[10]

These first hostile blasts found Elizabeth shivering from a real 'Ruth fever', which turned out to be the start of a five-week bout of severe flu. Sick and low, she joked plaintively to Tottie:

'I think I must be an improper woman without knowing it, I do so manage to shock people. Now *should* you have burnt the 1st vol. of Ruth as so *very* bad? even if you had been a very anxious father of a

1 Linsey Row, Chelsea, around 1820.
Drawing by W. W. Burgess.

2 Hannah Lumb.

3 Heathside, Elizabeth Stevenson's childhood home.

4 King Street, Knutsford.
Drawing by A. R. Quinton.

5 Sandlebridge.

6 Brook Street Chapel.

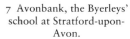

7 Avonbank, the Byerleys'
school at Stratford-upon-
Avon.

8 The Revd William Turner.

9 Elizabeth in 1829.
Thorneycroft's copy of bust
by David Dunbar.

10 Miniature of Elizabeth
by W. J. Thomson, 1832.

11 William Gaskell, photographed on holiday in Scotland by Rupert Potter.

12 Cross Street Chapel.

13 Marianne, Meta and Flossy
in 1845. Pastel by C. A. Duval.

14 Elizabeth in 1854.
Pastel by Samuel Laurence.

15 'Abermouth Sands'. Sketch of Silverdale by Meta Gaskell.

16 Lindeth Tower, Silverdale.   17 The drawing-room of 42 Plymouth Grove.

18 Valentine drawn by George Smith for
Elizabeth in 1864.

The text reads:

More more, he cried, e'er Phillis breath'd her last,
Three Volumes more, I want them quick and fast
Trollope's too long: Macdonald slow and tame
There's only you can raise the Cornhill's fame.

Muti has charms, no doubt, and Elsie too
But listen to your Smith and Elder – do
March is upon us; Copy's wanted sore
Oh! be our Valentine, and send us more.

St Valentine's Day
1864

19 Mary Mohl.

20 The ending of *Wives and Daughters*.

21 Watercolour of Elizabeth by Meta, 1865.

22 The Lawn, Holybourne.

family? Yet *two* men have; and a third has forbidden his wife to read it; they sit next to us in Chapel and you can't think how "improper" I feel under their eyes.' (L223)

'But some people like it,' she added hopefully. Friends in Manchester and elsewhere soon rallied to support her, although Richard Cobden had warned Grace Schwabe that Ruth would be thought 'dangerous company for unmarried females even in a book',[11] The list of requests for the book at the Portico Library was so long that a second copy had to be ordered.[12] Elizabeth herself called it a prohibited book in her own house, although she planned to go through it quietly with Marianne. There were some surprises. Whereas Annie Austin's parents 'thought Ruth so disgusting that they were unable to finish it', the strictly proper Unitarian ministers' wives, Mrs J. J. Tayler and Mrs Tagart, thoroughly approved and gave the novel to their daughters.[13]

Each letter of encouragement was 'such a relief', as she told Mary Green (who assured her that 'Harry has not cried so much for many years').[14] London friends wrote swiftly – Forster, Dickens, Anna Jameson, Maurice, Hallam. Although he found things to complain of, William Rathbone Greg sat up until one o'clock in the morning reading *Ruth*. Archdeacon Hare, hearing of its fate at the hands of 'virtuous friends', retorted, 'Well, the Bible has been burnt.'[15] The support helped, but in March Elizabeth still felt like St Sebastian. It seemed typical that all the comforting letters, which she had packed up and sent to London for Emily Shaen to read, should get lost in the post, while 'every letter of reprobation and blame comes to me, straight as an arrow'. She was hurt that 'good kind people – and *women* infinitely more than men' were against her. By now she did, however, feel she had 'put the small end of the wedge in', a phrase she used in early March to both Anna Jameson and Mary Rich. To the latter she sighed: 'I am in such scrapes about Ruth . . . I can't think how it is that I who am such an arrant coward, *must* always go headlong into people's black books; and good people's too.'[16] But by April she was able to see the arguments as evidence of her book's power. It had at least made people 'talk and think a little on a subject which is so painful that it requires all one's bravery not to hide one's head like an ostrich and try by doing so to forget that the evil exists'.

Two treasured letters came later. One was from her 'hero', Charles

Kingsley, who wrote in July, admitting rather comically that he had only read a little, 'though of course I know the story'.[17] Kingsley, whose own novels *Yeast* and *Alton Locke* are so full of misery, found *Ruth* too painful – as he had *Uncle Tom's Cabin, Othello* and *The Bride of Lammermoor*, none of which he could finish. (He was almost certainly the friend referred to in Ludlow's review: ' "I don't think I shall go on with it," said one very dear friend to us, after reading the first twenty pages, "I am sure it is not going to be pleasant." ') He was still indignant at the abuse Gaskell had received and wrote to assure her that 'pure and pious women' of his acquaintance admired it, and that whatever snobs and bigots might say, 'English people in general have but one opinion of "Ruth", and that is one of utter satisfaction.'

A week earlier Gaskell had heard from a heroine, Elizabeth Barrett Browning, to whom she had written after begging an autograph from John Kenyon. By chance, her letter arrived in Florence just as Barrett Browning finished reading *Ruth*. She wrote back at once, praising its 'purity', its style and truth, but echoing Brontë's plea:

'I am grateful to you as a woman for having treated such a subject – Was it quite impossible but that your Ruth should *die*? I had that thought of regret in closing the book – Oh, I must confess to it – Pardon me for the tears' sake!'

Her husband, she said, though not a 'thick and thin novel reader like me', was now deep in the book and shared all her feelings.[18]

By late spring the major journals had endorsed Mrs Gaskell's cause, applauding her courage at tackling a subject usually thought 'inconsistent with good taste' and backing her attack on the double standard.[19] She was particularly pleased with Ludlow's piece in the *North British Review* (despite his views on unmarried women writers), since he emphasized Ruth's redemption through motherhood: 'Satan sent the sin – God sends the child.'[20] Elizabeth was delighted to be 'so completely understood' and used copies of the review to convert friends who had 'extremely objected to Ruth'.[21] As Charlotte Brontë had anticipated, plenty of comparisons were made with *Villette*, the most famous being by G. H. Lewes in his article '*Ruth* and *Villette*'. Asking, 'Should a work of Art have a moral?' Lewes compared Gaskell's open moral aim with Brontë's '*morale en action*', and contrasted her 'strong and genial humour' to Charlotte's anger, 'glory' and power. He concluded that no two books could be more different: 'we are comparing sunlight with moonlight, passion with affection'.[22] Charlotte had also foreseen that many reviewers would seize on Thurstan Benson's lie as 'the weak part of the book – fix and cling there – In vain is it explicitly shown that this step was regarded by the author as an error, and that she unflinchingly follows it up to its natural and fatal consequences – there – I doubt not – some critics will stick like flies caught in treacle.'[23] Stick they did, in journal after journal, although some, like Lewes, saw that the lie was itself 'forced by the untruths of convention'.

All over the country *Ruth* was debated in drawing-rooms, clubs, churches, chapels – even Oxford colleges. Josephine Butler, later the bravest of all opponents of the double standard in the campaign to repeal the Contagious Diseases Acts, was a young wife in Oxford in 1853 and bitterly remembered the dons' pious insistence that no pure woman should know of such things. She heard one young man saying 'he would not allow' his *mother* to read *Ruth*. The staggering hypocrisy tallied with her experience when she tried to raise the case of a 'very young girl' seduced by a college fellow and was warned by a university sage to keep silent because 'it was dangerous to rouse a sleeping lion'.[24]

Elizabeth had roused the lion and it roared around her. Even her supporters argued. Should Benson have lied? Should Ruth have died? Should she even, as the Bonamy Prices and others felt, have married Bellingham? Had the author been too bold – or too timid? A. H. Clough spoke for the latter camp when he found Ruth's inner humiliation repellent and thought the novel 'rather cowardly – and "pokey" in its views'.[25] Harriet Martineau felt the same, telling Susanna Winkworth that it was a thoroughly poor book, which she was sorry Mrs Gaskell should have written.[26] Harriet wrote tartly to Fanny Wedgwood about both *Villette* and *Ruth*. The former (as she hurtfully stated in the *Daily News*) was '*marvellously* powerful but grievously morbid, and not a little coarse'. She longed for a woman with Brontë's power to raise women out of the 'subjective slough':

' "Ruth" won't help us, all strewn with beauties as it is, it is sadly feeble and *wrong*, I think. Amidst much wrong, I think making Mr Benson such a nincompoop fatal. What a beautiful "Cranford" Mrs Gaskell has given us again.'[27]

341

To many readers – then and since – *Cranford* was Elizabeth's natural level. She was out of her depth in *Ruth*.

The respectable condemned her immorality, the liberal praised her courage, the radical regretted her feebleness. On balance, however, praise was loudest, and *Ruth* raised Gaskell's reputation to new heights. But it took her a long time to see this. Slowly she regained her equilibrium and her sense of humour. By the middle of the year, in smart society, she could be 'clever satirical' and say to Sir Francis Doyle 'she wished people would not look at her, as if she were the author of Ruth'. She loved his reply: 'Can't you tell them, my dear, that you're Ruthless?'

[17]

Finding Space

Elizabeth's next novel, *North and South* was conciliatory rather than confrontational, but it still explored the problem of women's place in the world, this time with a middle-class heroine. It was her first attempt at a weekly serialized novel and led to prolonged battles with Dickens for space in *Household Words*. Towards the end of her writing, in 1854, she was also hunting for space in a different sense, for places to write away from the bustle of Manchester and family life. And while she planned, wrote and tussled with Dickens, three women – Charlotte Brontë, Mary Clarke Mohl and Florence Nightingale – influenced her thinking about women's role and about the clash of independence and domesticity, the quest for purpose and the need for love.

At the end of 1852, when Elizabeth told Tottie that *Ruth* was utterly off her mind and gone to the printers, she mentioned that Charlotte Brontë was ill, '*very* ill I'm afraid'. She had a good mind to go and see her uninvited: 'However I don't mean to stir from home this long time when I get back, but write, write, write. I really do mean to do something good and virtuous.' She did not go to Charlotte, but she did start to write. Ironically, given her state of mind over *Ruth*, one of the first things she sent to Dickens was 'The Great Cranford Panic'. Dickens, delighted, welcomed it in words that would have choked him eighteen months later: 'As to future work, I do assure you that you cannot write too much for *Household Words*, and have never yet written half enough.' He ended at his most flirtatious: 'I receive you, ever (if Mr Gaskell will allow me to say so) with open arms.'[1] More Cranford stories followed, and it was not until May that she finally

343

decided on 'something good and virtuous' and sent him an outline of her next novel. His response was wholehearted. The subject she had chosen, industrial conflict, was, he said, 'certainly NOT too serious, so sensibly treated' for *Household Words*.[2] He added that he himself 'had similar reasons for giving it some anxious consideration'. (A year later he wrote *Hard Times*.) She should send the papers as she wrote them and he would think of a name which might fit, if hers needed improving.

The idea of another book on Manchester had been simmering in her mind since the furore over *Mary Barton*, when friends suggested she should write something to show the masters in a better light. At that point she had felt this would have to be done by someone else:

'In the first place whatever power there was in Mary Barton was caused by my feeling strongly on the side which I took; now as I don't feel as strongly (and as it is impossible I ever should,) on the other side, the forced effort of writing on that side would be \end in/ a weak failure.' (L119)

She had also felt that if she picked out one benevolent mill-owner, who seemed to her good, but was judged by businessmen to be a failure, she would be doing 'an injury instead of a service'. Samuel Greg, for example, could 'almost be made the hero of a fiction on the other side of the question', but the failure of his schemes had been 'a stinging grief' to him. Over the past four years the industrial scene had calmed. Her friendships with engineers like the eminent William Fairbairn and James Nasmyth, inventor of the steam-hammer in 1839 (whose commercial partner at the huge Bridgewater foundry in the 1840s was William Gaskell's cousin Holbrook) had made her even more conscious of the energy and imagination of Manchester. At the same time her belief that capitalism could be combined with care had been encouraged by initiatives like the school at Price's candle-factory at Vauxhall, and the innovations of Salis Schwabe at his Rhodes works. Schwabe seemed to have succeeded where Greg failed. Frances Bunsen, Baron Bunsen's wife, noted on her first visit to Manchester in 1849:

'The calico printing at Rhodes and numberless arrangements for the comfort and intellectual furtherance of the workpeople in that industrial village, constructed by Mr Schwabe, was a sight to move the feelings of all.'³

All this, and the campaigns of the Christian Socialists, a major interest of Elizabeth in the early 1850s, made her think that there might be a way that domestic values could soften mercantile life. In June 1853 she visited the Spottiswoode's printing works in London, where masters and workers shared prayers, meals and outings: 'in short they are like a large & happy family'.

As the spring of 1853 grew warmer Elizabeth's whole outlook became more optimistic. In her February gloom she told Tottie forlornly that she saw no hope of getting to London 'this winter, spring or summer'. There had been changes at Plymouth Grove: Meta had gone to Rachel Martineau's school in Liverpool and Rosa Mitchell had left, with the prospect of a good school post. Marianne had left Mrs Lalor's before Christmas and now stepped into the breach to teach Flossy and Julia. Elizabeth worried about this at first, but by April it was clear the arrangement was a great success, Marianne being 'a most gentle and patient teacher'.

The sky lightened, the horizon widened. Her flu was over, *Ruth* was finding better reviews and suddenly there was the chance of a new adventure. On 7 April she told Lady Kay-Shuttleworth that it was 'between a Possibly & a Probably' that she and William would be in London at Whitsun. Three days later she took up her letter again:

'April 10th. Since writing my last sentence it is become "between a possibly and a probably" that we go to Paris on May 12 or 13th! I have never been there; and we plan to take Marianne . . . I don't know if she or I are the most delighted with this sudden plan; which after all can hardly be called a plan after all [*sic*], only an idea.' (L229)

It would be her first trip abroad since Heidelberg twelve years before. She had always envied Tottie and the Winkworths their time on the Continent and from now on travel became a passion. Until the end of her life she went abroad almost every year, most often to France, but also to Germany, Switzerland and Italy. At least one of her daughters usually went with her while William took his holidays alone. In 1861 she explained that 'his own womankind wd any of them, be *thankful* to go with him, but he says he needs "entire freedom of responsibility" which he could not have if he had the charge of any of us, and of our luggage'. The truth may also be that without him *she* had entire freedom, luggage or not.

They did, however, make this first Paris trip together. And at the end of April, before they left, there was another pleasure, a visit from Charlotte Brontë. Charlotte was uncertain of her future. The previous December Arthur Bell Nicholls, whom she had known as a curate at Haworth since 1845, had suddenly declared his love. Like John Thornton, Gaskell's hero in *North and South*, this rather stern, silent man was suddenly disabled by passion. Charlotte described him as:

'shaking from head to foot, looking deadly pale, speaking low, vehemently yet with difficulty – he made me for the first time feel what it costs a man to declare affection where he doubts response. The spectacle of one ordinarily so statue-like, thus trembling, stirred, and overcome, gave me a strange kind of shock.'[4]

If she was disturbed by the spectacle, her father was outraged: 'the veins on his temple started up like whipcord'. Shaken, Charlotte promised that she would give Nicholls a distinct refusal the next day.

Arthur Nicholls had resigned his curacy and left the village. Since then Charlotte had been in low spirits and poor health, and had accepted with relief an invitation from her publisher, George Smith, to spend a month in London. On her way back she stayed at Plymouth Grove. Elizabeth was once again amazed at the extreme shyness that she had first seen in 1850. Charlotte shivered at the sight of a strange face. She could not bear to be the centre of attention, but when the Winkworth sisters sang Scottish ballads, 'she forgot herself, and rose and crossed to the piano, where she asked eagerly for song after song'.[5] She agreed to go to their house next day and sing more, but the thought of meeting a third sister proved too much and they walked up and down the street, Charlotte remorseful, Lily soothing, until they gave up and went home. There were many such incidents. Julia remembered that once when Mrs Sidney Potter called, Miss Brontë abruptly vanished, to emerge later from behind the drawing-room curtains.[6] At a dinner party she shrank into silence until guests ignored her and argued fiercely about Thackeray – William had been 'outraged' by the morality of his lecture on Fielding. Charlotte, devoted to but infuriated by Thackeray, 'threw herself warmly into the discussion: the ice of her reserve was broken'.[7]

Elizabeth said that during this stay her former respect for Charlotte turned to liking, liking to love:

'I thoroughly loved her before she left, – and I was so sorry for her! She has had so little kindness & affection shown to her; she said that she was afraid of loving me as much as she could, because she had never been able to inspire the kind of love she felt.' (L230)

In the face of William's kindness, Elizabeth's warmth and the liveliness of Flossy and Julia, Charlotte's self-consciousness fell away. She wrote from Haworth: 'The week I spent in Manchester impressed me as the very brightest and healthiest I have known for these five years past.'[8]

Did they discuss their next books as well as the reviews of *Ruth* and *Villette*? Almost as soon as Charlotte left Elizabeth sent off her outline to Dickens.

In early May Elizabeth set off with William and Marianne for Paris. There she met another woman of genius, but a genius with people, not on the page, Mary Clarke Mohl. Clarkey, as her friends called her, could not have been more of a contrast to Charlotte Brontë. She wore an air of freedom that seemed unattainable for women in British society. In 1854 she was nearing sixty.[9] She looked extraordinary. She was tiny, with shining eyes and wild, unfashionably curly hair – Guizot remarked that she and his Skye terrier must share the same *coiffeur*. She was at the hub of French political and literary life and at her informal Friday salons cabinet ministers mixed with scientists, German theologians and Italian poets with English lords. She read voraciously, from metaphysics to botany, and had gained her place through vivacity, intelligence, impulsive sympathy and a sometimes acid wit. Her friend the scientist Ampère noted cryptically that 'her great charm lay in the absence of it. I never knew a woman so devoid of charm in the ordinary sense of the word and yet so fascinating. She was hardly a woman at all.'[10] Florence Nightingale, whom Clarkey supported in all her battles with her family and who loved her dearly, explained that 'she never had a breath of posing or "edifying" in her presentation of herself, even when it would have been most desirable. She was always undressed – naked in full view. A little clothing would have been decent.'[11]

Mary Clarke Mohl's background was Scottish Whig. Her maternal grandmother, Mrs Hay, an important figure in her life, had been at the centre of radical Edinburgh in its eighteenth-century heyday; through her Mary knew Elizabeth's friends Mrs Fletcher and the Davys. In 1801, when Mary was eight, her mother moved to France for her health and although Mary endured one miserable year of English schooling and spent four or five months in England with her sister every summer, France was her home for the rest of her life. They had lived in the south until 1813, when they moved to Paris. Chafing against the role of dutiful daughter to an invalid mother, Mary wanted to paint, to write or to act, but finally found her *métier* when Mme Récamier gave them rooms above her own in the Abbaye de Bois. Mary attended her salon, becoming the pet of the elderly Chateaubriand, and soon began to hold a small salon of her own. For sixty years, from the 1820s to her death, she numbered among her friends writers like Stendhal, Mérimée, Victor Hugo, Sainte Beuve, de Tocqueville, Renan, Turgenev and, from across the Channel, Harriet Martineau, the Thackerays, the Brownings and George Eliot.

For many years she was passionately, jealously in love with the medieval scholar Claude Fauriel, who happily shared her life though not her bed. In 1847, four years after Fauriel died, she married his younger friend, the German orientalist Julius Mohl. She was fifty-four; Julius was forty-seven. (At the wedding Ampère was ordered to blow his nose loudly when she had to state her age.) It was a companionable, sexless marriage. When Julius was exhausted by her energy, he retreated to his library. When Thomas Trollope visited, he discovered him among his books, 'built into walls around him, as to suggest almost inevitably the idea of a mouse in cheese, eating out the hollow it lives in'.[12]

In May 1853 Elizabeth Gaskell found herself unexpectedly swept into the colourful ambience of 121 rue du Bac, as Mme Mohl explained to Elizabeth Reid:

'I had Mrs Gaskell to lionise for a fortnight, luckily I had no cold then and it was a great pleasure . . . I am so fond of her that I invited her to come and stay with me and to bring her nr. 2 daughter Meta when she comes, principally as Marianne is not that interesting with nothing of the beaming countenance of the mother. To my taste she is the most agreeable literary lady I have yet seen. Mrs Gaskell has a great quantum of good sound sense and discrimination, a great addition to talent and by no means a necessary accompaniment and no vanity. It is a healthy sound mind & temper. She was staying with Mrs Schwabe who had the measles and could show her nothing which was an absolute piece of good fortune to me as it made me see so much of her.'[13]

Poor Grace Schwabe. (A few weeks later Florence Nightingale was tucked up in the Mohl's back room, tenderly cared for by Julius, measles having cut short her scheme to train with the Sisters of Charity in Paris.)

The Mohls' world was irresistible to Elizabeth, with its brilliant conversation, scholarship, openness and oddity. This first acquaintance was the start of an enduring friendship. Elizabeth sent *Cranford* (which Julius read 'instead of doing his work in the evening').[14] A kitten named Cranford arrived from Paris at Plymouth Grove, and Mary Mohl found a translator for the book, her friend Louise Swanton, married to the painter Hilaire Belloc.[16] Elizabeth had found a new network. She was soon writing letters of introduction for William Rathbone Greg to the historian E´mil Souvestre and in 1861 Greg in turn helped Mme Mohl with her book on Mme de Sable´ although she (rightly) told Elizabeth that she liked 'my bad English better than Mr Greg's good'.[16] On her visits to Paris Elizabeth met Rosa Bonheur, whose spirit she admired as much as her art, explaining enthusiastically to John Forster how Bonheur had dressed as a man to paint horses in the livery stables. Most important of all, the Mohls introduced her to the American sculptor William Wetmore Story and his wife, Emelyn. Emelyn described Clarkey vividly, remembering how she used 'to drop out of an omnibus, often into a mud-puddle, at our door':

'I can see her now, just arrived, her feet on the fender before the fire, her hair flying, and her general untidiness so marked as to be picturesque – since she showed a supreme indifference to the details of dress. Her talk was all her own; nobody was like her for a jumble of ideas and facts, which made her mind much like her clothes, topsy-turvily worn.'[17]

The Mohls quickly influenced Elizabeth's writing. Their voices can be heard in three pieces written before she became exclusively embroiled in *North and South*: 'My French Master', 'Modern Greek Songs' (an account of Fauriel's collection) and 'Company Manners'.

The last piece, based on Victor Cousin's articles on Mme de Sablé in *Revue des deux mondes*, shows Gaskell's astonishment at the difference between society at the rue du Bac and stuffy social gatherings in England, and at the status of intellectual women in France. Despite her friendship with Elizabeth Reid, founder of Bedford College, Mme Mohl was bemused by the British passion for women's colleges; if a Frenchwoman wanted to hear a lecture, she simply went to the Sorbonne with the men. Quizzing her on her salon, Elizabeth caught her irreverent tone perfectly. The 'gentleman' remarks mildly that Mme de Duras and Mme Récamier missed many celebrities by their rule of not inviting strangers:

' "Bah!" said the lady, "Celebrities! what has one to do with them in society? As celebrities, they are simply bores. Because a man has discovered a planet, it does not follow that he can converse agreeably, even on his own subjects; often people are drained dry by one action or expression of their lives . . . The writer of books, for instance, cannot afford to talk twenty pages for nothing, so he is either profoundly silent, or else he gives you the mere rinsings of his mind." '[18]

While Mary delivered such barbs, Julius looked on and added his comments, more kindly, but no less witty.

When the Gaskells returned from Paris, Marianne dashed back to her music lessons and William to his 'congregational duties'. He was always burdened by work. During this year it was finally decided that Manchester New College should move to London and become purely a theological college, with J. J. Tayler as principal, training students for the ministry – the new Owens College, opened in 1846, would carry on its more general teaching role in Manchester. William's teaching load was thus lightened slightly, but the move provided more cares for him in his role as a trustee. Meanwhile his own parish work was ever increasing, and would expand still more in 1854 when John Robberds died and he became senior minister.

In the spring of 1853 Elizabeth did not return to any such 'duties'. She stayed in London. Fired by France, she was already planning a second trip and at dinner with Lady Coltman she grilled Henry Hallam about his holiday in Normandy the previous year. A surviving scrap of paper shows her careful notes on 'Mr Hallam's scheme of a tour of Normandy'. She had decided on her summer plans – a circuit from Le

Havre, through Rouen, Lisieux and Caen to Bayeux and Coutances and then on to Mont St Michael. Within a week Hallam sent a detailed letter from his travelling partner, Boileau, advising her to buy Murray's handbook, suggesting hotels and discussing the hire of a carriage and the problems of trains.[19]

London was the usual flurry. Names are not so much dropped as hurled into her letters. To Emily: 'I should so like to come and know a little of Mazzini, but there is a great dinner-party here, made for me – Macaulay, Hallam, Sir Francis Palgrave and Lord Campbell.' To F. J. Furnivall: 'IF I do get to Mr Ruskin's class, I shan't have a minute to spare for anything else I'm afraid – I EXTREMELY want to go. But this week is in a mist.' To Marianne, from Crix: 'dressed for dinner: Sir Charles and Lady Trevelyan, Monckton Milneses, Milnes Gaskells, Dean of St Paul's & Mrs Milman, Wm Duckworths – Lady Coltman thought the party flat, but I did not.' She had promised to see Maria James: 'oh! *she* is such a charming person . . . Ly Coltman is vexed (in her pretty way) that I don't stay *there*, and I have so many calls to pay: & shall *utterly* offend the Carlyles, if I don't give them a day, they have said so much about it. I really think if you don't want me at home, darling I must stay on to Tuesday or Wednesday week (7 or 8) & then go straight to Miss Brontë's.'

In the end she postponed her visit to Haworth because Charlotte was ill. Instead she and William took Florence and Julia to the Schwabes' mansion in North Wales, Glyngarth, on the Menai Straits, while Marianne and Meta went to London. At the end of July they left the younger girls in Wales and met their two older daughters at Beechwood, the Duckworths' house near Southampton, where the nearby New Forest glades inspired Elizabeth's description of Helstone in *North and South*. From Southampton they sailed to Normandy. When Meta was back at school, Charlotte wrote: 'This summer's tour will no doubt furnish a lifelong remembrance of pleasure to her and Marianne.'[20] 'An Accursed Race', published two years later, opens with a similar Normandy holiday, and in the autumn of 1853 France prompted four contributions to *Household Words*: 'Traits and Stories of the Huguenots', 'My French Master', 'Bran' and 'The Scholar's Story'. The last two were versions of old Breton ballads in octosyllabic couplets, translated by William, with an introduction to the second by Elizabeth.[21]

In September Elizabeth finally visited the Brontë's. When she wrote to suggest a date, Charlotte was away, but Patrick opened the letter and sent a warm, formal note of welcome. As soon as she got home Charlotte wrote: 'Come to Haworth as soon as you can; the heath is in bloom now; I have waited and watched for its purple signal as the forerunner of your coming.'[22]

Elizabeth had been looking forward to seeing the heather at its height, but the moors around Haworth were blasted by a thunderstorm two days before she arrived and instead of being a 'blaze of purple glory' were 'all of a livid brown colour'. The dreariness fitted her preconceived vision of the Parsonage. Indeed everything was made to fit, even her arrival on a 'dull, drizzly, Indian-inky day', amid the wind that she always associated with restless passion:

'In I went – half blown back by the wild vehemence of the wind which swept along the narrow gravel walk – round the corner of the house into a small plot of grass enclosed within a low stone wall, over which the more ambitious grave-stones towered all round.

. . . The wind goes piping and wailing and sobbing round the square unsheltered house in a very strange unearthly way.' (L242-3)

In two long letters, one later included in the *Life*, she described every detail, as if knowingly recording it for posterity (and sure her reports would be circulated, as indeed they were).[23] She noted the furniture, the prints, the food, the servants, Tabby and Martha. She described Charlotte's neatness and punctuality and her restless pacings, still keeping to the habit she had developed of walking up and down with her sisters as they discussed their writing night after night. Elizabeth felt the shadows of Emily and Anne as she listened to 'that slow, monotonous, incessant walk in which I am sure I should fancy I heard the steps of the dead following me'.

Now only Charlotte remained, alone with her father. Elizabeth was fascinated by Patrick Brontë, whom she was meeting for the first time: 'a tall, fine looking old man, with silver bristles all over his head; nearly blind; speaking with a strong Scotch accent (he comes from the North of Ireland), raised himself from the ranks of a poor farmer's son'. She was struck by his courtesy and elaborate, old-fashioned compliments, but since she had decided in advance that he was oppressive and potentially violent, that was what she found. As she told John Forster, 'I was sadly afraid of him in my inmost soul; for I caught a glare of his stern eyes over his spectacles at Miss Brontë once or twice which made me know my man.' He was a fierce conservative; took the side of masters against men; was much to be respected but ought never to have married. And, she added, to account for her fear ('rather an admiring fear after all'), Charlotte had told her that her father never dressed in the morning without putting a loaded pistol in his pocket, as regularly as he put on his watch: 'There was this little deadly pistol sitting down to breakfast with us, kneeling down to prayers at night to say nothing of a loaded gun hanging up on high, ready to pop off on the slightest emergency.'

Everything combined to complete the picture. The two women battled against the wind on Penistone moor, where 'the sinuous hills seem to girdle the world like the great Norse serpent'. As they walked Charlotte told such wild tales of the ungovernable local families who lived in lonely houses on the moor that *Wuthering Heights* seemed tame by comparison. In the evenings, when Patrick retreated to smoke his clay pipe, they sat by the fire and talked: of Elizabeth's meeting in London with Harriet Beecher Stowe, of Charlotte's absurd dread of being accused of plagiarism in *Jane Eyre*. They talked too of more personal matters: Charlotte's childhood, her time in Brussels, the deaths of her sisters and Branwell, her feelings towards Mr Nicholls. 'We were so happy together,' Elizabeth remembered, 'so full of interest in each other's subjects.' For her part, Charlotte wrote:

'After you left, the house felt very much as if the shutters had been suddenly closed and the blinds let down. One was sensible during the remainder of the day of a depressing silence, shadow, loss and want. However, if the going away was sad, the stay was pleasant and did permanent good.'[24]

During their long walks Elizabeth had become convinced that Charlotte and Arthur Nicholls should marry. After she left, believing that the chief reason for Mr Brontë's 'violent and virulent opposition' was Nicholls's lack of money, she set out at once to remove this obstacle. Knowing Charlotte would be too proud to accept a literary pension, she asked Richard Monckton Milnes if he could obtain something for Nicholls. He must keep the scheme secret, she insisted: 'if my well-meant treachery becomes known to her I shall lose her friendship, which I prize most highly'. She enjoyed the conspiracy and also tried to help Charlotte to get away from Haworth so that the couple could meet, providing the address of Mrs Dove, her Bloomsbury landlady.

While this private drama was unfolding, Elizabeth was also engrossed by a public one involving F. D. Maurice. Raised a Unitarian, Maurice had been a magnet to controversy since 1830 when his refusal to subscribe to the Thirty-nine Articles (like Mr Hale in *North and South*) prevented his graduation from Cambridge. He then developed a theology of his own, closer to the Church of England, and became professor of divinity at King's College, London, in 1846. He was still viewed with deep suspicion by Anglicans, especially after he founded the Christian Socialist movement with Kingsley and Ludlow in 1848, and in 1853, when he published his *Theological Essays*, the Church establishment pounced. The *Essays*, they declared, were wholly unorthodox – he admitted his disbelief in the eternity of hell – and he was dismissed from King's. Both Elizabeth and Charlotte, who admired Maurice greatly, were outraged. Elizabeth exchanged anxious letters with John Ludlow and F. J. Furnivall and gave pamphlets to everyone she met 'because it is one of the subjects uppermost in my mind, and I am constantly hearing, & consequently often repeating instances of people who have owed more than they can well speak of without breaking down to Mr Maurice's writings or Mr Maurice's self'. Religious debate and intolerance, as well as the problem of Charlotte's marriage, was thus 'uppermost in her mind' when she started writing her novel at the close of this year.

Christmas was coming. Elizabeth dashed off to Knutsford, sending back a barrage of instructions to Marianne: to order some leather for a box for her own present; to send a small pattern of silk for a dress; 'to think what Flossy & Julia would like for Xmas presents. I do so want to hear that they did not catch cold yesterday'; to give Agnes 'the enclosed clothing tickets' and ask her to see if 'Scattergood (widow living in clean cellar in Stopford court), *could* pay even 2d a week'; to remind Margaret 'to order this next Friday pieces of beef for our poor people' (here follows a list of the weight for each family) and arrange Christmas dinner for the Sunday-school children. Had she finished covering her white satin shoes? And could she 'fix with Hearn on Friday what gown I'm to wear blue or lilac'?

Marianne then went to London (for a rest, perhaps). Her mother sent her reports of Manchester parties with less enthusiasm than usual. The Ewarts' dance (to which she did not go) was probably 'large, vulgar and overdressed'. Dinner with the Unitarian families – Greenwoods, Marslands, Potters – was not only large but dull: 'everybody out of tune with each other and with the piano'. She was impatient to clear some time and 'write, write, write'.

With the new year of 1854 came greetings from Dickens, promising that a business letter from Wills would follow 'involving a proposal which I earnestly hope you will consider favourably and accept'.[25] She consulted Forster and sent him her outline. Reassuring as ever, he found it 'by far the best material you have yet worked with' and urged her on: 'now I say very earnestly go on with this story whether it be for Dickens or not'.[26] She decided it would be for Dickens and after a short trip to Paris got down to work.

Elizabeth was apprehensive about writing a serial, but in February Dickens told her not to worry about dividing the story into parts. She should write as she pleased and he would decide on the breaks. By March she had made a start. 'We read a little of her book,' noted Katie Winkworth.[27] By this time Dickens's own plans were beginning to alarm her. He seemed to be stealing her material, just as he had pinched her story of 'the face'. In January he had visited the Lancashire town of Preston, paralysed in the fourth month of a controversial weavers' strike. The owners had closed their mills to prevent the strike from affecting them piecemeal, and whether it was a lock-out or a strike was hotly argued. Dickens blamed intransigents among the masters and agitators among the workmen. In response to debates in London as well as events in the north he began to write *Hard Times*. Hearing that it was due to start in *Household Words* in April, Elizabeth wrote worriedly to Forster. This time he could not reassure her because he simply did not know:

'As to the content which Dickens' story is likely to take I have regretted to see that the manufacturing discontents are likely to clash with part of your plan, but I know nothing yet from him as to how far he means to use that sort of material. Nor do I think he knows himself . . . I am your witness if necessary, that your notion in this matter existed before and quite independently of his.'[28]

He suggested she ask Dickens directly, which she did, when she sent 'Company Manners' at the end of April. Dickens promised he had 'no intention of striking', although he would deal with the 'monstrous claims at domination' made by a certain class of manufacturers, and the way in which it was made easy for working men 'to slide down into discontent under such hands . . . but I am not going to strike, so don't be afraid of me'.[29] She should read the first two numbers and see for herself. Although he answered breezily enough, from this point a slight coolness crept into his manner. Even before any copy arrived, the course of *North and South* was not set fair.

While Elizabeth was still planning her book, she heard news of Charlotte Brontë which made her forget her work. Over the past six months Charlotte and Arthur Bell Nicholls had corresponded and met, at first secretly and then, having confronted her father, openly. In January Nicholls stayed nearby and Charlotte's feelings turned to esteem, 'and if not love – at least affection. Still papa was very, very hostile – bitterly unjust.'[30] Nicholls persevered and the Revd Brontë grudgingly conceded. The opposition did not come only from Patrick. On 18 April Charlotte wrote to Elizabeth: 'I cannot deny that I had a battle to fight with myself; I am not sure yet that I have even conquered certain inward combatants.' Finally, she said, she hardly knew how, 'I find myself engaged.' The only things she sounds pleased about are the gladness of the local people and the promise given by Mr Nicholls that he would prove his gratitude to Patrick Brontë 'by offering faithful support and consolation to his age'. Her tone is painfully subdued:

'I could almost cry sometimes that in this important action in my life I cannot better satisfy papa's perhaps natural pride. My destiny will not be brilliant, certainly, but Mr Nicholls is conscientious, affectionate, pure in heart and life. He offers a most constant and tried attachment – I am very grateful to him. I mean to try and make him happy, and papa too.'[31]

This could not have been a more private letter, yet Elizabeth immediately sent it 'in strict confidence' to Monckton Milnes and repeated its contents to Forster. One of her fears was personal, the dread that Nicholls, a Puseyite, would forbid her friendship with Charlotte. 'I am terribly afraid he won't let her go on being intimate with us, as heretics,' she wrote. She had wanted the marriage, but in the light of Charlotte's joyless surrender her doubts surfaced. She tried to persuade herself that although Mr Nicholls seemed stern and bigoted, the marriage might work. After all, Mr Nicholls loved Charlotte 'vehemently', had known her brother and sisters and had loved her before she was famous. It was now that she made the comment, which tells us as much about herself as her friend, that perhaps what Charlotte needed was an 'exacting, rigid, law-giving, passionate man'.

When she wrote these words, she was brooding on her own inflexible but passionate hero, John Thornton. In the last paragraph of her letter she asked Forster if it might be a good idea to introduce another woman into *North and South*, in love with Thornton and jealous of Margaret, perhaps as a housekeeper or a companion for Mrs Thornton. She would be an orphan from a retired country village: 'the kind of wild wayward character that grows up in lonesome places, which has a sort of Southern capacity of hating & loving'.

The idea was dropped (Emily Shaen pointed out there were a great many characters already). Then, at the beginning of May, Charlotte Brontë came from her 'lonesome places' to stay at Plymouth Grove. While she was there, an odd scene occurred, the sort of talk Mary Clarke Mohl liked best 'as women talk most openly in the dimly-lighted bedroom at curling-time'.[32] One day, on leaving Charlotte's room, Elizabeth whispered to Catherine Winkworth that she should say something about the engagement. Katie, unsure quite what to say, murmured awkwardly that she had heard Charlotte was ' "not going to be alone any more". She leant her head on her hand and said very quickly: "Yes, I am going to be married in June." ' There was a pause and then Charlotte burst out, 'But Katie, it has cost me a good deal to come to this.' Mr Nicholls was kind and reliable, but, she admitted, far from intellectual:

' "Such a character might be less amusing and interesting than a more impulsive and fickle one; it might be dull!"
"Yes, indeed" said Lily.'[33]

Katie put the two writers in their places by pointing out that a dull, steady man, if less fun for an evening, might be better for life. He would provide a stable centre and anyway, the steadiness might allow one to be fickle oneself:

' "Oh Katie, if *I* had ever said such a wicked thing", cried Lily; and then Miss Brontë: "Oh Katie, I never thought to hear such a speech from *you*!" '

Both were greatly amused. They talked on, Lily reassuring Charlotte by telling her how tender the apparently severe William could be as a nurse and how loving he was to his children. But, Katie concluded, remembering *Villette*, 'I *guess* the true love was Paul Emmanuel after all, and is dead; but I don't know, and don't think that Lily knows.'

After Charlotte was married on 29 June 1854, Elizabeth never saw her again. She had to turn down an invitation to Haworth the following year and felt hesitant about writing. Their last exchange of letters concerned the early chapters of *North and South*. Charlotte admired them, although she thought Mr Hale's religious doubt a difficult subject and had 'groaned at first'. She said she knew, however, that Elizabeth felt no bitterness towards the Church but was merely defending those who differed from it and 'felt it a duty to leave her fold . . . Well – it is good ground, but still rugged for the step of Fiction; stony – thorny will it prove at times – I fear.'[34] Elizabeth sent a long reply, chiefly for the benefit of Mr Nicholls, but it was never answered.

The opening of *North and South* was indeed thorny ground. At the time of Charlotte's visit in May Elizabeth was depressed about her novel. She felt it was slow and sluggish and did not want to show it to Forster because it was 'flat and grey – with no bright clear foreground as yet . . . Oh dear! I can't get Mr Gaskell to look at it, & it is no use writing much longer.' She seemed to have no time even to reply to letters, as she told Mary Green, 'but it shan't go on an hour longer unless some of the many unforeseen interruptions of my life break in'.[35]

The chief interruption was scarlet fever, which had broken out in Greenheys at the beginning of that month. Elizabeth packed Hearn, Marianne and the girls off to the sea at Poulton, and badgered William to leave Manchester, 'by assuring him he shall have no peace or comfort at home'. Eventually he agreed to 'bachelorize off comfortably guided by the wind of his own daily will', going to Dumbleton, Oxford and then London.

She stayed behind alone. Since she had told her friends she was

leaving, no one knew she was there and although the house was lonely
without the girls, she enjoyed her freedom. She wrote exuberantly to
Tottie:

'Nature intended me for a gypsy-bachelor; that *I* am sure of. Not an
old maid for they are particular & fidgetty, and tidy, and punctual –
but a gypsy-bachelor. I get up early. I breakfast with a book in my
hand. I go out and feed all the animals.' (L301)

She could eat when and where she liked, like Sancho Panza. She could
tend her chickens and plant cabbages, like Cincinnatus. She could
answer her post, feeling like 'an ass between a great number of bundles
of hay, with so many invitations here, there and everywhere'.

She was forced out of her gypsy life by Emily Shaen, who came up to
Manchester to see her sisters and swept her off to London. There she
joined William and, to his alarm, leapt into a round of social calls. He
had had enough already. The Winkworths found him 'desperately
tired of gaiety' though 'very merry despite his fatigue'. He kept his
head low: 'Mr Gaskell spent the morning lounging about and talking
to us, Lily going about.'[36] Lily did not forget her book, however, and
John Forster was invited to dinner specifically to talk about it. Then
she fell ill, and complained bitterly: 'I have not written one line of
"Margaret" for three weeks for headaches and dizziness.' Much of the
talk that May, as well as her illness, made for depression – the Crimean
War had just begun. In late March England and France had declared
war on Russia in defence of the Turks (and of their own trade routes
to the East and naval supremacy in the Mediterranean). The Russian
base at Sebastopol was now under heavy bombardment, and allied
casualties were high. Thoughts of the war would dog Elizabeth
throughout the writing of her novel.

June flew past. She went to Leighton Buzzard to see Stevenson
relatives, and to Betley Hall in Staffordshire to stay with Ellen Tollett,
a new friend she had met the previous year at Teddesley. The Tolletts
were cousins of the Nightingales and close friends of the Wedgwoods
and Darwins; there were seven remarkable sisters, all highly educated
and independent. In their youth Emma Wedgwood (Charles Darwin's
future wife) called them 'a group of clever, spirited girls', and Charles
himself thought so highly of one of them, Georgina, that he sent her
part of the manuscript of *On the Origin of Species*, to correct his errors
of style.[37]

Elizabeth's circles were constantly widening: in the summer of 1854 the cabbages and chickens of Plymouth Grove were forgotten as she moved from place to place. By late August, however, she was clearly searching for bolt-holes to write in. At the end of that month she went with Meta to the Isle of Man, entirely on impulse. Meta sent Marianne a hilarious account of how they arrived with nowhere to stay and were directed all over the island before finding completely unsuitable lodgings. The rain poured down, the house was full of wailing children, Meta tried to sketch, her mother to write. Elizabeth felt entirely cut off: 'Do you know they even get their *cabbages* from Liverpool,' she wrote in a letter for Julia's eighth birthday.

Everywhere she went she took her manuscript with her. In May she told Forster she had '76 pages'. In mid-June she sent over a hundred to Dickens, who read them, he said, 'with all possible attention and care. I have shut myself up for the purpose and allowed nothing to divide my thoughts. It opens an admirable story, is full of character and power, has a strong suspended interest in it.'[38] (This was either tact or wishful thinking: *North and South* was a fine psychological novel, but it lacked the suspense required for a successful serial.) In a long letter he explained that he had asked the printers for a cast-off, to estimate the space her foolscap pages would fill, and had divided the copy she had sent into the first six numbers. But he was adamant that the second section (which described Mr Hale's decision to leave the Church) should be firmly compressed, since this episode, 'where the dialogue is long – is a difficult and dangerous subject'.

Elizabeth totally ignored him. In late August, when Wills sent proofs, Dickens was horrified to find the text 'as it originally stood, and *unaltered by you*'. As it had to go to press immediately she must alter the proofs and 'will you be so kind as to do so at once'.[39] She did not. To make matters worse, the printers' estimate was wrong: the book was going to be far too long. All through the summer, while Elizabeth was paying her polite visits, she and Dickens wrangled over length, over who should write the sentences at the close of each division, over the advertising, over the name. It is not clear who suggested 'North and South', but Dickens certainly preferred it as more 'expressive of the opposite people brought face to face by the story'.[40] After she finished the book, perhaps remembering the complaints about the death scenes in *Mary Barton* and Dickens's laments over her sad endings, Elizabeth jokingly suggested that 'Death and Variations' might have been better, since 'there are 5 deaths, each beautifully suited to the character of the individual'.

At one point she sensibly suggested that Dickens should see the whole book before he started to print; he needed a serial for September and could not wait. From July to October he was in Boulogne, firing endless letters across the Channel to Wills and Gaskell. He was furious with her and with the printers:

'If I had known how it was to turn out, that when they said in Whitefriars "white" they meant "black", or when they said "Ten" they meant "Twenty", I could not, in my senses, have accepted the story . . . I am unspeakably vexed by all the needless trouble and bewilderment. There is no more reason for it than there is for a calomel pill on the top of the Cross of St Pauls.'[41]

On 2 September the first instalment appeared. It soon became clear that in serial terms *North and South* was not a hit. Sales of *Household Words* dropped and Dickens declared he was not at all surprised. He put the blame squarely on Mrs Gaskell's 'wearisome' novel.[42]

Mrs Gaskell was still being difficult. Her novel was spilling over its allotted bounds and by the end of October she was a whole episode behind Dickens's plan. Their dealings became so fraught that William Gaskell stepped in and persuaded Dickens to increase the columns in each number from twelve to sixteen. *Hard Times* had never exceeded eleven. Dickens had no patience, despite his explosion to Forster only a few months earlier over the agony of writing for weekly parts:

'the difficulty of space is CRUSHING. Nobody can have any idea of it who has not had an experience of patient fiction writing, with some elbow room always, and open places in perspective. In this form, with any kind of regard to the current number, there is absolutely no such thing.'[43]

He had wrestled and overcome. Why couldn't Mrs G.? But she was used to plenty of elbow room and could not or would not adapt.

When publication began, the wearisome novel was far from finished. In early October, looking for somewhere to write in peace, Elizabeth took her foolscap sheets 'ready paged' to the Nightingales at Lea Hurst, near Matlock in Derbyshire. The large house (not large at all, said Florence – it only had fifteen bedrooms) gazed out across the Derwent valley as if, thought Elizabeth, it were floating on air. From its battlemented roof 'one can see the clouds careering round one; one seems on the Devil's pinnacles of the Earth'. She told Katie:

'It is getting dark. I am to have my tea, up in my turret – at 6, – And after that I shall lock my outer door & write. I am stocked with coals and have candles up here; for I am a quarter of a mile of staircase & odd intricate passage away from everyone else in the house. Could solitude be more complete!' (L308)

At Lea Hurst Gaskell met another woman whose real-life story influenced the final stages of her work. Her arrival coincided with the end of Florence Nightingale's holiday, and in her Elizabeth found a woman who would make no compromises between genius and domestic ties. Florence was now thirty-two. The previous year, after fourteen years of frustration (including eight years of fighting with her family), she had finally cut free. In July 1853, to the accompaniment of tears, rage and fainting fits on the part of her mother, Fanny, and older sister, Parthenope, she became superintendent at 'the Institution for the care of Sick Gentlewomen in Distressed Circumstances' in Harley Street (or, in her own words, 'a Sanatorium for sick governesses run by a Committee of fine ladies').[44]

A year later, Florence was ready to move on, having stunned her committee of 'Fashionable Asses' (as Clarkey called them), and been accepted as a saint by her patients. At the height of the cholera epidemic of 1854 she went as a volunteer to the Middlesex Hospital, which had been cleared of its usual patients to take in emergencies. Many were prostitutes. They died in her arms, night after night, delirious, drunken and screaming with pain. On hearing her stories, Elizabeth explained to Katie how Florence was up day and night receiving the women as they 'were brought in from their "beat" along Oxford St . . . undressing them – & awfully filthy they were, & putting on turpentine *stupes* &c all herself to as many as she could manage – never had a touch even of diarrhea'.

Like all who met Florence Nightingale, Elizabeth was spellbound. She told Katie of her learning, her Egyptian travels, her brief training at Kaiserwerth and Paris. She was struck by her beauty – her chestnut hair and grey eyes – and by her wicked humour: 'she has a great deal of fun, & is carried along by that'. A great mimic herself, she delighted in Flo's impressions of the grateful governesses in Harley Street who were so flattered at having '*Lady* Canning & *Lady* Monteagle to do this &

that' or of a tipsy nurse-cum-prostitute at the Middlesex who boasted proudly, as she was carried in with cholera, that 'but a week go I was in silk and satins; in silk and satins dancing at Woolwich'. The humour suggested a certain detachment, though, and beneath the self-sacrifice Gaskell spotted steely single-mindedness.

At first she was all admiration: 'Is it not like St Elizabeth of Hungary! The efforts of her family to interest her in other occupations by allowing her to travel &c – but the clinging to one object!' But as she stayed longer at Lea Hurst, a change set in – partly because she was a captive audience for the moans of Fanny and Parthe, partly because of her own sharp encounters with Flo. Perhaps, she thought, Miss Nightingale was *too* single-minded. Parthe, whom Florence had dubbed the 'Devourer' when she thwarted her plans by her hysterical illnesses, could also be seen as the Devoured: 'She is devoted – her sense of existence is lost in Florence's. I never saw such adoring love.' Parthe, she added, 'says F. does not care for *individuals* – (which is curiously true) – but for the whole race as being God's creatures'. Although she may have suspected that Parthe's self-annihilation was spiked with bitterness, and her tones of 'intense affection' cloaked a jealous sense of exclusion, her remark intrigued Elizabeth, whose general social concern always sprang from individuals, especially those nearest to her. She mused on this to Emily:

'That text always jarred against me, that "Who is my mother and my brethren?" – and there is just that jar in F.N. to me. She has no friend – and she wants none. She stands perfectly alone, half-way between God and his creatures . . .

. . . She and I had a grand quarrel one day. She is, I think, too much for institutions, sisterhoods and associations, and she said if she had influence enough not a mother should bring up a child herself: there should be crêches for the rich as well as the poor. If she had twenty children she would send them all to a crêche, seeing, of course, that it was a well managed crêche. That exactly tells of what seems to me *the* want – but then this want of love for individuals becomes a gift and a very rare one, if one takes it in conjunction with her intense love for the *race*: her utter unselfishness in serving and ministering.' (L319–20)

This ambivalent judgement was made at the turning-point of Florence Nightingale's life. On 9, 10 and 13 October, during Elizabeth's first days at Lea Hurst, *The Times* published William Howard

Russell's devastating accounts of the Crimea. Suddenly, to the total surprise of her family, Florence returned to London. While Elizabeth was writing her first admiring letter, Flo was secretly organizing a party of nurses and writing to her friend Sidney Herbert, Secretary for War. The cabinet confirmed her appointment in the Crimea on the 18th. Fanny and Parthe rushed to town, leaving Elizabeth behind, and so she was the one who wrote to tell Parthe that Flo's pet owl, Athena, forgotten in the hurry, had been found dead. When Florence heard the news, she burst into tears, the only time she showed any emotion before she left for Turkey on the 21st.

Over the past decade the endless family scenes, her sense of God's 'call' and horror of her 'dreaming' had hardened Florence Nightingale's resolve. In a note to herself in 1846 she had scribbled: 'I feel as if all my being were gradually drawing together to one point.'⁴⁵ In the same year she wrote to her dearly loved cousin, Hilary Bonham Carter:

'Are one's earthly friends not too often Atalanta's apple, thrown in each other's way, to hinder that course, at the end of which is laid up the crown of *righteousness* – & so, dearest, it is well that *we* sh'd not eat too much of one another.'⁴⁶

Family ties, friendship, love – all must be pushed away: all were part of the dreaded 'devouring'. In 1849 she finally refused to marry Richard Monckton Milnes, who, as Elizabeth noted, had been 'at her feet for nine years'. A subsequent near breakdown in Egypt intensified her belief that her only salvation was denial of private feeling.

Such self-isolation intrigued and appalled Elizabeth Gaskell. At one stage Florence had been strongly influenced by Henry Manning and had thought of converting to Catholicism. Towards the end of *North and South*, when Gaskell's heroine Margaret Hale is at her darkest point, she too longs to cut herself off from feeling or to lose herself in a faith. The language of her thoughts echoes closely Elizabeth's letters from Lea Hurst:

'If I were a Roman Catholic and could deaden my heart, stun it with some great blow, I might become a nun. But I should pine after my kind; no, not my kind, my love for my species could never fill my heart to the utter exclusion of love for individuals. Perhaps it ought to be so, perhaps not; I cannot decide tonight.' (Ch. 46)

Although Gaskell described Nightingale's tireless efforts in the Crimea as 'a visible march to heaven', and warmly supported her work in future years, the whole of her own fiction – and especially *North and South* – opposes the route that Florence had chosen, the subordination of relationships to causes and of people to ideas.

[18]

North and South:
'Tender, and Yet a Master'

Elizabeth stayed at Lea Hurst until late October 1854, alone in the vast house, taking long walks, gathering mushrooms and writing. The end of *North and South* was in sight, as she told Emily:

'I've got to (with Margaret – I'm off at her now following your letter) when they've quarrelled, silently, after the lie and she knows she loves him, and he is trying not to love her; and Frederick is gone back to Spain and Mrs Hale is dead and Mr Bell has come to stay with the Hales, and Mr Thornton ought to be developing himself – and Mr Hale ought to die – and if I could get over this next piece I could swim through the London life beautifully into the sunset glory of the last scene. But hitherto Thornton is good; and I'm afraid of a touch marring him; and I want to keep his character consistent with itself, and large and strong and tender, and *yet a master*. That's my next puzzle. I am enough on not to hurry.' (L321)

But she did have to hurry. Over the next month, after a short visit to her cousin Frederick Holland at Ashbourne Hall, she had little time for letter-writing.

Back at Plymouth Grove she dashed on to the end. On 17 December Katie Winkworth reported that Lily was writing furiously, thirty pages a week, and hoped to finish in ten days. Dickens had relented and begun to praise her, but, said Katie, 'I hope she won't be "wiled by his fause flattering tongue" into thinking him true and trustworthy, like Mr Forster'.[1] Elizabeth was relieved by his letter. By now she was weary of her book and found it hard to judge it clearly, telling Dickens: 'I dare say I shall like my story, when I am a little further from it; at present I can only feel depressed about it, I meant it to have been so

366

much better.' Sending her latest batch of thirty-three pages, she explained that it was very compressed, but 'Mr Gaskell has looked the piece well over' so there should be no corrections and 'therefore I never wish to see its face again'. She had given up: Dickens could shorten it as he wished, he must please himself.

On Christmas Eve she was in the final throes. She had not written to Tottie for two months and was stung with reproach,

'but I believe I've been as nearly dazed and crazed with this c—, d— be h— to it, story as can be. I've been sick of writing, and everything connected with literature or improvement of the mind; to say nothing of deep hatred to my species about whom I was obliged to write as if I loved 'em.' (L325)

Her handwriting had collapsed, her spelling had gone. 'Seriously,' she groaned, 'it has been a terrible weight on me and has made me have some of the most felling headaches I ever had in my life.' And when she did raise her aching head, all she saw were accounts of the Crimea. In Scutari the very bricks of the hospital were carriers of death, impregnated with germs from the sewers beneath; on the heights of Balaclava, in the depths of winter, men lay in the mud without blankets, their crushed limbs protruding through their flesh; in the harbour below, the once clear waters were sullied by innumerable corpses. The worst phases of this war were being played out as she worked. Every story, as she rightly said, must 'make one's blood run cold at the rotting away of those noble glorious men'. Thirty thousand British soldiers would die, many from disease, before peace was declared.

Her book seemed trivial in comparison, yet she battled on, and the final episode of *North and South* eventually appeared in *Household Words* on 27 January 1855. Dickens wrote to congratulate her and as a conciliatory gesture added £50 to the £250 which was due. While she had driven him to fury, he grudgingly admired her spirit, as stubborn as that of her heroine. He knew, he said, that it had been an anxious labour which she had come to dislike, but 'it seems to me you have felt the ground thoroughly firm under your feet, and have strided on with a force and purpose that MUST now give you pleasure'.[2] They had argued over style as well as space, and in early March, when he could (almost) laugh at this impossible woman, he told Wilkie Collins – only half jokingly:

'The best of it was that she wrote to Wills, saying that she must particularly stipulate not to have her proofs touched, "even by Mr Dickens." That immortal creature had gone over the proofs with great pains – had of course taken out the stiflings – hard plungings, lungeing and other convulsions – and had also taken out her weakenings and damagings of her own effects. "Very well" said the gifted man, "she shall have her own way, but after it's published show her this Proof, and ask her to consider whether her story would have been the better or the worse for it." '[3]

In his view she had won: she had had her own way. In her view she had lost: he had ruined her novel. She lamented to Maria James that *Household Words* had agreed to extend the serial from twenty to twenty-two episodes, 'with a kind of Che Sara Sara resignation on their part, & a perpetual grumbling. So my poor story is like a pantomime figure with a great large head and a very small trunk. And it might have been so good!'[4] Form, so important to her as a writer, had been sacrificed to time; now it was 'unnatural' and 'deformed' (a telling choice of adjectives) and she was determined *never* to write for *Household Words* again.

When *North and South* appeared in volume form, she expanded the last few chapters and explained in a prefatory note why the serial version 'was compelled to hurry on with an improbable rapidity towards the close'. But just as she changed her mind about writing for *Household Words*, she softened, slightly, even about the conclusion. Maybe the pressure had forced her into something more spontaneously 'right' than she suspected. She told Anna Jameson, whose advice she had taken: 'now I am not sure if, when the barrier gives way between 2 such characters as Mr Thornton and Margaret it would not go all smash in a moment, – and I don't feel certain that I dislike the end as it now stands'.

North and South does not open in Gaskell's usual fashion with a walk through a landscape into the story. It begins in mid-scene, in an interior, with one young woman calling to another:

' "Edith!" said Margaret gently, "Edith!"
But as Margaret half suspected, Edith had fallen asleep.'

NORTH AND SOUTH: 'TENDER, AND YET A MASTER'

While her cousin sleeps curled up on the sofa, in a 'soft ball of muslin and ribbon and silken curls', Margaret listens to women in the next room, discussing Edith's wedding, and broods on her own past and her future. She is already slightly apart. *North and South* is Margaret's voyage out, away from the London drawing-room and Hampshire parsonage to the industrial north. She turns her back on a marriage like Edith's when she rejects a proposal from the barrister Henry Lennox. She leaves the country parsonage when her father rejects the Church, unable any more to live a lie by accepting the Thirty-nine Articles against his conscience. Neither father nor daughter feels able to follow the paths expected of them. Cut adrift, feeling the waters close over her old life, Margaret painfully enters a different society, the northern town of Milton. In the end her place, like her cousin's, will be determined by whom she marries. But when she chooses, she will be awake, not asleep.

North and South is part *Bildungsroman*, part industrial novel. Gaskell had seen numerous idealistic young women, suffocated by the prospect of what her heroine comes to see as 'the eventless ease in which no struggle or endeavour was required', in which one could so easily become 'sleepily deadened into forgetfulness'. She had noticed how such women from the south were excited yet disturbed by Manchester: Annie Shaen in 1849, Charlotte Froude in 1850, Adelaide Procter, who came to stay in 1851. Her book had a direct application, expressing her hope that women might assimilate to the new economic order not by changing the conventional pattern of their lives entirely and abandoning ideas of love and marriage, but by extending the domestic range of reference. Even so, when she wrote about Margaret's time in Milton, she was also exploring her own ambivalence towards the industrial world; at one point she quailed at condemning Margaret to live in the heart of the city for ever. There were two big factory fires in Manchester in 1854 and they may have prompted this question to Katie: 'What do you think of a fire burning down Mr Thornton's mills *and house* as a *help* to failure? Then Margaret would rebuild them larger & better & need not go & live there when she's married.'[5]

Gaskell began with her heroine; in her mind the novel remained 'Margaret Hale'. At the same time she returned to the ethics of commercial life, a preoccupation since the early 1840s, when Carlyle had proclaimed:

'We call it Society, and go about professing openly the totalest separation . . . Our life is not a mutual helpfulness; but rather, cloaked under due laws-of-war, named "fair competition" and so forth, it is a mutual hostility. We have profoundly forgotten everywhere that *Cash-payment* is not the sole relation of human beings; we think, nothing doubting, that *it* absolves and liquidates all engagements of man.'[6]

Carlyle's martial diction, his contrast of past and present and his automatic exclusion of women (linguistic convention reflecting social assumptions) are all concerns of *North and South*. By 1854 Gaskell no longer felt, as she had implied in *Mary Barton*, that mutual awareness would remove confrontation – the battle-lines were too firmly drawn – but she wanted to suggest that dialogue could soften hostility and counter alienation. The corner-stone for a new ethic must be respect based on sympathy: an emotional recognition of the other that would get rid of reductive abstractions like 'men', 'masters', 'traitors', 'hands', 'ladies', 'gentlemen'. The implications (like her quest for the causes of suffering in *Mary Barton*) extended beyond industrial disputes.

North and South links the themes of love and class war in a quite different way from Gaskell's first novel, recognizing the seductiveness of power as well as the need for humility. The combative relationship of Margaret Hale and the mill-owner John Thornton (a prickly, urban male as his name suggests) is far from an exact analogy to the class relations of industrial capitalism.[7] It does, however, provide an intensely intimate, accessible way of arguing the need to tear down the high, thorny barriers between self and others. The novel considers a variety of such barriers, not only between the sexes and the classes but also between cultures and faiths – Margaret's brother Frederick marries a Catholic and she herself befriends a poor Methodist, Bessy Higgins. After Bessy's death, we are told, 'Margaret the Church-woman, her father the Dissenter, Higgins the Infidel, knelt down together. It did them no harm.' The romantic novel, with its traditional plot of troubled love and closure in marriage, could dramatize conflict and conciliation on many levels, personal, social and theological.

Romantic convention had already been used in this way in the two long stories that immediately preceded *North and South*: 'My French Master' and 'Morton Hall'. Both encompass civil war and revolution and end in marriages that unite the old landed order with the new mercantile power, but their heroines do not enter the new world directly, whereas in *North and South* the sheltered girl with a feudal background is brought physically into the streets of the industrial town. Margaret grows to self-awareness against this clash of cultures and at the end she invests in the future emotionally and tangibly, by marrying Thornton and by using the legacy of 'old money' left her by her godfather Mr Bell to save Marlborough Mills and ensure that Thornton's reforming 'experiments' will continue.

History, Gaskell suggests, is cyclical as well as progressive. In 'Morton Hall' the marriage of land and trade had resolved an antagonism dating back to the Commonwealth and Restoration, a period frequently invoked in *North and South*'s discussion of authority, individualism, rebellion and loyalty. Nothing is clear-cut. John Thornton (in a hidden allusion to Carlyle's *Cromwell*, of 1845) admires Oliver Cromwell's leadership:

' "Cromwell would have made a capital mill-owner, Miss Hale. I wish we had him to put down this strike for us."

"Cromwell is no hero of mine," said she, coldly, "But I am trying to reconcile your admiration of despotism with your respect for other men's independence of character." ' (Ch. 15)

Margaret herself has a dual inheritance: when her father is in doubt about leaving the Church, he finds reassurance in the words of a Puritan divine ejected in 1662, but her mother is descended from the aristocratic Beresfords, whose annual toast was the Cavalier cry, 'Church and king and down with the rump'.

While Gaskell draws on history, she is aware of its contradictory legacy and sceptical of the past as prophecy. She is equally sceptical of Utopias, whether it be Thornton's mercantile dreams or Bessy's apocalyptic visions. The novel rejects absolutes in favour of accommodations and seeks a better present rather than a millennium. It notes established patterns, and points to the gradual changes that come with each generation. Thus both Mr Hale's children extend their father's private act of 'speaking out' according to personal conscience into public gestures: Frederick by leading a mutiny on behalf of ill-treated sailors, Margaret by impulsively defending both workers and master on grounds of common humanity.

North and South develops the themes of social and religious conflict of *Mary Barton* and 'Morton Hall'. At the same time it develops the exploration of inner conflict – anger, desire, suppression and lies – begun with Mary and John Barton and continued in *Ruth*. Margaret suffers not only from her encounter with Milton but from her own denial of her body, constrained by notions of 'maidenly dignity'. These constraints are partly seen as virtues; at the end, when she declares her love, she still turns to Thornton with 'a face of glowing shame'. But while she feels something of the same shock and ambivalence dramatized in *Ruth*, she lives through the crisis to become a unified, not split, personality. The romantic plot provided the vehicle Gaskell needed to deal with a woman's 'fall' – from icon to sexual being – without the dangerous figure of an actual 'fallen' woman. She no longer had to split her heroine into 'good' and 'bad' – Mary and Esther, Jemima and Ruth; although she dallied with the idea, there was no need for that other character, openly in love with Thornton and driven by 'Southern jealousy'. The figure of Margaret was strong enough to combine passionate sensuality and pure idealism.

The romantic, intensely physical tension between Margaret and Thornton becomes a way of suggesting other oppositions – between nature and industry, sympathy and authority, passion and reason. From the moment Margaret arrives in Milton physical currents vibrate through the text. Gradually the city takes on a material shape, turning from a leaden cloud on the horizon into a maze of 'straight, hopeless streets' and then to a human swarm. Going out in search of a servant, Margaret falls in with crowds of working girls 'rushing along, with bold, fearless faces, and loud laughs and jests' who comment on her dress, touch her shawl and gown. The men too accost her and remark on her looks. She feels naked in the 'disorderly tumult' and fear brings out 'a flash of indignation which made her face scarlet, and her dark eyes gather flame'. Only after she meets Bessy and her father, Nicholas Higgins, on one of her walks does the threatening crowd resolve itself into individuals. The city has attained a personal face.

In a similar way *North and South* literally 'embodies' social and economic exploitation – in the factory, on the land, in the law, army or navy. It is the sight of a sailor being flogged to death that drives Frederick Hale to mutiny. It is sympathy for Bessy – a girl of nineteen like herself, dying of consumption, her lungs ruined by fluff from the carding room – that makes Margaret feel the cruelty of industry. It is the thought of Nicholas as a farm labourer that opens her eyes to the real nature of the rural south. Nicholas cannot find work after leading the strike at Thornton's mill, but wants to support the children of his neighbour Boucher, a man he had forced to join the union, beginning a process of despair which led to Boucher's suicide. Farm work is Nicholas's last option, yet when Margaret imagines him working the land, the countryside no longer seems a picturesque sketch or 'a village in a poem – a poem by Tennyson', as she described Helstone to Mr Lennox. Instead it is a site of bodily and spiritual oppression:

'You would not bear the dulness of the life; you don't know what it is; it would eat you away like rust. Those that have lived there all their lives are used to soaking in the stagnant waters. They labour on from day to day, in the great solitude of steaming fields – never speaking or lifting up their poor, bent, downcast heads.' (Ch. 37)

This is the hardship of Kingsley's *Yeast*: the industrial 'North' and the rural 'South' are the same country. But it is also the inner landscape of women's oppression – a 'dulness' that devours and corrodes, an immersion in 'stagnant waters'.

The bodily pressure of the streets, the pain of illness, the horror of Boucher's body on the stretcher, bloated and dripping, the stifled desire of Margaret and Thornton: all insist on *physical* awareness. The close interweaving of bodily and emotional responses with criticism of social codes is seen in a small detail – the imagery of hands. When Henry Lennox takes 'sudden possession' of Margaret's hand, she rejects him by 'quietly but firmly, seeking to extricate her hand from his grasp'. When she arrives in Milton, she constantly washes her hands in an effort to remain 'clean' and undefiled. When Thornton watches her, he is mesmerized by her hands and arms:

'She looked as if she was not attending to the conversation, but solely busy with the tea-cups, among which her round ivory hands moved with pretty, noiseless daintiness. She had a bracelet on one taper arm, which would fall down over her round wrist. Mr Thornton watched the replacing of this troublesome ornament with far more attention than he gave to her father. It seemed as if it fascinated him to see her push it up impatiently until it tightened her soft flesh; and then to mark the loosening – the fall . . . She handed him his cup of tea with the proud air of an unwilling slave; but her eye caught the moment when he was ready for another cup; and he almost longed to ask her to do for him what he saw her compelled to do for her father, who took her little finger and thumb in his masculine hand, and made them serve as sugar-tongs.' (Ch. 10)

Margaret's 'hand' is still the possession of her father. Her role is decorative and domestic; she serves her father, willingly and with love. But this little scene with its suggestions of bondage and release, of domination and submission – the bracelet on the soft flesh – has other implications.

The initial antagonism between Thornton and Margaret is heightened by her repeated failure to shake his proffered hand. Following southern convention, she merely bows, but he 'felt the omission and set it down to pride'. The handshake, if given, would have revealed her hidden strength, as the local doctor notes, ruefully shaking his ringed fingers: 'Who would have thought that little hand could have given such a squeeze? But the bones were well put together, and that gives immense power. What a queen she is!' Her refusal to give her hand, in both senses, to Thornton is paralleled by his refusal to allow personality to his 'hands' – a term of disembodiment to which Margaret strongly objects. The handshake is the first symbolic contact between masters and men, when Higgins accepts the offer of work, 'for the sake of the childer':

' "So, measter, I'll come; and what's more, I thank yo'; and that's a deal fro' me," said he, more frankly, suddenly turning round and facing Mr Thornton fully for the first time.

"And this is a deal from me," said Mr Thornton, giving Higgins's hand a good grip.' (Ch. 39)

A sophisticated social argument is thus built from bodily gesture.

The body is the common denominator which defies abstractions. Thornton must eat with his workers before he can understand them. As Mr Bell says, each man dies alone, after his own fashion, but,

'the philosopher and idiot, publican and pharisee, all eat after the same fashion – given an equally good digestion. There's theory for theory for you!' (Ch. 43)

'Indeed I have no theory; I hate theories,' answers Thornton. Thornton the master and Higgins the worker claim to be equally contemptuous of theory – Nicholas complains he cannot read the book his employer Hamper gives him, with its jargon of capital, markets, risk and labour: he prefers to speak from direct experience. Both, however, unknowingly live by theories, making men into cyphers:

'The workmen's calculations were based (like too many of the masters') on false premises. They reckoned on their fellow-men as if they possessed the calculable powers of machines, no more, no less; no allowance for human passions getting the better of reason.' (Ch. 28)

Once again political and personal are linked. Margaret Hale and John Thornton both have their fixed ideas about the world; both, in different ways, make no allowance for 'human passions getting the better of reason'. Their love is not blocked, as in more conventional novels, by circumstances or by the intervention of others; they are their own enemies, kept apart by pride, and by a clash of deeply internalized values. Margaret's code stresses sympathy, but denies the feelings of her own body. Thornton's code suspects tenderness as weakness and holds rules, 'justice', control, to be prime virtues. Thornton

'had tenderness in his heart – "a soft place" as Nicholas Higgins called it; but he had some pride in concealing it; he kept it very sacred and safe, and was jealous of every circumstance that tried to gain admission. But if he dreaded exposure of his tenderness, he was equally desirous that all men should recognise his justice.' (Ch. 39)

North and South often contrasts, and sometimes blurs, maternal, sexual and social tenderness, and also evokes a specific kind of erotic tension through its continual use of linked images of domination and submission – queen and vassal, master and men, God and saint. Such imagery powerfully suggests the contrary human desires for separateness and intimacy, for selfhood and loss of self.

Some modern psychologists derive a similar dynamic of desire from infant experience. They argue that while girls identify with the mother's body, boys, in defining themselves as different (as they must necessarily do), grow up to repudiate intimacy and stress independence; this leads to an emphasis on reason, individualism and power that pervades the whole culture.[8] Sometimes the repressed desire for contact can find no outlet except in sudden outbursts of irrationality and violence (as in Gaskell's riot, mutiny, sudden gesture of 'baffled passion'). On the other hand the contrary 'female' desire for connection with others can lead to self-annihilation (the ultimate loss of self, like Bessy's religious fervour and longing for death). Ideally sexual union can satisfy the opposing needs to assert and surrender, while 'love', translated into social terms, recognizes the selfhood of others, defuses tension and provides new, more open political structures.

Although Gaskell would certainly not have phrased her argument like this (or made such crude male/female divisions), the interwoven narratives of *North and South* dramatize similar deep oppositions. Thornton and his mother (who has adopted the masculine code of the industrial north) almost personify 'separation'. In a key discussion of the word 'gentleman' (a contribution to a long debate which ran from the 1840s to the end of the century) Thornton objects that 'gentleman' only describes a person in relation to others,

'but when we speak of him as "a man" we consider him not merely with regard to his fellow-men, but in relation to himself – to life – to time – to eternity. A castaway lonely as Robinson Crusoe – a prisoner immured in a dungeon for life – nay, even a saint in Patmos, has his endurance, his strength, his faith, best described by being spoken of as "a man".' (Ch. 20)

While this expresses the individualism of the *laissez-faire* industrialist (and the bourgeois novel, with its prototypical hero, Crusoe), it is a solipsistic, lonely view, that of a soul adrift. The saint before God appears as isolated as the prisoner or the castaway.

By contrast Margaret shows the weaknesses and strengths of 'connection', the impulse to identify with others. She has to learn to stand alone, to see herself and others clearly. At the beginning, although outwardly strong, she is inwardly unseeing, 'childlike', 'inexperienced', constantly surprised by people – by Henry Lennox's proposal, by her father's religious doubt. Her first awareness of her sexual power comes in a guilty dream of Lennox falling to his death. Awakening, she decides that 'if the world was so full of perplexing problems she would trust, and only ask to see the one step needful for the hour'.

Her steps are unsure, her path full of pitfalls. In Milton Thornton and his mother affront her less because they are 'shoppy' than because they deny the sympathy she has been brought up to think of as essentially human. She cannot see that Mrs Thornton's self-confidence is a false front, that she fears company and appears aggressive because she is shy. Ashamed of her husband's debts and suicide, she invests all her hopes in her son. She is strung taut as a wire, and her drawing-room is a model of icy discomfort, full of unread books, its furniture veiled by netting, its flowered carpet covered by glazed and colourless linen drugget, its alabaster ornaments protected by glass shades: 'Everything reflected light, nothing absorbed it.' The room feels 'as if no one had been in it since the day when the furniture had been bagged up with as much care as if the house was to be overwhelmed with lava, and discovered a thousand years hence'. Her son's circling relationship with Margaret is keenly evocative of the same dangerous battened-down forces, seen in his reluctance, his pride, his urge to make excuses to see the woman who causes him pain, the way 'the careful avoidance of his eyes betokened that in some way he knew exactly where, if they fell by chance, they would rest on her'.

The tension in the love story mirrors, and is mirrored by, the pent-up feelings of the working class. When Margaret is trapped at the mill during the strike, she first urges Thornton to speak to the crowd who have battered down the heavy gates and poured into the yard. When they turn on him like 'beasts' at the sound of his voice, she rushes to intervene, throwing her arms around him to shield him. She is wounded by a flying stone. It is this moment of sudden physical contact in the middle of public violence which makes Thornton suddenly aware of his feelings. The writing links Margaret's rash act and Thornton's arousal to the battering down of the gates and the rising feelings of the crowd. The sexual language applies equally to mob, hero and heroine:

'Margaret felt intuitively, that, in an instant, all would be uproar – that first touch would cause an explosion . . . in another instant, the stormy passions would have passed their bounds, and swept away all barriers of reason, or apprehension of consequence.' (Ch. 22)

The passage refers to her feelings when the crowd surge through the gates and surround Thornton, but her impetuous embrace, the blow, her swooning and the 'thread of dark-red blood' on her white skin which wakes the mob from their 'trance of passion' suggest the breach of a different kind of barrier.

The following day, having misinterpreted her act as one of personal feeling, Thornton impulsively declares his love. To Margaret it feels like a second assault, a different kind of blow. She retorts that her concern was merely generalized 'womanly instinct' – 'any woman, worthy of the name of woman, would come forward to shield, with her reverenced helplessness, a man in danger from the violence of numbers' – but the shock of his declaration is described in imagery which recalls the desire/repulsion language of *Ruth*. Afterwards, as the conviction dawns that he loves her, 'she shrank and shuddered as under the fascination of some great power, repugnant to her whole previous life':

'The deep impression made by the interview was like that of a horror in a dream; that will not leave the room although we waken up, and rub our eyes, and force a stiff rigid smile upon our lips. It is there – there, cowering and gibbering, with fixed ghastly eyes, in some corner of the chamber, listening to hear whether we dare to breathe of its presence to anyone. And we dare not; poor cowards that we are!' (Ch. 25)

After this rejection Thornton will not speak again, his silence enforced first by pride and then by mistaken jealousy of her brother, Frederick, whom he sees with Margaret near the station. Since Frederick is under threat of court martial, she cannot reveal his identity, and lies when questioned about him. When she leaves Milton, Thornton still thinks she loves another. He watches her go and 'though his heart beat thick with longing words' he says nothing:

' "No!" said he, "I put it to the touch once, and I lost it all. Let her go, – with her stony heart and her beauty; – how set and terrible her look is now, for all her loveliness of feature! She is afraid I shall speak what will require some stern repression. Let her go." ' (Ch. 43)

The danger of 'stern repression' is a constant theme. Both Thornton and Margaret – like the masters and the workmen – are prisoners of their codes, immured within stone walls of pride and misunderstanding. At one point Margaret refers to a Nuremberg merchant who kept his retarded son in an attic 'to save him from temptation and error'. When the son was freed, he proved morally and practically incompetent, and had to be saved from starvation by the council (an image which could apply as much to contemporary women as to factory hands). This image of imprisonment and destructive over-protectiveness is part of a different argument, not about self-control but control over others, a critique of the infantilization of the workers. Margaret has challenged Thornton, remembering her conversations with

378

Nicholas Higgins, that 'the masters would like their hands to be merely tall, large children . . . with a blind, unquestioning obedience'. Thornton argues that they *are* like children and need a 'wise despotism' to guide them, but on hearing her Nuremberg story, changes his position and rejects the implied responsibility for his work-people outside factory hours as interference with their individual rights. Mr Hale suggests, instead, that the 'wise parent humours the desire for independent action' and that what is lacking is the 'equality of friendship between the adviser and advised class'.

North and South has been called paternalistic, and the social experiments that Gaskell admired, and that Thornton introduces under the influence of Margaret and Higgins, undoubtedly are, but the novel is wary of the analogy between the family and the workplace (or society as a whole). The wise parent in this novel lets the child go, providing support while respecting the drive to autonomy. The protective family model of social relations implied in *Mary Barton* is replaced by one of mutual recognition between adults.

Although Margaret has always shown independence of thought, she finds it hard to be alone, and this is vividly conveyed by her grief at her exclusion from her mother's sickroom. Watching her mother, she learns the stoic strength of the apparently weak and comes to understand how love can be as powerful as conscience in overthrowing conditioned beliefs. Despite her deference to the social order Mrs Hale defends Frederick's mutiny against the official 'lie' that he is a 'traitor of the blackest die'. Her anger takes surprising form for such a mild, well-mannered woman:

' "I took the paper in my hands as soon as I had read it – I tore it up to little bits – I tore it – oh! I believe, Margaret, I tore it with my teeth. I did not cry. I could not. My cheeks were as hot as fire, and my very eyes burned in my head." ' (Ch. 14)

This maternal fury prompts Margaret to articulate the central belief of the novel, that 'loyalty and obedience to wisdom and justice are fine; but it is still finer to defy arbitrary power, unjustly and cruelly used – not on behalf of ourselves, but on behalf of others more helpless'. Her eyes are opened to the arbitrary power of South as well as North. Frederick's court martial would be held in a court where 'authority weighs nine tenths in the balance and evidence forms only the other tenth'. The old authority of the bishop, the law, parliament or the army is just as harsh as the new, simply more elegantly clothed. Although his army life may seem nothing but picnics and band concerts, Edith's husband, Captain Lennox, like the northern mill-owner, prefers unquestioning obedience in his troops to 'hedge-lawyers', who 'questioned and would know the reason for every order'. The early manufacturers with their naked disregard for their workers' rights are no different from the landed gentry Mrs Hale's servant Dixon remembers so proudly:

' "Bless you child! I like to see you showing a bit of spirit. It's the good old Beresford blood. Why, the last Sir John but two shot the steward down, there where he stood, for just telling him that he'd racked the tenants, and he'd racked the tenants till he could get no more money off them than he could get skin off a flint.' " (Ch. 16)

Thornton is doing nothing new in bringing in the army to quell rioting strikers, or in using his powers as a magistrate for personal ends.

The novel constantly forces its heroine to come face to face with brutal realities and arbitrary power. But its central 'romance' is also at odds with 'reality'. In stripping the illusions from the eyes of Margaret and Thornton Gaskell examines the values (and deceptions) inherent in her chosen genre and in the older forms of Romance that lie behind it, questioning the literary conventions of female purity and masculine aggression. In *North and South* she invokes legend, fairy tale and oriental, classical, medieval and Renaissance romance consciously and critically. The chapter headings mingle the language of romance with that of the industrial problem and religious quest: 'Haste to the Wedding', 'Roses and Thorns', 'Wrought Iron and Gold', 'Masters and Men', 'What Is a Strike?', 'Expiation', 'Ease not Peace'. Her literary allusions and epigraphs reach back from Tennyson and Coleridge to ancient ballads and to Spenser, Tasso and Dante (whom Margaret is reading when she comes to Milton). The use of medieval romance to depict contemporary problems was typical of her time: of the history paintings of Ford Madox Brown, the art of the Pre-Raphaelites, the poetry of Tennyson, the theories of Ruskin. Yet Gaskell was wary of medieval nostalgia; ultimately she believed in progress rather than return to pre-industrial innocence.

One of Margaret's ruling illusions is that there can be a 'chivalric' order in industry, a term which her father corrects to 'Christian'. She is proud of her 'high, maidenly dignity' and takes her motto from the troubadour poet, Eustace des Champs, 'Fais ce que dois, advienne que pourra'. Even as a girl she is 'romantic', full of restless energy. She loves to escape outdoors, 'with the soft violence of the west wind behind her', and envies the 'wild adventurous freedom of the poachers' life'. She is identified with strong, regal heroines: with Badoura, Princess of China, from the *Arabian Nights*; with Vashti, Zenobia, Cleopatra and the 'fleet-footed' Camilla. All their histories link strife and love. Her distance from the Harley Street materialism is shown when she stands in the drawing-room like a princess in Edith's Indian shawls, entranced not by their price but by their scent, softness and colour.

When she first meets Thornton, she is wearing such a shawl, which 'hung about her in long heavy folds, and which she wore as an empress wears her drapery'. As she removes it he sees her 'full beauty . . . her round white flexile throat rising out of the full, yet lithe figure; her lips, moving so slightly as she spoke'. As yet her sensuality is unrealized. She meets his gaze 'with quiet maiden freedom'. He knows she would reject him 'as a queen would a vassal'. Like a virgin queen, Margaret inspires unlikely men: Henry Lennox, who describes himself as 'a man not given to romance in general – prudent, worldly, as some people call me – who has been carried out of his habits by the force of a passion'; or her godfather Mr Bell, who promises to be 'her preux chevalier, sixty and gouty though I be'. The blunt, self-contained Thornton becomes as dizzy and weak as a medieval squire, 'blinded by passion'.

Thornton – with his strong features, sudden smile and natural 'mastery' – is surrounded by an aura of romance of a different kind. He has been reared in dreams of power: ' "Her merchants be like princes," said his mother, reading the text aloud, as if it were a trumpet call to invite her boy to the struggle.' This is a new version of epic narratives older than the medieval tales, of the heroic deeds of Homer, which Thornton reads with Mr Hale, or of Norse legends. Thornton attributes his proud individualism to the 'Teutonic blood' of Darkshire: 'Our glory and our beauty arise out of our inward strength, which makes us victorious over material resistance, and over greater difficulties still.' Mr Bell, with a hidden pun, has to admit to Thornton that Milton, city of the future, does reverence the past: 'You are regular worshippers of Thor.'

When John Thornton talks to Mr Hale, always conscious of Margaret in the background, he vaunts his pride in Milton's achievements, explaining

'the might of the steam-hammer, which was recalling to Mr Hale some of the wonderful stories of subservient genii in the Arabian Nights – one moment stretching from earth to sky and filling all the width of the horizon, at the next obediently compressed into a vase small enough to be borne in the hand of a child.' (Ch. 10)

The sexual metaphor is inescapable, but it is the equally male metaphor of battle that is emphasized, as Thornton insists that there are many men 'who could spring into the breach and carry on the war which compels, and shall compel, all material power to yield to science'. This reminds Mr Hale of the 'hundred captains' of *The Ballad of Chevy Chase*, a connection bewildering to Margaret but apt in its recognition of the same proud nationalism and masculine aggression. Thornton makes the early manufacturers sound like robber barons, men who used to 'ride to the devil in a magnificent style – crushing human bone and flesh under their horses' hooves without remorse'. Now, he says, the forces of masters and men are better balanced and 'the battle is pretty fairly waged between us'.

Both John Thornton and Nicholas Higgins employ this martial imagery. Higgins says he will stand by the union like a soldier at his post and Bessy declares: 'It's like the great battle o' Armageddon, the way they keep on, grinning and fighting at each other, till even while they fight, they are picked off into the pit.' There was nothing romantic about a real nineteenth-century battlefield: Elizabeth looked up from writing to imagine men rotting on the Balaclava heights. Mr Hale and Margaret are both jokingly identified with pacifism. When she defends North against South, Mr Bell complains that 'her residence in Milton has quite corrupted her. She's a democrat, a red republican, a member of the Peace society, a socialist', but Margaret's concern is for the *victims* of progress, not its heroes. She asks: 'in the triumph of the crowded procession, have the helpless been trampled on, instead of being gently lifted aside out of the roadway of the conqueror, whom they have no power to accompany on his march?'

Although Margaret questions Thornton's Teutonic heroics, she clings to her own Romance ideals. Her fall from the status of troubadour heroine comes when she lies to the police, to defend

382

Frederick, who has returned under threat of court martial, to see his dying mother. At the station he pushes a man who recognizes him, who later dies from his fall: when questioned, Margaret denies that she was there. She is overwhelmed with shame and her identity is shaken. She has denied her guiding principle of truth, of speaking out. The discovery that Thornton knows she has lied, and has used his power as a magistrate to save her the ordeal of appearing at the inquest, makes matters worse: 'no more contempt for her! – no more talk about the chivalric! Henceforward she must feel humiliated and disgraced in his sight.' Her fall from the high moral ground is also, very noticeably, a fall into the world of sensation. With disgrace comes desire: 'What strong feeling had overtaken her at last?'

Thornton also sees Margaret's untruth in terms of blemished Romance, and, since he believes it covers a secret liaison, brackets falsehood with sexuality:

'he, while he blamed her – while he was jealous of her – while he renounced her – he loved her sorely, in spite of himself. He dreamt of her; he dreamt she came dancing towards him with outspread arms, and with a lightness and gaiety which made him loathe her, even while it allured him. But the impression of this figure of Margaret – with all Margaret's character taken out of it, as completely as if some evil spirit had got possession of her form – was so deeply stamped upon his imagination, that when he wakened he felt hardly able to separate the Una from the Duessa; and the dislike he had to the latter seemed to envelop and disfigure the former.' (Ch. 40)

In *The Faerie Queene* Una, the One Truth, is impersonated by the vile Duessa, daughter of Falsehood, who 'full well did know/To be most fit to trouble noble knights/Which hunt for honor'. In Duessa's train rides the hag Ate, bringing anarchy and unrest, battle and death.

But while the lie demolishes chivalric notions of Truth and Purity, it heightens the relevance of the religious Romance of the questing soul. At the moment Margaret utters her lie to the policeman at the door Thornton is upstairs discussing religion with her father. As she falls in a faint Mr Hale is talking

> Of death and of the heavy lull
> And of the brain that has grown dull.
> (Ch. 35)

In this conversation Thornton appears less like a merchant prince or worshipper of Thor than a type of Christian knight: 'Man of action as he was, busy in the world's great battle, there was a deeper religion binding him to God in his heart, in spite of his strong wilfulness, through all his mistakes, than Mr Hale had ever dreamed.' Meanwhile Margaret's long swoon resembles a psychic death from which she must awake reborn. Focusing on her sensuality, her relaxed mouth and her lips, Gaskell quotes Dante's *Vita Nuova*, Sonnet 15:

> E par che de la sua labbia si mova
> Un spirito soave e pien d'amore
> Chi va dicendo a l'anima: sospira!

'A soft spirit of love seemed to come from her lips, saying to the soul: breathe!' – she will recover through learning to love.

The lie that makes Margaret recognize her need for Thornton also makes her accept the real; she sees that her 'preux chevalier of a brother' has 'turned merchant, trader!' On the day that her father leaves for Oxford with Mr Bell, not knowing she will never see him again, she feels a burst of happiness, the sense that all her personal cares have been stuffed into a dark cupboard and that now she can take them out and 'mourn over them, and study their nature, and seek the true method of subduing them into the elements of peace'. She takes hope from the stirring words not of a fourteenth-century poet but of a sixteenth-century saint, St Francis de Sales, whose book she opens by chance (as Maggie Tulliver stumbles upon Thomas à Kempis in *The Mill on the Floss*). De Sales rejects the self-flagellation which would command the heart to die of shame – 'meurs de honte, aveugle, impudent, traistre et desloyal à ton Dieu' – and directs her instead to seek the light, and to find a way out of the pit through appealing to God's mercy; to be resolute but follow the path of humility. 'Courage, soyons meshuy sur nos gardes, Dieu nous aydera.'[9]

At this point Mr Hale dies. Margaret is now, as the chapter title tells us, 'Alone! Alone!' She must leave Milton, return to London and (in the expanded volume edition) to Helstone. She loses hope in the south, when the London dinner-party conversation denies the hidden existence of the city's toiling masses. She loses any remaining faith in rural innocence when she hears of the horrific superstition which has led to the roasting of a cat. The alterations at Helstone parsonage thrust her childhood into the past:

'A sense of change, of individual nothingness, of perplexity and disappointment, overpowered Margaret. Nothing had been the same; and this slight, all-pervading instability, had given her greater pain than if all had been too entirely changed for her to recognise it.' (Ch. 46)

By now she mourns the loss of Thornton as well as of her parents. She is in the mood Tennyson describes in *In Memoriam*, stunned by 'The steps of Time – the shocks of Chance – the blows of Death'. Utterly alone, oppressed by mutability, she longs for something 'Everlasting', which will involve total surrender. Dante is invoked again:

'I am so tired – so tired of being whirled on through all these phases of my life, in which nothing abides by me, no creature, no place; it is like the circle in which the victims of earthly passion eddy continually. I am in the mood in which women of another religion take the veil. I seek heavenly steadfastness in earthly monotony.' (Ch. 46)

But she cannot quell the call of individual love: she is roused by the voices of children at play outside her window, just as Dorothea Brooke, in *Middlemarch*, will be roused from a similar despair by seeing a man with a bundle on his back and a woman carrying a baby. The children's voices are pointers to the future. Margaret learns to accept the inevitability of change. If the world stood still, she thinks, it would become 'retrograde and corrupt'.

The death of Mr Bell seals her solitariness. There is no hope now of a reunion in Spain with her brother, or of Mr Bell telling Thornton the reason for her lie. By the sea at Cromer she decides to take her life 'into her own hands' and when she comes to London, she takes up social work. (Her return to health is suggested by the reappearance of humour in the text; Aunt Shaw insists she take a footman with her to the slums, while Edith fears that she may become 'strong-minded', abandon jokes and wear dust-coloured clothes.)

During this phase of numbness and recovery Thornton has also been caught in a Dantesque circle, seemingly without a goal, described with almost Dickensian vigour:

'Meanwhile at Milton the chimneys smoked, the ceaseless roar and mighty beat and dizzying whirl of machinery struggled and strove perpetually. Senseless and purposeless were wood and iron and steam in their endless labours; but the persistence of their monotonous work was rivalled in tireless endurance by the strong crowds, who, with sense and with purpose, were busy and restless in seeking after – What?' (Ch. 50)

The hero and heroine must redefine their quests and their goals. Only when Thornton's mill fails and he steps down from being a 'master', only when Margaret has abandoned the chivalric past and engaged with the present are they reunited. Hearing of his reforms and of his failure, she approaches Thornton not as queen to vassal, or maiden to knight, but as a partner in business. They meet as equals, conscious of their faults. The barriers give way 'all smash in a moment'.

North and South is an invigorating, stirring read; we care about its forceful, troubled characters. The fusion of politics and love is too simple, but Gaskell knows this: she never expected that all the old battles could be ended by a marriage. All she shows, at the end, is that Margaret and Thornton are awake – to each other and to the realities they face, as Thornton laughingly imagines Aunt Shaw's horror at 'That man!' and Margaret his mother's indignant tones as she says 'That woman!'. This is one of the earliest novels of industrial alienation, tellingly linked to the plight of nineteenth-century women. Its reading of the dialectics of history, class and sexual politics exposes the exploitation which underpins both the romance of progress and the nostalgia for tradition: the protective carapace of 'culture' is painfully thin, whether in the individual or the mob, and the novel's very physical vocabulary gives a bodily weight to the virtue of 'tenderness', 'a soft place', an openness to suffering. The problem for us all, not only for Thornton and Margaret, is how to identify with the needs of others yet remain strong as an individual, how to become, in other words, 'tender and yet a master'.

19

The Life of Charlotte Brontë

As she finished her 'wretched' story at Christmas 1854, Elizabeth planned her next flight from Manchester. Mme Mohl, she explained to Tottie, had asked her to stay three times that year, 'and three times it had to be given up. Now she peremptorily commands us to come in February . . . I think we shall go and escape the reviews, hang 'em.' She would take Meta with her, as Mary Mohl had also earlier commanded, and would stay about three weeks, 'during which time reviewers are earnestly requested to say all they have got to say about N&S'.[1]

Packing the revised ending for the volume edition of *North and South* in her luggage, she left Manchester on 8 February. After four days in London, where she stayed in Bloomsbury Square, and Meta was 'swallowed up' by the Austins, they took the train from London Bridge. Elizabeth wrote a final letter to Marianne, full of exhausting instructions and laments about William's bad cold, the awkward time of sailings from Folkestone, the ruin of Meta's new petticoats in the wash: 'I am puzzled. What with a new end to my book, new flannel petticoats, & bad tides I'm altogether in a maze.' Even after she arrived in Paris she found it hard to settle, wished she was in London, and was in a 'terrible fidget' about William's health until Marianne reassured her.

Meta, however, was in ecstasies from the start. Mary Mohl had arranged sessions at an atelier and, she told Marianne excitedly,

'There is going to be a dance here tonight – everything is in confusion – the great red cushions of the salon being beaten & shaken till the room is clouded with dust. They have been polishing the dining-room-floor, till I anticipate a *fall* in every waltz. It is so funny the way in wh. Mme Mohl has asked people to come in my name – Mrs Hollond (whom I have never seen) was invited "because it wd give Miss Gaskell so much pleasure" – and Mlle Gaskell has a prominent part in most of the invitation notes . . . Tomorrow we dine at the Scheffers, to meet Mme Viardot, & Mrs Holld – & afterward go on to the Geoffroi St Hilaires' – where I am afraid we shall have to talk zoologically – & be kissed.' (L331–2)

(The unseen Mrs Hollond was called upon to take Elizabeth's manuscript back to London.)

The dance was a great success despite dust and dangerous polish: 'Great preparations were made; ices, & a man to wait, & galette ad lib; much to Meta's joy. She danced all evening; the rooms were crowded and I can't tell you half the people. No Tourghieneffs. No end of Americans.' A political gathering at the Thierrys' was then followed by 'a magnificent party on Tuesday for grandeurs, title & dresses', but, wrote Elizabeth, 'except for eyes it was very dull'. Elizabeth and Meta took walks on the *quais*, visited artists' studios and went to concerts. One evening was spent with old Lady Elgin, whom they liked for her love of 'wild stories'.

They spent hours at the Hôtel de Cluny, visited the Maison des Diaconesses and called on the Duc de Broglie and his daughter, so like her famous grandmother, Mme de Staël, 'with the same dark red hair, dark red fiery eyes etc'. Elizabeth also cannily fitted in a meeting with Hachette, who bought options on French translations of her works.[2] The only thing wrong was the food – not quality, but quantity. At the Jardin des Plantes there were 'cups of rich chocolate & cream cakes, which made Meta wish she could have kept either her good dinner, or her good tea to another day, for she is perpetually hungry'. (She was very like her mother in this respect.) 'We hardly ever have more than twice to eat in the day. Breakfast, tea & bread & butter. *Then* 6 o'clock dinner, & *nothing* whatever after, even when we go to theatre.'

Starving or not, they regretted having to leave so soon. Elizabeth did not go directly home but stayed with friends: Wedgwoods, Shaens, Bonamy Prices, Lady Coltman. In London, on 4 April 1855, she received a letter from John Greenwood, the Haworth stationer who supplied the Brontë sisters with such mysterious quantities of paper. He told her that Charlotte was dead.

*

388

Charlotte Brontë had died at the Parsonage on 31 March. She was thirty-eight. After terrible bouts of sickness, probably connected with pregnancy, she began coughing and vomiting blood. For weeks she was unable to eat. In the third week of March she revived slightly and asked for food and stimulants. It was too late; exhausted, she sank slowly into death.[3]

Elizabeth had known nothing. She wrote at once to Patrick Brontë, to Thackeray, Charlotte's flawed idol, and to Greenwood:

'My dear Sir
I cannot tell you how VERY sad your note has made me. My dear dear friend that I shall never see again on earth! I did not even know she was ill. I had heard nothing of her since the beginning of December when she wrote to a mutual friend saying that she was well, and happy. I was meaning to write to her this very day, to tell her of the appearance of a copy of my new book, whh I was sending to her. You may well say you have lost your best friend; strangers might know her by her great fame, but we loved her dearly for her goodness, truth and kindness, & those lovely qualities she carried with her where she is gone.' (L335–6)

Asking about Charlotte's illness, she used words she would repeat, with variations, to many people many times, in the next two years: 'I want to know EVERY particular . . . You would oblige me *extremely* if you could, at your earliest leisure, send me every detail.' And, in the next letter, '*Anything* else you can ever remember to tell me about her will be most valuable.'

To Elizabeth, Charlotte's death seemed 'as sad as her life'. Within a week of hearing the news she wrote touchingly: 'it is no use regretting what has passed; but I do fancy that if I had come, I could have induced her – even though they had all felt angry with me at first – to do what was so absolutely necessary for her very life'.[4] This regret intensified her later determination: unable to save Charlotte in life, she would save her reputation in death.

She was not yet thinking of writing anything, even another novel. *North and South* had drained her and at the moment she was merely arranging new editions of earlier works with Chapman.[5] She told John Furnivall, who had forwarded a proposal from Macmillan, that she had 'nothing to say': 'I doubt if I shall ever write again for publication, but nobody knows; not I, certainly, whether I shall keep to this idea, or write a Dictionary, or some other good sensible voluminous work.' For the next two months, however, she brooded, and kept up her correspondence with Greenwood. At the end of May she wrote to Charlotte's publisher, George Smith, hoping that he might have a copy of the portrait of her by Richmond, or would let a daguerreotype be taken. (The portrait belonged to Nicholls and his refusal to let it be copied became a bone of contention.) By the time she wrote to Smith an idea had formed. Some day, if she lived, and 'no one is living whom such a publication would hurt', she would publish what she knew of Miss Brontë, 'and make the world (if I am but strong enough in expression) honour the woman as much as they have admired the writer'.

This was the first of many letters charting the progress of *The Life of Charlotte Brontë* stage by stage.[6] In 1855 George Smith, son of the founder of Smith, Elder, was thirty-one, a stout, genial man with a 'pretty, Paulina-like little wife' and a baby daughter – and, Elizabeth noted, a keen eye for business. After he published the *Life*, he became her own publisher and friend. Her lively letters to him are among her most engaging. (Luckily, he did not obey the instructions she gave him in 1856. If she put a star on the front, she said, 'you may treasure up my letter; otherwise *please burn them*, & *don't* send them to the terrible warehouse where the 20000 letters a year are kept'.

She took Smith into her ring of trusted confidants, sending on a letter from Greenwood and telling him sadly of her estrangement from Charlotte:

'She often asked me (after her marriage last year) to go over & see her; I never went, partly because it required a little courage to face Mr Nicholls, as she had told me he did not like her intimacy with us as dissenters, but she knew he *would* like us when he had seen us. Now I intend to go over for one day to see Mr Brontë, and also to see her husband, & where she is laid.' (L346)

She explained too that it was because she found herself forgetting the names and dates Charlotte had spoken of that she wanted to write down everything she remembered about 'this dear friend and noble woman' before its vividness had faded from her mind,

'but I *know* that Mr Brontë, and I *fear* that Mr Nicholls, would not like this made public, even though the more she was known the more people would honour her as a woman, separate from her character as authoress. Still my children, who all loved her would like to have what I could write about her; and the time may come when her wild sad life, and the beautiful character that grew out of it may be made public.' (L347–8)

The deliberate concentration on the woman, as opposed to the writer, was already present. Later that year, when she read the letters to Ellen Nussey (Charlotte's friend from childhood, but never privy to her thoughts on writing, literature or art), the division crystallized: 'I am sure the more fully she – Charlotte Brontë – the *friend* the *daughter* the *sister* the *wife* is known – and known where need be in her own words – the more the highly will she be appreciated.' The concentration on private life, relationships and character rather than on public achievement would make Gaskell's book both convention-ally yet subversively 'feminine', a contrast to the current model lives (by male authors) of successful men. At the end of the century Margaret Oliphant, who was twenty-nine when the *Life* appeared, remembered its impact and suggested that Gaskell

'originated in her bewilderment a new kind of biography. The cry of the woman almost distressed as well as puzzled the world . . . The *Times* blew a trumpet of dismay; the book was revolution as well as revelation . . . That cry shattered indeed altogether the "delicacy" which was supposed to be the most exquisite characteristic of womankind. The softening veil is blown away when such exhibitions of feeling are given to the world.'[7]

It was, Oliphant said, a plea for 'every woman dropped out of sight'.

Elizabeth was wrong about Patrick Brontë. In Yorkshire Patrick, Arthur Nicholls and Ellen Nussey had been reading the press accounts of Charlotte – Harriet Martineau's moving but inaccurate tribute in the *Daily News*, mistaken reports of the family's Irish past in the *Belfast Mercury* and the outright attack in *Sharpe's London Magazine*. Incensed by this last, Ellen suggested that they should commission a reply, perhaps from Mrs Gaskell. Arthur Nicholls demurred, explaining that Charlotte herself would have kept a dignified silence and that Mr Brontë had laughed more than he had for months at the things said about him.[8] But then Patrick wrote directly to Elizabeth. In view of the falsities put out by 'a great many scribblers', he said, and fearing that ill-qualified writers might venture to write Charlotte's life, he could see no better plan than to ask an established author to 'write a brief account of her life and to make some remark on her works. You seem to me to be the best qualified for doing what I wish should be done.' If she would agree, Nicholls and he would give her whatever information she needed. The book would appear under her name and all royalties would be hers. 'Could my daughter speak from the tomb I feel certain she would laud our choice.'⁹

Elizabeth, astonished, accepted at once. As soon as he heard from her Mr Brontë sent a long letter, giving an outline of his own life and his children's, and a separate sheet of dates (which proved to be full of errors). Elizabeth had already written to Smith, enclosing the first letter she had received, 'most unexpectedly'. While Mr Brontë was alive, she felt that she would have to omit some details of Charlotte's home life, but her task now had the ultimate womanly sanction – duty: 'I am very anxious to perform this grave duty laid upon me well and fully.' The next day she told Marianne, slipping the news into a torrent of chatter about Flossy's French muslin sleeves and the regiment stationed nearby: 'It makes me have to write to Mme Mohl today to get an address.'

Everything had to be done 'today'. Despite her urgent desire to go to Haworth, she and Meta had promised to go to the Tolletts at Betley Hall and the Hathertons at Teddesley. Life in Manchester itself was 'so complicated full of engagements' that it was not until 23 July that she went to Yorkshire. On a day of broiling heat she and Katie Winkworth toiled up from Keighley station. At the Parsonage she explained that her book would have to be as much about Charlotte's family life as her work and that she would have to record 'the circumstances which made her what she was'. The two men agreed, Patrick 'not perceiving the full extent of the great interest in her personal history felt by strangers', Nicholls only too aware of the danger of gossip. He acknowledged grudgingly that if a life was to appear, it had better be authorized. 'His feeling was against its being written; but he yielded to Mr Brontë's impetuous wish.' After they talked he brought down a handful of Charlotte's letters to Emily, Patrick, Branwell and her aunt. It was an emotional scene; both Mr Brontë and Mr Nicholls cried sadly. ('I like Mr Nicholls,' Elizabeth decided.) As she left, Patrick Brontë's last words were 'No quailing, Mrs Gaskell! No drawing back!'

Too late for their train, Elizabeth and Katie slept at a Skipton inn, so tired that they overslept and missed the first train home. As if in a Gaskell novel, after the tension of the visit the weather broke – weeks of heat gave way to pouring rain. They arrived in Manchester at eight that night, 'wet, tired, cold and hungry'.

Elizabeth had already begun her quest for material and people. Epistles were arriving from Patrick Brontë, with more hopelessly unreliable dates. She asked George Smith if he knew the address of Mr Taylor '(the "Yorke" family of Shirley)', and said she was on the track of 'Miss "Temple" of Jane Eyre'. This was Jane Thompson, who had taught at Cowan Bridge and was now, by an odd coincidence, married to a clergyman who held a living on the estate of one of Elizabeth's friends. Her next step, on Mr Nicholl's advice, was to write to Ellen Nussey about her letters and request a meeting.

Arrangements for the summer had already been made. William was off to Switzerland with his friend William James, the Unitarian minister from Bristol. Elizabeth was heading for Fox How, then Silverdale and finally Glasgow, where she and Marianne would go to the British Scientific Association. Nevertheless she continued to pursue her search. In the Lake District she saw Harriet Martineau and bore away more letters. From Silverdale in August she made a brief dash to the Kay-Shuttleworths' at Gawthorpe and scribbled a note from there to Mary Green agreeing to have the Green girls to stay, and apologizing for her haste: 'Upwards of 300 letters to read through & copy what is written in 2 days, & every day a journey to take till I land at Silverdale on Monday must be my excuse.'[10] She wrote to Greenwood, asking him to copy the memorial tablet in Haworth Church, tried to trace the families where Charlotte had been governess and sought local publications on 'the peculiar customs &c character of the population towards Keighley'.[11] This background information would create the evolutionary 'habitat' of her heroine in the early chapters.

Meanwhile another theme ran through the summer, the distant rumour of war. The 51st Lancashire Regiment was stationed in Manchester, due to go to the Crimea. In early July Tottie was told that Plymouth Grove was 'deep in military affairs', since one officer '*will* know us and will call and will be civil and ask us to presentations of colours, and balls (to which I own we go) more than I like, as Miss Meta and one of the officers are a little too thick in the dancing line'.

Eight dances in one evening was too strong, 'drawing down upon the young lady a parental rebuke'. The Crimea, however, made mockery of balls. Their friend Captain Duckworth was one of thousands who died there of cholera, and Elizabeth begged Marianne, then in London, to tell her what people there were saying of 'this terrible news about the war . . . *every scrap you hear*'.

She also wrote to Parthe Nightingale, asking for news of Florence, who lay desperately ill in Constantinople. Miss Nightingale was now the poor man's idol and Elizabeth told Parthe that 'babies ad libitum are being christened Florence here; poor little factory babies, whose grimed stunted parents brighten up at the name'. This letter was sent two days before the Haworth visit; the two heroines, one dead, one apparently lying on the point of death, became curiously bracketed and contrasted in Elizabeth's mind, with their powerful intellects, and different versions of self-sacrifice and duty. On New Year's Day 1855 she had written to Katie:

'What would Miss B. say to Florence Nightingale? I can't imagine! for *there* is intellect such as I never came in contact with before in woman! – only two in men – great beauty, and of her holy goodness who is fit to speak?' (L327)

Florence recovered from her fever, and just over a year later Elizabeth was corresponding eagerly about the Nightingale Fund with Monckton Milnes (whose new baby was another Florence). In the same week that she was attending a huge meeting held in honour of Florence's public work she wrote the opening pages of the *Life*, her tribute to Charlotte's private heroism.

In September 1855 Elizabeth and Marianne paid their planned visit to Glasgow, where they stayed with the artist Charles Wilson, who was married to a Stevenson cousin. William was attending the British Association meeting and they went along too, without tremendous enthusiasm. Elizabeth told Maria James that Marianne enjoyed her visit to Scotland more than the Scientific Association itself, 'and so did I, I must confess. Scientific language is quite new to me; and yet some knowledge of it is required to understand all the papers.'[12] From Glasgow, her head spinning with scientific terms, Elizabeth went on to stay in Dunoon, Argyleshire, with her half-sister Catherine, whom she had not seen for twenty-four years. There she met her stepmother again; as she traced the youth of Charlotte Brontë she confronted the ghosts of her own past.

At Dunoon a chance meeting with William Scoresby, the vicar of Bradford, who was staying nearby, provided more anecdotes about 'the extraordinary character of the people around Haworth'. Back home in the autumn, she continued to gather material. There were, of course, constant diversions, like unexpected visits from Monckton Milnes and Maria Chapman ('the Anti-Slavery Mrs C'), who arrived just as Milnes left when she thought she had a quiet space before her. 'So you see,' she sighed to Mary Green, 'my life seems worked up into other people's, & as if I had no time for anything, just now, anything belonging to myself, I mean.'[13] She did, however, find time to write some fiction, adapting 'Martha Preston' as 'Half a Lifetime Ago' for *Household Words*. This plunged her into another taut correspondence with Dickens about space, divisions and corrections. (Now was the time of his outburst to Wills: 'Mrs Gaskell – fearful – fearful! If I were Mr G. O Heaven how I would beat her!')[14]

All this took time and effort. Still, she had visited Miss Wooler, Charlotte's teacher at Roe Head and lifelong friend, had read Ellen's 350 letters and plied George Smith for his papers. In late October she reported that she had almost enough material to make a volume the size of Carlyle's *Life of Sterling* (1851) – an arresting comparison, as Angus Easson points out, in view of Carlyle's conclusion:

'Like other such lives, like all lives, this is a tragedy; high hopes, noble efforts; under thickening difficulties and impediments, ever-new nobleness of valiant effort; – and the result death . . . "Why write the Life of Sterling?" I imagine I had a commission higher than the world's, the dictate of Nature herself, to do what is now done.'[15]

November and December brought two more parcels of letters, a bundle from Miss Wooler and the valuable series from W. S. Williams, the kindly and sympathetic reader for Smith, Elder who had 'discovered' *Jane Eyre* and kept Charlotte well supplied with new books. Elizabeth had also contacted several schoolfellows, including Mary Taylor in New Zealand. Mary sent the only letter she had kept, Charlotte's vivid description of the first visit to George Smith's office. Like Elizabeth, she thought Charlotte oppressed by her father and told

Ellen Nussey: 'I can never think without gloomy anger of Charlotte's sacrifices to the selfish old man.' She added a note of warning:

'But how on earth is all this to be set straight! Mrs Gaskell seems far too able a woman to put her head into such a wasp nest, as she would raise about her by speaking the truth of living people. How she will get through with it I can't imagine.'[16]

When she neared the end of writing, Elizabeth quoted this to George Smith, escalating the danger from a 'wasp nest' to 'a nest of hornets'. But at this stage she had no such qualms. She was covering the ground as well as the correspondence and had already seen Cowan Bridge, Roe Head and Oakwell Hall. By next July she was able to say she had been everywhere Charlotte had lived apart from 'her two little pieces of private governess-ship'.

Marianne and Meta copied the piles of letters as they arrived and Snow Wedgwood, staying in October and November, was also commandeered. 'I am rather sick of writing,' Snow told her sister, 'as I have been copying for Mrs Gaskell.' That morning's bundle had already taken two hours, and the work was broken up by huge meals: 'I never did see such a house as this for perpetual feeding.'[17] (Some letters, she remembered later, were too intimate for publication.) The previous day she had copied Charlotte's 'warm *éloge*' on Plymouth Grove. Elizabeth read it aloud, '& Mr G. was so much amused at Miss Bronti's [sic] saying that the family consisted of 4 little girls all more or less pretty and intelligent, he asked if "less" was not dashed under'.

By 20 December the house was not only buried in papers but swamped by visitors. Writing to her old friend of Newcastle days, Harriet Carr (discovered again after so many years and now Harriet Andersen), Elizabeth explained that between returning from Scotland and Christmas 'we had nineteen people staying in the house! So I think you may imagine the necessarily quick succession . . . all this gaiety was but bad for the work I have in hand.'[18] Although she had hoped to write a quarter of the book by Christmas, she had to confess to Ellen Nussey (who had sent an account of Anne Brontë's death and was threatening to come and stay) that she had not yet written a word. 'It would not be right,' she wrote, 'to conceal from you the actual state of nothingness in which the Memoir is at present.'

Occasionally the affairs of the wider world broke in. On New Year's Day 1856, at Tottie's request, she signed the petition to amend the law on married women's property, organized by Barbara Leigh Smith. She was sceptical: 'I don't think it is very definite, and *pointed*; or that it will do much good.' In her view no legislation, on its own, would end the tyranny of husbands (adding: 'Mr Gaskell begs Mr Fox to draw up a bill for the protection of *husbands* against wives who will spend all their earnings'). Having signed, because 'our sex is badly enough used and legislated *against*, there's no doubt of *that*', she then set about her life of the dutiful daughter and wife. By February two chapters were drafted. In March she went to stay with elderly friends, Samuel Alcock and his wife Susanna, John Robberds's sister, at the peaceful, ancient Burrow Hall in Lancashire (in the same parish as the Clergy Daughter's School at Cowan Bridge). Marianne was housekeeping at home, while Meta had gone to stay in Canterbury with her friend Louey Jackson, the ward of Dean Stanley, and was going on from there to spend Easter with Charles Darwin at Down.

Meta and Marianne had both been helping their mother with her work. Writing from the peace of Burrow Hall, Elizabeth told Harriet Andersen how hard she found it – reading all the letters, amending, making extracts:

'And I never *did* write a biography, and I don't exactly know how to set about it; you see you have to be accurate and keep to facts; a most difficult thing for a writer of fiction. And then the style too! that is a bugbear. It must be grander and more correct, I am afraid. But in all matters of style and accuracy I have a capital helper in my husband, who has an admirable knowledge of language, and an almost fastidious taste as to style. I sometimes tell him he does not read books for the subject but for the style.'[19]

As she wrote – and William corrected – she sent batches of copy to George Smith for comment. In April she thanked him for a note which 'has "heartened me", as we say in the North, extremely, for I was & am very anxious to do it thoroughly *well*'. She was vexed, she said, when reading it over, that her English was so bad: 'But it *shall* be good before I have done.'

She still, however, had one essential trip to make. She must go to Brussels. In March she had organized her passage and lodgings and collected introductions.[20] At the end of April she spent a week in London with Meta, Flossy and Julia before she left. She took Meta to see Monckton Milnes's collection of Blake manuscripts, and scurried round to the Wheelwrights' to check on Charlotte's Brussels days. Most of her time, though, was devoted to Flossy and Julia, who were to be shown London 'in true Country cousin sense of the expression', plus Windsor, Hampton Court and Kew. Their arrangements were dogged by trouble, and on 6 May, the day she set off, she told Marianne: 'so many other things have gone wrong that I am in despair & can hardly keep from perpetually crying which is partly being so overtired'. With a single companion, Eliza Thornborrow, she took the night boat from Dover to Ostend.

Two days before, Sunday, 4 May, had been National Thanksgiving Day for the end of war in the Crimea. Back in Manchester William had preached a sermon on making peace with the enemy and later that summer he sent Mr Brontë a copy. A long reply came back about the chaos of licentiousness which could 'banish liberty and conscience from the world'. 'We often wonder,' Patrick added, 'how Mrs Gaskell is getting on with her mournful but interesting task.'[21]

In Brussels that May Mrs Gaskell stumbled on the saddest and most mournful secret of all. She stayed with Mme Haydon at 47 avenue Soison d'Or, Porte Louise, and went at once to call on the Hegers in the nearby rue Isabelle. Mme Heger, having read an unauthorized French translation of *Villette* and hearing that Elizabeth was a friend of Charlotte, refused to see her, or have anything to do with her. Constantin Heger, on the other hand, received her warmly and won her liking and respect. While she was there, he showed her (or read her) Charlotte's letters. These proved passionate, despairing and self-exposing. The early ones were proud: if she thought Monsieur might write to her '*out of pity*', Charlotte wrote, 'I should feel deeply wounded.' But then her pride had given way:

'Day and night I find neither rest nor peace. If I sleep I am disturbed by tormenting dreams in which I see you, always severe, always grave, always incensed against me . . . If my master withdraws his friendship from me entirely I shall be altogether without hope; if he gives me a little – just a little – I shall be satisfied – happy; I shall have a reason for living on, for working.'[22]

It is now generally accepted that Gaskell knew the contents of all the letters to Heger. Even if she did not see every word, she immediately understood their essence; their mood was so close to Brontë's fiction, particularly Lucy Snowe's love for Paul Emmanuel in *Villette*. The revelation dismayed her, while confirming something she seems already to have sensed. The previous summer, while hunting for material on Charlotte, she had begun one of her strange supernatural stories, designed for the Extra Christmas issue of *Household Words*. It was based on the tale from the south of France, heard in Lady Elgin's 'vast, half-lighted room' in Paris, and transferred to the north of England.[23] Uncannily, as if by intuition, it seized on something hidden in the life Elizabeth was planning to write. It is the story of a gentle and pious girl, Lucy, haunted by a sexual double, a tragically ironic consequence of her grandmother's curse on her father. She sees behind her in the mirror 'another wicked, fearful self, so like me that my soul seemed to quiver within me, as though not knowing to which similitude of body it belonged'. The man who loves her has the same experience:

'I saw behind her another figure – a ghastly resemblance, complete in likeness, so far as form and feature and minutest touch of dress could go, but with a loathsome demon soul looking out of the grey eyes, that were in turn mocking and voluptuous. My heart stood still within me; every hair rose up erect; my flesh crept with horror.'[24]

Lucy's ancestors (like the Brontës') are Irish: she comes from the wilds of north Lancashire, the Trough of Bowland, an area of 'rocky and bleak hills' famous for witch-hunts. The 'Grandmother Witch', said Elizabeth, was her own invention. The story was postponed because of work on the *Life*, but completed in 1856 while she was actually writing the biography. She called it 'The Poor Clare'. For the ending – the death of the grandmother, now a penitent in Antwerp – Elizabeth drew on a story heard on her trip to Belgium, of the Poor Clares 'ringing the bell in extremity of famine'.[25]

Charlotte Brontë's life already fell easily into the patterns of Gaskell's fiction, with its suffering daughters, profligate son and stern father, and its emphasis on upbringing and environment, female endurance and courage, but she could not let it resemble 'The Poor Clare'. Part of her mission was to defend Brontë against the accusations of sensuality levelled at her novels: the story of her starved love must not be told. The biography, supposedly so devoted to showing Charlotte's inner life and 'the circumstances which made her what she was', thus involved a suppression which matched Charlotte's own. When Gaskell came to write this episode, she depicted only a diligent, grateful pupil. Mme Heger's antipathy was put down to religious difference, and Charlotte's terrible depression in 1845 was explained by a heightened and foreshortened account of Branwell's decline.[26]

When she was back in England, Constantin Heger sent Elizabeth cautious, anodyne extracts, with examples of *devoirs* by Charlotte and Emily. She discovered that his own replies to Charlotte had disappeared, probably burnt by Charlotte before her marriage. She was now understandably anxious to see *The Professor*. She was writing fast, twenty pages on one rainy day alone, but she needed to read that unpublished novel. She told Smith: 'perhaps all my alarm as to the subject of it may be idle and groundless; but I am afraid it relates to M. Héger, even more distinctly & exclusively than Villette does'. She was finding Arthur Nicholls difficult and feared he would not allow her to see the manuscript. So, at the end of July she went to Haworth with a formidable ally, Sir James Kay-Shuttleworth. Where she had asked politely and been refused, Sir James simply bullied and 'coolly took actual possession of many things while Mr Nicholls was saying he could not possibly part with them'.

They brought away not only *The Professor* and the pencilled opening of 'Emma', the novel Charlotte had begun before her marriage, but also, 'by far the most extraordinary of all, a packet about the size of a lady's travelling writing case, full of paper books of different sizes'. These were the priceless 'Gondal' and 'Angria' manuscripts. Elizabeth had promised to return them within ten days and in her haste, finding the reading difficult even with a magnifying glass, did not appreciate their full significance. She thought them 'the wildest & most incoherent things . . . They give one the idea of a creative power carried to the verge of insanity.' 'Just lately,' she commented, 'Mr Milnes gave me some MS. of Blake's, the painter's to read, – & the two MSS (his & C.B.'s) are curiously alike.' She wanted Smith to photograph a page for the *Life*.[27]

To her relief the small books held greater surprises than *The Professor*: when she managed to prise this manuscript away from Sir James, she found no dangerous clues to the Heger affair. The only remaining problem, it seemed to her, was that Sir James seemed determined to edit it for publication, something Charlotte would have hated. Elizabeth herself, over-sensitive about Charlotte, felt that some changes must be made as the text was 'disfigured by more coarseness, – & profanity in quoting texts of Scripture disagreeably than in any of her other works'. Worried letters went to George Smith, Emily Shaen and Arthur Nicholls. Nicholls disliked the idea of any revision and since neither he nor Patrick found anything to shock them, he prepared the text for publication himself.

It was now August. Elizabeth (optimistically) judged that she was about halfway through and would be finished by Christmas. But she was still seeking new information. In June, with Smith, she had visited the Chapter Coffee House, where Charlotte and Anne stayed on their first trip to London – had Smith managed to talk to the coffee house waiter yet? Could he please ask George Henry Lewes (*'not from me'*) about the correspondence over *Shirley*? This was important because Elizabeth knew that Charlotte felt Lewes had betrayed her trust by revealing her sex in his review. In September, when Lewes sent these letters with his own comments, she overcame her distrust of him in admiration of his frankness and generosity. The packet included Charlotte's famous note:

TO G. H. LEWES, ESQ

I can be on my guard against my enemies,
but God deliver me from my friends.
'CURRER BELL'

During the summer Elizabeth pursued every avenue, even writing to Jemima Quillinan, the daughter of Wordsworth's son-in-law, about Branwell's letters to Wordsworth.[28] Most discoveries led to revisions. The little 'Gondal' books, for example, with their glimpses of Charlotte as a twelve-year-old, meant rewriting about forty pages, but at the same time, while staying with her Holland relations in Worcestershire, she covered 120 new sheets. She told Emily:

'I used to go up at Dumbleton & Boughton to my own room, directly after 9 o'clock breakfast; and came down to lunch at ½ p 1, up again, & write without allowing any temptation to carry me off till 5 – or past; having just a run of a walk before 7 o'clock dinner. I got through an immense deal; but I found head & health suffering – I could not sleep for thinking of it. So at Broad-Leas (the Ewarts) I only wrote till lunch.' (L411)

William joined her when she stayed at Broad-Leas in Wiltshire and together they took drives over Salisbury Plain, with its wide, misty views and 'great sweeps of green turf, like emerald billows stretching off into the blue sky miles & miles away'. It was a brief holiday, without the 'sick wearied feeling of being overworked; & Mr Gaskell being very jolly'. Even writing to Emily, though, was 'trenching on my precious Brontë time' and the work took its toll. At the end of September Elizabeth had a long fainting fit '("quite promiscuous" as servants say,) consequent doctor, *consequent* illness, consequent ordering to sea side & prohibition of reading or writing, receiving or answering letters'. She blamed the doctor, not herself: the seaside stay meant an even greater pile of letters awaiting her return.

By early October the biography had reached 1845 and she now aimed to finish in February. Every stage threw up new queries. As Marianne had explained to Ellen Nussey in July, 'Mama is afraid she is very troublesome, but things occur to her often when she is writing, that she wants to know, often more to fill up the picture in her own mind, than for any publishing purposes.' Thus, when she reached the Brussels period, she fired off a letter to Laetitia Wheelwright. Could she tell her 'their exact position in the school – their duties & occupations – if they had a bedroom to themselves – even the school-hours – all these details would be invaluable'. When she reached the publication of *Jane Eyre*, she asked Ellen Nussey how Branwell had responded and then tackled George Smith:

'My dear Sir,
Business first and pleasure afterwards. Questions.

When, *exactly*, was Jane Eyre published? Can you tell? It was in Sepr, 1847. Beginning, middle or end? Which was the first review, giving note as it were of its signal success?' (L424)

More requests followed, and an apology – 'I am writing in a terrible hurry as usual' – before a page of gossip, 'which of course, is a woman's pleasure'. She was indeed in such a hurry that she made a note on her manuscript, 'to come in here as soon as I have heard from Mr Smith', and later inserted thirteen separately numbered pages.[29]

The manuscript of the *Life*, now in the John Rylands Library, tells its own story. Some pages flow on untouched, others are heavily scored, with insertions scribbled on the back. Few lack corrections of punctuation, grammar and style in William's neat writing. Often other hands appear – those of Marianne and Meta copying in letters while their mother continues the narrative. Sometimes the gaps left for the daughters were too short and the final lines of a letter are crushed and cramped. Many of these letters were edited on the page itself, as Elizabeth explained to Smith when he asked her to cut some personal details:

'I had often to trust long pieces of copying letters to one of my daughters, & I told her just to write straight on, and I should take out what it was undesirable to have published when I read it over with Mr Gaskell . . . I should certainly have scored out, so that no one could have read it through my marks all that related to any one's appearance, style of living &c, in whose character as indicated by these things the public were not directly interested.' (L429)

This editing, of course, also edited Charlotte's character – we miss some of her humour, and much of her tartness.[30]

In November a new threat loomed which might render all this careful scoring out redundant. Henry Chorley warned Elizabeth that copyright in unpublished letters belonged to the executors, and that therefore 'Mr Nicholls *may*, if he likes turn sharp round on you, and not merely protest but *prohibit*'. She had long found Nicholls a 'terrible tickle person to have to do with'. He made difficulties about the Richmond portrait; he insisted that only he, Mr Brontë and Smith should see the manuscript. (Elizabeth resorted in desperation to *reading* it to Ellen Nussey, who had supplied so many letters.) This final obstacle of the copyright was too much: 'Oh! if once I have finished this biography, catch me ever writing another!' Nicholls too was suffering. In early December he formally assigned his interest in Charlotte's manuscript writings to Elizabeth Gaskell, 'in so far as it relates to the publication of the Biography of my wife which you are engaged in writing'.[31] But he wrote angrily to George Smith:

'I trust I shall not be required to do anything more in a matter which from beginning to end has been such a source of pain and annoyance to me; as I have been dragged into sanctioning a proceeding utterly repugnant to my feelings – indeed nothing but an unwillingness to thwart Mr Brontë's wishes could have induced me to acquiescence in a project, which in my eyes is little short of desecration.'[32]

Dickens was not the only one who smarted under Mrs Gaskell's stubborn determination to get what she wanted.

A final problem remained. In October she had asked Smith: 'Do you mind the law of libel, – I have three people I want to libel – Lady Scott (that bad woman who corrupted Branwell Brontë), Mr Newby, & Lady Eastlake.' The first and last were 'not to be named by name, the mean publisher to be gibbetted'. Lady Scott, as Lydia Robinson, had been the cause of Branwell's dismissal and disgrace. Newby was the unscrupulous publisher who had tried to pass the novels of Anne and Emily off as works of the more famous Currer Bell. Lady Eastlake had written the damning review of *Jane Eyre* in the *Quarterly* implying that it was not only by a woman but by one of doubtful character. Neither Gaskell nor Smith showed concern about her description of the harsh conditions at Cowan Bridge, which would later lead to furious denials and threatened lawsuits. Nor did they worry much about the picture of old Patrick Brontë, although he sent Elizabeth a pamphlet about himself in November, full of mistakes, he said, since 'it appears to make me a somewhat extraordinary and eccentrick personage'. In his own view 'the truth of the matter is – that I am, in some respects, a kindred likeness to the father of Margaret Hale in "North and South" – peaceable, feeling, sometimes thoughtful'.[33] This was hardly how Elizabeth (or Charlotte) had seen him.

In December Smith wrote a firm letter about her treatment of individuals. On Boxing Day Elizabeth replied. She agreed, reluctantly, that he could cut her comments on Newby and (although these slipped through) could alter clues to Lady Scott's identity. About Lady Eastlake she said nothing. Her only disguise (a suggestive one) was in retaining the male gender even when she knew the reviewer was a woman. The attack on the *Quarterly* was her great defence of Charlotte, rising through a flight of rhetorical questions to identification with the suffering Christ himself: 'Who is he that should say of an unknown woman: "She must be one who for some sufficient reason has long forfeited the society of her sex"?' Had the reviewer, she asks, experienced such a 'wild and struggling and isolated life', or known trials like those 'close following in dread march through this household, sweeping the hearthstone bare of life and love', while striving to accept it as the will of God?

'If through all these dark waters the scornful reviewer has passed clear, refined, free from stain, – with a soul that has never in all its agonies, cried "lama sabacthani", – still, even then let him pray with the publican rather than judge with the Pharisee.' (II, ch. 3)

She was loathe to let this go. Nor would she lose her comments on that 'bad heartless woman', Lady Scott.

Reading Elizabeth's letters, one cannot help feeling that she knew the risks, yet was wilfully determined to press ahead. In 1857, when she accused Smith of not warning her about libel, he resisted the tempation of sending her a copy of his December letter: 'I simply made the best excuse I could, expressed my regret and took my scolding, in short, "lying down".' He knew she remembered perfectly well.[34]

In early January 1857 Elizabeth wrote to Emelyn Wetmore Story in Rome:

'I want just, if I can, to leave England on the day of publication of my book: this will be, I expect, one day in the first half of February . . . I have still 200 pages to write, but they begin to print to-morrow.' (L434)

She exaggerated a little, but still, such confidence astounds. She had long set her sights on this finishing date. The previous autumn she had begun to look beyond her hard labour, towards escape, freedom and fun. She wrote nostalgically to the Storys:

'I like to think of *our* Sunday breakfasts in Paris, and your Sunday bunches of violets, and the dear little girl, and the magnificent baby, and the Italian nurse, and the Etruscan bracelets, and the American fish-rissoles; and then of Mr Story, high and far above all, with his — Island ghost-story and his puns. Oh, weren't we happy!' (L416)

The Wetmore Storys had alternated between Europe and America for the past ten years. In the summer of 1856, after several months at home, they had moved to Rome 'for good'. In this autumn letter Elizabeth mentioned, as 'the vaguest idea in the world', that she, Marianne and Meta might visit them there at the winter's end.[35] If, as she hoped, she finished in February, 'I should like to be off and away and out of reach of reviews, which in this case will have a double power to wound.' If critics were disparaging, she would know she had not done Charlotte justice.

As soon as the end was in view she asked Smith, Elder to start printing so that proofs could be corrected as she wrote. In January 1857 Plymouth Grove thought of little else. Elizabeth briskly sorted out an estrangement between her two oldest daughters: she could not bear, at the end of writing this tragic tale of sisterhood, to think of them quarrelling: 'it is so dreary to see sisters grow old (as one sometimes does) not caring for each other, & forgetting all early home-times'. Ellen Nussey came to read (or hear) the manuscript and gave her approval.[36] Elizabeth herself fell ill, and so that Meta (the real heroine of this month) could copy without interruption, Marianne was summoned home:

'Will you look after Julia's two ends, i.e. hair, & *bowels*? Hearn came home too late last night to curl former, & Meta has been writing almost day & night for me, & putting children to bed &c, and has not done it. She wanted *to*, but I said she had better not. The late omnibus will do for you, love, – & we shall look for our darling at 6 o'clock tomorrow eveng . . . I am *so* tired of this writing, & so is poor Meta – it makes her out of spirits, – & she has strained her back so with lifting children's bath.' (L435)

Letters sped south to Smith, signed 'Believe me in the greatest haste . . .' Last minute additions were posted to W. S. Williams (after months of inquiries Elizabeth had discovered from Charlotte's preface to *Wuthering Heights* that Emily returned as a pupil when Charlotte taught at Roe Head, 'which exactly fills up a little blank and accounts for what wanted accounting for'. On 6 February Elizabeth checked illustrations and sent a sketch of Haworth Parsonage. The next day, in a formal note to Laetitia Wheelwright, she stated simply: 'I have today finished my Life of Miss Brontë; and next week we set out for Rome.' (L443)

At the end of the bound manuscript of *The Life of Charlotte Brontë* are two loose sheets of quotations, perhaps copied by Elizabeth to guide her thoughts.[37] Two are from the *Quarterly Review* of 1856. The first opens: 'Get as many anecdotes as possible, if you love your reader and want to be read, get anecdotes! Character manifests itself in little things, just as a sunbeam finds its way through a chink.' The second notes that 'a tender tie between biographer and hero' is found in all the greatest lives.[38] These extracts, which combine Gaskell's belief in stories and in sympathy as routes to understanding, are followed by Southey's words about his respect, as a reviewer, for authors' privacy, also quoted in the *Life* itself: 'In reviewing anonymous works myself, when I have known the authors I have never mentioned them, taking it for granted they had sufficient reasons for avoiding the publicity.' The final quotation is from an Anna Jameson letter, remarking on 'the truth of that wonderful infinite life – in which there seems to have been so little of external fact or circumstance and such a boundless sphere of feeling and intellect crammed into a silent existence'.

Anonymity and fame, a 'crammed', silent existence and a boundless, infinite art – Southey and Jameson point directly to the core of the book. They lead, in particular, to a pivotal point, Gaskell's comment on the publication of *Jane Eyre* in 1847:

'Henceforward Charlotte Brontë's existence becomes divided into two parallel currents – her life as Currer Bell, the author; her life as Charlotte Brontë, the woman. There were separate duties belonging to each character – not opposing each other, not impossible, but difficult to be reconciled.' (II, ch. 2)

Behind this lingers another statement by Southey, his brutal advice to Charlotte ten years before:

'Literature cannot be the business of a woman's life, and it ought not to be. The more she is engaged in her proper duties, the less leisure will she have for it, even as an accomplishment and recreation.' (I, ch. 8)

Gaskell wanted to make the praise of Charlotte Brontë, the woman, match that of Currer Bell, the author. But beneath the surface woman and writer are held in balance from beginning to end. Art too demands its 'proper duties'.

With all its silences, large and small, *The Life of Charlotte Brontë* is profoundly expressive. Gaskell used her novelist's skill to create the atmosphere, setting and character which would frame Charlotte's own words in her letters. While it remains a 'factual' account, detail is imperceptibly used (as in her fiction) to construct her central theme, the conflicting yet *converging* lives of woman and artist. For example, she turns aside from Charlotte's own account of the inspired, spasmodic composition of *Jane Eyre* to repeat a story told by others of how the servant Tabby, now over eighty, jealously guarded her old household tasks, like peeling potatoes. As her sight was failing, she often left in the black specks, or 'eyes'. 'Miss Brontë was too dainty a housekeeper to put up with this', but could not bear to hurt Tabby's feelings, so she would quietly carry off the bowl and, 'breaking off in the full flow of interest and inspiration in her writing, carefully cut out the specks in the potatoes, and noiselessly carry them back to their place. This little proceeding may show how orderly and fully she accomplished her duties, even at those times when the "possession" was upon her.

Any one who has studied her writings, – whether in print or in her letters; any one who has enjoyed the rare privilege of listening to her talk, must have noticed her singular felicity in the choice of words.' (II, ch. 1)

The jump is deliberate, and brilliant. The picture of Charlotte with her sharp knife poised remains behind that of Charlotte with her pen; her housekeeping and her writing are both 'silent duties', distinguished by scrupulous care.

Gaskell's fictional urge is also felt in the narrative. Although the book is peppered with judgements, the terrible plot-line of the Brontës' fate is never obscured. (She had strong reservations, for instance, about Emily's selfishness in her last illness, but it is impossible to read the account of Emily's stubborn death without emotion.) From beginning to end she holds to a sure imaginative shape. The opening lines guide the reader from the modern railway and the changing town of Keighley up to the sinuous wave-like hills, the wild bleak moors, 'oppressive for the feeling which they give of being pent-up by some monotonous and illimitable barrier'. In their midst is Haworth, with the Parsonage and the church. On the church wall is a terrible record of loss: the memorial to Charlotte's mother, sisters, brother. Set slightly apart, on its own, is a separate tablet – in memory of Charlotte Brontë.

The early movement of the book is one of memory, reaching back to Haworth's wild, strange past and the love of Patrick Brontë and his young wife. The mother's death is followed by the regime of Aunt Branwell, the terrible schooldays at Cowan Bridge and the move to Roe Head. All the time a different momentum is building: the urge to expression. The children write their strange little books: Branwell sends his verses to Wordsworth, Charlotte asks advice of Southey. Their hopes are crushed and despair breaks in as Charlotte and Emily go to Brussels and Branwell sinks deeper into disgrace. Yet here, at the exact centre of the book, comes the achievement itself, introduced by Charlotte's own words: 'One day in the autumn of 1845, I accidentally lighted on a MS. volume of verse, in my sister Emily's handwriting.' Volume I of the *Life* ends with the *Poems of Currer, Ellis and Acton Bell*; volume II begins with the rejection of *The Professor* and the acceptance of *Jane Eyre*. The formal structure of the book, which has passed without notice, has a periodic, female rhythm: two volumes, each with fourteen chapters – the waxing and waning of the moon, key symbol of *Jane Eyre*. And when we reach the publication of *Jane Eyre*, Gaskell breaks her careful pattern of reporting, comment and letters to insert a small dramatized scene. It is, she is swift to say, exactly as Charlotte told her: 'I wrote down her words the day after I heard them.'

' "Papa, I've been writing a book."

"Have you, my dear?"

"Yes, and I want you to read it."

"I am afraid it will try my eyes too much."

"But it is not in manuscript: it is printed."

"My dear! you've never thought of the expense it will be! It will be almost sure to be a loss, for how can you get a book sold? No one knows you or your name."

"But, papa, I don't think it will be a loss; no more will you, if you will just let me read you a review or two, and tell you more about it."

So she sate down and read some of the reviews to her father; and then, giving him the copy of "Jane Eyre" that she intended for him, she left him to read it. When he came into tea, he said, "Girls, do you know Charlotte has been writing a book, and it is much better than likely?" '
(II, ch. 2)

After this muted victory comes a brief, extraordinary flowering: *Wuthering Heights, Agnes Grey, The Tenant of Wildfell Hall*. Charlotte and Anne visit London. Then tragedy drowns the triumph. Death takes Branwell, then Emily, then Anne. Although she is now famous, fêted in London and abroad, Charlotte is alone with her father and her memories. She paces the parlour at night; she writes *Villette*. The narrative circles round to a second marriage at the Parsonage, her own, and returns at last to the church and the graveyard, beneath the rim of the hills.

The Life of Charlotte Brontë closes with a short chapter, two pages long. The manuscript pages are written in a firm, fast hand, with hardly a word crossed out, and the prose flows easily, apparently spontaneously, but the scene is carefully composed and the use of sources revealing. The conclusion opens with a quotation from Forster's *Life and Adventures of Oliver Goldsmith*, describing Gold-smith's funeral where the staircase is 'filled with mourners, the reverse of domestic: women without a home, without domesticity of any kind . . . outcasts of that great, solitary, wicked city'. This scene 'came into my mind', Gaskell writes casually, when she heard of Charlotte's funeral.

The overt connection with this crowd of weeping women is that Charlotte too was mourned by the poor. The two figures Gaskell picks out, however, are a village girl whom Charlotte helped after she was seduced and deserted, and a blind girl who begs to be guided across the moors to hear the words of interment; the unspoken suggestion is that Charlotte's writing, like her private kindness, touched women hurt by desire and blinded by fate.[39]

After Gaskell literally buries Charlotte, repeating the words by the graveside, 'Earth to earth, ashes to ashes', she writes: 'I have little more to say.' She quotes, instead, from Charlotte's friend Mary Taylor. Mary had emigrated to New Zealand in 1845 because 'she did not see why she was debarred from entering into trade because she was a woman'. Just before she went Charlotte was steeped in misery (attributed in the *Life* to Branwell's dismissal, but actually due to her feelings for Heger) and Mary had urged her 'very warmly' to leave home herself. The chapter which deals with this period contains Mary's description of the scene:

'Such a dark shadow came over her face when I said, "Think of what you'll be five years hence!" that I stopped, and said, "Don't cry, Charlotte!" She did not cry, but went on walking up and down the room, and said in a little while, "But I intend to stay, Polly." ' (I, ch. 13)

Mary's own comments (which follow directly in her letter to Elizabeth of January 1856 and in the original manuscript) were transferred at the last moment to these final paragraphs.[40] It was therefore with the figure of Heger in her mind, although not in public view, that Gaskell created her closing vision of her heroine. Charlotte did not leave home. She held fast to duty. In Mary's view,

'She thought much of her duty, and had loftier and clearer notions of it than most people, and held fast to them with more success . . . All her life was but labour and pain, and she never threw down the burden for the sake of present pleasure.' (II, ch. 14)

After quoting Mary's attack on those readers who greedily devoured Charlotte's novels and then blamed the spirit which created them – 'Why ask for a judgement on her from such a world?' – Gaskell turns away from 'the critical, unsympathetic public', who see only superficially. She appeals, rather, to a 'larger and more solemn' audience, who can 'look with tender humility upon faults and errors', who can admire extraordinary genius and reverence noble virtue. 'To that Public,' she concludes, 'I commit the memory of Charlotte Brontë.'

Here her book ends. But she had summoned into this brief conclusion another public still, the outcast women on the staircase. The move from Goldsmith's funeral to Brontë's is achieved with these words:

'Few beyond that circle of hills knew that she, whom the nations praised far off, lay dead that Easter morning. Of kith and kin she had more in the grave to which she was soon to be borne, than among the living.'

On her title page Gaskell placed an epigraph, deliberately echoed in the lines above:

> Oh my God,
> – Thou has knowledge, only Thou,
> How dreary 'tis for women to sit still
> On winter nights by solitary fires
> And hear the nations praising them far off.

The quotation comes from the bold, impassioned *Aurora Leigh*, only recently published.[41] Elizabeth Barrett Browning had also struggled with a dominating father, but had chosen *not* to stay. She eloped instead, to love, Italy and poetry. The biography of Charlotte Brontë as 'the friend, the daughter, the sister, the wife', a celebration of the stern duty of the family hearth, is thus framed, at its beginning and its end, by hints of rebellion and self-exile, by the 'solitary fires' of a different kinship, the sisterhood of women writers.

III

THE SOUNDS OF TIME
1857–65

On a summer's night, at the ebb of a spring-tide, you may hear the waves come lapping up the shelving shore, with the same ceaseless, ever-recurrent sound as that which Philip listened to, in the pauses between life and death.
And so it will be, until 'there shall be no more sea.'

Sylvia's Lovers, 1863

That dear, brilliant, ingenious creature, Mrs Gaskell.

Algernon Swinburne, 1865

20

Rome and Revisions

Plymouth Grove, Manchester
Monday, February 8th [9], 1857

My dear Mrs Story,
We are really truly coming to Rome!!!!!! We are starting off on Friday
next – the 13th . . .

Will you really receive us for a few days? And are we really coming –
and shall we truly see Rome? I don't believe it. It is a dream! I shall
never believe it, and shall have to keep pinching myself!

Yours ever, dear Mr & Mrs Story, affectionately

E. C. Gaskell

(L445)

The Life of Charlotte Brontë was finished. In a final letter, on the 11th,
full of rushed instructions about obtaining Circular Notes from the
bankers for her trip abroad, Elizabeth reminded George Smith that she
was the opposite of Miss Brontë. She never wanted to see or hear of
reviews: when she had done with a book she wished to 'shake off the
recollection thereof forever'.

In this case her wish was doomed, but the flight to Rome was like
bursting into summer after a long, hard winter. After spending only
three nights in Paris, the Manchester party sped to Marseilles and set
sail for Civitavecchia. Then came the first and only set-back: on their
second night at sea the ship's boiler burst and they had to return to
France. That boiler would later make its appearance in 'A Dark
Night's Work', on a voyage back from, not to, Civitavecchia, when
Ellinor Wilkins is watching the island of Elba receding from view,
flushed with the rosy light of sunset:

'Suddenly, there was a shock and sound all over the vessel; her progress was stopped; and a rocking vibration was felt everywhere. The quarter-deck was filled with blasts of steam, which obscured everything. Sick people came rushing up out of their berths in strange undress; the steerage passengers – a motley and picturesque set of people, in many varieties of gay costume – took refuge on the quarter deck, speaking loudly in all varieties of French and Italian patois. Ellinor stood up in silent, wondering dismay.' (Ch. 3)[1]

Ellinor's dismay is not at her own danger: if the sinking ship pulls her into the depths, she will never be able to free the old coachman, Dixon, wrongly charged with murder in England. Only she can save him, for only she knows that her father was the man who killed Mr Dunster, whose body has been unearthed from its shallow grave. 'A Dark Night's Work' is the only place in her fiction where Gaskell uses her Italian experience; the holiday which was so happy is set like a jewel in a sad, agonized story. All the time, while Ellinor is recovering in Rome, 'like a renewing of her youth', a cloud of horror, of accusation, waits to break in England.

On the voyage and in Rome Elizabeth did not sense the clouds gathering around *The Life of Charlotte Brontë*, which would build and break in her absence. Even the burst boiler proved all for the best – back in Marseilles they changed to a far superior steamer, the *Oran*, and sailed in luxury south towards the sun.

On board the *Oran* were Elizabeth, Marianne, Meta and Katie Winkworth (herself an established literary figure since her translation of the *Lyra Germanica* in 1856). With them were a Mr Hartnell and a Captain Charles Hill, a forty-year-old widower with two children, whom he had left in England, soon to figure large in Meta's life. Captain Hill (whose father was a distinguished major-general, Sir Dudley St Leger Hill) sounds something of a snob; in Rome he told Katie he was to be introduced to an American named Rogers, 'who was to remove all his prejudices and make him believe that Yankees could be gentlemen'. But he was undoubtedly dashing. He had belonged to the Madras Engineers since 1843, had been high in the Himalayas and 'known all the principal men of the Punjab – Lawrences, Edwardes etc.'[2]

The mood was romantic, the sea and sky a brilliant blue, the atmosphere dreamlike. They sailed past islands – Corsica, Gorgona,

Elba. They lounged on deck and looked and talked and at dusk leant over the stern and gazed at the trails of phosphorescence, flickering like the Milky Way in the sea. Mr Hartnell, Marianne and Elizabeth sang duets from Handel and Mendelssohn – until suddenly the stars were blotted out and the lightning flashed. Before they could snatch up their things and get below it was raining like a waterspout.[3]

On the night of 22 February the *Oran* moored off Civitavecchia. Next day, after tedious delays at the port, they drove towards Rome, looking out for the dome of St Peter's over every ridge. It was dark when they finally wound through the narrow streets: 'We came in close to St Peter's, and began exclaiming, as we recognised the places: Look! the Colonnade – the fortress – the Vatican – St Angelo! it seemed like a dream, seeing them dimly through the night.'[4] Here they separated, Katie to stay with Emma Shaen, Elizabeth and the girls with the Wetmore Storys, at the Casa Cabrale, 43 Via Sant' Isidoro.

William and Emelyn would not hear of them taking lodgings. They were ideal hosts, in their early thirties, with a large circle of friends. William, small and dark with a pointed beard and mobile, humorous face, was working on his sculpture of Cleopatra. Emelyn, with her mass of beautiful hair, was plump, impulsive, caressingly charming to all. They were both devoted to their little girl, Edith: their infant son, Joe, had died of fever in 1853, his loss covering Rome, in Elizabeth Barrett Browning's words, with 'ghastly flakes of death'.[5] In 1857, despite this shadow, their apartment was a place of exuberant sociability, a focus for artists, writers, actors and musicians. Since the 1840s American sculptors, in particular, had clustered in Rome, as English writers had in Florence. The Casa Cabrale was full of people from morning to night, gossiping about religion, love affairs, art and politics.

Elizabeth and her daughters shone in the warmth of this circle. And they were utterly seduced by Rome itself. Half a century later Meta remembered how they woke on their first morning and saw the city before them, 'all brilliant sunshine and colour and wild gaiety'.[6] It was Shrove Tuesday. William and Emelyn took a balcony on the Corso to watch the carnival. 'Suddenly against this turbulent background there stood out the figure of a young man just below the balcony, smiling up at my mother, whom he knew he was to see there and whom he easily distinguished from the others.' The young man caught some confetti which Elizabeth was dangling over the balcony on a long stick, and as he smiled she said, ' "Oh look what a charming face!" and Mr Story (I think it was) said "Oh, that's Charles Eliot Norton." '7

This scene too enters 'A Dark Night's Work'. Mrs Forbes has hired a balcony, 'as became a wealthy and respectable Englishwoman':

'The crowd below was at its wildest pitch; the rows of stately *contadini* alone sitting immovable as their possible ancestors, the senators who received Brennus and his Gauls. Masks and white dominoes, foreign gentlemen, and the riff-raff of the city, slow-driving carriages, showers of flowers, most of them faded by this time, everyone shouting and struggling at that wild pitch of excitement which may so soon turn to fury. The Forbes girls had given place at the window to their mother and Ellinor, who was gazing, half-amused, half-terrified, at the mad parti-coloured movement below; when a familiar face looked up, smiling a recognition; and "How shall I get to you?" was asked, in English, by the well-known voice of Canon Livingstone.' (Ch. 12)

Elizabeth, however, was no shrinking spirit like Ellinor, and the thirty-year-old Charles Norton – later a distinguished professor of art at Harvard – was very different from the mild Canon Livingstone. The Nortons were descended from old New England Puritans. Charles's father, Andrews Norton, professor of sacred literature at Harvard in the 1820s, was a biblical scholar, author of the controversial *Evidence of the Genuineness of the Gospels* (1837–41) and described as 'the hard-headed Unitarian Pope' in his bitter battle against the Transcendentalists (Emerson, his former pupil, was his fiercest opponent). Charles himself, though devoted to his father, was of the new generation, on good terms with Emerson and Lowell, a friend of Longfellow and Hawthorne.[8] After Harvard he worked for a Boston trading company in India and travelled in Europe and Britain. He had met Elizabeth briefly at the Procters' in 1850, and in 1854, on the publication of *North and South,* had written to tell her that *Cranford* had been his stern father's favourite book in his final illness. The meeting in Rome was significant in both their lives.

It would be too strong to say that Elizabeth fell in love with Charles. He was part of her Italian romance and she fell in love with the whole experience. In Rome, surrounded by people ten or fifteen years younger than herself, she felt released and exhilarated. Charles Norton was one of those people with an indefinable gift for friendship, to whom the most unlikely men and women – from Emerson to the young Henry James – poured out their feelings. John Ruskin, for example, became a devoted (and increasingly dependent) friend after they first met in 1855, calling Norton 'my first real tutor', and describing him as 'absolutely free from envy or ambition . . . a scholar from his cradle'.[9]

Charles Norton was, it has to be said, not only intellectually attractive. Ruskin bore witness too to 'the bright eye, the melodious voice, the perfect manner, the simple, but acutely flattering words'.[10] He certainly flattered Elizabeth, but his admiration was genuine. And he appealed to her because of his vulnerability as much as his confidence: he had damaged his spine during social work in Boston and some days was in such pain he could not go out. He lived with his mother and sisters, was at ease in the company of women and could talk to them about everything from Renaissance art to the ways of the Gaskells' dog, Lion.

Their philanthropic and cultural interests also coincided. Charles was steeped in Unitarian principles, a passionate abolitionist, actively concerned about the condition of the poor. He was also a writer, who had already published some of the articles which would make up his *Notes of Travel and Study in Italy* and just begun a translation of Dante's *Vita Nuova* (1859). But he was equally attuned to the new as well as the old, writing the first appreciative review of Walt Whitman's *Leaves of Grass* in 1855 and helping to get Clough's poetry published in America.

After they met on Shrove Tuesday Norton was endlessly attentive: almost every day he arrived at the Casa Cabrale with a huge bouquet of flowers. As he came to know Elizabeth well his admiration deepened to affection. He told Lowell she was like the best things in her books: 'full of generous and tender sympathies, of thoughtful kindness, of pleasant humour, of quick appreciation, of utmost simplicity and truthfulness'. With these went strong principle, tough purpose and 'straightforwardness of action, such as few women possess'.[11] He kept almost every scrap of paper she sent him, long tumbling letters from Manchester and even a scribble from Rome saying her headache was gone and, yes, she would like a drive. It is carefully marked, 'This is, I think, the first note I received from Mrs Gaskell.'[12]

Elizabeth's letters show how this holiday came to represent transient happiness and release from care. The following year she wrote: 'Oh, I so long for Italy and Albano that it makes me ill!' She could not bear to think of the Storys moving to a grand apartment in the Palazzo Barberini or even changing a single servant. She wanted everyone and everything to stay the same: 'Have you still Serafino? Our remembrances to Luigi and Clarke. Speak of us to Amante and Domenico. Have you still little birds for dinner, and the good "dolci", the creams of which it was necessary to be forewarned, lest we should eat too much previously?' In 1860 she wrote that Rome grew ever more vivid in her memory:

'Only the other night I dreamed of a breakfast – not a past breakfast, but some mysterious breakfast which neither had been, nor, alas! would be – in the Via Sant' Isidoro dining-room, with the amber sunlight streaming on the gold-grey Roman roofs and the Sabine hills on one side and the Vatican on the other. I sometimes think that I would almost rather never have been there than have this ache of yearning for the great witch who sits with you upon her seven hills.' (L642)

Charles was included in the ache of yearning. With his friend, the painter Hamilton Wild, he accompanied Elizabeth, Meta and Marianne on most of their outings. He was their guide to the art of Rome, and later of Florence and Venice, and they learnt from him, Meta said, 'more vividly than any book on art could teach, all the deep principles of painting and sculpture'.[13] He was a kind of perfect squire, as gallant to Marianne and Meta as to their mother (they wrote him affectionate letters all their lives). His last letter to Meta was written in July 1908, when he was eighty-one. It ends:

'With love to Julia as well as to yourself, my dear Meta, I am, and, so long as I shall have consciousness, shall remain

Your affectionate old friend
Charles Eliot Norton'[14]

At thirty, in 1856, Charles conveyed the excitement of the new world discovering the old. His encounter with Elizabeth Gaskell is a kind of Jamesian situation in reverse, not threatening but benign, with an eager young man in place of an innocent girl. In one of her fanciful moments, after visiting Oxford, Elizabeth told Charles how much she liked the associations of a life so different from Manchester, and, she presumed, from America. She believed, she said, that she *was* medieval, *un*-Manchester, un-American. She valued 'associations' as she loved fragrance in a flower – she was sure American flowers did not smell, nor birds sing. 'Now I like a smelling and singing world. Yes I do. I can't help it. I like Kings & Queens, & nightingales & mignionettes & roses. There!'

When Henry James wrote his memoir of William Wetmore Story, he was touched by the thought of Mrs Gaskell in Rome. This was partly, he said, because such 'clear echoes of a "good time" (as we have lived to call it)' reached him through her letters, and partly because she had been reading a forgotten novel (forgotten already when he wrote), *Tolla*, by the French writer Edmond About.[15] He imagined that she had explored Rome as he did on his first walk there, wondering which palace was the Palais Feraldi, where Tolla had 'lived, loved, wasted and died'. For Henry James, About's tragic story of lovers separated by their parents was 'the slim idyll of our fourteenth year', to be preserved, bound in ivory vellum and kept on a special shelf. For Elizabeth Gaskell it was the idyll of her mid-forties: she left her shabby old copy behind, to be bound in a 'pretty Roman binding', and never saw it again.

Tolla's elegiac mood, though, was hardly that of the holiday itself. From the moment of their arrival the Gaskell women were the centre of attention. Elizabeth was admired for her books and her charm, Marianne and Meta for their 'English freshness'. Katie Winkworth looked on with undisguised envy – she was staying with Emma Shaen, who was asthmatic and disliked going out. 'There is a great deal of gaiety, however, for those who go into it, and the Gaskells are overwhelmed with acquaintance and parties – no dancing of course, being Lent.' A week later the unhappy Katie was confined to the house with toothache while by contrast 'Mrs Gaskell and her daughters are "all the fashion here", constantly invited out, all the Embassies asking them to dinner, and the Roman Catholic dignitaries calling on them &c.'[16]

The Catholic attention was a bit overwhelming. Regular guests at the Storys' breakfasts included the languid poet, Aubrey de Vere, and the powerful Henry Manning, a convert since 1851. They were soon 'making the most tremendous set' at the Gaskell women, 'prayers being offered on their behalf, &c, &c, so far very unavailingly'.[17] The thought of this assault on a Unitarian minister's family is faintly comic, but it is hard to re-create the feverish tempo of the 1850s. There were waves of unlikely Catholic conversions; the new recruits were persistent and zealous and Rome itself gave them added fire. Unitarians were a particular challenge, at the opposite end of the spectrum from the Roman purple. Bessie Parkes, who was also in Rome this month, saw the contrast as almost reflected in the art encrusting the walls around them, finding similar antagonisms between Michelangelo's 'blotched, sketched, chopped creations and Raphael's perfect conceptions' as 'between the exceedingly absurd and vital Roman Catholic faith, and exceedingly rational Unitarianism with no vitality at all. Peter and John.'[18] (Bessie converted to the 'absurd' Roman Church in the 1870s.) In the same period Norton told James Lowell about the onslaught suffered by John Fields and his wife, then living on the corner of the Piazza Mignanelli and the Piazza di Spagna, close to Norton and the Storys, and 'undergoing a tremendous bombardment from a strong force of Catholic converts who are trying to compel them to yield to the claims of the true Church'. The attack was led by Aubrey de Vere and when force was needed, Henry Manning was called in, 'a wily and soft dialectician . . . he is called Apostle to the Genteels'.[19]

Norton had no time for the contemporary Roman Catholic Church, damning it as aggrandized and corrupt. And Elizabeth and her daughters also resisted its lure (although Marianne fell under Manning's spell on a later trip). They preferred to worship Rome itself. They saw all the sights: the Colosseum by moonlight; the Catacombs; the Sistine Chapel; the Raphaels in the Villa Borghese. They ascended the dome of St Peter's and watched tableaux vivants in the Palazzo Braschi. As the spring sun warmed they took drives to Albano across the Campagna, vibrant with lark-song. Elizabeth gathered anemones in the gardens of the Palazzo Doria and watched little green lizards basking on the stones.

They swam in a haze of new friends. On some nights they went to grand dinners or open evenings like those held by Mme Mohl's American friend Emma Weston. On others they gathered in Charles's apartments overlooking the Spanish Steps, where the splash of fountains mingled with their talk. Or they simply stayed in the Via Sant' Isidoro with 'the usual set': Storys, Norton, Wild and Mr and Mrs Fields. Jack Fields, who had made a large enough fortune by the age of forty to let his wife and himself lead a life of leisure, was less intellectual than the others, but was loved for his wit and childlike openness. He later visited Plymouth Grove: 'And oh! the talking, and the jokes & the fits of laughter.'

The talking was all. Often they sat in a circle and told stories, especially of mysteries and ghosts. Charles thought Elizabeth 'a wonderful story-teller, never exaggerating and always dramatic'[20] and Elizabeth later complained to Emelyn that she did not feel like *writing* any more short stories, but 'I could *tell* the stories quite easily. How I should like to do it to you and Mr Story and Edith, sitting over a wood-fire and knowing that the Vatican was in sight of the windows behind!'

Visiting celebrities joined them, like Harriet Beecher Stowe. ('Very commonplace,' grumped Katie, 'very abrupt and *distraite*, not popular here any more than in England.')[21] One evening Charles arrived at the Storys' to find them all sitting in the loggia with Mrs Stowe telling them stories about the indomitable freed slave Sojourner Truth. But he also reported how upset the American community (with plenty of southerners) was by the forthright author of *Uncle Tom's Cabin* and *Dred*: 'the American Eagle is ruffled here a good deal by Mrs Stowe's presence'.[22]

Other people dropped in, such as the pianist Edward Bache, who was giving a series of concerts, and Miss Crossman, who was obsessed with spirit rapping. There was also a 'very strong-minded young American lady who is studying in Mr Gibson's studio'.[23] This was the 25-year-old Harriet Hosmer, later a famous sculptor. Hatty was notorious for her wild ways, despite her dimpled face: in 1855 she persuaded Elizabeth Barrett Browning (to Robert's fury) to dress as a man so they could smuggle themselves into a monastery to see some paintings. A year earlier William Story described the group at Gibson's studio, 28 Corso: the 'harem (scarem) I call it – and the emancipated females who dwell there in heavenly unity'. These emancipated females included the actress Charlotte Cushman, the writer Grace Greenwood and Hatty herself:

'Hatty takes a high stand here in Rome, and would have the Romans know that a Yankee girl can do anything she pleases, walk alone, ride her horse alone, and laugh at their rules. The police interfered and countermanded the riding alone on account of the row it made in the streets, and I believe *that* is over, but cannot affirm. The Cushman sings savage ballads in a hoarse manny voice, and requests people recitatively to forget her not. I'm sure I shall not.'[24]

It was a long way, in all senses, from Cross Street Chapel Sunday School.

The Gaskells' intoxicated weeks in Rome reached a grand finale at Easter when they went to Good Friday mass in the Sistine Chapel and saw the Vatican by torchlight. The following Wednesday, 14 April, they said farewell. Mr Hartnell, their companion on the voyage out, had gone to Algiers, but Captain Hill joined them on a final month's tour of northern Italy. Charles Norton and Hamilton Wild came too. Leaving Rome behind, they wound slowly across the Campagna, where the anemones had given way to brilliant crimson and purple orchids. Then they turned towards the hills, to Viterbo, over the Apennines to San Quirico, and up to Siena. Determined to see all they could, they took a day-trip to Pisa by railway.

They travelled slowly, staying at rough country inns, feeling totally cut off from the world. Norton reported:

'One day, as we were travelling in Italy, Mrs Gaskell and her daughters and I were talking about the books we would choose if we were shut up in prison or on a desolate island. At last we agreed to choose one book by a living author, and when it came to Mrs Gaskell's turn to tell us what she had chosen she said "Modern Painters".'[25]

Elizabeth saw Rome, Florence and especially Venice through the filter of Ruskin's prose and Charles Norton's presence. But however gradual their progress, the Gaskells were now heading north, towards England. Elizabeth could no longer put the *Life* out of mind altogether. It had been published on 27 March, in two volumes, the first of her works to carry her name on the title page. On 16 April she read Charles Norton a letter from Patrick Brontë, who had perused the two volumes, he said, 'with a degree of pain and pleasure which can be known only to myself'.

'You have not only given a picture of my Dear daughter Charlotte, but of my Dear wife, and all my Dear children and such a picture, too, as is full of truth and life. The picture of my brilliant and unhappy son, and his diabolical seducer, are masterpieces.'[26]

Trouble lurked in this final phrase, and in the gentle words, 'There are a few trifling mistakes, which, should it be deemed necessary, may be corrected in the second edition.'

William had already replied, inquiring what the errors were and promising corrections. He did not tell Elizabeth of any other problems. Happily unaware, she arrived in Florence. Robert Browning paid a long call as soon as they arrived and Elizabeth took Katie Winkworth to meet his wife. Elizabeth Barrett Browning, however, scarcely spoke a word and Elizabeth desperately filled the silences by telling long stories about Charlotte Brontë, with Katie acting as chorus and the Brownings' friend Isa Blagden stopping the gaps by remarking on 'the delights of living in Italy instead of England in the style of artistic pleasure being the only thing in life'. Even Katie was driven to admit the evening was 'not particularly brilliant'.[27] Elizabeth and Charles tried to call again before they left, but the news of Mr Barrett's death had just reached the Casa Guidi; his daughter was devastated and would see no one.

From Florence Katie left for home, and the rest of the group crossed to Venice. Charles, who had lived there for some months, showed them the treasures of the city and on one dreamy Sunday took them across the lagoon to Torcello. In Manchester, in a foggy December, Elizabeth remembered the abandoned calm of the 'still, sunny, sleepy canal, – something like the Lady of Shalott, tho' how, why, & wherefore I can't tell'. A year later Charles wrote to remind her of the day and she replied with her own memories of gliding through canals gazing idly at the stars of Bethlehem, flowering in the cracks in the walls, and at the stones, carved and square cut, beneath the level of the banks – 'oh lovely, happy day'.

But in Venice the *Life* caught up with her again. Charles found a Tauchnitz edition in a bookshop – the first time she had seen the biography in print. She was still untroubled. During their wanderings in northern Italy the Gaskells' post was not forwarded, and for almost five weeks they received no letters. They heard no news, good or bad. Gossip, however, was humming in London, Rome and Paris. On 9 May Mary Mohl wrote anxiously (and a touch gleefully) to Elizabeth Reid:

'I have read Miss Brontë's life and think it admirable. I am expecting every day to hear from Mrs Gaskell but am every day disappointed.

She always intended coming here in May and Mrs Stowe, who saw her in Rome, says she must be at home before the end of the month. I'm told that wicked woman who caused so much harm to her brother is going to attack her for a libel.'[28]

A day after Mme Mohl wrote these words Elizabeth said goodbye to Charles Norton. Slowly she, Marianne and Meta moved homewards, through Verona, Milan and the Italian lakes to Nice, Marseilles and Paris. Their circle was complete. When they arrived at the rue du Bac on 26 May, they found over a hundred letters. By the evening of the 28th she was back at Plymouth Grove. On 16 June she would write to Ellen Nussey: 'I am in the Hornet's nest with a vengeance.'

The libel case had indeed been threatened by 'that wicked woman' Lady Scott. By now, in fact, it had already been dealt with. While Elizabeth was abroad, William Gaskell, George Smith and William Shaen, acting as the Gaskells' solicitor, had been fielding the on-slaught. William's work was particularly heroic, since from January he had been heavily involved as a trustee of Manchester College in a heated dispute about appointing James Martineau as a full-time tutor. The last thing he needed was more controversy. When she got home, Elizabeth thought he looked dreadful: he needed a holiday. She blithely suggested that perhaps he could stay with Charles Norton, who was returning to America? With understandable impatience William replied he 'could as soon go to the Moon'.

The first reactions to the *Life* had been good. In early April there was an emotional review in *The Times*, and Henry Chorley set the tone in the *Athenaeum* when he described himself as deeply moved by the sad record of 'self-denial and struggle, sustained to the last with courage, principle and genius, but without hope . . . As a work of Art, we do not recollect a life of a woman by a woman so well executed.'[29] Other reviews too were full of praise: the *Daily News*, the *Economist*, the *Spectator*, the *Saturday Review*, the *Leader*, the *New Monthly Magazine*, the *Globe*. On 15 April William wrote cheerfully to Ellen Nussey: 'All the notices I have seen have been favourable and some of the best, exceedingly so. I have had a considerable number of letters too from distinguished men expressing high approval.'[30] A second edition, a straightforward reprint, was announced on 9 May. Then, suddenly, came a letter from Lady Scott's solicitors announcing that legal action would follow unless all passages about her were with-drawn and a public apology made.

All unsold copies were called in and on 26 May, two days before Elizabeth returned, William Shaen sent a formal letter of retraction to the solicitors, Messrs Newton and Robinson of York, which they placed in *The Times* and the *Athenaeum*. Referring to 'a widowed lady', unnamed in the book, it withdrew all statements implying 'any breach of her conjugal, her maternal, or her social duties' and particularly any imputation of 'a guilty intercourse with the late Branwell Brontë'.[31] Such statements had been based on information which Mrs Gaskell had believed well founded but which had since proved 'not to be trustworthy'. Also published was a letter of acceptance from the York solicitors acknowledging Mrs Gaskell's good faith. The *Athenaeum*, feathers ruffled, apologized to its readers for misleading them in its review, due to a misplaced trust in biographers 'as accurate collectors of facts. This, we regret to state, Mrs Gaskell proves not to have been . . . biographers should be deterred from rushing into print with mere impressions instead of proofs, however eager and sincere those impressions may be.'[32] (This caused a rift between Elizabeth and the reviewer, Henry Chorley, which never quite healed.) One of the oddest reactions to all this was that of Patrick Brontë. Despite his praise of the portrait of the 'diabolical seducer', he presented Newton and Robinson (in a spirit of irony?) with a complete ten-volume set of Campbell's *Lives of the Lord Chancellors*, 'in recognition of legal services rendered to Bran-well Brontë'.[33]

The Scott–Gaskell battle was the choicest gossip of the month, and the buzz spread far and wide. Bessie Parkes, now in Paris, was dismayed. Barbara Bodichon had told her that the retraction 'is *Mr* Gaskell's; done in a fright', when Mrs G. could not be reached: 'altogether it is a pretty mess'. A pointless mess too, Bessie felt, since the original edition was all over the Continent, 'bought and read, right and left . . . Mr Enoch, at Galignani's, says that a great impetus to the sale has been given by the recantation.'[34]

A week later – preparing to descend on England – Mary Mohl pitched into the fray, elbows flying:

'I thought the whole book a masterpiece, and I do still, and when the present nonsensical fever is over, the whole public will be of my opinion. Distance plays the part of time in these matters and I can judge better from afar. I propose myself much fun in calling Lady Scott "the Immaculate" to all my religious friends, just like the Holy Virgin, and I have not said a word about the book to my people in any letter, that I may get all out at once and pounce on 'em like a cat.'³⁵

She loved Mrs Gaskell, she said, for the book's honest indignation. Anyway (though she practised it for her own interest), she despised worldly prudence as a virtue:

'I like her faults better than her virtues (of that sort), and you'll see if it does not add to her fame. The folk in Mayfair say "She's capable of anything (the Scott); she'll get the uppermost." No she won't, in the long run. I have not been so ardent about a game since '48 as I am at this Scott-versus-Gaskell, and I enjoy the idea of taking her part in England – not with an absurd zeal, which spoils everything, as Talleyrand says, but *sneeringly*.'³⁶

Elizabeth, however, had no heart for either fighting or sneering. She had already told George Smith on 3 June: 'I hate the whole affair, & everything connected with it.' It was clear, as the *Athenaeum* insisted, that *The Life of Charlotte Brontë* must be modified before it was circulated further. Long weeks of work lay ahead and the prospect was depressing, however supportive her friends were or however many letters she read from 'distinguished men'. These should have cheered her – a late one, in August, was from Charles Kingsley, and it suggested that she had succeeded in her principal aim. Kingsley was among those who had thought Charlotte Brontë's novels coarse; he had hardly looked into *Jane Eyre*, while ' "Shirley" disgusted me at the opening. How I misjudged her!' Mrs Gaskell had given 'the picture of a valiant woman made perfect by suffering':

'Be sure that the book will do good. It will shame literary people into some stronger belief that a simple, virtuous practical home life is consistent with high imaginative genius; and it will shame, too, the prudery of a not over cleanly though carefully white-washed age, into believing that purity is now (as in all ages till now) quite compatible with the knowledge of evil.'³⁷

Kingsley's was just the kind of response that feminists like Anna Jameson had hoped for. Jameson told Bessie Parkes that she had read the biography in Italy in May 'not so much read – as *devoured* it, with inexpressible pain and pleasure' and felt that much of its incalculable good would be in 'exciting the sympathy & waking up the attention of intelligent *men* – there can be no doubt – till men see the truth as regards us women no good can be done'.[38]

The reactions of Kingsley and Jameson are interesting in showing how Gaskell had pitched her book to suit the temper of the age. The most perceptive and generous response, however, came from George Henry Lewes. Lewes wrote from the Scilly Isles, where he was holidaying with Marian, declaring: 'I discharge my emotion through the penny post: at least such of it as was not discharged through wet eyes, and swelling heart as chapter after chapter was read.' Mrs Gaskell's book, he said, brilliantly created Charlotte's sad, noble life, and offered lessons in duty and self-reliance. But more than that,

'it also, thanks to its artistic power, makes us familiar inmates of an interior so strange, so original in its individual elements and so picturesque in its externals – it paints for us at once the psychological drama and the scenic accessories with so much vividness – that fiction has nothing more wild, touching and heart-strengthening to place above it.

The early part is a triumph for you; the rest a monument for your friend.'[39]

Lewes's verdict stands. It was this suggestive blend of inner and outer landscapes, always a potent technique in Gaskell's writing, that Virginia Woolf noted many years later: 'The *Life* gives you the impression that Haworth and the Brontës are somehow inextricably mixed. Haworth expresses the Brontës; the Brontës express Haworth; they fit like a snail to its shell.'[40]

Lewes did have one small objection. He felt he was misrepresented; he had not meant to be disrespectful to women in his remarks upon *Shirley*. Elizabeth made a minor correction in the third edition. His complaint was one of many. Patrick Brontë had already objected to the colourful account of his eccentricities, rages and austerity towards his daughters. (But he chuckled to a visiting Methodist minister, 'Mrs Gaskell is a novelist, you know, and we must allow her a *little* romance, eh? It is quite in her line. But the book is substantially true, sir, for all that. There are some queer things in it, to be sure – there are some about myself for instance – but the book is substantially true.')[41]

Elizabeth went back to Burnley to see the nurse, whose gossip she had earlier believed, and modified her description.

Letters rolled in. Mr Nicholls, who had read the book with 'inexpressible pain', wanted some passages removed. Harriet Martineau insisted that she was unfairly quoted in the dispute over *Villette* and was upset that even Elizabeth, who should have known better, had called her controversial book of 1851, *Letters on the Laws of Man's Nature and Development*, 'an error'. A furious argument ensued, not between Harriet and Elizabeth but between Harriet and Arthur Nicholls (an incredibly combative letter writer). Elizabeth knew they were having 'a warlike correspondence, *very* warlike, I imagine', but tried, as hard as she could, to stay out of it.[42] There were grumbles about the Haworth anecdotes. Two separate people swore that the meeting between Charlotte and Harriet Martineau had happened at *their* hous . The Brontës' servant Martha Brown wrote on behalf of relatives of the girl who was 'seduced': the word was changed to 'betrayed'. John Stuart Mill had to be pacified about the comments on 'The Enfranchisement of Women'. Even former Haworth servants were angry at the statement that there was 'plenty, and even waste' at the Parsonage: Mr Brontë sent a testimonial saying they were not wasteful.

In short, Elizabeth groaned, 'Every one who has been harmed in this unlucky book complains of some thing.' In mid-June she asked Smith wryly if she could please insert a preface. It had been sent from Paris, she said – presumably a joking suggestion from the Mohls:

' "If anybody is displeased with any statement or words in the following pages I beg leave to with-draw it, and to express my deep regret for having offered so expensive an article as truth to the Public."

It is clever, is it not?

Yours very truly & in great haste.' (L455)

However much she joked, the criticisms stung. Listing the catalogue of objections to Ellen Nussey, Elizabeth reverted to the justification she had used in earlier storms over *Mary Barton* and *Ruth*. She did not sign herself 'yours truly' lightly:

'I am writing as if I were in famous spirits, and I think I *am* so *angry* that I am almost merry in my bitterness, if you know that state of feeling; but I have cried so much since I came home that [*sic*] I ever did in the same space of time before; and never needed kind words so much, – & no one gives me them. I *did so try* to *tell the truth*, & I believe *now* I hit as near the truth as anyone *could* do. And I weighed every line with all my whole power & heart.' (L454)

Perhaps William had gone through too much in the Scott affair to offer 'kind words' in the face of her tears. Luckily, Lady Eastlake chose to stay aloof and silent about the comments on her review of *Jane Eyre*, but unexpected trouble came from a different direction, the supporters of W. Carus Wilson, founder of Cowan Bridge, the Lowood of *Jane Eyre*. Gaskell had blamed the school's harsh regime and inadequate food for the deaths of the elder Brontë sisters, Maria and Elizabeth, and for the ruin of Charlotte's own health, and had described Wilson himself as 'willing to sacrifice everything but power'.[43] On 4 April he wrote vehemently to the *Daily News*. His son-in-law published a pamphlet vindicating him, and lawsuits were mentioned. Although Elizabeth had collected evidence from former pupils and teachers, she was reluctant to name them for fear they would be abused; instead she decided on appeasement, toning down all references to the school. While she backed down, Arthur Nicholls took up the cause on Charlotte's behalf, asserting that the accounts in *Jane Eyre* and the *Life* were true of the time she was there, however much conditions might have changed since. The argument raged for weeks in the *Leeds Mercury* and *Halifax Guardian* until a final letter from Nicholls on 8 August.

The revisions took all summer. At the end of July Elizabeth retreated to Skelwith, where Julia and Flossy and Hearn were staying with the Prestons. A fortnight earlier she had felt so depressed that she asked George Smith if he could find someone else as editor, if she sent all the papers. He had not replied. Now, after a note from him, she resigned herself to finishing: 'so I set hard to work on my weary and oppressive task.' Final amendments were added even at proof stage. She had made many cuts, but also added a great deal of new material – letters from Charlotte to Martha Brown, new details sent by Mary Taylor, additional stories of the Keighley neighbourhood. When it was finally published in November, the third edition was longer than the first.[44]

Throughout everything Elizabeth had one firm supporter, Charlotte' father. In July Mr Brontë wrote to reassure her after a passionate article in the *Halifax Examiner* by William Dearden, objecting to the way his old friend was portrayed. Patrick was annoyed, and insisted that his first opinion was unshaken:

'And my opinion, and the reading World's opinion of the "Memoir", is that it is in every way worthy of what one Great Woman should have written of Another and that it ought to stand, and will stand, in the first rank of Biographies till the end of time.'[45]

In late August he wrote again: 'Why should you disturb yourself concerning what has been, is, and ever will be the lot of eminent writers?' Three thousand years ago Solomon had said, 'He that increaseth knowledge increaseth sorrow.' She had found it so, and so had his own daughter:

'You have had and will have much praise with a little blame. Then drink the mixed cup with thankfulness to the great Physician of souls. It will be far more salutary to you in the end, and even in the beginning, than if it were all unmixed sweetness.'[46]

An authorized biography is always difficult and a Victorian one was even more so. Discussing the *Life*, Arthur Pollard aptly cites Virginia Woolf's comment that Victorian biography was dominated by the idea of goodness, and quotes Carlyle's response to the criticism of Lockhart's *Life of Sir Walter Scott*, which was thought too indiscreet:

'How delicate, decent is English biography, bless its mealy mouth! A Damocles sword of *Respectability* hangs for ever over the poor English life-writer (as it does over English life in general), and reduces him to the verge of paralysis.'[47]

Modern readers may feel that Gaskell made Charlotte too good, too dutiful. Her contemporaries, including those who complained, tended to approve of the central portrait, but felt that the treatment of others was too outspoken – not nearly respectable enough. When the revised edition was published, the complainants were satisfied, but still, not everyone was pleased. From Wellington Mary Taylor wrote tersely to Ellen Nussey that Mrs Gaskell seemed a 'hasty, impulsive sort of person, and the needful drawing back after her warmth gives her an inconsistent look . . . As to the mutilated edition that is to come, I am sorry for it. Libellous or not, the first edition was all true.'[48]

Mary was not altogether right about the book – in some ways the third edition is stronger and more coherent – but she was not altogether wrong about the author. Elizabeth was hasty and impulsive, and she did sometimes seem inconsistent. She veered between feeling passionately about something, not caring whom she might offend, and desperately wanting to please and be liked. Friends noticed that her manners were not exactly insincere, but simply erratic. As her letters show, she responded to the moment. Arthur Clough was shaken at the Manchester Art Treasures Exhibition in November that year. Parthe Nightingale had been, and when a man asked if it was *the* Miss Nightingale, Elizabeth said yes. She knew it was not, since Fanny and Parthe were dining at her house, but 'when her companion expostulated, her reply was, "she could not bear to take away the poor man's faith" '. It made Clough, he said, feel very dubious about reading any biography by 'Mrs G'.[49]

Harriet Martineau, who liked Mrs G., wrote amusedly to Snow Wedgwood, while Elizabeth was still in Venice, about her own quarrels with the *Life*. William Gaskell promised that his wife would make amends and Harriet was sure that she would:

'But O! what a beautiful book it is! Mrs G's part is most charmingly done, I think, – allowance being made for sentiment now and then swamping conviction &c . . .

. . . I think my letter must gratify her on the whole, – I admire the book, – the doing of it, – so much! If not, I shall make myself easy, – well knowing the lady, and having been consulted and concerned in it, – She came over on purpose, you know, to consult with me, and see and hear what I could give her. She covered us all with kisses and wept when she went away, and asked, as the greatest favour, that she might write occasionally, to tell me how she went on. She never wrote a line, nor even sent me a copy!'[50]

When Gaskell was writing, she was always deeply preoccupied. In her work she was not inconsistent, sticking strongly to her purpose, although sometimes the wish for approval can be felt. *Ruth*, an immensely courageous book, was certainly affected by her anxieties about its reception. Even in the *Life* she is occasionally oddly evasive – less in the outright suppression of Heger, which was done deliberately, to protect Charlotte, than in her attitude to the Brontë sisters' writing. She manages to acknowledge their genius while making allowances for those who disapproved of their work. She explains, for example, that they wrote what they saw, obeying the stern dictates of their consciences:

'They might be mistaken. They might err in writing at all, when their afflictions were so great that they could not write other than they did of life. It is possible that it would have been better to have described only good and pleasant people, doing good and pleasant things (in which case they could hardly have written at any time): all I say is, that never, I believe, did women, possessed of such wonderful gifts, exercise them with a fuller feeling of responsibility for their use. As to mistakes, they stand now – as authors as well as women – before the judgement seat of God.' (II, ch. 2)

Charlotte Brontë herself had written shrewdly to Elizabeth in 1853, apropos of *Cranford*. Though she found it graphic and pithy, she thought it might be a touch *too* good and pleasant:

'A thought comes to me. Do you, who have so many friends – so large a circle of acquaintance – find it easy, when you sit down to write, to isolate yourself from all those ties, and their sweet associations, so as to be quite *your own woman*, uninfluenced, unswayed by the consciousness of how your work may affect other minds; what blame, what sympathy it may call forth? Does no luminous cloud ever come between you and the severe Truth as you know it in your own secret and clear-seeing soul?'[51]

Yet the secret truth of the soul is not objective. When Gaskell came to write about the Cowan Bridge days, she remembered that Charlotte had expressed regret that the school could be so immediately identified with Lowood: 'she also said that she had not considered it necessary, in a work of fiction, to state every particular with the impartiality that might be required in a court of law'. She felt that Charlotte might welcome the chance to correct the over-strong impression:

'though even she, suffering her whole life long, both in heart and body, from the consequences of what happened there, might have been apt, to the last, to take her deep belief in the facts for the facts themselves – her conception of truth for the absolute truth.' (I. ch. 4)

The revisions which Elizabeth made to satisfy the Wilson camp were an uneasy attempt to compromise between the truth of imagination and feeling and the 'impartial' accuracy required in a court of law.

1857 was an emotional year. In September, when the corrections to the *Life* were almost done, Elizabeth thought longingly of Rome. How far apart the group who had breakfasted together in Venice four months ago were now – Captain Hill was in Asia, Norton in America, and 'we Gaskells all now so stationary at home that Italy & everything seems like a dream.' Writing to William and Emelyn Story, she looked back across her 'terrible summer', as she later called it, to her idyllic spring:

'It was in those charming Roman days that my life, at any rate, culminated. I shall never be so happy again. I don't think I was ever so happy before. My eyes fill with tears when I think of those days, and it is the same with all of us. They were the tip-top point of our lives. The girls may see happier ones – I never shall.' (L476–7)

21

Art and India, Travels and Cash

In 1857 there were other reasons, apart from weariness and a wish to appease, why Elizabeth found revising *The Life of Charlotte Brontë* so oppressive. By midsummer she was exhausted by a perpetual stream of visitors to the Manchester Art Treasures Exhibition and, far more seriously, by Meta's affairs of the heart.

At the beginning the exhibition was an unmixed pleasure. It was the first great international show in Britain, a cultural triumph for the industrial north. Old Masters had been chosen from royal and private collections across the country and the British works, including many Turners, were a revelation. Hunt, Millais and other Pre-Raphaelites were among the living artists represented. It opened just before Elizabeth returned from Rome and within a week she was begging Charles Norton to come and see it; he eventually came in July. On the day she wrote, 3 June, she was going to the exhibition herself for the first time, with Harriet Beecher Stowe. But soon the pleasure became a burden; from May to October her spare rooms were full. At the end of September, with a fortnight to go, she wrote to Norton:

'There comes a ring – there comes a caller! – Our house has been fuller than full, day & night since you left, and this last fortnight it will be fuller than ever, as everyone will want to see the Exhibition before it closes. I am *very* fond of all the people who are coming; but so worn-out that it is hard word [*sic*] to lash myself up into properly hospitable feelings.' (L475–6)

She was constantly juggling with dates, trying, for example, to fit the George Smiths in before, or after, the Mohls and their niece Ida (promising Mrs Smith, who had been ill, that there were Bathchairs at the exhibition, which were a wonderful relief to the weary). She made some comically detailed arrangements, like these with Mrs Clive: 'I will come at ½ past 1, & ½ past 2 to the green seat in the transept *outside* the Hertford Gallery, & you will wear a lilac plaided silk; & a white bonnet, – just like a young lady answering a matrimonial advertisement.'

After long hot days of showing the same pictures over and over again to guests who did not have time to see them properly, she sympathized with Marianne's wail: 'Oh! are not you tired of being agreeable! I do so want leisure to sulk and be silent in.' Some visitors, though, were always welcome and she still begged her dear Tottie to come:

'We are worn out with hospitality – but I should make no stranger of you dear, but gape in your face if I chose. Oh I *am* so tired of it. X I mean, – I shd like it dearly if I weren't a hostess.' (L470)

However tiring her visitors were, they did not tax Elizabeth's emotions. Meta's romance with Captain Charles Hill, on the other hand, certainly did. He had remained with the Gaskells throughout their weeks in Italy, accompanying them home as far as Paris. A month after they came back he and Meta were engaged. He came to stay at Plymouth Grove at the start of July, but by then the country was rocked by news of trouble in India, where the pent-up resentment of years had exploded in the Bengal army, over interference with sepoy privileges and caste traditions, as well as rumours (true) that the new Enfield rifles were greased with the fat of the sacred cow and unholy pig. The Indian Mutiny (a loaded term) began at Meerut, on 10 May. Delhi fell quickly, as did Lucknow, where the garrison were trapped in the residency. Charles's furlough was recalled and a distraught Meta told Snow Wedgwood she was sure that 'she could not live through his absence'.[1]

An immediate wedding was planned, but when Elizabeth wrote to George Smith at the end of July she explained that 'after many preparations were made in a tremendous hurry, absorbing *all* my time, & making me very anxious and unhappy this plan has been given up'. The new idea was that either she or William would take Meta out to Egypt the following winter, where Charles would meet her. The couple would marry there, live in India for four years until Captain Hill's period of service finished and then return to England. Meanwhile the

Gaskells would try to find him a post: 'manager of railways, inspector of railroads etc'.

The engagement was a shock to Elizabeth, who later told Fanny Wedgwood that she was surprised by the speed of Meta's acceptance. Friends were bemused at Meta's rush to marry such a man. Effie Wedgwood felt sure it would not happen and her aunt Mrs Rich wrote noncommittally: 'It is not the kind of marriage I shd. have expected Meta to make.'[2] There was a sense of anxiety: had Meta leapt too quickly, perhaps to escape the pressure of life as Mama's amanuensis? She did not seem altogether happy. Always hungry, she now ate ravenously, as Mrs Rich noticed: 'Meta has grown very stout – & not improved in beauty as is generally said to be the case with engaged young ladies.'

Mary Rich also noted that Meta's affair had driven the Brontë trouble right out of Elizabeth's mind, and that she 'questioned me much about India of course'. Despite her dread of parting from Meta, the engagement had given Elizabeth another of her characteristic, swift extensions of interest. In March William had borrowed a selection of James Mill's *History of India* (1817) from the Portico, and by the summer Elizabeth was greedy for every detail: history, climate, politics, people. From July onwards, just as he had sent any scrap he could find about Charlotte Brontë a year before, the diligent George Smith was busy meeting this new demand. Smith, Elder happened to publish the *Bombay Quarterly*. 'Do you know India?' Elizabeth asked. 'How is it you publish an *Indian* newspaper?' She was grateful for his help:

'Thank you very much for every word, every sign of sympathy about India. From the depths of ignorance I am roused up to most vivid & intense interest. This daughter of mine is a most dear friend, more like a sister to me than anything else; and I like Capt Hill extremely; but the engagement is a most anxious one.' (L463)

In 1857 George published a translation of the *Autobiography of Lutfullah, a Mohammedan Gentleman* and Harriet Martineau's *British Rule in India*. Elizabeth gulped them both down. George knew ladies who had been there. Could they give her 'practical advice about the "outfit" and the journey'? Charles Norton was told: 'We have a great map of India and study it and learn geography.'

Although the thought of losing their daughter grieved William and

Elizabeth, they welcomed Captain Hill warmly and took an interest in his world and his family. His son came to stay with them for six weeks in his school holidays, an added burden for Elizabeth, but a great delight to Julia, who was about the same age and insisted (unsuccessfully) on being called 'Aunt'.[3] But all that summer the news from India was appalling. Cawnpore was taken by the rebels, after three weeks of terrible resistance. Captain Hill came back to Manchester on 13 August for his last ten days in England and on 22 August, the day before he was due to leave, the Gaskells heard that Colonel Ewart, his wife and small daughter had died in the Cawnpore massacre. William had just been staying with the Ewarts in Wiltshire: the terror was brought sharply home. The horrors of the mutiny eclipsed the lesser troubles of the *Life*, although these still had to be dealt with. Writing about a new Brontë upset involving William Dearden and Harriet Martineau, Elizabeth told Smith:

'I imagine people will abuse me to the end of the chapter. I only hope Mr Brontë won't be over-worried. Hitherto he has acted like a "brick". (I hope you understand slang?) Capt Hill goes today; and we are dreadfully in the dumps. Somebody is crying in every room. Moreover Col. Ewart & his wife (he in command 1st Native Infantry at Cawnpore) were our *very* dear friends, our only friends in India, & that horrid telegraph yesterday! Oh! I don't care what people say of me. I am a great deal better than they give me credit for, – & don't mind about anything but India. Can you make head or tail of this letter –

Yours very truly

E. C. Gaskell

P.S. Return Mr Nicholls' list of omissions & Mr Brontë's letter to me.' (L468)

The tension was too much. Travel was always Elizabeth's refuge and in the autumn, after the corrections to the *Life* were finished, she swept Meta off to Buxton. Here the tiring and the terrible abruptly gave place to the absurd. They had a special 'green card' from the Duke of Devonshire which permitted them to see Chatsworth, but after they were shown round by the housekeeper a footman suddenly appeared to announce that luncheon would be at two and their rooms were prepared. Astonishment mingled with dismay since they had only

439

their travelling dresses: 'Well! we thought it was a pity to miss seeing & doing many agreeable things for the sake of no gowns. – so we bravely consented to stay.' (Meta suggested they dress in the curtains of the four-poster bed – thick white satin stamped with silken rosebuds. Elizabeth said she felt like Cinderella.) In a daze they were whisked around endless improvements and innumerable fountains and driven back *through* the conservatory to dinner with the Duke. (Meta borrowed a dress, Elizabeth kept her grey carmelite, and black moiré.) The local MP was there, and Sir Joseph and Lady Paxton, who lived in the grounds, seemed somehow to be acting as hosts. Dinner was followed by a concert in the orangery from the private band. The Duke was deaf, but 'he can hear talking whenever music is going on, so he talked pretty incessantly'.

Elizabeth's impulsive expeditions were usually haphazard and serendipitous. Sometimes, as at Chatsworth, they turned out well, if bizarrely. Sometimes, as in the Isle of Man the previous year, they were disasters. One of the worst, again with Meta, was when they set off for Silverdale without booking lodgings and found everywhere full, or closed for the winter. Grange-over-Sands was full too so on they went to Furness. Next day, in driving rain, they ended up at Seascale on the bleakest stretch of the Cumbrian coast. The howling wind almost (but not quite) drowned the roar of the trains passing within ten yards of the house and Elizabeth told Marianne pathetically that they had to sleep together under piles of shawls with two great hot-water bottles. It was so dreadful that it was funny: 'I don't believe we shall be here long. We do so hate the place.'

Although often flustered by trains and times, Elizabeth liked travelling for its own sake. She never knew what might happen, even on the rumbling horse-drawn omnibus from Altrincham to Knutsford, where she read *Little Dorrit* over the shoulder of the man in front.

'Oh *Polly*! he was such a slow reader, *you*'ll sympathize, Meta won't, my impatience at his *never* getting to the bottom of the page . . . *We* only read the first two chapters, so I never found out who "Little Dorrit" is.' (L373)

When they got to Knutsford and she saw the man full face, 'I recognized Mr Seymour, & was sorry I had not moved' (probably to seize the book out of his hands altogether).

The flurry of journeys in the autumn of 1857 was clearly a device to cheer Meta, and the most successful was in November, when she and Elizabeth stopped at Oxford, on their way to stay with the Ewarts at Broad-Leas. They enjoyed it so much that they stayed again on the way back. Elizabeth was entranced by the beauty of the city in the pale autumn light:

'Any thing more lovely than that morning cannot be conceived, – the beech-leaves lay go den brown on the broad pathway; the leaves on the elms were quite still, except when one yellower than the rest came floating softly down. The Colleges were marked out clearly against the blue sky, and beautiful broad shadows made the lighter portions of the buildings stand out clear in the sunshine. Oh! I shall never forget Oxford.' (L481)

They met the Stanleys, Jowett, Mark Pattison, the Brodies and Matthew Arnold (getting ready for his inaugural lecture as Professor of Poetry). They saw Rossetti's murals at the Oxford Union, heard Arthur Stanley's lecture on 'The Eastern Churches' (which was boring) and explored the back rooms of New College (which were not). In the kitchen they learnt that a Mr Holland (no relation) was having 'all to himself, – stewed eels, minced chicken, beef steak with oyster sauce and College Puddings!' In the muniment rooms, 'in the secret places among the great deed Chests, we came upon a precious dozen of port, – each bottle with a paper-necklace, ticketing it as "very precious". In short it was very interesting, and not a little amusing.' The paper necklace on the port is typical of the joy with which Elizabeth always pounced on the small, odd detail rather than the grandeur of the whole. In 1858, for instance, she read Florence Nightingale's massive, solemn second volume of *Notes on Matters Affecting the Health, Efficiency & Hospital Administration of the British Army*, privately circulated, packed with statistics and tables. She got through it, she claimed, in one sitting between breakfast and lunch and liked it, she said, 'for such numbers of reasons. First, because you know of a varnish which is as good or better than blacklead for grates (only I wonder what it is).'

After Oxford, life telescoped to blacklead, petticoats, menus, flower-beds. Meta was calmer and happier although the news was still bad – 'Lucknow *not* relieved' – but the Indian obsession had ebbed, like a receding tide. Elizabeth had come to find it rather taxing. She had diligently ploughed through Sir John Kaye's books on the East

India Company and Sir John Malcolm's *Government of India* and now promised George Smith she would study Harriet Martineau deeply:

'Indeed we, as a family, are going through a whole course of Indian literature – Kaye & Malcolm to wit; but I'm afraid I read it for duty's sake, without taking as much interest as I ought to do, in all the out-of-the-way names & places, none of which give me any distinct idea.' (L483)

Turning from far to near, she donned her full domestic mode, envying Charles Norton's masculine ease and swiftly listing the important questions a woman had to settle in a morning. 'I really am going to write a proper stately letter,' she promised, 'full of news; only I have not got any news, and have a very runaway kind of mind.' If she had a library like his, oh, how she would write! Her letters would outdo Mrs Chapone, her fiction outshine *Rasselas*. 'But you see,' she explained, 'everybody comes to me perpetually':

'Now in this hour since breakfast I have had to decide on the following variety of important questions. Boiled beef – how long to boil? What perennials will do in Manchester smoke, & what colours our garden wants? Length of skirt for a gown? Salary of a nursery governess, & stipulations for a certain quantity of time to be left to herself. – Read letters on the state of Indian army – lent me by a very agreeable neighbour & return them, with a proper note, & as many wise remarks as would come in a hurry. Settle 20 questions of dress for the girls, who are going out for the day; & want to look nice & yet not spoil their gowns with the mud &c &c – See a lady about an MS story of hers, & give her disheartening but very good advice. Arrange about selling two poor cows for one good one, – see purchasers, & show myself up to cattle questions, keep, & prices – and it's not ½ past 10 yet!' (L489–90)

At the end of 1857 Elizabeth was very tired. She relapsed into illness, and Marianne (who blamed it on Meta's engagement) guarded her like a lion and protected her from visitors. But she was also restless. She needed to write, she could not bear to be inactive. Ellen Nussey guessed as much, though Elizabeth demurred: 'No I don't think it is the quiet and repose that tries me, on the contrary I am almost afraid of liking them too well, for I am inclined, either from laziness or depression, to refuse all invitations, and even to go out of the house as little as possible.' She thought her lethargy was a reaction to the summer. Towards the end of the exhibition she had kept thinking, 'Oh, in three weeks, in 3 days, in 3 hours I may give way to sorrowful thinking, the deadly feelings of fatigue.' Time and again she forced herself to be active and talkative, 'when I really *could* hardly do it'. Now she was paying the price. It was just as well, she thought, that she had had a quiet time to right herself in.

Slowly, after the exhibition closed in October, she had gone back to work. The *Life* had exhausted her – when she finished a book, she was convinced, like many authors, that she could never write another – and, as after *Mary Barton* and *Ruth*, she turned to short stories. She was now thinking more carefully about her future career (and although she would not have used the word, a career it certainly was). Over the past few years she had grown more professional, more canny about contracts, more wary of publishers. She was fed up with Dickens and disillusioned with Chapman. Her last exchange with Chapman and Hall over the cheap edition of *Cranford & Lizzie Leigh*, though phrased as a joke, was positively snappish:

'Please to remember that August is drawing very near to a close, and that you have confessed yourself "very much ashamed of the small amount you had to hand over &c" the last time; so that *this* time I am hoping for some improvement in either you or the undiscerning public.' (L406–7)

Also, she asked, what about *The Moorland Cottage*? It was nearly four years since she had heard of the book and after the first run of two thousand copies she was due half profits: 'Anxiously expecting yr answer & 100£ note, & regretting the day I was ever deluded into a "royalty" I remain dear Sir, Yours very truly, E. C. Gaskell.'

By contrast George Smith seemed a model publisher: charming, helpful – and ready to meet her terms. In 1856 he had offered £600 for the copyright of the *Life*. She had replied that while not wanting to seem 'having', as they said in Lancashire, really this book had cost her double the time and anxiety of *North and South*, for which she had received the same sum. On top of that the travelling and research had cost at least £100, although she might recoup that from the American and Tauchnitz profits. Smith promptly offered £800, which she equally promptly accepted. (£100 of this went to a new parish pump for Haworth.) The sales of the revised edition and the cheap editions which followed exceeded both their expectations. In March 1858 she was thrilled to be sent a cheque for another £200. She thought George Smith amazingly generous, especially since she knew what 'annoyance and vexation' the biography had cost him.

Smith had already approached her about taking over the existing copyrights, but apart from a few *Household Words* tales these were all tied up with Chapman and Hall. In fact she did not over-encourage Smith because she was also exploring other avenues. During the writing of the *Life* she had been approached by two American publishers, Ticknor & Fields and Harpers. Supported by Charles Norton, she began to think it might be more profitable to publish first in America, which might also spare her the first blast of reviews. She was pursued by Harpers' London agent, the 'rascally' Sampson Low, and in 1857 she edited (and 'Englished') Maria Cummins's *Mabel Vaughan* with an enthusiastic preface on the role of novels in Anglo-American friendship. In late October she sent Low 'The Doom of the Griffiths' for Harpers. But almost at once she heard rumours about Harpers' finances and asked Charles Norton to investigate.[4] Low had already sent the story to the States; it appeared in *Harper's* in January 1858. In embarrassment, she explained to Norton that she *had* wanted to get it back, but needed the money for the distress in Manchester since 'you Americans' were keeping cotton prices high:

'So don't give me up as a mercenary tricky woman, though I acknowledge I *should* like to out-dodge Mr Sampson Low if ever our wits came in contact. Are you never as wicked as this? I am sure if I were a servant, & suspected and things locked up from me &c, I should not only be dishonest, but a very clever thief.' (L488)

One idea suggested by Charles was that she should write for the *Atlantic*, the new magazine founded by James Russell Lowell. Elizabeth liked the notion (the contributors were very distinguished), but was distinctly put out by a letter insisting she would need to adapt her style for an American audience. She insisted in return

'that I *quite* understand an *Editor's* desire to please his readers, but that I *can* not (it is not *will* not) write at all if I ever think of my readers, & what impression I am making on them. "If they don't like me, they must *lump* me" to use a Lancashire proverb. It is from no despising my

444

readers. I am sure I don't do that, but if I ever let the thought or consciousness of them come between me & my subject I *could* not write at all.' (L503)

That was the end of *that*, at least for the time being.

So matters stood in May 1858. But by then, once again, Meta's engagement had swamped all other thoughts. After the relief of Lucknow the previous November the Indian situation calmed and the Gaskells used their contacts, through Lord Hatherton, to get Captain Hill the command of a regiment of sappers and miners at Dowlaisheram, where a huge irrigation project was under way. In January Marianne told Charles Norton that Hill 'seemed quietly settled down at Dowlaisheram and is making great improvements in the Station, from building a Roman Catholic Chapel, like the Church at Ambleside, to a billiard room like a Swiss chalet'.[5] Hardly 'quiet'. The Captain was flamboyant and ambitious; he hoped to go on from India to China. He wrote weekly to Meta and endeared himself to her mother by sending little presents to Hearn. His pay was good and Elizabeth told Ellen Nussey that as far as money was concerned their affairs were progressing well. But, she added, 'Mr Gaskell never names his name!'

William may have been suspicious of the glamorous officer. In early 1858, while staying with Captain Hill's sisters in Kent, Meta heard a rumour which disturbed her. Neither the sisters, nor outsiders, took it seriously: 'untruthfulness to a *small* degree in regard to money matters' according to Fanny Wedgwood.[6] Meta immediately wrote to India for reassurance. Weeks went by and Charles did not answer.

It was unfortunate that at Meta's lowest point Snow and Effie Wedgwood came to stay. Snow, cut off, as she herself acknowledged, by her almost total deafness, tended to magnify every drama and dispute; her Darwin aunts accused her of extreme over-reaction. She treated her women friends with violent affection and equally violent rejection, and now fixed her attentions on Meta, telling her confidante, Effie: 'I have gone so very near the precipice with Meta since you went, but I don't think I shall plunge in – not for fear of any bristling from *her*, but a prudential view to the future.'[7] Meta was vulnerable and already strongly attached to Snow, having written to her in January pleading forgiveness for her over-enthusiastic response to Snow's first novel, *The Old Debt*: 'I will not be thrown off – Snow – you *shan't* do it – I shall stick to you.'[8] Snow was convinced that Meta was oppressed

445

by her mother, that Elizabeth 'hated' Manchester and that her own mother, Fanny, 'hated' Elizabeth. Such undercurrents were dangerously unsettling when Meta was feeling so disillusioned with Charles Hill.

By May she began to feel she should call off the marriage, but must wait until Charles replied. She was ill and desperately unhappy. At the beginning of August she wrote to his sisters, who calmly replied that *they* had heard regularly by each mail: he was quite well, but complained of Meta's lack of confidence 'and said no marriage could be happy where the wife did not implicitly trust the husband'. Meta waited for two more Indian mails. Then she plucked up her courage and wrote to Charles's elder brother, Captain Dudley Hill, who said she was more than justified in breaking the engagement. When Fanny Wedgwood was staying with the Scotts in mid-August, she called at the Gaskells', to find Elizabeth in bed with back-pain and the house in disarray, 'and you know her constant attention to tidyness and comfort under all circumstances'. Elizabeth immediately told Fanny that the engagement was over: 'she spoke much of course of the intense relief that it was at an end . . . but that Meta still whenever they were alone was balancing whether she had done right in breaking her promise'. The girls came in: Meta looked sad and was silent and Marianne constrained. Even Flossy and Julia were silent and mouselike – but 'what a little beauty Flossy is'.[9]

That was the last of Captain Hill. In 1860 they heard that he was coming to England for six months to marry Matilda Wilson, daughter of the Finance Secretary to India. Meta hastily rearranged a visit to the Wedgwoods to avoid any chance of seeing him in London. In the event the marriage to Matilda was also called off when rumours reached the family, and once again Hill refused to reply to the charges against him. Meta was proved right in taking matters seriously: Matilda's brother-in-law, the economist Walter Bagehot, referred to '*both* pecuniary laxity and *systematic* profligacy' in connection with Hill, and another correspondent of the Wilsons mentioned 'amours and natural children', but said that 'the real cause of his unpopularity is gambling and running away without paying'.[10]

Meta did her best to forget Charles Hill, but it took her a long time to recover. The fire and verve went out of her and in the next two years she was often ill and tearful. She plunged fervently into good works: charities, ragged schools, teaching their servant Elliott to read.

Elizabeth admired her dedication, but was worried none the less, explaining in March 1859: 'She has gone back a year or two into her childhood, although professing to feel "very old" at twenty two Febry 5th, and declining to be called a *"young* woman", saying she is "middle aged".'

In March 1859 Snow, in callous mood, told Effie that she had just had a letter from Meta 'which she tells me in her own silly way is for "me & me only". It began: 'Not even you, Snow, can imagine what I have endured in the last year.'

'She says she is quite determined of one thing, *never, never, never* to enter into a second engagement – hohoho we know how much that means. What will you bet she ceases to be Meta Gaskell in a couple of years . . . It was a clever piece of second sight of yours that it would come to nothing.'[11]

But Meta never married. In future years, sneered at by Snow, she turned her passionate devotion on the more gentle Wedgwood sister, her 'own, dearest, darling, darling Effie'.[12] She was a gifted artist, a friend of Ruskin and Holman Hunt; a talented musician; a promising writer who had contributed a story, 'Helena Mathewson', to *Household Words* in 1857, but she would have no independent career. Her life was given to social and educational work in Manchester.

In September 1858, since Meta was still listless and languid, 'Mr Gaskell thought that complete and entire change of scene would be the best for her.' William's authority was useful, as Elizabeth had thought so all summer; she never entirely forgave herself for her blindness to Captain Hill's character and was stricken by Meta's suffering and the thought of the 'public-talking' that she had to hear. In May both she and Meta had been ordered 'tonics' and 'change of air', but they did not like to separate and relied on the practical Marianne to cheer them. They were going to Silverdale, but Elizabeth told Norton:

'If I can muster up enough money (but you see I am very poor, what with doctor's bills, half-got Indian outfit, inability to write, for want of health –) I would try & persuade Mr Gaskell, to take us three abroad, after we come back from Silverdale, and leave us (when the children would be settled at school) for a few weeks somewhere, – Rhine, Avranches, Normandy – &c &c. But Mr Gaskell dreads foreign diet like poison.' (L506)

447

If William's digestion prevented him, she would take the girls herself. And she would get the money. Quickly, and rather carelessly, she started *My Lady Ludlow* for *Household Words*.[13] The first episode appeared in June. While William tramped off for a walking tour with his brother Sam, Elizabeth wrote on in the tower at Lindeth Farm. Writing too could be an escape, and her story took her mind away from the present to the past. At the time she was helping Henry Green with his book on Knutsford history, and this, plus concern for her daughters may have led her to think of her own girlhood: although the story is set before she was born, she drew on memories of Avonbank and Warwickshire for Lady Ludlow's house, and of Knutsford for the Cranfordian story of eccentric, kind, sharp-tongued Miss Galindo.

If her writing had ever made Elizabeth feel guilty or seemed a distraction from motherly duties, it could also be a way of expressing her love, of bringing Meta back to happiness. She got her money for *My Lady Ludlow*. In fact she got it three times over. First from Dickens, then from Sampson Low, then from George Smith. Low published it as the first volume of the collection *Round the Sofa* the following year (the second volume contained 'An Accursed Race', 'The Doom of the Griffiths', 'Half a Lifetime Ago', 'The Poor Clare' and a new story, 'The Half-brothers'). In February 1859 Elizabeth warned Anne Robson:

'You will be seeing a book of mine advertized; but don't be diddled about it; it is only a REpublication of H W stories; I have a rascally publisher this time (Sampson Low, who publishes Mrs Stowe's books,) & he is trying to pass it off as new. I sold the right of republication to him in a hurry to get 100£ to take Meta abroad out of the clatter of tongues consequent on her breaking off her engagement.' (L530–1)

Smith, Elder also published the same set of stories that year as *My Lady Ludlow and Other Tales* and, to her fury, Harpers brought out a pirated edition of *My Lady Ludlow* in America, from which she earned nothing. She swore to have no more to do with them – though she later changed her mind.[14]

Once the cash was ensured, the trip was planned. They would go to the Belgian towns and the Rhine, with a month for sketching in Heidelberg. Meanwhile Silverdale was a calming retreat, although she described it to Frederick Furnivall as 'a charming primitive desert (butcher 15 miles off &c)'. They stayed there for six weeks, with Annie Austin as a friend for Meta, and were determined to 'all get as strong as horses'. Elizabeth described it graphically to Norton:

'We live in a queer pretty crampy house, at the back of a great farm house. *Our* house is built round a square court, – Stay. We have all that is shaded [here she draws a plan], the rectangular piece is *two* stories high, the little bit by the lane one story, said little bit being kitchen & servants' bed rooms; the houses [*sic*] is covered with roses, and great white virgin-sceptred lilies, & sweetbrier bushes grow in the small flagged square court, across which we merrily call for "hot water", "more potatoes" &c in very primitive fashion to the kitchen. It is well for our dinner when it does not rain, otherwise what is meant to be hot has to be carried carefully under an umbrella, if our visitors are *very* particular people.' (L504)

In the sandy soil around, she added, heathers and delicate wildflowers grew and hedgehogs and glow-worms abounded.

By now her fancy was flying freely. In the garden, she said, was an old square tower or ' "Peel" – a remnant of the Border towers'. In fact, as she well knew, this folly (where she wrote *Ruth*) was not even a century old. Silverdale was acquiring a fictional feel:

'I have had to dine 15 people, as hungry as hounds, on shrimps & bread & butter, – & when they asked for more had to tell them there was no bread nearer than Milnthorpe 6 miles off, and they had to come down to oat-cake, & be thankful!'

She told Norton of the view across the treacherous sands, and the guide who blew a ram's horn on foggy nights. In another letter she told him how their kitchen was filled by local boys and girls, a dwarf child (plus tame jackdaw) and three children of a drowned fisherman (one with a tame magpie); the birds sat on the children's heads, 'occasionally giving a plug or a dig into the thick curly hair, in a manner which I should not have liked, but it did not seem to disturb the appetites of the owners. It was very funny, & picturesque in the old kitchen here.' Even if the weather was wet, it was 'free & sweet-blowing, pattering rain', not like Manchester's 'sullen down falling inky drops'. Silverdale was a place of stories. Life, said Elizabeth, seemed simple compared with a great large town.

*

Following her escapist urge, at the end of September Elizabeth, with Marianne, Meta and (for the first time) Flossy, crossed the Channel. After three weeks Marianne returned to England and the remaining trio settled down in Heidelberg.

They already had several friends there, including Chevalier Bunsen and the family of Robert Mohl (Julius's brother), and to begin with they took rooms in the Prinz Carl Hotel, where Parthe Nightingale, now Lady Verney, was also staying. In 1855 Parthe had been morose about marriage. *North and South* was all very well, she thought, but Margaret would never be happy. Thornton was too old to mould and his mother would never forgive her for usurping her place and putting the mill in her debt. And anyway, she continued glumly, 'when do one's friends' marriages satisfy one? They are the most melancholy things generally one goes through.'[15] In June, however, Parthe herself had married. Her husband was Sir Harry Verney, a striking aristocrat of fifty-six, a Liberal MP and fervent Evangelical and so tall and handsome 'that people turned to look after him in the street as if he were a visitant from another world'.[16] Yet even here Parthe came second to her sister: Harry had been rejected by Flo the year before. From time to time in Elizabeth's letters from Germany we hear of him diligently dashing off to 'the Camp', anxious to tell Miss Nightingale how the men are managed '*in tents*' in Germany.

The Gaskells also made new acquaintances. Some were nice, like Franz von Schmidt, who told them about life in Hungary. Others were not, like M. Plarr: 'Oh, he is so tiresome and egotistical. We did nothing but talk of his plan for the "Triangulization of the Holy Land", whatever that may mean, – and staid till past 10, talking of nothing but that, & the geography of the Bible; to me too who know nothing about geography.'

In such varied company Meta recovered her spirits and the trip seemed worthwhile. But Elizabeth worried about money. The bills at the Prinz Carl came to a third more than her budget: 'this dispirits me, for extras *will* be required, let alone washing etc, etc.' On their second day

'Flossie & I were left in our bedroom counting up our money and doing our accounts; when loe & behold Mr Mohl was shewn in in a swallow tail coat & primrose coloured gloves. Flossie made a rush for

the next room when she was caught by the German washerwoman, &
sent back to have the bill paid.' (L893)

To cut costs they moved into rooms, and ordered meals for one instead
of three. (This was hardly starvation: Elizabeth, always precise about
menus, describes dinner for three as twenty to thirty potatoes in their
jackets, a dish of cabbage, four large sausages, a rib of roast beef and
an enormous rice pudding.)

Heidelberg in October was sociable but not madly gay. Instead of
parties they hired a piano, stayed in, read Boswell aloud and learnt
German. And, as in Rome, Elizabeth acquired a squire – no Charles
Norton this time but a solemn young man of twenty-two, Charles
Bosanquet, the son of a clergyman from Northumberland, related to
the London banking family, who had just graduated from Balliol and
was going to study law. Bosanquet (or Bosie, as they came to call him)
was also staying at the Prinz Carl and they met regularly at the
Bunsens', but he was lonely and asked if he might spend Sunday
afternoons with them, since these were especially dreary in a hotel.
Elizabeth agreed, 'for I saw that he was grave, serious, & ruling
himself by the Scripture law of conduct most strictly'. (She later
described him to Charles Eliot Norton as 'stern as an old Huguenot or
Covenanter'.)

The friendship with Charles Bosanquet casts light on Elizabeth's
faith – so integral to her life that she rarely writes about it – and shows
how Unitarians, despite their rising prominence in British life, were
still a sect 'everywhere spoken against'. Because the Gaskells went to
church on Sundays, Charles assumed they were Anglicans; this made
Meta uncomfortable and Elizabeth agreed to tell him they were not:

'At first he could hardly understand it, – he had evidently had some
unknown horror of Unitarians, – & gravely & seriously asked me "if
we believed in the Bible" – However I told him what I did believe –
(more I suppose what would be called Arian than Humanitarian,) –
and among other things said I had only one antipathy – and that was to
the Calvinistic or Low Church creed.' (L648)

The last statement was tactless, to put it mildly, since his father and all
his friends were Evangelicals. The stunned Charles set out to explain
their principal beliefs, all the time getting over the "shock" of coming
in contact for the first time with Unitarians'.

They did not know if he would ever appear again, but he did, coming twice a day to bring their English newspaper and find out their plans. Gradually they came to feel that his very gravity and piety were doing them good, especially Meta, 'bringing back the faith in *man*kind' which Captain Hill had shaken. ('Mind! there was no suspicion of "love" on either side,' added Elizabeth quickly.) The only drawback was his total lack of humour, which, she confessed, '*is a want*'. Her own faith did not rule out frivolity: she never felt the importance of being earnest. One day, after a trip to Mannheim with Flossy, she had a migraine and went to a confectioner's shop. There was no coffee, no cake, but she did get something for the headaches, mysteriously poured into a small liqueur glass: 'I drank it, – and lo! if it was not rum pure, it was *rum & peppermint*.' Flossy backed off, swearing she smelt like a cross between a pub and an apothecary, and on they went to the station, settling down to study Hendschel's *Telegraph* (the German Bradshaw):

'when lo & behold, Flossy whispered to me, me, smelling of rum – that Mr Bosanquet had come in! I tucked my head down over my book, & told F E. to take no notice; but he drew nearer & nearer, pretending to look at the affiches on the walls, till at last he came close, & said "Mrs G. can I assist you in making out yr train" – so I had to look up, & be civil, & let him take my (second) class tickets (whereupon he said it was thoroughly sensible, & I said nothing because of the rum, –).' (L519)

Charles turned a blind eye to the rum, and was so impressed by their theological conversations (and, when he came to Manchester, by William's sermons) that the following year he confided to Katie Winkworth 'his intense wish to enlighten "his friends" on the subject of Unitarianism'. His parents, however, were aghast at this flirtation with Dissent. They grudgingly gave him permission to visit Plymouth Grove, his father advising him 'to have no *doctrinal* (as distinct from *religious*) conversation'. There was a slight thaw – his stepmother sent a charming note and a present of game – but when the possibility arose of a meeting in London the frost set in again. Bosie appeared on the doorstep at Ashbourne where the Gaskells were staying *en route* for the capital, '& with EXTREME pain and awkwardness' explained that his father and mother '*do not wish to make any new acquaintance*', on

452

the grounds that his father was deaf and could not cope with new people:

'I cd hardly believe my ears, & Marianne & Meta would *not* believe it when I repeated it, – so the next day I said "Did I understand you rightly when I believed you said &c." – he looked miserable, but said *Yes*.' (L650)

Still, she was fond of Bosie, despite his parents, and they continued to meet and correspond. The friendship was one of the lasting fruits of this Heidelberg autumn.

Elizabeth had originally planned to move on from Heidelberg to Dresden. Already short of cash, she dashed off two stories for Dickens ('Right at Last' and 'The Manchester Marriage'), '& asked for immediate payment, to gratify this wish'.[17] On 4 November Ida Mohl wrote to her aunt in Paris: 'Mme Gaskell écrit quelque chose pour le Christmas number de Household Words – je ne sais que c'est – elle est très occupée – il faut que ce soit fini demain.'[18] Dickens turned up trumps and sent £40, which included an advance on a third story to be written when she liked, an act of generosity (or calculation) that placed a burden on Elizabeth for the next four years. In the end the intense cold scotched their Dresden plans anyway and they stayed put in Heidelberg for nine weeks, joined by Meta's friend Louey Jackson. By the time they left they knew nearly everybody in the town, 'from the man-milliner, who offered to drive us to his "Chasse" in the Black Forest, to Bunsen, – from Homrath the old Ferryman to the two English clergyman [*sic*] &c &c, such a good-bying as we had!' When they arrived home just before Christmas, she had been absent from Manchester – at Silverdale and abroad – for over six months.

Gaskell's letters from her German pension are sharp, pungent, story-filled: Sir Harry and his tents, M. Plarr's Triangulation, Robert Mohl's primrose gloves, Bosie and the rum. But within three months the German winter, like the Roman spring, had become idealized in memory, wonderful simply because so different. Even the cold had an *un*-Manchester quality:

'then came the most lovely poetical *wintry* November; clear deep blue sky, – white snow not very deep, except where it had drifted into glittering heaps, – icicles, a foot long, hanging on fountain & well, – trees encased in glittering ice – & weighed down with their own beauty, streets – walks – clear & clean – & the high peaked house tops so beautiful.' (L539)

In March 1859 she read in *The Times* that Tottie Fox, who had gone out to Rome the previous autumn, had married a 28-year-old artist, William Lee Bridell. She wrote at once to W. J. Fox: 'Never mind the House of Commons: it can keep – but my, our, curiosity CAN'T . . . Whole love story &c., &c., &c. Write for 26 hours consecutively, and you can't write enough.' Her letter crossed with one from Tottie, explaining that she had married suddenly and since Fox could not give her away, Robert Browning had taken his place and the Brownings had held a champagne supper to celebrate. She and her husband would return to England that summer, but for the moment had rooms in the Piazza Barberini, like the Storys. Elizabeth replied with delight, explaining how the news had spread like wildfire round the house and how she had dreamt for two nights of Tottie and her husband at Albano, in the gardens of the Villa Medici: 'Fancy your meeting your *fate* at Rome.'

She gave Tottie news of her family. Marianne was in Liverpool, staying with Henry Arthur Bright: 'She is very well and pretty jolly. *Only* Tottie, she never reads or settles to anything – but generally does the practical and polite and elder daughter things in the house. But I wish she would take up some steady employment and settle to it.' Meta was immersed in Greek and social work. Flossy was at a school in Knutsford run by the Green girls and Julia (nearly as tall as Flossy now) was at Rosa Mitchell's day school, 'very spirited and wilful, more like Meta in her naughty days than anything else'.

It seemed to Elizabeth that life had fallen into patterns which showed little sign of change. Earlier that year William had been offered the most senior Unitarian post in Britain, minister of Essex Street Chapel, London. He was 'urged and re-urged':

'But he declined and wisely and rightly I think. He could never get in London the influence and good he has here; and he is too old to be taken up by the roots and transplanted merely for an extra hundred or so a year. So he stays in X St and the people are very much pleased.' (L544)

He would have a new assistant and perhaps a longer summer holiday next year: 'So much for that.'

William had been at Cross Street for thirty years, since 1828, and would remain there for thirty more, until his death in 1888. In the spring of 1859 it was clear that the Gaskells were committed to Manchester, however much Elizabeth pined to get away. Since she returned from Germany, life had been quiet. She was touched by self-pity: 'I go on much as usual; swallowed up by small household cares: never feeling well in Manchester, and always longing for the country.'

William seemed reluctant to budge at all, let alone change jobs. He liked his routine: regular holidays with the Potters in Scotland, walking trips with Sam, visits to family and friends. Elizabeth, so restless herself, decided that 'he perpetually *wants* change and as perpetually rebels against it; I do believe he does like Manchester better than any other place in the world; and his study the best place in Manchester'. Recently his health had been poor and she felt that after so many years of hard work he *must* need a really long break. Even then she feared he would spend it in his study, 'out of which room by his own free will he would never stir'.

Elizabeth stirred, of course, but in 1859 money was tight. They thought of Paris and for once she advised restraint, feeling very proud of her new virtue: '*my* prudence (I have set up prudence, just as some people set up a carriage, and am *quite* as surprised at my new position as they are –) Well!' That year they stayed in Britain, visiting Louey Jackson in Canterbury, Frederick Holland at Ashbourne, staying with the Wedgwoods and spending three weeks in London in June. London was desperately hot, but Elizabeth enjoyed it, as always. Meta's art had drawn them both into a friendship with Ruskin and the Pre-Raphaelite painters. They saw Holman Hunt and 'got to know Rossetti pretty well', visiting his studio three times and meeting him socially. At parties she had a good deal of talk with him,

'always excepting the times when ladies with beautiful hair came in when he was like the cat that turned into a lady, who jumped out of bed and ran after a mouse. It did not signify what we were talking about or how agreeable I was; if a particular kind of reddish brown, crêpe wavy hair came in, he was away in a moment struggling for an introduction to the owner of said head of hair. He is not as mad as a March hare, but hair-mad.' (L580)

(Despite her lack of red hair, Rossetti adored Mrs Gaskell's vivacity and sent her lengthy letters about his new translations of Dante.)[19]

From London they went north. That summer Elizabeth chose Stevenson rather than Holland territory. Charles Bosanquet had made her think of the north-east: Flamborough (but the rooms were all full), Whitby '(not the town itself – we want something more primitive, cheaper and wilder –)', North Berwick, the Galloway coast, St Andrews. In March, after reading *Domestic Annals of Scotland* by Robert Chambers, whom she had met in Edinburgh in 1855, she had written to him saying that his book had warmed up her Scottish blood and she wanted her girls to know Scotland. Could he help? She was looking for somewhere about two hours by rail from Edinburgh, with wild sea, wild rocks, bracing air and 'pretty *sketchable* inland scenery':

'Indifferent to carpets, and such like luxuries.

Not indifferent to cleanliness and good air.

Price moderate; i.e. I should like *all* our expenses \ living & boarding/ to come to only about 8£ a week; and we *may* be nine persons part of the time, & are sure to be six.' (L548)

In the end, however, she settled on Auchenchairn, in Kircudbright-shire, on the Solway Firth.

By the time of that Scottish summer Elizabeth was able to face the thought of a new, long work. Cash played its part. She had been surprised that spring by a letter from Sampson Low offering what seemed to her an extraordinary £1,000 for a three-volume novel, and in June she wrote George Smith a 'rather disagreeable letter – disagreeable to write at any rate', telling him of the proposal: 'Now I am afraid I must own, 1,000£, does a little bit tempt me, it is such a great sum; but I do not like publishing with Messrs Lowe for one thing – and moreover *do* like publishing with you.' She knew Smith could not command such a big American sale, but she would far rather have £800 from him than £1,000 from them.

'so I have been weighing and balancing and never answering, till the other day this letter came which I enclose and I suppose I must decide. I have a story partly written. I doubt if it will reach 3 vols; and I have sometimes felt as if I should never dare to face the reviews again. But I should like to work away at it this summer.' (L558)

Smith replied at once. Within a fortnight she told James Fields, who approached her for Ticknor & Fields, that she had an offer of £1,000 from an English publisher, including the US copyright. At the end of that month, settling down in the peace of Auchencairn and thanking George Smith for a parcel of books, she promised:

'Oh! I will so try & write you a good novel; as good as a great nosegay of honeysuckle, just under my nose at present, which smells not only of honeysuckle, but of very good cake into the bargain.' (L563)

In Scotland, as in Silverdale, Elizabeth liked to pretend she was quite in the wilds, giving her address as 'Mr Turnbull's, Auchencairn, *By* (i.e. 22 miles off) Dumfries' and telling everyone that potatoes had to come from Castle Douglas, nine miles away, or that their groceries had missed the Kircudbright steamer so they had no candles and had to go to bed at sunset. The reality was not as wild as she had hoped: the huge, almost landlocked bay was nearly always dry and although there was a mountain behind with a 'rocky, heathery, ferny glen', little pools and birch trees, the path towards it was guarded by an enormous bull. They spent most of their time in the field between the house and the beach, 'which had a mossy bank on one side, with great beautiful trees, making armchairs of their roots'. Here they basked in the sun, 'often thinking we were reading or sewing, but generally finding out at the end that it had been a mistake on our parts'.

If she was stuck in a meadow, she could make up for it by the romantic associations of the district. The house itself

'had once belonged to a smuggler, in the palmy days of smuggling, close to all the scenery of Guy Mannering, and within a mile of the Maxwells of Orchardston, an ancestor of whom was the lost heir. Also it was in the Covenanter's country.' (L581)

The Maxwells of Orchardston were related by marriage to the Thomsons, the family of Elizabeth's stepmother Catherine.[20] She had met them when she stayed with her stepsister in Dunoon and had since seen Lady Matilda Maxwell in London; it may well have been they who found her this house in Walter Scott country, where she lazed on the mossy bank and began to think of her next novel. And it was through them, in 1855, that she had met William Scoresby, who was not only the vicar of Bradford, sparring-partner of Patrick Brontë and provider of rich Haworth anecdotes, but a former whaling captain and author of the wonderfully detailed work *An Account of the Arctic Regions, with a History and Description of the Northern Whale-Fishery.*[21]

Were these memories revived when she visited Orchardston? In the late autumn of 1859, ostensibly for Julia's health, Elizabeth took another sudden holiday. She went to Whitby, the small Yorkshire port which was Dr Scoresby's native town – and would be the setting for her next novel, *Sylvia's Lovers*.

22

Men, Women, Language and Power

The mid-1850s were dominated by the writing of *The Life of Charlotte Brontë*, but what looks like a great gap between Elizabeth Gaskell's novels – eight years from *North and South* to *Sylvia's Lovers* – was in fact a period rich in fiction. It was a time of stories, realistic and fantastic – 'The Poor Clare', *My Lady Ludlow*, 'Lois the Witch', 'The Grey Woman' and many more – in which she battled with disturbing questions of gender, faith, authority, power and pain. It was a time too when she pondered on the link between writing and the morality of private life, not only in connection with Charlotte Brontë but – more intensely still – in relation to her other great contemporary, George Eliot.

In a new wave of energy in late 1859 Elizabeth worked on several things at once. Two days before Christmas she wrote to Smith, who was scouting for his new *Cornhill Magazine*: 'I have three things begun (very bad management I know: but there are excuses for all things if you know them)'. The first was a long story, begun in mid-1857, which had now crept up to 120 pages, which she thought *'not good enough for the C.M.* – I am the best judge of that, please, – but might be good enough for *H.W.*' (This was 'A Dark Night's Work', which did not appear until 1863.) The second was a story of only forty pages: 'Begun and I think good.'¹ The third was her new novel: 'Now tell me please goodly and truly what you would like me to do.'

The day after Boxing Day she had her answer. She would send the shortest tale to the *Cornhill* in a fortnight – the magical 'Curious if True' – and finish the novel by September (wishful thinking). She was corresponding with Smith because the *Cornhill*'s editor, Thackeray, left the commissioning to his publisher, but she was unwilling, anyway, to come under the domination of another strong male editor. Her relationship with Dickens, always simmering, had recently boiled over in professional anger and private disapproval. In 1858 *My Lady Ludlow* had caused tension when she once again overran Dickens's word limit. In January 1859 he had published a short piece in the 'Chips' column of *Household Words*, called 'Character Murder', following up on one of the anecdotes in Gaskell's 'Disappearances' of 1851.[2] Elizabeth felt she had been misrepresented and wrote angrily to Wills, receiving a curt, noncommittal reply.

She was also upset by Dickens's separation from his wife and the rumours about his relationship with the young actress Ellen Ternan. He had issued wild press statements, and turned on old friends who interceded on Catherine's behalf, including the co-publishers of *Household Words*: in March 1859 Elizabeth received a circular announcing his intention of setting up a new journal. Wanting to detach herself, she offered to repay whatever she owed from her Heidelberg debt. But she feared Dickens would want her name on the list of contributors, as he 'happens to be extremely unpopular just now', owing to the publicity – fanned by himself – given to his domestic affairs. She told all this to Charles Norton, because by then she had embarked on 'a longish story', with the 'very weak vain little hope' that it might find a home in the *Atlantic*. The Boston journal would have been the right place if the story was 'Lois the Witch', set in New England, but, she lamented, 'I *know* it is fated to go to this new Dickensey periodical, & I do so hope to escape it.' She was right: 'Lois' ran in the new journal, *All the Year Round*, in October 1859. Later, relenting a little, she sent her dramatic dialect tale 'The Crooked Branch', which Dickens renamed 'The Ghost in the Garden Room', for the Extra Christmas Number.[3]

The new *Cornhill*, a monthly which would give her more space and more time, should have been a relief, but here too there were problems. Elizabeth had known Thackeray on and off for ten years, but had never felt at ease with him. First she took umbrage when he did not reply to a letter from their mutual friends, the Storys, suggesting that Meta and Annie Thackeray should meet (in the end they became lifelong friends). Worse, he did not answer her note about Charlotte's death, nor, she thought (wrongly), had he written to Patrick Brontë. For his part, Thackeray was mortified at the way she represented Charlotte's views of him in the *Life*.[4]

When Smith asked her to write for the *Cornhill*, he was astonished at her hesitation. She explained the tangled history and her belief that

'somehow or another my *luck* is against me in any intercourse with him, & being half-Scotch I have a right to be very superstitious; & I have my lucky & unlucky days, & lucky & unlucky people, – and my only feeling about not doing anything you ask me for the Magazine is because I don't think Thackeray would ever quite like it, & yet you know it would be under his supervision.' (L576)

She was sure that somewhere he had 'a noble & warm self, – only *I* can't get near it'. She promised to do her best, for the sake of Smith's kindness '(only I know he won't like it, & we shall come to grief somehow, –)'. 'Curious if True' appeared, without complaint from Thackeray, in the second number of the *Cornhill* in February 1860.

Elizabeth, a great supporter of new writers, constantly passed on possible *Cornhill* contributions or manuscript novels to Smith. Among her recommendations were Camilla Jenkins's *Cousin Stella*, William Wetmore Story's articles 'Roba di Roma' and Mary Mohl's piece on Mme de Sévigné. Among her warnings was one that Sir James Kay-Shuttleworth, due to have tea with the Smiths, had written a novel, *Scarsdale*: 'sooner or later, take my word for it, you or Mrs Smith will hear the subject gently touched upon'. And in 1858 she introduced him to an acquaintance, Hamilton Aidé, explaining with slight embarrassment that this was really a repayment for kindness shown them in Rome and Paris. All she could vouch for was that Aidé acted beautifully in private theatricals and sang enchantingly: 'you could not transact your business with him in a duett, could you?' Smith had doubts, and when Elizabeth finally read Aidé's *Rita* (in Bentley's Popular Novels series, *not* on the Smith, Elder list), she agreed. Her reason was interesting: 'I don't think it is "corrupting" but it is disagreeable, – a sort of dragging one's petticoats through mud.' It gave her 'a sort of distrust of his previous life'.

The relation of writing to personal life was a recurring theme. Five years earlier, when murmurs spread about Effie Ruskin's liaison with Millais, she was horrified that John Forster attached any blame to Ruskin and wrote a long, unkind letter full of hearsay about Effie (they had been to the same school, although at different times). Her defence of Ruskin is almost desperate: 'I can not bear to think of the dreadful hypocrisy if the man who wrote those books was a bad man.'

A similar note is heard in her letters about George Eliot, whose talent she had spotted at once. In 1857 she had practically ordered Charles Norton to read 'Scenes of Clerical Life', in *Blackwood's*: 'They are a discovery of my own, & I am so proud of them. *Do* read them. I have not a notion who wrote them.' It was in her efforts to find out that she allowed herself to be persuaded that the author was Joseph Liggins. In March 1859, hearing that a new book was due from the same writer, she sent a witty, barefaced request for a copy to John Blackwood. *Adam Bede* arrived by return of post. Thanking Blackwood, she explained that she too had been brought up in Warwickshire and could 'recognise the county in every description of natural scenery'. Next day she told Norton he must read it.

That June Elizabeth wrote directly to 'Dear Mr "Gilbert Elliot" ' (whether the name is a slip or a joke is not clear). In London, she said, she had been paid the greatest compliment of her life by being suspected of writing *Adam Bede*. She had denied it, but since the real author was at such pains to stay hidden, 'it would be very pleasant to blush acquiescence. Will you give me leave?'

'Well! if I had written Amos Barton, Janet's Repentance & Adam Bede I should neither be to have or to hold with pride & delight in myself – so think it is very well I have not. And please to take notice I knew what was coming up above the horizon from the dawn of the first number of Amos Barton in Blackwood. – After all it is a pity so much hearty admiration should go unappropriated through the world. So, although to my friends I am known under the name of Mrs Gaskell, to you I will confess that I *am* the author of Adam Bede, and remain very respectfully & gratefully

Yours
Gilbert Elliot.' (L559)

Within a few weeks she heard to her alarm that this flirtatious letter had probably gone not to a Warwickshire man called Liggins but to the 'strong-minded woman' Miss Evans, who had eloped with G. H. Lewes. Letter after letter rings with dismay. To George Smith: 'Oh dear – and *am* I to believe in Miss Evans?'

'I am *very* sorry, IF it is true . . . Do *you* really believe it? Please say. I do not think you do. It is a noble grand book, whoever wrote it – but

Miss Evans' life taken at the best construction, does so jar against the beautiful book that one cannot help hoping against hope.' (L566)

Frenetic inquiries continued. By October she was convinced; George Eliot's situation was miserable enough, she felt, but she believed there were many excuses: 'the worst is Mr Lewes' character & opinions which were (formerly *at least*) so bad'. (She had distrusted Lewes since before 1854, when she told Bessie Parkes and Barbara Leigh Smith what she had heard of his previous affairs, including the seduction of a young schoolteacher, left unsupported with an illegitimate child.)[5]

Yet despite her dismay, she continued to pester her friends for information. She wrote to Charles Bosanquet from Whitby: 'How could you find it in your heart to be so curt about Madam Adam?' Their evenings were long and gossip was scarce:

'send us PLEASE a long account of what she is like &c &c &c &c, – eyes nose mouth, *dress* &c for *facts* and then – if you would – your impression of her, – which we won't tell anybody. *How came she to like Mr Lewes so much?* I know he has his good points but somehow he is so soiled for a woman like her to fancy.' (L587)

But she told Harriet Martineau that 'after all one does get into a desponding state of mind about writing at all, after "Adam Bede" and "Janet's Repentance" choose (as the Lancashire people say,) whoever wrote them'. She would rather they had not been written by Miss Evans, 'but justice should be done to all; & after all the writing such a book should raise her in every one's opinion'. A woman who could write thus must have 'possibilities of greatness & goodness . . . I never can express myself metaphysically.'

Soon she wrote, straightforwardly and simply, to George Eliot herself, saying that since she had heard she was the author, she had read the books again, and wanted to tell her once more 'how earnestly, fully and humbly I admire them. I never read anything so complete, and beautiful in fiction, in my whole life before.' She apologized for her belief in Liggins, adding with tactless honesty: 'I should not be quite true in my ending, if I did not say before I concluded that I wish you *were* Mrs Lewes. However that can't be helped, as far as I can see, and one must not judge others.'

George Eliot had always admired Gaskell's writing. In 1856 she had ranked her with Harriet Martineau and Currer Bell, as one whose work stood out in contrast to the 'Silly Novels by Lady Novelists', and who suffered from male critics as a result. She had been hurt by Gaskell's support of Liggins and when she received this letter, she replied the same day. Her response was moving and dignified:

'My dear Madam
Only yesterday I was wondering that artists, knowing each other's pains so well, did not help each other more, and, as usual, when I have been talking complainingly or suspiciously, something has come which serves me as a reproof. That "something" is your letter, which has brought me the only sort of help I care to have – an assurance of fellow-feeling, of thorough truthful recognition from one of the minds which are capable of judging as well as being moved. *You* know, without my telling you, how much the help is heightened by its coming to me afresh, now that I have ceased to be a mystery and am known as a mere daylight fact. I shall always love to think that one woman wrote to another such sweet encouraging words – still more to think that you were the writer and I the receiver.'[6]

She had hoped, Eliot went on, that if her books did turn out to be worth something, Mrs Gaskell would read them, because she was conscious that her own feeling 'towards Life and Art' had 'some affinity with the feeling which had inspired "Cranford" and the earlier chapters of "Mary Barton".' She had read *Cranford* while writing the *Scenes*, and had turned back to *Mary Barton* on a dim, misty day on the Rhine while working on *Adam Bede*. She told her this, she said, to show what value her letter had: 'And I cannot believe such details are indifferent to you . . . I fancy, as long as we live, we all need to know as much as we can of the good our life has been to others.' Then she signed herself firmly, 'Ever, my dear Madam, Yours with high regard, Marian Evans Lewes'.

George Eliot and Elizabeth Gaskell would never meet, but these letters endure as a moment of profound recognition. By the end of the year Elizabeth confessed to Smith how she valued the woman she saw in the work, whatever her circumstances:

'Do you know I can't help liking her, – *because* she wrote those books. Yes I do! I *have* tried to be moral, & dislike her & dislike her books – but it won't do. There is not a wrong word, or a wrong thought in them, I do believe, – and though I should have been more "comfortable" for some indefinable reason, if a *man* had written them instead of a *woman*, yet I think the author must be a noble creature; and I shut my eyes to the awkward blot in her life.' (L594)

In the following spring she would shower him with excited thanks: 'Oh Mr Smith! your grandfather was a brick and your grandmother an angel . . . only think of having the Mill on the Floss the second day of publication, & of my very own.'

Why should Elizabeth have worried so about George Eliot? The answer, I think, lies in Eliot's words about their similar conception of 'Life and Art'.

One clue can be found in the writers they both admired: Ruskin, Scott, Wordsworth. When Eliot reviewed *Modern Painters*, III, in April 1856 (the one book that Gaskell said she would choose to solace exile or imprisonment), she admitted she would forgive Ruskin all his egotism and absurdity simply because he appreciated Scott's accuracy of place, period and local speech.[7] To George Eliot, Ruskin, like Scott, taught the truth of '*realism*', that truth and beauty were to be gained 'by a humble and faithful study of nature, and not by substituting vague forms, bred by imagination on the mists of feeling, in place of definite, substantial, reality'. Art of this kind, Eliot felt, could work change in the world: 'the thorough acceptance of this doctrine would remould our life . . . It is not enough simply to teach truth; that may be done, as we all know, to empty walls, and within the covers of unsaleable books; we want it to be so taught as to compel men's attention and sympathy.'[8] That 'we' would include Elizabeth Gaskell. The lesson of education through sympathy was one of the reasons why Elizabeth so liked 'Janet's Repentance', a story which celebrates the 'blessed influence of one soul upon another! Not calculable by algebra, not deducible by logic.' Through personal relationships or erotic love, Eliot suggests, ideas, which so often remain 'poor ghosts', are made flesh. 'Then their presence is a power, then they shake us like a passion, and we are drawn after them, as flame is to flame.'

Gaskell also admired 'Janet's Repentance' because it deals so graphically with women's vulnerability – with the problems of drink, of prostitution, of the bullying husband. It is full of anger, yet advocates stoicism. It depicts the solidarity of women and the rescuing power of love. These are themes which Gaskell herself had already explored, and would return to. She liked it too because of its egalitarian imperative, expressing Eliot's belief that through the realistic presentation of the life of the poor 'more is done towards linking the higher classes with the lower, towards obliterating the vulgarity of exclusiveness, than by hundreds of sermons and philosophical dissertations'.[9] This was precisely the aim of *Mary Barton*.

Eliot and Gaskell also stood close in their conviction that effective political change must be gradual, rooted in consciousness rather than imposed by legislation or forced by revolution. And accompanying this historical vision went a shared acceptance of inexorable laws of cause and effect. But here the writers differ, at least in their explanations, if not in the way they dramatize the operations of such laws in individual lives – in Ruth Hilton or Maggie Tulliver, John Barton or Mr Bulstrode. Eliot's explanation was primarily secular and specifically positivist. Gaskell's was primarily theological and specifically Unitarian, deriving from the deterministic notion of a divinely ordered scheme that incorporated evil as well as good: error and sin produced punishment, virtue reward.

After the 1840s, as she explored deeper into the 'causes of suffering' probed in *Mary Barton*, Gaskell sometimes chafed against the 'justice' of inevitable punishment meted out by an unrelenting God. Her unease is evident in *Ruth*, and in those stories which return to the text 'the sins of the fathers shall be visited upon the children'. She prefers the mercy of Christ to the law of the Father. The merciful message of 'Christ' is also retained, as a mystical idea made flesh, in the fiction of Eliot, the unbeliever. Both writers attempt to 'incarnate' in their characters the power – and intense difficulty – of self-denying love in opposition to stern authority. This, in turn, is related to their common belief in feeling as a guide to truth, and their insistence that priority be given to 'feminine' sympathy as opposed to 'masculine' judgement.

Some of Gaskell's indefinable discomfort that Eliot's books were written by a woman, not a man, may be explained by the sheer power of the mind she detected in them, the quality which made her use the word 'humbly' in her letter. Nothing shows this difference of mind – in terms of power of argument rather than imagination – so clearly as the essays which both women wrote in 1854, prompted by Victor Cousin's book *Madame de Sablé*: George Eliot's 'Woman in France' and Gaskell's 'Company Manners'. Where Eliot, writing in the intellectual, avant-garde *Westminster*, is piercingly analytical, sweeping across the whole field of history and ideas, Gaskell, addressing the family readership of *Household Words*, is personal, free-spinning, anecdotal.

Despite their differences these articles reveal another shared stance, a longing for women to have the intellectual and personal freedom of Mme de Sablé and her kind without losing what both novelists valued as special to their sex: a lightness, a lack of pomposity, an easy imaginative sympathy, above all a *language* of their own. In their memoirs, Eliot suggests, Frenchwomen of the seventeenth and eighteenth centuries, freed from any thought of a literary career, 'wrote what they saw, thought and felt, in their habitual language, without proposing any model to themselves, without any intention to prove that women could write as well as men, without affecting manly views or suppressing womanly ones'.[10]

In 'Woman in France' Eliot went further. After claiming that 'science has no sex' and that the reasoning faculties of men and women, properly used, 'must go through the same process and arrive at the same result', she declares that in art and literature, however, 'which imply the action of the entire being, in which every fibre of the nature is engaged',

'woman has something specific to contribute. Under every imaginable social condition, she will necessarily have a class of sensation and emotions – the maternal ones – which must remain unknown to man.'[11]

The only point on which Gaskell would differ (and one which George Eliot herself would modify in *Silas Marner*) is that she believed the 'maternal emotions' *can* be and are shared by men, and that if they would recognize and admit them, the world might be a different place. But neither Gaskell nor Eliot had an idealized view of women. The final vision they share is a bleaker one. In the fiction of both writers the maternal positive has a dark, sexual negative. If women can be creators, they can also be destroyers – or, more often, the destroyed.

Two of Elizabeth Gaskell's short works, *My Lady Ludlow* (1858) and 'Lois the Witch' (1859), show this polarity between female creativity and victimization very clearly. The former illustrates a gradual growth from patriarchal aristocratic power to a more democratic, outward-looking 'maternal' ethos. The latter shows a rigid religious society, ruled by Puritan elders, destroying itself by inward-looking fanaticism, making women its victims and scapegoats. While *My Lady Ludlow* celebrates the open, sympathetic vision found in the apparently unsystematic detail of women's letters, 'Lois' condemns the male 'texts' and authorities which are so often distorted to justify cruelty. Both stories open in the Warwickshire countryside, the scene of Eliot's and Gaskell's youth, but whereas in *My Lady Ludlow* Gaskell starts from the daily lives of women, in 'Lois' she suggests there is another mode of 'women's writing', moving from the real to the surreal that invades it. This was a voyage Eliot would take a year later, tentatively, in 'The Lifted Veil' (1860), and which would carry her, finally, to the engulfing seas of *Daniel Deronda*.[12]

My Lady Ludlow is the least regarded of Gaskell's longer works.[12] Yet this novella, often criticized for its shapelessness, is far cleverer and more experimental than first appears, as if Gaskell were trying to prove George Eliot's belief, expressed in 'Silly Novels', that women's writing could have

'a precious speciality, lying quite apart from masculine aptitudes and experiences. No educational restrictions can shut women out of the materials of fiction, and there is no species of art so free from rigid requirements. Like crystalline masses, it may take any form, and yet be beautiful – we have only to pour in the right elements – genuine observation, humour and passion.'[13]

My Lady Ludlow creates such a feminine fiction. It is flexible and detailed, and both its argument and its form arise naturally from the memories and daily lives of particular women. Formally, the experiment does not altogether work, but it is original and brave. The structure, like that of *Cranford*, has the unstable mobility and focus of memory. Doors open further and further into the past as each person's tale unreels. Even Lady Ludlow's melodramatic account of the fate of two young French aristocrats – which sets the trauma of revolution against the rhythm of gradual change – relies on piecing together the remembrances of different witnesses.

When this story was republished in *Round the Sofa*, where it is presented as the elderly Mrs Dawson's reminiscences, the perspective becomes still more subtle. The invisible female narrator attains personality and the written tale is seen to copy the loose, circling shape of conversational storytelling, of stories within stories. The effect is heightened by juxtaposition with the next piece in the collection, 'An

Accursed Race', a catalogue of persecutions recounted by Mrs Dawson's brother. The brother's contribution is a formal paper 'rather dry in itself' prepared for the Edinburgh Philosophical Society. The sister's narration, by contrast, is far from dry. It has all the variety of reminiscent speech: nostalgic, satiric, tragic and comic by turns. It can even encompass, as an image of the atrophying powers of the aristocracy, an evocative Lamb-like digression on scent, deftly tied, through the mention of a copy of Bacon's 'Essays on Gardens' lying on Lady Ludlow's table, to its own literary pedigree. Gaskell uses these blended modes, which make critics dismiss the piece as hybrid, to write of change, loss and the rebirth of hope. Through the events in a small village she presents a span of social, religious and economic history in which the old order slowly allows in the new.

Both Lady Ludlow and the other principal female character in the story, Miss Galindo, are single women, one a widow, the other a spinster, who care for the daughters of others. Lady Ludlow educates a group of needy young gentlewomen, Miss Galindo adopts the orphaned, illegitimate child of the man she once loved. Their maternal roles extend outwards to the community via Lady Ludlow's feudal responsibilities and Miss Galindo's bossy, well-meaning interference in village life. But when the story opens, Lady Ludlow is found clinging to remnants of a masculine authority, as if that were her true strength. In fact her power is already eroded: her husband has mortgaged Hanbury to cultivate his Scottish estates 'after some new fashion that required capital'; her beloved younger son has drowned at sea; her elder son is absent and will die on the Continent. The Gothic convention of the crumbling mansion and the aristocratic line falling into decay lies behind this tale: lacking an heir, the family has dwindled to a frail old lady with a gold-topped stick, who lives in a house full of relics while her estates fall into neglect. Even the medicines her wards prepare are mere placebos, 'but we were very careful in putting labels on them, which looked very mysterious to those who could not read, and helped the medicine to do its work'. Lady Ludlow's rule is built on the sands of ignorance and habitual submission.

She tries as hard as she can to insulate herself from change, snubbing the Baptist baker who buys land nearby, pretending that Miss Galindo's ward, the illegitimate Bessy, is invisible. Upset by the sermons of the new Evangelical clergyman, Mr Gray, she has the ancient Hanbury family pew glazed in. A window is left open so the service can be heard:

'But if Mr Gray used the word "Sabbath", or spoke in favour of schooling and education, my lady stepped out of her corner, and drew up the window with a decided clang and clash.' (Ch. 1)

A marvellous image, apt and strange, encasing and encapsulating.

No one can stay behind glass for ever: this story is yet another of Gaskell's variations on Snow White and Sleeping Beauty. As in the fairy tales, Lady Ludlow is awakened and brought back into the world by men, principally by the eager, consumptive Mr Gray. (The comic description of Hanbury's sequence of vicars is another nod towards *Scenes of Clerical Life*.) The men in this story effect change not through rational argument but through feeling. Lady Ludlow hotly disputes Gray's passionate objections when a local poacher is imprisoned, but she is piqued enough to seek out the Gregsons' hovel. The dismay she feels in this personal encounter with rural misery drives her to speak out against her fellow-magistrate, defying her peers and distinguishing between justice and 'law': 'Bah! Who makes laws? Such as I, in the House of Lords – such as you, in the House of Commons.'

Other men play their part in her awakening: the steward Mr Horner, with his tender hope of educating young Harry Gregson, the poacher's son; the boisterous, open-speaking Captain James, Lady Ludlow's dead son's friend, who dares to introduce new farming techniques. When these fail, he does even worse – he takes advice from the Dissenting baker from Birmingham with his efficient model farms. Despite Lady Ludlow's disapproval change cannot be balked. By the end Mr Gray has his village school, with Harry Gregson as star pupil, and the illegitimate Bessy, Miss Galindo's protégé, as his fellow-teacher and wife, while Captain James marries the baker's daughter. The farms and the village are, however gently, revolutionized. The final scene, a woman's tea-party, may seem trivial and domestic, but when Lady Ludlow takes her pocket handkerchief and lays it on her lap as a napkin, deliberately copying the baker's wife to save her from ridicule, we recognize a fundamental change – in the person and in the society. Nothing, and everything, has happened.

My Lady Ludlow is far from an unselfconscious effusion: within it even writing itself is suspected and redeemed. Gaskell, of course, makes fun of Lady Ludlow's certainty that literacy is doom:

' "Has your ladyship heard that Harry Gregson has fallen from a tree
and broken his thigh-bone and is like to be a cripple for life?"
"Harry Gregson! that black-eyed lad who read my letter? It all
comes from over-education!" '

Her story of the young aristocrats, Pierre and Virginie, in which a
servant's ability to read indirectly causes their deaths, is designed to
prove the equation, Rousseau + Education = Revolution. As suggested by the deliberately mysterious labels on the salt and water
medicines, literacy threatens because it destroys the *credibility* of the
powerful.

The argument about writing and power extends naturally from class
to gender. Lady Ludlow believes that women should cultivate a fine
old-fashioned hand, but their writing must remain decorative,
personal and social. They should not cross boundaries: when Miss
Galindo acts as a clerk, she sticks her pencil behind her ears and
whistles, in the vain hope that Mr Horner will not notice she is female.
But even she was nearly a writer once. As a girl she had been taught
music by Dr Burney:

' "And his daughter wrote a book and they said she was but a very
young lady, and nothing but a music-master's daughter; so why
should not I try?"
"Well?"
"Well! I got paper and half-a-hundred good pens, a bottle of ink, all
ready – "
"And then – "
"O, it ended in my having nothing to say, when I sat down to write.
But sometimes, when I get hold of a book, I wonder why I let such a
poor reason stop me. It does not others." ' (Ch. 9)

In Lady Ludlow's view it was just as well it did stop her. 'I am
extremely against women usurping men's employments, as they are
very apt to do.' The account of Hanbury's final transformation, and of
that significant tea-party, is given in a letter from Miss Galindo,
apparently artless and inconsequential, mixing births and deaths,
kittens and bulls, marriages and manners. Yet the 'heterogenous mass
of nonsense' (as Henry Holland described Gaskell's own letters)
contains all we need to know. Furthermore it loops back to the
narrator's opening memory of her girlhood: 'letters were letters then;

and we made great prizes of them, and read them and studied them like books'. It seems that Miss Galindo, who thinks she has nothing to say, is an authoress after all.

My Lady Ludlow replaces autocracy with association. It holds violence in its midst, but it is a gentle, rural, wished-for revision of history, deliberately removed from open hostility and suffering. Most of the stories Gaskell wrote in the 1850s and early 1860s reverse the pattern, presenting the threat and the darkness as the dominant force, returning relentlessly to an examination of power and the way it is imposed and accepted, with an almost sado-masochistic emphasis on domination and submission. Rules and ritual codify control. Institutions enforce and maintain it, relying on mystique to compel unquestioning acceptance. This is true of the law (in *My Lady Ludlow*, 'A Crooked Branch' and 'A Dark Night's Work') and of the priesthood (in 'Morton Hall' or 'Lois the Witch'). Behind them lie texts of 'authority' – the Statute Book, the slow-building common-law precedent, the Bible – and both the State and the Church can call on an ultimate sanction: the death of the body, the death of the soul.

Gaskell's critique is both social and personal. At one end of the scale, in 'An Accursed Race', she shows how superstitious prejudice is formalized by State and Church to the point of justifying the genocide of the Cagot race of western France. At the other end she examines the domestic hell of marriage, the lifelong cowing of a daughter. The Cagots were once thought to be lepers; Gaskell never loses her urge to speak, as she had in *Mary Barton*, on behalf of 'the leper, the outcast'.

In these stories women become 'natural' victims of the system their tacit obedience supports. Unless, that is, they have the courage to defy, and even then they may not survive. Like the fairy stories and folk-tales which so often underlie her work, Gaskell's is a fiction full of pain as well as love, annihilation as well as assertion of self. Physical and mental cruelty abound. In her Gothic story, 'The Grey Woman' (1861), a young German girl is married to a deceptively effeminate man, who offers her love and wealth only to entomb her (like Bluebeard) in a castle on the edge of a cliff.[14] Beneath his polite courtesy he is a brigand capable of torturing his victims on a heated iron floor; she learns the truth when he returns suddenly while she is searching his room for a letter – that womanly link with home. Hiding beneath the table, her hand touching that of a corpse flung on the floor, she hears that his first wife has already been murdered because she could not keep silent. Her servant, Amante, helps her escape and they travel by night and hide by day, disguised as man and wife; the husband pursues them, murdering an innocent woman whom he mistakes for his wife and leaving deadly notes promising vengeance. After years in hiding Amante is killed and her mistress finds a final refuge in a bigamous marriage to the gentle doctor who helped her in childbirth. She survives only by breaking the law which entraps her.

The heroine's very docility seals the fate she senses in her approaching marriage:

'I was bewitched – in a dream – a kind of despair. I had got into a net through my own timidity and weakness, and I did not see how to get out of it.'

So altered is she, so grey, that by the end her pursuing husband cannot recognize her. When she tells her story to her daughter in a letter, she gives herself no name, except that of Mother. The 'grey' woman literally embodies female suppression and entrapment – in her own numb, dreamlike state, in her marriage and even in her flight, when Amante hides her under a bridge: 'opening out her great, dark cloak, she covered up every light-coloured speck about us'. Once in safety, terrified to leave her room, she develops an agoraphobic fear of the wider world.

Again and again Gaskell shows women rendered helpless and denied speech. In 'The Crooked Branch' an old couple have to bear witness at the trial of the son who has betrayed and robbed them. The mother, already blind, is meek in the unseen presence 'of those whom she had been taught to respect', but when asked to condemn her son, 'her face worked – her mouth opened two or three times as if to speak – she stretched forth her arms imploringly; but no word came'. That night she dies, stricken by paralysis. Often women are forced to surrender not only their power of speech but their very identity. In 'Morton Hall' the proud Alice Carr is declared insane. In 'Lizzie Leigh' the father un-names his daughter for her sexual sin: 'he declared that henceforth they would have no daughter; that she would be as one dead, and her name never more be named'.

Men's obliteration of women, to the point of silence, torture and death, runs through Gaskell's stories from 'Clopton Hall' to those written in the last years of her life. Even in the gossipy article 'French

Life' (1864) she tells the true story of the Marquise de Ganges (again immured in a castle), who was hounded to death for her property by her husband and his two brothers. The Marquise was offered death by fire, steel or poison and, Gaskell writes, the poison was forced down her throat until 'her skin was blackened by the burning drops that fell upon it, and her mouth was horribly burnt'. Although she fled, dishevelled and in agony, to the women of the village who fought 'like lionesses', she was followed, stabbed repeatedly until the weapon broke in her shoulder and then viciously beaten by the worst of the brothers, the priestly abbé. After her inevitable lingering death, all the women of the town wear mourning.

There are, however, routes to survival – of the spirit if not of the body: the support of other women, servants, friends, mothers, and the shelter of nurturing men. Speech can be regained, authority challenged: Mary Barton speaks out in court in defence of Jem; Jemima challenges her father in defence of Ruth; Ellinor Wilkins braves the lover who abandoned her, now the judge in the case against her old servant; the mother of the Marquise de Ganges writes a pamphlet which brings her daughter's murderers to justice, speaking out for her child's burnt, silenced mouth. Defiance, as well as sympathy, is a central message of Gaskell's writing.

In the darker fiction the current of the past sweeping into the present does not flow gradually, gently, between banks of benign progress as it does in *My Lady Ludlow*. It surges and swirls and is full of menace, carrying the consequences, often literally, of 'the sins of the fathers' – like the murder in 'A Dark Night's Work' or the forgery in 'Right at Last'. Comforting images are overturned: the prodigal son, who is a life-giving figure in *Cranford*, comes back in 'The Crooked Branch' to rob his parents. In 'The Manchester Marriage' the longed-for wandering sailor returns as a dreaded revenant to find his wife peacefully married to another. Knowing that recognition would destroy her life and that of his child, he has no recourse but suicide.

Lives are controlled, Gaskell implies, not only by 'rational' institutions but through irrational structures of emotion. In many of Gaskell's short stories women themselves create misery through the very strength of their feelings, whether it be vengeful jealousy like Faith's in 'Lois the Witch' or possessive love like the servant Victorine's in 'Crowley Castle'. This female chain of consequence is expressed in the witch's curse. The law imposes retribution while the curse cries for pure revenge – in the words of Francis Bacon, 'Nay, rather, vindictive persons live the life of witches; who, as they are mischievous, so end they unfortunate.'[15] True, men can curse, as in the Celtic 'Doom of the Griffiths', but the female witch is the classic embodiment of this terrible power, a different brand of women's language. Gaskell shows that it may be a last response of the powerless, but it is the wrong response, and inevitably rebounds on the innocent. Thus Bridget Fitzgerald in 'The Poor Clare' unwittingly punishes her own granddaughter: before the curse can be lifted, Bridget must immolate herself, joining a silent order of nuns and starving to death, her last act being to nurse the man who harmed her.

The greatest of these dark stories is 'Lois the Witch', in which communal hysteria is suggestively fused with private sexual persecution and jealousy. Lois is the victim of public ignorance and fear of the unknown, but also of men's desire and women's vindictiveness; the heavy powers of Church and law collude with the witch's curse.

History provides the plot – a retelling of the Salem witch-hunt of 1692, with its terrible denouement and repentant coda. It provides models for the characters and details of the action and setting. It even hands down the words of the men involved, statements which stand like tablets of stone in the flight of the text.[16] The third-person narration contains cool authorial interventions reminding readers that they are looking back from an enlightened age to a benighted epoch of superstition and hysteria. In all these ways the story follows the rationalist analysis of witchcraft trials as examples of medical and priestly obscurantism that had engaged Unitarians in the 1830s – an approach evident, for instance, in Gaskell's chief source, *Lectures on Witchcraft* (1831) by Charles Upham, the Unitarian minister in Salem, in William Howitt's popular history of priestcraft (1833) and in Harriet Martineau's lucid article on Salem (1834).

Gaskell had long been fascinated by witch-hunts: she had borrowed Cotton Mather's name for her 1847 *Howitt's* articles and had mentioned the persecuted Lancashire witches in 'The Heart of John Middleton' in 1850, and in June 1856 we find an American correspondent promising to send information on the New England witch trials.[17] It may be that her interest was revived at this time by her friendship with William Wetmore Story and her reading of Nathaniel Hawthorne, both natives of Salem. (Hawthorne's ancestor John Hathorne appears in 'Lois the Witch' as one of the sternest persecutors.) But this story is no documentary. It depicts a cast of mind which might make itself manifest any time, anywhere, clothed in a shape to fit the age. All Gaskell's skills as a writer on the supernatural are employed in making this stalking phantom live: crossing the sea from old England to New England is a voyage from the 'normal' to a fearful psychic landscape.

In 1690 Lois Barclay, a vicar's daughter, comes to New England, obeying her mother's dying wish that she seek out her uncle, a schismatic settled in Salem: 'Solemnly did Lois promise; strictly she kept her word.' Ironically, she keeps her word too in fulfilling her mother's other wish, an unintentional curse: 'Oh Lois, would that thou wert dying with me!' She leaves Barford vicarage, its windows entwined with jessamine and sweet-brier – the 'mother's flowers' familiar from *Ruth* – and she leaves her suitor, Hugh Lucy, who has alarmed her by his impetuous passion. She is poised between mother and men, separated from childhood yet disturbed by the thought of sexual desire. Her inner balance is lost. And when she stands on Boston quay, 'steadying herself on stable land' after the rocking of the ship, she finds the land itself unstable, as full of perils as the sea. A forest encircles the settlement, a piercing wind blows, a sea mist mingles with her tears. She has found an ancient world, not a new: when Captain Holdernesse takes her to Widow Smith's house, she enters a room hung with skins, shells, wampum-beads, sea-birds' eggs, 'more like a museum of natural history' than a parlour.

The talk at once turns to threats to the colony: wild Indians in the woods, so disguised that the trees themselves seem to move; French Papist pirates ravaging the coast; the blood-chilling wail of a woman from the marsh, 'Lord Jesus! Have mercy upon me! Save me from the power of man, O Lord Jesu!' To a Puritan elder these are no natural terrors, but 'spiritual enemies in visible forms, permitted to roam about the waste places of the earth'. Drinking in their fear, 'half-incredulous, half-believing', Lois tells how, when she was four, she was cursed by a drowning witch, her grey hair streaming down her shoulders and her face bloody and black, her eyes glaring with fury. Lois's father, the parson, had not tried to save her,

' "and none shall save thee, when thou art brought up for a witch."
Oh! the words rang in my ears, when I was dropping asleep, for years
after. I used to dream that I was in that pond; that all men hated me
with their eyes because I was a witch.' (Ch. 1)

Immediately, lightly, fatally, Holdernesse jokes that he is sure there are
many young men whom Lois has 'bewitched' in England. Her beauty
is also a curse.

To reach Salem she must travel through encircling forests where fear
grows tall as trees, and the cries of strange birds ring like war-whoops.
This forest of the unknown with its rumours of human sacrifice is the
home of racial and sexual terror, lair of the cunning 'double-headed
snake' which lures white maidens to the tents of Indian men, 'adjuring
faith and race for ever'. Lois arrives unannounced – the mother's
letter, so significant in these stories, has gone astray and the person
who greets her is her cousin Manasseh, 'reading a great folio by the
fading light of day'. Her uncle is dying, she meets hostility and
suspicion from her aunt Grace and her cousins Faith and the 'freakish',
malevolent Prudence and slowly, as she strives to find a place in this
alien home, Manasseh fixes his desire on her. Outwardly sober and
brave, he is inwardly despairing, a man who has attempted suicide,
dreams dreams and sees visions. With his 'dark, fixed eyes, moving so
slowly and heavily, his lank, black hair, his grey coarse skin', he stalks
her like Death itself.

Another current of desire crackles in this pious house, where Grace
and Faith and Prudence sit and spin – Faith's unspoken love for Pastor
Nolan, who has left town after a doctrinal dispute. Excited by the talk
of English Hallowe'en customs (which makes Prudence condemn Lois
as a witch and claim to see the devil at her shoulder), Faith brews love
potions in the kitchen with the Indian servant Nattee. When Nolan
reappears, however, it is Lois who unconsciously 'bewitches' him.

The first half of the story brews a mixture of lust, superstition, racist
fear and religion. Manasseh's trust in God is little different from
Faith's trust in her potions; desire distorts his texts. Months before
Lois came, he claims, he was reading in the 'old godly books':

'I saw no letter of printer's ink marked on the page, but I saw a gold
and ruddy type of some unknown language, the meaning whereof was
whispered unto my soul; it was "Marry Lois! marry Lois!" . . . It is the
Lord's will Lois, and thou canst not escape from it.' (Ch. 2)

Inner and outer landscapes merge as superstition spreads in the winter months and Salem is 'snowed up and left to prey on itself'. Manasseh waits, muttering of 'submission'. At Christmas he tells Lois that in the woods, between sleeping and waking, he saw a spirit offer her two lots, or garments:

'and the colour of the one was white, like a bride's, and the other was black and red, which is, being interpreted, a violent death. And, when thou didst choose the latter, the spirit said unto me, "Come!" and I came, and did as I was bidden. I put it on thee with mine own hands, as it is pre-ordained, if thou wilt not hearken to me and be my wife. And when the black and red dress fell to the ground, thou wert even as a corpse three day old.' (Ch. 2)

This truly horrible, necrophiliac vision presages disaster. When the ice thaws in spring, disturbances begin. Pastor Tappau's children are convulsed and their Indian nurse Hota is tried as a witch. In the shadow of Hota's gallows, Lois carries a letter from Faith to Pastor Nolan, who is troubled by the delirium around him. Touched by her grave innocence, Gaskell says, 'Faith in earthly goodness came over his soul in that instant "and he blessed her unawares".' The allusion to the 'Ancient Mariner', who blesses the 'slimy things' that 'crawl with legs upon the slimy sea', is curiously disturbing, recalling the submerged monster imagery of sex in *Ruth* and *North and South*. It suggests that although Lois is innocent, there is some 'wild' element in women that both attracts and frightens men, some force that links them with dangerous depths, with the untamed and the primitive – with the Indians and the forest. Nolan's blessing, his touch on Lois's shoulder, is interpreted (rightly) by the jealous, watching Faith as an expression of unconscious desire.

At the service which follows Hota's execution, Lois is late and is forced into prominence. Suddenly, in the silence, Manasseh declares his visions of a fainting woman carried by angels to the land of Beulah:

'They shall kiss away the black circle of death, and lay her down at the feet of the Lamb. I hear her pleading there for those on earth who consented to her death. O Lois! pray also for me, pray for me, miserable!' (Ch. 3)

Pastor Tappau preaches on the multiple works of the devil. Prudence shrieks, lies in a fit and whispers the name of Lois, who stands as she did in her childish dream, 'with every eye fixed upon her in hatred and dread'. The crowd pulses around her while she stands 'quite still in the tight grasp of strange, fierce men'. Faith will not defend her now. Only Manasseh speaks out, passion driving him to the heresy of logic: if all is foredoomed and Lois has no free will, how can she be guilty? His reasoning is defined as unreason: his mother explains that he is mad, and bewitched.

Bound with cords, Lois finds herself in a square dark room with stone walls all around, the claustrophobic pit that lies beneath Gaskell's fiction from her earliest published writing, 'Clopton Hall'. Just as Charlotte Clopton devours her own flesh, so Lois becomes 'a girl thrown inward upon herself', brought back from the 'wild, illimitable desert' of her imagination only by the physical pain of the iron on her legs. Her hesitation before the words of forgiveness in the Lord's Prayer confirms her guilt, but when she is urged to confess and save her life, 'the truth came once more out of her lips, almost without exercise of her will. "I am not a witch," she said.'

Helplessly she thinks of Hugh Lucy, who 'might even now be sailing on the wide blue sea, coming nearer, nearer, every moment; and yet be too late after all'. But no one can save her. That evening Nattee, the Indian servant, is thrust into the cell, and to comfort her before they die together, Lois tells her the story of the crucifixion, the blood of the Lamb spilt to atone for the sins of men. She finds her own version of the Bible which had been used to condemn her; her last cry, before she swings in the air, is not on God or Christ, but 'Mother!'

When Hugh Lucy, who had indeed come too late, learns of Salem's recantation and Judge Sewall's annual day of penitence, he determines to pray for the judge yearly, 'that his sins may be blotted out and never more had in remembrance. She would have wished it so.' Salem's sins are forgiven through the intercession of Lois, the human sacrifice, the female scapegoat. Lois's father was a minister who would not save a witch; his daughter pays the price. Her story is an appeal against the hypocrisy of those who distort the word of God for their own, ill-understood ends – a prayer on behalf of women, a feminine rereading of the Litany from the Book of Common Prayer, issued in 1662, a generation before Salem:

'From all evil and mischief, from sin, from the crafts and assaults of the devil, from thy wrath, and from everlasting damnation,

Good Lord, deliver us.

From all blindness of heart; from pride, vain-glory, and hypocrisie, from envy, hatred and malice, and all uncharitableness,

Good Lord, deliver us.'

23

Interruptions

North-east from York across the Vale of Pickering the moors begin to rise, at first slowly and then abruptly. Beyond Pickering they climb steeply to the skies. Apart from the alien shapes and discs of Fylingdales the landscape is that which Elizabeth Gaskell saw when she travelled from York to Whitby early on the morning of Tuesday, 2 November 1859. On the heights time recedes, emptiness and distance reign. Away from the road the square-cut stones of the Roman Wade's Causeway still march towards the ancient border of the Picts. At Goathland, where George Stephenson built an experimental railway in 1836, a village has grown in the wild. Across the common from the inn, before heather and sheep take over again, stands an inland church where granite gravestones are decorated with anchors and ropes, memorials to men lost in Arctic gales sweeping the Greenland seas.

The moors have sudden hollows, pierced by waterfalls and streams, places of unexpected warmth where in spring the trees are green a month before their fellows on the hill. These are its secret, summer places. Elizabeth Gaskell came to the north Yorkshire coast in autumn, but she knew the warmth of the hollows beneath the purple crags, 'so that, while on the bare swells of the high land you shivered at the waste desolation of the scenery, when you dropped into these wooded "bottoms" you were charmed with the nestling shelter that they gave'. (*Sylvia's Lovers*, ch. 1). She knew too how nearer the coast the sea-wind cut into the shelter, stunting the trees, 'but still there was rich, thick underwood, tangled and tied together with bramble, and briar-rose, and honeysuckle'. In such a sensuous, spellbound valley her next heroine, Sylvia Robson, would bathe her feet in the stream on the way to Whitby market, the brambles catching at her kilted petticoat.

High above, the hills roll on, seemingly without end until a cleft opens to the south, the valley of the Esk, and a strange light glints in the east. The sky, already wide, opens into vastness. Below are the rolling backs of cliffs, dotted with farms. Beyond, sometimes a brilliant blue, sometimes a troubled, restless grey veiled with mists or 'frets', is the thin line of the sea.

When Elizabeth came here, the sea was not shining. Her fortnight in Whitby was wet and windy. But just as in 'Half a Lifetime Ago' she could imagine the Lakeland mountains she knew in summer, bleak and enshrouded in snow, so she could see Whitby in the sunshine, and could imagine it not as a growing resort but as the isolated whaling port of sixty years before, swathed in the smell of the melting sheds where the blubber and whalebone were taken. *Sylvia's Lovers* opens on a hot, early October day in 1796. Whalers returning from the Arctic lie offshore, and the press-gang also lies waiting, hidden by an angle of the cliff, hunting for men to fight the French. The view of Monkshaven that Sylvia sees evokes the fusion of closeness and extension that is the essence both of Whitby itself and of Gaskell's novel:

'The next turn of the road showed them the red-peaked roofs of the closely-packed houses lying almost directly below the hill on which they were. The full autumn sun brought out the ruddy colour of the tiled gables, and deepened the shadows in the narrow streets. The narrow harbour at the mouth of the river was crowded with small vessels of all descriptions, making an intricate forest of masts. Beyond lay the sea, like a flat pavement of sapphire, scarcely a ripple varying its sunny surface, that stretched out leagues away till it blended with the softened azure of the sky.' (Ch. 2)

Elizabeth and the girls arrived in Whitby early, to allow plenty of time to find lodgings. They eventually took rooms with a Mrs Rose in Abbey Terrace, a new development on the West Cliff built by the York railway king, Thomas Hudson, who was changing the appearance and status of the town. The Roses were an old local family and Elizabeth spent hours with Mrs Rose's mother, Mrs Huntrods, hearing her memories of the press-gangs of the 1790s, when she lived as a girl in one of the yards off Church Street, Whitby's cobbled main street running parallel to the harbour.[1]

From now on Whitby's history became her chief interest, and, as always, she talked to everyone she met. At the end of *Sylvia's Lovers* is a small scene which takes place sixty years after the close of the story, in other words in the year of her visit, 1859. Monkshaven is now a rising bathing-place, but, says the narrator, on a summer night when the long spring tides are ebbing, you can hear the same ceaseless, lapping waves that Philip Hepburn, Sylvia's husband, heard as he lay between life and death in Widow Dobson's cottage. Memories fade, but local people tell their tales. A visitor may still hear of a man who died of starvation while his hard-hearted wife lived 'not two good stone-throws away'. But what is the truth beneath the old gossip? What was this tragedy of ordinary lives? 'Not long since,' we are told,

'a lady went to the "Public Baths", a handsome stone building erected on the very site of Widow Dobson's cottage and, finding all the rooms engaged, she sat down and had some talk with the bathing-woman.' (Ch. 45)

The story the lady hears is strange and sad. She presses her questions: 'What became of the wife? . . . Miss Rose? . . . And the daughter?'

Even if the fictional scene never took place in life, we cannot fail to recognize this eager, absorbed, questioning woman. Over the next few months Elizabeth would combine the story of a crisis in the lives of a farmer's daughter, a harpooneer and a Whitby shop-man with the larger story of press-gangs and war. Her plot resembled that of a poem she had known since girlhood, Crabbe's 'Ruth', where 'gangs kept pressing till they swept the shore' and a young man was carried off on the eve of his marriage, leaving his bride prey to his rival, an obsessive religious suitor. Writing nearer the period, Crabbe appealed vehemently against the harsh press-gang laws and the wars that made them seem necessary, against a world 'where might is right and violence is law':

> Be not alarm'd, my child, there's none regard
> What you and I conceive so cruel-hard.
> There is compassion, I believe; but still
> One wants the power to help, and one the will;
> And so from war to war the wrongs remain,
> While Reason pleads, and Misery sighs, in vain.[2]

During her stay Elizabeth went out every day, despite the rain and an alarming collapse on Julia's part (briskly put down to 'bowels'). She and Meta (carrying her sketch-pad) wandered through the winding streets and cobbled alleys down to the narrow harbour. Across the bridge they climbed the steep steps to the old church standing bluff and square against the gales, its whitewashed galleries within swooping like sails over the dark box pews, its gravestones outside pitted by the wind. This was a churchyard 'rich in the dead', between the town and the sea:

'Masters, mariners, shipowners, seamen: it seemed strange how few other trades were represented in that great plain so full of upright gravestones. Here and there was a memorial stone, placed by some survivor of a large family, most of whom perished at sea: – "supposed to have perished in the Greenland seas", "Shipwrecked in the Baltic", "Drowned off the coast of Iceland". There was a strange sensation, as if the cold sea-winds must bring with them the dim phantoms of those lost sailors.' (Ch. 6)

Beyond the church Elizabeth and Meta explored the ruined Cistercian abbey of St Hilda, where high arches provide corners of calm, and the long naves are smooth with sheep-nibbled turf. On longer walks they followed the cliff road, since eaten by landslides, each fall letting fossils of past millennia tumble to the beach below. Past the Mulgate Inn they found two farms: one, combined with a farm near Sunderland where Elizabeth had once stayed, would become Haytersbank, the Robsons' home, the other Moss Brow, where the Corneys live.[3] Corney is a well-known Whitby name, and while she was there Elizabeth met John Corney, an old man who told her of the press-gang riot of 1793 and lent her his copy of Young's *History of Whitby*. Four years later she sent him an inscribed copy of her novel. She seems, indeed, to have questioned anyone who might help, from Mr Watson the Unitarian minister and Mrs Bradley the bookseller, down to fat old 'Fish Jane' on the harbour wall.

Back at Plymouth Grove she was exhilarated: she knew what her next book would be. Within a week she announced it to George Smith as one of the three things she was working on:

'3rdly The Specksioneer in 3 vols.
Published by Smith & Elder (it is to be hoped –)
not far on, but very clear in my head, & what I want to write more than any thing.' (L595)

Before she began, she wanted to know more. On 28 January 1860 William borrowed the *Annual Register* for 1793 from the Portico Library.[4] Over the next few months she consulted friends in the north and in London, ranging from John Corney in Whitby to Sir Charles Napier, once in command of the Channel Fleet, and General Perronet Thompson, uncle of Marianne's and Meta's friend Isabel Thompson and a stalwart Yorkshireman. He advised on the history, sent details of press-gang riots in Hull and later stopped her Yorkshire dialect from slipping across the Pennines into Lancashire.[5]

Elizabeth was immersing herself in a disturbed, catalytic period. In the 1790s fears induced by the Terror in France provoked the 'seditious meetings' legislation that was later adapted against Chartists and Unionists: the debates of Paine and Burke fired the people – pedlars carried *The Rights of Man* as well as *Pilgrim's Progress*. The fight for individual liberties exploded in riots against the press-gangs and in the historic mutinies at Spithead and the Nore in 1797.[6] All this lies behind the semi-comic arguments between Daniel Robson and Philip Hepburn about democracy and law, individualism and the national interest in *Sylvia's Lovers*:

' "But asking your pardon, laws is made for the good of the nation, not for your good or mine."

Daniel could not stand this. He laid down his pipe, opened his eyes, stared straight at Philip before speaking, in order to enforce his words, and then said slowly –

"Nation here! nation theere! I'm a man and yo're another, but nation's nowheere. If Measter Cholmley talked to me i' that fashion, he'd look long for another vote frae me. I can make out King George, and Measter Pitt, and yo' and me, but nation! nation, go hang!" '
(Ch. 4)

Elizabeth had a personal interest in the period, since two of her Stevenson uncles from Berwick-upon-Tweed, further north along the east coast, had been lost fighting the French at Dunkirk, while her father had experienced the violent hostility aroused by the Unitarians' support for the revolution and Paine. (Elizabeth would describe the vicar of Monkshaven as a 'kindly peaceable old man' but a vehement Tory who had 'two bugbears to fear – the French and the Dissenters. It was difficult to say of which he had the worst opinion and the most intense dread.' Probably the latter, since the French had the excuse of being Papists, while the Dissenters 'might have belonged to the Church of England if they had not been utterly depraved'.)

From November, to March 1860, while Elizabeth's mind was in the Whitby of the 1790s, daily life swirled around her as usual. In February she was earnestly telling Charles Eliot Norton about the model tenements Thurstan Holland and four friends were building in the East End. She told him too about a deeper concern which had worried her since the Captain Hill débâcle:

'My girls, my darlings, *are* such comforts – such happiness! Every one so good & healthy & bright. I don't know what I should do if one of them married; & yet it is constantly a wonder to me that no one ever gives them a chance.' (L598)

Dissenters were still suspect, as they had been sixty years before: she wondered if her daughters' lack of offers was because the young Unitarian men in Manchester were either good but uncultivated, or rich and insensitive, while the 'enlightened and liberal young men' outside Unitarianism (like Charles Bosanquet) were held back by bigoted fathers of the last generation. She was troubled:

'I think an unmarried life may be to the full as happy, *in process of time* but I think there is a time of trial to be gone through with *women*, who naturally yearn after children.' (L598)

The conjunction of her daughters' marriages and Thurstan's buildings was a link she would not quite let herself see. For the past year Marianne had been falling in love with this second cousin, whom she had known all her life as one of the rabble of Dumbleton children. Thurstan was now twenty-three and after Eton and Trinity, Cambridge, was studying for the Bar. A year earlier Elizabeth described him affectionately to Monckton Milnes as '*very* good, very intelligent, very gentlemanly, & very full of fun'. To begin with, Marianne's fondness was a family joke, an opportunity to tease her when Cambridge lost the boat-race in 1859: 'Aha!! Miss! Cambridge 100 yards behind Oxford – it is very well to *pretend* ignorance.' In fact this was the start of a protracted, eight-year romance, fiercely opposed by Edward Holland, Thurstan's father. The objection was on grounds less of consanguinity than of money – Thurstan was one of twelve children. It was made clear by both sets of parents that there was no future in the relationship: perhaps this was why Elizabeth described herself mysteriously in 1860 as 'silently and quietly most displeased with Thurstan'. A year later she told MA pointedly that 'it is the opinion here that E.T.H. is making up to Miss Darwin & that Dumbleton would not dislike it as he must "marry money".'

When she wrote to Norton, however, she placed no special emphasis on Marianne. She was planning a trip to Oxford with William, Marianne and Meta 'since the first two have never seen it'. She always enjoyed Oxford, as she told the Boston minister, Edward Hale: 'I like the society of Paris *very* best of all: & then Oxford, and then comes London.'⁷ On this visit she was enthralled by the passionate debate over the university's recent decision to allow professors to marry. In a hilariously complex letter, dealing with Max Müller (married as quickly as possible) and John Conington (too shy to ask), her particular concern was for the unfortunate Benjamin Jowett:

'Now Mr Jowett would like to marry; this is well known to his friends; not anybody in particular, but to have a home, for he is a very affectionate man, – & because he thinks a fellow's life too long continued induces selfishness & a shut-up heart &c.' (L609)

Hardly the usual picture of the egotistical Regius Professor of Greek.

From Oxford, with its donnish gossip, Elizabeth went to London, suffering from a terrible cold. The winter had been unusually severe, with biting winds, blizzards and weeks of frost. Now colds and flu were everywhere. Lady Coltman, the perfect hostess, had a stock of '*clean, large* thick pocket handkerchiefs on her table, being, she said, the "kindest attention she could offer to her friends just now," Mrs Clarke took one,' said Elizabeth, 'I another, & blew our noses just like two rival nightingales.' She still managed to visit model lodging-houses mentioned by Norton in a pamphlet and to see Tottie, now happily settled in England and painting and exhibiting with her husband.

As far as Elizabeth's circle were concerned, the topics of passionate interest that spring were two books. The first was *On the Origin of Species*, published on 22 November 1859, shortly after Elizabeth returned from Whitby. Battle had been joined at once between supporters and detractors of Darwin, and a war of words now raged in journals, lecture-halls and drawing-rooms; it would rise to a climax in the fierce confrontation between Bishop Wilberforce and Thomas Huxley at the British Association in Oxford in June. The other circus of war was *Essays and Reviews*, a volume of theological essays from seven contributors, including the Gaskells' Oxford friends Benjamin Jowett and Mark Pattison. Their broad church views, which included a denial of hell and (from some) an embrace of 'Darwinism' (a phrase coined by Huxley in April) outraged the Anglican establishment and led to two of the writers being tried for heresy in the ecclesiastical court. They were acquitted on appeal, but when Elizabeth visited London in March 1861, she reported that 'everybody' was still talking about the case.

Science and theology became entwined in all the arguments. At their heart lay two issues: the toppling of man's pre-eminence in the universe, no longer created in God's image but descended from apes, and the presence – or absence – of God in the process of creation. Darwin's vision of nature, as he himself saw, seemed analogous to human society, in which the weak so often went to the wall. It seemed hard, he wrote, looking on a sunny landscape or a tropical forest, to think of life as perpetual conflict:

'Nevertheless the doctrine that all nature is a war is most true. The struggle very often falls on the egg & seed, or on the seedling, larva & young; but fall it must sometime in the life of each individual, or more commonly at intervals on successive generations & then with extreme severity.'[8]

While Elizabeth was in London, she did not forget her own study of struggle, 'The Specksioneer'. At the British Museum and the Admiralty she sought details of the Whitby riot of 1793. The coast in the 1790s was divided into areas, with headquarters or 'rendezvous', usually set up at local inns, and she managed to obtain a copy of a long letter from Lieutenant Atkinson, keeper of the Whitby rendezvous in Haggersgate, who gave a graphic account of the uprising, the battering down of the doors and the fist-fights and vandalism that followed. Meanwhile her inquiries in the north were also bearing fruit. A York contact sent an extract from the 'Calender of Felons' tried at York Assizes. Among them was an old man accused, as Sylvia's father Daniel Robson would be, of inciting the rioters. His fate was recorded: 'William Atkinson, hanged, 13 April, 1793.'[9]

Elizabeth longed to start writing. But her cold refused to leave her and when she went on to stay with a friend at Winchester she collapsed with severe bronchitis. 'I was there for several weeks,' she told Hale, 'lying in bed, and looking out into the beautiful Cathedral Close, with the branches of its great trees sweeping slowly across my windows as the wind swayed them, and the sound of the chanted services in the Cathedral came to me faintly, morning & evening.'[10] As she slowly recovered she grew to love the quiet precincts, like those whose calm soothes Ellinor Wilkins in 'A Dark Night's Work'. Winchester would also provide temporary peace for Philip Hepburn, when he stays at 'the Hospital of St Sepulchre', based on the hospice of St Cross a mile outside the city. Elizabeth had almost finished collecting material for her novel and wrote impatiently from her sickbed to Marianne, who had been staying in Oxford with Goldwin Smith, professor of law and Balliol tutor:

'Oh! *please* ask the Tutor not to trouble himself or his friends about the press-gang affair. The Annual Register has been *care*fully looked over *months* ago, & it is of no use going over the ground again – and so many people are now at work for me, *in Yorkshire*, that I am sure to have my information sooner or later, without troubling any one further.' (L603)

At the beginning of April she came home, looking forward for once to having Plymouth Grove almost to herself. On 3 May Meta was due to leave on a sketching tour of the Pyrenees as companion to Catherine Darwin, Charles Darwin's older sister. Marianne was on a round of London visits. Flossy and Julia were at school. She told Norton that 'during their absence, & the comparative quiet of the house I mean to write *very* hard at my story; which *ought* to be done by Septr but owing to my illness, & subsequent weakness it won't I fear'.

On the day she made this resolution, 5 April, a parcel arrived from George Smith. It was *The Mill on the Floss*. 'I think it is so kind of you,' she wrote, '& am so greedy to read it I can scarcely be grateful enough to write this letter.' Did she read it greedily in the next two days, with its opening description of the broad Floss hurrying to the sea, where 'the loving tide, rushing to meet it, checks its passage with an impetuous embrace'? Was she struck by the pungent dialect? Or the layered, organic description of St Ogg's, 'one of those old towns which impress one as a continuation and outgrowth of nature', with its legend of the Virgin of the Flood, its citizens and shopkeepers, markets and farms, sectarian disputes and ingrown obstinacies? Perhaps. *Sylvia's Lovers* opens with a similar evocation of Monkshaven, the 'landing place of the throneless queen', where sea and land embrace. When Elizabeth dated the writing of her novel, she simply said: 'begun 8th of April'.

For a solid month she wrote. The house was peaceful and solitary and she told Norton she thoroughly understood 'the wisdom of French ladies going into rétraite'. Her letters were short and rather tired: 'My dearest Polly, Two lines to say nothing is happening.' The most newsworthy event was that one of their birds was sick and the 'Bird doctor' prescribed castor oil. Her work crept insistently into her casual chatter:

'And my book is really killing me, – i.e. I can't sleep at nights for thinking of my story. (*Have you written to Secretary Amateur Exhibition* in my name, about Meta's Florence; if sold, to whom?) I am glad you snubbed Sophy. My book is getting *on* famously.' (L910)

In May she started to feel the strain and think of holidays:

'My very dearest Polly,
It is hard work writing a novel all morning, spudding up dandelions all afternoon, & writing again at night . . . I see nobody, my employments being as aforesaid. I am getting on with my book; 117 pages done *of 570 at least*; and I've broken my back over dandelions. And I have not got a cook; and I don't know where we are to go to, any more than you do, and am too squeezed-dry of energy by the time I have done my book & my dandelions to see about either one thing or another . . .
. . . What do you think of *Heidelberg*?' (L614–15)

On 21 May William was sent down to the Portico to take out the two volumes of William Scoresby's *Arctic Regions* and *Northern Whale Fisheries*.[11] Elizabeth kept the books for three days, ransacking them quickly for the whaling anecdotes of Daniel Robson and the harpooneer, Charley Kinraid. But her first creative burst was fading. Domestic trials intervened. In the last week of May the house was robbed and the servants terrified, although the theft itself was on a *Cranford* level: 'Luckily, they *only* took a round of beef, lying in salt, & all the towels & dirty clothes out of the wash-house.' At the same time William was mysteriously cross and out of sorts, and a new cook arrived who confessed to a terrible temper.

While she dealt with the upsets, she wrote on, until a genuine crisis arose. She had 'got on splendidly with my new book that-is-to-be', had nearly finished the first volume and 'was full of it all', when on the morning of 6 June a letter came from Marianne, 'written in pencil & in bed from London, saying she was very ill, – supposed to be going to be small-pox'. Leaving frantic messages for William, Elizabeth dashed to the station. Fear of small-pox ruled out staying with friends:

'and it was Cup Day at Ascot, a thing which in my ignorance, I did not know would fill up every possible & hirable bed in London. I did not get there till ½ p. 7, & then began my search for a bed, – at last I got a garret in a back St, & then went to Marianne . . . It was *not* however small only *bad* chicken-pox.' (L631)

She nursed her daughter for ten days. Then, while Marianne went to convalesce with the Bonamy Prices at Brighton, Elizabeth sped up to irresistible Oxford, where she danced until four in the morning at Christ Church Ball.

A week or two later, when Marianne had recovered, they joined Hearn, Florence and Julia and set off for Heidelberg. Marianne was still weak and on the advice of a 'wise old German physician' was dispatched to the spa of Kreuznach, near Bingen, with Hearn to look after her and Elinor Bonham Carter to keep her company. Letters sped between the two towns, Elizabeth's pithy, exhausted yet rich with enjoyment. Julia had brought breakfast in bed:

'for oh! I was so tired! with packing, & callings and close air (at music at the Museum last night, – Dr Otto, Miss Kell & Mr Schwann being our chaperones –), and then I brushed Flossy's hair for an hour, & got clothes ready (such a heap!) for *our* Wasch Frau . . . There is no great amount of news going here . . . The Prussian Corps is going to have a great show on Friday – each student has subscribed 50 gulden; & they are to have an illumination, & an affair up the river, & music, & a procession, & no one knows what besides, – grandeur untold.' (L623)

Not much novel-writing was done.

It was a memorable holiday. They took long walks in the country, drank coffee in 'the pretty primitive "gast-hausen" ' and rowed on the river in the twilight. Several English friends were there, like Henry Roscoe, professor of chemistry at Owen's College, who had trained in Heidelberg. The troubles of home seemed very distant. On 25 July

William wrote to his 'dearest Lily' with the news that her cousin Frederick Holland, with whom they had so often stayed at Ashbourne, had died after great suffering, leaving his wife with seven children and 'the prospect of another in September'. Taking comfort in the thought that Frederick had 'fought his life battles well', William moved on to the health of his own family. He was drily sceptical about the regime at German spas: 'If I were asked, *professionally* I should say that the "cakes and coffee" of which letters have made mention, were not the most fit and proper dish.'

Although he was resigned to their staying until the cure was complete, William could not resist teasing. He wanted to fix his own holidays:

'I shan't be sorry when you are all on English ground again. Can you give me any idea when it is likely to be? . . . Another thing is to see that you don't knock *yourself* up with scientific pursuits and soaring too high and trying to make out what the sun is made of. (Tell Polly it is stron*tium* not *sium*.) With respect to your gout I never knew you wished it to be a secret – though it might show a want of *gout* in me to mention it – but Polly's pimples shall be sacred.'¹²

This rare letter, with its puns and gossip – of committees and dinners, of Florence Nightingale and Lord Clyde and a young Brahmin convert – lets us glimpse a William who is far from stiff, walking home in the rain (to save a cab fare) after a dinner with friends which ended with 'a few Christy minstrel songs'.

While she lapped up the news from home, Elizabeth dallied in Heidelberg, waiting for Marianne to recover and hoping that Meta – who was now in Switzerland – would join them. When she did return to Plymouth Grove, William had just left for his month in Scotland. Meta had come back the week before and they told each other their adventures 'with as much gusto as the one-eyed calendars in the Arabian Nights'.

Before she could get back to *Sylvia's Lovers*, she had to make plans for her daughters. Florence, now eighteen, had left school and Elizabeth was determined not to exploit her as secretary, housekeeper, teacher and confidante, as she was beginning (rather late) to realize she had done Marianne and Meta. It was decided that she would study French, German and music at home, with 'masters and regular reading', 'and we are reading with her Macaulay's Biographies &

Milman's Latin Xtianity'. Flossy (who was far from academic) detested her lessons. Lily ruefully came to the conclusion that she was 'very dainty-fingered, a beautiful ready workwoman, a capital shopper &c; and *prefers* doing all these sort of little housewife things to anything presenting the least intellectual *effort* or requiring perseverance'.

Meta was more of a problem. Still nervy and often ill, she was brooding on 'the life of an *amateur* and an *artist*'. She had brought back from her tour abroad folders of unfinished drawings which Elizabeth described as 'beautiful centres, really almost like Turner's, in the middle of a blank sheet of paper'. These intense details without context were so unusual (and so Meta-like) that viewers were puzzled. Meta was particularly stung when her ever tactless mother complained they were incomplete and Elizabeth felt guilty and troubled. As presented to Charles Norton, the question was 'Is she to draw to give pleasure to others, or to improve herself?'

'You see the complexity of the question, as to selfishness, Goethian theories of self-development. I believe it to be *right* in all things to aim at the highest standard; but I can't quite work it out with my conscience.' (L633)

(The question was hard to settle: in 1862, during intense relief work among the poor, Meta wrote despairingly to Effie Wedgwood about her passion for art and music: 'Oh Effie – *now* am I not as egotistical as any one could wish? What shall I *do*?')[13]

That summer the dilemmas of her family and her household absorbed Elizabeth more deeply than her book. Ordinary life beset her. Their housemaid, Mary, had a fiancé called Shaw, who had started a small mill in Huddersfield on borrowed capital, including the savings of the Gaskell's servant Elliott. But then:

'About a week ago Elliott came in crying – "May Mary go off for the day? Mary has heard that Shaw is dying." I went to her directly; she was as white as a sheet, but quite tearless, making the beds with vehemence, her eyes almost fierce; & her lips clenched. "Let me see the letter Mary while you go to get ready", and I read that in his own mill the machinery had caught him, & crushed him – some one else wrote "a very serious accident; all his cry is for you to come to him". We all speeded her off, and her letters are so pathetic. His right leg is crushed;

& tomorrow they decide if he can bear the amputation. He has no partner; his poor little humble mill must go to rack & ruin; but as Elliott says with tears "I should not care for the loss of my money a bit if he can only get better." And so I shall leave it, – for I know no more what it will please God to decree.' (L633–4)

Shaw did not die, nor lose his leg, but he was crippled for life.

The violent intrusion of accident into peaceful quotidian routines – the making of beds, the ordering of meals – always appals. A year later Elizabeth heard from Norton of the death of Mrs Longfellow, who was with her two youngest girls in the library sealing their newly cut curls in packets when the wax taper she was using set fire to her muslin dress. Desperate to get away from the children, she rushed into the study where Longfellow was sleeping on the sofa; he threw a rug from the floor around her, but could not save her. Elizabeth dreamt of this for days, 'the picture of the mother, the little girls, the pretty 'locks of hair' – the pleasant fearful occupation – and poor Mr Longfellow lying sleeping to waken up to such a dazzling flaming tragedy, – I can hardly bear to think of it'. The novel she was working on was built around exactly such sudden, brutal disruptions of the everyday, and on the impossibility of explaining to those involved why such disasters should happen under a supposedly beneficent God.

Yet ordinary life had to go on despite Mary's tragedy. In September Plymouth Grove was packed with visitors: her cousin Mary Holland (with whom she 'had a row' about a concert), Effie Wedgwood, Emma Shaen and the Fields, their American friends from Rome: 'he CHARMING she very nice, but almost entirely in her own room, & liking promiscuous teas, & odd foods, at odd times – and help in all her dressings &c.' In addition to difficult guests, William was absorbed in his ministry, his teaching and his many committees. Sunday schools and clothing clubs demanded time. Mary was still away, Marianne was still in Kreuznach and, even worse, Hearn was there with her and no one could find her housekeeper's keys. Elizabeth was rushed off her feet:

'Scanty time to wash ourselves – (tell Hearn I've my own doubts as to Julia's *ever* having washed since we left Germany, – and as for her hair! it *looks* all very well, & I have no time to enquire farther) . . . I have never had time to write to Mrs Laurence about mutton cutlet & risolle [*sic*]. In fact we are pretty nearly all worn out with dirt & work,

& being agreeable . . . Oh dear! poteration take the house,– Moreover
we can't get a *bit* of butter; – our butterwoman *won't* come, why we
can't make out . . . Tell Hearn *all* her wits are wanted in this desolate,
butterless, headless, washerwomanless, company full household.'
(L635–6)

Hearn returned to impose order and comparative calm, but weeks
passed, and still Elizabeth could not write. In November she was
briefly thrown back into the mood of *The Life of Charlotte Brontë*,
when she and Meta visited Patrick Brontë. She told him she had
hesitated before coming, 'feeling as if he might now have unpleasant
associations with her – which never seemed to have entered his
head'.[14] Patrick was bedridden, but stubborn and grandiloquent as
ever, waging an enjoyable war against Arthur Nicholls. Elizabeth told
W. S. Williams how possessive Nicholls was of Charlotte's memory,
even refusing to christen the Greenwoods' latest child Brontë. Patrick
had outwitted him, holding the christening secretly in his bedroom:

'When Mr Nicholls came upon its name upon the register book, Mr
Greenwood says that he stormed and stamped and went straight to the
Parsonage to Mr Brontë to ask him for his reasons in going so directly
against his wishes. Fortunately Mr Brontë had the excellent defence of
saying that if the child had died unchristened Mr Nicholls case would
have been extremely awkward, and that he had thus saved him from a
great scrape.' (L641–2)

(Theology could prove a useful ally in a private battle.)

At the close of 1860 Elizabeth was starting to despair: 'I seem to have
read and written nothing, ever since we came back from Heidelberg. I
must write though, and finish my book, about one quarter done.' As
she often did when she was feeling restless, she wrote a troubled short
story; the urgent, frightening 'Grey Woman', inspired by Heidelberg.

Spring came, with more visits to London and the south. Time flowed
away like sand. By April, a year after she had first put pen to paper,
'The Specksioneer' had run aground. To Charles Norton, on 6 April
1861, she wrote:

'I am sitting here by myself in the dining-room by the light of one
candle, – half disturbed and half-amused by the chatter of "the
children" in the next room – (Julia just come to wish me good-night, so

it is 9 o'clk) where Meta Florence & Julia have been sitting till now, when Julia the chatter-box and perpetual singer having gone to bed, sudden silence succeeds. I suspect that Meta has taken up either the 5th vol. of Modern Painters, or Tyndall on Glaciers, both of which books she is reading now, and Florence is probably reading the "Amber-Witch".' (L645)

William is out at the Lit. and Phil. planning the September meeting of the British Association for the Advancement of Science, and Elliott 'has just come in to ask me if Master would like some bread & milk when he comes home? So now you know the exact state of affairs on this Tuesday evening.'

The scene was peaceful, but her mood was not. That month wider issues began to fill her letters to Norton. During the past year tensions in America over abolition had reached a new intensity. In November 1860 the election of Abraham Lincoln had made it clear that after years of procrastination the North would finally take a stand against slavery, at least in the new states forming in the west. In April 1861 the South seceded to form the Confederacy. The North denied their right to do so. War seemed inevitable.

Boston friends like Edward Hale and Norton were fervent abolitionists, and Elizabeth tried hard to comprehend what was happening. Manchester mill-owners and merchants supported the South, locked in a bond of mutual interest with the cotton states. She herself supported abolition and the North, but loathed war. Dizzied by rhetoric from both sides, she begged for explanations, confessing to Hale that she found American politics 'most complicated'. Two months later, feeling as if she were 'dancing on eggs', she was still appealing to Norton: 'I don't mind your thinking me dense or ignorant, and I think I can be sure you will give me a quiet unmetaphorical statement of what is the end proposed in this war.'

Surely, she asked, the North must have seen that secession was inevitable. Might it not be that separation from the South was like getting rid of a diseased member? Amputation was drastic, but better than an infecting poison. And what would they do when they had conquered the South, as no one doubted they would? They would have to abolish slavery by force, becoming tyrants themselves. Her Unitarian belief in change through sympathy and argument was outraged at

496

the prospect of needless slaughter, of the splitting of families and the wreck of communities.

In an April letter to Hale, full of puzzled concern, Elizabeth also mentioned the long neglected novel. She was busy setting up a sewing machine for poor needlewomen and recovering from a sore throat – but she hoped to get back to work. She gave an additional, and revealing, reason for her tardiness: *Romola* was currently appearing in the *Cornhill*.

'I am going to finish my book, 3 vols, very soon; though after seeing what Miss Evans (George Eliot) does I feel as if nothing of mine would be worth reading ever-more and that takes the pith out of one. Then Meta says "But Mama remember the burying the one talent" – & I cheer up. I mean to get strong and do the best I *can*.'[15]

Unable to concentrate, she began to plan holidays: a long spell at Silverdale for herself, Meta and Julia, while Marianne visited friends, and – at last – a two-month break for William.

That April, adding to his already heavy work, William and John Beard had started the *Unitarian Herald*, with a circulation of five thousand, which they hoped to increase considerably. He seemed exhausted and Elizabeth felt he should go abroad. Fearing he might be lonely without companions, she suggested he visit the Storys. His face brightened, and then fell, as he declared he could not push himself on people he hardly knew. So she wrote herself, describing her husband of thirty years:

'Oh HOW I shall envy Mr Gaskell if he does reach you. I feel so sure you will like each other. He is very shy, but *very* merry when he is well, delights in puns & punning, & is very fond of children, playing with them all the day long, not caring for them so much when they are grown up, *used* to speak Italian pretty well, but says he can't now, 6 foot high, grey hair & whiskers & otherwise very like Marianne in looks. You'll think him stiff till his shyness wears off, as I am sure it will directly with you.' (L660)

William's holiday, begun on 3 July was exactly what he needed. He wandered blithely and erratically up and down northern Italy and spent ten days with the Storys in the Rhône valley. Little was heard of him until late August when he wrote from Newhaven, to his family's total surprise, saying he would not be back until September but was extremely well and happy and was enjoying English food and English sea.

While he was abroad, Elizabeth and the girls spent a month in Silverdale and then paid a short visit to Scotland. At Silverdale, looking out to the mountains and the sea, Elizabeth had started to write properly again. Once back in Plymouth Grove she had other concerns. In September the house was full of visitors for the British Association meeting. And in Manchester generally, and all over south Lancashire, the effects of the American Civil War were beginning to show. The blockade on the southern ports had stopped the flow of cotton and as stocks ran low, the old spectres of the 1840s appeared – short time, lay-offs, bread queues and soup-kitchens, fever and starvation. Elizabeth told Lady Kay-Shuttleworth that she could not help with the Institution for the Employment of Needlewomen or the Deaf and Dumb Memorial Annuities: 'this winter all our "charity must begin at home"; for I am afraid it is likely to be a very sad one in South Lancashire'. She feared right, and the hardship would be even worse next winter, in the terrible cotton famine of 1862–3.

In December 1861 it even seemed that Britain might be dragged into the conflict, on the side of the South. When Edward Hale sent his Christmas presents, William thanked him for the two barrels of apples 'rescued from Niagara', but added: 'I hope that no war may ensue to put an end to these friendly relations with America; which are the source of so much pleasure – and of barrels of American apples.'[16] He wrote lightly, but the reality was dark. Everyone at Plymouth Grove sent thank-you letters to Hale and everyone, except Julia, mentioned this fear. In Elizabeth's words, 'You don't know what an incubus this dread of a war with you is! I think of it almost the last thing at night, & the first in the morning.'[17]

The vision of young men dying in the Crimea had pursued her while she worked on North and South. Now the agony of America met her when she turned from this new novel, itself full of the distant thunder of guns in the French wars. The Civil War was yet another bitter example of a world 'where might is right and violence is law'.

Relief work left little time for writing. But at the end of 1861 Elizabeth was able to send the first two volumes of her novel to

George Smith. She waited anxiously for a response. None came. January passed and then, on 1 February 1862, a cryptic note arrived from Smith, Elder. Unable to bear the suspense, she wrote to the kindly W. S. Williams:

'My Dear Sir,
You must please consider this letter as *private* for I want to consult you about one or two things. In the first place, have you read my two vols of my new novel? If you have I am afraid you do not like them because you say nothing about them. If you *have* I should like to send you a sketch of the third vol: to make you see how everything in the first two "works up" to the events and crisis in that. But if you have *not* read it I should be very glad if you would tell me so, as I cannot help feeling a little disheartened by the ambiguous sentence in your note to-day, which I cannot interpret one way or another as to your having read it or not. If somebody (out of my own family) would be truly interested in my poor story it would give me just the fillip of encouragement I want.' (L675)

She told him Smith's silence made her fear he did not like it. He was no judge from an artistic point of view (an unnecessarily piqued remark) but they had made a bargain and she would feel sorry if he felt bound by it: 'I cannot help liking it myself, but that may be because firstly I have taken great pains with it, and secondly I know the end.'

Her pain becomes evident – 'Mind you I *don't* want you to read it, only to tell me whether you have or not' – before she turns swiftly to the second subject, a new escape, a new interruption. She had begun a series of articles on French life for *All the Year Round* ('while I was waiting for someone to like my book'), but these had become so engrossing that she now saw them as a whole, centred on a single much loved figure: 'Memoirs Elucidatory of the Life and Times of Madame de Sévigné'. Could Williams say how much of this ground Julia Kavanagh had covered in *French Women of Letters*? The idea gave her yet another excuse for putting the novel to one side. In late May, with Meta and Isabel Thompson, she set out on a carefully planned tour of Normandy to collect material. The memoirs, sadly, were never written, but Elizabeth's vivid, joyous letters from France, and the account of this holiday in her 1864 articles, 'French Life', show what a miraculous relief de Sévigné provided, both from Manchester's misery and from 'the saddest story I ever wrote'.

Williams and Smith had responded quickly to her February appeal. Smith was enthusiastic about the memoirs, but concerned to bring her to her main task. He sent the first two volumes to the printer and within a few weeks Elizabeth was writing to him more happily, discussing the title. If Smith came to stay for a week, William would teach him how to pronounce the outlandish 'Specksioneer'. What did he think of 'Philip's Idol'? But, she added (perhaps thinking of her rate of work), 'then again you may say people will call it "Philip's idle" '. 'Philip's darling' might sound better but did not mean the same. 'Monkshaven' might do – 'very stupid though'. Or perhaps 'Sylvia's Lovers'? As to length, she felt the last volume would be longer, but she could move some of the second volume into the first to balance the book. And could he please send the proofs to a friend in Vienna who wanted to translate it?

She was just under way again when another family drama sprang from an unexpected quarter – Marianne. Her sanguine, sensible, oldest daughter had spent the winter in Rome with Oxford friends, Mrs Dicey and her invalid son Alfred, later a distinguished legal scholar. Cheerful letters arrived until April, when Mrs Dicey sent a disconcerting note – Marianne had been seeing a suspicious amount of Henry Manning. Elizabeth could not bring herself to tell William until William Wetmore Story wrote to say that he feared Marianne really was on the verge of converting to Rome. Elizabeth immediately fell ill, retired to bed and wrote blazing letters to MA and the Storys. Marianne's was not posted, but the one to the Storys was, necessitating much subsequent backtracking and many apologies. Relieved that her daughter had not received the full blast, she wrote again to her 'dearest Polly'. Still far from calm, she warned her *not* to go near the Storys in case she saw Manning, and declared her intense relief that she had not been 'led off by excitement to go a few steps (as you think *only*) on a wrong & terrible way'.

Meta made matters worse by telling the Storys that her sister always had been susceptible to persuasive men – Charles Norton, James Martineau, Charles Kingsley. Trying to explain, Elizabeth revealed her own hurt: '(I write in *great* haste, so I may not measure my words *fully*.) Marianne has all her life been influenced by people, *out of her own family* – & seldom by the members of it, in anything like the same degree, in all matters of opinion.' Once home, the unfortunate Marianne, now a woman of twenty-five, was prescribed a course of reading and discussion with her father. It was not the wisest course, as Elizabeth admitted:

'I fear his *extreme* dislike & abhorrence of R.C-ism; & thinking all the arguments adduced by its professors "utterly absurd", makes *her* more inclined to take up its defence thinking it unjustly treated.' (L687)

She recognized with a sinking heart that while Marianne could see that all William said was 'very clear', she remained unconvinced. She was not abstract or logical but practical and emotional, and the rational Unitarian doctrines left her unmoved and unsatisfied.

The episode was soon over, but during it everyone at Plymouth Grove seemed to lose their sense of proportion except Marianne herself. William and Elizabeth presented a united front, acting in concert for the first time in a long while. Their anxiety (and anger) shows their intense identification with their faith, but it also exposes the limits of their tolerance and indicates how strongly they clung to their authority over their now adult daughters.

Marianne's yearnings soon found a less spiritual outlet. On her way back from Rome she stayed at Dumbleton, a perilous move given her state of mind and her feelings about Thurstan. In June Elizabeth took rooms in London for a few weeks, seeing friends and visiting the art exhibitions at the Crystal Palace and at private galleries, and in late July Thurstan's brother Fred, now an Anglican curate, came to stay a few doors away. Fred turned up every morning to discuss their plans, 'evidently most anxious to heal the old Thurstan breach', and soon Thurstan came himself, and took them all to the Eton boat-races. The rain pelted down, but there was more than thunder in the air. Elizabeth wrote with Bede-like feeling of the boats speeding into view,

'with shout & song & music down the dark river, into the bright coloured gleam of the fire works & coloured light, coming smoothly down with the current out of the darkness into the shining water, – into the darkness again.' (L929)

She was not alone in finding it romantic. From now on Marianne and Thurstan considered themselves engaged.

They kept their feelings secret and for a time relations between the two families remained cordial. Soon, however, a huge row erupted. Friends like the Wedgwoods blamed Elizabeth and the ill feeling took time to fade. In December, when Fred was working in Manchester,

Meta alluded bitterly to her family's 'expulsion' and told Effie that 'the Dumbletonians are now in my mind as "the Hollands and Fred" – he is much the best, – & agreeable too'.[18]

Amid such intense feelings Elizabeth found it hard to work steadily. She did manage to write when William was away on his wanderings, and on 28 August sent Dickens most of the manuscript of 'A Dark Night's Work'. Smith, Elder were beginning to press her, but when she sent back the revised proofs of the first two volumes, she still could not promise that the manuscript would be complete before the end of January. Her latest worry was that 'local causes' would absorb all her time. She wrote wearily that if the delay led to Ticknor & Fields pulling out of the deal for American rights, all she could do was ask Smith to deduct his loss from her royalties.

In Manchester local causes were indeed all-consuming. The mills had no American cotton, but the masters were reluctant to change their machinery to suit Indian supplies if there was hope of the Civil War ending. Elizabeth set up 'Sewing-schools' to provide part-time work and corresponded eagerly with Florence Nightingale, hoping that some of the laid-off mill-women might train as nurses.[19] She also involved philanthropists like Godfrey and Vernon Lushington from Liverpool, advising them to send contributions to William, who would pass them to the mayor for the great subscription for the whole of south Lancashire or, 'if you wished to give to Manchester *proper*', to Charles Herford for the District Provident Society, whose offices were now open from six in the morning until eleven at night. If they wished to give to 'any particular *class* of cases', Travers Madge, living right among the poor, would distribute money fairly.[20] She accounted for every cheque, down to 8d a week for an old woman. 'The poor old women' were her special concern:

'at present they have only the workhouse allowance; barely enough for the cheapest, poorest food – only just enough to keep life in. They have worked hard all their working years – poor old friendless women, and now crave and sicken after a "taste of bacon" or something different to the perpetual oat-meal.'[21]

By late summer the Plymouth Grove household had to check themselves from talking about the distress, 'which was literally haunting us in our sleep, as well as being the first thoughts on waking and the last at night'.

In late September Elizabeth went to Eastbourne, where there was rest '& the quiet time for writing'. Deadlines were looming. Dickens had asked for the conclusion of 'A Dark Night's Work' by the end of the month, but she wanted to finish *Sylvia's Lovers* first. She told Smith longingly:

'I wish North & South would make friends, & let us have cotton, & then our people would get work, and then you should have as many novels as you liked to take, and we should not be killed with "Poor on the Brain", as I expect we shall be before the winter is over.' (L698)

Back home, Elizabeth, Marianne and Meta were out from nine in the morning until 7.30 each evening, collapsing into bed too tired to eat. 'I can't tell you what a nightmare last winter was,' she told Norton next spring. Their work was dispiriting since in the face of desperate privation they met fraudulent claims and corruption: 'one *local* relief committee – consisting of small shopkeepers, were found to have supplied themselves with great-coats out of the Funds intrusted to them &c &c &c &c'.

The pace was too fierce. Marianne worked as hard, if not harder than Meta, but the latter was far less resilient. When Effie, with typically careless Wedgwood generosity, accidentally included her own riding-habit in a parcel of clothing, Meta was just about able to joke: 'we will not give it to the most starving Lady Godiva'. But death encircled them: 'Today is the grimmest, blackest November day possible – and inwardly, as well as outwardly, we are all most sad.' Rest was merely a 'weary collapse'.[22]

In early December Meta did finally collapse, and so did her mother, and when an invitation arrived from Philo Brodie asking them to stay in Worthing, William insisted they went at once. Once on the train their spirits rose and their health improved. Once off the train all Elizabeth wanted to do was write. She had reached the final chapters. The burning shores of the Levant had replaced the fecund northern seas and Philip Hepburn was drifting slowly homewards. The mood she was creating was penitential and strange. She wrote compulsively, although, Meta said, she was still not strong:

'sea air, and play with the baby, and rides in a lemon coloured cha'iot will, I hope, overbalance the fatigue of writing 10 pages a day of the tiresome book that is really "a story without an end".'[23]

The story would soon have an end, returning to the waves of Whitby, where it had begun. *Sylvia's Lovers* had taken three years to write, years eroded by illness and travel, by family crises, by war in America and hardship at home. The long gestation of this novel partly explains the change of tone in each volume: the vital, energetic realism of the first volume, written rapidly in the spring of 1860; the intensity of the second, full of death and loss, composed slowly during 1861; the spiritual allegory of the third, a desperate search for belief in a better world, written amid the shadows of the cotton famine. Yet through the many interruptions Elizabeth kept the world of Monkshaven intact and whole, entering it when she could. In early January 1863 she sent the final volume to George Smith. At last she had fulfilled her promise made at Auchencairn, in the honeysuckle-scented summer of 1859:

'Oh! I will so try & write you a good novel.'

[24]

Baffled Seas: *Sylvia's Lovers*

Something it is which thou has lost,
 Some pleasure from thine early years,
 Break, thou deep vase of chilly tears,
That grief hath shaken into frost!

Such clouds of nameless trouble cross
 All night below the darkened eyes;
 With morning wakes the will, and cries
'Thou shalt not be the fool of loss.'

Alfred Tennyson, *In Memoriam* (1850)

Sylvia's Lovers is a novel of longing for the irretrievable, in which energy and zest are slowly undermined and then suddenly destroyed. Gaskell's novel, like Tennyson's poem, sets the trackless sea, the returning ship and the watchers at the quayside – the longing for the return of the beloved – against the drear misery of 'the long unlovely street'. Both reject the consolation that ' "Loss is common to the race" – / And common is the commonplace'. Gaskell refuses to accept that the common *is* necessarily commonplace. Her rustic story dignifies common experience through the speech, customs and even objects of daily existence. Ballads and popular forms – secular and spiritual – are submerged in its depths. In its use of these the novel stays faithful to its period, for the first phase of the Napoleonic wars, unrepresented in the 'serious novel', gave rise to a wealth of broadsheets, prints, plays and songs – the contents of the pedlar's pack.[1]

Individual tragedy is thus blended with the people's story, lost in the official renderings of history. But there is deep sadness and perplexity in this novel. The title-page epigraph deliberately edits *In Memoriam*, to make a negative positive, or at least hopeful:

> Oh for thy voice to soothe and bless!
> What hope of answer, or redress?
> Behind the veil! behind the veil!

Gaskell omits the first line: 'Oh life as futile then, as frail'. Her contemporaries, though, would recognize it as belonging to the most pessimistic section of the poem, opening with the urgent 'Oh yet we trust that somehow good/Will be the final goal of ill', a trust that may be merely the 'dream' of the infant crying in the night, yearning to believe

> That nothing walks with aimless feet;
> That not one life shall be destroyed
> Or cast as rubbish to the void,
> When God hath made the pile complete.

Tennyson is dismayed at the spectre of nature, 'red in tooth and claw', and of her callous indifference: 'So careful of the type she seems,/So careless of the single life':

> 'So careful of the type?' but no,
> From scarpèd cliff and quarried stone
> She cries, 'A thousand types are gone;
> I care for nothing, all shall go.'

A decade after *In Memoriam* Darwin's theories of natural selection had made evolution seem more wasteful still. *Sylvia's Lovers* is an act of loving retrieval; gleaning the gossip of Sylvia and Philip from the bathing-woman and re-creating their world, the narrator asserts the lasting value of lost lives, like a geologist tracing fossils in the quarried stone. And yet, like Tennyson, despite her Unitarian optimism, Gaskell almost despairs in her attempt to fit the bewilderment of grief and the ravages of nature into the meliorist framework of history and a trust in divine providence.

To establish the pang of loss, she first had to establish the vitality of the lost, but she does this so effectively that she almost unbalances her novel. In *Sylvia's Lovers* the priorities of the world gradually give way to those of the spirit; much of its sadness stems from the departure of the romantic vivacity established at the start, when Sylvia chooses scarlet cloth rather than grey for her new cloak. Sylvia is wilful and spoilt, but she pulses with life. When she makes her defiant private purchase, amid the excitement of the whaling fleet's return to Monkshaven, she responds bodily – almost sexually – to the flux of emotions in the town. 'I can't help it,' she says, in answer to her cousin Philip's disapproval, when she clasps the hand of a young prostitute 'Newcastle Bess'. When joy turns to horror at the press-gang raid, she weeps with the crowd, and faints. Ominously, she is then carried into the claustrophobic back room of the Foster brothers' shop, where Philip works. Its window looks out (like the workroom in *Ruth*) on to a dark yard where poplars strain towards the light. But through the open door Sylvia can still glimpse the ships in the narrow harbour, moored on the 'dancing, heaving, river'.

Sylvia is drawn to that dancing, heaving river: to motion, distance, danger. And her heroine's choice is, one feels, Gaskell's own, however much she might resist it. She too likes the flux and romance of restless lives. She too might have chosen the scarlet cloak and not the grey. She too, as she tells us in 'Company Manners', preferred the wild tales in the dusky schoolroom to the solemnly sensible dinner-table talk. The vital current of this novel flows strong against its overt message of resignation, self-sacrifice and submission to the will of God.

The basic elements of the story, found in Crabbe's poem 'Ruth', rework two popular themes found in the prints and songs of the 1790s: 'The man seized by the press-gang on the day of his wedding' and 'The Sailor's Return'.[2] In Gaskell's version Sylvia Robson, a farmer's daughter, has been loved since she was twelve by her sober, Quaker cousin Philip Hepburn. He in turn is silently adored by the devout Hester Rose, who works with him in the shop, but Sylvia merely resents him as a moralizing voice of conscience. Her heart is won instead by the bold 'specksioneer', Charley Kinraid, a harpooneer on an Arctic whaler. When Charley is captured by the press-gang, Philip is a witness, but he suppresses the truth and lets Sylvia believe him dead. This lie unlooses their fates: it is not told for life-saving reasons, like Thurstan Benson's in *Ruth* or Margaret Hale's in *North and South*, but is akin to murder, killing Kinraid in fantasy and denying Sylvia's independent choice, destroying the very part of her he loves.

From this point disaster unreels: in 'the deep, passionate vengeance' of the people against the press-gang; in Daniel Robson's execution after he is accused of inciting the Whitby riot; in Sylvia's reluctant, despairing marriage to Philip; in the traumatic return of Kinraid. Private and public dramas of conflict and survival demonstrate fundamental polarities: the chapter where Kinraid meets Sylvia at Moss Brow and Philip tries to educate her is called 'Attraction and Repulsion'. This phrase calls to mind not only the opposition of physical laws but the revolutionary, Swedenborgian contraries of William Blake's *Marriage of Heaven and Hell*, begun in 1790 and completed in 1793, the year that *Sylvia's Lovers* opens:

Without Contraries is no progression. Attraction and Repulsion, Reason and Energy, Love and Hate are necessary to Human existence.
From these Contraries spring what the religious call Good & Evil. Good is the passive that obeys Reason. Evil is the active springing from Energy.
Good is Heaven. Evil is Hell.

Energy, of course, to Blake, was 'Eternal Delight'; Reason was the slayer of life and bodily passion. Gaskell, by contrast, preaches acceptance of the dictates of reason, law and God – but the pull of that Blakean fire is still felt in her book.

The argument of Gaskell's novels always proceeds through dialectic and *Sylvia's Lovers* is no exception. Its drama lies in the collision of opposites, its characters forming a sequence of reverse images and variations – Philip and Sylvia; Sylvia and Hester; Philip and Kinraid; Bell and Daniel Robson – suggesting permanent, almost genetic oppositions. To return to Gaskell's Darwinian metaphor, some types will adapt and flourish, others will not, but she does not interpret the 'survival of the fittest' in purely personal terms. She is painfully aware that the interests of the race may require the cruel obliteration of the individual – of soldiers in the French wars, or of men like Daniel Robson, who oppose the press-gang. Hence the debates about province versus nation, and the rights of the individual as opposed to the demands of the distant 'State'. The structural polarities of *Sylvia's Lovers* warn us that the real danger for both individual and society is imbalance, the extreme emotion which prevents clear sight; a love like Philip's can turn to possessive jealousy; a deep fellow-feeling for the oppressed, like Daniel's, into rash anger. Passion – a word that resounds through the novel – is the fatal flaw which disables these two men from adapting (as the opportunistic Kinraid does) to the flow of history. Daniel is condemned by the laws of the State, Philip by the equally inexorable laws of God. He lets his love overwhelm his judgement, veracity and religion. For him (as for Manasseh in 'Lois the Witch') his desire supplants his faith, as he acknowledges at his death:

' "Child," said he, once more. "I ha' made thee my idol; and, if I could live my life o'er again, I would love my God more, and thee less; and then I shouldn't ha' sinned this sin against thee." ' (Ch. 45)

The excessive, rule-breaking emotions of Daniel and Philip are also those of the community in which they live. *Sylvia's Lovers* opens, like *The Life of Charlotte Brontë,* by describing a unique place and society, an enclave even more isolated than Haworth, home of a 'wild North-Eastern people', where self-destructive passions flourish.[3] Cut off by the barrier of the moors, facing the open seas, Monkshaven is an amphibious town, with a strong touch of lawlessness. Even the Quaker Foster brothers have a secret passage for smuggled goods and Philip accepts this, uncomfortably aware from the start that he may not practise what he preaches. Sylvia, his prize, is also contraband, brought into his house under false pretences.

The Whitby on which this town was based had vanished by the time Gaskell wrote. In 1829 when she lived in Newcastle (Charles Kinraid's home town), the whaling fleets still set sail each spring, but the last whaler sailed from Whitby in 1837, and the railway soon made it easier to reach London by land than sea. Gaskell describes Monkshaven as changing even in the 1790s, its mansions on the heights and the Fosters' embryonic bank signalling a move towards the bourgeois. The romantic Charley, as much as the shop-man Philip, has begun to think in terms of status and money. When Charley proposes to Sylvia, he talks eagerly of 'seventy to ninety pounds a voyage' and his plans to become a ship's master. It is typical of Sylvia that she hardly listens (she would rather hear about love and adventure than worldly prospects) and dismisses his anxiety about Philip as a rival in a tone of contempt: 'He's so full o' business an t'shop, and o' makin money, and getting wealth.'

The French wars and the changing economy draw Monkshaven into the currents of national and international affairs; the town is evolving.

But the wider 'civilized' world turns out to have as dubious a relation to law, and to be as 'red in tooth and claw' as the isolated Yorkshire port; the lawless law of the age, embodied in the press-gang, causes Kinraid's capture and Daniel's death. In such a troubled, transitional time these characters are partly the casualties of history. As in *The Mill on the Floss*, the slow accretion of custom, of language, of ingrained attitudes gives way to both the tide of change without and the flood of passion within. Pretending to look back with the detachment of a more rational age (as in 'Lois the Witch'), Gaskell actually questions that age's assumptions of 'progress'. When she describes the cruelties of the press-gang, backed by militia with bayonets, she writes:

'Now all this tyranny (for I can use no other word) is marvellous to us; we cannot imagine how it is that a nation submitted to it for so long, even under any warlike enthusiasm, any panic of invasion, any loyal subservience to the governing powers.' (Ch. 1)

Yet she was writing against a background of the American Civil War, where brother was killing brother under exactly such loyal subservience.

The irony is conscious: when she tells of the prevarications of Dr Wilson, who preaches at the funeral of Darley, the sailor killed by the gang, the scene is tragic, but the vicar's confusion is comic: life is never straightforward. But, she adds,

'such discrepancies ran through good men's lives in those days. It is well for us that we live at the present time, when everybody is logical and consistent.' (Ch. 6)

The irony is less obvious, but still present, when she looks through the clarifying lens of time at individuals, as if self-awareness too was a product of evolution, a feature of period not personality.

'It is astonishing to look back and find how differently constituted were the minds of most people, fifty or sixty years ago; they felt, they understood, without going through reasoning or analytic processes; and, if this was the case among the more educated people, of course it was still more so in the class to which Sylvia belonged.' (Ch. 28)

Despite her 'astonishment' we feel that this still applies, as does the inability to analyse and identify with others: Philip cannot comprehend Kinraid, nor Hester Sylvia, and vice versa. And in any age such 'undeveloped' characters as Sylvia and her father will be taken aback by the consequences of their actions and find it hard to learn:

'In fact, Daniel was very like a child in all the parts of his character. He was strongly affected by whatever was present, and apt to forget the absent. He acted on impulse, and too often had reason to be sorry for it; but he hated his sorrow too much to let it teach him wisdom for the future.' (Ch. 22)

George Eliot makes Mr Tulliver and Maggie similarly unaware: Maggie Tulliver, she says, is 'unhappily quite without that knowledge of the irreversible laws within and without her'. Such laws might seem to render individuals impotent, their choices predetermined by an already written script. Both Gaskell and Eliot, however, present every decision as significant, no matter how small. Philip is longing to see Sylvia on New Year's Eve:

'At this hour, all the actors in this story having played out their parts and gone to their rest, there is something touching in recording the futile efforts made by Philip to win from Sylvia the love he yearned for. But, at the time, anyone who had watched him might have been amused to see the grave, awkward, plain young man studying patterns and colours for a new waistcoat, with his head a little on one side, after the meditative manner common to those who are choosing a new article of dress.' (Ch. 12)

Philip interprets events, past and present, in the light of his own obsession. His world hangs on Sylvia's smile. Hearing the story of old Alice Rose's marriage to a violent whaler in preference to the kindly Jeremiah Foster, he applies it to himself and Kinraid. He sees history as cyclical rather than progressive, wondering 'if the lives of one generation were but repetition of the lives of those who had gone before, with no variation but from the internal cause that some had greater capacity for suffering than others'. Such a vision undercuts any notion of benign progress. And in a sense Philip is right – the idea of reversion to type was also integral to Darwin's theories. Gaskell is retelling an ancient story, and the idea of the cycle is embedded in her countless images of death and resurrection.

The repetitive nature of human experience, a flowing and ebbing tide washing through time and circling the 'whole terraqueous globe', as Herman Melville so marvellously put it, imparts great power to the opening scenes, where women watch at the quayside for sons, brothers, fathers, husbands, lovers to return. Even before the press-gang strikes they wait in mingled excitement and dread. They fear the unknown, the toll taken by the 'terrible, dreary Arctic seas', the news that 'might rush in upon their hearts with the uprising tide'. Their rage when the gang seize their men has an ancient quality as if choreographed over centuries. First we see a crowd of 'wild, half-amphibious boys, slowly moving backwards'. When the gang are encircled, the late eighteenth-century mob retreats in time, back through the classical and the pagan, and reverts to the animal:

'pressing around this nucleus of cruel wrong, were women crying aloud, throwing up their arms in imprecation, showering down abuse as hearty and rapid as if they had been a Greek chorus. Their wild, famished eyes were strained on faces they might not kiss, their cheeks were flushed to purple with anger or else livid with impotent craving for revenge. Some of them looked scarce human; and yet, an hour ago, these lips, now tightly drawn back so as to show the teeth with the unconscious action of an enraged wild animal, had been soft and gracious with the smile of hope.' (Ch. 3)

Before this we have been shown another chorus, at once local and ancient, with the energy of a Bacchanal. A group of girls with flushed faces and careless dress have clambered on a pile of timber to see the ships come in:

'They were wild and free in their gestures, and held each other by the hand, and swayed from side to side, stamping their feet in time, as they sang —

Weel may the keel row, the keel row, the keel row,
Weel may the keel row that my laddie's in!' (Ch. 2)

'The Keel Row', with its jaunty tune and loving, opimistic lyrics, will be Charley Kinraid's motif; he is whistling it when he falls into the press-gang's trap. Up to that point the narrative is full of movement, song, dance and tale, for this is the world of the ballad, the hornpipe and the sailor's yarn, close to the land and at home on the sea. In the second volume, the 'pent-up' Whitby chapters, instead of songs we find invocations and ghost story, Gothic forms born of suppression; in the final penitential sequence (where Charley's men still sing 'The Keel Row' at the Battle of Acre) pantomimic portrayals of worldly glory – the panorama and the circus – battle against spiritual texts. Popular forms underpin the triple movement of the novel and biblical lore and folk tradition intertwine. For example, the action of *Sylvia's Lovers* is spread over seven years, from 1793 to 1800. This is an unusually long time for a Gaskell novel, but the chronology is related to its theme of separation and reunion. The seven-year span is frequently invoked: in Philip thinking of Jacob's 'twice seven years service' for Rachel, in Sylvia dreaming of the sailor lovers of ballad, in Philip again, reading of Guy of Warwick's return to his wife after 'seven long years' at the crusades.[4]

The free, rhythmic songs and stories of the opening spring from the lives of the people. They are part of a 'natural' organic culture which co-exists with, is ignored by and defies the regulated forms and texts imposed from above: the 'rule of law' in the Statutes, the rules of Mavor's spelling book which Philip gives Sylvia, the ruled lines of the Fosters' account books. In this community the old, customary oath that Sylvia exchanges with Kinraid is almost more valid than her formal church vow to Philip. When these farmers and sailors quote the Bible, they do not choose the authoritative edicts of prophets but the communally sung psalms. The sailors 'who go forth on the great deep', Gaskell tells us, sleep through the sermons but respond to the Book of Common Prayer, to the Litany, with its 'old, oft repeated words praying for deliverance from the familiar dangers of lightning and tempest; from battle, murder and sudden death', or to the great hymn of thanksgiving after the tempest, so suggestive of the story as a whole:

'We found trouble and heaviness: we were even at death's door.

The waters of the sea had well-nigh covered us; the proud waters had well-nigh gone over our soul.

The sea roared; and the stormy wind lifted up the waves thereof.

We were carried up as it were to heaven, and then down again into the deep: our soul melted within us, because of trouble;

Then we cried unto thee, O Lord: and thou didst deliver us out of our distress.'[5]

In *Sylvia's Lovers*, even more than in *Mary Barton*, Gaskell kept faith with the expression of the people. Speech, as William had insisted in his 'Lectures on Lancashire Dialect', has its own history and evolution, displaying regional, class and individual variants: Gaskell carefully gave Bell Robson Cumbrian forms to fit her origins. The manuscript reveals numerous alterations of word endings and technical details such as variations of the definite article – the, th', t' – and in the second edition she meticulously corrected the dialect wherever Lancashire forms had corrupted Yorkshire ('ne'er' to 'niver'; 'dost na' to 'dostn' t'). So precise was she that her idioms entered Wright's *English Dialect Dictionary* (such as: 'main an' ' – very; 'a coil' – a fuss; 'maskit' – infused; 't'fettling' – repairing), while other terms were included in locally compiled glossaries.[6]

Such details, imperceptible to most of her readers, were in tune with her determination to gather the 'unimportant' chaff and dust of past lives. Diction and syntax are carefully adapted to the speaker, reflecting relationships as well as origins: the intimate second person 'yo' as opposed to the formal plural 'ye', or the Quaker 'thee' and 'thou'.[7] Gradations are tenderly charted. Bell comes from a higher class than her husband (before her marriage she was a Preston, of that familiar Lakeland 'Statesman' class) and it irritates Daniel when she uses a word beyond his comprehension, like 'pretext', which he then promptly misuses. The misconception of meaning is more than merely verbal, as Sylvia recognizes when she wishes her mother had not spoken in favour of the grey cloak:

'Ay! but mother's words are scarce, and weigh heavy. Feyther's liker me, and we talk a deal o' rubble; but mother's words are liker to hewn stone. She puts a deal o' meaning in 'em.' (Ch. 2)

Daniel's 'deal o' rubble', gathered over a wandering life, has rough eloquence, like John Barton's Manchester speech, but his words spring from passion and his rash use of them is his downfall. Over a year before he spurs on the crowd in the riot. Bell blanches at his angry speeches about the press-gang:

'Ay, missus, yo' may look. I wunnot pick and choose my words, noather for yo' nor for nobody, when I speak o' that daumed gang. I'm noane ashamed o' my words. They're true, and I'm ready to prove 'em.' (Ch. 4)

Through the words native to them the inarticulate become articulate, even while they feel outcast from language. When the Robsons' farmhand Kester, who has loved Sylvia since she was a baby, visits her after her marriage, he recites the old sanding rhyme Gaskell heard at her own wedding, looking to the continuation of life through 'fruitful progeny':

'Theere, that's po'try for yo' as I larnt i' my youth. But there's a deal to be said as cannot be put int' po'try, an' yet a cannot say it, somehow. It'd tax a parson t' say a' as a've getten i' my mind. It's like a heap o' woo' just after shearin'-time; it's worth a deal, but it tak's a vast o' combin', an' cardin', an' spinnin', afore it can be made use on. If a were up to t' use o' words, a could say a mighty deal; but somehow a'm tongue-teed when a come to want my words most.' (Ch. 30)

Kester's image of the sheared wool, drawn from life, is as vivid as any poetry. Sylvia's resistance to literacy may be foolish, but it is also understood as loyalty to the unregulated oral vigour of her class. As such it contrasts to the upward aspirations of Philip, who reads aloud in a high-pitched voice 'which deprived words of their reality', or to the Foster brothers in their spotless, right-angled room, the smiles on their honest faces 'drawn to a line of exactitude', preparing their conversation 'like London diners-out of the last generation', intoning articles of trade like articles of faith. Jeremiah reads his Bible daily to the housekeeper: 'like many, he reserved a peculiar tone for that solemn occupation – and one which he unconsciously employed for the present enumeration of pounds, shillings and pence'.

The voices of the new bourgeoisie sound forced compared with Sylvia's 'natural' expression, but Gaskell respects these people too and does not mock them. As Philip points out, Sylvia's objection to printed books with their 'new-fangled words' confines her to the past. She must use her head as well as her heart and adapt to the wider culture, just as she must look at the globe to find other places than Greenland and the Arctic seas. And, as he sketches his map, she does begin to look outward, although still from the vantage of the local: 'even she became a little interested in starting from a great black spot called Monkshaven, and in the shaping of land and sea around that one centre'. Words also map the world. Every life, explains Philip, has its own language; hers of woman's work, his of the shop, that of the 'folks in fields' and the 'high English that parsons and lawyers speak'. *Sylvia's Lovers* is full of such vocabularies, creating a complex, developing and competing universe through the words of land, sea, trade, church, state and war.

Each sphere has its own rhythm, like that of the whaling fleet with the bustle of departure in spring when the ice-barrier breaks and the excitement of return in autumn, or that of the land, where the overall pattern of the year is inset with seasonal detail. The passing of the year itself is marked by the ritual of the New Year Fête, with the long-lived customs and games that Gaskell had recorded since her youth. These are solidly material worlds, of animals, food, furniture, implements of work, where even the tangible can express continuity and emotion, like the Corneys' counterpane, which has descended through the family since a time when 'patchwork was patchwork'. Alice Rose looks to the past, insisting that William Coulson mark her will with the sign of the Trinity, just as her father and her father's father did, but her small material bequests project her own life into the future. She leaves her settle, saucepans, dresser and kettle to Hester, and tells him:

'And thee shall have t' roller and paste-board, because thee's so fond o' puddings and cakes. It'll serve thy wife after I'm gone, and I trust she'll boil her paste long enough, for that's been t' secret o' mine.' (Ch. 7)

Traditional genres, like household possessions polished by use, are similarly used to carry meaning. Gaskell knows their crudity: Sylvia, who prefers pictures to words, ignores the text of the *Sorrows of Werther*, which has a place in every pedlar's basket, but smiles at 'the picture of Charlotte cutting bread and butter in a left-handed manner.' The familiar, statuesque poses of popular engravings become icons of longing for the lost, the central feeling of the novel. In Sylvia's memory the sight of her mother gazing across the fields into the sunset, 'searching through the blinding rays for a sight of her child, rose up like a sudden seen picture, the remembrance of which smote Sylvia to the heart with a sense of a lost blessing, not duly valued while possessed'. Later Philip will watch Sylvia herself standing in this pose, 'like a stone statue', gazing out at the sea where she thinks Kinraid lies drowned.

Such silent immobility is itself a sign of Sylvia's lost self. Before Kinraid's death she, like her lover and her father, is essentially mobile, a figure from a rustic print, but linked to music and dance. When she spins, her stance is specifically compared to the 'high culture' pose of the harpist, as she accompanies the 'pretty buzzing, whirring sound' with 'nimble, agile motion keeping time to the movement of the wheel'. And as she spins, or as she dances, as she ascends or descends the stairs, Philip sits watching, following 'the last wave of her dress'. She is the mobile body, he the still eye and restless mind.

A creature of ballad, Sylvia is drawn to the whalers, whose stories and songs, known since her childhood, create a world of strangeness and male daring which is the antithesis of the domestic hearth:

> And when we came to Imez
> Where the mountains flowed with snow
> We tacked about all in the North
> Till we heard a whalefish blow.[8]

Yet these heroes are also hunters, whose trade is killing, who identify with their knives, as big as a sickle: ' "Teach folk as don't know a whaling knife," cried Daniel. "I were a Greenland-man mysel'." ' There is more than a casual significance in the names Kinraid and Robson. Sylvia's mother is right to be wary of the harpooneer. William Scoresby had made special note of the 'maternal affection' of the mother whale, how she fought for her cub and exposed herself to attack, 'taking it under her wing; and seldom deserting it while life remains'.[9] But the women are won by the very violence of the men; 'Women is so fond o' bloodshed,' says Philip to Molly Corney. Sylvia's fascination with Charley begins before she sees him, with the travelling tailor's story of his fight against the press-gang, in which he kills two men, is wounded and left for dead. When she actually meets him at Darley's funeral, he looks like a corpse revived, a driven man who can defeat death itself, as the tailor Donkin says: 'He'll live! he'll live! Niver a man died yet, wi' such strong purpose of vengeance in him.' The whaling stories of Daniel and Kinraid are a male genre, where the ship which holds them (and, in Gaskell's telling, the whales they hunt) are always gendered as female. The stories themselves are a form of hunting: ' "Yo' may learn t' way of winnin' t' women," said Daniel, winking at the specksioneer.' The sensible Bell was won by these yarns: so will her daughter be.

When Kinraid enters, wildness floods the domestic. Mother and daughter are in the kitchen, their knitting-needles making 'a pleasant home sound'. As Bell dozes, Sylvia listens to 'the long-rushing boom of the waves, down below on the rocks, for the Haytersbank gully allowed the sullen roar to come up so far inland' and she springs to open the door 'with a lively, instinctive advance towards any event which might break the monotony'. The entry of Kinraid, we are told, is like breaking a smouldering lump of coal into sudden flame so that a dusky room is suddenly 'full of life, and light, and warmth'.

In this warm interior the men exchange tales of danger and cold. They speak of a region of timeless peril where the brief, violent struggle of whale and man takes place among icebergs which seem to have existed since the time of Adam, 'ne'er a bit bigger nor smaller in all those thousands and thousands o' years'. Three of their four tales are adapted from Scoresby, and since such heroic myths as his account of riding on the back of a whale are 'timeless', Gaskell can take her stories freely from future and past – the nineteenth or seventeenth century – and make them immediate, through the direct speech of Kinraid and Robson.[10] In the icy seas men seem expendable, forgotten, but the act of storytelling is itself an assurance of their survival. The personal, local voice, the wit and detail, define the teller as well as the tale: when Kinraid describes the berg which crashes into the sea, remaining grimly unscathed while whale and men go down, he adds that the Newcastle miners might find the boat if they dig deep enough, 'and I left as good a clasp knife in her as ever I clapt eyes on'.

The resurrective force of such stories is even clearer when Daniel describes a capsize. In Scoresby's grave account the whale did not sink, as usual, 'on receiving the wound', but 'only dived for a moment and then rose again beneath the boat, struck it in the most vicious manner with its fins and tail, stove it, upset it, and then disappeared'.[11] Daniel's retelling focuses not on the whale but on his shivering self, when she 'chucks me out into t' watter'. In the terrible cold he feels as if his skin were stripped from him, and 'ivery bone i' my body had getten t' toothache'. There is a roar in his ears, a dizziness in his eyes,

'an I thought I were bound for "kingdom come," an' a tried to remember t' Creed, as a might die a Christian. But all a could think on was, "What is your name, M or N"?' Ch. 9)

With the body *in extremis* there is no place for the anonymous formulas of the Catechism. Daniel's rescue and revival is a pagan rebirth, a return to the warm hearth, to the women's room where he now sits: 'they rubbed me as missus theere were rubbing t' hams yesterday . . . Talk o' cold!' he insists; 'it's little yo' women known o' cold!'

Kinraid, embodiment of fire as well as sea, counters Daniel's vision of cold with one of heat. In the southern seas an American whaler encounters a great ice wall, a challenge to the captain, who proclaims he will sail along it, looking for a break, 'till the day o' judgement'. After endless days and nights they see a cleft in the ice, its sheer sides plunging sharp down into the foaming waters:

'But we took but one look at what lay inside, for our captain, with a loud cry to God, bade the helmsman steer nor'ards away fra' th' mouth o' hell. We all saw wi' our own eyes, inside that fearsome wall o' ice – seventy miles long, as we could swear to – inside that grey, cold ice, came leaping flames, all red and yellow wi' heat o' some unearthly kind out o' th' very waters o' the sea; making our eyes dazzle wi' their scarlet blaze, that shot up as high, nay higher than th' ice around, yet never so much as a shred on 't was melted.' (Ch. 9)

The captain sees demons dancing within. Since his hubris has brought them there he must die. Bell is appalled: 'Eh, dear! but it's awful t' think o' sitting wi' a man that has seen th' doorway into hell.' But Sylvia is won by fire and ice.

The story binds the general theme of survival and death to the personal drama. Kinraid, the eternal survivor, will make 'a prosperous voyage' although he vows never to sail those seas again. Philip is like the captain, whose obsessive pursuit brings his doom, but he is also akin to the ice, 'pale', 'stiff' and 'cold', with a hellish heat in his heart. For Sylvia, who drops her work and gazes 'in fascinated wonder', the story works a sexual spell. Her later despairing yearning for the sailor who vanishes and returns is like the longing for the Demon Lover, who returns to claim his vows after seven years and finds his love a wife and mother:

> O whaten mountain is yon, she said,
> All so dreary wi frost and snow?
> O yon is the mountain of hell, he cried,
> Where you and I will go.[12]

Sylvia escapes this fate by refusing – unlike the mother in the ballad – to abandon her child. She does not, like Maggie in *The Mill on the Floss*, abandon herself to the waters, nor, finally, drown in the flood. But she glimpses the dreary mountain of hell, none the less.

Fire and ice, motion and stillness, temporal body and eternal spirit, weave and converge in Gaskell's narration. The main characters are each endowed with emotional climates and landscapes: Sylvia the farm, the dairy and the hearth, Philip the shop and the tighly closed room, Kinraid the rushing sea and northern ice. In the course of the book they enter each other's imaginative and spiritual territory, as in the wonderfully suggestive scene where Kinraid finds Sylvia in the barn with Kester, who is milking the cows, their breath mellowing the frosty air: the 'shippen' with its fragrant, milky, female warmth is the converse of his ship, ploughing the icy waters. In an earlier scene, when Philip teaches the rebellious Sylvia 'writing and ciphering', her hands become cramped and stiff; she would rather learn geography, at least that of Greenland, but he makes her write 'Abednego' over and over again – the name of the man who goes through the fire. When Kinraid's entry halts the lesson, Philip angrily stiffens himself 'into coldness of demeanour'; he is left in the cold, excluded from their quick, merry chatter by the fire, unable to hear or speak.

Later, at the New Year Fête, Philip is on the point of saying something 'explicitly tender' to Sylvia, when the spinning trencher separates them and he is once again

'left standing outside the circle, as if he were not playing. In fact, Sylvia had unconsciously taken his place as an actor in the game . . . He was wedged against the wall, close to the great eight day clock.' (Ch. 12)

Overhearing Molly Corney guess that Sylvia has kissed Charley in the other room, and seeing them at supper, sitting close together while he is pushed against the wall, he can only watch, while the clock ticks: 'It seemed to be Philip's luck this night to be pent up in places.'

Shut out from their warmth, leaving in a fury, Philip is flung into a landscape that is a spiritual equivalent of Kinraid's Arctic seascape:

'The cold sleet almost blinded him as the sea-wind drove it straight in his face; it cut against him as it was blown with drifting force. The roar of the wintry sea came borne on the breeze; there was more light from the whitened ground than from the dark laden sky above.' (Ch. 12)

The field paths would be a 'matter of perplexity' except for the glimpse of white through dark stone walls:

'Yet he went clear and straight along his way, having unconsciously left all guidance to the animal instinct which co-exists with the human soul, and sometimes takes strange charge of the human body, when all the nobler powers of the individual are absorbed in acute suffering.' (Ch. 12)

Philip's revenge comes when Kinraid is captured by the press-gang and rendered as immobile as he has been, 'still as any hedgehog', with only his eyes active, 'watchful, vivid, fierce as those of a wild cat brought to bay'. He too is an animal, trapped by suffering. Convincing himself that his promise to carry Charley's parting message to Sylvia is not valid, Philip sees the ship bearing his rival away as glorious: 'She had spread her beautiful great sails, and was standing out to sea in the glittering path of the descending sun.' The illusion is bitter. As he set out on that golden May morning, walking northward to take the boat to London on the Foster brothers' business, the calm sea was whitened by unseen rocks, 'but, otherwise the waves came up from the German Ocean upon that English shore with a long steady roll that might have taken its first impetus on the coast of "Norroway over the foam" '. Like Sir Patrick Spens in that ballad, he cannot keep out the force of the sea:

> He had not gone a step, a step,
> A step but barely ane,
> When a bolt flew out of the good ship's side
> And the salt sea it came in.[13]

After Kinraid vanishes the folk-songs fade. Sylvia is no longer Shakespeare's, whom all the swains adore, but the 'Sylvie' whose lover has left her, and who contemplates death by the riverside:

> And looking so sadly, and looking so sadly
> And looking so sadly upon its swift tide.[14]

For the first time in Gaskell's fiction, in contrast to the submerged lidless-eyed monster in *Ruth* or *North and South*, the face in the water represents an inescapable desire which was freely welcomed and whose loss is mourned. As Sylvia gazes at the fire, she thinks of her lover,

'lying somewhere, fathoms deep beneath the surface of that sunny sea on which she looked day by day, without ever seeing his upturned face through the depths, with whatsoever heart-sick longing for just one more sight she yearned and inwardly cried.' (Ch. 24)

She wants to resurrect him, to see him in the flickering firelight, 'his legs dangling, his busy fingers playing with some of her woman's work', and prays to 'some, any Power' to let her see him once again, 'just once – for one minute of passionate delight'. Joy is drowned. Revenge, the counter of love, dominates this central section of the novel. Imprisonment and death replace freedom and life in the uprisings against the press-gang, the terrible story of Daniel's trial and execution, the collapse of Bell, the marriage of Sylvia. Both father and daughter seem 'possessed'. Daniel's hanging renders Sylvia helpless, hopeless and as vengeful as he. All her words are of vehement, permanent denial: the phrases 'niver speak on 't', 'I'll niver forget' and 'I'll niver forgive' ring through scene after scene.

After Sylvia agrees to marry Philip, she is 'pent up' in her house in the narrow streets, 'stunned into a sort of temporary numbness'. Her lively nature is subdued: 'obedience to her husband seemed to be her rule of life at this period'. She escapes constantly to the cliffs and the 'mother-like' sea until she is literally 'confined': 'by and by, the time came when she was a prisoner in the house, a prisoner in her room, lying in bed with a little baby by her side – her child, Philip's child'.

As in *Ruth*, the child brings rebirth to the mother. Simultaneously the buried comes to life in dreams – Philip's dream of Kinraid returning 'stern and vengeful' and Sylvia's anguished, lifelike vision of her lover, from which she wakes stretching out her arms and crying 'in a voice full of yearning and tears, – "Oh! Charley! come to me – come to me!" ' The tension breaks in a bitter private quarrel over the making of Philip's tea, a brilliant example of the deep significance of the apparently trivial. Escaping to the cliffs again, Sylvia helps to pull the survivors of a wreck to shore, in a storm where 'it seemed as if all human voice must be lost in the tempestuous stun and tumult of wind and wave'. The repressed returns: one of these survivors is Kinraid.

The rescue is followed by the ghost-like apparition of Kinraid at Haytersbank, where Sylvia has gone to fetch lemon balm for her ailing mother, Bell: it is as if she created him by the very power of memory, a wraith of the past, like the lean cat who walks through her abandoned childhood home. He pursues her through the winding streets and together they confront Philip, but she chooses her child rather than either man. In her final speech to Kinraid the word 'never' tolls like a funeral bell. The marriage promise and the lover's oath are replaced by a new vow:

' "Hark!" said she, starting away from Kinraid, "baby's crying for me. His child – yes, it is his child – I'd forgotten that – forgotten all. I'll make my vow now, lest I lose mysel' again. I'll never forgive yon man, nor live with him as his wife again. All that's done and ended. He's spoilt my life, – he's spoilt it for as long as iver I live on this earth; but neither yo' nor him shall spoil my soul. It goes hard wi' me, Charley, it does indeed. I'll just give yo' one kiss – one little kiss – and then, so help me God, I'll niver see yo' nor hear till – no, not that, not that is needed – I'll niver see – sure that's enough – I'll never see yo' again on this side heaven, so help me God! I'm bound and tied, but I've sworn my oath to him as well as yo'; there's things I will do, and there's things I won't. Kiss me once more. God help me, he's gone!" ' (Ch. 33)

The end of this chapter, the second great crisis of the novel, comes straight from the stage. The manuscript shows that Gaskell worked on her draft with unusual care, heightening the speeches and rewriting the scene to insert virtual stage directions – when read aloud, the text, like a play-script, almost compels particular gestures, looks, actions, intonations. The quotations that follow show Gaskell's deletions – { } – and her insertions – \ /. For instance, Kinraid raises his arm to strike Philip, 'but Sylvia came {swift} between the blow and its victim'. And when Sylvia tells Charley that Philip is her husband:

' "Oh! \ thou/ false heart!", exclaimed Kinraid, \ turning sharp on her/, "If ever I trusted woman I trusted you, Sylvia Robson," He {turned from her} \ made as if throwing her from him/ with a gesture of contempt that stung her to life.'[15]

Popular melodrama and dialect speech are brilliantly combined to give Sylvia's decision a terrible poignancy as well as moral depth.

Sylvia's choice of child rather than sailor lover is followed by her own mother's death: she takes up the mantle of motherhood herself. Philip, the former Quaker, driven forth 'like Cain', enlists as a soldier under the name Stephen Freeman, dreaming of returning as heroic as Kinraid. From now on, as spirit and soul predominate over body and heart, the division between male aggression and female nurture becomes schematically stark.

At this point two chapters are juxtaposed. In 'Bereavement' Sylvia and her daughter Bella go to live with Alice and Hester Rose. Hester takes the place of male breadwinner, a virtual partner in the shop where 'she had long been the superintendent of that department of goods which were exclusively devoted to women'. There are elements of unease, but the women draw together in their love of the child. Just as Ruth educated herself for her son, so for Bella's sake Sylvia tackles the 'hard words' of church and chapel and old Alice, once so hostile, teaches her tenderly 'as if her pupil had been a little child'. They start from the beginning, with the book of Genesis. It is spring, with primroses in the hedgerows. Nature enhances the process of regeneration; when Hester falls ill, Sylvia takes her to 'drink milk warm from the cow'. The women, however, are not quite separate from the pain of men: Hester complains of a pounding in her head, 'as if there were great guns booming'.

The following chapter, 'The Recognition', takes place on the same day, 7 May 1799, where great guns are really booming by the glittering Mediterranean at the Siege of Acre. The unreality of this episode is always interpreted as an artistic lapse, a sign of haste, but Gaskell was too aware of language and genre for this to be a casual aberration and her reasoning in this scene is surely clear. Its obvious artifice denies the worth of heroic violence, however justified the cause. The wooden style is a deliberate contrast to the unfolding, casual 'feminine' realism of the previous chapter. The scenery is truly 'scenery', like the painted backdrop of a play or the fashionable panoramas of the day, with the reader placed firmly outside the action and invited to 'look again'. Gaskell even calls the town of Acre 'St Jean d'Acre', the title of a popular patriotic ballad celebrating the siege, thumped out on innumerable parlour pianos across Britain.

The use of the present tense in the description of Acre enhances the effect of demonstration and when Gaskell moves to the past tense to record the actual events, she retains an archaic formality: 'the besieged Turks took heart of grace'; the sailors march 'with merry hearts', singing 'The Keel Row' (a use of leitmotif typical of melodrama); the Pacha hurries to help 'with right hearty good will . . . but little recked the crew of the *Tigre*'. The language echoes the contemporary recitals of the exploits of 'Jack Tar' – another item among the pedlars' wares.[16] It reinforces Gaskell's point that in glorifying war men refuse to see its reality; 'and so they went on, as if it were some game of play instead of a deadly combat'.

In this artificial scene two moments stand out as 'real', written in the style of the novel as a whole. When Kinraid lies wounded, his throat parched,

'thoughts of other days, of cool Greenland seas, where ice abounded, of grassy English homes, began to make the past more real than the present.' (Ch. 38)

The past does becomes present as Philip, in an act of instinctive bravery, forgetful of himself, materializes like a dream to save Kinraid and utters words of spontaneous regret, 'I niver thought you'd ha' kept true to her!'

The sailor who tells Kinraid he was rescued by a spirit, not by flesh and blood, is partly right. The narration of Sylvia's life at Whitby, where she learns of Kinraid's marriage and hears from his new wife the almost incredible story of the rescue, remains rich in detail and dialect, but the description of Philip's progress is a spiritual allegory. Trailing northwards, given 'milk and home-brewed', by women at the wayside, he spends four months at the hospice of St Sepulchre. In its tomb-like tranquillity, weary of reviewing 'the mill-wheel circle' of his life, he picks up a chap-book version of *The Seven Champions of Christendom*, where he reads of the return of Guy of Warwick from the crusades.[17] Starving and travel-worn, unrecognized by his countess, Guy receives bread from her hands with the other beggars and is reunited with her only at his death.

A contrasting popular form is then introduced to mock the idealism of both the martial panorama of Acre and the Christian romance of the chap-book. When Philip returns to Monkshaven, its narrow streets are blocked by a circus parade, with trumpeters 'blaring out triumphant discord':

'In the chariot sate kings and queens, heroes and heroines, or what were meant for such; all the little boys and girls running alongside of the chariot envied them; but they themselves were very much tired, and shivering with cold in their heroic pomp of classic clothing.' (Ch. 42)

Philip notices nothing, for he has seen Sylvia laughing, with Bella in her arms. She will go in to the hearth, he is left out in the cold. 'The fable of the Countess Phillis, who mourned for her husband's absence for so long, is a fable of old times.'

Philip does, however, play out Guy's story, living as a hermit, sick and reclusive, in an out-house owned by Kester's sister. It is a time of famine and Sylvia makes her little daughter give the unrecognized, hungry father a bun, into which she thrusts a half-crown. This coin illustrates the complicated patterning of detail in the novel, linking the recurrent imagery of hunger and bread both to the crown coin that Kinraid and Sylvia divided between them when he left and to a second coin, pressed into Philip's hand by Kinraid, unknowingly, at Portsmouth, which Philip in turn passed on to his shipmate Jem. Jem, a dying man, is reunited with his wife and child. So is Philip. He ties Sylvia's half-crown on a black ribbon, a replacement for the 'brierrose' ribbon that he gave her at the New Year's Fête, which she then gave Kinraid and which identified Charley as 'dead' when his hat was washed up on the shore. At the end Sylvia takes the coin and ribbon from her husband's neck and hangs these tangled emblems of love around her own.

The final chapters are almost overwrought with such imagery. When Philip rescues his small daughter from the 'hungry waves', husband and wife are reconciled in forgiveness. As he dies (from an internal wound received from the rocks in the sea), he reviews his life. The stress is not on *what* he sees but the *form* it takes: almost a description of the method of *Pilgrim's Progress*, essential text of English Nonconformism.

'All the temptations that had beset him rose clearly before him; the scenes themselves stood up in their solid materialism – he could have touched the places; the people, the thoughts, the arguments that Satan had urged in behalf of sin, were reproduced with the vividness of a present time. And he knew that the thoughts were illusions, the arguments false and hollow; for in that hour came the perfect vision of the perfect truth: he saw the "way to escape" which had come along with the temptation.' (Ch. 45)

He sees the promised path of Christ and the terrible present 'when his naked, guilty soul shrank into the shadow of God's mercy seat, out of the blaze of his anger against all those who act a lie'.

Gaskell relents; Philip dies with a vision of heaven. Instead of the stern patriarch he finds a maternal haven; 'he remembered his mother, and how she had loved him; and he was going to a love wiser, tenderer, deeper than hers'. Yet Sylvia's story ends with a question: 'If I live very long, and try hard to be very good all that time, do yo' think, Hester, as

God will let me to him where he is?' The anticipated answer is 'Yes', but the chapter is not called 'Lost and Saved', as in the parables of the lost lamb or the prodigal son. It is 'Saved and Lost', looking back to the chapter 'Loved and Lost', where Sylvia thinks Kinraid dead, an unmissable echo of Tennyson's "Tis better to have loved and lost/ Than never to have loved at all'. The real affirmation is less the promise of religion than the power of temporal love.

In these final chapters, despite the tender depiction of maternal care and forgiveness, there is a terrible sense of enforced weeping. As at the end of *Ruth*, religion seems to forbid the exuberant and erotic and permit no fulfilment except through the dust and ashes of self-punishment. It is as if Gaskell had determinedly buried her scarlet cloak and unhappily put on the veil. The solace of heaven is somehow insufficient to compensate for pain and strife, which remains as inexplicable as they were when Dr Wilson preached at Darley's funeral. Reduced to mumbled platitudes – 'In the midst of life we are in death' – the vicar gives up in despair at 'the discord between the laws of man and the laws of Christ'. The dead sailor's father comes to church with 'a sore perplexed heart, full of indignation and dumb anger':

'And for the time he was faithless. How came God to permit such cruel injustice of man? Permitting it, He could not be good. Then what was life, and what was death, but woe and despair?' (Ch. 6)

It is not the sermon but the ancient ritual of burial that soothes the old man's grief. Approaching the graveside, he can only repeat again and again, 'It is the Lord's doing'. These words are also used by Bell Robson when Daniel is executed. They are taken from Psalm 118: 'This is the Lord's doing: and it is marvellous in our eyes.' We must trust the larger hope. No rational explanation *can* be given; any answer or redress remains behind the veil.

Sylvia's Lovers depicts an endless struggle amid the flux of time, like the battles of whalers and whales in the Arctic currents. Like Tennyson, Gaskell mourns even while she acknowledges historical necessity. The loss outweighs the gain. Like Matthew Arnold in 'Dover Beach', she leaves us with

> the grating over
> Of pebbles which the waves draw back, and fling
> At their return.[18]

In the circling tides of history the only certainty is uncertainty itself:

'on a summer's night, at the ebb of a spring-tide, you may hear the waves come lapping up the shelving shore, with the same ceaseless, ever-recurrent sound as that which Philip listened to, in the pauses between life and death.

And so it will be, until "there shall be no more sea".' (Ch. 45)

The mutual acknowledgement of guilt and forgiveness by Philip and Sylvia is profound and purgative, a private resolution outside the flow of history. And *Sylvia's Lovers* offers another consolation, that of art. Speech, songs and customs lie embedded in the strata of this book as in a rock facing the swirling sea. The story does not end with Philip's death, but with Bella's new life in America, learnt in casual gossip with the bathing-woman. As imagination resurrects the distant, silent people of the past we see their voyage as our own. The novel circles back to its beginning, to Sylvia's view of Monkshaven and the sea beyond:

'On this blue, trackless water floated scores of white-sailed fishing boats, apparently motionless, unless you measured their progress by some land-mark; but, still, and silent, and distant as they seemed, the consciousness that there were men on board, each going forth into the great deep, added unspeakably to the interest felt in watching them.' (Ch. 2)

[25]

Flossy and *Cousin Phillis*

Sylvia's Lovers was published by Smith, Elder, in three volumes, on 20 February 1863. It was the only book in which Elizabeth included a dedication, or rather two dedications. The British edition was inscribed devotedly (if cryptically);

> This book
> Is dedicated to
> MY DEAR HUSBAND
> By Her
> Who Best Knows His Value

The American edition read differently:

> This book is Dedicated
> To all my Northern friends
> with the truest sympathy of an
> English Woman; and in an especial
> manner to my dear Friend Charles Eliot Norton
> and to his Wife
> Who though personally unknown to me, is yet dear to me for his sake.

Charles wrote in April to say that he had read the novel with 'tender, respectful admiration':

'having had the happiness of knowing & loving you, and you having given me the book in a way that makes it very dear to me, – I have read it with such feeling as few other books have ever called out in me. It is impossible for me to say to you what I should like to say, – for the words do not convey when written the true impression of feeling.'[1]

529

The critics showed no such tenderness or respect. On the whole they praised the new novel for elevating the lives of ordinary people, but they were bemused by Gaskell's retreat to the past, in contrast to her earlier novels, and unnerved by her heavy use of local speech. Geraldine Jewsbury, in the *Athenaeum*, was typically equivocal. On one hand she declared that 'for true artistic workmanship we think "Sylvia's Lovers" superior to any of Mrs Gaskell's former works'.[2] On the other hand she saw what now seems the great strength of *Sylvia's Lovers* as a weakness, complaining of its being 'laid in humble life and narrated chiefly in the vernacular dialect'; this she judged 'a drawback to the comfort of the reader and fatiguing to the eye'. As for the characters, these were powerful, although Philip was too good to be true: 'There is no fault to be found with him except that he is detestable. Sylvia hates him and the reader sympathizes with her heartily.'

Other reviewers too had qualifications. The *Saturday Review* took Elizabeth sternly to task for lack of unity, superfluous characters and flagging pace towards the end, and found the marvellous descriptions of sea, town and farm merely 'tedious'.[3] Rather apologetically, its critic expressed 'a feeling of dissatisfaction'. The *Daily News* had no time for the book at all. Mrs Gaskell, it said, had a forceful style, narrative flair and descriptive ability:

'It would, however, require almost superhuman powers to invest with anything like interest a series of dreary images and comfortless events like that which forms the staple of the work before us . . . We do not mean to say that the grandest heroism and noblest virtues may not be exemplified in low life, but it is trying the patience of readers too far to compel them to wade through three volumes of unpronounceable *patois* and miserable incidents in order to follow the trail of persons who display a very ordinary amount of either heroism or virtue.'[4]

Elizabeth turned her back and went abroad. Her writing, however exhausting, had been an escape from Manchester's misery and now that the relief was being organized more efficiently and employment for the mill-girls was on the increase, she longed for the sun. She had £1,000 in her pocket from Smith, the full price of the copyright for her novel, enough to take her and her daughters to Italy. At the beginning of March she and Julia, now eighteen, went to Paris to stay with the Mohls, where Florence and Meta were to join them. Mary Mohl had no patience with Manchester workers. They had worn Elizabeth out, she said, and her daughters too: 'I would not stir a finger for them; they should learn to think for the morrow as other people do.'⁵ Her grumble was part personal: 'when friends take to being over-useful in any way the best plan is to consider them dead for they certainly forget one'.

Such blatant self-interest was a holiday in itself. Elizabeth could forget Manchester and ignore the reception of *Sylvia's Lovers*. As Mme Mohl said:

'She came here to avoid hearing about it, for she is not like me, a parvenu in literature, who likes to talk and hear talk of her newly acquired notoriety, whether good or bad. It bothers her, and she gets enormous compliments here which she don't know how to pocket and thank for.'⁵

Elizabeth pocketed the compliments, and delighted in the company. At the rue du Bac the familiar circles still met and crossed: British and European, Catholic and Protestant, cultural and political. The Mohls kept their old friends like Guizot, now seventy-six and charming as ever, and made new ones, like the 'very delightful' Ivan Turgenev. And here is another of those indirect connections, threads in a weave: Turgenev had visited Manchester in 1859: *Cousin Phillis* has the haunting quality of his 1860 story, 'First Love'; *Fathers and Sons*, translated into French in 1862, may have partly prompted *Wives and Daughters*.⁷ The names of Gaskell and Turgenev come close together in Mary Mohl's letters, but their lives and writings merely brush against each other, like frequenters of a salon who glance recognition but are not introduced.

Elizabeth in Paris, in escapist mood, was prepared to enjoy meeting everyone, French politician or Russian émigré, but almost at once she received a shock. Without consulting her parents, Florence, passing through London, had independently 'engaged herself', as Elizabeth put it, to a distant cousin, Charles Crompton, the son of a distinguished judge. Given the miserable confusion surrounding Meta's engagement and the courtship of Marianne and Thurstan, Flossy's *fait accompli* seems highly sensible. But Elizabeth was stunned: her daughter's sudden action seemed like desertion. She wrote at once to Flossy, William and Charles to ask if they should continue the Italian trip. All three said yes, so the holiday continued.

Flossy, at least, seemed quite unperturbed as they journeyed south to Marseilles. Before they left Paris, Charles de Montalembert, the militant Catholic historian, had suggested a possible route via Dijon. Elizabeth felt they lacked time to make the detour, but she included his notes, and his mournful account of the decline of the great Catholic families, in her articles on French life in *Fraser's* the following year. What she did not mention was that when they spoke, Montalembert was also reeling from a child's unexpected decision: his daughter had become a nun. Mary Mohl felt he had aged ten years:

'Few pity him; they say, "Well, he ought to have expected it". But he did not expect it. She was his companion, his playfellow, his secretary, his friend, his darling; always cheerful, always helpful. I believe he is hurt at her having the heart to leave him . . . the father was stronger in him than the fanatic, and I could almost have cried with him, I was so touched by his deep and smarting pain.'[8]

That autumn Gaskell would lay bare the baffled pain of a father in *Cousin Phillis*, in Farmer Holman's disbelief that Phillis could have left him to follow another, though for earthly, not religious love. He too should have expected it; but he did not. It is a theme which recurs in her writing, from *Mary Barton* to *Wives and Daughters*, a conflict stated bluntly in 'A Dark Night's Work':

'It was the usual struggle between a father and lover for the possession of love, instead of the natural and grateful resignation of the parent to the prescribed course of things; and, as usual, it was the poor girl who bore the suffering through no fault of her own.'

Montalembert lingered in Elizabeth's mind in Avignon, where they were delayed for twelve days while a mistral stopped sailings from Marseilles. She soon tired of reading *Eugénie de Guérin* by a blazing log fire, watching the wind whipping the acacia outside the inn window. To the landlady's alarm, she and her daughters wrapped up and stepped out, only to be 'taken and seized in a moment by the tyrant; all we could do was to shut our eyes, and keep our ground, and wonder where our petticoats were'. After beating their way through the town, they retreated to the fireside, where Elizabeth avidly read the history of the murdered Marquise de Ganges. She insisted on another expedition, across the Rhône suspension bridge shaking in the wind, to see the Marquise's portrait in a convent in Ville Neuve. She was painted in conventual dress, holding red and white roses:

'Her face was one of exquisite beauty and great peacefulness of expression – round rather than oval; dark hair, dark eyebrows, and blue eyes; there was very little colour excepting in the lips. You would have called it the portrait of a sweet, happy, young woman, innocently glad in her possession of rare beauty.' ('French Life', Part II)

Elizabeth was moved by the contrast between the peaceful face and the story of suffering. Still, she could seldom stay contemplative for long. For a minute or two, she said, her group were full of the Marquise, then, 'I am sorry to say, the carnal feeling of hunger took possession of us'. They sent their servant, in vain, 'in every direction to buy us a cake – bread – anything eatable'. Portraits stay framed in time, but life goes on. Next day, 17 March, a telegram came from Marseilles: 'A boat starts to-day for Civitavecchia.'

Avignon had provided an unexpected pause, time to recover slightly from the shock of Florence's engagement. Elizabeth told Mary Green that she was quite glad of the rest: 'as you may fancy we were all a good deal upset by the event of last week, – I hardly knew Mr Crompton.' William had stayed with him in Scotland; and Carry Crompton had visited Plymouth Grove the previous autumn, but she had never suspected an attachment. At first, she admitted, she was 'more surprised than pleased'.[9]

Her letters over the next few months show her striving to be pleased. She had persuaded herself that Flossy was delicate, dependent and quiet. In July she told Norton:

'You may be sure that what gives *them* pleasure makes me happy too. But I have had to take a good while to reconcile myself to the parting from this dear child, who still seems so much a child, & to want "mother's shelter" so much.' (L705)

When Charles brought Flossy and Meta over to Paris, he had proved very pleasant, and his parents wrote jovial letters, saying punningly that he was 'the Sun of the household' and had 'never given them a day's anxiety'. He was thirty, ten years older than Florence, the eldest of seven children, a rising barrister. Elizabeth did *try* to like him:

'*I* should have said *not* clever; but he was 4th Wrangler at Cambridge and is a Fellow of Trinity, and is getting on very fast in his profession;

so I suppose he has those solid intellectual qualities which tell in *action*, though not in *conversation*.' (L706)

Although she took refuge in his goodness (another 'solid' quality), there was always another 'but':

'But he has not imagination enough to be what one calls *spiritual*. It is just the same want that makes him not care for music and painting, – nor much for poetry. In these tastes Florence is his superior, although *she* is not "artistic". Then he cares for science, – in which she is at present ignorant.'

Still, she added tightly, 'His strong good, *un*sensitive character is just what will, I trust, prove very grateful to her anxious, conscientious little heart.' Poor Charles: he was generous and successful and made Florence (who was far from little, or anxious) very happy.

Elizabeth smothered her shock, but she could not quite recapture the thrill of her first Italian visit, even though she repeated its itinerary, pausing briefly in Rome before winding slowly up through Perugia, Assisi, Orvieto and Siena to Florence. She and her daughters stayed there, at the Casa Sandelli, until the end of May. They were warmly welcomed by British residents like the genial Thomas Trollope and found the city packed with visitors, some fleeing the heat of Rome, others the boredom of Britain. Elizabeth met old friends from home – the Brights, the Gregs and Stanleys – and acquaintances like Isa Blagden and Charlotte Cushman. 'All the world is here,' she declared. The news of the day was the marriage of Lady Augusta Bruce, daughter of Mary Mohl's old friend Lady Elgin, to Arthur Stanley, now dean of Westminster. Augusta and her sister Charlotte Locker were friends of Queen Victoria and the gossip was rather grand – which the chronicler of 'ordinary people' unashamedly liked:

'Mrs Charles Stanley (widow of the Bishop's son) is in this house on the same floor & we see a great deal of her . . . We do so delight in Lady Charlotte. She is so funny . . . and good natured & witty, & between her & the Stanleys we hear no end about the Prince of Wales' ménage.' (L931)

Hearn had come to take care of them, and they acquired a manservant, the same François who had scurried back and forth with daily notes from Charles Norton four years before. He seems to have travelled meanwhile, since to Elizabeth's frustration he fell ill with 'Eastern fever caught in the Holy Land', complicating their plans to go to Venice. None the less, by mid-May they were having a very good time. While Meta was 'gobbling up pictures', the rest of them left their piles of books unread 'since our friends have forced us out'. The heat was dizzying, and the air lay heavy under the colonnades. Elizabeth's mind hovered restlessly between Italy and England, Florentine festivals and Florence's wedding. She fussed about the Cromptons and worried about clothes, which in turn made her fret about money and work:

'It is fearfully hot & we envy the (Sainted!!!) Bishop of Siena who made a gift to the Virgin of all his clothes but I think I must tell Lady Crompton that I have made a gift of all my gowns if we stay there & *to-day Florence says she should like to stay at Hyde P. Sq. on her return.* So I shall stay. *Is Julia expected?* She would delight in it only is shy about not being asked – only our dress will be on its last legs & I shall have no money to refit *my poor old self* with in Paris. By the way *if* there is an article on *La Camorra* in the June Cornhill & *if* you come to Versailles would you ask Mr Smith for the money therefor & *bring it with you, but don't breathe to anyone* that the said article is mine.' (L933–4)

'La Camorra' never appeared in the *Cornhill* – instead of swelling her funds, it increased her worries. It was an article dealing with the darker aspect of Italy, the powerful Neopolitan secret society which she had already written about in 'An Italian Institution', published that March in *All the Year Round*.[10] This seems a strange topic for Elizabeth immediately after *Sylvia's Lovers*, but it deals with a similar institutionalized violence to that of the legal–lawless press-gang. It shows too another side of her tie to Italy, her support of the Italian nationalists. Over the years her closeness to the Shaens and other English friends of Mazzini had kept this enthusiasm keen. In 1860, while she was in Heidelberg, William put her name on a committee backed by Shaftesbury and Florence Nightingale to aid Garibaldi's sick and wounded troops, although, as he said, her name was all she could give since she had no time for practical help.[11] The following year, while struggling with the cotton famine and *Sylvia's Lovers*, she edited and wrote a preface to Colonel Vecchi's *Garibaldi on Caprera*.

(The proceeds, at Garibaldi's wish, went to found girls' schools in Italy.)[12] But she admitted to Henry Morley that although she was glad he liked it, 'I have no right to yr thanks, as the task of editing the book was imposed on me by force, not adopted of my own free will.'

She did write of the Camorra of her own free will, feeling fiercely antagonistic to the 'organised intimidation' and 'cruel tyranny' of the Bourbon rulers of Naples, who protected the brigands in return for their support as secret police. Ironically, when the Liberal city government imprisoned the leaders, the *camorristi* became political martyrs. Released on Garibaldi's entry into Naples, they swiftly took the city under iron control and for a time Garibaldi's popular magic turned them from robbers into police. But they soon reverted to crime and to their Bourbon allegiance.

Elizabeth wrote vividly of the gusts of politics and greed that tossed this violent band from one camp to another. Her material came from books and from friends, but she wrote in the first person as if she herself were the visitor to Naples, bewildered to find that when one paid a boatman, a cab-driver, a porter, 'even the itinerant orange-vendor, or the fabricator of cooling drink on the Chiaja', most of the money immediately slid into the pocket of a taciturn bystander. She was fascinated by the subject and had more to say, but by the time she sent this second article other writers had taken up the theme. George Smith turned it down, feeling it lacked novelty. This, she agreed, was understandable, but she was furious when he then sent it on to Froude, now editor of *Fraser's*, without asking her. She was mortified in case Froude thought he had to take it 'for old friendship's sake'. Elizabeth was already annoyed with Smith for keeping 'Dark' in the title of the volume edition of 'A Dark Night's Work' (it had been added by Dickens, to her intense irritation, when the serial began in *All the Year Round* in January). She had vowed that she would never publish with Smith again, '& this confirms me' (a very temporary vow). Marianne had acted as go-between: 'At any rate, dear, you did your best, but I am *very* angry with Mr Smith. *Don't you have anything more to do with it*, love.'

Her anger about 'La Camorra', this 'unlucky piece of work', reached its height when she was staying in Venice in early June. She was so flustered that she forgot to pay her bill at the Palazzo Zucchelli – a debt she was forgiven on condition she recommended the hotel to friends. It was time to leave Italy. Abruptly her mind jerked back from

Neapolitan conspirators and London publishers to Paris couturiers.
They would journey north, she thought, through Verona and Milan
and spend a night at the top of the St Gothard pass before reaching
Lucerne. Then they must head as fast as they could from Basle to Paris,
a trek of eighteen hours. On arrival there would be no time to rest, as
Marianne would meet them, having fixed up appointments with Mme
Lamy, for Flossy's trousseau.

Mme Lamy was an expensive dressmaker, but Elizabeth was
determined to grit her teeth and face the bills. For some strange reason
the Cromptons filled her with social dread. She admitted that
Marianne's visit to them sounded 'very pleasant', but,

'I confess I dread mine extremely. I feel sure I shall never get on, – and I
can never play proper I am afraid. & Florence is very shy of my going, I
can see – I'm sure she thinks we shan't suit. However I shall do my
best.' (L702)

She need not have worried. Charlie met them at Versailles and took
them to his parents' house in London; the fortnight's visit was enjoyed
by all and the two families became the closest of friends. Unlike his
wife, William, who met them in London, had never had any qualms
about the marriage. He thought it absolutely splendid, as he told
Susanna Winkworth. She was astonished at his high spirits, 'talking
most charmingly the whole time. He was so genial and effusive as I
have hardly ever seen him, regularly pouring out his heart.' (But,
typically, his enthusiastic talk was more of work than weddings.)[13]

The younger generation were settling into domesticity: Charles
Norton had a son that July; Charles Bosanquet had a daughter; Mary
Green became a grandmother. On 8 September Florence and Charles
were married by William at Brook Street Chapel, Manchester, with
only their families present. After a honeymoon in Wales – 'very happy
reading law, novels, driving, fishing & boating' – they came to stay at
Plymouth Grove. In the two weeks in Manchester, on home territory,
Elizabeth warmed to her son-in-law, who made heroically self-abasing
efforts to please: 'He is truly humble; & so exquisitely sweet-
tempered; so desirous of being a *son* to us; and a brother to the girls!'
The following February she wrote:

'My only fear is literally that he should spoil Florence; he is pretty
strict & self-denying towards himself but if he could dress her in

diamonds and feed her on gold, and give her the moon to play with, and *she wished for them* I don't think he would question the wisdom of indulging her.' (L725)

By then Florence was enjoying her independence and new-found affluence, showering her family with presents, but her mother still thought her very young for her age and sadly in need of 'daily elevation of her thoughts and aims'. Flossy had seemed a mere girl, and it was hard for Elizabeth to accept that she had grown into a woman without her noticing. Describing the ceremony, she told Norton:

'It was a very quiet wedding; a very serious one to me; for it was the first breaking up of a home; and the whole affair had appeared to me so very sudden; only I believe it was not; and that it really was for my child's happiness. I trust so. She had no doubts or fears; and she was in general an undecided person.' (L725)

A few days after that quiet wedding she replied to an inquiry from Smith about new material for the *Cornhill*. As usual she had 'ever so many things begun': Mme de Sévigné; some travel pieces which she might give to Froude to make up for the awkwardness over 'La Camorra'; a tale with the tantalizing title 'Two Mothers' (never finished). All these had been laid aside, however, while she worked on a story which she thought might do for the Christmas Number of *Household Words* (as she still stubbornly called *All the Year Round*). She had not yet spoken to Dickens, but was just thinking practically, hoping it might make up a volume with other uncollected *Household Words* pieces in which she held copyright.

Nothing she says about this new story makes it sound special. She has written about twenty pages out of a probable hundred; will it be too short for Smith's purposes? She mentions its title in passing – 'Cousin Phillis'.

The astonishment that often comes when turning from a person to their work is particularly strong with *Cousin Phillis*.[14] It seems extraordinary that the same woman we have just seen arguing with publishers, fretting about her in-laws and fussing about clothes could be the writer of such a quiet, perceptive, deeply considered tale. And yet it *is* linked to her life. *Cousin Phillis* is the story of a young woman whose love and suffering are invisible to a parent who believes her still a child. It expresses her renewed awareness of the gulf between pictured innocence and the unseen inner life, and returns to the scenes of her own childhood and the clash between rural Cheshire and the railway age. And it is full of her simultaneous nostalgia for the local and old and interest in ever broadening horizons, in the coming together of ancient and modern, whether it be in England or Italy, the land of Virgil and Dante, now criss-crossed by railways and riven by strife.

The story of Phillis Holman is simple, its movement slow, its crises of growth internal, like the unseen rings in a tree. It carries us inward, from the variegated surface to apparent stillness, and deeper still to the flow of growth. Gaskell lays no blame and forces no arguments, but her story brims with thought, holding up for examination a range of attitudes to faith, history, work, nature and women.

The narrator, Paul Manning, returns in memory to his youth, his first job as an apprentice engineer on the branch-line of a railway near a small country town. After a year a new spur takes him into the country and his mother asks him to visit her cousin, who is living nearby, married to a farmer and Independent minister, the Revd Ebenezer Holman. An innkeeper directs him to tall chimneys, rising above the hollyhocks and plum trees, and there at the side door, in the evening sun, he finds the Holmans' daughter, Phillis:

'I see her now – cousin Phillis. The westering sun shone full upon her, and made a slanting stream of light into the room within. She was dressed in dark blue cotton of some kind; up to her throat, down to her wrists, with a little frill of the same wherever it touched her white skin. And such white skin as it was! I have never seen the like. She had light hair nearer yellow than any other colour. She looked me steadily in the face with large, quiet eyes, wondering, but untroubled by the sight of a stranger. I thought it odd that so old, so full grown as she was, she should wear a pinafore over her gown.' (Part I)

The glance and the gaze, even more than the word, are the means of expression in this story. Paul's recollections, he says, 'rise like pictures to my memory'. His eye, lingering on Phillis's throat, wrists, skin, hair, on the body of a woman clothed as a child, bathes her from the start – like Ruth – in an ambiguous double aura of sensuality and purity, innocently erotic. As he leaves, she seems the glowing centre of a world at once Puritan and pagan:

'Inside the house sate cousin Phillis, her golden hair, her dazzling complexion, lighting up the corner of the vine-shadowed room.' (Part I)

Her mother explains that Phillis was seventeen 'last May-day', but checks herself, remembering the minister's disapproval of the term, the paradoxical festival of the Virgin and pagan fertility: ' "on the first day of May last," she repeated in an emended edition'.

Paul comes to love his retreats to the farm. He appreciates Cousin Holman's kindness and respects Farmer Holman's devouring appetite for knowledge, whether it be of agriculture, engineering or jurisprudence. His initial attraction to his cousin, as like her father in mind as in looks, is soon tempered by awe at her learning: 'A great tall girl in a pinafore, half a head taller than I was, reading books that I had never heard of.' And then, into the Holmans' slow-moving lives he brings a new stranger, his hero, the chief engineer Mr Holdsworth, a handsome, well-travelled, educated man of twenty-five. Holdsworth, who comes to recuperate from illness, brings fever to Phillis, the pleasure and pain of an unspoken love. And he brings too the restlessness of the wider world – to which he returns as abruptly as he came.

Cousin Phillis was written fast on the heels of *Sylvia's Lovers*. Unstable seas are exchanged for solid land: the seasons of the heart follow those of the earth. But this immaculate tale, heart-breaking in its restraint, still turns on a disappearance, a sudden void in a woman's life. In both works, almost as if she were rephrasing the contemporary debate between 'development' and 'catastrophe' theories of the geological formation of Earth itself, Gaskell counterpoints forces which forge lives, setting the gradual accumulation of years against the violent shock of the new. And in both she asks what values can sustain humanity through uncertainty, pain and change.

In many ways novel and story are complementary opposites. We see Sylvia's dreams and trials from within, but glimpse Phillis's joy and agony only obliquely, through Paul. *Sylvia's Lovers* is Romantic, as befits its period: *Cousin Phillis* is Pastoral, as befits its setting. In the novel, popular ballad and fable enrich spiritual drama. Here Virgil, Dante and Wordsworth deepen a rural tale. In both, conflicts of feelings are related specifically to language and form. While Sylvia scorns books, Phillis craves learning. Despite her name, she is no bucolic shepherdess, but a scholar in a garden. The Eden of Hope

Farm holds an Eve who reaches for the apple of knowledge and discovers desire; her devouring love begins as a hunger of the mind.

In describing Phillis's fall, Gaskell makes conscious use of the inherent paradoxes of classical and Christian pastoral. Nature here shows little of the predatory competition and random accident we find in *Sylvia's Lovers*. The model expressed by Hope Farm, like the faith held by the Holmans, does not derive from Lyell and Darwin but from the seventeenth and eighteenth centuries. It is that of the 'English Georgics' – from Pope's *Windsor Forest* to Thomson's *Seasons* – a teeming profusion which appears chaotic, but is ultimately inter-linked, harmonious and orderly: 'From stage to stage, the vital scale ascends.'[15]

Pastoral 'Nature' is inevitably female and, under God, its control and fertility are literally, under *man's* command. As minister and farmer, Holman guides his 'flock' and his plough with equal vigour: 'I try to keep the parish rod as well as the parish bull,' he tells Paul. Pastoral poets had shown women as worshipped, desired or mourned, but always as the objects of men's gaze; had lauded 'wild' beauty, but implied that land can be 'husbanded', society reformed, order imposed. By making Phillis the subject of her story instead of its object, yet following the tradition of seeing her through men's eyes, Gaskell gently questions the way 'man's control' is constructed and imposed, and probes the philosophy which underpins the whole. She shakes complacency by showing that the disorderly elements remain uncontrollable – thunderstorms strike the crops and passions under-mine the stable ground of habit and faith; the sunny arbours of Arcadia had always held the seeds of sorrow and of death.

Pastoral, too, celebrates the humble life and 'simple' passions, but always from above or from without; praises the contemplative retreat yet keeps its eyes on the busy world. Set in the thrusting Victorian age, *Cousin Phillis* looks over its shoulder to the previous century, and Paul's tender recollection of his vanished youth has an elegiac tinge. This is in part convention, and in part Gaskell's own nostalgia for the faith and practical skill which ruled her grandfather's acres. Hope Farm is recognizably the Sandlebridge she had loved since childhood, with its pillars above rusting gates topped with large stone balls, its grassy path bathed in the soft light of sunset, its oak shovel-board in the flagged kitchen. Elizabeth often yearned for its calm fruitfulness as she hurried through Manchester's dust – 'how I long for Knutsford strawberries!' she sighed to Mary Green in 1860[16] – but she wrote in full awareness of her distance from a rural childhood. Like pastoral writers from Virgil on she was now only a visitor to the country. And Knutsford itself was changing with the building of the railway, whose huge embankment scythed through cottages, cutting off Brook Street Chapel from the rest of the town. The station had been opened with great ceremony in May 1862.

Paul Manning works on such a railway and sees the country with the eyes of an urban boy from Birmingham, city of the Iron Masters. Holdsworth, his superior, has built railways in Italy, and will go on to penetrate the wilderness of Canada; however much Holdsworth loves Phillis, he is an Aeneas of the new age, who would leave Dido grieving on the shore to follow the commands of empire. There is no avoiding this invasion of the new, constantly associated with the railway; by George Eliot, whose Middlemarch rustics attack the surveyors with pitchforks, or by Thoreau, who watches the iron horse blaze through his Walden retreat, breathing fire and smoke, and muses: 'So is your pastoral life whirled past and away.'[17] Nineteenth-century pastoral was written in a true Age of Iron. The very land near Heathbridge seems to resist the coming of the train; Paul tells his father of 'the bogs, all over wild myrtle and soft moss, and shaking ground over which we had to carry our lines'.

This gives an undeniable impression of modernity – and men – forcing their will on the soft, reluctant earth. And when Paul first enters the farm, he feels that he has fallen into some hidden, ancient, female world. As Phillis brings him wine and cake he thinks of Rebekah at the well, and of Isaac waiting for a wife. A week later little has changed. Phillis still knits indoors, looking on a courtyard so full of flowers that, he says, 'I fancied my Sunday coat was scented for days afterwards by the bushes of sweetbrier and fraxinella that perfumed the air'. Style and tone imply the difference between town and country, boy and girl. Phillis at seventeen, lit by the sun, framed in the doorway or the shadowy room, is introduced in prose whose formal fall ('I see her now – cousin Phillis', 'Inside the house sate cousin Phillis'), could not be more of a contrast to the brisk opening of the story, giving Paul's view of himself at the same age:

'It is a great thing for a lad when he is first turned into the independence of lodgings. I do not think I ever was so satisfied and proud in my life as when, at seventeen, I sate down in a little three-cornered room above a pastry cook's shop in the country town of Eltham.' (Part I)

But the idea of the farm as a still, female oasis in a whirling world is swiftly contradicted: the clock ticks continually in its kitchen. The land, just as much as the railway, is ruled by men and has been since the time of Isaac and Rebekah. When Paul meets Holman, he thinks: 'I never saw a more powerful man – deep chest, lean flanks, well-planted head.' Farmer Holman is as patriarchal as Abraham. His harvesters progress with 'the primitive distinction of rank', the boy who chases sparrows coming last of all. He is an authoritarian and a realist, as concerned with a 'nasty, stiff, clayey, daubey bit of ground' as the engineers are, but one who merges practicalities and psalms, beating time to 'Come all harmonious tongues' with his spade, the implement of his work, standing bareheaded with his labourers and daughter in the tawny stubble field.

Like his industrial peers, Holman values knowledge and hard work. His texts are the Bible and the 'hard' pastoral of the *Georgics*, so accurate about weather signs at sunset, 'rolling and irrigation', choice of best seed, clearing of drains. He is no Wordsworthian romantic – far from prompting musings on simplicity, the local idiot, Timothy Cooper ('a downright lazy tyke' in Cousin Holman's view) rouses such fury at his bad workmanship that Holman cuts himself shaving. He keeps him on because he has a family ('More shame for him!' says Cousin Holman), but dismisses him when his patience snaps during Phillis's illness. The idiot, however, is reinstated when Holman hears how he guarded the bridge all day lest carts disturb Phillis's sleep. Suffering teaches him to value love as much as efficiency.

The men in this story all have the capacity to love, but all, without any ill intent, put it second to their work: they like 'masculine news' and dislike 'narratives which do not end in action'. We learn in passing that Paul's father, like Holdsworth, left a woman to pine and die when he went away to earn his bread without declaring his love. Men dictate the terms; this is simply the shape life takes. Women's lives, however independent their minds, are relative, defined by fathers, lovers, husbands. Phillis is the quiet, deep centre, but her story is seen through Paul's eyes.

Men see themselves as 'naturally' born to independence, both created to rule and allowed to transgress. Holman reassures the Heathbridge boys that if they did not run races and spill milk they would not be boys, but angels. (And, as the boys point out, they could not be that, for 'Angels is dead folk.') While most women remain angels in the home, men are physically, intellectually and socially mobile; they run races; they compete. Paul's job already places him above the status of his father, John, a self-taught mechanic and inventive genius, a man who works out his ideas not for money but from passion because, Paul tells us, 'until he could put them into shape, they plagued him by night and day'. Through Mr Manning Gaskell shows that the older, simpler order can co-exist with industrial progress. Like Holman, he combines an inquiring, creative mind with a sturdy Nonconformist faith, and like Holman, he loves his child, putting on his Sunday clothes and losing two days' work to bring Paul to Eltham.

There is respect and affection (and dry amusement) in Gaskell's portraits of these men and of the pride in work which can bridge classes and generations. Each is eager to learn the other's language. Holman asks Paul to translate mechanical terms and when Manning visits the farm, he 'learned the points of a cow with as much attention as if he meant to turn farmer'.

'He had his little book that he used for mechanical memoranda and measurements in his pocket, and he took it out to write down "straightback", "small muzzle", "deep barrel" and I know not what else, under the head "cow".' (Part II)

Manning is the kind of man who blithely takes a charred stick from the fire to draw his design for a new turnip-cutting machine on the beautifully scoured dresser (as James Nasmyth had once drawn diagrams for Elizabeth all over the walls of his room).[18] But Paul notices that Cousin Holman

'had, in the meantime, taken a duster out of the drawer, and, under pretence of being as much interested as her husband in the drawing, was secretly trying on an outside mark how easily it would come off, and whether it would leave her dresser as white as before.' (Part II)

Phillis does not reach for a duster. She is leaning on Holman's shoulder, 'sucking in information like her father's own daughter'. It is her mother who is left out, jealous until appeased by the minister's tactful change of subject. He and the ever observant Paul (in this respect a very 'feminine' narrator) are sensitive to such 'little shadows'. Phillis, always too engrossed by the matter at hand, notices nothing. *Cousin Phillis* is full of such undercurrents and ironies. The minister, for example, encourages Phillis's interest in classics and mechanics, but shakes his head at a longing for ribbons, welcoming the display of mind but not of body. The self-taught John Manning, on the other hand, regards her Latin and Greek as a passing phase, thoroughly unwomanly: 'She'd forget 'em, if she had a houseful of children.'

Paul can see that she would not forget. From the very beginning Gaskell presents this passion for learning as something which sets Phillis slightly at odds with her pre-ordained role. The interior of Hope Farm breathes a mingled air of serenity and labour, with its huge fireplace, its oven by the grate:

'and a crook with the kettle hanging from it, over the bright wood fire; everything that ought to be black and polished in that room was black and polished; and the flags, and window curtains, and such things as were to be white and clean, were just spotless in their purity. Opposite to the fire-place, extending the length of the room, was an oaken shovel-board, with the right incline for a skilful player to send the weight into the prescribed place. There were baskets of white work about, and a small shelf of books hung against the wall, books used for reading, and not for propping up a beau-pot of flowers. I took down one or two of those books once when I was left alone in the house-place on the first evening – Virgil, Caesar, a Greek grammar – oh, dear me! and Phillis Holman's name in each of them!' (Part I)

Everything is here: the black and white simplicity, the virtue of spotless purity; the precision of the craftsman which ensures the 'prescribed place' of the weight in the game. Only the books strike a jarring note, among the sewing and the flowers. They make Paul (whose only Latin is the significant *'tempus fugit'*) feel uncomfortably inferior; he abandons all romantic hopes. Much of the story's poignancy comes from the silence and denial not of Phillis but of Paul himself, the sense of missed opportunity, so lightly sketched in. Paul marries the daughter of his father's rich partner, but it is Phillis he sees with the eye of memory.

Phillis feels no contradiction between learning and love. She sees books as being as 'natural' as livestock and is surprised when Paul says he likes animals: 'Oh, do you? I am so glad! I was afraid you would not like animals, as you did not like books.' But she burns to use her head as well as her hands. Paul watches her peeling apples 'with quick dexterity of finger, but with repeated turnings of her head' to the book on the dresser beside her. She is impatient when thwarted by *The Inferno*, picked up cheap, a haphazard route to culture. She longs for someone to help her translate the difficult language:

' "Paring apples is nothing, if only I could make out this old Italian. I wish you knew it."

"I wish I did," said I, moved by her impetuosity of tone. "If, now, Mr Holdsworth were here; he can speak Italian like anything, I believe."

"Who is Mr Holdsworth?" said Phillis, looking up.' (Part II)

When Paul brings Holdsworth to the farm, to recover from fever, he not only helps with her Italian, but 'translates' Phillis to a different state. As the railway is built and the making of sheaves gives way to the gathering of apples, their friendship slowly ripens. Not a word of commitment is spoken. They do not touch except when Phillis rushes into the storm to save Holdsworth's surveying equipment and then feels his shirt, soaked in the summer downpour. But Phillis has been fatally struck by the lightning, while he escapes unscathed.

Holdsworth is no cool seducer, just a responsive man with careless-ness that comes from moving in a different orbit, as Paul acknowledges when Holdsworth teasingly accuses him of not thinking him good enough for the Holmans: ' "No", I replied boldly, "I think you are good; but I don't know if you are quite of their kind of goodness." ' He wears his hair in a foreign style and talks so differently, with his southern drawl and lazy levity, that the sober Holmans sometimes cannot follow his language. His stories cast a spell, as Farmer Holman admits:

'He makes Horace and Virgil living, instead of dead, by the stories he tells me of his sojourn in the very countries where they lived, and where to this day, he says – But it is like dram-drinking. I listen to him till I forget my duties, and am carried off my feet. Last Sabbath-evening he led us away into talk on profane subjects ill-befitting the day.' (Part II)

His appeal to Phillis is less like dram-drinking than dream-drinking. He brings that aura of a different sphere that is such a seductive charge for Gaskell heroines. Phillis thrills to an opposite, as Sylvia thrilled to Kinraid's ice and fire. In this too she resembles her father, a romantic beneath his buff coat, who 'had a fancy for the sea, like many other land-locked men, to whom the great deep is a mystery and a fascination'. Unfortunately, Holdsworth is also a romantic, whose illusions about women prevent him from seeing Phillis clearly. He values her intellect only for the piquancy it adds to her beauty and feels she would be better reading *I promessi sposi* than Dante. His choice of Manzoni's novel, a sacred text of Italian nationalism, shows both his familiarity with the broad international stage and his obtuseness about Phillis and her father, who would disapprove of novel-reading. But her own choice, *The Inferno*, is a dangerous text, in which her father's hero Virgil is no longer a pastoral sage but a guide to the underworld.

An argument about the crossing of boundaries and the definition of sphere is carried through the story by the metaphor of translation; Paul translating mechanics, his father learning farming terms, Phillis struggling with her Italian dictionary. The conservative faith in which Phillis grows up, however, resists strangers and change; even her father's quotation from the *Georgics* is condemned by a fellow-minister as 'vain babbling and profane heathenism'. Holman had resisted Holdsworth's stories, he says, in the same spirit with which Brother Robinson had told him that

'by learning other languages than our own, we were flying in the face of the Lord's purpose when He had said, at the building of the Tower of Babel, that He would confound their languages so that they should not understand each other's speech.' (Part IV)

Different kinds of men, and men and women, still do not understand each other's speech. They are trapped by the assumptions built into the language they use.

Phillis – like women in general – is trapped by a net of such assumptions, woven of the linguistic pastoral blurring of social and natural, the Romantic identification of women with 'nature' and the Victorian rhetoric of woman as child. Phillis reminds one, for instance, of the best known lines of Gray's *Elegy Written in a Country Churchyard*, describing the plight of many (male) scholars:

Full many a gem of purest ray serene
The dark, unfathomed caves of ocean bear;

Full many a flower is born to blush unseen
And waste its sweetness on the desert air.

As William Empson pointed out, Gray makes us feel the waste, but by comparing the social system to Nature he 'makes it seem inevitable, which it was not, and gives it a dignity which was undeserved. Furthermore, a gem does not mind being in a cave and a flower prefers not to be picked.'¹⁹ Gray's images imply that virtue goes with seclusion, that these sequestered souls are almost lucky to escape exposure of their virginal 'blush'.

Phillis is doomed to pain by the way those close to her define her as 'innocent' in this way. Although Holdsworth calls her a 'beautiful woman', he envisions her in roles which exclude autonomous feeling – a nature goddess, a Sleeping Beauty. He first glimpses her in the kitchen garden, among the strawberry beds and ripening peas. He watches her through the window, playing with her dog: 'I should like to have sketched her,' he says. After the storm, when she runs for shelter like a nymph, 'her long, lovely hair floating and dripping, her eyes glad and bright', he wants to draw her as Ceres, with wheat-leaves in her hair, to formalize her desirable 'wildness' (as Bellingham does Ruth's when he crowns her with water lilies). As he draws she comes to life: 'her colour came and went, her breath quickened'. Discomposed by his stare, with its force of physical possession, unable to meet his gaze, she quivers and leaves the room.

Before he leaves for Canada, he packs the nosegay of old-fashioned flowers she has given him (which remind him of childhood) and the abandoned sketch of her 'sweet, innocent face'. This, Paul notes, 'had not been successful enough for him to complete it with shading or colouring'. Holdsworth loves an image of innocence, not a living woman:

'God keep her in her high tranquillity, her pure innocence! – Two years! it is a long time, – But she lives in such seclusion, almost like the sleeping beauty, Paul . . . but I shall come back like a prince from Canada, and waken her to my love.' (Part III)

Denying the evidence of his eyes, and having *said* nothing, he can choose to believe her unawakened and can move on without guilt. (The princess was not known to be unhappy in her slumbers.)

Phillis, however, is already aroused. She is no Sleeping Beauty. Nor is she Ceres. She is more like Proserpine, pulled from the bright surface of the earth by desire. At Christmas, the turn of the year, she revives when Paul tells her of Holdsworth's intention to return. At Easter, when she believes herself loved, Paul watches her under the budding trees, secure in herself, 'unconscious of my gaze'. He too thinks her unaware. 'I think she hardly knew why she was so happy all the time,' he says, and compares her to a rose

'that had come to full bloom on the sunny side of a lonely house, sheltered from storms. I have read in some book of poetry –

> A maid whom there were none to praise
> And very few to love.

And somehow those lines always reminded me of Phillis; yet they were not true of her either.' (Part IV)

Wordsworth's Lucy, 'who dwelt among untrodden ways', like Gray's gem, or Paul's rose, is part of the natural world, even in death.[20] Her value lies in her importance to the poet: 'But she is in her grave and, oh,/The difference to me.' Phillis is a Lucy with intellect, heart and bodily yearning of her own. It is for *her* we feel, not her beholder. When Paul breaks the news of Holdsworth's marriage to a real Lucy, the Canadian Lucille Ventadour, and summer thunder crashes over the house, we see Phillis in tune with nature but apart. Her dry-eyed, silent hurt is all too human, a self-aware mixture of shame, mortified rejection and utter emptiness. The death of a dream.

Her father denies Phillis her own identity in a different way. An old-fashioned Puritan with regard to the senses, he is typically Victorian in his parental possessiveness and his belief (like Holdsworth's) that a 'good' woman's sexuality does not exist until awakened. Guessing the cause of her obvious misery, he is sure that the impetus to love must have come from without, if not directly from Holdsworth then from Paul, who has 'spoiled her peaceful maidenhood with talk about another man's love'. But Paul can see that while the father's love is deep, it is also blind:

'I could not help remembering the pinafore, the childish garment which Phillis wore so long, as if her parents were unaware of her progress towards womanhood. Just in the same way the minister spoke and thought of her now, as a child, whose innocent peace I had

spoiled by vain and foolish talk. I knew that the truth was different.'
(Part IV)

At this point Phillis enters, visibly changed from child to woman, from
a golden girl to a ghost from some tragic underworld. She is half
undressed, covered with a 'dark winter cloak, which fell in long folds to
her white, naked, noiseless feet. Her face was strangely pale; her eyes
heavy in the black circles round them.' Only now, to protect Paul, does
she speak out. Meeting her father's eyes, she says, 'I loved him, father!'
Paul watches a moth which has flown through the open window,
fluttering around the candle flame: 'I might have saved it,' he admits,
'but I did not care to do so, my heart was too full of other things.'

Holman's distress is like that of a jealous lover: he has seen his
daughter solely in relation to him, not as herself. Had they not made
her happy? Had they not loved her enough? A gulf has opened,
'probably the father and daughter were never so far apart in their lives,
so unsympathetic'. The division between the child, possession of the
father, and the woman, making her own choice, splits Phillis in two,
driving her to madness – like the delirium of Mary Barton, the fever of
Ruth. She suffers in body and mind, out of reach of the consolation of
her childhood faith. The picture Paul sees framed in an open door is no
longer a tranquil girl with a body full of promise, but a Dantean soul in
torment, Phillis tossing restlessly, shorn of her flowing hair, her shaven
head covered with wet cloths, moving backwards and forwards, 'with
weary never-ending motion, her poor eyes shut, trying in the old
accustomed way to croon out a hymn tune, but perpetually breaking it
up into moans of pain'.

The father's suffering mirrors the daughter's. While she moans
broken hymns, he wrestles with belief, goaded by his fellow-ministers,
sanctimonious Job's comforters, who suggest he is being punished for
making an 'idol of his daughter'. His certainties are shaken, but his
answer affirms his daughter's guiltlessness as well as his own: 'I hold
with Christ that afflictions are not sent by God in wrath as penalties
for sin.' 'Is that orthodox, Brother Robinson?' asks one of the
ministers. It is certainly not – Cousin Phillis, like Sylvia's Lovers, is a
fiction of the crisis of faith.

The Holman's servant Betty knows how to deal with Brother
Robinson and his like. "Od rot 'em!' she says, and sets about making
ham and eggs. 'They're a deal quieter after they've had their victual.'

Her brusque realism jolts Phillis back into life, just as Sally's did Ruth. After her recovery Phillis is indifferent when her father buys her the ribbons she once longed for, or her mother finds her Latin and Italian books, dusty with memories. She turns her face to the wall. Betty, laying the table for dinner, can stand it no longer. They have done all they could to cheer her; now she must help herself and think of others:

'If I were you I'd rise up and snuff the moon, sooner than break your father's and mother's hearts wi' watching and waiting till it pleases you to fight your own way back to cheerfulness. There, I never favoured long preachings, and I've said my say.' (Part IV)

The short sermon does its work. Soon afterwards Phillis asks Paul if she may visit his parents in Birmingham. She is looking outwards, stepping from the pastoral into the present:

'Only for a short time, Paul. Then — we will go back to the peace of the old days. I know we shall; I can and I will.' (Part IV)

Phillis is left at the turning point which all Gaskell heroines reach, when they see there is no recourse save their own will, and take their lives into their own hands. But her slight hesitation is infinitely sad. We know that there can be no true return to the old peace. Phillis has changed. Henceforth, in spirit if not in body, she is exiled from Eden.

Cousin Phillis has been called Gaskell's most 'perfect' story. It feels as natural in form as in content, its ending inevitable from its beginning. Disconcerting, then, but also exhilarating, that an uncollected letter should reveal alternative endings and show Gaskell less as spontaneous creator than as a harassed professional rapidly adjusting copy to deadlines.

The story appeared in the *Cornhill* from November 1863 to February 1864. On 10 December, she still had not written the ending. She had received the impression that Smith wanted the story to finish with the year, which would take it only to Holdsworth's departure. Although this would be a pity, 'since it is such a complete fragment', she was prepared to concede. In a rapid, sprawling script she dashed off two pages as a make-do conclusion. They deal with Holdsworth's marriage in a single sentence and then simply give up in despair:

'I had to tell Phillis this — I cannot bear to think of the piteous scene; all the more piteous because she was so patient. Spare me the recital.'[21]

George Smith spared Paul – and the reader.

In the same letter, still in the person of Paul, Gaskell sketched the ending she had originally planned, never written because Smith would allow her only four more issues. Her story, she said, had 'a sort of moral, "Tis better to have loved and lost, than never to have loved at all" ' (the implicit message too of *Sylvia's Lovers*). It was a story of growth through feeling. The last scenes would be set years later, after Holman had died. Paul, now married, returns to find Heathbridge struck by typhus and comes across Phillis using Holdsworth's old technical sketches to help her drain the marshy land. An independent single woman, working in harmony with the 'common labourers', she unites male knowledge with female love: Paul finds her with an orphaned child in her arms, 'and another pulling at her gown' – we hear afterwards that she has adopted them. If George Smith's guillotine had not come down, *Cousin Phillis* would not have ended at that poignant moment of poise, but would have circled back to a constant motif of Gaskell's fiction, filling the empty heart and hearth with the children of others.

26

Away from Manchester

On New Year's Day 1864 Elizabeth was still asking Smith when he needed the end of *Cousin Phillis*. In the past few months she had certainly been writing, but her energies were scattered: arranging for translations and American editions; sending corrections for the illustrated edition of *Sylvia's Lovers*; writing short pieces for quick money, like the comic 'Cage at Cranford' and 'Crowley Castle' for *All the Year Round*.

Relations with Smith, Elder had become rather tangled while Elizabeth tried to sort out her complicated publishing affairs. She was determined to make money from old work as well as new, but she was not quite as professional as she thought and found herself embroiled in an exhausting dispute with Chapman and Hall over *Cranford* and 'Lizzie Leigh'. These were out of print ('My dearest child, Cranford is worth gold,' she told Marianne. 'The only copy in the house is Hearn's') and Smith had long planned to reissue them. He had paid Elizabeth £100 for the privilege, but Chapman claimed the rights. Elizabeth declared herself in 'such a rage', swore she knew nothing of 'agreements' and had never heard a word of 'three months' notice'. The Cromptons, as lawyers, were called in to advise. Smith set up the plates for the new editions. Then, in December, William tidied his study. To George Smith:

'My dear Sir,
I am so *very* sorry; but Mr Gaskell in cleaning out his desk, (full of letters & papers) has found this *signed* agreement, – so we have been wronging Mr Chapman after all! I am very sorry. What can I do? *please* let me pay for the horrid old stereotypes, or whatever they are, –

I enclose your cheque for 50£ for you to take the money off for the stereotypes. I am trying to catch the morning post. *I will not write to Mr F Chapman till I hear from you.*

Yours most truly

E. C. Gaskell' (L721)

Dickens, Chapman, Smith – all her publishers from time to time had troubles with Mrs G.

George Smith was endlessly patient, but what he really wanted from Elizabeth was a new three-volume novel. It would not be long in coming. From the beginning of this year the themes of *Wives and Daughters* were springing in her mind, and the writing of that novel would run like a swift current through the last two years of her life. Although its course did not run smooth, her story swept her joyously back to the past and to the country, away from Manchester.

For over thirty years Manchester had been the pivot of Elizabeth's life. The winter of 1863–4 was a relatively quiet one, spent mostly at Plymouth Grove (quelling the Cross Street folk who muttered that the minister's wife took an uncommon number of holidays), but there were long visits from Flossy and from friends (a sister of Lady Brodie stayed six weeks). Entertaining must be done for visiting American preachers, Manchester guests and casual callers like Monckton Milnes. There were dinners and concerts and balls with the rich – and sewing-schools and Sunday schools for the poor.

Manchester was still a city of extremes. One moment Elizabeth would be pondering how to dress for an assembly (she thought her 'brown moiré, & new head-dress, for my *blue* is much too small for me, & the *grey* pelerine is not done') and telling Marianne that Mrs Pender, with whom they were to dine on Christmas Day, had worn £10,000 of diamonds and £400 of lace at a ball. In the next breath she could be thanking Charles Bosanquet for a subscription of £1, which had bought enough grey linsey for '6 good comfortable *shirts* – which have been distributed & caused great thankfulness'. As it had done from the time of her marriage, Elizabeth's life touched two different worlds.

Since 1832 Manchester had swelled from an industrial city, with a population of 180,000 in 1838, to a northern metropolis with over 350,000 inhabitants. It had engulfed the smaller manufacturing towns around its fringes and its tentacles reached deep into surrounding counties. The textile industry had spawned engineering works and chemical factories: the warehouses were modelled on Venetian palaces, a style dubbed 'Manchester palazzo'. (At least two were later converted without any sense of oddity into lavish hotels.) Even during the cotton famine when the city's very livelihood seemed threatened, grand buildings arose to assert its solid prosperity. New schools and hospitals displayed its social conscience and the Albert Memorial of 1862 proclaimed its national loyalty. But the City Council's decision in 1864 to build a vast new Town Hall protested its proud independence.

The Town Hall would eventually be designed in the Gothic style by Elizabeth's friend, the architect Alfred Waterhouse, and decorated with murals by Ford Madox Brown illustrating Manchester's history (a claim to Past as well as Present). The city had long been accepted as a fulcrum of the future, 'Invention, physical progress, discovery are the war-cries of today,' cried the *People's Journal* in 1847: 'Of this great movement Manchester is the centre. In that lies its especial importance. That work which it seems the destiny of the nineteenth century to accomplish is there being done.'[1] William Gaskell was one of the organizers of the 1861 meeting of the British Association for the Advancement of Science, which brought scholars from Oxford, Cambridge, Europe and America into its factory smoke. The Art Treasures Exhibition of 1857 and the weekly concerts of Hallé's orchestra, one of the finest and most innovatory in Europe, displayed it also as a centre of culture. Manchester wanted to be in the vanguard in every field.

Everything here seemed exaggerated: the poverty as well as the wealth. In 1854 the newly built Chorlton Union Workhouse boasted that it could house 2,500 people: it was always full. While the new Town Hall spires were rising, countless children still cut their teeth in over two thousand cellar-dwellings, where rats scurried and the walls were rank with slime.

Elizabeth despaired at the city's misery, but was still proud of its achievements. In 1864 she wrote a wonderful letter for Mme Mohl's nephew, enclosing notes of introduction to three men: Sir William Fairbairn, Mr Byers ('a German: a very benevolent, eccentric old bachelor', but head of the premier engineering works) and Charlie Crompton's younger brother, who was serving a year's apprenticeship. Then she made notes of 'the things best worth seeing in Manchester': Murray's spinning mill, where he could see the whole process 'with the *latest* improvements in the machinery required'; Hoyle's, where the cotton was printed:

' *"Whitworth's"* Machine[ry] Works, Canal St. Brook St or very near there. (The rifle works which have made Mr Whitworth so famous, are out of Manchester, and not easily shown). But these works are very interesting, if you do not get a stupid *fine* young man to show you over – try rather for one of the *working* men.

Sharp & Roberts, Bridgewater foundry. Good to see in the Railway-Engine line.

LOCKETTS, *Very* clever *small* machinery. For instance they engrave the copper roller used in calico-printing; made a machine for making (adul*terated* of course,) raw coffee? berries, when people began doubting *ground* coffee.' (L229–30)

Those coffee berries are a touch obscure, but the enthusiasm is crystal clear.

Unitarians had been at the helm of the industrial expansion, and were now steering the city's new corporatism: William Gaskell's flock included mayors and councillors, bankers and barons of industry. William, on the whole, was happier with the grey linsey shirts than the diamonds and lace, but he sat on the rich men's committees and joined them in their clubs. Since the 1840s he had added to his Cross Street duties and teaching an array of other tasks: chairman of the Portico Library, council member of the Lit. and Phil., trustee of Manchester College, committee member of the very active Manchester and Salford Sanitary Association. Each took a great deal of time and one can see why Elizabeth felt his work was hard (on her as well as on him). She dutifully supported the Sanitary Association and even sold autographed letters from distinguished literary friends on behalf of its Boston equivalent. But she was somewhat brisk when Charles Norton too started dwelling on the subject: 'How *very* interesting that report of the Sanitary Commission is? it tells one so very much one wanted to know. I want you please to write me a *war* letter.'

There seemed no end to the list of her husband's commitments: no wonder he lacked time to find her contracts. Yet he roused her tenderness as much as irritation. Although William was a powerful, dedicated man, he could be blessedly human. He was grumpy if visits from Elizabeth's smart friends interrupted his work and he fussed about his diet, but he still made dreadful puns, teased his daughters and sometimes gossiped as keenly as his wife. 'And how are *you* at keeping a secret?' he asked her slyly in 1860. 'Mr Greenwood is going to be married! Who to? Why, Miss Taylor sister of the one whom his brother married. Of course you mustn't let it out to Dr Roscoe that you have heard this.'[2] He devoured the latest travel books and relaxed with the *Police Gazette*. (He was gripped by the notorious case of Constance Kent.) He had his spots of weakness too, like keeping all the 'love letters' from swooning women in his congregation (which Margaret Shaen saw as appalling vanity).[3]

William's work, however, was his real love. His students' pictures of him teaching home missionary classes in the cramped attic room above an old warehouse in Marsden Square, or at Owen's College, are full of affection, whether he is quoting poetry at length or quipping, when his chair crashes over as he leaps up to protest at some howler, 'Mr So-and-So, *the very chair can't stand it!*'[4] He told Susanna Winkworth animatedly in 1863 that he was 'almost worked to death, and has no time for reading, but is otherwise jolly. His Missionary College is his closest work, but also Owen's College and Working Men's, and everything is going so well, he can't find it in his heart to give anything up till he can find a successor.'[5] He did not try hard to find one.

William's '*terribly* hot' study at Plymouth Grove, where he pains-takingly wrote his sermons, read reports and received his stream of callers, was the boiler room of this energy. In 1865 Elizabeth wrote a graphic letter to his sister Nancy, in which frustration and fondness vie for equal place, describing her husband, his work and his health. He was now sixty and she admitted that he was touchy when his liver complaint was troubled by east winds or cold weather, but 'in general I should say he is *much* more cheerful & happy in his mind than he used to be, when he was younger'. Despite his cheerfulness she remained convinced he did too much, and still complained that 'it is almost impossible to push, pull, or stir him from home':

'I never know what makes him so busy; as if we any of us ask him he always says "it's only so much extra fatigue going over all I have got to do." I *fancy* a great many people refer to him on business or family difficulties; and besides the necessary thinking this requires, he writes letters *very* slowly and very neatly and correctly, so that replying to these letters takes up a great deal of time.' (L758)

For four hours on three days a week he taught at the Home Mission Board; once a week he lectured at Owen's College, in 'the six *winter &* *bad weather* months of the year':

'That takes up two long hours; and on a Monday too which is often a hard day with committees &c, but you might as well ask St Pauls to tumble down, as entreat him to give up this piece of work; which *does* interest him very much, & which no one could do so well certainly; only it comes at such an unlucky time. Then, there is the plaguing Unitarian Herald; which takes up six or seven hours a week, (*at the office*) & a great deal of odd time at home.' (L758–9)

His family wished he would leave at least the *Herald* to younger men, but, she concluded, 'I think he really *likes* all these things; he meets with people he likes; and all the subjects he is engaged on interest him very much.' Her real grievance follows: 'And when he *is* at home, we only see him at meal-times, so that it is not the giving-up of the *family* life to him, that it would be to many men.'

Between the lines we see William dodging the invasive rays of her intense (but spasmodic) interest. Perhaps for Nancy's benefit, she writes as if she were a patient wife, always waiting at home but pushed to the sidelines. Yet in the last decade she had spent as much, if not more time away than at Plymouth Grove. And her returns often coincided rather noticeably with his departures, or vice versa. Undoubtedly she was piqued that William's absorption in his work excluded her: undoubtedly she felt hurt that he preferred to go away alone, not only on foreign travels but even on his annual stays with the Potters in Wales or Scotland. 'Mrs Potter says she has often asked me (in letters to him,) to accompany him,' she told Nancy, 'but if she has, he has never told me of it.' But although she would have liked to go with him, especially to Rome, she pushed him just as keenly to go by himself. For his own good, she said (and meant), but also for as long as possible. William and Elizabeth had stayed close, but were now almost closest when apart.

In late 1863, as soon as Florence and Charles were married, Elizabeth started plotting again on William's behalf. The Storys had asked him to Italy that summer, but Flossy's wedding prevented it.

Now they asked again: his work, he said, made it impossible. Elizabeth negotiated secretly with Cross Street Chapel, and with John Relly Beard as representative of the Home Missionary College, for her husband to have six week's leave *directly* after the January examinations'. 'Mr dear Dr Beard,' she wrote, 'I want you to enter into a conspiracy against Mr Gaskell; and like all conspirators you must be so kind as to do your work quietly & silently.' At the same time she made arrangements with the Storys. Their apartment was full of American relations, so he would stay nearby and spend the days with them:

'I shall send him en garçon, for I dare say that he would feel more independent in an hotel without me, and with no tie to bring him back from his Forums, or the old book-stalls of the Piazza Navona, until the pangs of hunger remind him that there is such a thing as dinner.' (L714)

Her affection is obvious, but that 'I shall send him' shows who is in charge. The following February she told Charles Norton that Mr Gaskell was leaving for Rome on the 22nd 'for six weeks or two months!!'

William Gaskell gave his life to Manchester and never wanted to leave. Elizabeth preferred to be somewhere else: *anywhere* else, one sometimes feels. When she told Norton of William's holiday, she was away again. Meta had been ill and she had brought her up to Edinburgh for 'bracing air'.

Edinburgh was a tonic for herself as well as her daughter. She addressed her letter to Charles conspicuously: 'at Dr Allman's (The Professor of Natural History)'. George Allman, professor of zoology at Edinburgh since 1855, was married to her old Crix friend, Louisa Shaen. Elizabeth immediately brought her far-flung network of friendships into play, asking Norton if he could find volume I of Daniel Eliot's work on birds in Boston, since Allman needed it and could not get it through Trubner's. Perhaps Louis Agassiz, professor of natural history at Harvard, who knew Allman, could help?

She wanted to give the book to Allman as a present: she was enchanted by him. He was so 'charmingly wise and simple', full of deep thought, and also 'like a child for unselfconscious and sweet humility'. Allman and his milieu brought out all her eager curiosity. Although when she was in Glasgow eight years before, she claimed not to understand scientific language, she was always intrigued by new branches of knowledge. William regularly took home the *Athenaeum* (the journal which reported the British Association) from the Portico and in the 1860s scientific discoveries were still topics of general conversation, only gradually being corralled into specialisms. Elizabeth had known many scientists, from the aristocratic amateur Lord Francis Egerton, patron of Manchester science, to her close friend Benjamin Brodie, professor of chemistry at Oxford. In Manchester she met practical inventors like Fairbairn and Nasmyth, theoretical and experimental physicists like James Joule, analytical chemists like James Allan and Edward Schunk and dynamic teachers like Henry Roscoe, who breathed new life into the school of chemistry at Owen's College. Since the 1830s she had admired the self-taught artisans, the naturalists like Job Legh of *Mary Barton*. They still abounded: five hundred amateurs gathered to form the short-lived Banksian Society in Manchester in 1860. But she had encountered nothing quite like the natural history department of Edinburgh.

George Allman was a marine zoologist with a genius for detail whose most important work was a highly technical monograph on hydrozoa; his research never took him far from home. The tradition of his department was broader. In the sonorous words of the official history written for the British Association in 1921:

'Most distinctive of the product of the University is the series of naturalist travellers who have left her walls to gather knowledge in the ends of the earth.'[6]

In an age when travellers sent specimens by the ton back to Britain from all corners of the earth, Edinburgh's worldwide collection of flora and fauna was regarded as outstanding. Edinburgh students had covered the globe: Mungo Park, James Bruce, William Balfour Baillie (naturalist on the Niger expedition of 1854) in Africa; Alexander Dalrymple in the South Seas; William Scoresby in the Arctic. The Franklin expeditions were staffed by Edinburgh naturalists; Sir John Richardson had studied there and so had Richard Spruce, who had just returned to Britain in 1864 after spending nearly fifteen years collecting botanical specimens from the head waters of the Amazon and the heights of the Andes.

Perhaps most significant for Elizabeth, the best known scientific traveller of them all, her relation Charles Darwin, had studied medicine in Edinburgh in the late 1820s, skipping the grisly operating rooms to collect cuttlefish and sea slugs on the Firth of Forth or to argue evolution with Robert Grant and the members of the Plinian Society. From Edinburgh Darwin went to Cambridge and then, in 1831, set sail on his world-circling voyage on the *Beagle*. Elizabeth had been fascinated by such travellers in her youth, as she explained in 'Company Manners'. She had seen Darwin from time to time and was a friend of his family. If the 51-year-old Allman, though charming, had hardly cut a heroic figure even in his youth, Charles Darwin certainly had. In these two or three weeks in Edinburgh, one strand of her next novel began to evolve in her mind.

From Scotland Elizabeth went to London to see Flossy's house in Oxford Terrace, Hyde Park. She returned to Plymouth Grove in early March and for the next six weeks, while William was abroad, she worked happily on her French articles for Froude's *Fraser's Magazine* and tinkered with 'Two Mothers'. And she also brooded on her novel. By the time her husband returned from Rome, 'a different creature in consequence', she had worked out her ideas. In late April she took a short holiday and on 3 May, a week after she came home, she wrote to George Smith:

'I threw overboard the story of the "Two Mothers" because I thought you did not seem to like it fully – and I have made up a story in my mind, – of country-town life 40 years ago, – a widowed doctor has one daughter Molly, – when she is about 16 he marries again – a widow with one girl Cynthia, and these two girls – contrasted characters, – not sisters but living as sisters in the same house are unconscious rivals for the love of a young man, Roger Newton, the second son of a neighbouring squire or rather yeoman. He is taken by Cynthia, who does *not* care for him – while Molly does.' (L731)

The bones of *Wives and Daughters* are then swiftly sketched out: the spoilt elder son's moral weakness and clandestine marriage; the disappointed father; the stalwart support of Roger and his 'fast and loose' engagement to Cynthia, whose affections turn elsewhere and who makes Molly her confidante. The simple plot outline is like the anatomical drawing Gaskell had recommended in her advice to Herbert Grey in 1859: one must draw a proper skeleton before clothing it with muscle, flesh and drapery. At this stage only one of the characters is fleshed in:

'Roger is rough, & unpolished – but works out for himself a certain name in Natural Science, – is tempted by a large offer to go round the world (like Charles Darwin) as a naturalist, – but stipulates to be paid *half* before he goes away for 3 years in order to help his brother.' (L732)

As she worked, Gaskell varied her plan slightly, and placed the two central families – the Gibsons and the Hamleys (no longer Newtons) – in their precise position within the multi-layered society of Hollingford, but that society was already familiar and clear:

'You can see the kind of story and – I must say – you may find a title for yourself for *I* can not. I have tried all this time in vain. I think it will be in 3 volumes, – but I never can tell before hand – Please how much of *my* writing is 24 pages of the Cornhill? And by what day of the month *must* you have the next month's MSS to print, in case I am driven very hard?' (L732)

She would certainly be driven hard. She had committed herself to unceasing work for at least a year, racing to keep up with monthly deadlines. She was keen to begin, had perhaps already begun. Her first chapter, describing the twelve-year-old Molly Gibson's trip to the garden party at Cumnor Towers, is aptly called 'The Dawn of a Gala Day'. Almost like a dream, working outwards from the bed of the doctor's small daughter waking on a fine summer morning, the map of *Wives and Daughters*, the 'little straggling country town' fading into the countryside close to the lodge of the great park, spread out before her. She stepped swiftly and easily into this country of the mind and wrote with deep enjoyment until late June. Then, when Julia finally left school, her own daughters absorbed her attention again and her novel had to take second place.

Julia, she told Charles Norton, was 'full of promise, – the merriest grig, the most unselfish girl by *nature*, that I ever knew', with a strong sense of religion as a counterweight to her high spirits. As for Flossy, Elizabeth had not only come to terms with the marriage, but was already taking Charles's side in the partnership: 'Dear little Florence is curiously unchanged by marriage in many ways; takes her place as *third* daughter at home, runs errands &c, but is a little bit tyrannical over her sweet-tempered husband in her own house.' The negatives of the previous year had become positives. The qualities she saw in

Charles – 'not clever' at first glance, with solid virtues which told in action and not in conversation, a man who preferred science to music and art and embodied common-sense goodness rather than 'spiritual' imagination – were given to her new hero, Roger Hamley.

If Elizabeth had no worries about Flossy and Julia, she was troubled about Marianne and Meta. That summer Marianne and Thurstan had finally announced their engagement, but when Elizabeth thanked Smith for his congratulations at the end of July, she added: 'It has been a good deal of worry; which we, not being in love, have felt a good deal more than the parties concerned.' Edward Holland was still obdurately opposed, but Marianne was now thirty and as she and Thurstan had been attached for six years, her parents felt it was absurd to wait any longer. Elizabeth feared that Edward might cut off Thurstan's allowance: 'we are in the middle of a pretty little family "tiff", – which will, I suppose, die out in time, but is unpleasant in the interval'. The following year the Hollands reluctantly gave their blessing and after that the only worry was financial, since Thurstan had to make his way slowly at the Chancery Bar: at the moment he had only £300 allowance and the most the Gaskells could afford to add was £100. 'They are in very good heart and have been very constant to each other,' she said in early 1865, adding disarmingly: 'and we don't mind a long engagement for we shall keep our child that much the longer'. In time the money problems too were overcome: Marianne and Thurstan were married in 1866, eight years after they first fell in love.

If anything, in the summer of 1864 Elizabeth was more concerned about Meta, who had not recovered from her winter fever and was again ordered bracing air. 'We talk of Switzerland,' she scribbled rapidly to Norton, 'going to a high Alpine pension, & living there for a month or six weeks quietly. Carriage come in, everyone in, goodbye.'

That carriage had rolled up to the door of Cowley House, now being substantially extended for Benjamin and Philo Brodie. Elizabeth was impressed: 'Wayland – the sculptor at the Assize Courts is here, carving cornices etc etc.' She had just spent a week with Flossy and Charles in London and was now snatching a glimpse of her university friends. It was a final dip into the Oxford which had given her so much pleasure since her visit in 1857. But her stay was brief. That afternoon she was going to Stanton Harcourt and next morning she was due to see the newly discovered Vandyke of Sir Kenelm Digby in the Bodleian. Then off to the station, Manchester and work.

The Brodies were full of holiday plans and pressed her to go with them. Writing to Marianne from Cowley House on a dismal Sunday morning before church, with the summer rain streaming, Elizabeth wondered if they might accept Philo's invitation to Wales, or perhaps look further, to the Tyrol or Pyrenees. Her desire for a holiday became as fixed as her need to write. Ideally, she thought, she could combine the two. At the end of July she begged Smith to advance her £100. The day before, watching Meta reeling with headaches, she and Marianne had decided that they *must* take her to the Alps while William was in Scotland, 'coute qui coute, pretty literally'. Julia, Flossy and Thurstan could come too, to 'a cheap unknown-*ish* place'. There they would live quietly, '& I should write hard'.

In August she achieved her aim, taking all four daughters, plus Charlie and Thurstan, to Pontresina and Glion, six thousand feet up in the Grisons above Lake Geneva. Until early September they spent the time walking, talking, reading and writing. They did not even stir as far as Vevey, four miles from Glion, and her travelogue this time was one of omissions. 'I think never did such a party go to Switzerland and travel about less,' she told Nancy later. 'We never saw Mt Blanc nor the Jung frau nor Monte Rosa nor the Matterhorn . . . nor Lausanne, Geneva, Interlaken, Lauterbrunnen etc etc.' Sadly the holiday did least good for the person it was most designed for. Meta had loved the Alps since her sketching tour with Catherine Darwin and in future years she and Julia, keen hill-walkers like their father, became enthusiastic mountaineers (they were the first women to cross one of the difficult Swiss passes), but this summer in Pontresina she was felled by migraines. Anxiously, Elizabeth appealed for help to a London doctor, Mr Erlichson, who was staying in the hotel.

Despite the very real pain in her spine, Meta's problem, as her mother knew, was as much nervous as physical: she cried hysterically at times. Elizabeth, who had only recently written in *Cousin Phillis* of 'brain-fever' related to thwarted love, unfulfilled talent and family tensions, publicly traced the onset of the illness to Meta's alarm over Marianne and Cardinal Manning and to the heavy relief work of 1862. She conveniently forgot Captain Hill. Nor did she raise Meta's lack of a career or acknowledge that her own powerful personality might create pressures on her daughters – much as they loved her and freely as they seemed to talk to her.

Back in England Meta stayed under Erlichson's care, and spent

October and November in Brighton, having warm sea-water douches on her spine. The doctor's prescription was a progressive, outdoor alternative to the sofa and the darkened room: 'a great deal of open air, 6 hours a day – but no fatigue, early hours, *a great deal of meat* to eat, bitter beer, a little society, but not large assemblies, as much change as possible, and tonics'. But it was still typically Victorian in that the approach to women's nervous ailments was negative rather than positive: 'She is *not* to read deep books, she is *not* to visit the poor, she is *not* to be worried &c.' Even Meta's self-enhancing role as solver of family problems was deliberately checked. 'All this she knows & grieves over. But just now she seems very much better.'

These words were written in February 1865, when Elizabeth sent Norton her regular family bulletin. '*I am in the dining-room, by myself. It is after our usual Sunday Evening tea; Mr Gaskell is preaching at X St Chapel, – all just as usual.*' Marianne and Thurstan were next door in the drawing-room. After describing Meta's poor health, Elizabeth confessed that she herself was feeling low and convalescent. That autumn, she said, she had been almost confined to the house for three months, feeling very weak, and had begun to despair of ever getting out:

'But now, thank God! I am a great deal better; nearly quite strong again, I shall be when *light* comes back. I am always influenced so much by darkness, or cloudy skies.
I really *am*; it is not fancy.' (L745)

It was partly true – her depression was certainly seasonal, affected by winter gloom – but the physical problems did not stem from cloudy skies so much as from her weak heart. After the exertions of the cotton famine, Mary Mohl had said:

'Mrs Gaskell had a constant headache for six months at Manchester, which went away as soon as she was here, but returns in the night very often, when she wakes in a bustle to hurry off to the committees and poor folk. And she still faints for a quarter of an hour when she is in Manchester and hurried or too late.'[7]

Yet she still hurried. And even when she took to her couch, she did not stop working. In December, in the middle of the time when she told Norton she was 'very weak', she wrote briskly to George Smith asking for two copies of the text so far printed of *Wives and Daughters*. One was for Anna Mohl, to translate into German. The other was for herself 'as I had not one either in MSS or print, and had forgotten all the names'. She was writing blithely, ill or not, and her zest shines off the pages. She was also writing fast. The story itself never feels rushed, but the manuscript is dotted with small inconsistencies. Some she found herself, some were caught by Smith, but several slipped through into the *Cornhill*. And she did forget the names: the elder Miss Browning, for example, could have chosen to be Sally, Clarinda or Dorothy.[8]

If her illness did not slow down her writing, one imagines it must at least have kept the house quiet. Apparently not. She may have longed to join Meta by the sea and resented being stuck within the doors of Plymouth Grove, but she kept those doors open:

'I long, shall long, have longed, and will ever long till I get it, for a whiff of Brighton air. But our house has been full, & I have had to play chaperone, and now Meta is leaving Brighton, and Florence & Mr Crompton come here on Saturday – so alas!' (L740)

Elizabeth was fifty-three. She was driving herself to the limit and only resting (and then not completely) when her body forced her to. Her work and her social life proceeded at a fearsome pace. She took little exercise now – the days of stiff walks in the Lake District or on the Derbyshire moors were long over – and she also ate what doctors today would think a fatal diet for someone with a heart condition, rich in starch and sugar and cholesterol. But she loved good food. In her view it was a much needed fuel and she sometimes blamed her collapses on lack of it. She insisted that each illness had a specific cause. Above all, she persisted in blaming Manchester. First it was the winter smog and dark. Then, when she fell ill in summer, she blamed the Plymouth Grove drains. The remedy was simple – to get away.

In the autumn of 1864 Elizabeth conceived a plan. She would buy a house in the south. Not to live in straight away, but in a couple of years' time. She found a perfectly unselfish justification: it would be 'for Mr Gaskell to retire to and for my unmarried daughters'. This was not a phoney excuse: she did genuinely want to winkle William out of Cross Street and to save Meta and Julia from the Manchester life she herself had found so oppressive. They would be nearer Marianne and Flossy, and William could work (but less) in London. She must, however, have known in her heart that her schemes were wishful thinking: that William would stay and work in the city he loved until he dropped, and that Meta and Julia, if they did not marry, would stay to look after him and make their lives there.

It is too simple to say that this house was a physical manifestation of her desire for escape. It *was* a present to her husband; but it was also something which she could 'present to' William, springing it upon him as concrete (or bricks and mortar) evidence of her independent achievement. It was more than 'a room of her own', it was a whole house of her own, won and paid for by her writing. The house she eventually chose, appropriately enough, was in the home county of Jane Austen, whose guiding presence hovers behind *Wives and Daughters*.

Once she had made up her mind, Elizabeth closed her eyes and steamed ahead. She started looking at properties and in December she thanked George Smith gratefully for his offer of £100 for the copyright of *North and South*, which he wanted to reprint:

'Only please I don't want the money now; only to know how much I may reckon upon, for the purchase of the (impossible) house. Oh! What a fool I was to let the East Grinstead house slip through my fingers!' (L740)

William Shaen already held £600 on her behalf towards the 'nest egg for the house'. The subterfuges she had used to plot William's holidays paled in comparison with this new conspiracy: this time her husband must be kept *completely* in the dark.

By February 1865 Elizabeth had realized that *Wives and Daughters* would stretch to about 870 pages of her writing. She told Smith that she was finding the story tricky to tell:

'I could make it longer I have so much to say yet; but oh! I am so tired of spinning my brain, when I am feeling so far from strong! However my brains are as nothing to yours! How do you manage! I hate intellect, and literature, and fine arts, and mathematics! I begin to think Heaven will be a place where all books & newspapers will be prohibited by St Peter: and the amusement will be in driving in an open carriage to Harrow, and eating strawberries and cream for ever.' (L746)

She was not entirely joking. As spring approached her energy level rose – and so did her desire for strawberries and cream and her urge to get away. A fortnight later she was in Cambridge, flinging her next episode into the post and asking if a printed copy of the last MS could be sent on to her at the Mohls':

'I want the *catch-word* of what I wrote last . . . Also – in the last piece sent (April or May part I *think* the latter) – there is a word omitted in describing the band at the Ball; – I did not know what instrument to put in; and wise people tell me "CLARIONET". Also – please *entirely* take out the words "HE IS A PRINCE AMONG MEN" – also I think in the same *May* part; but it is in a speech of *Cynthia's* (and *extremely* out of character) to her mother after the latter has been rude to Roger.' (L748)

Leaving such tasks to her publisher, she set off for Paris.

During the last decade France had been one of her favourite escapes. Her delight in these holidays and her deep love of French seventeenth-century history and literature are evident in several short stories and in the 1864 'French Life'. These long articles (nearly eighty pages in book form) were written in the shape of an apparently spontaneous diary for 1862 and 1863, describing trips with 'Mary and Irene' – Meta and Isabel Thompson, who went with her to Paris and Normandy in 1862. Far from 'artless', they draw on memories (or lost diaries) from 1855 and 1857 as well as later stays and, like the letters of her heroine Mme de Sévigné, they blend the light and inconsequential with real knowledge and sharp judgement. *Fraser's* readers would have found a wealth of information mixed with entertaining stories and character sketches of a wide range of people, from famous hostesses to the farm-servants of Brittany.

The most vivid figure, however, is the author herself. In one episode 'Mary and Irene' are sketching at St Germain. She is bored. Typically, she hunts for sustenance: 'I could not find a confectioner's, nor, indeed, would it have been of much use, for French confectioners only sell sugary or creamy nothings, extremely unsatisfactory to hungry people.' She goes boldly into a restaurant ('the Café Galle, I think it was called,' she adds thoughtfully, for the benefit of anyone else in the same plight), and (although it is against the rules) persuades Madame to give her a basket of delicious ham rolls and fresh strawberries. The sketchers eat, but then, disappointingly, 'relapse into silence and hard work':

'It was rather dull for me; so I rambled about, struck up an acquaintanceship with one of the gardeners, and with a hackney-coachman, who tried to tempt me into engaging him for a *course* to Versailles by Marly-le-Roi – the Marly, the famous Marly of Louis XIV, of which the faint vestiges alone remain in the marks of old garden plots. I was tempted.' (Part I)

She would always be tempted. Froude asked if she wanted her name attached to the articles.[9] She said no, but she could not escape being spotted. Henry Arthur Bright asked Monckton Milnes if he had seen Mrs Gaskell's 'pleasant articles': 'I felt sure they were hers, & taxed her with it the other day at Manchester.' Anyone who knew her would have felt the same.

She was in high spirits when she arrived in Paris once again, on 12 March. She had planned the trip in darkest December and Mary Mohl had been longing to welcome her: 'What a gossiping we'll have, shan't we?' she had written.[10] For the first three weeks Elizabeth felt extremely well, saw all the people she knew and wrote away in the grand salon of the rue du Bac – standing up, using the mantelpiece as a desk – and her novel is sprinkled with French phrases and allusions.

She slipped happily into the Mohls' routine. Regular as clockwork, she told Emily Shaen, Julius had hot chocolate in the library at 6.30 and Mary had tea at seven. Elizabeth (late) came down for coffee at eight in the smallest and shabbiest of the sitting-rooms, where 'we live and eat all day'. After a long gossipy breakfast (with Mary still in her curlers) she took up *Wives and Daughters* and wrote (as well as she could with Mary's talking), 'till "second breakfast" about 11. Cold meat, bread, wine and water and sometimes an omelette – what we should call lunch, in fact, only it comes too soon after my breakfast, and too long before dinner for my English habits.' Then she would try to write again, interrupted by callers, and in the afternoon she took a walk on her own. They dined at six sharp. Afterwards the Mohls went to sleep, and so did she. At eight exactly Julius woke and brought the ladies a cup of very weak tea. (But to Elizabeth's dismay, there was nothing to eat after dinner, 'not even if we have been to the play'.) After her tea Mary roused herself and was 'very amusing and brilliant; stops up till one, and would stop up later if encouraged by listeners'.

The indefatigable Mary Clarke Mohl was now in her seventies and had recently been ill: a week earlier she had called herself 'so weak, so thin, so languid and often incapable'.[11] For all that, mused Elizabeth, she saw a great many people and generally had a dinner party of ten or twelve every Friday, after which she 'received'. Evening was the time for social life: 'everybody stays up the first half of the night, as I should call it'. Guizot, Mignet and Montalembert came to dine, the last talking passionately in support of the North in the American Civil War, and abusing British apathy.

Most evenings, however, the Mohls went out. After their nap and tea, they and Elizabeth would put on their finery

'and just cross the court-yards even in snow, or step to the Porter's Lodge opening into the Rue du Bac, and send him for a coach. We "jigget" to some very smart houses (for all Mme Mohl's friends are very smart people and live in very grand houses) curtsey as low as we can to the Master of the house, and shake hands with the Mistress, sit down and in general have a great deal of very beautiful music from the masters of the Conservatoire, quartettes and quintettes; make a buzz of talk, look at fine dresses, and I come home hungry as a hawk about one a.m.' (L750–1)

Fortunately for the starving Elizabeth, she was often asked out to dine by herself: once at 'a real Russian dinner'. This was a menu to appreciate, at least after the first course of mutton soup and 'sour kraut' ('very nasty and horrible to smell'). Then it improved: fish balls and rissoles ('very good'); caviare and smoked fish; sweetbreads; eels chopped with mushrooms, lemon juice and mustard; 'rôti of some common sort'; Russian partridge fed on the sprouts of young pine trees ('and taste strong of turpentine') and finally, for dessert, 'a sweet soup, ball of raisins and currants, like plum-pudding, boiled in orange-flower water. I think that was all – it was all I took at any rate.'

After at least two of these evenings (perhaps not after that dinner) Elizabeth hurried back to her room, wrote furiously and walked to a distant post-box after midnight, with an envelope addressed to the *Pall Mall Gazette*. She was supplying George Smith's new newspaper with 'A Column of Gossip from Paris': a blend of *bon mots* and *bon sang* – the sculptor Duchess di Colonna (about to send a bust of the Gorgon to the London Exhibition); the notoriously fast Princess Metternich; the singer Adelina Patti.[12] The Hollingford of *Wives and Daughters*,

which she was describing daily in the Mohls' apartment, with its
copses and hedgerows, its doctor and squire, was more than geogra-
phically remote.

After three weeks of fine living Elizabeth fell ill. The cold crisp
weather gave way to an early April heatwave and 'the close overpowering heat & the real want of food and lowness of diet' left her weak
and depressed. She made her adieus to the Mohls on 20 April.
Recovering with Flossy in London, she moped to Marianne: 'I almost
get out of spirits about ever being fit for anything again.' 'I broke down
in Paris,' she told George Smith. He and his wife should not bother to
call: 'I am not strong enough to see anyone just yet. – Oh for a house in
the country.'

Characteristically, that moan to Marianne about never being fit for
anything is embedded in a letter which seems, at first glance, to hum
with vitality. Bristling instructions about servants ('*Pray* let Jane go as
soon as you can get rid of her . . . About Lizzie – I am vexed . . . Don't
THINK of getting her a silk gown . . .') flow into a passionate
discussion of clothes:

'No morning gowns are trimmed at the bottom in Paris. The *only* kind
I saw was like a spiked VV *petticoat* of darker silk below; which was
done (*I think*) with *lined* RIBBON – (& got dirty directly I should
fancy.) Mme Lamy said she was not trimming any more *morning*
gowns\ skirts/; and all the *walking* gowns here strike me as *very* long
after Paris; tho' their *evening* gowns are (far) longer than English.
Florence says the cord wears out directly. *Pray* don't have your skirt
trimmed, unless you put the ribbon vandykes – (a good way up –) not
at the bottom so as to look *loose like a petticoat* do you understand?'
(L753)

On she rushes, pursuing the same subjects with equal fervour in her
next day's letter. The energy is that of fever: the care for detail is out of
control. Even she recognized this: 'I was so weak, I had to keep lying
down in the midst, & I don't know what I said.' But one can see her
strength as well as weakness, her buoyant resilience and absolute
determination to control every aspect of her life, even from a distance,
from her servants' habits, cleanliness and 'rough manners' to her adult
daughters' clothes. And every time she mentions her illness her pen
swoops, as if driven, to the house in the country. While in London she

must see as much about houses as she can. Thurstan, Marianne and Meta were roped in to search across the home counties from Putney, Wallingford and Sunninghill, near Windsor, to as far afield as Arundel in Sussex.

Day by day, despite bad nights, Elizabeth felt better (helped by Meta's medicinal brandy and 'Mr Mellor's tonics'). She was able to see the Sunninghill house herself, but not strong enough, apparently, to face Mary Holland at Plymouth Grove: 'She did so snub me that day at Knutsford!' She delayed her return until 6 May, when cousin Mary was safely gone. She had been away two months.

Once she came home she was determined to concentrate on *Wives and Daughters*. At the moment she was keeping ahead. She had finished the August number and since she expected the story to run until December, that meant only four more issues to write. Marianne had left to spend the summer in the south, Meta was still unwell, Hearn was depressed and friends were due, but 'I must set to and write hard at it; & I shan't do anything else for the next 6 weeks, except house-keep, & nursing, & cheering up Hearn'. For a short time her life returned to the rhythm of her first exuberant dash at *Sylvia's Lovers*. Marianne received short letters, free of strain. The dog was ill, the newly calved cow was ill. 'You see I have nothing else to tell you. We are living the quietest of quiet lives.' Or, 'Where *is* Meta's hat? I have no news to tell you. I am writing away, but I hate my story, because I am not to have more money for it, I believe.'

That was written in jest, but laced with truth. Smith was paying her £2,000 for the copyright, good money by current standards, but nothing to the £7,000 which Lewes had obtained from the *Cornhill* for George Eliot's *Romola* in 1862. Elizabeth may not have known of that payment, but she was certainly sore later that summer when Smith paid Wilkie Collins £5,000 for *Armadale*, also for the *Cornhill*. In June she needed that money more than ever; she was at last on the verge of finding her house. Marianne and Meta were chasing two more advertisements, one at Great Bookham and one at Alton, in Hampshire. The second came up trumps.

On 18 June William went to London. (Elizabeth bought him a ticket for the Handel Festival to keep him there until 1 July.) 'And then,' she told Charles Norton gleefully, 'I did a terrible grand thing! and a secret thing too! only you are in America and can't tell. I bought a house and 4 acres of land in Hampshire, – near Alton.' She had not seen it herself, but from her daughters' description it sounded ideal. It was at Holybourne, a small village set in chalk hills a mile and a half from Alton, on the ancient Pilgrim's Way from Winchester to Canterbury. The house was called the Lawn. Until fifty years before it had been the White Hart, part inn, part farm, a stopping-place for the coaches. Its Georgian façade concealed a much older structure, with an oak-panelled hall leading from the front door, under a covered conservatory, right through the house to the back. Tall French windows opened from the elegant ground-floor rooms on to a sweeping lawn, and upstairs there were ten bedrooms, enough for family and guests. Behind lay kitchen gardens, and a paddock reached by a rustic bridge over a small stream, the Bourne, which rose in the churchyard and flowed through the bottom of the garden.

The Lawn was substantial and charming, but at £2,600 it was expensive. She had saved over half, and George Smith lent her a final £1,200 on an 'equitable mortgage'. Had he known, this would have been another shock to William, who sternly disapproved of debt. Elizabeth planned to pay Smith off by degrees and 'Mr Gaskell is *not to know till then*, unless his health breaks down before'.

It was madness to embark on the complicated purchase of a house at the other end of England while she was in the middle of a complex novel. Until the end of the summer the Lawn was less of a secret delight than an added strain. First she had to find another £500 to furnish it (the present furniture was apparently 'hideous') and then to hunt for a tenant who might take it for the next three years, until the loan was repaid. What was more, her existing house was creating problems. In late June and early July the heat of Manchester was intense. No breeze blew to disperse the pall of smoke – or the smell of the Plymouth Grove drains. The sultry summer rain only made things worse. Everyone in the house fell ill and 'the pestiferous smell' lingered on well into the autumn. By then Elizabeth had worked out (in detail, naturally) exactly what was wrong. One drain took waste to a cesspool in the yard, one ran beneath the house to a separate cesspool in the field: adjoining both drains was the cistern under the pantry which fed the scullery tap, where they washed all the pans and plates. It was certainly a hazard. Even when the scullery tap was turned off, a leak remained. Everything must be mended and the flag-stone 'CEMENTED *down*'. Elizabeth was almost overwhelmed. Under the combined onslaught of heat, drains, house-buying and writing, she collapsed again.

In mid-August she confessed: 'I've done nothing but lie on a sofa and be X this last 3 weeks. I don't sleep, that's the worst.' She was not ill enough, though (or was determined not to be), to cancel her coming weekend with Meta at Fryston, the home of Lord Houghton (Monckton Milnes), even if it was 'as muggy and damp as this, in a low flat country all intersected with dykes'. She was desperately behind with the novel and feared she might not be able to bear the journey, or the 'being agreeable', but go she did, taking her manuscript with her and writing as hard as she could 'before breakfast & late at night'. The rest of the day she sparkled and beamed, responding lightly or earnestly as need required to the procession of people who streamed through the house:

'Judges, Marshals, Mr FitzStephen, Mrs Borter & Edith, Mr & Mrs Lowe, Mr Cholmondely, Sir John Lowther, Mr Kitson (brother to your old schoolfellow) Mr Wickham, Mr & Mrs Parker, Mr Swinburne ('Atalanta in Calydon') Mrs Blackburn & Miss Blackburn, Miss Newton (a cousin of my lords), Mr & Mrs Maurice (rev. F.D.) & all their men & maids. Oh! & School inspectors & three or four clergymen, Dr & Mrs Vaughan etc.' (L937-8)

Swinburne may have struck an odd note with the school inspectors and Christian Socialists but not with Elizabeth. Remembering this week, he wrote: 'no one, I think, in so short a time, ever impressed or charmed me more'.[13] She never lost her interest in new artists and writers, however different their views, their lives and their aesthetics were from her own.

Fryston was a plunge back into society, a brief encounter with old friends like the Maurices and acquaintances from many sides of her life. But even here the house was on her mind: she stayed an extra day hoping for a letter to say the valuer had been. As soon as she returned to Manchester she wrote frantically to Marianne. It was broiling hot and Meta and Julia were playing croquet with Emily Greg. She was bothered. Her sleepless nights had begun again. They were about to have the drains up. Her book was dreadfully late. The owners of the Lawn, Mr and Mrs White, were causing delays. Finding a new tenant was harder than she thought although she was answering advertisements in The Times and the Farnham Hampshire Herald and employing agents in Alton and Manchester. A new deadline was announced; the Whites would leave on 29 September and she wanted to furnish immediately: 'I very much regret it has all to be settled just now, when I *must* save all my health & strength for writing.' She was beginning to doubt herself: '*it's an unlucky* house & I believe I was a fool to set my heart on the place at all'.

She sounds in a panic. Marianne had just made a fruitless journey from Dumbleton to Hampshire about furniture. In her mother's view this was 'spilt milk, spilt fatigue & disappointment & money. (By the way are the Kath. Dock dividends due yet? I want them sadly; *& you must want some more money I am afraid?*)' It was too much for her although she had no fewer than three lawyers to help – Charlie Crompton, Thurstan and William Shaen – and, as usual, was relying heavily on her daughters. This itself caused tensions. In July Charlie cleverly swept Flossy out of reach, on a two-month tour of the Italian and Swiss lakes. Now Thurstan put his foot down, pointing out that Marianne had not been well, and furthermore she was supposed to be spending the holidays with him. Elizabeth let out an ungrateful wail:

'I *am* so badly behindhand in *Wives and Daughters*. All these worries about Alton do so incapacitate me from writing. Now I must do it all myself – I mean about Alton etc. Indeed I see Thurstan grudged me the time you could have given me & you would have had to return before much of the *work* was done.' (L937)

Since Marianne must do less, 'after much cogitation' Meta and Hearn (presumably no longer needing nursing or cheering) were dispatched to measure and purchase everything necessary: she must stay and write. Annoyingly, the delegation of tasks did not work. Meta appealed for help and inevitably Elizabeth went herself. On Friday, 1 September, she bought a two-day excursion ticket and settled herself in the 9.30 train for London. Meta and Hearn were on the platform at Euston. They went straight to Heals, a few minutes away, where Meta flourished an alarming-sounding 'tabular statement' of rooms, spaces, contents and colours. All the bedroom furniture was bought. Next day they dashed to the City, way past St Paul's, to find cheap carpets: a failure, 'coarse common things – not really cheaper'. In the flurry Meta was nearly crushed by two lorries in Cheapside and was just saved in time by a 'very kind man'. Shaken, they cabbed back to Shoolbreds (carpets); Heals again; Copelands in Bond Street (china and glass). At last, at eight o'clock, they returned to the Crompton-less Oxford Terrace for dinner, '*dead-beat*'.

Even Elizabeth called it 'a long *crazing* day of furnishing'. But it was done and her brisk descriptions suggest she thoroughly enjoyed it. No mention of illness. She was especially pleased since George Smith had large discounts at '*his* shops – he ships off so much'. She used his name without compunction: 'I am the less scrupulous since I heard of Wilkie Collins' £5,000.' And at Oxford Terrace they learnt that they had a tenant, Mrs Moray: '*such* a relief'. Her troubles seemed past.

Three days later, back in Manchester, Elizabeth wrote: 'Oh dear! I *am* nearly killed, but the *stress* of everything is nearly over.' Marianne, who had seen letters saying her mother was 'nearly killed' for at least fifteen years, would not have been unduly worried. Nor would she have been surprised when, as if by a reflex action, the letter turned immediately to holidays. These months are exhausting to behold. Elizabeth simply could not keep still. Now she had been roused by Flossy's letters from Switzerland. At first she thought they might all go for a month, then that Marianne might go alone and the rest must stay at home: she could not leave until Alton was settled. With great resolve she refused all invitations (even Miss Marshall's Archery Meeting and Ball, which Julia had been greatly looking forward to) and turned down offers to stay with Georgina Tollett and the Nightingales '(and this I *did* regret)'. Despite these sacrifices she was still bothered by visitors like Fanny Wedgwood and cousin Mary. Even a nice American, she sighed, 'sadly interrupted my writing'.

She did need a holiday. All summer her mind had been racing faster and faster, and in the first week in September her letters are frenetic, as if she could not stop the flow of ink. The long, repetitious screeds to Marianne became hectic and anxious once more. What furniture do the tenants need? What earthenware, china and glass? What state is the garden? '*I wish you could hurry on all enquiries about Mr Christian. What family has he? What children? Would he keep up garden etc pretty well?*' At this point she realized that she must get away:

'You see we are so worn out – what with these horrid drains etc. that we do want a holiday, quite away if we can, from care about the house for 3 weeks or a month.' (L940)

On 5 September she decided to go abroad. On the 9th William came home from Scotland. Three weeks later Elizabeth was across the Channel; so much for her lament that 'his family' never saw him.

But William had been in her mind. In the midst of one of her letters to Marianne comes a sudden halt: 'I *must* go and write for the P.M.G.' Smith had requested her to send another letter-article '*by return* of post – simply impossible – but has to be written *today*'. Almost unbelievably, during the height of the novel-writing and tenant-hunting, she had been sending regular contributions to the *Pall Mall Gazette*. Called 'A Parson's Holiday', these were fictional letters to the editor about a Dissenting minister struggling to take an annual break from his congregation. The holidays described, though, are Elizabeth's own, in Silverdale and in Europe, and the parson's town is not Manchester but her fictional home, another Cranford, Eltham, Hamley or Hollingford.

She wrote five of these pieces. All are absolutely delightful, untroubled, joyfully comic – dashed off the top of her head as if she had not a care in the world. She enjoyed the jokes and she let one character, the local nurse, deliver a firm literary judgement. Mrs Dunne is a stout Anglican, with strong views on Dissenters, women and books. She has her say about biographies and warns us roundly about the conjunction of books and motherhood – and the solemnity of endings:

'My ladies never reads, and never is read to, except out of the Holy Bible on a Sunday, which does not try the head. You may be sure, sir, if you've got a life of Mrs Anybody it will end in a death; and deaths is pathetic; and my ladies must not have their feelings touched, because of the milk.'[14]

At the end of September, planning only a short holiday, thinking she would return in a few weeks, Elizabeth packed her bags, including her manuscript. The doors of Plymouth Grove shut behind her. She turned out of the drive, as she had a thousand times before, and drove through the familiar streets, past the shops of the London Road into the city centre – not as far as Cross Street, but to the station. As the train gathered speed and headed south, it passed through the stations of Stockport and Macclesfield. Knutsford and Sandlebridge lay unseen, a few miles to the west. Smoke was replaced by clear skies, as factory chimneys and warehouses gave way to the trees and pastures of the Cheshire plain. Mrs Gaskell had said goodbye to her husband and her home. She was away from Manchester.

27

Wives and Daughters:
Windows and Clothes

'To begin with the old rigmarole of childhood.' This is the first, throwaway line of *Wives and Daughters*. Like a microscope focused on one cell among many, or a telescope trained on a star whose light is long past when it reaches us, the lens of a childish formula reaches across time and space:

'In a country there was a shire, and in that shire there was a town, and in that town there was a house, and in that house there was a room, and in that room there was a bed, and in that bed there lay a little girl; wide awake and longing to get up, but not daring to do so for fear of the unseen power in the next room.' (Ch. 1)

The magical repetition condenses Gaskell's usual opening, through countryside, streets and houses, into a single 'Abracadabra'. The little girl who longs to get up is Molly Gibson. The invisible power is her lovingly tyrannical servant, Betty, who has cared for her since she was four. But another unseen power waits in a metaphorical next room: that of the grown-up world. The novel follows her initiation into its mysteries and her discovery of herself.

Molly grows up happily with her widowed father, cared for by Betty, her governess, Miss Eyre, and her mother's old friends the Misses Browning until she is nearly seventeen, when Mr Gibson is horrified to find that Mr Coxe, one of the apprentices, has fallen in love with her. To protect her he sends her to stay with his friend Squire Hamley and his invalid wife. The Hamleys too have children, two sons currently at Cambridge: Osborne, a poet, expected to get a fellowship, and Roger, more interested in bugs than books. While Molly is away, her father, seeing a solution to guarding his daughter, drifts into marriage with Mrs Kirkpatrick, genteel ex-governess to the Cumnors, the family who rule the little town of Hollingford. With the coming of her stepmother Molly's life changes. A stepsister, Cynthia, returns from school in France; Osborne Hamley returns from Cambridge not a hero but a failure and in debt, and his brother, Roger, her confidant and friend – no more, or so she thinks – falls in love with Cynthia.

In the first chapter all this lies unseen in the future. Molly is only twelve. Today she is going to a garden party at the Towers for the helpers at Lady Cumnor's charity school. She must dress up. She runs to her new straw bonnet, outwardly plain but with quilling inside, that she has made herself 'with infinite pains' and a hidden blue bow, her first bit of grown-up finery. When the church bells ring out six o'clock, 'as they had done for hundreds of years', she jumps to open the windows. Columns of smoke show that housewives are making breakfast for the breadwinners of the family, but she has no eyes for the larger pattern: 'All she thought about it was, "Oh! it will be a fine day! I was afraid it never never would come; or that if it ever came, it would be a rainy day." '

It will be a fine day, at the end of the story, but Molly is not ready, yet, to move out of childhood; as the next chapter-heading warns, she is 'A Novice amongst the Great Folk'. At the Towers smooth-looking velvet lawns are criss-crossed by hidden ha-has and sunlit spaces are offset by 'the dark gloom of the forest trees beyond'. For this girl on the verge of puberty, in her simple white dress, the melting of cultivation into wildness has 'an inexplicable charm'. She sighs with indrawn breath at the lush flowers and fallen blossoms. But in the hothouses, where plants are forced, she tires and cannot breathe. Like a babe in the wood, she falls asleep under a tree, to be woken by the voices of strangers, one of them 'the most beautiful person she had ever seen' – Clare, Mrs Kirkpatrick – in whose care she is placed. Left in Clare's room, Molly is forgotten. She oversleeps. More ordeals follow: the going down to dessert, the teasing of Lord Cumnor, imitating the 'deep voice of the fabulous bear', the mirrors and curtains and pictures in gilded frames, the vast floor she must traverse to say goodbye to her ladyship: 'forty feet away – a hundred miles away! all that blank space had to be crossed; and then a speech to be made!' With a brave, angry effort she shakes off Clare's hand and speaks out for herself, but weeps with relief when returned to her father.

The fairy-tale rigmarole of awakening and transformation, the crossing of that space between the child and the adult, could apply to any girl at this chrysalis stage: whether she be a Sleeping Beauty, as Lord Cumnor calls Molly (or 'the Seven Sleepers, and any other famous sleeper that came into his head') or a Cinderella as her stepsister Cynthia will call herself. Fairy tales and proverbs ripple beneath the surface of their story: the Three Bears, the man in the moon, the Babes in the Wood, diamonds and toads, the Frog King, the Arabian Nights. Yet the day at the Towers is preceded by an ironic account of the Hollingford hierarchy and followed by a detailed description of Molly's education. The mixture of allegory and realism, and the blended images of class and sex, prepare us for a story that can be read in different ways. Private and public lives are equally governed by visible and by unseen powers, and it is the latter, whether unquestioned assumptions or unspoken desires, which are the most powerful of all.

The date of Molly's visit to the Towers is 'five and forty years ago' and the main action runs roughly from 1827 to 1830. The dates blur at the edges, partly from carelessness but partly because Gaskell wants to show how one era blends into another. *Wives and Daughters* begins 'in those days before railways', but near the end, with an anachronistic slide, Lady Cumnor deposits her daughter at 'the railway station on the new line between Birmingham and London', a line which actually opened in 1837. If Molly stands on a threshold, so does the nation, on the brink of the railway age and the penny post, of Catholic emancipation and the extension of the franchise. Molly is the same age as the author, and this is the real, remembered world of Gaskell's own childhood. The story is set in the Midlands, where she went to school, but Hollingford is clearly Knutsford and the Cumnors are based on the Egertons of Tatton Park, who dominated the little town.[1] As she conjured up this earlier era, Gaskell was addressing her contemporaries: the middle-class daughters of the 1820s, most of whom had long been wives; the sons, like her own cousins, who were now men of power – merchants, lawyers, landowners, MPs. By examining the world which formed them she could make them question the values governing their lives and the present age.

This makes *Wives and Daughters* sound a serious book, which it is, but it is also immensely funny, and very moving, because it shows underlying structures of thought as they surface in manners, speech, dress and action. The subtitle is 'An Everyday Story', a sly phrase since everyday life does not have a 'story', although we all invent our own, dramatizing the past, speculating on the mysterious (as the Hollingford ladies gossip hopefully about the Byronic-looking Mr Gibson being the illegitimate son of a duke) or fantasizing about the future. Even Miss Phoebe Browning finds her heart fluttering when her old friend Mr Gibson says he is contemplating marriage: 'Like the Caliph in the Eastern story, a whole lifetime of possibilities passed through her mind in an instant.' Could she leave her sister, she wonders. Gaskell addresses her fondly but firmly, as if she were indeed a character in the *Arabian Nights*: 'Attend, Phoebe, to the present moment, and listen to what is being said before you distress yourself with a perplexity that will never arise.' Reality may disappoint, but it is our duty to clear away fictions and live in the cold light of day.

The novel's structure follows an everyday pattern – childhood, education, falling in love (for girls), finding a *métier* (for boys). Parents die, babies are born. Love stories end in marriage, then, probably, there will be children and so the story will begin again. The plot too looks mundane enough – at least to start with – but gradually, with that familiar shift towards genres which can more easily encompass the transgressive and symbolic, *Wives and Daughters* begins to change. The first secrets we learn are those of character – Mr Gibson's romantic memories of a mysterious Jeanie, Mrs Kirkpatrick's concealed materialism. Soon concealment starts to shape the plot itself, like a contemporary sensation novel, hanging on sexual and financial misdemeanour. The first secret, which explains Osborne's failure and debt, is his clandestine marriage to a French nursemaid, Aimée. The second is Cynthia's relationship with Mr Preston, the Cumnors' insinuating young land-agent, who is blackmailing her with compromising letters to keep a promise of marriage given at sixteen in return for a loan. Molly, brought up to tell the truth, finds herself bound by promises to hide it. Yet she too has a secret, one which she cannot even tell herself, her love for Roger. Without villains, murders, bigamies or adulteries Gaskell's novel, just as much as Mary Braddon's *Lady Audley's Secret*, shows how fatal lies and silences can be.

Wives and Daughters is an acute dissection of family tensions and a fine study of individual psychology, especially in its understanding of the pain and confusion of Molly, Mr Gibson and Squire Hamley, but the tone is kept light because in addition to the dark secrets of sensation novels and fairy tales, Gaskell makes dazzling use of another genre of duplicity, the comedy of manners. Lady Harriet, the sharpest of the Cumnors, evokes this mood when she hears of the scandal surrounding Mr Preston and Molly (who is trying to retrieve Cynthia's letters). In her view Cynthia is probably the real culprit because she 'always looks like a heroine of genteel comedy; and those ladies were capable of a good deal of innocent intriguing, if I remember rightly'. As for Molly, 'why the child is truth itself'. The shades of Sheridan and Goldsmith hover over the plot, appropriate to Hollingford's eighteenth-century inheritance. Mr Preston, a man on the make, is welcome in all the great houses since he is a good shot and an excellent games-player:

'He taught young ladies to play billiards on a wet day, or went in for the game in serious earnest when required. He knew half the private theatrical plays off by heart, and was invaluable in arranging impromptu charades and tableaux.' (Ch. 13)

The narrator sees behind the screens (and sometimes lets the reader see and sometimes not). Moreover she not only sees but *understands* what is going on, as in this little nod to the side: 'It is odd enough to see how the entrance of a person of the opposite sex into an assemblage of either men or women calms down the little discordances and the disturbance of mood.' Such comments, which recall Jane Austen's more epigrammatic asides, assume that the reader shares a worldly wisdom born of experience that the young heroine lacks. At one point Molly thinks Osborne Hamley much improved:

'no longer sarcastic, or fastidious, or vain or self-confident. She did not know how often all these styles of talk or behaviour were put on to conceal shyness or consciousness, and to veil the real self from strangers.' (Ch. 29)

That is the voice of someone who has watched and listened to people for a long time, with sympathy as well as amusement, who knows that speech and manners are more often the clothes than the windows of truth.

The balance between comedy and depth is maintained through the heroine's mediating consciousness. Jane Austen does the same, especially in *Persuasion*, but Molly's mentality is that of mid- rather than early nineteenth-century fiction. While *Wives and Daughters* was appearing, the *Cornhill* carried Anne Thackeray Ritchie's light-hearted article, 'Heroines and Their Grandmothers'. 'Why do women now-a-days write such melancholy novels?' she asked – the heroines of Maria Edgeworth and Jane Austen would never recognize their grand-daughters' 'soul-writhings and heart-troubles'. Among the afflicted are 'Cousin Phillis, or Margaret Hale, or Jane Eyre, or Lucy Snowe, or Dinah or Maggie Tulliver's distractions or poor noble Romola's perplexities'. She sighs for good old-fashioned girls, with all their faults:

'they fainted a good deal, we must confess, and wrote long and tedious letters to aged clergymen residing in the country. They exclaimed "ha!" when anything surprised them and were, we believe, dreadfully afraid of cows, notwithstanding their country connections.'[2]

The banter makes a point: *Wives and Daughters* is not a melancholy novel (whereas *Mansfield Park* is), but Molly's troubled introspection places her firmly in the 1860s.

The novel is also typical of its decade in a different way: its use of science as another form of storytelling. Like her naturalist hero, Roger Hamley, by focusing on the individual specimen Gaskell analyses general patterns without surrendering complexity. She detects slow patterns of growth and change invisible to the casual eye, notes how people relate to their environment and what protective colouring they adopt and shapes her observations into a framework of 'development'. Fiction and natural science, she suggests, share a morality implicit in their method. When Molly is weeping under the ash-tree over her father's remarriage, Roger finds her because he has left the path to find a rare plant that he has spotted, 'with those keen bright eyes of his'. He approaches his goal 'with light and well planted footsteps':

'He was so great a lover of nature that, without any thought, but habitually, he always avoided treading unnecessarily on any plant; who knew what long-sought growth or insect might develop itself in that which now appeared but insignificant?' (Ch. 10)

He offers sympathy to Molly hesitantly because he has not yet 'got hold of the end of the clue', but when he does give advice it is not in general terms, but through a story of a girl in a comparable situation, who 'thought of her father's happiness before her own'. The narrative technique works (despite its very male assumptions about womanly self-sacrifice). Molly is 'interested in this little story of Harriet'.

His second mode of comfort also makes her look outwards. Having retrieved his sling-net, full of 'imprisoned treasures of nastiness', unattractive-looking bugs dredged from ditches and ponds, he skilfully nets Molly:

'That evening he adjusted his microscope, and put the treasures he had collected in his morning's ramble on a little table; and then he asked his mother to come and admire. Of course Molly came too, and this was what he had intended. He tried to interest her in his pursuit, cherished her first little morsel of curiosity, and nursed it into a very proper desire for further information. Then he brought out books on the subject, and translated the slightly pompous and technical language into homely every-day speech.' (Ch. 10)

Time passes without Molly noticing: 'she had been refreshed by a new current of thought'. And although the fellowship of science is male, the language applied to Roger in these first encounters is maternal: 'cherishing', 'nursing', 'homely'.[3] Like Molly's doctor father, he seeks to protect and nurture as well as define and diagnose.

Scientists begin with detail and structure, searching inward as well as out: Darwin's early interest in comparative anatomy prompted the long work which led eventually to *On the Origin of Species*.[4] The three scientists in this novel, Lord Hollingford, Mr Gibson and Roger, all share an interest in comparative osteology and it is a paper on anatomy (a contribution to the debate between Cuvier and Geoffroi St Hilaire) that first wins Roger an international reputation. Six years later George Eliot would make another anatomist, Bichat, the inspiration for Lydgate's search for the 'primal tissue' and a model of the impassioned imagination that 'reveals subtle actions inaccessible by any sort of lens'.

Yet in *Middlemarch*, as in *Wives and Daughters*, the actual men concerned lack any true insight into their own emotions. Indeed they are fundamentally suspicious of feeling. Despite his sympathy, Roger thinks Molly's grief 'exaggerated'. Lord Hollingford is tongue-tied on all subjects except science, while Mr Gibson opposes any demonstration of emotion on the then fashionable grounds that 'uncontrolled feeling' endangers health. They cannot help Molly discover the inner life of painful, private experience. The precise observations of science are inadequate unless complemented by the fluid suggestion of metaphor.

Gaskell claims simply to look, like Roger Hamley, into a pool which others might pass by: the everyday life of families in a country district. But she knew that her dull-looking specimens would turn out to be rich and rare.

Truth, she implies, is often revealed indirectly when we least expect it; understanding is a matter of interpreting clues and we often misread these because we are so busy with our own stories. From beginning to end of *Wives and Daughters* people overhear and eavesdrop, intercept or read other people's letters. Rumours abound and the messenger gets the blame – whether it be the maid carrying Mr Coxe's notes to Molly, or Molly herself retrieving Cynthia's letters from Preston. Molly learns both Osborne's secret and Cynthia's when she accidentally overhears conversations. Truth in *Wives and Daughters* still lies 'behind the veil', but the veils are not the inexplicable mysteries of pain and chance invoked in *Sylvia's Lovers*. They are the veils of *human* behaviour. As Molly tells Roger:

'perhaps all our earthly trials will appear foolish to us after a while; perhaps they seem so now to angels. But we are ourselves you know, and this is *now*, not some time to come, a long, long way off. And we are not angels, to be comforted by seeing the ends for which everything is sent.' (Ch. 11)

The question posed is not the 'why' but the 'how' of existence.

Real understanding requires context as well as content. *Wives and Daughters* is rich in both, a study of the delicate yet powerful interplay of nature and nurture, and of the combined pressures of class and culture. These strands are woven into a densely patterned tapestry. We can choose to unravel a single thread, but at the risk of diminishing the complex whole. *Wives and Daughters*, for example, is a fable of a girl's adolescent awakening, as the opening suggests, a story of female 'wildness and cultivation', of nature tamed, exploited, husbanded, explored. Following from its powerful portrayal of the position of women, we can trace its acute dissection of marital and parental relationships, its commentary on the interrelationship of heredity, upbringing and education. In broader terms we can analyse it as a post-Darwinian study of historical development, competition and adaptation, in the antagonism of the 'new' Whig Cumnors and the Tory Hamleys, a topical contribution to the debates leading up to the second Reform Act of 1865. Or, to take another contemporary theme, it can be interpreted as a narrative of nineteenth-century social and national development, employing the metaphor of sexual selection, its marriages linking the landed interest (already allied to 'trade') to the professional classes, and uniting the nationalistic British to Europe and to their previous enemies, the Catholic French.

All these readings are equally valid, but inevitably partial. And still more are possible. *Wives and Daughters* is also, for instance, a study of the power-shifts in British society: of the rise of aggressive middlemen like Preston, the emergence of a scientifically led intelligentsia, the resurgence of the legal and financial establishment of the south. The industrial capitalists of the north, who dominated *Mary Barton* and *North and South*, are notably absent here, a recognition, perhaps, that by the 1860s economic power was again based firmly in the south. As in the 1820s aspiring eyes and empty purses looked not to Drumble but to London.[5] And one could see the novel too as an interesting example of the limits of mid-Victorian thinking about race (even among committed abolitionists) in the patronizing stereotypes and music-hall jokes applied by Mr Gibson to the African peoples Roger encounters on his expedition.

Gaskell is aware that the society she describes is founded upon exploitation and empire, but she depicts a world seen through the eyes of characters whose horizons are national and local. Within these horizons, and within their houses, she dramatizes their struggles for power and for control of the resources – material and emotional – on which their lives depend. Her deeper interest, however, is in an underlying battle of values, of self-interest and self-sacrifice.

If we pick out a particular thread, that of money, we can see how it weaves into all the other strands, the psychological drama, the analysis of class, of the role of women, of altruism and egotism, truth and lies. Money had always been a force in Gaskell's novels, but *Wives and Daughters* could almost have been written on banknotes (and in a way it was, for each sheet went to pay for the Lawn and her own move south). Notes of all denominations flutter through these pages, tokens of paternal or husbandly provision. Even small sums are significant: the price of tea is a bond between the Misses Browning and Lady Harriet. The stakes at *vingt-et-un* cause much debate – should they be 3d or 6d? Molly has no turn for gambling: Cynthia stakes high and is 'at one time very rich', but ends in debt to Molly, claiming to have forgotten her purse.

The coinage has more than face value. Molly does not care if she wins at cards: she is wretched because Cynthia has 'won' Roger's attention. Cynthia cannot pay because she is saving to buy off Preston. (Eventually she repays him with interest, carefully calculated at five per cent.) Everything that matters most has a price: Cynthia's beauty, Osborne's love poems, Squire Hamley's beloved trees and the drainage works which represent his emotional investment in his land. Land is entailed, lives are insured; we are at the start of an actuarial age. The competing moralities here are neatly represented by Mrs Gibson and her husband. What is the point, she says, of visiting a patient who is dying anyway: 'Does he expect a legacy, or anything of that kind?' Mr Gibson, on the other hand, may joke to his apprentices about the motto 'kill or cure' that it would not do to 'make away with profitable patients' who pay two-and-sixpence a visit. 'But you go every morning, sir, before breakfast,' says the puzzled Mr Wynne, 'to see old Nancy Grant, and you've ordered her this medicine, sir, which is about the most costly in Corbyn's bill?'

This conflict of self-interest and altruism in relation to money finds a different expression in the contrast between Mrs Gibson and Mrs Hamley, where it forms part of a critique of the role and expectations of women. Before she marries, when she is staying at the Towers, Clare admires a muslin-dressed looking-glass (a perfect image), and laments that for a schoolteacher this highly desirable object is so hard to maintain:

'Now here, money is like the air they breathe. No one even asks or knows how much the washing costs, or what pink ribbon is a yard. Ah! it would be different if they had to earn every penny as I have! They would have to calculate, like me, how to get the most pleasure out of it. I wonder if I am to go on all my life toiling and moiling for money? It's not natural. Marriage is the natural thing; then the husband has all that kind of dirty work to do, and his wife sits in the drawing-room like a lady.' (Ch. 9)

Even so marriage does not stop her counting and calculating (or, more often, miscalculating). She is always 'rapidly balancing advantages and disadvantages'. After her little dinner party for Roger and Osborne Hamley, a ploy to win the latter for Cynthia, she is too engrossed in her worsted work to see Molly's misery: 'her work had been intricate up to this time, and had required a great deal of counting; so she had no time to attend to her duties'. She protests when Mr Gibson accuses her of 'trading' in her daughter's affections, but trading in Cynthia's only assets, her beauty and charm, is exactly what she does.

By contrast Mrs Hamley brings wealth to her marriage rather than seeks it. A London merchant's daughter, well educated after a Rousseau-esque fashion, she suppresses her own interests, her enjoyment of society, art and music, out of love for her farmer husband. True, she does sit in the drawing-room like a lady, but her life is a living death. She becomes an invalid, pouring her emotion into her eldest son; the doctor, Mr Gibson, can see that some 'incalculable harm was being done'. The over-romantic Osborne is as much a product of her self-suppression as Cynthia is of her mother's manipulations. At different times both women act as mothers to Molly. They embody two options open to her: to scrabble for life like Cynthia or to fade away like Mrs Hamley's dead daughter, Fanny.

While preferring Mrs Hamley, Molly has a tough sense of self-preservation. When she is in despair and Roger assures her that she will be happier by and by if she thinks of others rather than herself, she instinctively objects:

' "No I shan't!" said Molly, shaking her head. "It will be very dull when I shall have killed myself, as it were, and live only in trying to do, and to be, as other people like. I don't see any end to it. I might as well never have lived." ' (Ch. 11)

We need a strong sense of self to survive. The deeply held view that the chief role of women is to serve, please and succour is potentially lethal if taken to extremes. Paradoxically, the self-interested Mrs Gibson has also absorbed this ideology as well as Mrs Hamley; the belief that women must please others lies at the heart of her strategy. While Molly is always 'Molly', her stepmother changes her name like her clothes, always preferring the fanciest – Clare, Hyacinth, Mrs Kirkpatrick and Mrs Gibson (rather a come-down). She shifts position constantly, like the sunflower which Mary Wollstonecraft saw as an image of female dependence. Her stratagems, pretences and pretensions provide the best jokes of the novel – especially since they hardly ever work. ('If there is one thing that revolts me, it is duplicity,' she remarks indignantly at Osborne's death, on learning that the prime target of her marital campaigns had been married all the time.) Comic it may be, but such silliness is dangerously corrosive; her husband becomes embittered and her daughter's 'instinctive' habit of charming everyone she meets is revealed as a pathetic recompense for the emotional deprivation of her childhood, which has crippled her own capacity to love.

But where do such values and habits of behaviour come from? What is it that makes women either predators or prey? All the characters in *Wives and Daughters*, even Betty, the servant, and Miss Eyre, Molly's governess, or the vicar (whose mental indolence leads him to 'utter platitudes in the most gentlemanly manner'), are given depth by Gaskell's fundamental concern as to how personalities are formed. This was a subject over which she had long brooded, both in the context of the Unitarian belief in human perfectibility and as a mother, as shown by her painstaking diary entries on the infant Marianne and Meta.

Heredity and parental influence play their part, but so does education, a central subject in the early chapters of this novel. In Osborne and Roger Hamley, for example, she follows a standard Unitarian line in attacking the priority given to classics and literature over mathematics and science. But at least it was recognized that boys *should* be educated, while with girls, as Harriet Martineau complained fiercely in the *Cornhill* in November 1864, there was 'no tradition, no conviction, no established method, no imperative custom'.[6] *Wives and Daughters* suggests that moral principles are learnt at home (as Molly imbibes them from her father, and Cynthia does not from her mother), but it also stresses the need for formal education. Women's minds are too often starved, while ingrained assumptions can make the most loving parent an oppressor. These are Mr Gibson's instructions to Miss Eyre:

'Don't teach Molly too much: she must sew, and read, and write, and do her sums; but I want to keep her a child, and, if I find more learning desirable for her, I'll see about giving it to her myself. After all, I'm not sure that reading or writing is necessary. Many a good woman gets married with only a cross instead of her name; it's rather a diluting of mother-wit to my fancy; but, however, we must yield to the prejudices of society, Miss Eyre, and so you may teach the child to read.' (Ch. 3)

The joke works against him, since he *is* yielding to the real prejudices of society, by keeping his daughter a child and placing female literacy, if laughingly, only in relation to marriage. Molly has dancing lessons, of course, but 'only by struggling and fighting hard' can she persuade her father to let her learn French and drawing. Learning thus becomes an object of desire: 'being daunted by her father in every intellectual attempt, she read every book that came in her way, almost with as much delight as if it had been forbidden'.

'Reading', in all senses, is a clue to the argument of Gaskell's later works – *Sylvia's Lovers*, *Cousin Phillis* and *Wives and Daughters*. In this last novel it is used indirectly as a key indicator of attitudes. At some point almost everyone offers a text. 'Ah here is a nice book,' says Clare to Molly on that first day at the Towers: both her snobbery and inauthenticity are suggested by her choice, *Lodge's Portraits*. (Its full title, not cited in the story, is *Portraits of Illustrious Personages of Great Britain. Engraved from Authentic Pictures.*) In contrast, Mr Gibson belittles the polite pomposity of the Towers, by joking that he should have read a few chapters of *Sir Charles Grandison* before he came 'to bring myself up to concert pitch'. Mrs Hamley, the sofa-bound romantic, gives Molly Felicia Hemans, the most popular woman poet of the day ('somewhat too poetical for my taste,' Walter Scott told Joanna Baillie in 1823, 'too many flowers and too little fruit').[7] On the other hand Lady Harriet, who sees through all façades, refers her to Maria Edgeworth's *Castle Rackrent* with its sharp analysis of class, while the stubbornly provincial, old-fashioned Miss Browning stands by the 'British Essayists' – Steele, Addison, Johnson and Goldsmith – who present 'town' as the centre of dissipation, 'corrupting country wives and squires' daughters'. The dictatorial Lady Cumnor gives Cynthia a double wedding present: a velvet-bound Bible and prayer book for show, and a set of household account books for substance (in which she writes 'with her own hand' the proper weekly allowance of groceries. So it goes on.

On her first visit to Hamley Hall Molly herself chooses Scott's *Bride of Lammermoor* and wallows in Osborne's poetry. Creating an ideal, imaginary Osborne, she thinks Roger plain and clumsy until he shows his very different, 'scientific' vision of life and morality. His proffered texts are Cuvier's *Le Règne Animal*, which sets humanity in the context of other species, and Huber's *New Observation on Bees*, from which she learns that although superficially bees may all look alike, there are two hundred species in England alone. As Mentor to her Telemachus he brings a wider world view; the scientific fraternity to which he belongs is democratic and international, encouraging exploration and discovery. She is eager to learn and, like Phillis Holman, she falls in love with her teacher.

Molly reads for the love of it – and later for love of Roger. Mrs Gibson, on the other hand, values learning only if it may catch a husband for her daughter. The only time she opens a scientific work is to look up Osborne's heart disease in the medical encyclopedia, to see if it might be fatal, in which case she should turn her attentions to Roger. Her one burst of scholarly enthusiasm occurs when Lord Hollingford (a catch indeed) dances with Molly and finds her easy to talk to, 'well read, too – she was up in *Le Règne Animal* – and very pretty'. Swift to spot a trend, she murmurs that it was a pity that Cynthia 'preferred making millinery to reading; but perhaps that could be rectified'. The next morning Cynthia, pretending to read a three-day-old newspaper, is startled by her mother directing her to take up a book and 'improve herself':

' "Why don't you keep up your French? There was some French book that Molly was reading – *Le Règne Animal*, I think.'

"No! I never read it!" said Molly, blushing, "Mr Roger Hamley sometimes read pieces out of it, when I was first at the Hall, and told me what it was about."

"Oh! well. Then I suppose I was mistaken. But it comes to all the same thing." ' (Ch. 26)

Cynthia dutifully (if cynically) unearths Voltaire's *Le Siècle de Louis XIV*, but this, Molly sees, is just to keep her mother quiet and cover her own thoughts.

It is a supreme irony that Mrs Gibson should be a teacher. As the Cumnors' governess, all she teaches Lady Harriet is how to gossip about flirtation, making her clever pupil cynical of love. As a schoolteacher, she hates her work, loathes girls 'as a class' and though she has clearly used the ubiquitous *Mangnall's Questions* for rote-learning, she still cannot remember the name of 'the heathen deity whose office it was to bring news' (her patron deity). She is hard put to remember the name of any author except Sterne, but she has, however, absorbed the idea (displayed more seriously in Mrs Hamley) that love of poetry is evidence of tender female sensibilities. When Cynthia

engagingly confesses to Roger that she is a dunce at science, her
mother jumps in to assure the poetic Osborne (her current target) that
'her memory for poetry is prodigious':

' "I have heard her repeat the 'Prisoner of Chillon' from beginning to
end."
"It would be rather a bore to have to hear her, I think," said Mr
Gibson, smiling at Cynthia, who gave him back one of her bright looks
of mutual understanding.' (Ch. 24)

(Byron's poem has nearly four hundred lines.)
   Mrs Gibson's own private reading is far from improving. When she
is a schoolteacher, one of her small 'sins to be concealed' is 'the dirty
dog's-eared delightful novel from the Ashcombe circulating library,
the leaves of which she turned over with a pair of scissors'. Underneath
the fashionable surface such a woman is very tacky indeed: she buys
new dresses for show but 'her stock of underclothing was small, and
scarcely any of it new'. Her reading and her language are like her
clothes; in public she abhors vernacular proverbs and, even *in
extremis*, reaches for the grandest word. Faced with Cynthia's reputation as a jilt, she asks how her daughter could get herself

' "into such an imbroglio" (Mrs Gibson could not have said "mess"
for the world, although the word was present to her mind).' (Ch. 50)

Such diction, which she thinks makes her seem genteel, actually
identifies her with the apprentice Mr Wynne, who makes Mr Gibson
wince with ' ., 'May I assist you to potatoes' instead of 'may I help
you', or with Lady Harriet's maid, who asks Molly to tell her when to
arrange her hair

' "preparatory to luncheon". For, if Lady Harriet used familiar
colloquialisms from time to time she certainly had not learnt it from
Parkes, who piqued herself on the correctness of her language.'
(Ch. 58)

   In 1863 Gaskell had written a wonderful short satire for *Fraser's*
called 'Shams'.[8] Her male speaker, a deep-eyed Conservative, lambasts
many of the affectations exposed in this novel: false scholarship, the
aping of gentility, the double standard applied to '*fast*' and '*slow*' girls
(the first might amuse a fellow for half an hour but are not for
marrying, the second are ignored until a chap needs a decent wife). But

his own language is the greatest sham, pompous, patronizing, and self-congratulatory and dotted with foreign clichés to show what a cultured soul he is. Once again we must look beneath the surface.

As in *Cousin Phillis*, language in *Wives and Daughters* is the colouring of the species, sometimes a camouflage, sometimes a badge of aggression, a cloak of defence. When Molly objects to Lady Harriet calling the Misses Browning 'Pecksy and Flapsy' (the two girl robins in Mrs Trimmer's children's story), protesting that she speaks about her class 'as if it was a strange kind of animal', Lady Harriet replies, 'Don't you see, little one, I talk after my kind, just as you talk after your kind. It's only on the surface with both of us.' Doubtless, she adds, the 'good Hollingford ladies' (a give-away phrase in itself) 'talk of the poor people in a manner which they would consider as impertinent in their turn', but she admits that her own blood has boiled at the laden diction of one of her aunts:

'Any one who earns his livelihood by any exercise of head or hand, from professional people and rich merchants down to labourers, she calls "persons". She would never in her most slip-slop talk accord them even the conventional title of "gentlemen"; and the way in which she takes possession of human beings, "my women", "my people" – but, after all, it is only a way of speaking.' (Ch. 14)

In this novel dress, food, furniture, houses, bouquets of flowers – all so lovingly described – are all 'a way of speaking'. Unthinking conventions are suspect, as in the recurrent argument (resembling that in *Persuasion*) about the merits of poetry and prose. This sets the 'rational' eighteenth century of the *Spectator* and Johnson's 'dixonary', as the Squire calls it, against the diluted version of Romanticism popular in the 1820s, and contrasts the prosaic detail of science (or realism) to the unthinking lyrical effusion. As Mr Gibson says, 'One gets a great deal of meaning out of Roger's words', while Osborne, who writes of 'the time of roses', has no idea when they actually bloom:

' "I believe my movements are guided more by the lunar calendar than the floral. You had better take my brother for your companion; he is practical in his love of flowers. I am only theoretical."

"Does that fine word 'theoretical' imply that you are ignorant?" asked Cynthia.' (Ch. 28)

Poetic vagueness hides inattention. Mr Coxe's 'eternal passion' for Molly is exposed as calf-love by his lazy conventions: 'she was fair, not pale, her eyes were lode-stars, her dimples marks of Cupid's finger, &c'. Reading this, Mr Gibson vows to replace the Shakespeare in the surgery library by 'Johnson's Dictionary' and writes a terse Latin prescription for a dose of modesty, respect and silence. It is the emotion itself, not its object, that inspires Mr Coxe, and it is no surprise when he falls equally in love with Cynthia. When Roger is reduced to flowers, moons and stars in his letters to Cynthia, we guess that their love is false. His truer self is expressed in his discussion of places, flora and fauna, books and ideas – the passages Cynthia does not read. She smiles at the compliments, until Molly asks where Roger is:

'Where? Oh, I didn't look exactly – somewhere in Abyssinia – Huon, I can't read the word, and it doesn't much signify, for it would give me no idea.' (Ch. 37)

The words that do 'signify' are different for each person, each class, each discipline. *Wives and Daughters* affirms the values of directness, the language of friendship rather than romance. It has a special place too for pungent local speech – Betty's dialect words like 'scomfished', and old proverbs with the patina of time – the verbal equivalent of the coarse strong-smelling cheese that Mrs Gibson banishes to the kitchen in favour of ill-made French omelettes. Since *Mary Barton*, Gaskell had been fascinated by the way that speech, which should be an open window, a means of communication, was so often a barrier; to live in harmony and grow in understanding we must constantly interpret and translate. After Osborne dies, Molly tells Squire Hamley about his secret marriage and reads him Aimée's letters, translating her 'innocent sentences of love' into colloquial English:

'little sentences in "little language" that went home to the Squire's heart. Perhaps, if Molly had read French more easily, she might not have translated them into such touching, homely, broken words.' (Ch. 53)

Just as Roger had translated the intellectual language of science into 'homely everyday speech' for her, so Molly now translates the language of feeling for the grief-stricken father; both find the sense beneath the style.

There are times, however, when language fails altogether, as Molly knows when she sees the Squire with his dead son: 'possibly her presence might have some balm in it; but uttering of words was a vain thing'. People with the gift of sympathy will 'read' and communicate without speech; Molly can 'read her father's face like an ABC' and when Aimée arrives after Osborne's death, she does not need to speak 'except that at such moments the eyes speak solemnly and comprehensively. Aimée read their meaning.'

Our deepest feelings lie below words. The most frequent 'literary' scenes in this novel are not of people actually reading, but *pretending* to read, falling asleep over a book, dreaming of their own fears and desires, often by an open window; such scenes are particularly associated with Molly.

Molly is our detective in a novel of secrets, but she is a perpetual third, a constant messenger. She silences her natural voice. Watching her father become bitter in his marriage, she wonders whether silence is right, or whether she should tell her stepmother some 'forcible home truths'. Her strongest virtues are those that she is told to suppress: her anger and outspokenness. As a child she is a tomboy, getting stains on her dress by climbing up into the cherry-tree to read. When she defends timid Miss Eyre, the jealous Betty likens her to a hen sparrow or a vixen defending their young. But such maternal wildness and giving way to 'passion' is reproved by Miss Eyre; Molly thinks it hard 'to be blamed for what she considered her just anger'. Thus begins a process of taming which she outwardly accepts but inwardly resists.

To describe her heroine's unconscious growth Gaskell needs a different form of narrative. Although the novel remains entirely credible in 'realistic' terms, it can also be followed, in detail, as a symbolic account of Molly's inner life, a psycho-drama complete with characters, plots and props, which we understand almost without thinking in the way we apprehend the underlying 'meanings' of Snow White, or Beauty and the Beast. There are five plots in Molly's story: the power of the father; the absent mother; the arrival of the stepmother with her 'webs and distortions of truth'; the acceptance of the sexual double, 'the bad sister'; and the awakening of the sleeping self.

Almost the first thing we know about Molly is that she is 'motherless'. Her father is all in all to her. As a girl she fantasizes about fastening a chain between them 'and we could never lose each other', but as she grows older her feelings become harder to express. When he tells her of his coming marriage, speech deserts her:

'She did not answer. She could not tell what words to use. She was afraid of saying anything, lest the passion of anger, dislike, indignation – whatever it was that was boiling up in her breast – should find vent in cries and screams, or worse, in raging words that could never be forgotten. It was as if the piece of solid ground on which she stood had broken from the shore, and she was drifting out into the infinite sea alone.' (Ch. 10)

She 'did not care to analyse the sources of her tears and sobs'; she feels that he is angry with her, that he prefers another, that she has lost his love.

The pain lessens as Molly recognizes that a new bond need not necessarily break an old and later we see the situation in reverse and feel the tug of separation from the father's end of the chain. Just as Molly had despaired at the thought of his new wife, so Mr Gibson is overwhelmed at the rumours that Mr Preston is Molly's lover. He grips her arms until she gives a 'little involuntary sound of pain' and looks at 'her soft bruised flesh, with tears gathering fast to her eyes to think that he, her father, should have hurt her so'. Although Molly denies the relationship, Mr Gibson has to face her maturity and the loss of his 'child'. At the end he watches her when she cannot eat on the day Roger leaves:

' "Lover *versus* father!" thought he, half sadly. "Lover wins." And he, too, became indifferent to all that remained of his dinner. Mrs Gibson pattered on; and nobody listened.' (Ch. 60)

Despite his tenderness, Mr Gibson thinks of love in male terms, of possession and competition. The love of the absent mother is of a different quality, self-sacrificing and mutually life-giving – Molly's last memory of her mother is of her holding out her arms, already numb in death, to be warmed by her child. When Miss Browning refurnishes her father's bedroom, her eyes fill with tears at the banishment of that scene. But the mother is eternally reborn: eventually this symbolic figure will reappear in Aimée, who turns from being a passive object of love (Aimée), 'submissive to Osborne's will', into an actively loving mother, returning from the brink of death when her son is placed in her arms, and bringing new life to Hamley Hall.

To grow up, Molly *must* separate from her mother. When her stepmother enters her house, she begins to think not of her mother's body, in death, but her own, in life. Dressed for the wedding, she is startled when she looks in the mirror: ' "I wonder if I'm pretty," thought she. "I almost think I am – in this kind of dress I mean, of course. Betty would say, 'Fine feathers make fine birds'." ' In perfect accord with the realistic plot, her own bedroom is now redecorated, and at the same time as her little 'white dimity bed' (which had been her mother's before she was married) is consigned to the lumber-room two things happen: Mrs Hamley, her 'good mother', dies and Cynthia arrives. The atmosphere is subtly sexualized by this 'bad sister', a fatherless counter to the motherless Molly. As her name suggests, she is the inconstant moon to Molly's steady sun. 'You are good,' says Cynthia:

'At least, if you're not good, what am I? There's a rule-of-three sum for you to do! But it's no use talking; I am not good, and I never shall be now. Perhaps I might be a heroine still, but I shall never be a good woman, I know.' (Ch. 19)

Through Cynthia, Gaskell can leave Molly innocent yet show a girl fully aware of her developing sexual power: the reader can enjoy both the 'good' and the 'bad', Molly with her 'delicate neatness' and Cynthia with her 'tumbled gowns'. Their doubleness is suggested by Molly's immediate response to her stepsister: she 'fell in love with her, so to speak, on the instant' and 'would watch her perpetually as she went about the room, with the free stately grace of some wild animal in the forest'. It is natural that Roger Hamley should fall in love with both of them. At one stage Gaskell called her own Marianne both 'Molly' and 'Cynthia'.[9] They are halves of a whole.

Cynthia continually plots her future life – her marriage to Roger as an escape from Preston, her fantasy of going to Russia as a governess. She can see herself as a heroine, capable of one effort and then a relapse: 'a moral kangaroo!' Molly does not even know she has a story. Cynthia is Cinderella, who wants to go to the ball; Molly is Sleeping Beauty. Yet she grows as she 'sleeps', and her unrecognized desires and confusions are expressed, above all, in those repeated images of her half reading, half dreaming by an open window. Squire Hamley pulls her away from *The Bride of Lammermoor* to walk round his estate: she sees nothing because her mind is full of

'Ravenswood' and 'Lucy Ashton' – and of the Squire's chance remark that people had expected her father to marry again. When Mr Gibson comes to announce his marriage, she is asleep over her book by the window.

Both these scenes are associated with her feelings for her father, but a different sequence runs alongside. Shortly before Mr Gibson breaks his news, she is sitting upstairs at Hamley Hall, 'losing herself in the dreamy outlooks into the gardens and wood, quivering in the noon-tide heat'. The house is so still, we are told, it might have been the 'moated grange'. Like Tennyson's Mariana, she is waiting for the lover who cometh not. Time is suspended, sounds blurred. Flies buzz within, bees buzz without, and the words of Osborne's poem that she is trying to learn by heart lose their meaning through repetition. Suddenly sounds break in from outside: the snap of a gate, wheels crackling on dry gravel, horses' hooves. A loud cheerful voice penetrates to Molly's room, 'coming up through the open windows, the hall, the passages, the staircase, with unwonted fullness and roundness of tone'. From Squire Hamley's greeting she knows it must be Roger, whom she has not yet met. Doors shut and only the 'distant buzz of talking' can be heard. Molly returns to her poem.

The extremely suggestive imagery of an unfocused, sensual inner world suddenly assaulted from outside and then closing in upon itself again reappears in a more disturbing form later when Molly returns from a country walk to hear that Roger, on the eve of departing for Africa, has told Cynthia he loves her:

'She felt as if she could not understand it all; but as for that matter, what could she understand? Nothing. For a few minutes, her brain seemed in too great a whirl to comprehend anything but that she was being carried on in earth's diurnal course, with rocks, and stones, and trees, with as little volition on her part as if she were dead. Then the room grew stifling, and instinctively she went to the open casement window, and leant out, gasping for breath. Gradually, the conscious-ness of the soft peaceful landscape stole into her mind, and stilled the buzzing confusion.' (Ch. 34)

We recognize that open window, towards which Gaskell's heroines, particularly Ruth, fling themselves in moments of mingled desire and despair. Here and in the scene at Hamley Hall, Molly surrenders to a male view of women and romance – Scott, Tennyson, Osborne,

Wordsworth – which overwhelms, entraps and threatens to kill her.
Scott's Lucy merges with Wordsworth's: romantic fantasy gives way
to death.

In contrast to the buzz of confusion within, the landscape Molly sees
through the window 'hums' with life. She sees the cottagers' smoke,
showing that evening meals are being made 'for the husband's
homecoming' (a carefully balanced opposite of the opening view from
her childhood window). She hears the sound of children laughing. Like
Margaret Hale in *North and South*, she is pulled back from solipsistic
misery by the sound of children's voices, an assurance of the continuity
of life – but not entirely. Hearing steps on the stairs and thinking that
Roger has left without saying goodbye, she lays her head on the
window-sill and cries. Molly will not admit she loves him, but while he
is in Africa, 'lost in the mysterious darkness of distance', she thinks of
him in 'the soft darkness of her room'. 'Just anger' and sympathy force
Molly into action on Cynthia's behalf, at the risk of her own
reputation. Lady Harriet overturns the gossip about Molly and Mr
Preston, using Phoebe Browning as 'Sancho Panza to my Don
Quixote', but Molly's own story is still denied; she seems to be always
controlled by others. A great fear of death, a 'rush of senseless terror'
at the annihilation of the self overwhelms her when she sees Osborne's
corpse; like Mary Barton, Ruth and Phillis, under internal pressure she
collapses with fever.

Roger returns to find her slowly recovering. She is still in a white
dress, still reading dreamily by the open window. Soon afterwards
they look down together at Cynthia and her new fiancé, the London
lawyer Mr Henderson. Later, through that open window, Molly
overhears Mrs Goodenough speculating that Mrs Gibson is now
plotting that she, instead of Cynthia, should marry Roger Hamley.
Self-consciousness swamps her and she determines to avoid him, 'and,
when she was with him, she must be as natural as possible, or he might
observe some difference; but what was natural?' They meet again at
the Towers, where Lady Harriet has persuaded Molly to stay while her
father and Mrs Gibson are away at Cynthia's wedding. There, among
the fraternity of scientists gathered by Lord Hollingford, they learn to
speak again 'naturally' as friends. When Molly goes to Hamley Hall, at
his invitation, to try and soothe matters between Aimée and the Squire,
they begin to understand their own feelings, although these are not
openly expressed, except through Molly's parting gift of a rose.

Roger returns to Africa without speaking directly to Molly; instead he reaches a tacit agreement with her father. While both men respect her independence of choice, women are still 'wives' or 'daughters'. When Roger finally leaves, on a rainy day, Molly is engaged in 'women's work', making a worsted-work cushion for Cynthia: 'One, two, three. One, two, three, four, five, six, seven; all wrong; she was thinking of something else and had to unpick it.' And when Mrs Gibson calls her to the window, to see Roger standing patiently, staring at the house, she finds it hard to dodge her stepmother's flailing arms to wave goodbye; not until she retreats can Molly quietly move 'into her place'. She must wait for space to be left for her. We sense that Molly will win through one day. But that ending was never written. The final words of Elizabeth Gaskell's fiction are those of Mrs Gibson, returning us from the open window to female silence, sleep and clothes: 'And now cover me up close, and let me go to sleep, and dream about my dear Cynthia and my new shawl!'

[28]

Endings

For eighteen months thousands of readers followed Molly's progress in the *Cornhill*. *Wives and Daughters* was proving Mrs Gaskell's most popular work since *Cranford*. Many, like Mary Mohl, adored it from the start:

'I have this very evening read the last number of the *Cornhill*, and am as pleased as ever. The Hamleys are delightful, and Mrs Gibson! – oh, the tricks are delicious . . . Everyone says it's the best thing you ever did. Don't hurry it up at the last; that's a rock you must not split on.'[1]

As she neared the end of her story in September 1865, Elizabeth was in a hurry. But she was determined not to show it in her writing, as she had in the abrupt conclusion of *North and South* ten years before. Roger must travel to Africa and back, before he proposed to Molly.

She was pleased with her book, and knew it was good. With its du Maurier illustrations, it sat proudly in the *Cornhill*, beside the work of the best of her contemporaries. George Smith, 'the prince of publishers', rivalled Dickens's *All the Year Round* in providing first-class fiction. And Smith had not one but two serialized novels in each monthly issue. In 1864 *Wives and Daughters* overlapped with Trollope's *The Small House at Allington* and Thackeray's last, unfinished historical novel *Denis Duval*. In 1865 it shared the lead with Wilkie Collins's sensational *Armadale*.

Gaskell does not take one's breath away at her breadth and penetration as George Eliot does, nor can she match the visionary intensity of Charlotte Brontë, but her unforced storytelling power and impassioned sympathy create an unrivalled range of fully imagined worlds. Over the years she consciously extended her craft, exploring the use of different genres, the variety and nuance of language. Her humour, which can be biting, more often displays an endless, quick amusement at quirks of speech, oddities of behaviour, small snobberies and false logic. But it was anger at the inequities of society that drove her to write her first novel and this never left her. Although in her last work she writes about drawing-rooms rather than tenements, her insistence on clear vision and on the duty to assert 'truth', however uncomfortable, makes *Wives and Daughters* as political, in a broad sense, as *Mary Barton*. She believed vehemently that 'the power of sympathy depended on the power of imagination',[2] and she never ceased to speak for the outcast, or to defy the internalized ideologies, including those of religion, that were used to justify oppression. Sometimes the links Gaskell makes between domestic and political relationships seem naïve, but they are challenging none the less. She was well aware that her prescription for social and personal evils – the replacement of rigid rules by 'loving attention', a discriminating, flexible sympathy – would never be easy to follow. She lived, after all, in the middle of an industrial city, at a time of bitter class conflict in Britain and of wars and revolutions abroad.

Gaskell's own uncertainties give her writing a strange, individual tone. As she traced the struggles of her heroines and asserted the need for women's autonomy, she also advocated self-sacrifice. As she fought against the silencing of women, she also confronted, within herself, the effects of their dependency: the stultifying guilt attached to sexuality, the buried defiance and anger, the despairing impulse to self-annihilation. Such feelings were so deep and insistent that often she could only express them through the symbolic language of ghosts and dreams. Her fiction is far from cool. It is coloured by her sensuality, her delight in the ridiculous, her reluctant but compulsive fascination with pain, her urgent questioning of religious belief and historical necessity. When the 22-year-old Henry James reviewed *Wives and Daughters* for the *Nation* in 1866, he wrote:

'Mrs Gaskell's genius was so composite as a quality, it was so obviously the offspring of her affections, her feelings, her associations, and (considering that, after all, it was genius) was so little of an intellectual nature . . . But genius is of many kinds, and we are almost tempted to say that that of Mrs Gaskell strikes us as being little else than a peculiar play of her personal character.'[3]

Surveying her career and its controversies, he thought she displayed, 'considering her success, a minimum of head'.

James was not mindlessly applying the current stereotype of a typically intuitive female writer: he explained that this was not to value Gaskell's intellect the less, but her character the more. I think he was right. She was a clever, widely read woman, whose intellect is underestimated because it is submerged rather than obtrusive. Her thinking, however, was not abstract or codified: she enacts and embodies rather than argues. And she cannot always answer the questions which disturb her.

There was always a strain of restlessness and longing in her. From 1860, when Julia went to school with the Greens and she paid more visits to Knutsford, she drew increasingly on her youth – in 'A Dark Night's Work', in Cousin Phillis and in Wives and Daughters. When Frederick Greenwood outlined the conclusion to this last, unfinished novel in the Cornhill, he said that what promised to be the crowning work of a life was now 'a memorial to death'. Yet it is also a memorial to life, especially to the early years which fed Elizabeth Gaskell's imagination. It summons up the warmth and gossip of Knutsford, but also the tense isolation of her stays in Chelsea and the subjective confusion of adolescence. It brings together the deep themes which flow through all her stories: the 'mother want', the troubled second marriage, the beloved man who disappears overseas, the stifled sexuality, the divided self, the dread of death, the struggle with a loved but fallible father.

The repeated confrontation with the father becomes, in Gaskell's work, a parable of the male drive to possess and infantilize women, part of a critique of vertical structures of power that extends from the home to the masters' dealings with the workers, the State's relationship to the people, and the vengeful Old Testament 'law' in contrast to the mercy of Christ. We have no way of telling if it draws on the pain of private experience. But one enduring theme, the death of the child, certainly does. If Elizabeth's son Willie had lived, he would have been twenty-one in 1865. When she sent a letter of condolence to Robert Gould Shaw's mother after his death in the American Civil War in

1863, she wrote with deep emotion, as if her own loss had happened yesterday and nothing could ever compensate:

'I know as well as any one that he died nobly doing his duty, "laying down his life for others"', thus showing the greatest love possible; but O! dear friend, I know what it is to lose a child, and I do feel for you.' (L710)

The numb grief, expressed so rawly in *Mary Barton*, is still felt in the heart-broken Squire Hamley, turning away from the body of his dead son and taking no more notice of Molly 'than he did of the moon, looking through the unclosed window, with passionless stare'.

After Willie's death Elizabeth often endured deep depressions, triggered by overwork, illness and winter darkness, but these were offset by other periods of intense happiness and by her constant energetic interest in life. Her most marked characteristic, evident in her writing as well as her life, was a total immersion in the experience of the moment. Her complete absorption in the task she was doing, the story she was telling, the person she was talking to – even the meal she was eating or the dress she was making – formed a large part of her often mentioned charm. She could be stubborn, prejudiced, overwhelming and erratic, but people forgave her because she was so clearly *involved*. When Fleeming Jenkin and Annie Austin were married in 1859, they wrote to her jointly, sure of that interested response. 'We want to be congratulated,' they said, and as Julia and Meta had not done them justice,

'we appeal confidently to you – tell us that our wedding cake is admirable, that our little country wedding is the beau ideal of weddings and we shall be so pleased and believe every word of it.'[4]

In the last two years of her life, despite the strain she was under, that responsiveness was much in evidence. It endeared her to younger writers like Swinburne, or John Addington Symonds and Catherine North, whom she met at Pontresina and whose joint Christmas story she was soon warmly recommending to George Smith. It caught the attention of Anne Thackeray Ritchie, who saw her in 1862, in the dining-room at Palace Green, talking to Thackeray and 'looking up at him laughing, inquiring, responding, gay yet definite'.[5] And with that interest in others went great kindness. When Thackeray died on

Christmas Eve 1863, she immediately sent a motherly letter inviting Annie and her sister to stay.

Annie was an acute observer, despite her notorious scattiness, and she left a vivid picture of Elizabeth as a storyteller. In particular she remembered her voice:

'a delicate enunciation, singularly clear and cultivated, a harmonious note moved by a laugh now and then, and restrained by a certain shyness, that shyness which belongs to sensitive people who feel what others are feeling almost too quickly, and are at times suddenly hindered by the vibration.'[6]

It was a gusty morning in the autumn of 1864. At George Smith's house in Hampstead, while the children played in the garden and the wind whistled round the house, Mrs Gaskell told stories to a circle of women, a succession of tales, 'of Scotch ghosts, historical ghosts, spirited ghosts with faded uniforms and nice old powdered queues'. The wind died and they went outside and sat under a tree, and the listeners asked for more stories and Elizabeth found more to tell: 'legends of smugglers as well as ghosts, adventures too, stories with weather in them, wild snowstorms rising and dying away'. Then at last the women's stories had to stop. Leslie Stephen came walking down the garden arm in arm with Thurstan Holland, 'and the talk became general, and reality began when the story-telling came to an end'.

Compared with her own father, who had 'laid down his weary pen at last', Annie thought Elizabeth did not seem weary at all. On the contrary, 'she was at work and play almost to the last'. Most people noticed her energy rather than her tiredness, like Mary Mohl:

'If you had known what a heart she had! But no one did. One who gave so much had a right to expect a good deal in return, and she got it and enjoyed it. She was a singularly happy person, and her happiness expressed itself in an inexhaustible flow of high spirits. She looked happy.'[7]

But she was not inexhaustible.

She could still bubble euphorically, but in September 1865 she was physically, mentally and emotionally tired. Weariness made her nostalgic for times which seemed free from care, and she looked back especially to her weeks in Rome in 1857 and her 'dear Americans'. She had never entirely lost her tenderness for Charles Eliot Norton. 'My dear Mr Norton,' she wrote in February 1865, 'To think that you will really touch this bit of paper! It has suddenly struck me as so odd and strange.' Charles had just had a daughter, named Sara. He wanted to call her after Elizabeth, but she was unable to reply in time, a lapse she deeply regretted, saying she would have liked it very much, and 'Elizabeth', though not pretty itself, had 'very pretty abbreviations and pet names'. His next daughter, born in 1866, was named Elizabeth Gaskell Norton; her family called her Lily.[8]

Two weeks after her mother died, Meta told Charles Norton that she had wanted him to be among the first to know because 'she was so faithful to you – so unswerving in her affection, not only to you, but to all that she had known through you; in her burning adherence to the side of the North, and her longing for freedom and right to triumph in her "dear America" '.[9] That September, before she left Manchester, Elizabeth often thought of Rome. James Lowell had sent her his *Fireside Travels* and when she thanked him, she told him how the Storys had talked about him and how Charles had recited the yet unpublished 'I only know she came and went' in evenings in his rooms in the Piazza di Spagna. Three American visitors had arrived in Manchester that month; she hoped they were the swallows that presaged summer:

'Now, said we the Americans will be coming over, and travelling about again, & perhaps we may see some of our own people. "Our own people" being the Nortons, the Fields, Mr Hamilton Wilde – (where is he? oh where?) dear Romans of old.' (L776)

Telling Charles of these hopes, in her last letter to him, she added sadly: 'But life never flows back, – we shall never again have the old happy days in Rome, shall we?' With a mental shrug she turned briskly to other subjects and her new house, her present for William. A fortnight later she left Plymouth Grove for the last time.

On the way south Elizabeth visited the Tolletts at Crewe. There she heard that Judge Crompton was ill, but to her fury her letters of sympathy – and a letter from Marianne to her – never reached their destinations: it made her 'strongly suspect the tipsy Crewe butler'. Then she went on to London, staying briefly at the Grosvenor (managing to reduce the bill by 'various contrivances'), but she was ill and irritated and slept so badly that she persuaded Julia and Meta to

go on to Newhaven at once, for that precious 'breath of sea-air'. She
was jumping with impatience. Newhaven would not do either; the inn
was filthy and the town was crammed with cross-Channel passengers.
The sea-air must have worked, though, since for once she slept like a
top, from eight at night until eight the next morning and awoke
starving, to complain that 'we had no breakfast so to speak, but 2
mutton chops a piece & bitter beer'. She wanted to move on. Straight
after breakfast 'we met Mrs Milner-Gibson, just arrived from Dieppe
on the stairs. She advised us to come to this hotel.' A day later they
were in France: at fifty-five she had lost none of her impulsiveness.

On 6 October Elizabeth wrote to Marianne from the Hôtel de Paris,
Dieppe, dealing first with the problems she had left behind. 'I *am* so
sorry about the smell,' she began, before launching into a detailed
review of the Plymouth Grove plumbing. 'However one does not
expect to write about *drains* from Dieppe.' In high spirits she described
their journey, their hotel – and, naturally, their food. Their crossing
had been perfect, smooth as a lake, and she was almost sorry it was
over:

'We have a pleasant sitting room au premier, *two* double-bedded
rooms, (one opening out of the sitting room, –) breakfast (coffee bread
& butter in our room) lunch any time we like – chocolate, cold meat,
bread & butter Neufchatel Cheese & grapes – in the Salle à manger at
a little table, & dinner at the table d'hote (10 persons only 1 gentleman
which Julia finds dull –) soup, fish, 2 meats, pudding & desert – for 9
francs a piece, *service* included. Bougies, wine & fire extras. We are 2
minutes from the sea, & the house is as sweet as a nut.' (L778)

For half a franc they could go into 'the Establissement' nearby and
hear a shocking band and read newspapers. Everything was shutting
up for the winter, but the air and sky were splendid and she felt like a
different creature: 'I shall write to Papa next, – about the drains.'

While Julia sighed and longed for Switzerland, her mother was
completely content. Meta vouched for the fact that for the next few
weeks her sleeplessness and faintness disappeared. Elizabeth told
George Smith Dieppe got more and more charming as the weather
became rougher and wilder '& the people (smart ones I mean,)
disappear'. Not all of them vanished: 'We are becoming highly
authorial (if there is such a word), in this hotel. Mrs Crowe; and a M.
Alfred de Bréhat who has sent me his romans as a compliment to the

author of Ruth (pronounced Roit).' She had never heard of him and left his novels unopened on the table while she wrote her own. Another guest was Mme Gosch, the wife of the Danish envoy in London, to whom Mrs Milner-Gibson had given them a note of introduction, but, Elizabeth declared airily, 'the Gaskell hatred of society prevails' (a new characteristic) '& we have not delivered it'.

They liked Dieppe so much that they stayed an extra week. The new house seemed entirely manageable from across the Channel. Hearn sent word that a soup-tureen lid and a chair had been broken in carriage, but '*all else right*'. At last, after taking Julia to Rouen to see the cathedral, Elizabeth set off for England and at the Hôtel des Bains in Boulogne she scribbled a note:

'My dear Thurstan,
Please we are hoping to see you on the 28th\at *The Lawn*/ – you won't mind everything being rough. We can give you bread & cheese & cold meat, and "Alton Ale" & tea & bread & butter & "excellent milk" (Hearn says) & a hearty welcome. Come sooner if you can. I want all sorts of advice about the garden &c &c – No time for more from your ever affec cousin.

E. C. Gaskell' (L779–80)

'All else' suddenly did seem right.

A couple of days later she saw the Lawn for the first time, driving up from Alton station, a mile and a half away. She wrote at once to William, with obvious glee at her truthfulness, 'to tell him we had "crossed the channel" – (I did not say where from or to where) and were now spending the remainder of our time & money at a little village on the borders of Hampshire'.

Charwomen had been cleaning the house for five weeks – which seems excessive – but it was still not quite ready. Trees overshadowing the dining-room windows must be cut down, little bits of joinering were needed and all the woodwork wanted painting, but 'the wet weather is *so* against this'. The 'upholstering woman' had not turned up and Meta and Julia were packed off in the rain to bring her up from Alton by main force. The Heals list had been left in Manchester 'and until we have the thing *complete* it is no use making our dear "*lists*" '. The carpets could not be put down until the upholstery was done, 'so you see we seem rather at a stand still, which is *very* provoking'.

The prospective tenant, Mrs Moray, was a problem too, since her offer of rent was lower than expected. Elizabeth put her off until she could get 'masculine advice' from Thurstan and wondered if she should find another tenant:

'But we don't know who to leave in charge of the house when we go? &c &c &c, and you know I'm an old fidget, and if we *don't* let it! – It will be so nice, & so complete. We long for you to see it so much. Every day we like it better & better even in the midst of all the *half* furnished state, painters & charwomen . . . Oh I must tell you something. Last night the ringers rang the 3 church bells, and then came to say they had been ringing for our arival [sic] (we had never heard the bells) & I had to give them 2s-6d. Hearn liked it tho'. She seems very well now; I am giving her sherry every day, twice.' (L781)

The old fidget sounds busy and cheerful. She badly wanted Florence to come, as well as Marianne, especially since Flossy was 'quite knocked up' by helping Lady Crompton in the judge's final illness. (He had died on 30 October, and Elizabeth felt 'so sorry to think we shall never see the dear kind judge again'.) Unable to bear being 'at a stand still', she thought she would work: 'I am going to finish my story while here if I can – but I am constantly called off just now. Only I may as well make use of this waiting time.'

Inevitably, the manuscript was put aside in favour of unpacking and cleaning and sorting and arranging. Ten days later everything was almost as Elizabeth wanted; she could look around with pride. It had been tiring, but she had said over and over again 'that she felt better than she had for years, & years younger . . . & she was more than ordinarily happy & full of spirits'.[10] The house was very nearly in her full possession; William Shaen was due to come down the next week to complete the final purchase. On Saturday, 11 November, she wrote to him 'full of life and spirits' and adding: 'it is so nice to think we shall see you on Wednesday'. He had just finished reading her letter on the Monday morning when Thurstan Holland walked through the door, to tell him that Lily was dead.[11]

Florence and Charles had come down on Saturday – Elizabeth having persuaded Charles he needed country air after being closeted in a house of mourning. On Sunday, 12 November, they spent a lazy morning and in the afternoon Meta and Charlie went for a walk while Elizabeth took Flossy and Julia to church, half a mile up the lane. Even the clergyman, said Meta, 'noticed how particularly well mama was looking'. After church Elizabeth happily showed a poor widow from the village her house and her 'pretty new furniture', and then walked in the garden with Charlie. Dusk fell early now. Everyone met for early tea in the drawing-room at five o'clock and sat round the fire talking 'most cozily and happily', discussing plans to lend the house to Lady Crompton for a rest.[12] Elizabeth was telling Charlie about a conversation she had had with the judge a short time ago, about going to Rome, city of her dreams. The judge, she was just saying, had said, 'I want Lady Crompton to have something pleasant to look forward to after I'm gone. She can go to Rome when . . .'[13]

Elizabeth's last clear word was 'Rome'. The rest of the sentence, 'when I am dead', seemed to those listening to hang in the air as she stopped and fell forward, with a slight gasp, into the arms of Meta, sitting next to her on the sofa. At first they thought she had fainted, or at worst had a stroke. The girls tried to give her some brandy and ran to bring a hot-water bottle for her feet. Charlie and a servant rushed to fetch the doctor. 'We tried everything, with growing terror,' said Meta. But it was too late. When the doctor came, nearly an hour later, he said that he could have done nothing – she had died almost instantly. 'She had always wished and often spoken of her wish to die a sudden painless death like this,' wrote Thurstan, 'and we all believe that her end was peculiarly happy.'

Meta was the only one to break down physically. Florence and Julia stayed calm. Then someone had to tell Marianne and William. Charlie left for Manchester by the first train on Monday, pausing in London to tell Thurstan. A telegram had already been posted up for William at the Portico, but he was at a minister's meeting in Altrincham. Another telegram was sent to him there, saying that Charlie Crompton was in Manchester, 'So he knew that something bad had happened'. His fellow-minister Samuel Steinthal brought William back to face the news, and he and Charlie travelled up to London by the night mail, arriving at Alton at noon the next day. At the Lawn, Elizabeth's secret house where her body now lay, William's usual reserve gave way, as William Shaen told Catherine Winkworth:

'The girls feared he would shut himself up, but he has not; he has wept a great deal and found much relief in talking to them and hearing all she had lately been saying and planning. And he wishes as far as possible to carry out just what she has planned, and has taken to the place. So I hope it will end in their going to it at once without letting it.'[14]

It was a passing thought, a desire to stay with his wife as long as possible. But this was her dream, not his: William did not move south. A fortnight later Meta wrote: 'Papa is wonderfully calm.' He took solace in his work and his faith. Ten years later he wrote to the widow of John Relly Beard: 'I know from experience what your feelings at present must be . . . but we do not sorrow as those who are without hope.'[15]

Like her father, Meta took refuge in belief in an afterlife where there would be no more parting. But, she said, 'For me it has changed the face of the world forever.' In years to come new editions and translations of Elizabeth's books continued to fill the shelves of Plymouth Grove. Her portraits and, for some years, her funeral mask looked down from the drawing-room walls, but there was no living, volatile presence to pounce, fuss, give orders, gossip, make them laugh – or, sometimes, despair – and spirit them off or disappear herself at a moment's notice to distant places. From 1865 onwards Mrs Gaskell's daughters had to make their lives after new patterns.

Her husband, however, resumed his familiar routine. William worked on in Manchester, busy with his minister's duties, his teaching, his committees and his 'plaguing *Unitarian Herald*'. He still ordered new travel books and scientific works for the Portico and lectured on Crabbe and Burns and the Lancashire dialect. He remained as much in demand as a teacher as when Elizabeth had boasted to Mary Howitt in 1838 of the deputations of workmen arriving on the Dover Street doorstep asking him to lecture on 'The Poets of Humble Life'. In 1874, thanking Henry Arthur Bright for a new book, he wrote: 'my interest in Burns is not at all less than it used to be . . . Unfortunately, as I get older my time for recreation among the poets gets less, and I sometimes think I will shake myself free from some of my work, but when I come to decide what it shall be, I feel at a loss, and so "power on".'[16] William was greatly respected in Manchester; in 1878, on the fiftieth anniversary of his coming to Cross Street, over a thousand people came to pay tribute to him at a special soirée at the Town Hall. The speeches were long, but the atmosphere was hardly formal: the

party on the platform were greeted with loud cheers and the singing of
'Auld Lang Syne'.

When he travelled south to meetings as a trustee of Manchester
College, he stayed with Florence or Marianne. In March 1866, after he
had been ill and was on his way to convalesce in Hastings, he wrote a
note to Marianne at Dumbleton. Few of his personal letters survive
and this one is irresistibly William-like.

'Railway, between Stafford and Rugby

My dearest Polly,
I got off very comfortably at 9½, Florence accompanying me to the
station and so far I have got *on* very comfortably. I have the middle
seat with my back to the engine, which exactly suits me, and my three
fellow passengers like true Englishmen never open their lips or the
windows either which is also to my liking. I have begun a similar
scribble – under similar difficulties to Meta . . .

. . . I have picked up my crumbs very much during the last two days,
and when Mr. Mellor came to say "Go-o-o-o-d by-y" last night, he
said I looked quite different . . . We are now slackening speed for
Rugby and I must attack my sandwiches *and* my brandy and water . . .
When I was taking my ticket, a poor man, that I didn't know, spoke to
me very nicely and said he hoped I was better. Everybody, certainly,
has been exceedingly kind. There came more blancmange from Mrs
Carver, and an offer of jelly yesterday.

Leighton Buzzard

I've finished my sandwiches, & my brandy and water (rather strong of
the latter), and have just been indulging in a bit of your ginger, which I
found very toothsome and pleasant . . . As we are not likely to have
any adventures between this and London, I think I had better make a
finish of my scrawl.

Your loving Papa
Wm. Gaskell'[17]

Despite his high position, the Revd Gaskell was completely without
pomposity. When she was eight, Beatrix Potter, who grew to love him
dearly on those annual Potter holidays in Scotland and the Lakes,
knitted him a huge comforter as a birthday present. He was suitably
grateful: 'Big as I am,' he wrote, 'I know I could not have done it one-

tenth as well. Every time I put it round my neck, which during the winter will be every day, I shall be sure to think of you.' He died on 12 June 1884, aged eighty-eight, and two days later Beatrix wrote in her journal: 'Four o'clock Saturday afternoon. Mr Gaskell is just being buried beside his wife. We have sent some flowers.'[18]

Meta and Julia kept house for their father, and were even more actively (or at least more consistently) involved in Cross Street and community work than their mama. They fought for women's higher education, acted as governors for Manchester High School for Girls, founded the Manchester Social Club and turned the open space opposite Plymouth Grove into a recreation ground. Elizabeth's royalties were ploughed back into Manchester charities, but not into feminist battles, since they opposed the suffrage movement as a diversion from more urgent, practical campaigns.

The two sisters were inseparable, at home and on holiday. They were great climbers, but on their first trip to Switzerland after Elizabeth's death Meta told Norton:

'There is a great deal that is keenly painful in going abroad again. It was such a special delight of Mama's to guide us and plan our tours; and it seems to bring back the very freshness of one's grief each time that one remembers that she will not be with us.'[19]

In future years they often went abroad, but they still liked to retreat to Silverdale, where they built a house called The Shieling. They were strong single women of the kind their mother had admired, but they knew how to enjoy themselves and their friends included artists, writers, musicians and even the odd anarchist. (They once introduced Annie Ritchie to Kropotkin, with hilarious results.) Annie loved staying with them:

'O what kind ladies!
O what a delicious dinner!
O what a nice room!
... Meta met me at the station in a beautiful brougham. Pheasant, jelly, Apollinaris for dinner, champagne on the side table . . . The sun is shining, the air is delicious! I like the climate of Manchester!!'[20]

Although they lived well and were always busy, Meta remained nervous, dependent on her younger sister's unstoppable vitality. After Julia's death in 1908 she turned two houses in Plymouth Grove into a nursing home in her memory, but she was lost without her sister and from then on her health was poor until she died five years later, in 1913.

The independent Flossy, whom Fanny Wedgwood had thought such a beauty, had died over thirty years before in 1881, aged only thirty-nine; she and Charlie had no children. Thurstan and Marianne had three, but Thurstan also died young, in the same year as William. The strong, sensible Marianne, 'more like an eldest son than a daughter', survived them all. She lived on in Worcestershire until 1920, a lively, sociable woman, even in her eighties.

When Marianne died, over half a century had passed since her fiancé Thurstan took Elizabeth Gaskell's coffin north to Knutsford on Thursday, 16 November 1865.

By then obituaries had appeared in the national papers and many more were to come. In the *Pall Mall Gazette*, on 15 November, Richard Monckton Milnes remembered Mrs Gaskell as a 'genial and deightful' person as well as a fine writer.[21] The *Examiner*, in a long and moving notice, spoke of her charm 'which no one could resist' and her constant encouragement of young authors.[22] Other notices appeared that week in the *Saturday Review*, the *Reader*, the *Spectator*, and the *Illustrated London News*. Her old friend and critic, Henry Chorley, described her in the *Athenaeum* as, 'if not the most popular, with small question, the most powerful and finished female novelist of an epoch singularly rich in female novelists'.[23] Chorley had been wary of Elizabeth since they crossed swords over *The Life of Charlotte Brontë*, and he added a tart rider to his praise, noting her sense of 'mission' and 'intense but prejudiced desire to right what is wrong':

'As a woman she was enthusiastic and inconsiderate – thus frequently unjust; in her own family she was deservedly beloved and cherished; one by the outer world to be missed, as all genuine and individual literary workers must and should be.'

It was her sense of mission, on the other hand, that had endeared her to many, especially to the poor of Manchester. The Unitarian *Inquirer* and *Herald* noted that on Monday, 13 November, unaware that Elizabeth had died the evening before, some parish workers were reading *Mary Barton* to a group of working women who met every week at Lower Mosley Street Sunday School; they still recognized the life described in that novel as their own. They had stopped at chapter 3, the death of the mother.[24] All the tributes are laced with Victorian sentiment, but often the conventional phrases ring true, as they do in Thurstan's words to Charles Eliot Norton, written the Saturday after her death:

'I feel her loss very deeply, for all who knew her well must have loved that kind sympathetic heart which shared every one's joys and griefs, that fresh intellect, that powerful imagination, that kindly interest that she took in everyone about her.' (L971)

And he ended the letter in good Gaskellian form: 'I have been obliged to write very hurriedly.'

That Sunday a crowded Cross Street Chapel heard William's assistant James Drummond, preach a funeral sermon. His theme was 'The Holiness of Human Sorrow', which should be seen, he said, not as 'the punishment of man's guilt but the quickening of his nature'.[25] This had been Elizabeth's view too; despite Drummond's masculine grammar, his remark may have made a few people shift uncomfortably in their pews, remembering their burnt copies of *Ruth*. After *Ruth* Elizabeth had fought shy of strict Unitarian piety, of the kind represented by Marianne's teacher, Mrs Lalor: '10 to 1 I should flame up against her.' The Manchester papers all carried notices of her death, but they remembered the rows over *Mary Barton* as well as the applause.[26] As Elizabeth had said to Tottie Fox in 1850, 'One of my mes is, I do believe, a true Christian – (only people call her socialist and communist).'

The Manchester farewell was for the writer and the minister's wife, but the ceremony at Knutsford was for the woman. On the afternoon of Friday, 17 November, Henry Green read Elizabeth Gaskell's burial service in the sloping graveyard at Brook Street, beside the chapel built two hundred years before, asserting the right of all to state their beliefs according to their conscience. Around Elizabeth's open grave clustered memorials to earlier Colthursts, Swintons and Hollands: her Sandlebridge grandparents, her uncle Peter, her 'more than mother', Hannah Lumb, who took her in when she was one. In death she returned to the people who gave her, as she grew up among them, her faith and her habit of stories.

As was common at that date, only men came to the funeral; the daughters stayed at home. William was supported by his brothers,

Sam and Robert. Charlie and Thurstan were there, with a few old Manchester friends and Henry Arthur Bright from Liverpool. And of all people, among the mourners was one of her protégés, Hamilton Aidé, who had walked across from Tatton. He was the man who wrote so badly but sang so beautifully, to Elizabeth's huge amusement. She would have liked that.

First Publication of Elizabeth Gaskell's Works

This lists the first appearance in print of Gaskell's known works during her lifetime. Items not conclusively identified appear in square brackets. (For a few other, more dubious attributions see John Geoffrey Sharps, *Mrs Gaskell's Observation and Invention*, Appendix VIII, 605–12.) Works published individually in volume form (either on first appearance or after periodical publication) are indicated in bold type. Collections of stories are not included, apart from *Round the Sofa*, which constitutes a 'new' work since Gaskell gave it a narrative frame, and included the previously unpublished 'Half-brothers'.

1837 January 'Sketches among the Poor, No. 1', *Blackwood's Edinburgh Magazine*, XLI

1839 Notes on Cheshire customs, in 2nd edition of William Howitt, *Rural Life*

1840 Description of Clopton Hall, in William Howitt, *Visits to Remarkable Places*

1847 June 'Life in Manchester: Libbie Marsh's Three Eras', *Howitt's Journal of Literature and Popular Progress*, I
September 'The Sexton's Hero', *Howitt's Journal*, II
[December 'Emerson's Lectures', *Howitt's Journal*, II]

1848 January 'Christmas Storms and Sunshine', *Howitt's Journal*, III
October **Mary Barton**

1849 July 'Hand and Heart', *Sunday School Penny Magazine*, II
July 'The Last Generation in England', *Sartain's Union Magazine*, V

1850 February 'Martha Preston', *Sartain's Union Magazine*, VI
March–April 'Lizzie Leigh', *Household Words*, I
November 'The Well of Pen-Morfa, *Household Words*, II
December **The Moorland Cottage**
– 'The Heart of John Middleton', *Household Words*, II

1851 February–April 'Mr Harrison's Confessions', *Ladies Companion and Monthly Magazine*, III
June 'Disappearances', *Household Words*, III
December 'Our Society at Cranford', *Household Words*, IV

1852 January 'A Love Affair at Cranford', *Household Words*, IV
January–April 'Bessy's Troubles at Home', *Sunday School Penny Magazine*, NSII
March 'Memory at Cranford', *Household Words*, IV
April 'Visiting at Cranford', *Household Words*, V
June 'The Shah's English Gardener', *Household Words*, V
December 'The Old Nurse's Story', *Household Words*, Extra Christmas Number

1853 January ***Ruth***
– 'Cumberland Sheep Shearers', *Household Words*, VI
– 'The Great Cranford Panic', *Household Words*, VI
April 'Stopped Payment at Cranford', *Household Words*, VII
May 'Friends in Need', *Household Words*, VII
– 'A Happy Return to Cranford', *Household Words*, VII
June ***Cranford*** (British publication in book form)
October 'Bran', *Household Words*, VIII
November 'Morton Hall', *Household Words*, VIII
December 'Traits and Stories of the Huguenots', *Household Words*, VIII
– 'My French Master', *Household Words*, VIII
– 'The Squire's Story', *Household Words*, Extra Christmas Number
– 'The Scholar's Story', *Household Words*, Extra Christmas Number

1854 February 'Modern Greek Songs', *Household Words*, IX
May 'Company Manners', *Household Words*, IX
September–January 1855 ***North and South***, *Household Words*, X (British publication in book form, 1855)

1855 August 'An Accursed Race', *Household Words*, XII
October 'Half a Lifetime Ago', *Household Words*, XII

1856 December 'The Poor Clare', *Household Words*, XIV
– [A Christmas Carol, *Household Words*, XIV]

1857 February ['The Siege of the Black Cottage', *Harper's Monthly Magazine*, XIV]
– ***The Life of Charlotte Brontë***
September Preface to Maria Susanna Cummins, *Mabel Vaughan*

1858 January 'The Doom of the Griffiths', *Harper's Monthly Magazine*, XVI
June 'An Incident at Niagara Falls,' *Harper's Monthly Magazine*, XVII

June–September   *My Lady Ludlow*, *Household Words*, XVIII (US
publication in book form)

November   'The Sin of a Father', *Household Words*, XVIII (retitled
'Right at Last' when published in the Sampson Low collection *Right at
Last, and Other Tales*, 1860)

December   'The Manchester Marriage', *Household Words*, Extra
Christmas Number

1859 March   *Round the Sofa*, I: *My Lady Ludlow*; II: 'An Accursed Race',
'The Doom of the Griffiths', 'Half a Life-time Ago', 'The Poor Clare',
'The Half-brothers'

October   'Lois the Witch', *All the Year Round*, I

December   'The Ghost in the Garden Room', *All the Year Round*, Extra
Christmas Number (retitled 'The Crooked Branch' when published in
Right at Last, and Other Tales, 1860)

1860 February   'Curious if True', *Cornhill Magazine*, I

1861 January   'The Grey Woman', *All the Year Round*, IV

1862 February   Preface to C. Augusto Vecchi, *Garibaldi at Caprera*
May   'Six Weeks at Heppenheim', *Cornhill Magazine*, V

1863 January–March   'A Dark Night's Work', *All the Year Round*, VIII
(British publication in book form, April)

February   *Sylvia's Lovers*

– 'Shams', *Fraser's Magazine*, LXVII

March   'An Italian Institution', *All the Year Round*, IX

November–February 1864   *Cousin Phillis*, *Cornhill Magazine*, VIII (US
publication in book form, 1864; British 1865)

– 'The Cage at Cranford', *All the Year Round*, X

December   Obituary of Robert Gould Shaw, *Macmillan's Magazine*, IX

– 'How the First Floor Went to Crowley Castle', *All the Year Round*,
Extra Christmas Number (collated with unpublished manuscript by A.
W. Ward as 'Crowley Castle' in *The Works of Mrs Gaskell*, Knutsford
VII (London, 1906)

1864 April–June   'French Life', *Fraser's Magazine*, LXIX

August–January 1866   *Wives and Daughters*, *Cornhill Magazine*, X
(British publication in book form, 1866)

1865 March   'Columns of Gossip from Paris', *Pall Mall Gazette*, I

August–September   'A Parson's Holiday', *Pall Mall Gazette*, II

Notes

FREQUENTLY CITED SOURCES

Some archives and works are abbreviated throughout, as listed below. Otherwise, a full reference is given the first time a work or source is cited in each chapter; thereafter it is in a short form.

For Gaskell's publications which appeared first in periodical form, page numbers are given for the collected Knutsford edition, rather than for the separate issues of each periodical.

Archives and Unpublished Works

Brotherton	The Brotherton Special Collection, Brotherton Library, University of Leeds
Edinburgh	The National Library of Scotland, Edinburgh
Girton	Bessie Rayner Parkes Papers, Girton College, Cambridge
Hall	Hall typescript, Manchester Central Library, MS823,894G69, using transcripts from Edward Hall Collection, Wigan Archives, Leigh, d/dzEHC
Harvard	The Houghton Library and Reading Room, Harvard University
Holloway	Reid Papers, Royal Holloway and Bedford New College
Jamison	Letters in possession of Dr R. R. Jamison
John Rylands	The John Rylands Library, Deansgate, Manchester
Keele	Wedgwood and Mosley Papers, Keele University Library
Manchester	Manchester Central Reference Library
Pierpont Morgan	The Pierpont Morgan Library, New York
Princeton	Princeton University Library, New Jersey

Sharps Collection	MSS in the possession of J. G. Sharps
Smith	Sophia Smith Collection, Smith College Library, Northampton, Mass.
Winkworth	Susanna Winkworth and Margaret Shaen (eds), *Letters and Memorials of Catherine Winkworth*, 2 vols (privately circulated, Clifton, 1883–6; the only publicly available copy in Britain is in Manchester Central Library)

Published Sources

AYR	*All the Year Round*
Brill	Barbara Brill, *William Gaskell, 1805–1884* (Manchester, 1984)
BST	Brontë Society *Transactions*
CH	*Elizabeth Gaskell: The Critical Heritage*, ed. Angus Easson (London and New York, 1992)
Chadwick	Mrs Ellis H. Chadwick, *Mrs. Gaskell: Haunts, Homes and Stories* (London, 1910, 2nd ed, London,1913)
Easson	Angus Easson, *Elizabeth Gaskell* (London, 1979)
GSJ	*Gaskell Society Journal*
GSN	*Gaskell Society Newsletter*
HJ	*Howitt's Journal of Literature and Popular Progress*
HW	*Household Words*
Knutsford	*The Works of Mrs Gaskell*, ed. A. W. Ward, Knutsford, 8 vols (London, 1906)
L, *Letters*	*The Letters of Mrs Gaskell*, ed J. A. V. Chapple and Arthur Pollard (Manchester, 1966)
Nonesuch	*The Letters of Charles Dickens*, ed. W. Dexter, Nonesuch Edition, 2 vols (London, 1938)
Pilgrim	*The Letters of Charles Dickens*, V: *1847–49*, ed. Graham Storey and K. J. Fielding, and VI: *1850–52*, ed. Graham Storey, Kathleen Tillotson and Nina Burgis, Pilgrim Edition (Oxford, 1985, 1988)
Portrait	J. A. V. Chapple, assisted by J. G. Sharps, *Elizabeth Gaskell: A Portrait in Letters* (Manchester, 1980)
Shaen	Margaret Shaen, *Memorials of Two Sisters: Susanna and Catherine Winkworth* (London, 1908)
SHB	*The Brontës: Their Lives, Friendships and Correspondence*, ed. T. J. Wise and J. A. Symington, Shakespeare Head Brontë, 4 vols (Oxford, 1932, reprinted in 2 vols, 1980)

Sharps	John Geoffrey Sharps, *Mrs Gaskell's Observation and Invention: A Study of her Non-biographic Works* (Fontwell, Sussex, 1970)
Simpson	M. C. M. Simpson, *Letters and Recollections of Julius and Mary Mohl* (London, 1887)
Waller	R. D. Waller, 'Letters Addressed to Mrs Gaskell by Celebrated Contemporaries', *Bulletin of the John Rylands Library*, 19 (1935), 102–69
Whitehill	Jane Whitehill (ed.), *The Letters of Mrs Gaskell and Charles Eliot Norton, 1855–1865* (Oxford, 1932)

I LEARNING VOICES: 1810–48

1 Far and Near

1 ECG to Harriet Carr, 20 October 1831, Brotherton. The transcription is my own, but see the useful annotations of J. A. V. Chapple, 'Before "Crutches and Changed Feelings"; Five Early Letters by Elizabeth Gaskell (née Stevenson)', *GSJ*, 4 (1990), 1–27.

2 ECG to Harriet Carr, 31 August 1831, Brotherton.

3 A clear introduction to Unitarianism at this date is given by R. K. Webb, in *Harriet Martineau: A Radical Victorian* (London, 1960), ch. 3. Webb quotes a splendid Methodist hymn, 'Stretch out thine arm, thou Triune God! The Unitarian fiend expel, and chase his doctrines back to Hell' (71).

4 John Locke, *An Essay Concerning Human Understanding*, bk 1, ch 4, section 12.

5 Quoted in Webb, *Harriet Martineau*, 80.

6 William Hazlitt, 'Mr Coleridge', *Selected Writings'*, ed. Ronald Blythe (Harmondsworth, 1970), 236–7.

7 Manchester Literary and Philosophical Society, *Memoirs* (Manchester, 1785), VI, quoted in Robert H. Kargon, *Science in Victorian Manchester: Enterprise and Expertise* (Manchester, 1977), 6.

8 For a comparable position see Harriet Martineau's letter to Henry Atkinson, 1851, in Harriet Martineau, *Autobiography* (London, 1877), I, 539. Webb, in *Harriet Martineau*, 68, quotes Thomas Belsham's very relevant sermon 'On the Importance of Truth'.

9 R. V. Holt, *The Unitarian Contribution to Social Reform*, 2nd edn. (London, 1958), 332.

10 E. S. Holland, *A History of the Family of Holland of Mobberley and Knutsford*, ed. W. Fergusson Irvine (privately published, Edinburgh, 1902), 70; Henry Holland, *Recollections of Past Life* (London, 1872), 7.

11 E. S. Holland, *The Family of Holland*, 70.
12 See *Annual Biography and Obituary* (1829).
13 Mary Ann Galton, *Life of Mary Anne Schimmelpennick* (London, 1858), I, 216, quoted in Brian Simon, *Studies in the History of Education, 1780–1870* (London, 1960), 63.
14 William Stevenson, *Remarks on the Very Inferior Utility of Classical Learning* (Manchester and London, 1796), 30. Cf. the attitude of Mrs Thornton in *North and South*: 'Classics may do very well for men who loiter away their lives in the country or in colleges; but Milton men ought to have their thoughts and powers absorbed in the work of today' (ch. 15), although her son John Thornton (and Gaskell) did see value in classical learning.
15 *Annual Obituary* (1829). William's sudden change of course on the eve of his marriage may have been more responsible than it seems, for the Dissenting Academies were facing hard times. At Manchester in 1797 Joseph Astley wrote to Charles Wellbeloved: ('there are many who think very despairingly of the future situation of the College — partly, perhaps, in consequence of the general Fate which similar institutions have generally met with' (quoted in D. L. Wykes, 'Sons and Subscribers', in Barbara Smith, ed., *Truth, Liberty, Religion: Essays Celebrating Two Hundred Years of Manchester College*, Oxford, 1986, 45).
16 In 1866 Meta Gaskell told Charles Eliot Norton that her mother's second name, Cleghorn, was given in memory of the daughter 'of a Mrs Cleghorn who had been very good to mama's mother; and just as mama was born this Miss Cleghorn died, and the little baby was called after her — at the poor mother's request' (quoted in J. A. V. Chapple, 'Cleghorn Again', *GSN*, 8, August 1989, 10).
17 *Annual Obituary* (1829).
18 Quoted in Henry Cockburn, *Life of Lord Jeffrey* (Edinburgh, 1852), I, 131.
19 For a description of this circle see: Henry Cockburn, *Memorials of His Times* (Edinburgh 1856); Mrs Fletcher, *Autobiography*, ed. Mary Richardson (Edinburgh, 1875), 56–92; and also Karl Miller, *Cockburn's Millennium* (London, 1975), 24–30. Eliza Fletcher, wife of the reformer Alexander Fletcher, was a close friend of the *Edinburgh Review* circle. A feminist and a radical, she held an informal salon in Castle Street. Elizabeth Gaskell came to know her in 1848, when Mrs Fletcher said she had both 'loved and reverenced' William Stevenson in the time of her early married life (*Autobiography*, 237). Gaskell's cousin Henry Holland, who arrived in Edinburgh in 1806 and belonged to the same circles, also describes the political, literary and scientific excitement of the city and writes that 'the society of Edinburgh at this time was not surpassed by that of any city of similar rank in Europe' (*Recollections*, 81).
20 For his *Edinburgh Review* contributions see the *Wellesley Index to*

Victorian Periodicals, 1824–1900 (Toronto, 1966), I, 430–8, William Stevenson's publications include *A System of Land Surveying* (1805, 1810), *A General View of the Agriculture of Surrey* (1809), *A General View of the Agriculture of Dorset* (1812), *A Historical Sketch of Discovery, Navigation and Commerce* (1824) and *A Life of Caxton* (1828). He also contributed most of the material for the *Annual Register* for several years, reviewed for periodicals such as the *Westminster Review* and *Gentleman's Magazine* and wrote lengthy articles for *Brewster's Encyclopedia* and *Blackwood's Magazine*. He has been described as contributing to Campbell's and Yorke's *Lives of the Admirals* (1814), but this is another William Stevenson.

21 *Annual Obituary* (1829).
22 Notes written by Clement Shorter, Brotherton.
23 All quotations from Mary Anne are from the Brotherton transcript, which is based on Meta Gaskell's transcript, Harvard, bMS Am 1088/4490.
24 See Sarah Whittaker to John William Whittaker, n.d., Hall, 35a. The Edward Hall Collection, Wigan Archives, contains 1,500 letters, covering 1809–29, being the correspondence of the Revd John William Whittaker (addressed as William by his family), whose mother was the sister of Dr Peter Holland's second wife, Mary Whittaker. Edward Hall edited a selection of these in an unpublished typescript, 'Cranford Again; The Knutsford Letters 1809–24' (Manchester Central Library). My references are to this more accessible source, which, like the originals, does not always give precise dates. For a description of the collection and its relevance see Geoffrey Sharps's meticulous note, spread over two pages, Sharps, 302–3.
25 Abigail, like many unmarried daughters of her class, had moved around the country staying with relations. She may at first have lived not at the Heath but at nearby Heath House — once the home of the famous 'Highwayman Higgins' on whom Gaskell based 'The Squire's Story'.
26 Sarah Whittaker to John William Whittaker, n.d., Hall, 20.
27 Gaskell, 'The Last Generation in England', *Sartain's Union Magazine*, V (July 1849), reprinted in *Cranford*, World's Classics (Oxford, 1972), 161–8, to which subsequent citations refer.
28 Sarah Whittaker to John William Whittaker, n.d., Hall, 8.
29 Margaret Ganz, *Elizabeth Gaskell: The Artist in Conflict* (New York, 1969), 8.
30 Mrs Sarah Whittaker to John William Whittaker, n.d., Hall, 97.
31 Hall, 73, n. 1; Elizabeth Whittaker to John William Whittaker, n.d., Hall, 124.
32 Henry Holland, *Recollections, passim*.
33 Catherine Whittaker to John William Whittaker, n.d., Hall, 14.
34 Martha Sharpe to John William Whittaker, January 1821, Hall, 109.

35 Quoted in Philip Ziegler, *The Sixth Great Power: Barings, 1762–1929* (London, 1988), 93. Sam nearly went bankrupt in 1818, and Emily Winkworth later referred to him as having been 'enormously rich but lost all his money at once' (letter to Eliza Paterson, May 1848, Winkworth, I, 146). See also Catherine Whittaker to John William Whittaker, n.d. [1818], Hall, 93.

36 Sarah Whittaker to John William Whittaker, 30 September 1812, Hall, 34; Martha Sharpe to John William Whittaker, January 1814 and March 1815, Hall, 51, 64.

37 John Stevenson to ECG, 1820, Sharps Collection. It appears that Elizabeth kept up a regular correspondence with her cousin Isabella from Berwick, of whom John was also obviously very fond.

38 Marianne Gaskell to Clement Shorter, 1914, Brotherton. John was registered as a mariner in the service of the East India Company. He was not an actual employee: the company was gradually losing its monopoly, but all seamen in ships to India still had to register under their regulations: W. Gérin, in *Elizabeth Gaskell* (Oxford, 1976), 33–4, notes that the company records show that William Stevenson paid a bond of £500 to guarantee John's conduct.

39 John Stevenson to Hannah Lumb and Abigail Holland, 1820, Sharps Collection.

40 Katherine Thomson, *Recollections of Literary Characters and Celebrated Places* (London, 1854), I, 101–3.

41 Henry Green, *Knutsford: Its Traditions and History* (Macclesfield, 1859), 114. Gaskell herself asserts the authenticity of this story, and of that about the cat who ate the lace, in 'The Last Generation', 163.

42 Gaskell, 'The Last Generation', 163.

43 Thomas Satterthwaite to his cousin, 1821, Hall, 93, 133 n. 1.

44 A point increasingly recognized by critics. See, for example; Edgar Wright, *Mrs Gaskell: The Basis for Reassessment* (Oxford, 1965); Coral Lansbury, *Elizabeth Gaskell: The Novel of Social Crisis* (London, 1975); and Patsy Stoneman, *Elizabeth Gaskell* (Brighton, 1987). Stoneman draws on feminist psychoanalytic writings and criticism to give a convincing account of Elizabeth's attitude to her parents and to Hannah Lumb.

2 Books and the World

1 Sharps Collection, A letter from John Stevenson to ECG, 21 December 1826, notes: 'You have read *Sandford and Merton*.' Molly Gibson in *Wives and Daughters* is upset when the Misses Browning are called Flapsy and Pecksy after the girl robins.

2 Harriet Martineau, *Autobiography* (London, 1877), I, 34.

3 Richard Edgeworth and Maria Edgeworth, *Practical Education* (London, 1795), III, 292–3.

4 Quoted in A. W. Ward. Introduction to Knutsford, I, xxi.

5 Lindley Murray, *English Grammar* (1795). See Amy Cruse, *The Englishman and His Books in the Early XIX Century* (London, 1930), ch. 5, 'The Schoolroom'. (Cruse's book, though sixty years old, is enormously enjoyable and informative and, despite its title, just as concerned with the Englishwoman and *her* books.)

6 Quoted in Chadwick, 33.

7 Easson calls this 'not everybody's childhood reading' (21), but Cruse, in *The Englishman and His Books*, 91, notes that when Thomas Day, the author of *Sandford and Merton*, was looking for suitable children's literature, among the only things he could find were 'a few passages in the first volume of Mr Brooke's *Fool of Quality*', so the 'old uncles and aunts' may have thought the same.

8 Catherine Whittaker to John William Whittaker, n.d., Hall, 59.

9 Martha Sharpe to John William Whittaker, n.d., Hall, 146–7. The information about Mrs Leigh was provided by Joan Leach.

10 Mary Wollstonecraft, *A Vindication of the Rights of Women* (1792), 3. See also Catherine Macaulay, *Letters on Education* (1790), and Wollstonecraft, *Thoughts on the Education of Daughters* (1787). Hannah More had been writing on girls' education since the 1770s, but her *Strictures on the Modern System of Female Education* was not published until 1799. See Josephine Kamm, *Hope Deferred: Girls' Education in English History* (London, 1965), 124. See Kamm, 112–51, for a detailed examination of these arguments and sources, and Jane Rendall, *The Origins of Modern Feminism: Women in Britain, France and the United States, 1780–1960* (London, 1985), for a useful summary of the main lines of the debate.

11 William Turner to Mary Turner, 29 January 1812, Newcastle City Library. See J. A. V. Chapple, 'Elizabeth Gaskell and the Turner family', in Charles Parish (ed.), *The History of the Literary and Philosophical Society of Newcastle upon Tyne* (Newcastle, 1990), II, 108–9.

12 Anna Laetitia Barbauld, *A Legacy for Young Ladies* (London, 1826), 53.

13 Harriet Martineau, 'Middle-class Education in England', *Cornhill Magazine*, X (November 1864), 556.

14 Dr Gregory, *A Father's Legacy to His Daughters* (London, 1774), 28.

15 Hannah More, *Essays for Young Ladies* (London, 1777), 145.

16 Gaskell mentions spending five years at school in L97 and 197. Until recently (see *Portrait*, 7) the dates were taken to be 1822 to 1827, but a letter of 14 June 1826 from Jane Byerley (Sharps Collection) suggests that she had already left school. Details about the Byerleys and their school are

taken from Phyllis Hicks, *A Quest of Ladies* (Birmingham, 1949). For topographical details and disposition of rooms at Barford and Avonbank see Edward Chitham, 'Elizabeth Stevenson's Schooldays', *GSJ*, 5 (1991), 1–15.

17 The music books are in the Gaskell Collection, Manchester Central Library.

18 See also *The Life of Frances Power Cobbe as Told by Herself*, ed. B. Atkinson (London, 1894), I, 66.

19 A suggestion made by A. B. Hopkins, *Elizabeth Gaskell: Her Life and Work* (London, 1952), 38–9, and W. Gérin, *Elizabeth Gaskell* (Oxford, 1976), 28.

20 Mrs William Parkes, *Domestic Duties: or Instructions to Young Married Ladies, on the Management of Their Households and the Regulation of Their Conduct in the Various Relations and Duties of Married Life* (London, 1825), 375.

21 Ibid, 2–3.

22 Quoted in Hicks, *A Quest of Ladies*, 116.

23 Parkes, *Domestic Duties*, 36.

24 Mary Ann Evans to Maria Lewis, 16 March 1839, *The George Eliot Letters*, ed. G. S. Haight (London and New Haven, 1954), I, 22.

25 Sarah Whittaker to John William Whittaker, 18 April 1820, Hall, 100.

26 William Stevenson, review of Charles Mills's *History of Chivalry*, *Westminster Review* (5 January 1826), 80–1.

27 William Stevenson to ECG, 28 July 1827, Sharps Collection. Knutsford Public Library possesses two books inscribed 'Elizabeth Cleghorn Stevenson' (which suggests that she continued her languages and classical studies after leaving school), a French–Italian dictionary, *Le Maître italien* and *Lives of the Roman Emperors*, with the date 1826 written in her hand.

28 Easson, 21.

29 Martha Sharpe to John William Whittaker, Hall, n.d., 149.

30 Quoted in Cruse, *The Englishman and His Books*, 75.

31 This commonplace book is described in an unpublished typescript of the 1930s by Jane Coolidge (later Jane Whitehill) in the Brotherton Special Collection, but its present whereabouts are not known.

32 ECG to Harriet Carr, 20 October 1831, Brotherton. See J. A. V. Chapple, 'Before "Crutches and Changed Feelings": Five Early Letters by Elizabeth Gaskell (née Stevenson)', *GSJ*, 4 (1990), 10.

33 See the article by Barbara Brill and Alan Shelston based on their study of the Portico Library records of William Gaskell's borrowings (over seven hundred books) from 1849 to 1860; 'Manchester; "A Behindhand Place for Books": The Gaskells and the Portico Library', *GSJ*, 5 (1991), 27–37. Barbara Brill has also most generously kept me in touch with her further work in the library. My own reading of the Portico's fascinating manuscript

catalogues has been especially fruitful in throwing light on the Gaskells' interest in science and travel. In 1856, the year that *Perversion* was borrowed, for example, among the many works William took out were: Alexander Bain, *The Senses and the Intellect*; Alexander Ross, *Fur Hunters of the Far West*; Revd E. Hughes, *Two Summer Cruises on the Baltic; The Last of the Arctic Voyages* (the hunt for the Franklin expedition); Revd J. Porter, *Four Years in Damascus*; Richard Burton, *Pilgrimage to Old Medina and Mecca*; Francis Bailey, *Journal of a Tour in Unsettled Parts of America*; and James Hamilton, *Wanderings in North Africa*.

34 Jane Byerley to ECG, 14 June 1826, Sharps Collection.

3 Changing Places: 1826–31

1 Martha Sharpe to John William Whittaker, n.d., Hall, 109.

2 Gaskell, 'The Shah's English Gardener', *HW*, V (19 June 1852), Knutsford, VII, 591–603.

3 Gaskell, 'The Last Generation in England' *Cranford*, World's Classics (Oxford, 1972), 164.

4 The old lady's stories are used in 'Disappearances' (*HW*, III, 7 June 1851, Knutsford, II, 410–21) and 'The Last Generation'.

5 Martha Sharpe to John William Whittaker, n.d., Hall, 119.

6 Martha Sharpe to John William Whittaker, n.d., Hall, iii, n. 2.

7 William Stevenson to ECG, 2 July 1827, Sharps Collection, quoted in *Portrait*, 5.

8 John Stevenson to ECG, 8 and 17 June 1827, Sharps Collection.

9 For both Samuel Hollands see A. H. Dodd, *The Industrial Revolution in North Wales* (Cardiff, 1951), 166, 214–16, 219, 326, and *The Memoirs of Samuel Holland* (Merioneth Historical and Record Society, Extra publications, Series 1, 1952). Sam became a prominent figure in North Wales and a Liberal MP. See H. L. Malchow, 'Ffestiniog to Westminster', *Gentleman Capitalists: The Social and Political World of the Victorian Businessman* (London, 1991), 17–77.

10 Gaskell's music books, Gaskell Collection, Manchester Central Library.

11 ECG to Harriet Carr, 31 August / 1 September 1831, Brotherton. All the quotations from this correspondence in this chapter are from three letters: 18 June 1831 and 31 August / 1 September 1831 (both from Woodside, Liverpool) and 20 October 1831 (from the Heath, Knutsford), transcribed in J. A. V. Chapple, 'Before "Crutches and Changed Feelings": Five Early Letters by Elizabeth Gaskell (née Stevenson)', *GSJ*, 4 (1990), 6–15.

12 John Stevenson to ECG, 30 July 1828, Sharps Collection.

13 Fifty letters exchanged between William Stevenson and William Blackwood are in the National Library of Scotland. See J. A. V. Chapple, 'William

Stevenson and Elizabeth Gaskell', *GSJ*, 1 (1987), 1–9, and National Library of Scotland, *Catalogue of Manuscripts Acquired since 1925* (Edinburgh, 1968).

14 See L415 and the will of William Stevenson, Somerset House, proved 15 June 1829, as described in W. Gérin, *Elizabeth Gaskell* (Oxford, 1976), 37. His salary started at £200 and rose to £350.

15 John Stevenson to ECG, 15 August 1828, Sharps Collection.

16 Catherine Stevenson to Hannah Lumb, 18 June 1829, Brotherton.

17 Jane Byerley to ECG, 4 November 1829, Sharps Collection.

18 Henry Holland, *Recollections of a Past Life* (London, 1872), 165, 176. He had become a member of the Royal College of Physicians the previous year and modestly resolved to 'keep my practice within 5000*l* a year' and to spend his leisure in travel.

19 Jane Byerley to ECG, 4 November 1829, Sharps Collection.

20 Henry Holland, *Recollections*, 8–9.

21 See J. H. Clapham, *Economic History of Modern Britain*, 2nd edn. (Cambridge, 1970), I, 3–8.

22 See R. Welford, *Pictures of Tyneside, or Life and Scenery on the River Tyne Sixty Years Ago* (Newcastle, 1881), containing thirty-three engravings from drawings by J. W. Carmichael, 1828–9. See also S. Middlebrook, *Newcastle-upon-Tyne: Its Growth and Achievement* (Newcastle, 1950), 182–229.

23 See the letters from James Aspinall Turner (1834) and Ann Turner (1836) quoted in J. A. V. Chapple, 'Elizabeth Gaskell and the Turner Family', in Charles Parish (ed.), *The History of the Literary and Philosophical Society of Newcastle-upon-Tyne* (Newcastle, 1990), II, 113–16.

24 Harriet Martineau, *Autobiography* (London, 1877), I, 32.

25 See Chadwick, 145–72, for a description and photograph of the house in 1910. Meta Gaskell's annotations denying the resemblance between Turner and Mr Benson (Chadwick, 158) are in the Brotherton.

26 See R. S. Watson, *History of the Newcastle Literary and Philosophical Society* (Newcastle, 1897), 223, and Appendix B, 341.

27 I. Inkster and J. Morrell (eds). Introduction to *Metropolis and Province: Science in British Culture, 1780–1850* (London, 1983), 14; Derek Orage, 'Rational Dissent and Provincial Science: William Turner and the Newcastle Literary and Philosophical Society', in ibid, 212.

28 Quoted in Watson, *History*, 164, 146–7.

29 Jane Marcet, *Conversations on Natural Philosophy* (1824) and *Conversations on Vegetable Physiology* (1829). Mary Somerville presented her paper 'The Magnetic Properties of the Violet Rays of the Solar Spectrum' to the Royal Society in 1826. In 1835 she and Caroline Herschel were the first women elected to the Royal Astronomical Society. Gaskell

admired both Marcet and Somerville, and letters from them are to be found in the Autograph Collection in John Rylands. For Sarah Losh see R. Welford, *Men of Mark Twixt Tyne and Tweed* (London, 1897), III, 92.

30 Watson, *History*, 102–3, 177. For the story of *Milo* see also Welford, *Men of Mark*, III, 104.

31 See Middlebrook, *Newcastle-upon-Tyne*, 173–5.

32 For identification of the Carr family see Chapple, *GSJ* (1990), 1–2.

33 See Watson, *History*, 107.

34 ECG to Anne Burnett, *c.* 1830, Brontë Parsonage Museum, Haworth, quoted in *Portrait*, 11–12.

35 Meta Gaskell to Clement Shorter, 25 November 1909, Brotherton.

36 Mrs Fletcher, *Autobiography*, ed. Mary Richardson (Edinburgh, 1875), 56–92. (See Ch. 1, n. 19)

37 For example, Gérin, *Elizabeth Gaskell*, 43. For brief details of W. J. Thomson's life see D. Foskett, *British Miniature Painters* (London, 1936), I, 548, and G. Reynolds, *English Portrait Miniatures* (London, 1988), 160, and compare with the *Dictionary of National Biography* entry for Dr Anthony Todd Thomson. *The Royal Scottish Academy 1826–1916: Complete List of Exhibited Works* (Edinburgh, 1917), 400, lists an exhibited portrait of 'Mrs Gaskill' in 1834. Whether this is the Manchester University miniature or another portrait is not known.

38 See S. Shapin, 'Edinburgh and the Diffusion of Science in the 1830s', in Inkster and Morrell, *Metropolis and Province*, 157–9, and D. A. de Giustino, *Conquest of Mind: Phrenology and Victorian Social Thought* (London, 1975). For the relation to mesmerism and the search for 'truth' see R. K. Webb, *Harriet Martineau: A Radical Victorian* (London, 1960), 235–6.

39 ECG to Harriet Carr, 31 August / 1 September 1831, Brotherton. See Chapple, *GSJ* (1990), 8. The works of Gall and Spurzheim first appeared in English in 1815 and the third ('greatly improved') edition of Spurzheim's *Phrenology* was published in 1826.

40 ECG to Anne Burnett, *c.* 1830, quoted in *Portrait*, 12.

41 William Gaskell, *Sermon at the Funeral of the Revd William Turner* (Manchester, 1859).

42 Ramsay Muir, *A History of Liverpool* (London and Liverpool, 1907), 27.

43 ECG to Harriet Carr, 31 August / 1 September 1831, Brotherton. See Chapple, *GSJ* (1990), 7.

44 Ibid.

45 Ibid, 10–11.

46 See R. J. Morris, *Cholera: 1832: The Social Response to an Epidemic* (London, 1976), 79.

47 ECG to Harriet Carr, 20 October 1831, Brotherton. See Chapple, *GSJ* (1990), 14.

4 Love, Marriage and Manchester

1 William Gaskell's 'Two Lectures on the Lancashire Dialect' were bound into the 1854 edition of *Mary Barton*. See also John Levitt, 'William Gaskell and Lancashire Dialect', *Journal of the Lancashire Dialect Society*, 32 (1982), 36.44.

2 'The Rev. W. Gaskell's Literature Class (From a Correspondent)', *Manchester Guardian* (19 June 1884). See also W. E. Adams, *Memoirs of a Social Atom* (London, 1903), who describes William as 'the most beautiful reader I have ever heard'. His delight in language was not confined to English: 'to hear Mr Gaskell read and pronounce Greek was a delicious pleasure' (Adam Rushton, *My Life as Farmer's Boy, Factory Hand, Teacher and Preacher*, Manchester, 1909). Both are quoted in Brill, 77, 74.

3 For information on William Gaskell's life see: Brill; *Dictionary of National Biography*; obituaries in the *Manchester Guardian* (12 June and 7 July 1884), *Unitarian Herald* (27 June 1884), *Academy* (12 June 1884) and *Unitarian Monthly* (July 1910); and A. W. Fox, 'The Rev. William Gaskell, MA', *Papers of the Manchester Literary Club*, 63 (1937), 275–9.

4 Private information quoted in Coolidge typescript, Brotherton.

5 See Brill, 22.

6 Edmund Potter was the grandfather of Beatrix Potter, who knew William well when she was a child. Brill (115) has a photograph of them together. See *The Beatrix Potter Journal*, 1881–97, ed. Leslie Linder (London, 1966).

7 See D. L. Wykes, 'Sons and Subscribers', in Barbara Smith (ed.), *Truth, Liberty, Religion: Essays Celebrating Two Hundred Years of Manchester College* (Oxford, 1986), 58–68.

8 William Gaskell's speech at the Commemoration of his Fifty Years as a Minister, 1878, John Rylands.

9 J. G. Robberds (1789–1854) came of a Huguenot family from Norwich, like the Martineaus. Unlike William, who prepared his sermons carefully, he preached extempore, and he was known for his geniality and conciliatory approach in disputes. See W. Gaskell, *Funeral Sermon on the Death of J. G. Robberds* (Manchester, 1854), and J. J. Tayler, memoir attached to J. G. Robberds, *Christian Festivals and Natural Seasons* (London, 1855).

10 William Gaskell to Eliza Gaskell, 'Tuesday evening' [20 March 1832], Brotherton. Elizabeth's note, written at the foot of this letter, is in LI.

11 Emily Winkworth to Catherine Winkworth, May 1848, Winkworth, I, 146. A short account of Eliza's life is given in E. S. Holland, *A History of the*

Family of Holland of Mobberley and Knutsford, ed. W. Fergusson Irvine (privately published, Edinburgh, 1902), 83–5.

12 All quotations from Gaskell to Harriet Carr are from letters of 3 May and 8 August 1832. See J. A. V. Chapple, 'Before "Crutches and Changed Feelings": Five Early Letters by Elizabeth Gaskell (née Stevenson)', *GSJ*, 4 (1990), 16–17.

13 Quoted in J. A. V. Chapple, 'Elizabeth Gaskell and the Turner Family', in Charles Parish (ed.), *The History of the Literary and Philosophical Society of Newcastle-upon-Tyne* (Newcastle, 1990), II, 109.

14 ECG to Harriet Carr, 8 August 1832, Brotherton. See Chapple, *GSJ* (1990), 19.

15 The custom of sanding, which lasted well into this century, is also described by Elizabeth's friend Henry Green in *Knutsford: Its Traditions and History* (Macclesfield, 1859). See also Chadwick, 186–9.

16 William Gaskell to Eliza Gaskell, 16 September 1832, Brotherton. An accurate transcription by J. A. V. Chapple appears in 'The Gaskell Honeymoon', *GSN*, 9 (March 1990), 5–7. Elizabeth added a note to his letter: see L2.

17 ECG to William Turner, 6 October 1832, Newcastle Literary and Philosophical Society Library, quoted in Chapple, in Parish (ed.), 108, and partially quoted in *Portrait*, 18.

18 A. C. Smith, 'Mrs Gaskell and Lower Mosley Street: A Centenary Address', *Sunday Schools Quarterly*, II, no. 4 (January 1911).

19 Sarah Stickney Ellis, *The Daughters of England* (London, 1842), 6–7.

20 ECG to William Turner, 6 October 1832, quoted in Chapple, in Parish (ed.), 108.

21 J. Aston, *A Picture of Manchester* (Manchester, 1816). See also R. Dennis, *English Industrial Cities of the Nineteenth Century: A Social Geography* (Cambridge, 1984), 72.

22 Friedrich Engels, *The Condition of the Working Class in England*, ed. E. Hobsbawm (London, 1969), 79.

23 Quoted in Shaen, 24.

24 James Butterworth, *A Complete History of the Cotton Trade* (1823); James P. Kay, *The Moral and Physical Condition of the Working Classes Employed in the Cotton Manufacture of Manchester* (London, 1832); Thomas Carlyle, *Chartism* (1839). (See Gary S. Messinger, *Manchester in the Victorian Age*, Manchester, 1985, 5, 12, 40, 90.)

25 'Notes of an Octogenarian Minister', *Christian Life* (17 December 1910). For accounts of Cross Street see: Thomas Baker, *Memorials of a Dissenting Chapel* (London, 1884); Benjamin Nightingale, *Lancashire Nonconformity* (Manchester, 1893), V; Alexander Gordon, *What Manchester Owed to Cross Street Chapel* (London, 1923); Herbert McLachlan, 'Cross Street

Chapel in the Life of Manchester', *Proceedings of the Manchester Literary and Philosophical Society*, 84 (1939–41); and Lester Burney, *Cross Street Chapel and Its College, 1786–1915* (Manchester, 1983).

26 Valentine Cunningham, *Everywhere Spoken Against: Dissent in the Victorian Novel* (Oxford, 1975), 131–2.

27 An account of the religious and social background is given by Monica Fryckstedt in *Elizabeth Gaskell's 'Mary Barton' and 'Ruth': A Challenge to Christian England* (Uppsala, 1982), 17–73. Fryckstedt and Cunningham, in *Everywhere Spoken Against*, both point out that during the span of William's ministry his congregation actually included fifteen MPs, seven mayors and numerous magistrates.

28 Quoted in Shaen, 26.

29 See: Messinger, *Manchester*, 36–53; R. J. Morris, *Cholera: 1832: The Social Response to an Epidemic* (London, 1976); Kay, *The Working Classes of Manchester*; and William Axon, *Annals of Manchester* (Manchester, 1888).

30 See Revd Herbert E. Perry, *A Century of Liberal Religion and Philanthropy in Manchester: Being a History of the Manchester Domestic Mission Society, 1833–1933* (Manchester, 1933), 5–6.

31 See Lester Burney, *Cross Street Chapel Schools, 1734–1942* (Didsbury, 1977), and A. C. Smith, *Sunday Schools Quarterly* (1911).

32 The sonnet is printed in A. W. Ward, Biographical Introduction to Knutsford, I, xxvi–xxvii.

5 Finding a Voice

1 Gaskell, *My Diary: The Early Years of My Daughter Marianne*, ed. Clement King Shorter (privately published, 1923), 1. The entries run from 10 March 1835 to 28 October 1838.

2 This opening has been read in a more negative way as a hidden proscription against women's writing; the mother must die before the daughter can read her words. See Margaret Homans's suggestive Lacanian study, *Bearing the Word: Language and Female Experience in Nineteenth Century Women's Writing* (Chicago and London, 1986), 162–3.

3 Gaskell, *My Diary*, 7.

4 Ibid.

5 Gaskell, 'Christmas Storms and Sunshine', *HJ*, III, New Year's Day Number (1848), Knutsford, III, 196–205.

6 Gaskell, *My Diary*, 32.

7 Ibid.

8 Homans, in *Bearing the Word*, 36, analyses the influence of Wordsworth's 'Intimations of Immortality'.

9 Gaskell 'Sketches among the Poor, No. 1', *Blackwood's Edinburgh Magazine*, XLI (January 1837), reprinted in the Biographical Introduction to Knutsford, I, xxii–xxiii, and as Appendix 2 in the Penguin Classics edition of *Mary Barton*, ed. Stephen Gill (Harmondsworth, 1970), 469–72.

10 George Crabbe, 'The Parish Register' (1807), lines 1–2.

11 See Howard Mills, Introduction to *George Crabbe: Tales, 1812, and Other Selected Poems* (Cambridge, 1967), xxix.

12 William Wordsworth, Preface to the *Lyrical Ballads*, *Wordsworth's Poetical Works* (Oxford, 1974), 735.

13 Quoted in Brian Maidment, *The Poorhouse Fugitives: Self-taught Poets and Poetry in Victorian Britain* (Manchester, 1987), 240.

14 *English Chartist Circular*, I (1841), 162, quoted in Martha Vicinus, *The Industrial Muse: A Study of Nineteenth-century Working-class Literature* (London, 1974), 2.

15 Gaskell, *My Diary*, 26.

16 Homans, in *Bearing the Word*, 168–9, notes that 'the word "confinement" holds a crucial place' in the diary.

6 Beginnings

1 The will of Hannah Lumb, proved in London, 17 August 1837 and 30 December 1837.

2 See Friedrich Engels, *The Condition of the Working Class in England*, ed. E. Hobsbawm (London, 1969), 79.

3 ECG to Mrs Darbishire, n.d., Princeton, AM 21097.

4 *Unitarian Herald* (27 June 1884).

5 J. R. Beard (ed.), *Collection of Hymns for Private and Public Worship* (London, 1837). See Brill, 48–50. Cf. William's 'Manchester Song', used as the epigraph to chapter 6 of *Mary Barton*, of which these are the first and last verses:

> How little can a rich man know
> Of what the poor man feels
> When Want, like some dark demon foe,
> Nearer and nearer steals.
>
> *He* never saw his darlings lie
> Shivering, the flags their bed;
> *He* never heard that maddening cry,
> Daddy, a bit of bread.

6 William Gaskell, *Temperance Rhymes* (London and Manchester, 1839). See also Brill, 51–2, and *Alliance News* (22 September 1910).

7 William Wordsworth to William Gaskell, 22 July 1840, John Rylands, MS 730/110, quoted in Waller, 133.

8 Quoted in Brian Maidment, *The Poorhouse Fugitives: Self-taught Poets and Poetry in Victorian Britain* (Manchester, 1987), 297. See also his whole section 'The Metropolitan Response', 281–320, and its useful introduction, 281–9. The section includes extracts from Byron, Carlyle, Southey, Gilfillan, Engels, Howitt and Kingsley as well as other critics and reviewers.

9 Joan Leach, 'The Gaskells and Poetry', GSN, 4 (August 1987), 24.

10 *Manchester Guardian* (19 June 1884).

11 Quoted in Maidment, *The Poorhouse Fugitives*, 304–5, For Elizabeth's relationship with the Howitts see Mary Howitt, *An Autobiography*, ed. Margaret Howitt (London, 1889).

12 See Carol Martin, 'Elizabeth Gaskell's Contribution to the Work of William Howitt', *Nineteenth-century Fiction*, 40, no. 1 (July 1955), and William Howitt, *Visits to Remarkable Places: Old Halls, Battle Fields and Scenes Illustrative of Striking Passages in English History and Poetry* (London, 1840), 135–9, Gaskell's piece is reprinted as 'Clopton House' in Knutsford, I, 502–8.

13 Gaskell, 'Clopton House', 506.

14 Ibid, 507.

15 William Howitt to ECG, 30 January 1839, Harvard, fMS Am 1943, 1 / 133. In the same letter William Howitt mentions that he and Mary 'were much interested in your account of the customs and superstitions of Cheshire, which, with your permission, I shall transfer to another ed. of "Rural Life".'

16 Gaskell, 'The Doom of the Griffiths', *Harper's Monthly Magazine*, XVI (January, 1858), Knutsford, V, 237–86.

17 Gaskell, 'The Well of Pen-Morfa', *HW*, II (16–23 November 1850), Knutsford, II, 242–6.

18 Gaskell, 'Lizzie Leigh', *HW*, I (30 March–13 April 1850), Knutsford, II, 206–41.

19 See Sally Stonehouse, 'A Letter from Mrs Gaskell', *BST*, 20 (1991), 217–22. I use the transcription by J. A. V. Chapple in 'Two Unpublished Gaskell Letters from Burrow Hall, Lancashire', *GSJ*, 6 (1992), 71.

7   Light and Darkness

1 Quoted in Barbara Smith (ed.), *Truth, Liberty, Religion: Essays Celebrating Two Hundred Years of Manchester College* (Oxford, 1986), 246.

2 Quoted in James Drummond and C. B. Upton, *Life and Letters of James Martineau* (London, 1902), I, 112.

3 Quoted in ibid, 154.

4 See R. J. Webb, 'The Gaskells as Unitarians', in Joanne Shattock (ed.), *Dickens and Other Victorians* (Basingstoke, 1988), 145–70.

5 The emphasis in the early 1840s on feeling as opposed to rational inquiry was not confined to Unitarianism. Cf. George Eliot's famous statement of 1843: 'speculative truth begins to appear but a shadow of individual minds, agreement between intellects seems unattainable, and we turn to the *truth of feeling* as the only universal bond of union' (*The George Eliot Letters*, ed. G. S. Haight, London and New Haven, 1954, I, 161–2).

6 William's sermon on his golden jubilee at Cross Street (*Unitarian Herald*, 9 August 1878) is quoted in R. J. Webb, in Shattock (ed.), 151–2. See also Webb for a careful analysis of the allegiances of the Gaskells' friends.

7 Drummond and Upton, *James Martineau*, 154–5.

8 *The Life of Frances Power Cobbe, as Told by Herself*, ed. B. Atkinson (London, 1894), I, 96, noted by Brenda Collom, who wonders if the story is 'Libbie Marsh's Three Eras' (*Gaskell Society Christmas News-sheet*, 1991).

9 Susanne Winkworth to Selina Winkworth, 17 February 1851, Winkworth, I, 272.

10 I. G. Sieveking, *Memoir and Letters of Francis W. Newman* (London, 1909), 104–6.

11 Mary Robberds to William Turner, 18 October 1840, quoted in J. A. V. Chapple, 'Elizabeth Gaskell and the Turner Family', in Charles Parish (ed.), *The History of the Literary and Philosophical Society of Newcastle-upon-Tyne* (Newcastle, 1990), II, 112.

12 See J. W. Cross, *George Eliot's Life* (London, 1885), I, 93–4.

13 Quoted in Basil Willey, 'Francis Newman', *More Nineteenth Century Studies: A Group of Honest Doubters* (London, 1963), 11.

14 See Sieveking, *Francis W. Newman*, 61.

15 Adam Sedgwick, *Memoirs*, I, 303, quoted in O. J. R. Howarth (ed.), *The BAAS: A Retrospect, 1831–1921* (London, 1922), 102–3. See also R. Angus Smith, *A Centenary of Science in Manchester* (London, 1883), and Robert H. Kargon, *Science in Victorian Manchester: Enterprise and Expertise* (Manchester, 1977).

16 Thomas Southwood Smith, *The Divine Government*, 4th edn. (London, 1826), 109, quoted in Adrian Desmond and James Moore, *Darwin* (London, 1991), 217; William Gaskell in the *Unitarian Herald*, 30 September 1864, quoted by R. J. Webb, in Shattock (ed.), 149.

17 See Winkworth, I, 36, and Shaen, 11.

18 In the *Letters* the letter to Anne Robson is dated 'Late 1841', but the editors have now redated it a year earlier. See *Portrait*, 26 n. 10.

19 ECG to Fanny Holland, 9 March 1847, Brotherton.

20 See Elie Halévy, *A History of the English People, 1830–1841* (London, 1927), 278.

21 Quoted in R. Challinor, *A Radical Lawyer in Victorian Britain: W. P. Roberts and the Struggle for Workers' Rights* (London, 1990).

22 Quoted in Asa Briggs, *Victorian Cities* (Harmondsworth, 1968), 134.

23 See Norman McCord, *The Anti-Corn Law League, 1838–1846* (London, 1958), 99.

24 Ibid, 101.

25 ECG to John Pierpont, 12 June 1841, Pierpont Morgan, MA 1756 R–V. Partially quoted in *Portrait*, 29–30.

26 Archibald Prentice, *History of the Anti-Corn Law League*, 2 vols (London, 1853); Joseph Adshead, *Distress in Manchester: Evidence (Tabular and Otherwise) of the State of the Labouring Classes in 1840–2* (London, 1842). There are innumerable contemporary accounts of the distress in these years, but see especially: Edward Baines, *The Social, Educational and Religious State of the Manufacturing Districts* (London, 1843); Edwin Chadwick, *Report on the Sanitary Condition of the Labouring Population* (London, 1843); Leon Faucher, *Manchester in 1844* (translated by a member of the Manchester Athenaeum, with many annotations; London and Manchester, 1844); Benjamin Love, *The Handbook of Manchester* (Manchester, 1842); Revd Richard Parkinson, *On the Present Condition of the Labouring Poor in Manchester* (Manchester, 1841); and William Cooke Taylor, *Notes of a Tour in the Manufacturing Districts of Lancashire* (London, 1842).

27 Friedrich Engels, *The Condition of the Working Class in England*, ed. E. Hobsbawm (London, 1969), 93–4.

28 *Reports of the Ministry to the Poor, in Manchester* (Manchester, 1840), 23–4, quoted in Monica Fryckstedt, *Elizabeth Gaskell's 'Mary Barton' and 'Ruth': A Challenge to Christian England* (Uppsala, 1982), 93. See also Revd Herbert E. Perry, *A Century of Liberal Religion and Philanthropy in Manchester: Being a History of the Manchester Domestic Mission Society, 1833–1933* (Manchester, 1933), 15.

29 ECG to John Pierpont, 12 June 1841, Pierpont Morgan, MA 1756 R–V.

30 Mary Howitt, *An Autobiography*, ed. Margaret Howitt (London, 1889), I, 65.

31 Quoted in Drummond and Upton, *James Martineau*, 179.

32 Prentice, *History*, I, 296–8.

33 Ibid, 374. Catherine Winkworth noted in her journal: 'we have been much troubled by beggars who sometimes come 30 at a time!' (Winkworth, I, 60–1) The Winkworths laid in a large stock of bread and coppers, distributing them from the dining-room window.

34 Gaskell, 'The Sexton's Hero', *HJ*, II (4 September 1847), Knutsford, I, 490–501. See A. W. Ward, Introduction, lxxi–lxxii, who suggests it may be based on an anecdote by Thomas Gray.

35 Gaskell, 'The Sexton's Hero', Knutsford, I, 497.

8 Emerging from Shadows

1 See James Drummond and C. B. Upton, *Life and Letters of James Martineau* (London, 1902), I, 117.
2 Maria Edgeworth to Mary Holland, 27 December 1848, John Rylands, MS 732/52. See Waller, 9.
3 ECG to Fanny Holland, 9 March 1847, Brotherton.
4 Ibid.
5 The epigraph, from J. L. Uhland's poem 'Auf der Überfahrt' (1826), appeared in the original German opposite the preface to the first edition:

> Nimm nur Fährmann, nimm die Miethe,
> Die ich gerne dreifach biete!
> Zween, die mit nur überfuhren,
> Waren geistige Naturen.

See Introduction to Knutsford, I, xlix.
6 An anonymous review of Chadwick's biography, thought to have been written by Meta Gaskell, says that the novel was begun in the spring or summer of 1846, and was chiefly written after Julia's birth in September. See Sharps, 551.
7 John Evans, *Lancashire Authors and Orators* (Manchester, 1850), 97–9.
8 Travers Madge (1823–66) was never satisfied, and his restlessness led to a breakdown in 1850. He joined the Methodists in 1853 and became an Anglican in 1864. See Brooke Herford, *Travers Madge: A Memoir* (London, Manchester and Norwich, 1867). For excellent concise accounts of Madge and Wright see Easson, 27, 39.
9 Thomas Wright (1789–1876). See [T. Wright Mcdermid], *The Life of Thomas Wright, of Manchester, the Prison Philanthropist* (London, 1876).
10 ECG to Fanny Holland, 9 March 1847, Brotherton.
11 Ibid.
12 William Gaskell to ECG, 25 July 1860, Brotherton.
13 See Susanne Brookshaw, *Concerning Chopin in Manchester* (privately published, Manchester, 1951), 10–13.
14 Gaskell, 'Modern Greek Songs', *HW*, IX (25 February 1854), Knutsford, III, 471–90.
15 Edward Herford to Catherine Winkworth, 27 August 1856, Winkworth, II, 67.
16 Shaen, 23.
17 Ibid, 24.
18 Susanna Winkworth to Emily Winkworth, 1846, Winkworth, I, 106–7.
19 Ibid. See also Susanna Winkworth's MS notes on *Mary Barton*, Brotherton.

20 Susanna Winkworth to Catherine Winkworth, 1846, Winkworth, 1, 105; Emily Winkworth to Susanna Winkworth, 12 October 1848, ibid, 159.
21 Susanna Winkworth to Emily Winkworth, 20 September 1846, ibid, 117.
22 Quoted in Louise Collis, *Impetuous Heart* (London, 1971), 55, quoted in Brian Masters, *The Life of E. F. Benson* (London, 1991).
23 See Pauline Nestor, *Female Friendships and Communities: Charlotte Brontë, George Eliot, Elizabeth Gaskell* (Oxford, 1985), 76–82.
24 Ibid, 81.
25 Catherine Winkworth to Eliza Paterson, May 1846, Winkworth, I, 146; Emily Winkworth to Susanna Winkworth, 12 October 1848, ibid, 158.
26 Emily Winkworth to Catherine Winkworth, 3 May 1848, ibid, 145. (Shaen, 30–1, omits the shocking reference to Goethe.)
27 Geraldine Jewsbury to Jane Carlyle, n.d. [1845], *Selections from the Letters of Geraldine Endsor Jewsbury to Jane Welsh Carlyle*, ed. Mrs Alexander Ireland (London, 1892), 180. Norma Clarke writes eloquently about this group in *Ambitious Heights: Writing, Friendship, Love: The Jewsbury Sisters, Felicia Hemans and Jane Carlyle* (London, 1990). See also Susanna Howe, *Geraldine Jewsbury: Her Life and Errors* (London, 1935), 55–60.
28 Geraldine Jewsbury to Jane Carlyle, n.d. [1849], *Selections from the Letters*, 347–8.
29 Ella Hepworth Dixon, *As I Knew Them* (London, 1930), 14.

9 Into Print

1 See C. R. Woodring, *Victorian Samplers: William and Mary Howitt* (Lawrence, Kansas, 1952), 109–10. For the Howitts' circle in the 1840s see Woodring, chs 5 and 6, 'International Relations' and 'The Ravenous Forties'. Their interest in Swedenborg's ideas led them to resign from the Society of Friends in 1847.
2 Gaskell: 'Life in Manchester: Libbie Marsh's Three Eras', *HJ*, I (5 June 1847), Knutsford, I, 459–89; 'The Sexton's Hero', *HJ*, II (4 September 1847), Knutsford, I, 490–501; and 'Christmas Storms and Sunshine', *HJ*, III, New Year's Day Number (1848), Knutsford, II, 196–205.
3 Mary Howitt, *An Autobiography*, ed. Margaret Howitt (London, 1889), II, 42–3.
4 *HJ*, I (2 January 1847), 1–2.
5 Quoted in Mary Howitt, *Autobiography*, II, 43.
6 See E. M. Wilbur, *A History of Unitarianism* (Boston, 1945), I, 383.
7 Mary Howitt to ECG, 20 October 1849, John Rylands, MS 730/43.
8 ECG to Leigh Hunt, n.d., John Rylands, MS 730/47/48. See Waller, 127–8. Gaskell sent Leigh Hunt the story reprinted as 'Libbie Marsh's Three Eras' in 1851.

9 [Gaskell], 'Emerson's Lectures', *HJ*, II (11 December 1847), from which
subsequent quotations are taken. This has never been verified as Gaskell's
and has the byline 'Our Manchester Correspondent', but a postscript to
William Howitt's letter of 17 November 1847 adds: 'The impressions made
by Emerson's lectures would be very acceptable. We have seen nothing of
the kind yet.'

10 For Emerson's tour see Ralph L. Rusk, *The Life of Ralph Waldo Emerson*
(New York, 1949), 333–4, and for the Gaskells' attendance see
Winkworth, I, 130–2.

11 Catherine Winkworth to Eliza Paterson, late May 1847, Winkworth, I,
123.

12 *HJ*, II (6 November 1847), 303.

13 Revd Herbert E. Perry, *A Century of Liberal Religion in Manchester; Being
a History of the Manchester Domestic Mission Society, 1833–1933*
(Manchester, 1933).

14 Catherine Winkworth to Susanna Winkworth, 16 November 1847, Shaen,
26–7.

15 Elizabeth Barrett Browning to Mary Russell Mitford, 13 December 1850,
The Letters of Elizabeth Barrett Browning, ed. Frederic G. Kenyon
(London, 1898), I, 471.

16 William Howitt to an unknown correspondent, quoted in *Manchester
Guardian*, see Chadwick, 239. The undated cutting is in the Shorter
Collection, Brotherton.

17 Mary Howitt, *Autobiography*, II, 28.

18 Arthur Waugh, *A Hundred Years of Publishing: The Story of Chapman and
Hall* (London, 1930), 27–9. For indispensable background see also John
Sutherland *Victorian Novelists and Publishers* (London, 1976).

19 See L69 and Shaen, 39.

20 Elizabeth Barrett Browning to Mary Russell Mitford, 13 December 1850,
Letters of Elizabeth Barrett Browning, I, 471–2.

21 William Howitt to ECG, 17 November 1847, John Rylands, MS 730/44.

22 Mary Howitt to ECG, 9 January 1848, John Rylands, MS 730/45.

23 Mary Howitt to unknown correspondent, n.d., Nottingham County
Library, MSS DD976/20/2.

24 Catherine Winkworth to Emma Paterson, 7/9 October 1848, Winkworth, I,
155–8.

25 See Susanna Winkworth to Catherine Winkworth, 22 September 1849, ibid,
207.

26 Catherine Winkworth to Emma Paterson, 27 October 1848, ibid, 159, and
Shaen, 29–30.

27 Emily Winkworth to Catherine Winkworth, 3 November 1848,
Winkworth, I, 161. (Shaen, 31, tactfully leaves out 'or I'm a blackie!')

II SPEAKING OUT: 1848–56

10 Exposure: *Mary Barton*

1 A useful general discussion of these novels may be found in Joseph Kestner, *Protest and Reform: The British Social Narrative by Women, 1827–1867* (London, 1985). See also Easson, 60–72, and Michael Wheeler, 'Two Tales of Manchester Life', *GSJ*, 3 (1989), 6–28.

2 Gaskell, Preface to *Mary Barton*, Knutsford, I, lxxiv.

3 See Mat Hompes, 'Mrs E. C. Gaskell', *Gentleman's Magazine*, CCLXXIX (1895), 124.

4 A point ably demonstrated by Stephen Gill in his introduction to the Penguin Classics edition of *Mary Barton* (Harmondsworth, 1970).

5 George Eliot, 'The Natural History of German Life', *Selected Essays, Poems and Other Writings*, ed. A. S. Byatt and Nicholas Warren (Harmondsworth, 1990), 110. Gaskell presents her themes in the way George Eliot describes Dorothea's sudden perception of Casaubon's character in *Middlemarch*; 'an idea wrought back to the directness of sense, like the solidity of objects'. For a close analysis of Gaskell's documentary use of the Reports of the Mission to the Poor in Manchester, 1839–42, see Monica Fryckstedt, *Elizabeth Gaskell's 'Mary Barton' and 'Ruth': A Challenge to Christian England* (Uppsala, 1982), 90–7.

6 The plan for *Mary Barton* (Brotherton) is reproduced in the Penguin Classics edition, Appendix 1, 467–8, and in Sharps, Appendix 1, 551–62. Sharps also includes the long note on the 'Conclusion still to be written' (Forster Collection, Victoria and Albert Museum). For a study of the differences between the plan and the novel see Edgar Wright, *Mrs Gaskell: The Basis for Reassessment* (Oxford, 1965), 231–2, and Brian Crick, 'The Implications of the Title Changes and Textual Revisions in Mrs Gaskell's *Mary Barton*', *Notes and Queries*, CCXXV (December 1980), 514–19.

7 See, for example, Arthur Pollard, *Mrs Gaskell: Novelist and Biographer* (Manchester, 1965), 42.

8 Patsy Stoneman, in *Elizabeth Gaskell* (Brighton, 1987), 65–86, explores this aspect, with an interesting reading of the Frankenstein allusion.

9 Mary Howitt, *An Autobiography*, ed. Margaret Howitt (London, 1889), II, 66.

10 Herbert Grey, *The Three Paths* (London, 1859). This author's second novel was *The Voyage of the Lady* (London, 1860). Margaret Homans, in *Bearing the Word: Language and Female Experience in Nineteenth Century Women's Writing* (Chicago and London, 1986), 171–3, mistakenly attributes the works to Marianne Gaskell, who was acting as her mother's secretary in writing this letter, without supporting evidence apart from the

appearance of the name on the title page as 'Herbert Grey, M.A.' (MA being Gaskell's nickname for Marianne). Marianne, in fact, was the least literary of all the Gaskell sisters.

11   Fame and New Friends

1 [Henry Fothergill Chorley], review, *Athenaeum* (21 October 1848), 1050–1; [John Forster], review, *Examiner* (4 November 1848), 708–9; unsigned review, *Literary Gazette* (28 October 1848), 706–8. For a selection of reviews see *CH*, 59–191.

2 Maria Edgeworth to Lucy Holland, 27 December 1848, John Rylands, MS 732/52. See Waller, 108–11.

3 Note from Arthur B. Potter to Clement Shorter, 14 July 1914, Brotherton, commenting on Gaskell's letter of 1852 to Sir John Potter, in which she apologizes for the distress caused to his sister-in-law and claims not to have based the murder upon that of Ashton (L130).

4 Edward Chapman to ECG, n.d., Brotherton.

5 Thomas Carlyle to ECG, 8 November 1848, John Rylands, MS 730/14.

6 Geraldine Jewsbury to Arthur Clough, 27 January 1849, *The Correspondence of Arthur H. Clough*, ed. F. L. Mulhauser (Oxford, 1957), I, 234.

7 Unsigned notice, *Manchester Guardian* (28 February 1849), 7 (see *CH*, 119–20); unsigned review, *British Quarterly Review*, IX (February 1849), 117–36.

8 Samuel Bamford to ECG, 9 March 1849, John Rylands, MS 730/4. See Waller, 107.

9 Francis Espinasse, *Literary Recollections and Sketches* (London, 1893), 263, quoted in Rosemary Ashton, *G. H. Lewes: A Life* (Oxford, 1991), 80.

10 See Pilgrim, V, 479n.

11 Dates are problematic here. L43, dated 2 April, makes it clear Gaskell is still in Manchester. However, the editors of the Pilgrim letters assume the 31 March dinner took place, basing this on a letter of Jane Carlyle to Jeannie Welsh which describes meeting Gaskell at a Dickens dinner (*Jane Welsh Carlyle: Letters to Her Family, 1839–63*, ed. L. H. Huxley, London, 1924, 325–8). This letter is dated 'Holy Thursday', which they, like Huxley, took to be the Thursday of Holy Week, i.e. 5 April. But Jane Carlyle mentions having already met Gaskell at her house (her first visit there was in mid-April) and the style of the dinner and the guests suggest that she is describing the lavish dinner for *David Copperfield* (12 May). I have assumed that 'Holy Thursday' was therefore Ascension Day (17 May). Professor K. Fielding, joint editor of *The Collected Letters of Thomas and*

Jane Welsh Carlyle (Durham, NC, 1970–), has kindly investigated the matter and confirmed that this is the probable date.

12 Hensleigh Wedgwood (1803–81) was the son of the potter Josiah, and a distinguished philologist, author of the *Dictionary of English Etymology*. Fanny (1800–1809) was the daughter of Sir James Mackintosh. Snow (1833–1912), who was severely deaf, became an accomplished writer and committed feminist.

13 Quoted in J. Collingwood, *John Ruskin*, 7th edn (London, 1911), 101.

14 Emily Winkworth to Catherine Winkworth, 8 May 1849, Winkworth, I, 176, and Shaen, 40. Emily's letters (Winkworth, 175–89), although not always correctly dated, give interesting details of the London visit. See also Shaen, 39–43.

15 E. W. Malleson, *Elizabeth Malleson, 1828–1916* (printed for private circulation, 1926), 40.

16 Eliza Bridell-Fox, 'Memories', *Girls' Own Paper*, IX (19 June 1890), 659. See also Mary Howitt, 'Stray Notes', *Good Words* (1895), 604.

17 Bridell-Fox, 'Memories', 659.

18 Ibid.

19 Emily Winkworth to Catherine Winkworth, 8 May 1849, Winkworth, I, 179. (Shaen, 39, omits 'Lily is deep in love'.)

20 Quoted in James A. Davies, *John Forster: A Literary Life* (Leicester, 1983), 108. See E. Johnson, *Charles Dickens* (London, 1953), 597. Peter Ackroyd's *Dickens* (London, 1990) contains a splendid portrait of Forster.

21 *The Letters and Private Papers of William Makepeace Thackeray*, ed. Gordon N. Ray (London, 1945), II, 252, quoted in Davies, *John Forster*, 93.

22 [William Rathbone Greg], review, *Edinburgh Review*, LXXXIX (April 1849), 402–35; [William and Mary Turner Ellis], initialled review, *Westminster and Foreign Quarterly Review*, LI (April 1849), 48–63; [Charles Kingsley], review, *Fraser's Magazine*, XXXIX (April 1849), 429–32. For a similar view to *Fraser's* see also *North British Review*, XV (1851), 424–7.

23 Jane Carlyle to Jeannie Welsh, 'Holy Thursday' [1849], *Letters to Her Family*, 326–7. Dickens had sent Rogers a copy of *Mary Barton* in February (Pilgrim, V, 479).

24 Charlotte Brontë to Patrick Brontë, 26 June 1851, SHB, III, 252. For Gaskell's visit see Shaen, 39. Emily says 'Macreadys', but Macready was still in America.

25 Emily Winkworth to Catherine Winkworth, 18 May 1849, Shaen, 42–3. Whewell took to Gaskell and wrote on the same day, pointing out resemblances between *Mary Barton* and Goethe's *Hermann und Dorothea* (12 May 1849, John Rylands, MS 731/107).

26 Jane Carlyle to Jeannie Welsh, 'Holy Thursday' [1849], *Letters to Her Family*, 326.

27 Emily Winkworth to Catherine Winkworth, 12 May 1849, Winkworth, I, 187.

28 Charles Dickens to Thomas Talfourd, 14 May 1849, Pilgrim, V, 538–9.

29 Autograph Collection, John Rylands, MS 732. It contains over two hundred letters.

30 Henry Crabb Robinson, MS, Dr Williams Library. See Pilgrim, V, 539n.

31 Charles Cowden Clarke and Mary Cowden Clarke, *Recollections of Writers* (London, 1878), 91–3.

32 A. C. Hare, *The Story of My Life* (London, 1896–1900), II, 224–7.

33 A. Stanton Whitfield, *Elizabeth Gaskell* (London, 1929), 25.

34 J. A. Froude to ECG, 5 January 1862, John Rylands, MS 730/30.

35 Susanna Winkworth to Emily Winkworth, 8 June 1849, Winkworth, I, 190–1.

36 ECG to Mrs Scott, n.d., in Michael Silverman, *Manuscripts*, Sale Catalogue 5 (1991), item no. 13.

37 Harriet Martineau, 'A Year at Ambleside', *Sartain's Union Magazine*, V (29 July, 1849).

38 Max Müller to ECG, 14 August 1864, John Rylands, MS 731/70/71. See also Froude's letter from Skelwith, n.d., MS 730/35.

39 Mrs Fletcher, *Autobiography*, ed. Mary Richardson (Edinburgh, 1875), 237–9. Mrs Fletcher was given a copy of *Mary Barton* by W. E. Forster (who married Mary Arnold) in December 1848, and discovered Gaskell's identity through a mutual Manchester friend, Miss Beever, who lived in the Lake District.

40 See *The Correspondence of Henry Crabb Robinson with the Wordsworth Circle*, ed. E. J. Morley (Oxford, 1927), II, 698, 700, 705.

41 Autograph Collection, John Rylands, MS 731/110. See Waller, 133.

42 Stephen Winkworth to Catherine Winkworth, 4 August 1849, Winkworth, I, 194.

43 Arthur Clough to Anne Clough, 10 February 1849, *Correspondence of Arthur H. Clough*, I, 238.

44 Gaskell, 'Hand and Heart', *Sunday School Penny Magazine*, II (July–August, October–December 1849), Knutsford, III, 536–56. In January she had, however, declined Eliza Cook's request to write *Eliza Cook's Journal*, which started in April 1849. See Waller, 147–8.

45 Gaskell, 'The Last Generation in England', *Sartain's Union Magazine*, V (July 1849), reprinted in *Cranford*, World's Classics (Oxford, 1972), 161–8.

46 Gaskell, 'Martha Preston', *Sartain's Union Magazine*, VI (February 1850), not reprinted in Knutsford. (By a strange coincidence 'Martha Preston' is

NOTES

immediately followed by 'February' in Harriet Martineau's series 'A Year at Ambleside'.)

47 Gaskell, 'Half a Lifetime Ago', HW, XII (6–20 October 1855), reprinted in *Round the Sofa* (1859), as Mrs Preston's tale, and in Knutsford, V, 277–325.

48 Gaskell, 'Martha Preston', *Sartain's Union Magazine*, VI, 131.

12   A Habit of Stories

1 ECG to Mary Green, January 1853, Jamison.

2 Emily Winkworth to Susanna Winkworth, 12 October 1848 and 21 September 1849, Winkworth, I, 158, 205.

3 Gaskell, 'Company Manners', HW, IX (20 May 1854), Knutsford, III, 491–503.

4 Charles Dickens to ECG, 21 December 1851, Pilgrim, VI, 558. (There are twenty-eight letters from Dickens to ECG and two to William Gaskell in John Rylands, MS 729/1–31.)

5 Charles Dickens to ECG, 13/14 March 1852, Pilgrim, VI, 625.

6 See Wedgwood Papers, University of Keele, I am grateful to Professor K. J. Fielding for directing me to this particular circle of gossip. See also his article, 'Froude's Revenge, or the Carlyles and Erasmus A. Darwin', *Essays and Studies*, XXXI (1978), 75–97.

7 See Martineau Papers, University of Birmingham, HM 350–4, 431–9. In HM 352 (L909) Gaskell explains: 'I did not see the date of Mrs Bracebridge's letter; indeed it was only a *copy* that I saw, shown me by my cousin Captain Holland . . . he & his wife came here to Knutsford from Lord Belpers; and this letter from Mrs Bracebridge had (as I understood) been received by one of the party (Lady Sitwell I think) during their stay.'

8 R. K. Webb, *Harriet Martineau: A Radical Victorian* (London, 1960), 207–8. See also *Selected Letters of Harriet Martineau*, ed. Valerie Sandars (London, 1991).

9 Geraldine Jewsbury to Jane Carlyle, 1849, *Selections from the Letters of Geraldine Endsor Jewsbury to Jane Welsh Carlyle*, ed. Mrs Alexander Ireland (London, 1892), 337.

10 Gaskell, *The Life of Charlotte Brontë*, I, ch. 12.

11 A. C. Hare, *The Story of My Life* (London, 1896–1900), III, 117–23.

12 Augustus Sala, *Belgravia*, IV, quoted in Peter Ackroyd, *Dickens* (London, 1990).

13 Charles Dickens to ECG, 25 November 1851, Pilgrim, VI, 546.

14 See also Martineau Papers, University of Birmingham, HM 352.

15 Charles Dickens to ECG, 9 January 1850, Pilgrim, VI, 6.

16 Charlotte Brontë to ECG, 1 February 1849, SHB, II, 305.

17 Charlotte Brontë to W. S. Williams, n.d. [20 November] and 24 November 1849, ibid, III, 40, 45.

18 See V. Wheatley, *Harriet Martineau* (London, 1857), 282. For Martineau's own account see her *Autobiography* (London, 1877), II, 323–8.

19 Charlotte Brontë to Ellen Nussey, 26 August 1850, SHB, III, 148.

20 Ibid.

21 Charles Dickens to ECG, 31 January 1850, Pilgrim, VI, 21–2.

22 Charles Dickens to ECG, 5 February 1850, ibid, 29.

23 Charles Dickens to ECG, 4 February 1850, ibid, 27.

24 Charles Dickens, *HW*, I (30 March 1850), 2.

25 For the list of contributions see Anne Lohrli, *'Household Words': Table of Contents, List of Contributors and Their Contributions* (University of Toronto Press, 1973). 'Lizzie Leigh' appeared in *HW*, I (30 March–13 April 1850), and under Dickens's name in *Harper's* I (June 1850); it is reprinted in Knutsford, II, 206–41.

26 Charles Dickens to ECG, 3 July 1850, Pilgrim, VI, 121.

27 Gaskell, *The Moorland Cottage* (London, 1850), Knutsford, II, 267–383.

28 Transcript of letter from Mrs W. E. Forster, 30 December 1850, Brotherton.

29 Charlotte Brontë to ECG, 4 January 1851, SHB, III, 194. See also Charlotte Brontë to ECG, 22 January 1851, ibid, 204.

30 Gaskell, 'The Heart of John Middleton', *HW*, II (28 December 1850), Knutsford, II, 384–409.

31 Charles Dickens to W. H. Wills, 12 December 1850, Pilgrim, VI, 231.

32 Charles Dickens to ECG, 17 December 1850, ibid, 238.

33 See Gaskell, *The Life of Charlotte Brontë*, I, ch. 1.

34 Charles Dickens to ECG, 6 March 1850, Pilgrim, VI, 55; Charles Dickens to W. H. Wills, 28 February 1850, ibid, 50.

35 Charles Dickens to ECG, 14 March and 17 December 1850, ibid, 64, 238.

36 Charles Dickens to ECG, 20 December 1850, ibid, 243.

37 Gaskell, 'Disappearances', *HW*, III (7 June 1851), Knutsford, II, 410–21.

38 *The Moorland Cottage* is almost an outline for the characters in *Wives and Daughters*, written fifteen years later and transposed to a richer countryside. The Squire, Mr Buxton — who is proud of his yeoman stock but careless of his land, and dotes on his son and is devoted to his gentle, ailing wife — is a pattern for Squire Hamley, his wife for Mrs Hamley and his son Frank for Roger, while Maggie's spoilt brother Edward is echoed, with the form of his misdemeanour changed, in the other Hamley son, Osborne. The contrasting heroines of the 1850 story, Maggie Browne and Mr Buxton's niece Erminia, one dark and sophisticated, the other blonde and Paris educated, also point the way forward to Molly Gibson and her stepsister, Cynthia.

39 Gaskell, 'Curious if True', *Cornhill Magazine*, I (February 1860), Knutsford, VII, 259–77.
40 Charles Dickens to ECG, 25 November 1851, Pilgrim, VI, 545–6.

13 Daily Life

1 Geraldine Jewsbury to Jane Carlyle, December 1850, *Selections from the Letters of Geraldine Endsor Jewsbury to Jane Welsh Carlyle*, ed. Mrs Alexander Ireland (London, 1892), 383. For the dinner (with Dickens) see Jane Carlyle to John Forster, December 1850, *New Letters and Memorials of Jane Welsh Carlyle*, ed. Thomas Carlyle and Alexander Carlyle (London, 1903), II, 26. See also Pilgrim, V, 238–9.
2 ECG to Lucy Holland, n.d., Princeton, AM 19536.
3 Geo. H. Larmuth and Sons, Auctioneers, *Sale Catalogue: Re the Late Miss M. E. Gaskell, 84, Plymouth Grove, Manchester* (Manchester, 1914), now in Manchester Central Library.
4 ECG to Mary Holland, n.d., Princeton, AM 20124.
5 Gaskell, *My Diary: The Early Years of My Daughter Marianne*, ed. Clement King Shorter (privately published, 1923), 28.
6 ECG to Caroline Davenport, n.d., Princeton, AM 20064.
7 Gaskell, 'French Life', *Frazer's Magazine*, LXIX (April–June 1864), Knutsford, VII, 604–80.
8 Easson, 25–6, translated from Fanny Lewald, *England und Schottland*, 2 vols (Brunswick, 1851–2). See also Susanna Howe, *Geraldine Jewsbury: Her Life and Errors* (London, 1935), 133, and Peter Skrine, 'Fanny Lewald and Mrs Gaskell', *GSJ*, 4 (1990), 52–7.
9 Catherine Winkworth to Emma Shaen, November 1850, Winkworth, I, 263.
10 Catherine Winkworth to Susanna Winkworth, 1 January 1852, ibid, 325.
11 Charlotte Brontë to ECG, 12 January 1853, SHB, IV, 34.
12 Charlotte Brontë to George Smith, 1 July 1851, ibid, III, 255.
13 Charlotte Brontë to Mrs Smith, 1 July 1851, ibid, 254.
14 Charlotte Brontë to ECG, 6 August 1851 and n.d. [1851], ibid, 269, 271.
15 ECG to Maria James, in Michael Silverman, *Manuscripts*, Sale Catalogue 5 (1991), 8, item no. 12.
16 The Gaskell *Letters* identify the recipient as 'unknown', but see H. McLachan, *Records of a Family* (Manchester, 1935), 30–2. For the rumour of their departure see Catherine Winkworth to Susanna Winkworth, February 1851, Winkworth, I, 275.
17 Quoted in Waldo Dunn, *James Anthony Froude: A Biography* (Oxford, 1961), 165, 167.
18 Jane Carlyle to Thomas Carlyle, 12 September 1851, *New Letters and*

Memorials, II, 29. For Jane Carlyle's stay see also L102, Winkworth, I, 297, Waller, 112–13, and Jane Carlyle's letters, John Rylands, MS, 730/12/13.

19 Susanna Winkworth to Catherine Winkworth, 23 December 1851, Winkworth, I, 321.

20 Catherine Winkworth to Emily Shaen, 10 November 1851, ibid, 299.

21 Catherine Winkworth to Emma Shaen, 25 November 1851, ibid, 317.

14   Making Safe: *Cranford*

1 Gaskell, 'The Last Generation in England', *Cranford*, World's Classics (Oxford, 1972), 164.

2 Marianne Gaskell to Charles Norton, 25 January 1858, Harvard, bMS Am 1088/3489.

3 Gaskell, 'Mr Harrison's Confessions', *Ladies Companion and Monthly Magazine*, III (February–April 1851), Knutsford, V, 405–91.

4 Charles Dickens to ECG, 4 December 1851, Pilgrim, VI, 548–9.

5 Charles Dickens to ECG, 21 December 1851, ibid, 558.

6 The Cranford stories appeared in *Household Words* in the following sequence, and were subsequently divided into chapters in the 1853 single-volume publication. Chapter references in my text belong to Knutsford, II, 1–195.

IV 13 December 1851, 'Our Society at Cranford'
　　3 January 1852, 'A Love Affair at Cranford'
　　13 March, 'Memory at Cranford'
V 3 April, 'Visiting at Cranford'
VI 8 and 15 January 1853, 'The Great Cranford Panic'
VII 2 April, 'Stopped Payment at Cranford'
　　7 May, 'Friends in Need'
　　21 May, 'A Happy Return to Cranford'

7 Coral Lansbury, in *Elizabeth Gaskell: The Novel of Social Crisis* (London, 1975), sees these conventions as one of *Cranford*'s weaknesses.

8 Charles Dickens to John Forster, 9 March 1852, Pilgrim, VI, 623. Interesting readings of *Cranford* include: Nina Auerbach, *Communities of Women* (London and Harvard, 1978); Martin Dodsworth, 'Women without Men at Cranford', *Essays in Criticism*, 13 (1963) 132–45; and Margaret Tarratt, 'Cranford and the Strict Code of Gentility', *Essays in Criticism*, 18 (1968) 152–63.

9 John Forster to ECG, 9 March 1853, Brotherton. When it appeared in book form, Forster's praise of *Cranford*'s nostalgia and tenderness was echoed in reviews, such as [Henry Fothergill Chorley], review, *Athenaeum* (25 June

1853), 76, and an unsigned review, *Examiner* (23 July 1853), 467–8 (see *CH*, 194–7).

10 See Knutsford, II, xv.

11 Charles Dickens to ECG, 1 December 1852, Pilgrim, V, 812.

15 Overlapping Circles

1 'Bessy's Troubles at Home', *Sunday School Penny Magazine*, II (January–April 1852), Knutsford, II, 514–35.

2 ECG to Agnes Sandars, Wednesday [?27 January 1852], autograph letter signed in possession of Mrs Susan Kearney, transcribed in 'An Unpublished Gaskell Letter', *GSN*, 10 (August 1990), 4–9.

3 See Catherine Winkworth to Eliza Paterson, 27 February 1852, Winkworth, I, 332. Gaskell's letter to Agnes Sandars (see n. 2) gives a full account of the dresses and jewellery and the tenants' farewell.

4 See Gaskell, 'The Shah's English Gardener', *HW*, V (19 June 1852), Knutsford, VII, 591–603.

5 Samuel Greg (1804–76) was an enlightened factory-owner, who established an industrial community called Goldenthal, or Happy Valley, complete with schools, library and playroom. He was distraught when his workers still went on strike, and gave up the mill, which was managed for a time by his brother, the critic William Rathbone Greg (1809–81). Both brothers have been suggested as models for John Thornton in *North and South*; see Valentine Cunningham, *Everywhere Spoken Against: Dissent in the Victorian Novel* (Oxford, 1975), 133–7.

6 For a description of Park Hall see Janice Kirkland, 'Mrs Gaskell's Country Houses', *GSN*, 2 (August 1986), 10–11.

7 For Wright see L170–8, 181. For the Wilson brothers' school at Price's candle factory (which she initially called Palmers) see L184 and ECG to Charles Dickens, 23 May, late May–early June and 29 June 1852, Pilgrim, VI, 681, 686, 702.

8 Susanna Winkworth to Catherine Winkworth, 15 May 1852, Winkworth I, 346.

9 Emily Shaen to Catherine Winkworth, July 1852, ibid, 348.

10 Chadwick, 328–35.

11 Catherine Winkworth describes this trip in some detail (letter to Emily Winkworth, 3 August 1852, Winkworth, I, 352–8). See also Eliza Bridell-Fox 'Memories', *Girls' Own Paper*, IX (19 June 1890), 660.

12 My description of this event and the quotations are taken from Gary S. Messinger, *Manchester in the Victorian Age* (Manchester, 1985), 133–9.

13 Charles Dickens to Angela Burdett Coutts, 2 September 1852, Pilgrim, VI, 752–3.

14 Quoted in Messinger, *Manchester*, 138.
15 Gaskell, 'The Old Nurse's Story', *HW*, Extra Christmas Number: 'A Round of Stories by the Christmas Fire' (1852), Knutsford, III, 422–45.
16 Charles Dickens to ECG, 6 November 1852, Pilgrim, VI, 799.
17 Charles Dickens to ECG, 9 November 1852, ibid, 800.
18 Charles Dickens to ECG, 4 December 1852, ibid, 815.
19 Charles Dickens to ECG, 6 December 1852, ibid, 817. See also Charles Dickens to ECG, 17 December 1852, ibid, 823.
20 John Forster to ECG, 12 November 1852, Brotherton.
21 ECG to Mary Green, November 1852, Jamison.
22 Catherine Winkworth to Emily Shaen, 22 November 1852, Winkworth, I, 369.
23 Charlotte Brontë to Ellen Nussey, 22 November 1852, SHB, IV, 20.
24 See Professor Chapple's neat summary in *Portrait*, 133–4, and his reference, Anne Henry Ehrenpreis, 'Elizabeth Gaskell and Nathaniel Hawthorne', *Nathaniel Hawthorne Journal* (1973).
25 For general background see Jane Rendall, *The Origins of Modern Feminism: Women in Britain, France and the United States, 1780–1960* (London, 1985), and *Equal or Different* (Oxford, 1987).
26 Dinah Mulock to ECG, 19 April [1851], John Rylands, MS 731/72. See Waller, 146.
27 See Sheila Herstein, *A Mid-Victorian Feminist: Barbara Leigh Smith Bodichon* (New Haven and London, 1985), 56–7.
28 See William Axon, *Annals of Manchester* (Manchester, 1888).
29 For Gaskell's correspondence with Mill see L563–4, 567–9.
30 Charlotte Brontë to ECG, 20 September 1851, SHB, III, 277–8.
31 Geraldine Jewsbury, *Marian Withers* (London, 1851), III, 124–5.
32 Florence Nightingale to Mary Mohl, *Ever Yours, Florence Nightingale: Selected Letters*, 3 September 1867, ed. Martha Vicinus and Bea Nergard (London, 1990), 39. See Cecil Woodham-Smith, *Florence Nightingale, 1820–1910* (London, 1950), 79, and Florence Nightingale, 'Cassandra', in R. Strachey, *The Cause* (London, 1928), 395–418.
33 Virginia Woolf, *A Room of One's Own* (London, 1946), 104.
34 Both Anglican and Catholic lay sisterhoods expanded in the 1840s and were the subject of fierce debate over the next two decades. See Pauline Nestor, *Female Friendships and Communities: Charlotte Brontë, George Eliot, Elizabeth Gaskell* (Oxford, 1985), 5–9, and Nina Auerbach, *Communities of Women* (London and Harvard, 1978).
35 Gaskell, 'Morton Hall', *HW*, VIII (19–26 November 1853), Knutsford, III, 446–89.
36 Gaskell, 'My French Master', *HW*, VIII (17–24 December 1853), Knutsford, II, 506–31.

37 John Ludlow, review, *North British Review*, XIX (1853), 151–74. See Gaskell's letters to Ludlow in Cambridge University Library, Ad. 7348/10/115–28, and J. Miriam Benn, 'Some Unpublished Gaskell Letters', *Notes and Queries*, CCXXV (December 1980), 507–14.

38 Josephine Butler, *Women's Work and Women's Culture* (London, 1869), xvi. See J. Uglow, 'Josephine Butler, from Sympathy to Theory', in Dale Spender (ed.), *Feminist Theorists* (London, 1983), 153.

39 Quoted in J. A. V. Chapple, 'An Anglo-American Story', *Brontë Society and Gaskell Society Joint Conference Papers* (1990), 96.

40 ECG to Mary Green, 15 October 1855, Jamison, quoted in ibid.

41 ECG to Maria James, 3 December [1855], Pierpont Morgan, MA 2696.

42 Geraldine Jewsbury to Jane Carlyle, n.d. [1849], *Selections from the Letters of Geraldine Endsor Jewsbury to Jane Welsh Carlyle*, ed. Mrs Alexander Ireland (London, 1892), 342.

43 Joseph Kestner, *Protest and Reform: The British Social Narrative by Women, 1827–1867* (London, 1985), 144. Eliza Meteyard, *Lucy Dean*, *Eliza Cook's Journal*, 2 (16 March–20 April 1850). One of the best general surveys remains the section on needlewomen in Wanda Neff, *Victorian Working Women: An Historical and Literary Study of Women in British Industries and Professions, 1832–1850* (London and New York, 1929). The literature is interestingly dealt with by Kestner, 81–90, 102–9, 144–51, and a short background is also given by Monica Fryckstedt, *Elizabeth Gaskell's 'Mary Barton' and 'Ruth': A Challenge to Christian England* (Uppsala, 1982), 143–8, and Aina Rubenius, *The Woman Question in Mrs Gaskell's Life and Works* (Harvard, 1950), 188–9. Key fictional works include: Elizabeth Stone, *The Young Milliner* (1843); Charlotte Elizabeth Tonna, *The Wrongs of Women* (1843–4); Camilla Toulmin, 'The Orphan Milliners', *Illuminated Magazine* (April 1944); Frances Trollope, *Jessie Phillips* (1844); G. W. M. Reynolds, 'The Seamstress', *Reynolds's Miscellany* (August 1850); and 'Ellen Linn the Needlewoman', *Tait's Edinburgh Magazine* (August 1850).

44 W. R. Greg, 'Prostitution', *Westminster Review*, 53 (1850), 448–506. See the useful discussion of these sources in Rubenius, *The Woman Question*, 188–9.

16 *Ruth*: Nature, Lies and Sacrifice

1 ECG to Mary Green, ? January 1853, Jamison.
2 Charlotte Brontë to ECG, 26 April 1852, SHB, III, 332.
3 Chevalier Bunsen to Susanna Winkworth, 3 February 1853, Shaen, 99.
4 See the analysis of Gaskell's 'ideological confusion' in Patsy Stoneman, *Elizabeth Gaskell* (Brighton, 1987), 99–197, Michael Wheeler, 'The Sinner

NOTES

as Heroine: A Study of Mrs Gaskell's *Ruth* and the Bible', *Durham University Journal*, 68 (1975), 148–61, and B. Crick, 'Mrs Gaskell's *Ruth*', *Mosaic*, 9 (1977–8), 85–104.

5 Cf. Stoneman, *Elizabeth Gaskell*, 103.

6 George Eliot to Mrs Peter Taylor, 1 February 1853, *The Letters of George Eliot*, ed. G. S. Haight (London and New Haven, 1954), II, 85–6.

7 John Forster to ECG, 21 December 1852, Brotherton. See also his letter of 17 January 1853.

8 [Henry Fothergill Chorley], review, *Athenaeum* (15 January 1853), 76–8. (For the varied but generally favourable response to *Ruth* see CH, 200–371.)

9 Unsigned review, *Sharpe's London Magazine*, II (15 January 1853), 125–6.

10 [Margaret Oliphant], 'Modern Novelists – Great and Small', *Blackwood's Edinburgh Magazine*, LXXVII (May 1855), 554–68; unsigned article, *Christian Observer* (July 1857).

11 Richard Cobden to Grace Schwabe, 21 March 1853, John Rylands, MS 730/25. See Waller, 118.

12 Portico Library Archives, Manchester.

13 Catherine Winkworth to Eliza Paterson, 9 February 1853, Winkworth, I, 382–3.

14 Mary Green to ECG, n.d. [February 1853], Brotherton.

15 See Brotherton.

16 ECG to Mary Rich, 10 March 1852, Keele, MS 58-32354.

17 Charles Kingsley to ECG, n.d. [June 1853], John Rylands, MS 730/57, transcribed in *Charles Kingsley: Letters and Memorials*, ed. Mrs F. E. Kingsley (London, 1855), 294.

18 Elizabeth Barrett Browning to ECG, 15 July [1853], John Rylands, MS 730/9. See Waller, 138–45.

19 See, for example, *Prospective Review*, IX (May 1853), 222–47, *Putnam's Monthly Magazine*, 1 July 1853), 535–8, [J. R. Beard], *Tait's Edinburgh Magazine*, XXIV (April 1853), 217–20, and *Gentleman's Magazine*, XL (July 1853), 82–3.

20 John Ludlow, review, *North British Review* XIX (1853), 155.

21 ECG to John Ludlow, n.d. [1853], Cambridge University Library, Ad.7348/10/116.

22 G. H. Lewes, '*Ruth* and *Villette*', *Westminster Review*, NS3 (1853), 474–91.

23 Charlotte Brontë to ECG, February 1853, SHB, IV, 49.

24 Josephine Butler, *An Autobiographical Memoir*, ed. George W. Johnson and Lucy A. Johnson (London, 1909), 31.

25 Arthur Clough to Blanche Smith, 15 April 1853 and n.d. [19 April 1853], *The Correspondence of Arthur H. Clough*, ed. F. L. Mulhauser (Oxford, 1957), II, 415, 418.

652

26 See Susanna Winkworth to Emma Shaen, n.d. [March 1853], Winkworth, I, 395.

27 Harriet Martineau to Fanny Wedgwood, n.d. [March 1853], *Harriet Martineau's Letters to Fanny Wedgwood*, ed. Elisabeth Arbuckle (Stanford, 1983), 125.

17 Finding Space

1 Charles Dickens to ECG, 13 April 1853, Nonesuch, II, 457.

2 Charles Dickens to ECG, 3 May 1853, ibid, 459.

3 Frances Bunsen, *A Memoir of Baron Bunsen* (London, 1868), II, 341.

4 Charlotte Brontë to Ellen Nussey, 15 December 1852, SHB, IV, 29.

5 See Gaskell, *The Life of Charlotte Brontë*, I, ch. 12.

6 See Chadwick, 286–7.

7 See Gaskell, *The Life of Charlotte Brontë*, I, ch. 12.

8 Charlotte Brontë to ECG, April 1853, SHB, IV, 64.

9 There are many descriptions of Mary Clarke Mohl, and among the liveliest is Cecil Woodham-Smith's in *Florence Nightingale, 1820–1910* (London, 1950), 26–31. For fuller treatments see the (unreliable) Kathleen O'Meara, *Madame Mohl: Her Salon and Her Friends* (London, 1885), Mary Simpson's invaluable *Letters and Recollections of Julius and Mary Mohl* (London, 1887) and Margaret Lesser's vivid *Clarkey: A Portrait in Letters of Mary Clarke Mohl* (Oxford, 1984).

10 Quoted in Woodham-Smith, *Florence Nightingale*, 26.

11 Quoted in ibid, 26–7.

12 T. A. Trollope, *What I Remember* (London, 1897), quoted in Lesser, *Clarkey*, 118.

13 Mary Mohl to Elizabeth Reid, 17 [May 1853], Holloway.

14 Mary Mohl to ECG, 6 May 1853, Brotherton.

15 Mary Mohl to ECG, November, 1855, Simpson, 126–7.

16 Mary Mohl to ECG, 2 June 1861, ibid, 184.

17 Quoted in Henry James, *William Wetmore Story and His Friends* (Edinburgh and London, 1903), 365.

18 Gaskell, 'Company Manners', Knutsford, III, 495.

19 Gaskell's notes of 30 May on Hallam's tour are in John Rylands, MS 730/39; Hallam to ECG, 4 June 1853, John Rylands, MS 730/38.

20 Charlotte Brontë to ECG, September 1853, SHB, IV, 84.

21 Gaskell: 'An Accursed Race', HW, XII (25 August 1855), Knutsford, V, 218–36; 'Traits and Stories of the Huguenots', HW, VIII (10 December 1853), Knutsford, II, 490–505; 'My French Master', HW, VIII (17–24 December 1853), Knutsford, II, 506–31; 'Bran', HW, VIII (22 October

1853); and 'The Scholar's Story', *HW*, Extra Christmas Number: 'Another Round of Stories by the Christmas Fire', (1853), not reprinted in Knutsford.

22 Charlotte Brontë to ECG, September 1853, SHB, IV, 84.

23 See Emily Winkworth to Susanna Winkworth, 30 August 1850, Winkworth, I, 250.

24 Charlotte Brontë to ECG, 25 September 1853, SHB, IV, 96.

25 Charles Dickens to ECG, 21 April 1854, Nonesuch, II, 554.

26 John Forster to ECG, 16 January 1854, Brotherton.

27 Catherine Winkworth to Susanna Winkworth, 20 March 1854, Winkworth, I, 431.

28 John Forster to ECG, 18 March 1854, Brotherton.

29 Charles Dickens to ECG, 21 April 1854, Nonesuch, II, 554.

30 Charlotte Brontë to ECG, 18 April 1854, SHB, IV, 112.

31 Ibid, 116.

32 Gaskell, 'Company Manners', 496.

33 Catherine Winkworth to Emma Shaen, 8 May 1854, Winkworth, I, 437–40, and Shaen, 113–18.

34 Charlotte Brontë to ECG, 30 September 1854, SHB, IV, 153–4.

35 ECG to Mary Green, May 1854, Jamison.

36 Catherine Winkworth to Susanna Winkworth, 28 May and 7 June 1854, Winkworth, I, 441, 443.

37 See Emma Darwin, *A Century of Family Letters (1792–1896)*, ed. Henrietta Lichfield (London, 1915), I, 52, and G. N. Brown, *This Old House: A Domestic Biography: Living Conservation at Betley Court* (Betley, 1987), 78–81.

38 Charles Dickens to ECG, 15 June 1854, Nonesuch, II, 561–3.

39 Charles Dickens to ECG, 20 August 1854, ibid, 581.

40 Charles Dickens to ECG, 26 July 1854, ibid, 570–1.

41 Charles Dickens to ECG, 24 August 1854, ibid, 583.

42 Charles Dickens to W. H. Wills, 14 October 1854, ibid, 598.

43 Charles Dickens to John Forster, February 1854, ibid, 543.

44 Florence Nightingale to Mary Mohl, 9 April 1853, *Ever Yours, Florence Nightingale: Selected Letters*, ed. Martha Vicinus and Bea Nergard (London, 1990), 65.

45 Quoted in Woodham-Smith, Florence Nightingale, 62.

46 Florence Nightingale to Hilary Bonham Carter, 26 April 1846, Vicinus and Nergard, *Ever Yours*, 32.

18   *North and South*: 'Tender, and Yet a Master'

1 Catherine Winkworth to Susanna Winkworth, 17 December 1854, Winkworth, II, 472.

2 Charles Dickens to ECG, 27 January 1855, Nonesuch, II, 618.
3 Charles Dickens to Wilkie Collins, 24 March 1855, ibid, 645.
4 ECG to Maria James, n.d. [1854], Brotherton.
5 Two factories were destroyed by fire in March and April 1854. See William Axon, *Annals of Manchester* (Manchester, 1888), 265.
6 Thomas Carlyle, *Past and Present* (1843), bk 3, ch. 2, quoted in Easson, 77.
7 For criticism of the inadequacy of Gaskell's economic and political argument see: Deirdre David, *Fictions of Resolution in Three Victorian Novels: 'North and South', 'Our Mutual Friend' and 'Daniel Deronda'* (London, 1981); John Lucas, 'Mrs Gaskell and Brotherhood', in David Howard et al. (eds), *Tradition and Tolerance in Nineteenth-century Fiction* (London, 1966), and *The Literature of Change: Studies in the Nineteenth Century Provincial Novel* (Brighton, 1977); and Raymond Williams, *Culture and Society, 1780–1950* (London, 1958).
8 See, for example: Nancy Chodorow, *The Reproduction of Mothering* (Berkeley, 1978); Dorothy Dinnerstein, *The Mermaid and the Minotaur* (New York, 1976); P. Schaffer, *Mothering* (Cambridge, Mass., 1977); and Jessica Benjamin, 'Master and Slave', in Ann Snitow et al. (eds), *Desire: The Politics of Sexuality* (London, 1984).
9 St Francis de Sales (1567–1622), *An Introduction to the Devout Life*, III, ix. (See the World's Classics edition *North and South*, ed. Angus Easson, Oxford, 1973, 345n. The Oxford text of De Sales is more accurate than the Knutsford.)

19 *The Life of Charlotte Brontë*

1 ECG to Maria James, n.d. [January 1855], Brotherton. For selected reviews of *North and South* see *CH*, 330–71. It is interesting that several contemporary critics, including Henry Chorley and Margaret Oliphant, commented on the difficulty of resolving industrial and social troubles through a fictional romance: [Henry Fothergill Chorley], review, *Athenaeum* (7 April 1855), 403; [Margaret Oliphant], 'Modern Novelists – Great and Small', *Blackwood's Edinburgh Magazine*, LXXVII (May 1855), 554–68.
2 See L333, 433, 438. Hachette had the right to decide on translation within a specified time, and paid 1.5 francs per page.
3 Charlotte's death, credited on the death certificate to tuberculosis, has been the subject of intense speculation. Doubts have been cast on her pregnancy (although it was accepted by her husband and father) and it has been suggested that the intense sickness may have represented an unconscious rejection of the foetus. See W. Gérin, *Charlotte Brontë: The Evolution of Genius* (Oxford, 1967), 564–7, and Rebecca Fraser, *Charlotte Brontë*

(London, 1988), 483.

4 It has been suggested that Gaskell used the term 'induced' technically, referring to inducing Charlotte's baby prematurely, but despite her knowledge of midwifery this seems highly unlikely. See Anna Unsworth, 'Mrs Gaskell and Charlotte Brontë', GSN, 8 (August 1989), 17–18.

5 A cheap edition of Cranford, and a collection of tales.

6 The timetable, very clear from the letters, is described in the excellent chapter on the Life in Easson, 126–59.

7 Margaret Oliphant, 'The Sisters Brontë', Women Novelists of Queen Victoria's Reign (London, 1897), quoted in Alison Kershaw. 'The Business of a Woman's Life: Elizabeth Gaskell's Life of Charlotte Brontë, BST, 20 (1990), 11–24. Kershaw also provides an illuminating comparison between the Life and the 'male' best-seller of 1857, Samuel Smiles's Life of George Stephenson.

8 Ellen Nussey to Arthur Nicholls, 6 June 1856, and Arthur Nicholls to Ellen Nussey, 11 June 1856, SHB, IV, 189–90.

9 Patrick Brontë to ECG, 16 July 1855, ibid, 190–1. For Patrick Brontë's letters to Gaskell during this period see (the highly partisan) John Lock and W. T. Dixon, A Man of Sorrow: The Life, Letters and Times of the Rev. Patrick Brontë, 1777–1861 (London, 1965).

10 ECG to Mary Green, 17 August 1855, Jamison.

11 Her principal sources were Scatcherd's History of Birstall (Leeds, 1830), John Newton's Memoirs of the Life of William Grimshaw (published by Greenwood, Haworth, 1854) and Joseph Hunter's Life of Oliver Heywood (1842).

12 ECG to Maria James, 3 December [1855], Pierpont Morgan, MA 2696.

13 ECG to Mary Green, 15 October 1855, Jamison.

14 Quoted in A. B. Hopkins, Elizabeth Gaskell: Her Life and Works (London, 1952).

15 Thomas Carlyle, Conclusion, Life of Sterling (Edinburgh edn, 1902), 235–6, quoted in Easson, 136.

16 Mary Taylor to Ellen Nussey, 19 April 1856, SHB, IV, 198.

17 Snow Wedgwood to Effie Wedgwood, 3 November 1855, Keele, W/M MSS 324. See also J. A. V. Chapple, 'An Author's Life: Elizabeth Gaskell and the Wedgwood Family', BST 17 (1979), 288–9.

18 ECG to Harriet Andersen, 15 March [1856], transcribed in J. A. V. Chapple, 'Two Unpublished Gaskell Letters from Burrow Hall, Lancashire', GSJ, 6 (1992), 71. See also Sally Stonehouse, 'A Letter from Mrs Gaskell', BST, 20 (1991), 217–22.

19 Chapple, GSJ (1992), 71. Chapple also identifies the Alcocks.

20 For arrangements concerning the Brussels trip see ECG to Fanny Holland, n.d. [?13 March 1856], in ibid.

21 Patrick Brontë to William Gaskell, 23 July 1856, in Lock and Dixon, *A Man of Sorrow*, 501–2.

22 Charles Brontë to Constantin Heger, January 1845, SHB, II, 23 (trans). Gaskell used extracts from the first two letters, but nothing from the third and fourth. See Gérin, *Charlotte Brontë*, Appendix A, 171–2. In L401 Gaskell refers to 'receiving M. Heger's confidence and *hearing* her letter,' (my italics).

23 See Adeane Notebook, Brotherton, quoted in J. A. V. Chapple, 'Elizabeth Gaskell's "Morton Hall" and "The Poor Clare"', BST, 20 (1990), 47–9.

24 Gaskell, 'The Poor Clare', HW, XIV (13–27 December 1856), reprinted in *Round the Sofa* (1859), as Signor Sperani's story, and in Knutsford, V, 329–90.

25 See Adeane Notebook (see n.23).

26 See Gérin, *Charlotte Brontë*, 573.

27 See Fanny E. Ratchford, Introduction to *The Brontë Web of Childhood* (New York, 1941), x.

28 ECG to Jemima Quillinan, 4 August 1856, Dove Cottage Museum, Grasmere, quoted in Stephen Gill, 'A Manuscript of Branwell's with Letters of Mrs Gaskell', BST, 15 (1970), 408–11.

29 See MS of *The Life of Charlotte Brontë*, John Rylands, fol. 347, marked 'to be inserted between 347–8'. For this and the moving of passages for greater effect see Easson, 145–6.

30 Comparison with the full letters, even in the often untrustworthy texts of the Shakespeare Head Brontë, makes clear this kind of omission, for example from the letter about the first visit to George Smith, as well as the cutting of tart remarks about Sir James Kay Shuttleworth, or 'embarrassing' stories, like Thackeray's admission about crying over *Jane Eyre*. See Alan Shelston's discussion of the Kay Shuttleworth omissions and of Gaskell's reticence, in deference to Nicholls, in her presentation of William Weightman and the proposals of marriage from Henry Nussey and James Taylor in the Introduction to *The Life of Charlotte Brontë*, Penguin Classics (Harmondsworth, 1975), 32–4. It should also be noted that many of Ellen Nussey's letters were censored *before* they were given to Gaskell.

31 Arthur Nicholls to ECG, December 1856, Brontë Museum, Haworth (5–9, 105c), quoted in 'The Gordon Bequest', BST, 19 (1986), 41.

32 Arthur Nicholls to George Smith, 1 December 1856, John Murray Archives, London, quoted in Fraser, *Charlotte Brontë*, 490.

33 Patrick Brontë to ECG, 3 November 1856, in Lock and Dixon, *A Man of Sorrow*, 503.

34 See L. Huxley, *The House of Smith Elder* (printed for private circulation, 1923), 77. See also A. B. Hopkins, *Elizabeth Gaskell: Her Life and Work* (London, 1952), 222–3.

35 See Henry James, *William Wetmore Story and His Friends* (Edinburgh and London, 1903), 321, 354.

36 Ellen Nussey approved at the time, but later felt aggrieved that she received no payment and had not been adequately acknowledged (even though she made Gaskell represent her by her initial only in the text). She tried for many years, without success, to have her collection of Brontë letters published separately. See SHB, IV, 247–92.

37 MS of *The Life of Charlotte Brontë*, John Rylands.

38 *Quarterly Review*, XCVIII (1856), 297, 300.

39 These two girls were mentioned by Patrick Brontë in one of his early letters to Gaskell (27 August 1855). See Lock and Dixon, *A Man of Sorrow*, 499–500.

40 MS of *The Life of Charlotte Brontë*. See Easson, 141–2, and Joan Stevens, who first drew attention to this moving of the text in *Mary Taylor: Friend of Charlotte Brontë* (Auckland and London, 1972), 161–2.

41 Elizabeth Barrett Browning, *Aurora Leigh* (1857). See Kershaw, BST (1990), 11.

III THE SOUNDS OF TIME: 1857–65

20 Rome and Revisions

1 Gaskell, 'A Dark Night's Work', *AYR*, VIII and IX (24 January – 21 March 1863), Knutsford, VII, 404–590.

2 Details of Captain Hill's career are given in *Madras Military Fund Officer's Families, Cadet Records* and *Military Records*, India Office Library. See *Letters*, vol. XIII of *The Collected Works of Walter Bagehot*, ed. N. St John Stevas (London, 1986), 572–3 n. 2. Katie's comments are from Winkworth, II, 111; her letters from Rome (109–41) are full of details of this holiday.

3 Catherine Winkworth to Susanna Winkworth, 2 March 1857, Winkworth, II, 109–10.

4 Ibid, 111.

5 See Margaret Forster, *Elizabeth Barrett Browning* (London, 1988), 285–7.

6 Meta Gaskell to Sara Norton, n.d. [1910], quoted in the Introduction to Whitehill, xix. The Houghton Collection, Harvard, has numerous letters from Meta and Marianne to Charles Norton.

7 Meta Gaskell to Charles Norton, n.d., quoted in the Introduction to Whitehill, xix.

8 See K. Vanderbilt, *Charles Eliot Norton: Apostle of Culture in a Democracy* (Cambridge, Mass., 1959). Norton edited Emerson's and Lowell's letters, and his own letters are regarded as one of the most valuable accounts of the Boston and Cambridge 'intellectual aristocracy'.

9 John Ruskin, *Praeterita*, III, vol. XXXV of *The Works of John Ruskin*, ed.
   E. T. Cook and Alexander Wedderburn (London, 1908), 579, 520. In
   Praeterita Ruskin wrote of a romantic first meeting with Norton in a boat
   on Lake Geneva, in terms very like Gaskell's first sight of him; Norton,
   more prosaically, pointed out that they actually met in the drawing-room at
   Denmark Hill the year before (see *The Correspondence of John Ruskin and
   Charles Eliot Norton*, ed. J. Bradley and I. Ousby, Cambridge, 1987, 21).
10 Ruskin, *Praeterita*, III, 520. See *Portrait*, 103.
11 See Meta Gaskell to Charles Norton, *The Letters of Charles Eliot Norton*,
   ed. Sara Norton and M. A. de Wolfe (London, 1913), I, 155; Charles
   Norton to James Lowell, 20 June 1857, ibid, 171.
12 See the Introduction to Whitehill, xxii.
13 See ibid. See also *Charles Eliot Norton, Notes of Travel and Study in Italy*
   (Boston, 1860).
14 Charles Norton to Meta Gaskell, 24 July 1908, *Letters of Charles Norton*,
   II, 409.
15 Henry James, *William Wetmore Story and His Friends* (Edinburgh and
   London, 1903), 354–5, 359–61; Edmund About, *Tolla* (Paris, 1856).
16 Catherine Winkworth to Susanna Winkworth, 20 March 1857,
   Winkworth, II, 122; Catherine Winkworth to Charles Herford, 25 March
   1857, ibid, 129.
17 Catherine Winkworth to Susanna Winkworth, 21 March 1857, ibid, 126.
18 Bessie Parkes to Elizabeth Parkes, 21 April 1857, Girton, BRP II/7.
19 Charles Norton to James Lowell, 1 January 1857, *Letters of Charles
   Norton*, I, 159; Charles Norton to Arthur Clough, 4 April 1857, ibid, 166.
20 Charles Norton to Mrs Andrews Norton, 1 March 1857, ibid, 162.
21 Catherine Winkworth to Susanna Winkworth, 12 March 1857,
   Winkworth, II, 122.
22 Charles Norton to Mrs Andrews Norton, 15 March 1857, *Letters of
   Charles Norton*, I, 163.
23 Catherine Winkworth to Susanna Winkworth, 12 March 1857,
   Winkworth, II, 120.
24 Quoted in James, *William Wetmore Story*, 255.
25 Charles Norton to Mrs Andrews Norton, 2 July 1857, *Letters of Charles
   Norton*, I, 174.
26 Patrick Brontë to ECG, 2 April 1857, in John Lock and W. T. Dixon, *A
   Man of Sorrow: The Life, Letters and Times of the Rev. Patrick Brontë,
   1777–1861* (London, 1965), 504.
27 Catherine Winkworth to Susanna Winkworth, 29 April 1857, Winkworth,
   II, 140.
28 Mary Mohl to Elizabeth Reid, 9 May 1857, Holloway.
29 [Henry Fothergill Chorley], review, *Athenaeum* (14 April 1857), quoted in

Alison Kershaw, 'The Business of a Woman's Life: Elizabeth Gaskell's Life of Charlotte Brontë, *BST*, 20 (1990), 14. For a selection of reviews see *CH*, 372–431, and also Easson's useful survey of the public response, *CH*, 35–8.

30 William Gaskell to Ellen Nussey, 15 April 1857, SHB, IV, 221.
31 *The Times*, 30 May 1857.
32 *Athenaeum*, 6 June 1857.
33 See Lock and Dixon, *A Man of Sorrow*, 507.
34 Bessie Parkes to Elizabeth Parkes, 10 June 1857, Girton, BRP II/10.
35 Mary Mohl to Elizabeth Reid, 16 June 1857, Holloway.
36 Ibid.
37 Charles Kingsley to ECG, 4 August 1857, John Rylands, MS 730/584, transcribed in SHB, IV, 222–3.
38 Anna Jameson to Bessie Parkes, 20 May 1857, Girton, BRP VI/20.
39 G. H. Lewes to ECG, 15 April 1857, John Rylands, MS 731/61, in *The George Eliot Letters*, ed. G. S. Haight (London and New Haven, 1954), II, 316.
40 V. Woolf, 'Haworth, 1904', in Michèle Barrett (ed.), *Virginia Woolf: Women and Writing* (London, 1979), 121, quoted in Kershaw, *BST* (1990), 23.
41 See Lock and Dixon, *A Man of Sorrow*, 515.
42 The 'warlike correspondence' can be read in the Martineau Papers, University of Birmingham. Some of these correspondences continued long after the revised edition appeared. See Gaskell's own exchange with J. S. Mill after she read *On Liberty* in 1859 (L563–4, 567–9) and SHB, III, 277–8, IV, 233–6.
43 Matters were further complicated because Mary Mohl was related to the Carus Wilson family, but since she was having an argument with them about some property, she did not care how Gaskell attacked them.
44 For the revisions and additions see *The Life of Charlotte Brontë*, ed. Alan Shelston, Penguin Classics (Harmondsworth, 1975), Appendix A. This contains the two rewritten chapters on Cowan Bridge and the Branwell Brontë–Robinson affair. The notes to this edition indicate all other significant emendations.
45 Patrick Brontë to ECG, 30 July 1857, in Lock and Dixon, *A Man of Sorrow*, 509.
46 Patrick Brontë to ECG, 24 August 1857, in ibid, 511.
47 Thomas Carlyle in the *Westminster Review* (January 1838), 299, quoted in Arthur Pollard, *Mrs Gaskell: Novelist and Biographer* (Manchester, 1965), 145.
48 Mary Taylor to Ellen Nussey, 28 January 1858, SHB, IV, 229.
49 Arthur Clough to Charles Norton, 23 November 1857, *The*

Correspondence of Arthur H. Clough, ed. F. L. Mulhauser (Oxford, 1957), II, 536.

50 Harriet Martineau to Snow Wedgwood, 4 May 1857, *Harriet Martineau's Letters to Fanny Wedgwood*, ed. Elisabeth Arbuckle (Stanford, 1983), 153.
51 Charlotte Brontë to ECG, 9 July 1853, SHB, IV, 76–7.

21 Art and India, Travels and Cash

1 Meta Gaskell to Snow Wedgwood, 1 July 1857, Keele, W/M MSS 324.
2 Mary Rich to Fanny Wedgwood, 6 August 1857, Keele, W/M MSS 360.
3 See Marianne Gaskell to Charles Norton, 8 September 1857, Harvard, bMS, Am 1088/3488.
4 Maria Susanna Cummins's *Mabel Vaughan* was published by Sampson Low in September 1857, 'The Doom of the Griffiths' was sent to Sampson Low on 26 October 1857. See letters from Marianne Gaskell to Charles Norton (20 October) and from Low to ECG (29 October), Harvard, bMS Am 1088/3491 and Autograph File. The story appeared in *Harper's*, XVI (January 1858).

Other *Harper's* stories which have been attributed to Gaskell are 'The Siege of the Black Cottage' (XIV, February 1857) – now identified as by Wilkie Collins (see Angus Easson, 'Elizabeth Gaskell and Wilkie Collins: An Attribution Corrected', *Notes and Queries*, CCXXV, June 1980, 210–11) – and, more plausibly, despite its subject matter, 'An Incident at Niagara Falls' (XVII, June 1858).
5 Marianne Gaskell to Charles Norton, 25 January 1858, Harvard, bMS, Am 1088/3489.
6 Fanny Wedgwood to Snow Wedgwood, 20 August 1858, Keele, W/M MSS 268.
7 Snow Wedgwood to Effie Wedgwood, 28 May 1858, Keele, W/M MSS 375.
8 Meta Gaskell to Snow Wedgwood, 23 January 1858, Keele, W/M MSS 375.
9 Fanny Wedgwood to Snow Wedgwood, 20 August 1858, Keele, W/M MSS 268.
10 Walter Bagehot to Matilda Wilson, 7 February 1861, *Letters*, vol. XIII of *The Collected Works of Walter Bagehot*, ed. N. St John Stevas (London, 1986), 572–3, n. 2.
11 Snow Wedgwood to Effie Wedgwood, 21 August 1859, Keele, W/M MSS 324.
12 Meta Gaskell to Effie Wedgwood, 7 January 1862, Keele, W/M MSS 408.
13 As Sharps points out, 276–7, Gaskell is particularly careless about names in this story, Lady Ludlow's living son being called Rudolph, then Ughtred, the Baptist baker being first Mr Lambe then Mr Brooke, the son of Morin,

in the story of the revolution, being alternatively Jean and Victor. For her casual use of names generally see Sharps, Appendix VII, 596–604.

14 *My Lady Ludlow* appeared in *HW*, XVIII, in fourteen episodes (19 June–25 September 1858). Gaskell told Norton she hoped for £150 from Low, not £105 – a misprint in L513. The pirated edition, *My Lady Ludlow: A Novel*, was published by Harpers, 1858. For the split with Harpers see Marianne Gaskell to Charles Norton, 27 January 1859, Harvard, bMS Am 1088/2644.

15 Quoted in Elizabeth Haldane, *Mrs Gaskell and Her Friends* (London, 1930), 104–7.

16 See Cecil Woodham-Smith, *Florence Nightingale, 1820–1910* (London, 1950), 304.

17 'Right at Last' was given the title 'The Sin of a Father' in *HW*, XVIII (27 November 1858); Knutsford, VII, 278–9), and renamed when published in the Sampson Low Collection *Right at Last, and Other Tales* in May 1860; 'The Manchester Marriage', *HW*, Extra Christmas Number: 'A House to Let' (1858), Knutsford, V, 492–523.

18 Idah Mohl to Mary Mohl, 4 November 1858, Coolidge typescript, Brotherton. Jane Coolidge copied the Mohl letters before they were destroyed during World War II. See Sharps, 299.

19 Dante Gabriel Rossetti to ECG, 18 July 1859, 17 December 1861 and n.d., John Rylands, MSS 730/86/87/88.

20 Catherine Stevenson, Elizabeth's stepmother, had returned to Kircudbrightshire after William Stevenson died; her brother Anthony Todd Thomson's first wife (before Katherine Byerley) was Christine Maxwell. For Gaskell's acquaintance with the Maxwells see L872, 387, 880 and New York Public Library, MSS 64, 7, 4–4, 1007.

21 This was the Revd William Scoresby (1789–1857); his father, William Scoresby, was also an Arctic navigator and scientist. Gaskell had met him at Orchardstown while staying with her stepsister at Dunoon. The relevant books are *An Account of the Arctic Regions, with a History and Description of the Northern Whale-fishery*, 2 vols (Edinburgh and London, 1820), and an abridgement of vol. II, *The Northern Whale-fishery* (London, 1849).

22 Men, Women, Language and Power

1 Gaskell, 'A Dark Night's Work', *AYR*, VIII and IX (24 January–21 March 1863), Knutsford, VII, 404–590, and 'Curious if True', *Cornhill Magazine*, I (February 1860), Knutsford, VII, 259–77.

2 For these allegations and history of earlier correspondence in *HW* see Sharps, 122–3.

3 Gaskell, 'Lois the Witch', *AYR*, I (October 1859), Knutsford, VII, 110–208, and 'The Crooked Branch', ('The Ghost in the Garden Room'), *AYR*, Extra Christmas Number; 'The Haunted House' (1859), Knutsford, VII, 208–58. Some of the dialect speech was borrowed directly from her friend Georgina Tollett's manuscript 'Country Conversations', not published until 1881 (privately published London), and reissued as *Country Conversations: The Humour of Old Village Life in the Midlands* (London, 1923). See A. W. Ward, Introduction to Knutsford, VII, xxv, and Sharps, 327–8.

4 See *The Letters and Private Papers of William Makepeace Thackeray*, ed. Gordon N. Ray (London, 1945), I, xciv n.

5 See Bessie Parkes to Barbara Leigh Smith, 18 November 1863, Girton, BRP, V/123 Appendix B, and unpublished typescript by Bessie's daughter, Marie Belloc Lowndes.

6 George Eliot to ECG, 11 November 1859, *The George Eliot Letters*, ed. G. S. Haight (London and New Haven, 1954), III, 198–9.

7 See Ruskin, *Modern Painters* (1856), III, ch. 16, section 29, quoted in Eliot's article in the *Westminster Review* (April 1856) in *Selected Essays, Poems and Other Writings*, ed. A. S. Byatt and Nicholas Warren (Harmondsworth, 1990), 377.

8 George Eliot, *Selected Essays*, 368–9.

9 George Eliot, 'The Natural History of German Life', *Selected Essays*, 110.

10 George Eliot, 'Woman in France: Madame de Sablé', *Selected Essays*, 9.

11 Ibid, 8.

12 Gaskell, *My Lady Ludlow*, *HW*, XVIII (19 June–25 September 1858), Knutsford, V, 9–217.

13 George Eliot, 'Silly Novels by Lady Novelists', *Selected Essays*, 162.

14 Gaskell, 'The Grey Woman', *AYR*, IV (5–19 January 1861), Knutsford, 300–361.

15 Francis Bacon, 'On Revenge', *Oxford Book of Essays*, ed. John Gross (Oxford, 1991), 4.

16 The story is based on the account given in Charles Wentworth Upham, *Lectures on Witchcraft: Comprising a History of the Delusion in Salem, in 1692* (Boston, 1831). Gaskell follows this closely, in several places to the extent of merely adapting Upham's words: for example, the son hiding his mother in the marsh, and the crushing to death of Giles Corey. An Indian slave, Tituba (Hota) was accused first, and the disturbances began in Revd Samuel Parrish's house (Pastor Tappau); another minister, George Burroughs (Pastor Nolan), was one of the victims. Historical characters introduced by Gaskell include Cotton Mather, Justice Samuel Sewall, Jonathan Corwin and John Hathorne (Nathaniel Hawthorne's ancestor).

17 John Gorham Palfrey (letter to ECG, 21 June 1856, John Rylands, MS 731/81) writes of there being only one copy of Robert Calef's *The Wonders of*

the Invisible World (1700) in Britain, and promises to send material from America.

23 Interruptions

1 For Gaskell's visit see the introductions to *Sylvia's Lovers* by Ward (Knutsford, VI) and Thomas Seccombe (Bell edn, London, 1910), and Chadwick, 352–60. The local works on which she drew were George Young: *A History of Whitby and Streoneshalh Abbey* 2 vols (Whitby, London and Edinburgh, 1817), and *A Picture of Whitby and Its Environs*, 2nd edn (Whitby, 1840), and the guide by F. K. Robinson, *Whitby: Its Abbey and the Principal Parts of Its Neighbourhood* (Whitby, 1860). See Sharps, 373–421.
2 George Crabbe, *Tales of the Hall* (1819).
3 Gaskell said she did not intend Haytersbank for any particular place (L537). However, George du Maurier, the illustrator, was advised by a friend to take Whitby as a model, and found the descriptions uncannily accurate. See Edith Sichel, *The Life and Letters of Alfred Ainger* (London, 1906), 280.
4 Portico Library Archives, Manchester.
5 General Thompson's letter about riots in Hull is quoted in full by A. W. Ward in Knutsford, VII, xxiii–xxvii.
6 See N. Rance, *The Historical Novel and Popular Politics* (1975), and Terry Eagleton, '*Sylvia's Lovers* and Legality', *Essays in Criticism*, 26 (1976), 17–27.
7 ECG to Edward Hale, 14 December 1860, Smith, Box 24/588.
8 R. C. Stauffer (ed.), *Charles Darwin's Natural Selection* (Cambridge, 1975), 175–6, quoted in Adrian Desmond and James Moore, *Darwin* (London, 1991), 450.
9 Atkinson's letter and the York Calendar are quoted in full by A. W. Ward in Knutsford, VII, xxiii–xxvii.
10 ECG to Edward Hale, 14 December 1860, Smith, Box 24/588.
11 Portico Library Archives, Manchester.
12 William Gaskell to ECG, 25 July 1860, Rutgers University Library, MS 9253/3, transcribed in Brotherton.
13 Meta Gaskell to Effie Wedgwood, 25 January 1862, Keele, W/M MSS 408.
14 Meta Gaskell to Emily Shaen, n.d. [6 November 1860], SHB, IV, 239.
15 ECG to Edward Hale, 22 April 1861, Smith, Box 24/588.
16 William Gaskell to Edward Hale, 13 December 1861, Smith, Box 24/588.
17 ECG to Edward Hale, 14 December 1861, Smith, Box 24/588.
18 Meta Gaskell to Effie Wedgwood, 19 December 1862, Keele, W/M MSS 408.
19 See Gaskell's letters to Florence Nightingale, in Brotherton and Smith.

NOTES

20 ECG to George and Vernon Lushington, May 1862, Gaskell/Lushington Letters, Manchester, MS 823, 894 B1264. Letter 1.

21 ECG to George and Vernon Lushington, April [1862], Gaskell/Lushington Letters, Manchester, MS 823, 894 B1264, Letter 2.

22 Meta Gaskell to Effie Wedgwood, 2 November 1862, Keele, W/M MSS 408.

23 Meta Gaskell to Effie Wedgwood, 19 December 1862, Keele, W/M MSS 408.

24 Baffled Seas: *Sylvia's Lovers*

1 For the wealth of popular representations of the Napoleonic wars, from melodrama and satire to Staffordshire Toby Jugs of 'The Sailor's Return', see: H. F. B. Wheeler and A. M. Broadly, *Napoleon and the Invasion of England*, 2 vols (London, 1908), especially ch. 9, 'Literary and Artistic Landmarks', II, 195–255; Betty T. Bennet, *British War Poetry in the Age of Romanticism, 1793–1815* (London, 1976), which includes some appalling repetitive verse; J. Ashton, *English Caricature and Satire on Napoleon the First*, 2 vols (London, 1884); and F. J. Klingberg and S. B. Hustvedt, *The Warning Drum: The British Home Front Faces Napoleon* (Berkeley and Los Angeles, 1944).

2 See the illustrations in J. R. Hutchinson, *The Press Gang Ashore and Afloat* (London, 1913).

3 See Edgar Wright, *Mrs Gaskell: The Basis for Reassessment* (Oxford, 1965), 78–9, and also Andrew Sanders's excellent chapter 'Suffering a Sea-change', in *The Victorian Historical Novel, 1840–1880* (London, 1978), 197–228.

4 The seven-year motif is found in ballads and folk-songs, from 'The Demon Lover' to the eighteenth-century 'Young and Single Sailor':

> 'Oh, young man, I have a sweetheart
> And seven long years he's away from me
> And seven more I will wait for him,
> And if he's alive he will return to me.
>
> Oh, seven years makes an alteration,
> Perhaps he's drowned and is now at rest,
> Then no other man shall ever join me.
> For he's the darling boy that I love best.'

5 'A Hymn of Praise and Thanksgiving after a Dangerous Tempest', Book of Common Prayer, quoted in Sanders, 'Suffering a Sea-change', 197.

6 Joseph Wright, *The English Dialect Dictionary*, 6 vols (London, 1898–

1905): *A Glossary of Words Used in the Neighbourhood of Whitby*
(Whitby, 1855). See Sanders, 'Suffering a Sea-change', 145–55, and Sharps,
416–17. The MS of *Sylvia's Lovers* in Brotherton shows many changes to
the definite article, for example fol. 48, and other minute alterations,
particularly in Daniel's and Kester's speech, for example, 'himself' to
'hissel', 'before' to 'afore' (fol. 59), 'must' to 'mun' (fol. 60), 'there' to
'theer' (fol. 68), 'myself' to 'mysen' (fol. 78). Gaskell's dialect has recently
begun to attract the attention of linguists, who find it corresponds closely to
the regional boundaries established in the *English Dialect Survey* (Gunnel
Melcher, 'Mrs Gaskell and Dialect', paper presented at the Gaskell and
Brontë Societies' Joint Conference, Scarborough, 1991).

7 See Patricia Ingham, 'Dialect as Realism: *Hard Times* and the Industrial
Novel', *Review of English Studies*, 37 (1986), 519–23. See also Wendy
Craik, *Mrs Gaskell and the English Provincial Novel* (London, 1975).

8 'The Whale-catchers', *The Penguin Book of English Folk-songs*, ed. R.
Vaughan Williams and A. L. Ward (Harmondsworth, 1959), 100.

9 It may be significant that Gaskell had trouble finding the right name for
Kinraid – her fierce crossings-out make the MS almost indecipherable; until
the New Year's Fête he seems to have been first Alick, then Sandy
Macphraille.

10 William Scoresby, *An Account of the Arctic Regions, with a History and
Description of the Northern Whale-fishery* (Edinburgh and London, 1820),
II, 471. Gaskell drew her stories from two chapters in Scoresby, *The Arctic
Regions*, II; 'Anecdotes Illustrative of Peculiarities in the Whale Fishery',
and 'Anecdotes Illustrative of the Dangers of the Whale Fishery'. The latter
includes 'Dangers from Ice', 'The Nature of the Climate' and 'The Whale'.
The capsize concerned the *Aimwell* of Whitby on 26 May 1910, whereas
the story of riding on the back of a whale is an almost legendary tale of the
famous Dutch harpooneer Vienkes in 1660, taken by Scoresby from a
French translation of a Dutch work, the *Histoires des pennes*. Kinraid's
story of the southern ice is not from Scoresby.

11 Scoresby, *The Arctic Regions*, II, 101.

12 'The Demon Lover', *English and Scottish Ballads*, ed. Robert Graves
(London, 1957), 28.

13 'Sir Patrick Spens', ibid, 19.

14 'As Sylvie was walking', *Penguin Book of English Folk-songs*, 14.

15 MS of *Sylvia's Lovers*, Brotherton.

16 See the description of the pantomime *The Mouth of the Nile*, which ran for
forty nights at Sadler's Wells in 1798–9, in Wheeler and Broadly,
Napoleon, 225–7.

17 In his notes to the World's Classics edition of *Sylvia's Lovers* (Oxford,
1982) Sanders points out that Guy is not one of the seven patron saints of

Europe in *The Seven Champions*, but suggests that a popular chap-book might bind two such stories together.

18 Matthew Arnold, 'Dover Beach' (written in 1850), but not published until 1867). There is no evidence to show that Gaskell read this – like the motif of the returning sailor, found here and in Tennyson's *Enoch Arden*, the image is common to the period – but letters from Arnold in the John Rylands Library show that he did send her early drafts of some of his poems.

25 Flossy and *Cousin Phillis*

1 Charles Norton to ECG, 23 April 1863, Whitehill, 100.
2 [Geraldine Jewsbury], review, *Athenaeum* (28 February 1863). For a sample of critical responses see *CH*, 432–55.
3 Unsigned review, *Saturday Review*, XV (4 April 1863), 446–7.
4 Unsigned review, *Daily News* (3 April 1863), 2.
5 Mary Mohl to Elizabeth Reid, 28 February 1863, Holloway.
6 Mary Mohl to Mrs Nassau Senior, 3 March 1863, Simpson, 202.
7 See Leonard Shapiro, *Ivan Turgenev: His Life and Times* (Oxford, 1978), 128; Patsy Stoneman, *Elizabeth Gaskell* (Brighton, 1987), 171.
8 Mary Mohl to Mrs Nassau Senior, 23 February 1863, Simpson, 200–201.
9 ECG to Mary Green, 18 March 1863, Jamison.
10 Gaskell, 'An Italian Institution', *AYR*, IX (21 March 1863), Knutsford, VI, 531–40.
11 William Gaskell to ECG, 25 July 1860, Brotherton.
12 C. Augusto Vecchi, *Garibaldi on Caprera* (Cambridge and London, 1862), vii.
13 Susanna Winkworth to Catherine Winkworth, 4 June 1863, Winkworth, II, 391.
14 Gaskell, *Cousin Phillis*, *Cornhill Magazine*, VIII (November 1863–February 1864), Knutsford, VII, 1–109.
15 James Thomson, 'Autumn', *The Seasons*. See John Chalker, *The English Georgic* (London, 1969), 129.
16 ECG to Mary Green, 8 July 1860, Jamison.
17 Henry David Thoreau, *Walden* (Harmondsworth, 1983), 161, 167.
18 Mr Manning was evidently modelled on the engineer James Nasmyth (William Gaskell's cousin Holbrook Gaskell was his commercial partner). Nasmyth not only mocked apprentices wearing gloves (as Manning does), but in 1856 gave 'a lesson in geology' at his Patricroft works to Elizabeth,

Marianne and Selina and Catherine Winkworth, 'illustrated with impromptu diagrams drawn on the wall alternately with a piece of white chalk and a sooty fore-finger' (Catherine Winkworth to Emily Shaen, 18 March 1856, Winkworth, II, 18).

19 William Empson, *Some Versions of Pastoral* (London, 1935), 4.
20 For an interesting reading of the Lucy theme see Stoneman, *Elizabeth Gaskell*, 165–6.
21 ECG to George Smith, 10 December 1863, Edinburgh, MS 23181, fols 180–5, quoted in J. A. V. Chapple, '*Cousin Phillis:* Two Unpublished Letters from Elizabeth Gaskell to George Smith', *Études anglaises*, XXIII (1980), 183–7.

26   Away from Manchester

1 Quoted in Robert H. Kargon, *Science in Victorian Manchester: Enterprise and Expertise* (Manchester, 1977), 3–4.
2 William Gaskell to ECG, 25 July 1860, Brotherton.
3 Margaret Shaen to Elizabeth Haldane, 28 August 1930, Edinburgh, MS 6036f, 53, 54v.
4 See: Brill, 74–8, J. J. Wright, *Young Days* (London, 1899); and Adam Rushton, *My Life as Farmer's Boy, Factory Hand, Teacher and Preacher* (Manchester, 1909).
5 Susanna Winkworth to Catherine Winkworth, 4 June 1863, Winkworth, II, 391.
6 C. G. Knott et al. (eds), *Edinburgh's Place in Scientific Progress* (Edinburgh and London, 1921), 113.
7 Mary Mohl to ECG, 28 December, 1864, Simpson, 217.
8 See MSS of *Wives and Daughters*, John Rylands. For a useful summary of inconsistencies see Sharps, 490.
9 See the letters from Froude, 5 and 20 March 1863, John Rylands, MS 730/33/34.
10 Mary Mohl to ECG, 28 December 1864, Simpson, 218.
11 Ibid.
12 Gaskell, 'Columns of Gossip from Paris', *Pall Mall Gazette* (25 and 28 March 1865). A third article, 'A Letter of Gossip from Paris', on 25 April, has been attributed to Gaskell, but its title, its date, her illness and its style and subjects, which include music-halls, make this unlikely.
13 Algernon Swinburne, autograph letter signed (one sheet only, no addressee, no date), Berg Collection, New York Public Library.
14 Gaskell, 'A Parson's Holiday', *Pall Mall Gazette* (21 August 1865), 3.

27 *Wives and Daughters:* Windows and Clothes

1 See Joan Leach, 'Hollingford alias Knutsford', *GSN*, 5 (March 1988), 8–10.
2 Lady Ritchie, 'Heroines and Their Grandmothers', *Cornhill Magazine*, II (1865), 630–4.
3 Cf. Patsy Stoneman, *Elizabeth Gaskell* (Brighton, 1987), 177–8.
4 Angus Easson's excellent notes to the World's Classics edition of *Wives and Daughters* (Oxford, 1937) trace the connections between Roger's pursuits and Darwin's early career (including his interest in anatomy and in bees). They are also invaluable for placing the literary references in the text.
5 See Martin Wiener, *English Culture and the Decline of the Industrial Spirit, 1850–1980* (Harmondsworth, 1985).
6 Harriet Martineau, 'Middle-class Education in England: Girls', *Cornhill Magazine*, II (November 1864), 549. The Report of the Commission on Public Schools, 1864, had found nine leading public schools deficient in everything but classics and sport: Rugby (to which Squire Hamley sends his sons) was the exception. Gaskell's discussion of education appeared in the *Cornhill* episodes from August to October 1864, Martineau's articles, the first on boys, the second on girls, in October and November. The following year saw a public inquiry into the state of education for the middle classes.
7 Walter Scott to Joanna Baillie, 18 July [1823], *The Letters of Sir Walter Scott*, ed. J. J. C. Grierson (London, 1935), VIII, 52–3.
8 Gaskell, 'Shams', *Fraser's Magazine*, LXVII (February 1863), not reprinted in Knutsford.
9 In letters of 1859 and 1860 Marianne had the most nicknames of all the girls, but Gaskell usually addresses her as Polly or MA, sometimes as Minnie or Mima.

28 Endings

1 Mary Mohl to ECG, 28 December 1864, Simpson, 218.
2 Meta Gaskell to Charles Norton, 2 July 1867, Harvard, bMS Am 1088/ 2613.
3 [Henry James], review, the *Nation* (February 1866), reprinted in Henry James, *Literary Criticism: Essays on Literature: American Writers, English Writers*, ed. Leon Edel (Cambridge, Mass., 1984).
4 Fleeming Jenkin and Annie Austin to ECG, 7 March 1859, Harvard, Autograph File, quoted in *Portrait*, 159–60.
5 Lady Ritchie, 'Mrs Gaskell', *Blackstick Papers* (London, 1908), 214–15.
6 Ibid, 212–13.
7 Quoted in Chadwick, 437.
8 This is the name she used, and that given by Whitehill (119), but she seems

initially to have been called Elizabeth Cleghorn Norton. See J. A. V.
Chapple, 'Cleghorn Again', *GSN*, 8 (August 1989), 10. See letters from
Meta Gaskell to Charles Norton, 5 July 1866 and 28 March 1867,
Harvard, bMS Am 1088/2609 and 26012. In the latter she thanks him for a
locket containing 'dear little Lily's hair'.

9 Meta Gaskell to Charles Norton, 24 November 1865, Harvard, bMS Am
1088/2607.

10 Thurstan Holland to Charles Norton, 18 November 1865, Harvard, bMS
Am 1088/3484, reprinted as Appendix F in the *Letters*, 970–1.

11 William Shaen to Catherine Winkworth, 15 November 1865, Winkworth,
II, 428–9.

12 Meta Gaskell to Ellen Nussey, 22 January 1866, Brotherton.

13 William Shaen to Catherine Winkworth, 15 November 1865, Winkworth,
II, 428.

14 Ibid, 429.

15 Meta Gaskell to Charles Norton, 24 November 1865, Harvard, bMS Am
1088/2607; William Gaskell to Mrs Beard, John Rylands, Unitarian College
Collection. See also Brill, 104.

16 William Gaskell to Henry Arthur Bright, 16 December 1874, University of
California, Los Angeles, MS 100/box 54.

17 William Gaskell to Marianne Gaskell, 24 September 1868, Harvard, bMS
Am 1088/2645, Brotherton transcript.

18 *The Beatrix Potter Journal, 1881–97*, ed. Leslie Linder (London, 1966),
quoted in Brill, 115–16.

19 Meta Gaskell to Charles Norton, 12 August 1868, Harvard, bMS Am
1088/2620.

20 Anne Ritchie to Richmond Ritchie, 14 November [1891], *Letters of Anne
Thackeray Ritchie*, ed. Hester Ritchie (London, 1924), 215.

21 Lord Houghton (Richard Monckton Milnes), notice, *Pall Mall Gazette*, II
(14 November 1865), 10.

22 Unsigned notice, *Examiner* (18 November 1865), 726.

23 [Henry Fothergill Chorley], notice, *Athenaeum* (18 November 1865), 689–
90.

24 *Unitarian Herald* (17 November 1865), 366–7. This has been attributed to
Mrs Charles Herford, but it is signed with the initial M, and Angus Easson,
among others, surmises it might be by James Martineau. See *CH*, 506–7.

25 James Drummond, 'The Holiness of Human Sorrow, a sermon preached at
Cross Street Chapel, Manchester, on Sunday, 19 November 1865, on the
occasion of the sudden death of Mrs Gaskell', John Rylands and
Manchester Central Library.

26 See *Manchester Guardian* (14 November 1865), *Manchester Courier* (15
November 1865) and *Manchester City News* (18 November 1865).

Index

INDEX

Blackwood's 40, 101, 187, 338, 462
Blagden, Isa 425, 534
Blake, William 397, 508
Blanc, Louis 226, 231
Bloomfield, Robert 116
Bodichon, Barbara (*née* Leigh Smith):
ECG's attitude to Lewes 463; feminism
221, 312; married women's property
petition 397; on Scott–Gaskell battle
427; Parkes friendship 311, 312;
Unitarian background 7, 311
Bombay Quarterly 438
Bonham Carter, Elinor 491
Bonham Carter, Hilary 364
Bonheur, Rosa 349
Bosanquet, Charles (Bosie): charity
subscription 554; ECG's letters 232,
233, 240, 463; fatherhood 537;
friendship with ECG 451–3; religion
451–3, 486
Boucherett, Jessie 35
Boucicault, Dion 303
Bracebridge, Charles and Selina 242
Braddon, Mary 581
Bradford, John 111–12, 160
Bradford, Julia 111–12
Bradley, Mrs (Whitby bookseller) 484
'Bran' 351
Bréhat, Alfred de 607
Bremer, Fredrika 44, 142, 170, 271
Brewster, Harry 164
Bridell, William Lee 454
Bridell-Fox, Charlotte *see* Fox
Bright, Henry Arthur 310, 454, 569, 611, 616
Bright, John 145, 304
British Association for the Advancement of
Science: Glasgow meeting 393, 394;
journal 560; Manchester meetings 134,
555; Wilberforce–Huxley confrontation
488; William's involvement 89, 271,
394, 496, 555, 560
British Quarterly 215, 218
Brodie, Benjamin 560, 563–4
Brodie family 441, 554
Brodie, Philo 503, 563–4
Brontë, Anne 249, 352, 396, 404, 409
Brontë, Branwell: Charlotte's letters 392;
death 353, 409; disgrace 400, 404, 408;
Jane Eyre publication 402; letters to
Wordsworth 401, 408; Scott affair 404,
427
Brontë, Charlotte (Currer Bell): attitude to
writing 311–12; Cove visit 302; Cowan
Bridge School 35, 249, 393, 397, 404,
408, 431; ECG comparison 46, 317,

340–1, 601; death 388–9; ECG
relationship 166, 236, 247–9, 272–3,
343, 346–7, 352–3, 390–1; Eliot's
admiration 463; father 11, 249, 404;
'Gondal' books 400, 401; health 266,
343, 351; Heger relationship 398, 400;
heroines 583; *Jane Eyre* 247, 314, 353,
395, 402, 404, 407, 409; letters 224,
244, 431; *Life* 94, 390–411; marriage
72, 79, 346, 356–8; *Moorland Cottage*
reaction 252; on *Cranford* 434; on *Ruth*
323–4, 340; on women's role 314–15;
on women's suffrage 313; portrait 390,
403; private life and work 390–1, 459;
The Professor 400, 409; *Shirley* 247–8,
314, 401; shyness 220, 249, 346; stone
proverb 253; *Villette* 266, 272, 308,
322, 328, 340, 341, 358, 398, 409, 430;
visits to Gaskells 272–3, 396
Brontë, Elizabeth 431
Brontë, Emily: Charlotte's account 352;
Charlotte's letters 392; death 408;
father 249; novels 404; poems 409; Roe
Head school 406
Brontë, Maria 431
Brontë, Patrick: attitude to writing of *Life*
390–3, 401, 404; Charlotte's death 389;
ECG's first meeting 352–3; ECG's
portrayal 249; Nicholls relationship
356, 495; response to *Life* 424–5, 427,
429, 431–2, 439; Scoresby relationship
457; wife's death 408; William's sermon
398
Brontë sisters 44
Brooke, Henry 30
Brougham, Henry, 1st Baron 10, 17, 62,
68
Brown, Ford Madox 380, 555
Browne, Hablot Knight (Phiz) 225
Browning, Elizabeth Barrett: *Aurora Leigh*
33, 411; ECG's relationship 226, 340,
425; father 11, 425; health 265; Howitt
relationship 171; Mohl friendship 348;
monastery visit 423; on *Mary Barton*
182, 183; on *Ruth* 340; quoted 417
Browning, Robert: ECG visit 425; Forster
friendship 183, 223; Howitt relationship
171; Mohl friendship 348; *Ruth* reading
340; Tottie's wedding 454; work 264;
young lover 170
Bruce, Lady Augusta 534
Bruce, James 560
Bryant, J.F. 111, 115
Buckland, George 141
Bulwer-Lytton, Edward George Lytton, 1st
Baron Lytton 42, 43, 223, 303, 304

672

Englishwoman's Journal 311
Evans, John 155
Evans, Mary Ann *see* Eliot, George
Ewart, Colonel 439
Ewart family 355, 401, 439, 441
Ewart, Mary 215, 216, 228, 243
Ewart, William 304
Examiner 215, 222, 223, 338, 614

Fairbairn, William 344, 555, 560
Farmer's Journal 10
Fauriel, Claude 348, 349
Fergusson (nurse) 152, 157
Ferrier, Susan 42–3
Fielden family 74, 87
Fielding, Henry 39, 41, 346
Fields, James 456
Fields, John (Jack) and Mrs 422–3, 494, 606
Fletcher, Angus 277
Fletcher, Eliza 64
Fletcher, John 39
Fletcher, Margaret *see* Davy
Fletcher, Mary 232, 277, 279, 306, 348
Forster, Eliza (*née* Colburn) 223
Forster, John: *Cranford* response 292; Dickens' friendship 183, 225, 289, 299; ECG friendship 222–4, 233, 237, 273, 289, 299; ECG's letters 79, 237, 280, 349, 356; *Examiner* reviewer 215; influence 182–3, 223, 273; *Life of Goldsmith* 410; *Mary Barton* 182–3, 186, 215, 222–3; *North and South* 357, 358, 359, 360, 366; Ruskin–Millais affair 461; *Ruth* 278, 305–6, 307, 337, 338, 339
Forster, Mary, *née* Arnold 252
Fox, Eliza (Tottie, later Bridell-Fox): career 45, 487; ECG's letters 45, 78, 84, 93, 133, 155, 167, 212, 227, 236, 247, 249, 251, 259, 264, 276, 278, 306, 308, 312, 338, 345, 359, 387, 393, 437, 615; friendship with ECG 166, 167, 221–2, 267, 270–1; lifestyle 265, 345, 487; marriage 47, 454, 487; married women's property petition 78, 396; *Mary Barton* response 212; Silverdale holiday 301, 303; visits 233, 246, 299, 437, 487; women's movement 311
Fox, W. J. 47, 170–1, 221, 222, 454
Franklin, Sir John 560
Fraser's Magazine: 'French Life' articles 532, 561, 568–9; Froude's editorship 536, 538, 561, 569; *Mary Barton* review 189, 224; 'Shams' 592
Freiligrath, Ferdinand 170

'French Life' 263, 473–4, 499, 568
Froude, Charlotte (*née* Grenfell) 229–30, 231, 237, 248–9, 369
Froude, Georgina 229
Froude, James Anthony: Darbishire family tutor 228–30; family background 228–9; *Fraser's Magazine* 536, 538, 561, 569; holiday 232; intellect 132; Manchester departure 274–5; marriage 230, 231; mesmerism interest 230; works 228–9, 231
Froude, Richard Hurrell 228
Fuller, Margaret 170
Furnivall, Frederick J. 351, 354, 389, 449

Gallenga, Antonio 161
Galt, John 21–2
Galton, Mary Ann 9
Galton, Samuel 9
Ganges, Marquise de 474, 532–3
Garibaldi, Giuseppe 535–6
Garrison, Lloyd 170
Gaskell, Anne *see* Robson
Gaskell, Anne (wife of Robert) 109
Gaskell, Eliza *see* Holland
Gaskell, Elizabeth Cleghorn (Lily, *née* Stevenson): adoption 12–13, 24–5; Alton house 572–6, 606; anti-slavery campaign 318–19; appearance 63, 65, 87, 162, 227, 234, 266; attitude to George Eliot 462–6; attitude to women's rights 311–17; attitude to writing 236, 249–50, 311–12; Aunt Lumb's death 106–7; autograph letter collection 226; birth 4–5, 11, 12; Brontë comparison 317, 340–1, 601; Brontë meeting 247–9; Brontë relationship 347; brother's loss 53–4; childhood 13–26; children 91–2, 105–7, 126–7, 146, 150–1, 155; Christian Socialism 225, 231, 265, 310, 345; clothes xii, 354, 201, 269, 299–300, 312, 535, 554, 571; death 609–10; death scenes 153, 360–1, 604; diary 93–100; Dieppe visit 607–8; Edinburgh visits 64–5, 559–61; education 27–38, 44–5; Eliot comparison 465–7, 601; European holiday 142–4; family life 151–2; farm 84–5; father's death 54–5; father's influence 40–1, 187; finances 450–1, 453; Flossy's engagement 531, 533–4; Free Library opening 304–5; friendships 160–7, 275–6; funeral 615–16; ghost stories 227–8, 239, 244–5, 306–7, 605; grammar 158, 397; Haworth visit 352–3; health 186–7, 233, 264–6, 309, 338,

INDEX

Gaskell, Meta (Margaret Emily, daughter):
Adam Bede authorship enquiries 243;
Alton house 608; birth 97, 106, 107,
108, 126–7; Bosie friendship 451–3;
childhood 151–2, 159; dancing 387–8,
393–4; death 614; ECG's plans for
566–7; education 157–8, 268, 270,
345; engagement 437–49, 531, 564;
Esmond enthusiast 305; Free Library
opening 304; friends 219, 265, 445–7,
455, 460; Great Exhibition 273;
Haworth visit 495; health 493, 559,
563, 564–5, 572; holidays 303, 351,
360, 450–1, 483, 497, 607; house
hunting 572; Italian trips 416–17,
420–1, 426, 535; letters to 160; life
613; London visits 301; Manchester
cotton famine work 503, 564; misses
Marianne 267; Mohl's summons 348,
387; mother's death 609–11;
mountaineering 564, 613; moving house
259–60; Normandy tour 499; Norton
correspondence 420, 606, 613; nursing
316–17; on ECG's Edinburgh visit 63,
65; Oxford visit 487; Paris visits 387–8,
530, 568; Pyrenean sketching tour 489;
reading 496; relationship with sister
405–6; romances 393–4, 416, 437;
temperament 137, 270; work 447, 454,
493; work for mother 396, 397, 402–3,
406, 492, 575
Gaskell, Robert (brother-in-law) 109, 616
Gaskell, Samuel (Sam, brother-in-law):
brother's wedding 79–80; doctor 83,
105, 109; ECG's funeral 616; holidays
448, 455; Lunacy Commission 219;
Marianne's health 105, 109; visits 83
Gaskell, Revd William: appearance 70,
155–6, 302, 497; British Association 89,
394, 496, 555, 560; Brontë *Life* 426–7,
431, 433; Chapman and Hall contract
553; committees 300; corrects ECG's
grammar 397, 402; Cross Street Chapel
75, 86–9, 260, 454–5, 554, 556, 559,
611; dialect lectures and notes 72, 186,
202, 223, 513–14, 611; dislike of
foreign food 447–8; Domestic Home
Mission 141; Elizabeth's death 610–11,
615–16; family background 73;
fatherhood 95, 96–7, 109, 137, 159,
267, 358; finances 108, 260; Flossy's
wedding 537; Garibaldi committee 535;
Great Exhibition 273–4; health 270,
387, 448, 455, 557; holidays 345–6,
393, 447–8, 455, 492, 497, 558–9, 576;
hymns 113–14, 175; letters 492,

612–13; Lit. and Phil. 134, 300, 556;
literature classes 72; London trips 184,
273–4, 301, 359; Manchester life 84;
Manchester New College 129, 156;
marriage 71–80; *Mary Barton*
publication 184, 186; meets Elizabeth
70; Meta's engagement 445, 447; *North
and South* 361; overwork 274; Oxford
visit 487; poetry 100–4, 113–14; poetry lectures 100,
115, 156, 611; Portico Library 43–4,
300, 485, 556, 560, 611; relationship
with Elizabeth 71–2, 77–8, 117, 137–8,
160, 251, 259–60, 358, 556–9, 610–11;
Ruth publication 338; sanitary reform
89, 556; Scott libel affair 426–7, 431;
sermons 155–6, 300, 398, 452, 557;
Silverdale holiday 301–3; *Sylvia's
Lovers* dedication 529; teaching 136,
156, 162, 300; temperament 556–7;
temperance movement 319–20;
Temperance Rhymes 113–14, 125;
wedding trip 80–2; Wiltshire visit
401–2; work 274, 350, 494, 556–9,
566–7, 611
Gaskell, William (Willie, son) 150–5,
603–4
Geological Society 134
'Ghost in the Garden Room, The' 460
Globe 426
Goethe, Johann Wolfgang von 144, 167,
493
Goldsmith, Oliver 28, 41, 222, 410, 590
Gore, Catherine Grace Frances 44
Gothic fiction 118, 120, 143, 469, 472
Gray, Thomas 41, 72, 547–8, 549
'Great Cranford Panic, The' 343
Great Exhibition 271, 273–4, 279
Green, Annie: ECG's letter 225; school
454, 603; visits 265, 299, 306, 393
Green, Ellen: school 454, 603; visits 265,
299, 306, 393
Green family 277
Green, Henry 23, 74, 339, 448, 615
Green, Mary: daughters 265, 393; ECG's
letters 308, 318, 322, 339, 358, 395,
533, 542; grandmotherhood 537; *Ruth*
response 339
Greenwood, Frederick 603
Greenwood, Grace 423
Greenwood, John 388–9, 390, 393
Greg, Emily 574
Greg family 87, 110, 160, 277, 300, 534
Greg, Mary (*née* Needham) 160, 181, 193,
216
Greg, Robert Hyde 277

678

INDEX

Illustrated London News 614
'Indian Mutiny' 437, 439, 445
Inquirer 267, 614
Irving, Washington 112
Isaacs, Charlotte (née Holland, cousin, daughter of Swinton) 55, 69, 266
'Italian Institution, An' 535

Jackson, Louey 397, 453, 455
James, Henry 93, 419, 421, 602–3
James, Maria 319, 351, 368, 394
James, William 393
Jameson, Anna: Brontë Life 407, 428–9; ECG relationship 219–20, 311, 407; ECG's letters 339, 368; feminism 219–20, 311; Howitt friendship 171
Jeffrey, Francis, Lord 10, 225
Jenken, Fleeming 604
Jenkins, Camilla 461
Jerrold, Douglas 225, 251, 299
Jewsbury, Geraldine: appearance 168; correspondence 244; ECG's letters 15; Forster relationship 223; friendship with Jane Carlyle 167–8, 244, 259, 276; Froude's disapproval 274–5; Half-sisters 185; lifestyle 167–8; Mary Barton response 217, 259; on ECG 259; on middle-class women's lives 313; on seamstresses 320; reviews 231, 530; visitors 233, 266; Zoë 168
Jewsbury, Maria Jane 167
Johnson, Samuel 42, 590, 593, 594
Jones, John 114
Joule, James 560
Jowett, Benjamin 441, 487, 488

Kant, Immanuel 130
Kavanagh, Julia 44, 499
Kay, Dr James P. see Kay-Shuttleworth, Sir James
Kay-Shuttleworth, Sir James (formerly Dr James Kay): advice to ECG 266; Brontë Life assistance 400; Brontë's visits 248; cholera epidemic 88, 247; description of Manchester 86; ECG's visits 248, 393; Manchester health report 86, 141; marriage 247; novel 461; opinions of 248
Kay-Shuttleworth, Lady: Brontë gossip 249; ECG's letters 147, 212, 315, 318, 345, 498; Gaskell's visits 248, 393; marriage 247–8
Kaye, Sir John 441–2
Keats, John 147, 327
Kemble, Fanny 226

Kennett family 20, 37, 53
Kenrick, John 156
Kenyon, John 225, 226, 340
Kingsley, Charles: Brontë Life response 428–9; Christian Socialism 231, 354; Froude friendship 229; influence 500; Mary Barton response 189, 224; publishers 183; Ruth response 339–40; Yeast 340, 373
Kingsley, Fanny 229
Knutsford: changes 542; Cranford model 13, 23, 235, 245; description 15–16; ECG's funeral 615; ECG's home 13–19, 25, 41, 277, 541; ECG's wedding 80; history 448; Holland family 8; 'Last Generation' source 14, 234–5, 239, 279–80, 298; school 454; Swinton family 8; Wives and Daughters 603
Kossuth, Lajos 277
Kropotkin, Prince Peter 613

Ladies Companion 268
Lady's Magazine 38
Lafayette, Marie Joseph, Marquis de 43
Lalor, Mrs (teacher) 267–8, 269, 308, 345, 615
Lamb, Charles 168, 223, 292
Lamont, Julia 216
Lancashire Public Schools Association 156
Landon, Letitia 38
Landor, Walter Savage 42, 223
'Langham Place Group' 311
language see dialect, speech
Langland, William 202
Langton, William 141
'Last Generation in England, The' 14, 48, 234–5, 239, 279–80, 282, 298
Lauderdale, James Maitland, 8th Earl of 11
Leader 426
Lea Hurst 362–4, 366
Lee, James Prince, Bishop of Manchester 234, 235, 265
Lee, Susannah 234, 235
Leeds Mercury 431
Leisler family 88
Lemon, Mark 299
Lewald, Fanny 266
Lewes, G.H.: Brontë correspondence 401; ECG's attitude 219, 243, 401, 463; living with Marian Evans 243, 462; Manchester lectures 218; Romola copyright 572; Ruth and Villette 340–1; Shirley remarks 401, 429; Shylock performance 219

681